HORIZON
FIVE YEAR
CUMULATIVE
INDEX

*VOLUME I, NUMBER 1 — VOLUME V, NUMBER 8 * SEPTEMBER 1958 — NOVEMBER 1963*

"So essential did I consider an index to be to every book that I proposed to bring a bill into Parliament to deprive an author who publishes a book without an index of the privilege of copyright, and moreover, to subject him for his offense to a pecuniary penalty."

LORD CAMPBELL
Lives of the Chief Justices of England
Preface to Volume III

This five-year Cumulative Index covers the first 32 issues of HORIZON, A Magazine of the Arts produced by American Heritage Publishing Co., Inc.

Part One, the General Index, includes all places, names, subjects, authors, and titles which have appeared in the issues from September, 1958, through November, 1963, completely indexed as a single unit.

Part Two is a separate Index of the Illustrations in these issues, beginning on page 80.

The eminent critic John Mason Brown has reported that he is "dazzled and delighted at the range of subjects covered" in HORIZON. The Index is not only a guide to those subjects, it is also a map of HORIZON's wide-ranging exploration of the "long cultural adventure of modern man."

Additional copies of the five-year Cumulative Index are available for $3.00 each. Annual Indexes are also available at $1.00 for each year's volume of six issues, beginning with September, 1958. (N.B.: Volume V has eight issues — September, 1962, through November, 1963.) Orders should be directed to the magazine's Sundry Department at 239 Great Neck Road, Great Neck, Long Island, New York.

Beginning with the May, 1961, issue, HORIZON has been indexed in the *Readers' Guide to Periodical Literature.*

GENERAL INDEX

To Subjects, Authors, Names, and Places

An Index to Illustrations Begins on Page 80

A

AALTO, ALVAR, Mar 61, 36, Jul 62: 8
ABBAS I, SHAH OF PERSIA (ABBAS THE GREAT), Mar 61: 28, May 61: 25–26, Jan 63: 62, 72
  Painting of, Jan 63: 69
ABBAS II, SHAH OF PERSIA, May 61: 27, 28
ABBASID CALIPHATE OF BAGHDAD, Sep 62: 75, 77, Nov 63: 26
ABBEY THEATRE, Mar 59: 87
ABBOTT LABORATORIES, Sep 58: 110
ABD AL-RAHMAN I, EMIR OF CÓRDOBA, Sep 62: 75
ABD AL-RAHMAN II, EMIR OF CÓRDOBA, Sep 62: 77–78
ABD AL-RAHMAN III, EMIR AND CALIPH OF CÓR-DOBA, Sep 62: 78–79
"ABDUCTION OF REBECCA, THE," painting by Delacroix, May 61: 74; illus, May 61: cover, 3
ABDUL AZIZ, May 59: 131
ABDUL HAMID II, May 59: 59, 135
À BECKETT, GILBERT ABBOTT, Mar 60: 129
ABEL, NIELS HENRIK, Mar 62: 75
ABERCORN, DUKES OF, May 63: 95–96
"ABOLITION OF MAN, THE," essay by C. S. Lewis, May 59: 127
"À BOUT DE SOUFFLE," motion picture, Nov 61: 116
"ABOUT-FACE IN POLAND," article by Dore Ashton, May 61: 20–23
ABRAHAM, Nov 59: 119
ABRAM, MORRIS B., Sep 61: 13
ABRAMOVITZ, MAX, Jul 62: 5, 8, 10
  Photograph of, Jul 62: 7
ABSTRACT EXPRESSIONISM, Sep 58: 44–45, 109, 134–35, Jan 63: 73–74
  Art of This Century gallery and, May 59: 11
  Chance as principle of creation, Sep 60: 30–32, 121–24
  Chase Manhattan Bank collection, Nov 60: 4–11
  European reactions to, Nov 59: 32, 41, 120–21
  Figure painting by Elmer Bischoff, David Park and Richard Diebenkorn, Jul 60: 16–24, 114–16
  Gottlieb, Adolph, as exponent of, Mar 59: 135
  Hofmann, Hans, and, Jul 61: 13, 16
  On Long Island, May 63: 9
  Noguchi, Isamu, quoted on, Mar 60: 112
  Nudes of, Sep 63: 96
  Rebellion against, Jul 62: 12–25
  In San Francisco Bay Region, Jan 59: 13–14
  Search for successor to, Jan 63: 16–25, 105
  Selz, Peter, quoted on, Sep 60: 122
"ABSTRACT IMAGIST" PAINTING, Jan 63: 25
ABU BEKR, Jan 59: 130
ABULCASIS, Moslem physician, Sep 62: 80
ABUNDANCE ECONOMY, Jul 60: 65–72
ABU SIMBEL, EGYPT
  Ancient temples at, Jul 60: 8, 10, 14, 124–25
  Threat to, from Aswan Dam, Jul 60: 8–10
"ABU SIMBEL: THE SEAL ON THE GATE OF EGYPT," article by Étienne Drioton, Jul 60: 10–15, 124–25
ABYSSINIAN HOAX, by Horace de Vere Cole and others, Jan 61: 66–68, 72
ACACIUS THE BEARKEEPER, Nov 63: 10
"ACADEMESE," Jul 63: 37–39
"ACADEMIC MARKETPLACE, THE," book by Theodore Caplow and Reece J. McGee, quoted, Sep 62: 19
ACADEMICS, in poetry, vs. Beat Generation, Sep 61: 116–21
ACADÉMIE FRANÇAISE, Sep 60: 69, May 62: 60

ACADÉMIE GONCOURT, Sep 62: 112
ACADEMY OF AMERICAN POETS, Jul 63: 69, 70, 72
ACADEMY OF FINE ARTS, INSTITUTE OF FRANCE, Mar 60: 54
ACADEMY OF MUSIC, New York City, Nov 58: 118–19
"ACCENT," magazine, Jan 62: 13
ACCIDENT, as principle of artistic creation, Sep 60: 30–32, 121–24, Mar 61: 45–46, Jan 63: 77
ACCRA, BRITISH WEST AFRICA, American consulate building, Jan 60: 119
ACHAEANS, Jan 61: 80–81
  Use of wheeled vehicles by, in war, Sep 58: 148–49
ACHAEMENID DYNASTY, of Persia, Jan 63: 43–49, 52 (chart), 58, Sep 63: 86, Nov 63: 15
  Goldsmiths of, Nov 62: 104, Jan 63: 53
ACHAIA, PRINCIPALITY OF, Nov 63: 31
ACHELOUS, river-god, Jan 60: 134
ACRAGAS. See AGRIGENTA
ACRE, PALESTINE
  Siege of, in 1291, Mar 61: 60
  In Third Crusade, Jan 59: 87–90, 130, 131
ACROPOLIS, of Athens, Jul 61: 42–43
ACTION PAINTING (see also ABSTRACT EXPRESSIONISM) Sep 58: 44, 109, 110
ACTON, LORD. See DALBERG-ACTON, JOHN EMERICH EDWARD
"ACT ONE," book by Moss Hart, quoted, Jul 62: 40
"ACTOR PREPARES, AN," book by Constantin Stanislavsky, Nov 62: 106–7
ACTORS STUDIO, THE, and proposed theatre, Nov 62: 106–8
"ACTORS STUDIO GOES LEGIT, THE," article by Robert Hatch, Nov 62: 106–8
ACTOR'S WORKSHOP, San Francisco, Jan 59: 22
"ACTS OF THE APOSTLES," cartoons for tapestries, by Raphael, Jul 61: 89, 94
"ACT WITHOUT WORDS 1," play, Sep 60: 114
ADA, of Caria, Mar 59: 47
ADAM, JAMES, Mar 62: 62–63
ADAM, ROBERT, Mar 62: 61, 62–63, 67, May 63: 35
  Portraits of, Nov 58: 60, Mar 62: 62
  Works by. See ILLUSTRATIONS INDEX
ADAM and EVE, Hebrew myth about, Nov 63: 42
"ADAM AND EVE," painting by Jan Mabuse, Jul 63: 93
ADAMOV, ARTHUR, Eugène Ionesco quoted on, May 61: 93
ADAMS, ANSEL, wilderness photographs by, Mar 60: 16–24
ADAMS, DIANA, Nov 59: 54
ADAMS, FRANKLIN PIERCE (F. P. A.), Jul 62: 37, 38, 39, 40
  Caricature of, Jul 62: 41
ADAMS, HENRY
  Letter to Isabella Stewart Gardner, quoted, Jul 59: 28
  Quoted: on historians, Mar 59: 5–6; on medieval churches, Jul 61: 49; on Rome, Jan 60: 22; on State, War and Navy Building, Jan 60: 121
  In South Seas, Jan 60: 125
ADAMS, JAMES TRUSLOW, Sep 63: 101
ADAMS, J. DONALD, Jan 60: 7
ADAMS, JOHN, quoted
  On education of his sons and grandsons, Sep 61: 17
  On Philadelphia, Jul 63: 9
ADAMS, JOHN QUINCY (1767–1848)
  Childhood of, May 60: 34, 36
  Portrait of, May 60: 32
ADAMS, LÉONIE, May 60: 22, Jul 63: 70, 72
  Photograph of, May 60: 23
ADAMS, MARK, Jan 59: 14

ADAMS, SHERMAN, Sep 61: 9
ADDAMS, CHARLES, May 63: 18
  Photograph of, May 63: 18
  Wyeth, Andrew, quoted on, Sep 61: 99
ADDISON, ADELE, Jan 62: 9, 13
ADDISON, JOSEPH, May 61: 66, Nov 63: 43–44
  On ballooning, quoted, Sep 58: 116
  Cato, Mar 62: 56
  Portrait of, Nov 63: 45
"ADDRESS FROM THE CLASS OF 1944 TO THE CLASS OF 1963, AN," article by Henry Anatole Grunwald, May 63: 86–89
ADEMUWAGUN ADESIDA II, DEJI OF AKURE, portrait of, Mar 63: 59
ADLER, EDWARD, Sep 62: 65
  Photograph of, Sep 62: 64
ADLER, LUTHER, Sep 58: 44, Sep 62: 65
  In *Golden Boy,* Jan 61: 32
ADLER, MORTIMER J., Sep 58: 98, 103, 133, 134
  Photographs of, Sep 58: 98, 99
ADLER, STELLA, Jan 62: 104
ADMIRALTY ISLANDS, Americanization of Manus, May 60: 122–23
"ADORATION OF THE MAGI," painting by Ghirlandaio, Nov 60: 30; illus, Nov 60: 26–27
"ADORATION OF THE MAGI, THE," illumination by Jean Fouquet, May 61: 103, 104, 113
ADRIAN, May 61: 103, 104, 113
ADRIANOPLE, BATTLE OF, Nov 63: 11
"ADRIFT ON A SEA OF GORE," article by Saul Bellow, Mar 59: 109–11
"ADULT PRODIGY," article by Robert Hatch, Jul 63: 84–91
ADVENTURE, why men seek it, Sep 58: 6–13, 135–39
"ADVENTUROUS ANGELS, THE," article by Peter Lyon, May 59: 4–19
"ADVERTISEMENTS FOR MYSELF," book by Norman Mailer, Jul 60: 120
ADVERTISING (see also CHANNELS; CRITIC'S VIEW: ADVERTISING; CRITIC'S VIEW: CHANNELS)
  Vs. artist, Sep 60: 38
  By banks, Mar 61: 121
  Billboard industry, May 61: 4, 5, 18
  Billboards of U.S. and U.S.S.R. compared, Jul 62: 118–19
  As characteristic industry of abundance economy, Jul 60: 69
  Communications satellites and, Jan 62: 20
  Communications Theory, Mar 60: 48–49
  Endorsements, Jul 60: 122
  François, André, art of, May 59: 116–17
  Love in, Nov 59: 113–17
  Mass media and imaginary audience, Mar 60: 46–51
  "Momism" in, Mar 59: 134
  Mutilation of English language by, Jul 63: 36
  Nonconformists and, Mar 59: 112
  By Olivetti enterprises, Nov 59: 48–49
  Radio vs. television, Nov 61: 102–3
  As reflection of American society, Nov 62: 114
  Television commercials, Jul 60: 6, 122
  Togetherness cult and, Nov 58: 30–31, 33, 146, 147
  Ungerer, Tomi, Jan 61: 128, 134
  By Washington, D.C., hotels (Madison and Georgetown Inn), Mar 63: 116
  "Word from Our Sponsors, A," miniature satirical revue, Jul 61: 77
"ADVERTISING AGE," magazine
  "Profile of the 'Advertising man'" in, Jul 61: 118–19
  Quoted, Mar 62: 112–13; on LeRoy Collins, Mar 63: 114
"ADVISE AND CONSENT," motion picture, compared with novel, May 62: 116–18

"ADVISE AND CONSENT," play, May 62: 117
AE. See RUSSELL, GEORGE WILLIAM
AEGEAN ISLANDS, Mar 61: 22
AEGINA MARBLES, Sep 59: 30–49
AELIAN, on Tuscans, quoted, May 60: 74
AENEAS, possible sculptural representation of, May 59: 123
"AENEID," epic poem by Vergil, survival of, Nov 62: 76, 80
AERONAUTICS (see also AIRLINES)
　Adventure in, Sep 58: 10–11
　Aeronautical Research Associates of Princeton, Sep 59: 27, 118–19
　Ballooning, Sep 58: 114–28
　Daniel Guggenheim Fund for Promotion of, May 59: 7, 8
　First instrument flight, May 59: 8
　"Law of diminishing transportation" and, Sep 58: 152
　Princeton University Department of Aeronautical Engineering, Sep 59: 26
AEROSTATION. See BALLOONING
AESCHYLUS
　Persians, quoted, Sep 63: 85
　In Renaissance curriculum, Jan 60: 62
　In Sicily, Sep 61: 24
　Survival of plays by, Nov 62: 76, 80
AETHELWALD, Nov 62: 94
AËTION, Mar 59: 55
"AFFAIR, THE," novel by C. P. Snow, Sep 60: 118
AFFLUENT SOCIETY, May 61: 118
"AFFLUENT SOCIETY, THE," book by J. K. Galbraith, quoted, Nov 63: 103
AFGHANISTAN, Minaret of Jham, Nov 59: 42–43
AFGHANS, in Persia, Jan 63: 72
AFRICA (See also NORTH AFRICA; SOUTH AFRICA, UNION OF)
　Archaeological and anthropological discoveries, Mar 62: 9–11
　Burton, Richard Francis, in, Jul 63: 110, 112–14, 116
　Dance of, Jul 59: 49–55; Giovanni-Antonio Cavazzi quoted on, Mar 63: 40
　Dinesen, Isak, quoted on, Sep 59: 111–12
　Exploration by Portuguese of west coast south of Cape Bojador, Nov 60: 76–83
　History of, Mar 63: 38–59, 105–6
　Livingstone, David, in, Sep 58: 135–36
　And man's passion for ivory, May 60: 89–90, 93, 94
　White man as portrayed by artists of, Sep 60: 12, 13–14, 22–23
"AFRICAN GENESIS," book by Robert Ardrey, excerpt from, Nov 61: 38–41
"AFRICA: THE FACE BEHIND THE MASK," article by Basil Davidson, Mar 63: 38–59
　Comment on, Mar 63: 105–6
AFRO (AFRO BASALDELLA), painting by, at UNESCO headquarters, Sep 59: 18
"AFTER ABUNDANCE, WHAT?" article by Eric Larrabee, Jul 60: 65–72
"AFTER-DARK SATIRE GOES TO TOWN," article by H. E. F. Donohue, Jan 62: 66–71
"AFTER MANY A SUMMER DIES THE SWAN," novel by Aldous Huxley, quoted, Jan 60: 11
"AFTERNOON OF A FAUN," ballet, Nov 59: 56
AGATE, JAMES, on Peter Ustinov, quoted, Nov 58: 137
AGATHIAS, Nov 63: 33
"AGE OF ANXIETY," symphony by Leonard Bernstein, Jul 59: 22, Jan 60: 79
"AGE OF ANXIETY, THE," poem by W. H. Auden, Jul 59: 22
AGE OF REASON. See ENLIGHTENMENT, THE
"AGE OF REASON, THE," book by Harold Nicolson, article excerpted from, Mar 61: 114–19
AGINCOURT, BATTLE OF, Sep 60: 61
AGNEW, HAROLD, Sep 58: 133
"AGON," ballet, Nov 59: 56, Jan 61: 44, 47, 48, 49
AGORA, of Athens, Jul 61: 42–43
AGOSTINO DI DUCCIO, sculpture by, Sep 60: 70
AGOULT, MARIE D', Nov 61: 36
　In painting by Joseph Danhauser, May 61: 84–85
AGRA, INDIA, Mar 61: 32
AGRICULTURE
　Effect on population increase, Jan 59: 93
　Man's first revolution, from food-collecting to food-producing, Sep 62: 4–9
　In Moslem Spain, Sep 62: 82
　Wheeled vehicles in, Sep 58: 149–50
AGRIGENTA (ACRAGAS), ITALY, Sep 61: 23, 24, 28
AGRIPPINA THE ELDER, coin portrait of, Sep 63: 39; illus, Sep 63: cover, 3
AHERNE, BRIAN, Sep 63: 77 (note), 80
AHLSTRÖM INDUSTRIAL TRUST, Jul 63: 63
AHMED I, OTTOMAN SULTAN, Sep 59: 59–60, 63
AHMED III, OTTOMAN SULTAN, May 59: 60
"AH, WILDERNESS!" play, New London, Conn., background of, Mar 60: 26–40
"AÏDA," opera, Leontyne Price in, Mar 61: 72

AIKEN, CONRAD, May 60: 48, Sep 61: 117, Jul 63: 70
　Limericks by, Nov 63: 100–1
AILEY, ALVIN, May 63: 49, 108
"AIMEZ-VOUS BRAHMS?" novel by Françoise Sagan, motion picture based on, May 62: 116
"AIR-CONDITIONED NIGHTMARE, THE," book by Henry Miller, Nov 61: 105
AIR FORCE ACADEMY. See UNITED STATES AIR FORCE ACADEMY
AIRLINES
　Advertising by, Jan 62: 113
　"Little Flight Music, A," Mar 62: 100–1
"AIR RAID," radio play, Jan 60: 54
AIR RAID SHELTER, on Long Island, Nov 62: 115
AIX-EN-PROVENCE, FRANCE, Mar 59: 85
AKHNATON, colossus of, Nov 58: 13; illus, Nov 58: 4
AKIHITO, with bride, photograph of, May 60: 7
AL-, in Arabian names. See second element of name
ALABAMA, state song, quoted, Nov 61: 119
ALABAMA, UNIVERSITY OF, Mar 60: 70
"ALADDIN," television production, Jan 59: 139
ALAIN-FOURNIER, HENRI, Jul 62: 59
ALAMEDA, CALIF., Coast Guard swimming pool at, Jan 60: 121
ALARIC, KING OF THE VISIGOTHS, Mar 63: 4, May 63: 77, 79–80
ALBA, DUKE OF. See ALVA
ALBEE, EDWARD, Sep 60: 56, Sep 61: 79, May 62: 112, Jul 62: 94, Sep 62: 34, Nov 62: 108
　American Dream, The, Jul 61: 116, 117, Sep 62: 34–35 (illus), 37
　Death of Bessie Smith, The, Jul 61: 116–17, Mar 63: 108
　Photograph of, Sep 61: 78
　Sandbox, The, Sep 62: 34–35 (illus), 37, 38–39 (illus), 40
　Who's Afraid of Virginia Woolf? Mar 63: 107–8, Sep 63: 98–99
ALBEMARLE, LORD, Nov 58: 56
ALBERS, ANNI, Nov 61: 61
　Design by, Nov 61: 70
ALBERS, JOSEF, Nov 61: 61, 64, 73, 74
　Photographs of, Nov 61: 58, 75
　Works by. See ILLUSTRATIONS INDEX
ALBERT, ARCHDUKE OF AUSTRIA, Nov 62: 38, 41
ALBERT, PRINCE CONSORT OF ENGLAND, as collector of paintings, Jul 63: 107
ALBERTI, LEON BATTISTA, Jan 60: 66, Jan 62: 27
　Quoted: on cities, Jul 59: 14; on "universal man," Jan 60: 73
ALBERTO-CULVER COMPANY, May 63: 112–13
"ALBERT SCHWEITZER," motion picture, Jul 61: 107
"ALBERT'S SON," painting by Andrew Wyeth, Sep 61: 3, 98; illus, Sep 61: cover
ALBERTUS MAGNUS, Mar 63: 5
ALBRIGHT, IVAN LE LORRAINE, Jan 59: 105
　Painting by, Jan 59: 102
ALBRIGHT, WILLIAM F., Nov 59: 6, 119
ALCMAN, quoted, Sep 63: 85
ALCOHOLIC BEVERAGES. See FOOD and DRINK
ALCOHOLISM, in United States, Nov 63: 106
ALCUIN, Sep 59: 126
ALDERNEY, ENGLAND, Mar 61: 32
ALDREDGE, THOMAS, Nov 60: 118
ALDRICH, THOMAS BAILEY, Jul 59: 133
ALDRIDGE, JOHN W.
　Party at Cranton, The, Sep 60: 119
　On Salinger, J. D., quoted, May 62: 101–2
ALEATORY MUSIC, Jan 63: 77, 78
ALEKHINE, ALEXANDER, Jan 62: 114, 116, 118, 119, 120
　Photograph of, Jan 62: 114
ALEMBERT, JEAN LE ROND D', Mar 61: 118, Nov 61: 35
ALENÇON, 1ST DUKE OF (JOHN), Mar 62: 90, May 63: 94
ALEXANDER I, CZAR OF RUSSIA, meeting with Napoleon at Tilsit, Sep 63: 28–32
ALEXANDER III, POPE, Nov 58: 106
ALEXANDER VI, POPE, Sep 58: 47, Jan 62: 32
　In painting by Pinturicchio, Jan 62: 32, 38
ALEXANDER VII, POPE, Jan 62: 45
ALEXANDER OF APHRODISIAS, Mar 63: 99
ALEXANDER SEVERUS, ROMAN EMPEROR, Nov 63: 63
ALEXANDER THE GREAT, Sep 58: 87, 141, Nov 63: 15, 20, 63
　Coin portrait of, Nov 63: 63
　Descent into sea, Nov 58: 68, 70
　Encounter with Diogenes, Mar 63: 10–13
　Invasion of Persia, Jan 63: 49
　On Persians, quoted, Jan 63: 53
　Portraits by Lysippus, Jan 59: 99
　Portrait sculpture of, Mar 59: 28
　At Sardis, Sep 63: 86, 88
　Two worlds of, Mar 59: 28–59

　Visit to Ilium described by Plutarch, Jan 61: 91
"ALEXANDER THE GREAT," motion picture, May 61: 53, 55, 57
ALEXANDRIA, EGYPT, Mar 60: 113–14
　Byzantine control lost, Nov 63: 26
　Durrell, Alexander, quoted on, Mar 60: 114, 115, 116, 117
　Fabri, Felix, in, Mar 60: 91
　Founding of, Mar 59: 40, 42
　Library at, Nov 62: 78
"ALEXANDRIANS OF LAWRENCE DURRELL, THE," article by Gilbert Highet, Mar 60: 113–18
ALEXIS I, CZAR OF RUSSIA, Sep 59: 62
ALEXIS PETROVICH, son of Peter the Great, Sep 59: 80
ALEXIUS I COMNENUS, BYZANTINE EMPEROR, Nov 63: 28
ALFONSO I, KING OF LEÓN AND ASTURIAS, Sep 62: 75
ALFONSO VI, KING OF LEÓN AND CASTILE, Sep 62: 88
ALFONSO X, KING OF LEÓN AND CASTILE, illus from works by, Sep 62: 83–86
ALFONSO XIII, KING OF SPAIN, May 61: 126
ALGIERS, and Battle of Lepanto, Jul 63: 53, 58
ALGONQUIN HOTEL ROUND TABLE, Jul 62: 36–41
ALHAMBRA, Granada, Spain, May 62: 15–16
ALICE, sister of Philip II of France, Jan 59: 87
"ALICE'S ADVENTURES IN WONDERLAND," book by Lewis Carroll, Nov 60: 97, Jul 61: 113
ALIENATION THEORY, of Bertolt Brecht, Mar 61: 44, 46
ALI PASHA, Turkish commander at Battle of Lepanto, Jul 63: 50, 53, 57, 58
　Imaginary portrait of, Jul 63: 57
ALISON, ARCHIBALD, on 18th-century neoclassicism, quoted, Mar 62: 50, 55
"ALL BUT LOST ART OF HANDWRITING, THE," article by Wolf von Eckardt, Sep 59: 124–28
ALLECTUS, Sep 63: 40
"ALLEGORY OF LOVE, THE," book by C. S. Lewis, May 59: 66
"ALLEGRA KENT," article by Robert Emmett Ginna, Nov 59: 52–56
ALLÈGRE, schoolteacher imprisoned in Bastille, Jan 60: 88, 128
ALLEN, DONALD, *The New American Poetry: 1945–1960,* Sep 61: 116–17
ALLEN, FREDERICK LEWIS, Nov 60: 119
ALLEN, GEORGE H., Nov 58: 30–31
ALLEN, GEORGE V., in painting by Robert Sivard, Nov 63: 91
ALLEN, HERVEY, Mar 63: 28
ALLEN, REGINALD, Jul 62: 11
ALLEN, STEPHEN, Jan 59: 8, 11
　Portrait of, Jan 59: 9
ALLEN, VIOLA, Mar 60: 32
ALLEN, VIVIAN BEAUMONT, Jul 62: 7
ALLEN, WOODY, May 63: 46
　Photograph of, May 63: 47
ALLEYN, EDWARD, Jan 60: 92–93
"ALL FALL DOWN," motion picture, Jan 62: 104, Mar 63: 35
"ALL-OUT IN THE DESERT," article by John Knowles, Jul 62: 108–11
ALMANZOR (AL-MANSUR), Sep 62: 82, 87
ALMA-TADEMA, LAWRENCE, painting by, Mar 60: 64
ALMOHADS, Moroccan dynasty, Sep 62: 84, 89
ALMORAVIDS, Sep 62: 88
ALPHABET, Ghana claim to invention of, Jan 63: 116–17
ALPHAND, ADOLPHE, May 63: 71–72, 73
"ALPHONSO XII," S.S., bullion salvaged from, Nov 58: 77
ALPS, tourism and, Mar 59: 83–84
ALSACE, and Thirty Years' War, Nov 62: 34, 36, 41
ALSOP, JOSEPH, Mar 60: 49
——— and STEWART ALSOP, on 1948 Presidential election, quoted, Mar 60: 49
ALSTEDT, JOHANN HEINRICH, Mar 60: 101, 102
ALTAI TRIBESMEN, Jan 60: 112
ALTDORFER, ALBRECHT, paintings by, Mar 60: 12, Sep 63: 15
ALTICK, RICHARD D., *The Scholar Adventurers,* Mar 59: 107 (note)
ALVA (or ALBA), DUKE OF (FERNANDO ÁLVAREZ DE TOLEDO), Sep 58: 19
　Attitude toward Russia, Sep 59: 60
ALVARADO, PEDRO DE, portrayed in Codex, Sep 60: 25
ALYATTES, KING OF LYDIA, Sep 63: 85, 88
"AMADIS DE GAUL," romance of chivalry, Nov 61: 106, 109, 110
AMAGANSETT, N.Y., May 63: 7 (map), 9, 13
AMATEUR CHAMBER MUSIC PLAYERS, Nov 62: 44–45
"AMATEURS ALL," article by Oliver Jensen, Jul 62: 96–97

AMAZONS, studied by Richard Francis Burton, Jul 63: 116
AMBER, Bronze Age trade in, Jul 60: 90
AMBLER, ERIC, Nov 58: 137
"AMBOINA, NATURAL HISTORY OF," by François Valentijn, Jan 60: 130
AMBOS MUNDOS HOTEL, Havana, Jan 59: 84
AMBROGIO, abbot of Camaldoli, Jan 60: 62, 64
AMBROGIO DA MILANO, Jan 60: 68
AMENHOTEP III, KING OF EGYPT, Jan 61: 85
AMERICAN ACADEMY OF ARTS AND LETTERS, Jul 63: 70, 75
AMERICANA HOTEL, New York City, Mar 63: 115–16
AMERICAN AIRLINES, terminal at New York International Airport, Sep 59: 19
AMERICAN BOWLING CONGRESS, Mar 63: 92
AMERICAN CIVILIZATION
  Advertising as reflection of, Nov 62: 114
  Art and the economy, Sep 60: 33–40
  Art as status symbol, May 63: 90–91
  Assault on English language, Jul 63: 33–48
  Bowling goes bourgeois, Mar 63: 89–95
  Changes in goals of, Nov 62: 5–6
  Children of today, Mar 62: 40–41
  "Come, Girls, Art Can Be Fun!" Sep 61: 64–65
  Coming generation of genius, Mar 62: 70–75
  Cult of unthink, Sep 58: 38–45, 134–35
  Culture of non-hotel, Mar 63: 115–17
  Easterners and Westerners, Jul 59: 121–25
  Future class system, May 59: 20–23
  Gardens in America, May 59: 31, 52–53
  Grand Tour period, Nov 59: 100
  Liberalism and personal ethics, Mar 63: 60–61
  Liberals and reactionaries, Jul 61: 66–69
  Love according to Madison Avenue, Nov 59: 113–17
  As Mencken would find it today, Nov 60: 70–71
  Mores at mid-century. See "AMERICAN MORES AT MID-CENTURY"
  Motion picture versions of, May 59: 99, 100–1
  Nonconformism, Mar 58: 112
  Poker, and American character, Nov 63: 56–62
  Privacy lost, Jul 60: 4–7, 120–22
  Research and its economics, Sep 63: 60–63
  Richesse oblige, Nov 58: 148
  As seen by Robert Osborn, Sep 60: 41–48
  Streets of America contrasted with those of Italy, Nov 61: 120–28
  Supermarkets, Mar 58: 110–11
  Taxation, Federal, vs. the individual, Nov 62: 118–19
  Togetherness cult, Nov 58: 30–33, 146–47
  Tyranny of teens, Jan 58: 137–39
  Ugliness of man-made America, May 61: 4–19
  U.S. and U.S.S.R. compared by English traveler, Jul 62: 112–19
AMERICAN COLONIES, wilderness of, Mar 60: 14–15
"AMERICAN COMMONWEALTH, THE," book by James Bryce, May 59: 23
AMERICAN COUNCIL OF LEARNED SOCIETIES, president of, quoted, Sep 62: 17
AMERICAN COUNCIL ON EDUCATION, report by John W. Gustad, quoted, Sep 62: 19
AMERICAN DENTAL ASSOCIATION, Nov 60: 123
"AMERICAN DREAM, THE," play, Sep 61: 79, Jul 62: 94, Sep 62: 34–35 (illus), 37
  Reviewed, Jul 61: 116, 117
AMERICAN EDUCATIONAL RESEARCH ASSOCIATION, official magazine of, quoted, Jul 63: 38
AMERICAN EDUCATION WEEK, 1959, Mar 60: 71
AMERICAN FOUNDATION FOR THE STUDY OF MAN, Nov 59: 119
"AMERICAN GOTHIC," play, Mar 60: 98, 120
AMERICAN HISTORICAL ASSOCIATION, Watumull Prize awarded by, Jul 63: 68
AMERICAN INSTITUTE OF PUBLIC OPINION, Sep 59: 25, 118
AMERICANIZATION, of other cultures, May 60: 6–9, 122–23
AMERICAN LANGUAGE (see also ENGLISH LANGUAGE)
  Peter Ustinov quoted on, Nov 58: 139
AMERICAN LITERATURE (see also authors by name)
  Adler, Edward, Sep 62: 64–65
  Algonquin Round Table, Jul 62: 36–41
  Barth, John, Jan 63: 36–37
  Battle of the bards, Sep 61: 116–21
  And cult of unthink, Sep 58: 38–42
  Dickinson, Emily, Jul 61: 100–5
  First novels of 1958, Mar 59: 14–17, 117–19
  Ford Foundation aid to creative writing, Jan 62: 8, 12
  Frontier deculturation, Sep 62: 94–95
  Frost, Robert, Nov 58: 34–35
  Hemingway, Ernest, interview, Jan 59: 82–85, 132–35
  Joan of Arc in, Mar 62: 97–98
  Kazin, Alfred, interview, Jul 62: 98–103
  MacLeish, Archibald, interview, Jan 60: 48–56
  Miller, Henry, Nov 61: 104–5

  O'Neill, Eugene, New London youth of, Mar 60: 25–40
  Pound, Ezra, Jan 61: 116–18
  Prizes and prize winners, Jul 63: 68–75
  Salinger, J. D., May 62: 100–7
  San Francisco Bay region, Jan 59: 16–19
  "Selling" of authors, Jul 60: 120–21
  Spectra hoax, May 60: 42–48
  Updike, John, Mar 62: 84–85
  Vanity Fair, magazine, Jul 62: 33–36
  Williams, Tennessee, memorandum from Seneca to, May 59: 54–55
  Williams, William Carlos, Mar 59: 60–61
AMERICAN MACHINE & FOUNDRY COMPANY, Mar 63: 92, 94
"AMERICAN MORES AT MID-CENTURY," series of articles by Eric Larrabee
  "After Abundance, What?" Jul 60: 65–72
  "Cultural Class War, The," Jan 60: 4–11
  "Imaginary Audience, The," Mar 60: 46–51
  "Our Face to the World," May 60: 4–9, 122–23
  "Wreck of the Status System, The," Nov 59: 20–25, 128
AMERICAN MOTORS, "junk" offer by, Nov 62: 114
AMERICAN MUSIC CENTER, Jan 62: 9
AMERICAN OPERA FESTIVAL, Jan 60: 14, 123
AMERICAN PRESIDENT LINES BUILDING, San Francisco, Jan 59: 8, 11
AMERICAN REVOLUTION
  Debates of Fox, Burke and Lord North on, May 60: 99–100
  Franklin letter concerning peace treaty, facsimile, Sep 59: 135
"AMERICANS, THE," book of photographs by Robert Frank, Mar 61: 14
AMERICAN SCHOOL FOOD SERVICE ASSOCIATION, Mar 60: 71
AMERICAN SCHOOLS OF ORIENTAL RESEARCH, Sep 63: 85
AMERICAN SHAKESPEARE FESTIVAL THEATRE, Stratford, Conn., Jul 59: 44, May 60: 28, Jan 63: 108
  Scenery used at, Sep 62: 110–11
AMERICA'S CUP, "Amateurs All," by Oliver Jensen, Jul 62: 96–97
AMES, MRS. ELIZABETH, Mar 63: 32
AMIS, KINGSLEY, Jan 63: 86
  Lucky Jim, Sep 60: 119
  New Maps of Hell, quoted, Mar 63: 79
AMMAN AND WHITNEY, Mar 59: 123, Jul 60: 123
AMMIANUS MARCELLINUS, on Persians, quoted, Jan 63: 50
AMORY, CLEVELAND, Nov 59: 23
  On Isabella Stewart Gardner, quoted, Jul 59: 32, 134
AMOS 'N' ANDY, on radio, Nov 61: 103
AMRAM, DAVID, Jan 60: 51, Mar 61: 14, Sep 61: 86, May 62: 82
  Photograph of, May 62: 83
AMSTERDAM, NETHERLANDS, Jul 61: 58–59
  American abstract expressionism in, Nov 59: 120
  C. 1620, Nov 62: 40
  Messianic year of 1666 in, Mar 60: 125
  Peter the Great in, Sep 59: 74; painting of, Sep 59: 70–71
  In 17th century, Sep 58: 20, 22, 33
  Skyscraper plans for, Nov 60: 16
AMSTERDAM AGREEMENT, Mar 59: 80
ANACHARSIS, on Homer's birthplace, quoted, Jan 61: 91
ANASTASIA, sister of Theodora, Nov 63: 10
ANASTASIUS I, BYZANTINE EMPEROR, Nov 63: 11
"ANATOMY OF A MURDER," motion picture, Sep 60: 88
"ANATOMY OF A MURDER," play, Jul 60: 93
"ANATOMY OF PARADISE," book by J. C. Furnas, Jan 60: 126
ANAXAGORAS, Jul 60: 103, 117
ANCESTOR CULT, in Africa, Mar 63: 44, 106
ANCRAM, EARL OF (ROBERT KERR), Jul 61: 90, Jul 63: 94
ANDALUSIA, Moslems in, Sep 62: 72–93
ANDERSEN, HENDRICK CHRISTIAN, Mar 63: 6
ANDERSON, BOYD, Mar 59: 123
ANDERSON, DILLON, Sep 61: 9
ANDERSON, JOHN MURRAY, Jan 61: 49
ANDERSON, JUDITH, Jul 60: 93
ANDERSON, LENNART, painting by, Sep 63: 94
ANDERSON, LINDSAY, Jan 63: 26
ANDERSON, MARIAN, concert in Topeka, Kans., Sep 59: 89
ANDERSON, MAXWELL, May 61: 56, Jul 62: 40
  Joan of Lorraine, Mar 62: 98
  Quoted by Archibald MacLeish, Jan 60: 49
ANDERSON, T. J., photograph of, Mar 63: 29
"ANDERSONVILLE TRIAL, THE," play, Jul 60: 93
ANDERSSEN, ADOLPH, Jan 62: 117
"AND GOD CREATED WOMAN," motion picture, May 60: 49
"AND NOW THE ATONAL AD LIB," article by Alfred

  Frankenstein, Jan 63: 76–81
  Comment on, Jan 63: 105
ANDREAE, JOHANN VALENTIN, Mar 63: 75–76
ANDREWS, EDWARD, May 62: 118
ANDREWS, JULIE, May 61: 103, 113
"ANDREW WYETH," interview by George Plimpton and Donald Stewart, Sep 61: 88–101
ANDREYEV, LEONID, He Who Gets Slapped, Jan 60: 123
ANDRONICUS, FLAVIUS, Mar 63: 98
ANDROUET DU CERCEAU, JACQUES THE YOUNGER, Sep 60: 66
"ANGEL BABY," motion picture, Jan 62: 103
ANGELICO, FRA (GIOVANNI DA FIESOLE), Jul 59: 30, Nov 60: 28, Jan 62: 31, Jul 63: 107
  Paintings by, Nov 60: 35, Jan 62: 32, 40
ANGELL, NORMAN, The Great Illusion, Mar 63: 6
ANGELS, and their antecedents, Nov 60: 26–49
ANGIVILLER, COMTE D', Sep 60: 72
"ANGKOR," article by Santha Rama Rau with photographs by Ernst Haas, Jan 59: 60–81
ANGLICANS (see also EPISCOPALIANS)
  And freedom of thought, Sep 63: 8–9, 107
ANGOLA
  Design by Louis Kahn for U.S. Consulate in Luanda, Sep 62: 60
  Forced-labor system in, Mar 63: 106
ANGRY YOUNG MEN, of Britain
  Beat Generation vs., Sep 58: 135
  And English Stage Company, Jan 63: 28–29, 31, 32
ANGST, Jul 59: 22
ANIMALS
  Domestication of, Sep 62: 7
  Draft, prehistoric, Sep 58: 147–48
  Infrared sense in, Nov 63: 50
  As motifs in ancient cultures of Near East, Nov 62: 102–4
  Sources of ivory, May 60: 90–94
  Sources of mermaid legend, Jan 60: 134–35
ANIMISM, in Africa, Mar 63: 106
ANJOU, DUKE OF, See RENÉ I
"ANNA CHRISTIE," play, Sep 58: 143, Mar 60: 32
ANNA COMNENA, Nov 63: 28
"ANNA KARENINA," novel by Tolstoy, Jan 62: 62
ANNA VICTORIA, PRINCESS OF SAXONY-HILDBURG-HAUSEN, Mar 62: 50
ANNE, QUEEN OF ENGLAND, Sep 61: 69, 71, 73, 75, 76, Jul 63: 96
  In painting by Godfrey Kneller, Sep 61: 72
"ANNÉE DERNIÈRE À MARIENBAD, L'," motion picture, May 62: 81
ANNE OF AUSTRIA, QUEEN MOTHER OF FRANCE, Sep 60: 67, Jul 63: 80, 82
  Portrait of, Sep 60: 66
ANNE OF BOHEMIA, QUEEN OF ENGLAND, May 63: 99
ANNE OF DENMARK, Jul 61: 80
ANNIGONI, PIETRO, Jan 59: 99
  Paintings by, Jan 59: 104, Jul 63: 93
"ANNOTATED INDEX TO THE CANTOS OF EZRA POUND," book by J. H. Edwards and W. W. Vasse, Jan 61: 116
"ANNUNCIATION," painting by Fra Angelico, Nov 60: 28; illus, Nov 60: 35
"ANOTHER UNCLE EDITH CHRISTMAS STORY," story by Robert Benchley, Sep 58: 130
ANOUILH, CATHERINE, Nov 60: 54
ANOUILH, JEAN, Nov 58: 62, Nov 60: 50–55, 126–27
  Ionesco, Eugène, quoted on, May 61: 91
  Lark, The, Mar 62: 99
  Photograph of, Nov 60: 50
  Waltz of the Toreadors, The, Mar 61: 46
ANSHEN, ROBERT, Jan 59: 8, 11
  Portrait of, Jan 59: 9
ANSHEN & ALLEN, Jan 60: 121
  Building designed by, Jan 60: 25
ANSHUTZ, THOMAS POLLOCK, Jul 63: 18
ANSIDEI MADONNA, painting by Raphael, Sep 61: 77
ANSKY, S. (SOLOMON RAPPOPORT), The Dybbuk, Jan 61: 32–33
ANSPECHER, FLORENCE, Nov 60: 117
ANTARCTIC EXPEDITIONS
  To Cape Crozier, 1911, Sep 58: 8, 138
  Of Scott, Robert Falcon, Sep 58: 9, 139
ANTHEMIUS OF TRALLES, Nov 63: 12
ANTHONY, IRVIN, The Saga of the Bounty, Sep 63: 42
ANTHROPOLOGY
  In Africa, Mar 63: 40, 43
  Man, nature, and miracle, Jul 60: 25–32
  Man's family tree, Mar 62: 6–7
  Man's first revolution, from food-collecting to food-producing, Sep 62: 4–9
  Man's need to adapt himself to changing world, Nov 62: 5–9
  Man's weapons instinct related to war, Nov 61: 38–41

Silent Language, The, book by Edward T. Hall, Mar 60: 122–23

Time of man, Mar 62: 4-11

White man as seen by artists of colored races in early contacts, Sep 60: 10–29

"ANTIGONE," play by Jean Anouilh, Nov 60: 52, 54, 126, 127

ANTI-INTELLECTUALISM
In American arts, Sep 58: 38–45, 134–35
In American education, Nov 58: 32–33

ANTIKYTHERA, GREECE, underwater archaeological discoveries at, Nov 58: 72

ANTINOÜS, Jan 62: 45, May 62: 3, May 63: 34, 35, 37
Sculpture of, May 63: 34

ANTIOCH, during Crusades, Jan 59: 87

ANTIOCHUS, KING OF SICILY, Sep 61: 26

ANTIOCHUS III, KING OF SYRIA, Sep 58: 140, 141

ANTIPATER, Nov 62: 88

ANTI-SEMITISM, in role of Shylock, Jan 60: 89–96

ANTOINE, ANDRÉ, Sep 61: 102

ANTONINUS, BROTHER, Jan 59: 18

ANTONINUS PIUS, ROMAN EMPEROR, Sep 63: 38

ANTONIONI, MICHELANGELO, Nov 62: 110
L'Avventura, Sep 61: 110, 112

ANTONY, MARK. See MARK ANTONY

"ANXIETY," woodcut by Edvard Munch, May 60: 113

ANYTUS, Jul 60: 100, 102, 104, 117

ANZARUT, RAY, Nov 59: 124

"APARAJITO," motion picture, reviewed, Jan 61: 115

"APARTMENT, THE," motion picture, Jan 61: 123

APHAIA, Aegina temple of, Sep 59: 32

APHRODISIAS, ancient city in Asia Minor, Mar 63: 96–101

APHRODITE
Description of, by Ezra Pound, Jan 61: 118
Temple of, at Aphrodisias, Mar 63: 100

APOLLINAIRE, GUILLAUME, May 59: 121
On Seine River, quoted, Jul 62: 60

"APOLLO," ballet, Nov 59: 56, Jan 61: 44, 46, 47

APOLLO BELVEDERE, sculpture, Jan 62: 48; illus, Jan 62: 47

APOLLONIUS, Belvedere Torso, Jan 62: 32; illus, Jan 62: 36

"APOLOGY," of Plato, Jul 60: 102, 103, 104

"APOLOGY," of Xenophon, Jul 60: 102, 103, 104

"APOLOGY FOR GLUTTONS, AN," article by Patrick Leigh Fermor, Jan 63: 34–35

APPIA, ADOLPHE, Sep 62: 110, 112, May 63: 41

"APPLE, THE," play, Mar 62: 109, Sep 62: 37

"APPLE CART, THE," play, Nov 58: 136–37

APPLIED SCIENCE CORPORATION, Princeton, N.J., Sep 59: 27, 118–19

APSARASES, Nov 60: 30–31

APULEIUS, LUCIUS, survival of works by, Nov 62: 87, 89 (illus), 91, 94

AQUILEIA, BATTLE OF, Jul 63: 3

AQUINAS, THOMAS, Mar 63: 5, Sep 63: 9, 107
On the devil, quoted, Nov 59: 58

ARABA, WADI EL, archaeological discovery of copper in, Nov 59: 9–10

ARABIA
Archaeological possibilities in, Nov 59: 119
Burton, Richard Francis, in, Jul 63: 112

"ARABIAN NIGHTS' ENTERTAINMENTS," translations of, Jul 63: 110, 116–17

ARABS
In Africa, May 60: 89–90
Bargaining of, May 59: 136
Capture of Palestine, Nov 63: 26
Invasion of Persia, Jan 63: 52–53, 60
In Sicily, Sep 61: 22, 24, 28, 32
In Spain. See SPAIN, Moslems in

ARAGON, LOUIS, Mar 59: 70

ARBELA, BATTLE OF, Mar 59: 40, 47, 49

ARBUTHNOT, F. F., Jul 63: 117

"ARCANA," composition by Edgard Varèse, Jul 59: 20

ARCANGELI, ALDO, Mar 59: 122

ARCHAEOLOGY
Aegina marbles, Sep 59: 30–49
In Africa, Mar 63: 40, 43
Ancient sites used for performances and festivals, Jul 62: 26–31
Angkor, Jan 59: 60–81
Aphrodisias, Mar 63: 96–101
Arles, France, Roman remains at, Jul 59: 98, 129, 130
Barberini vase. See Portland vase
Bible as divining rod, Nov 59: 4–10, 118–19
Bronze Age commerce and travel, Jul 60: 84–91, 113
Çatal Hüyük, Turkey, Sep 62: 8; sculptures, Nov 63: 66–67; wall paintings, Sep 62: 11, 12
Cave-dwellers of Safadi and Abu Matar, and their ivory figurines, Jan 62: 72–75
Cave of Tiberius, May 59: 102–7, 122–24
Cities, earliest, Jul 61: 38–41

Curses of Esarhaddon, Sep 59: 103–5
Ephesus, Sep 58: 85–87, 140–42
Etruscans, May 60: 56–79
Gaul, sanctuaries in southern part of, Jul 59: 92–93, 95
Homeric Age as related to Mycenaean remains, Jan 61: 73–99
Marlik Tepe and its gold treasures, Nov 62: 100–4
Minaret of Jham, Nov 59: 42–43
Near East, evidence of man's transition from food-collecting to food-producing, Sep 62: 4–9
Neolithic village, Jul 61: 36–37
Nile River monuments threatened by Aswan Dam, Jul 60: 8–15, 124–25
Paleolithic cemetery and cave, Jul 61: 34–35
Pazyryk burial vault discoveries, Jan 60: 110–12
Piraeus, Greece, ancient Greek sculpture unearthed at, Mar 60: 6–11
Pompeii and Herculaneum, their burial and discovery, Mar 62: 42–69
Portland vase, Nov 63: 63–65
Rock paintings of Sahara, May 59: 70–83, Sep 62: 11, 12, Mar 63: 43
Rome, excavations under Basilica of St. Peter, Jan 62: 26, 29
San Men Dam, China, and rescue of cultural remains above, Jan 61: 4–13, 124
Sardis, Sep 63: 82–89
Sumer, new treasures from Nippur, Nov 61: 84–87
Sumerian love songs, Jul 63: 108–9
Underwater discoveries, Nov 58: 66–77
Wheeled vehicles, Sep 58: 146–51

ARCHER, WILLIAM, Jan 62: 108
In caricature by Max Beerbohm, Jan 62: 107

ARCHERY, Zen style, Jan 59: 75

"ARCHIBALD MacLEISH: ON BEING A POET IN THE THEATER," interview by Donald Hall, Jan 60: 48–56

ARCHILOCHUS, quoted, Sep 63: 85

ARCHIMEDES, Mar 62: 73
Portrait of, Sep 61: 26

ARCHITECTS' COLLABORATIVE, THE, Nov 61: 70
Building designed by, Nov 61: 72

"ARCHITECT'S HERO: LOUIS KAHN," article by Albert Bush-Brown, Sep 62: 57–63

"ARCHITECTURAL FOLLIES IN AMERICA," book by Clay Lancaster, excerpt from, Mar 59: 136

"ARCHITECTURAL FORUM," magazine, quoted on Federal construction, Jan 60: 119

ARCHITECTURAL LEAGUE OF NEW YORK, and street furniture, Nov 59: 108–9

"ARCHITECTURAL REVIEW, THE," journal, quoted on "things outdoors," Nov 59: 108

ARCHITECTURE (see also CHURCHES and SYNAGOGUES)
Angkor, Jan 59: 60–81
Avant-garde or blind alley? Mar 62: 30–39
Of banks, Mar 61: 120–21
Baroque, Jul 60: 35, 42, 50; illus, Jul 60: 34, 51–57; Saarinen, Eero, quoted on, Jul 60: 82
Bauhaus, Nov 61: 58–75
Blenheim Palace, Sep 60: 68–77
Boston City Hall design, Jan 63: 10–15
Bowling establishments, Mar 63: 90–91, 94
Brighton Pavilion, Nov 62: 20–31
Castles of Ludwig II of Bavaria, Jan 61: 34–43
City. See CITIES, Origins, transformations, and prospects of
Classical revival of 18th century, Mar 62: 62–63
Competitive economy and, Sep 60: 37–38, 39
Couvent Sainte-Marie de la Tourette, by Le Corbusier, Mar 61: 34–41
Dome, significance in Byzantium, Nov 63: 12, 15, 20
Domestic: in California, Jan 59: 8, 10; contemporary American, Mar 59: 113–14; development in Europe, Nov 58: 39, 41–42; effects of Togetherness cult, Nov 58: 32, 147; of Goff, Bruce, Nov 61: 42–47; suburban, May 61: 19; of Wright, Frank Lloyd, Sep 60: 99, 102, 127, 128
Effect of victory at Lepanto, Jul 63: 60
Elephant of Paris, Mar 59: 136
England's noble houses, Nov 58: 38–61
Fantasy creations by painters, Sep 63: 10–27
Fashion cycles in, Mar 59: 63, 66–67, 113–14
Gastronomic approach to, Jan 63: 35
Georgian, Nov 58: 42
Ghana claim to origin of, Jan 63: 117
Hadrian's Villa, May 63: 32–39
"High modern," Sep 59: 4–21
Homes of John F. Kennedy and Barry M. Goldwater contrasted, Sep 63: 102–3
International style, Sep 59: 6
Kahn, Louis, Sep 62: 57–63
Lincoln Center, New York City. See LINCOLN CENTER FOR THE PERFORMING ARTS
Of Louvre, Sep 60: 59–69, 72, 81–85

Metropolitan Opera House, old and new, Nov 58: 28–29, 117–20
Monuments for our times, May 61: 41–49
Moore, Henry, quoted on, Nov 60: 114
Nervi, Pier Luigi, Mar 59: 18–25, 121–24
Paris, Haussmann's rebuilding of, May 63: 50–75
Persian, Jan 63: 44, 51, 57; mosques, Jan 63: 57
Privacy lost in, Jul 60: 5
Resort hotels, Jan 61: 102–12
Roads and, Jan 62: 94–95
Saarinen, Eero, Jul 60: 76–83, 123
Of San Francisco Bay Region, Jan 59: 8–12
Second Empire style, May 63: 68
Skyscrapers in Europe, Nov 60: 12–16, 124–25
Soane, John, Nov 63: 72–83
Spanish Arab, and Great Mosque at Córdoba, Sep 62: 75
Stained-glass revival in religious architecture, Sep 62: cover, 3, 22–32
Street furniture, Nov 59: 105–12
Suburban, May 61: 19
Tange, Kenzo, Sep 61: 58–63
Towers, mass and class appeal of, Jan 60: 9
U.S. government buildings, Jan 60: 18–27, 119–21; of State Department, Jul 61: 30–31
Urban redevelopment, Eero Saarinen quoted on, Jul 60: 82, 123
Vaux-le-Vicomte, castle of Nicolas Fouquet, Jul 63: 76–83
Water as the wine of, May 62: 10–33
World's Fair plan of Victor Gruen, May 60: 80–87
Wright, Frank Lloyd, war on fine arts by, Sep 60: 96–103, 127–28
At Yale University, May 59: 84–87

"ARCHPOET, THE," article by Francis Russell, Nov 60: 66–69

ARCIMBOLDO, GIUSEPPE, painting by, Nov 60: 2, 3

ARCOLA, BATTLE OF, May 61: 70

ARCTIC EXPEDITIONS, Watkins and Peary, Sep 58: 10, 138

ARDEN, JOHN, Jul 62: 91–94, Jan 63: 26, 32, 33
Photograph of, Jan 63: 30

ARDREY, ROBERT
"How Can Man Get Along Without War?" excerpt from *African Genesis,* Nov 61: 38–41
Shadow of Heroes, Jan 62: 103

ARDYS, KING OF LYDIA, Sep 63: 85

ARENSBERG, WALTER CONRAD, May 60: 43

ARGENTO, DOMINICK, Jan 60: 15, 123

ARGENVILLE, DEZALLIER D', May 62: 14

"ARGO," sculpture of, in Cave of Tiberius, May 59: 123, 124

ARGONAUTS, Jul 60: 85, 86

ARGYLL, 11TH DUKE OF (IAN DOUGLAS CAMPBELL), photograph of, Nov 61: 26

"ARIADNE AUF NAXOS," opera, Igor Stravinsky quoted on, Sep 58: 84

ARIAS, ANTONIO, portrait by, Nov 61: 108

ARIOBARZANES, Mar 59: 43

ARIOSTO, LODOVICO, Nov 61: 111, Mar 63: 27

"ARISE, YE PLAYGOERS OF THE WORLD," article by Robert Hatch, Jul 61: 116–18

ARISTANDER, Mar 59: 30, 38

ARISTEAS, Mar 63: 98

ARISTOPHANES
Clouds, Jul 60: 117
Lysistrata, Jan 63: 29
In Renaissance curriculum, Jan 60: 62
Survival of plays by, Nov 62: 76
Wasps, Jul 60: 102

ARISTOPHANES OF BYZANTIUM, on *The Dyskolos* of Menander, quoted, Jul 59: 80

ARISTOTLE, Jul 60: 103, Nov 60: 18, 19
Alexander the Great and, Mar 59: 32, 33, 47, Mar 63: 12–13
Arab translations of works by, Sep 62: 89
And modern science, Jul 61: 5–6, 8
New painting as overthrow of, Sep 60: 122
Poetics, Nov 62: 86
Quoted, Jan 59: 27; on drama, May 62: 38; on gods, Mar 61: 90; on Greek Mysteries, May 63: 115; on Sicilian tyrants, Sep 61: 24; on Tyrrhenians, May 60: 74
In Renaissance curriculum, Jan 60: 62

ARITHMETIC. See MATHEMATICS

ARIZONA, suburban developments at Phoenix, May 61: 19

ARIZONA, UNIVERSITY OF, Mar 60: 70

"ARKANSAS BOYHOOD, AN," paintings by Carroll Cloar, Nov 58: 78–81

ARKWRIGHT, RICHARD, Erasmus Darwin quoted on cotton mills of, May 59: 94

ARLANDES, MARQUIS D', Sep 58: 114, 117

"ARLES," article by Allan Temko with paintings by Vincent Van Gogh, Jul 59: 90–105, 129–32

ARLISS, FLORENCE, photograph of, Sep 63: 78

ARLISS, GEORGE, Sep 63: 75, 76, 80
Photograph of, Sep 63: 78

ARMISTEAD, ELIZABETH, May 60: 100, 125
ARMISTEAD, HORACE, Sep 62: 110
ARMOR, medieval, Nov 58: 106, 107
ARMORY SHOW OF 1913, Sep 60: 102, Nov 61: 10
ARMSTRONG, LOUIS, photograph of, Mar 61: 19
ARMSTRONG, W. H., "Mr. Eliot Revisits the Waste Land," poem by, Jan 63: 92–93
ARMSTRONG-JONES, ANTHONY (EARL OF SNOWDON), Jan 63: 38
ARMY, U.S., "Militant Liberty" program, Nov 58: 147
ARNHEM, NETHERLANDS, monument at, May 61: 42; illus, May 61: 44
ARNOLD, MATTHEW, May 61: 81
Quoted: on man (from "The Future"), Jul 62: 88; on Oxford, Jan 63: 86; on Shelley, May 61: 58
ARONSON, BORIS, Jul 59: 42, Jan 62: 14
Stage design for *J.B.,* Jan 60: 50, 51
ARONSON, DAVID, Jul 62: 25
Painting by, Jul 62: 25
ARQUETTE, CLIFF, *Charley Weaver's Letters from Mamma,* Jul 60: 121
ARRABAL, Sep 62: 34, 36
ARRIAN (FLAVIUS ARRIANUS), quoted
On Alexander the Great, Mar 59: 40
On military divers, Nov 58: 71
ARRIGHI, LUDOVICO DEGLI (VICENTINO), Sep 59: 127
ARRINGHIERI, ALBERTO, portrait of, Mar 61: 71
ARSUF, BATTLE OF, Jan 59: 90
ART (see also DRAWING; PAINTING; SCULPTURE)
Of African cultures, Mar 63: 40, 43, 44–59
In Age of Leisure, Nov 63: 109
Angels and their antecedents, Nov 60: 26–49
Artist in our time, Jan 63: 73–75, 105
Attitudes toward nature in, Mar 60: 13–14
Auctions at Sotheby's, Nov 62: 58–67
Avant-garde or blind alley? Mar 62: 30–39
Birth of an art form, Jan 59: 144
Byzantine, Nov 63: 25, 28, 31, 33
Catalan, Mar 59: 78, 126
Chance as principle of creation, Sep 60: 30–32, 121–24
Chinese imperial art treasure, Jan 61: 14–25
Christian: at Arles, France, Jul 59: 131; Gilson, Etienne, quoted on, Nov 58: 115; Malraux, André, quoted on, Nov 58: 15–16, 112–14
"Come, Girls, Art Can Be Fun!" Sep 61: 64–65
And economics, Sep 60: 33–40
Effect of victory at Lepanto, Jul 63: 60
Effects of Grand Tour of 18th and 19th centuries, Nov 59: 94–96
And European unity, Mar 63: 8, 9
Ford Foundation and, Jan 62: 4–15
Forgery in, Mar 59: 105, 109
Guggenheim family as sponsors of, May 59: 4–19
"Happening" as form of, Nov 62: 114
Hellenistic, Nov 63: 25
History of, drawings by Michael Thaler, Jan 61: 120–21
Influence of colleges and universities on, Jan 62: 11
Ivory in, May 60: 89–95, 120–21
Joan of Arc in, Mar 62: 97, 99
Kennedy look in the arts, Sep 61: 4–17
Louvre, history and treasures of, Sep 60: 57–85
And mass culture, Jan 62: 4–11
Memorandum to the President from the Secretary of Arts and Leisure, Nov 62: 18–19
Metamorphosis of the Gods, book by André Malraux, discussed, Nov 58: 4–17, 112–17
Of N'debele people of Transvaal, Nov 60: 56–65
Persian, Jan 63: 49, 51–52, 53, 72; carpets, May 59: 44, Jan 63: 51, 72; miniatures, Jan 63: 57, 62, 67–69
Polish, May 61: 20–23
Of Pompeii and Herculaneum, and classical revival of 18th century, Mar 62: 42–69
In San Francisco, Jan 59: 4–23
Stained-glass revival, Sep 62: cover, 3, 22–32
As status symbol, May 63: 90–91
Wedgwood, Josiah, and his circle, May 59: 92–94
What Is Art? by Tolstoy, quoted, Nov 60: 56
Whistler, James McNeill, quoted on, Jan 60: 5
White man as portrayed by artists of colored races in early contacts, Sep 60: 10–29
Wirkkala, Tapio and Rut Bryk, Jul 63: 62–67
"ART AGAINST THE GRAIN," article by Frank Getlein, Jul 62: 12–25
"ART BY ACCIDENT," article by Leonard B. Meyer, Sep 60: 30–32, 121–24
ARTEMIS, of Ephesus, Sep 58: 85–87, 141, Mar 59: 30
ARTEMIS, TEMPLE OF, at Sardis, Sep 63: 86; illus, Sep 63: 88
ARTEMISIUM, GREECE, underwater archaeological discoveries at, Nov 58: 76
"ARTFUL BANKER, THE," article by Peter Lyon, Nov 60: 4–11
ARTHURIAN LEGEND

In *Camelot,* May 61: 104, 113
Versions of James Knowles and Thomas Malory, May 60: 115–18
"ARTIST FROM THE OUTBACK," article by Alan Moorehead, Sep 62: 96–104
"ARTIST IN OUR TIME, THE," article by Murray Kempton, Jan 63: 73–75; comment on, Jan 63: 105
ARTISTS' COLONIES
Huntington Hartford Foundation, Mar 63: 27, 32
MacDowell Colony, Mar 63: 26–33
Yaddo, Mar 63: 27, 32
"ARTIST SPEAKS FOR HIMSELF, THE," series of interviews
Balanchine, George, Jan 61: 44–56
Chayefsky, Paddy, Sep 60: 49–56
Gould, Glenn, Jan 62: 88–93
Hemingway, Ernest, Jan 59: 82–85, 132–35
Ionesco, Eugène, May 61: 89–91, 93, 95, 97
Kazin, Alfred, Jul 62: 98–103
MacLeish, Archibald, Jan 60: 48–56
Moore, Henry, Nov 60: 102–15
Noguchi, Isamu, Nov 60: 104–12
Rivers, Larry, Sep 59: 94–102
Saarinen, Eero, Jul 60: 76–83, 123
Wyeth, Andrew, Sep 61: 88–101
"ART NEWS," magazine
Critical jargon appearing in, Jul 63: 38
Quoted: on collection of Isabella Stewart Gardner, Jul 59: 27; on Museum of Non-Objective Art, May 59: 10
"ART OF GOING IT ALONE, THE," article by Saul Bellow, Sep 62: 108–10
"ART OF LOVE," poems by Ovid, Nov 58: 108
"ART OF THE HOAX, THE," article by Gilbert Highet, Jan 61: 66–72
ART OF THIS CENTURY, gallery in New York City, May 59: 11
"ART OF TRAVEL, THE," book by Henry James, quoted, Mar 61: 24
ARUNDEL, 14TH EARL OF (THOMAS HOWARD), Jul 59: 30, Jul 61: 80, 91, Jul 63: 93, 94, 96
ARUNDELL, ISABEL. See BURTON, MRS. RICHARD FRANCIS
ARZACHEL (AL-ZARKALI), Toledan Tables of, Sep 62: 80, 92
ASBELL, BERNARD, articles by
"Glenn Gould," Jan 62: 88–93
"Mrs. Landon's Harp," Sep 59: 86–91, 122–23
ASCALON, in Third Crusade, Sep 59: 130, 131
"ASCENSIONS AEROSTATIQUES LES PLUS REMARQUABLES," panorama from, Sep 58: 114–15
"ASCENT OF F-6," play, Sep 62: 41
ASCH, NATHAN, Ernest Hemingway quoted on, Jan 59: 133
ASCLEPIUS, Jul 60: 103, 104
ASHANTI KINGDOM, of Africa, Mar 63: 41 (map), 56
ASHBERY, JOHN, Sep 61: 119
ASHLEY, WILLIAM JAMES, Sep 63: 101
ASHMOLE, ELIAS, Nov 63: 73
ASHTON, DORE, "About-Face in Poland," article by, May 61: 20–23
ASHTON, FREDERICK, Sep 60: 94
ASHURBANIPAL, KING OF ASSYRIA, Sep 59: 103
Known world of, Jul 60: 85
ASHURNASIRPAL, KING OF ASSYRIA, Jul 61: 39
Statuette of, Jul 61: 38
ASIMOV, ISAAC, Jan 59: 28
ASPDIN, JOSEPH, Mar 59: 20
ASPEN, COLO., Walter Paepcke at, Sep 58: 96–103, 133–34
ASPREMONT, JOFFROI D', Nov 58: 105
ASSASSINS, Mar 61: 52, 54
"ASSISTANT, THE," novel by Bernard Malamud, Jul 62: 102
ASSOCIATION OF AMERICAN UNIVERSITY PROFESSORS, *Bulletin* of, quoted, Sep 62: 17
ASSOCIATION UTOPIAS, Mar 63: 78
ASSY, FRANCE, Notre-Dame-de-Toute-Grâce, Sep 62: 24
ASSYRIA
Aramaean invasion and conflict with Urartu, Nov 62: 102
Cities of, Jul 61: 38–41
Curses of Esarhaddon, Sep 59: 103–5
Lydian appeals to, Sep 63: 85
Wheeled vehicles used by, Sep 58: 148–49
Winged spirits of, Nov 60: 27
ASTAIRE, ADELE, Sep 58: 59
ASTAIRE, FRED, Sep 58: 59, Jan 61: 48, May 63: 111
ASTOR, JOHN JACOB, on buying land, quoted, Jul 59: 10
ASTOR, NANCY LANGHORNE, visit to Stalin, Nov 58: 20
"ASTRÉE, L'," chronicle, Jan 62: 58
ASTROLABES, Sep 62: 80, 81 (illus), Nov 62: 59
ASTRONOMY
In Moslem Spain, Sep 62: 80, 92
Space and the spirit of man, Jan 59: 26–31, 122–23

Volvelles, Mar 63: 3
ASTYAGES, KING OF THE MEDES, Jan 63: 43
ASWAN DAM, ancient monuments threatened by, Jul 60: 8–15, 124–25
Proposed U.S. contribution to preserve, Sep 61: 14
"AS YOU LIKE IT," play by Shakespeare
Guthrie, Tyrone, quoted on performance of Edith Evans in, Jan 61: 30–31
Source of, Nov 60: 98
"ATALA," romance by Chateaubriand, May 61: 67
"ATELIER TO THE EMPIRE," illustrated feature, Mar 63: 96–101
ATERGATIS, Semitic goddess, Jan 60: 134
ATHENAEUM CLUB OF PHILADELPHIA
And of Boston, compared, Jul 63: 12–13
Literary award given by, Jul 63: 68
ATHENODOROS, May 59: 104, 124
ATHENS, ANCIENT
As city, Jul 61: 42–43
Peloponnesian War, Thucydides' account, Jan 60: 41–45
Trial of Socrates, Jul 60: 100–4, 117
ATHENS, BARONY OF, Mar 63: 31
ATHENS FESTIVAL, Jul 62: 30
ATHERTON, GERTRUDE, *Black Oxen,* quoted, Jul 62: 37
"AT HOME THROUGH THE AGES," drawings by Philippe Julian, Mar 63: 80–83
ATKINSON, BROOKS, quoted
On Beatty, Warren, Jan 62: 104
On Hurst, David, Jan 61: 101
On Jacobs, Jane, Jul 62: 50
On *J.B.,* Jan 60: 49, 51
On Jens, Salome, Jan 62: 103
On Scott, George C., Jul 60: 93
ATLANTIC BLUE RIBAND, Jan 59: 42
ATOMIC ENERGY
James Forrestal Research Center, Sep 59: 26
Rocks as source, Jan 59: 94
ATOTAS, tomb inscription of, May 62: 49
"AT THE TIP OF CAPE COD," article by Robert Hatch, Jul 61: 10–29
ATTILA, KING OF THE HUNS, encounter with Pope Leo I, May 63: 76–80
ATTIS, Sep 63: 84
ATWATER, RICHARD, translation of Procopius by, quoted, Nov 63: 10
ATYS, KING OF LYDIA, May 60: 61
AUBERJONOIS, FERNAND, articles by
"Gislebertus Hoc Fecit," Sep 61: 46–48, 57
"Missing Mourners of Dijon, The," Sep 58: 62–63
AUBERT, GEORGES, Nov 62: 57
AUBREY, JOHN, biography of William Harvey, quoted, May 63: 115
AUBUSSON, PIERRE D', Mar 61: 56
Portrait of, Mar 61: 49
AUCHINCLOSS, DOUGLAS, comment on *Honest to God,* book by John A. T. Robinson, Sep 63: 8–9
AUCTIONS, at Sotheby's, London, Nov 62: 58–67
AUDEN, W. H., Jan 59: 19, Jul 63: 70
"Age of Anxiety, The," Jul 59: 22
On invitation to Kennedy inaugural, quoted, Sep 61: 5
Narration for *The Play of Daniel,* Nov 60: 94; quoted, Nov 60: 95
Phi Beta Kappa poem, quoted, May 63: 86
Photograph of, Nov 60: 90
Thomas, Dylan, quoted on, Sep 58: 84
———— and CHRISTOPHER ISHERWOOD, *Ascent of F-6,* Sep 62: 41
AUDINCOURT, FRANCE, church of Sacré Coeur, Sep 62: 24; illus, Sep 62: 25
AUDLEY END HOUSE, Nov 58: 41 (illus), 51
AUDREY, SAINT, May 60: 128
AUDRY, COLETTE, Jul 63: 74
AUDUBON, JOHN JAMES, Mar 60: 15
AUGUSTA, PRINCESS OF WALES, Jul 63: 105
AUGUSTINE (354–430), SAINT, Nov 59: 57, Jan 60: 68, Jan 63: 58
City of God, The, Nov 62: 81
Commentary on Psalms on palimpsest, Nov 62: 90; illus, Nov 62: 77
Confessions, quoted, Mar 60: 14
AUGUSTUS II, KING OF POLAND, Sep 59: 74
AUGUSTUS III, KING OF POLAND, Mar 62: 50
AUGUSTUS, ROMAN EMPEROR, Nov 58: 111, May 60: 126, Nov 62: 88, Mar 63: 99, Sep 63: 33, 38, 89
At Arles, Jul 59: 130
Autobiography of, Nov 62: 90; illus, Nov 62: 79
Coin portraits of, Sep 63: 36, 39
Law regarding manumission, May 62: 44
Statues of, Jul 59: 98, 129, Sep 60: 70 (illus), Jan 62: 46 (illus)
AUGUSTUS WILLIAM, PRINCE OF PRUSSIA, Nov 58: 86, 143–44
Portrait of, Nov 58: 89
AUMALE, DUC D', Nov 61: 88, Jul 62: 61, 64

"AU MOULIN ROUGE," poster by Picasso, Nov 61: 9
AURELIAN, ROMAN EMPEROR, Sep 63: 40
 Coin portrait of, Sep 63: 36
"AURORA'S WEDDING," ballet, Jan 61: 27
AURTHUR, ROBERT ALAN, Sep 60: 51
AUSTEN, JANE, Mar 60: 127
"AUSTERLITZ," motion picture, Jul 61: 97
AUSTERLITZ, BATTLE OF, Sep 63: 30, 31
AUSTRALIA
 Arrival of James Cook in, Sep 60: 11
 Art in, Sep 62: 97–98
 New York City Ballet tour, Nov 59: 54
 Painting of Sidney Nolan, Sep 62: 96–104
AUSTRALOPITHECUS AFRICANUS, Nov 61: 38, Mar 62: 10–11
AUSTRIA
 As member of Holy Alliance, Mar 63: 5
 In Napoleonic Wars, Sep 63: 30
 Organ (musical instrument) in, Mar 60: 74
 And Thirty Years' War, Nov 62: 33–41
 World War I aftermath, Jan 59: 115, 117, 119, 121
AUTO-BEATNIK POETRY, May 62: 96–99
AUTOGRAPHS
 On menu of Escoffier, May 61: 128
 Morrison, Alfred, collection of, Nov 60: 97
AUTOMATION
 In banks, Sep 62: 120
 Calculating machine invented by Pascal, Jan 63: 97, 99; illus, Jan 63: 95
 In hotels, Mar 63: 115–17
"AUTOMOBILE GRAVEYARD, THE," play, quoted, Sep 62: 36
AUTOMOBILES
 Advertising of, Nov 59: 117, Mar 63: 114
 Fashion cycles in design of, Mar 59: 67, 115–17
 Ford, Henry I and Henry II, dialogue on, Nov 58: 36–37
 Italian, Nov 61: 125
 Junking of, as policy, Nov 62: 114
 "Law of diminishing transportation" and, Sep 58: 152
 Production of, scarcity ideal in, Jul 60: 69
 As "status symbols," Nov 58: 147, Nov 59: 25
 Trojan horseless carriage, Jul 60: 118–19
 Of wealthy, Nov 58: 148
"AUTUMN," painting by Poussin, Mar 61: 93
AUTUN, FRANCE, sculptures of St. Lazare Cathedral, Sep 61: 46–57
"AVANT-GARDE OR BLIND ALLEY?" article by James Marston Fitch, Mar 62: 30–39
AVEMPACE, Sep 62: 88
AVENZOAR, Sep 62: 89
AVERCAM (AVERCAMP), HENDRICK VAN, Sep 58: 26
AVERROËS, Sep 62: 88, 89
 Portrait of, Sep 62: 79
AVERY, MILTON, Jan 59: 105, Jul 61: 28, Jan 62: 8, Jul 62: 15, 20
 Paintings by, Jul 61: 28, Jul 62: 20
 Portrait of, Jul 61: 28
AVERY, SEWELL, Jul 60: 69
AVIATION, See AERONAUTICS; AIRLINES
AVICEBRÓN, Sep 62: 88, 89
AVICENNA, Sep 62: 89, Jan 63: 53
AVIENUS, GENNADIUS, May 63: 79
AVON RIVER, Clifton Bridge over, Jan 59: 36–37
"AVVENTURA, L'," motion picture, Sep 61: 110, 112, May 63: 112
"AWAKE AND SING," play, Nov 62: 106
AXUM, Abyssinian warrior, Mar 63: 53
AYERS, LEMUEL, Jul 61: 98
AYLESFORD, 11TH EARL OF (CHARLES IAN FINCH-KNIGHTLEY), Mar 60: 73
AZECHI, UMETARO, May 60: 114
 Print by, May 60: 107

B

BAALBEK FESTIVAL, Jul 62: 30
BABUR, EMPEROR OF INDIA, Mar 61: 31
 Gardens of, May 59: 27, 44
BABYLON, Jul 61: 41
 Alexander the Great in, Mar 59: 51
 Hanging Gardens of, May 59: 26, 32
BABYLONIA
 Cities of, Jul 61: 38–41
 Fish deities of, Jan 60: 131, 134
BACCARAT, FRANCE, church of St. Rémy, Sep 62: 24; illus, Sep 62: 22
"BACCHANAL WITH A LUTE PLAYER," painting by Poussin, Mar 61: 80
"BACCHANTES," play by Euripides, Sep 63: 84
BACH, JOHANN SEBASTIAN, Jul 60: 62, 64, May 63: 115
 Balanchine, George, quoted on, Jan 61: 47, 48

Beecham, Thomas, quoted on, Mar 62: 103
 Goldberg Variations: copy owned by Rudolf Serkin, Sep 61: 86; Gould, Glenn, quoted on, Jan 62: 89
 Influence on Chopin, May 63: 110
 Organ music of, Mar 60: 74, 79, 80
 Schweitzer, Albert, quoted on, Mar 60: 76
"BACHELOR PARTY, THE," television play and motion picture, Sep 60: 49, 55
BACHMANN, GIDEON, Mar 61: 100
"BACK STREET," motion picture, May 63: 110–11
"BACK TO THE NUDE," article by John Canaday, Sep 63: 90–96
BACON, FRANCIS, Sep 59: 121, Nov 59: 60, Jul 61: 5–6, May 63: 29, Sep 63: 99–100
 New Atlantis, The, Mar 63: 75
 Portrait of, Nov 60: 19
 Quoted: on education, Nov 60: 19–20, 23; on gardens, May 59: 24, 28; on money, May 59: 7
BACON, PEGGY, on Heywood Broun, quoted, Jul 62: 39
BACON, ROGER, Sep 58: 116, Mar 63: 5
 And world's most mysterious manuscript, Jan 63: 4–9
BACTRIA, Mar 59: 47, 52, 58
BADDELEY, HERMIONE, May 63: 108
"BAD SEED, THE," play, Mar 60: 120
BAEZ, JOAN, Sep 62: 66
 Photograph of, Sep 62: 67
BAGBY, PHILIP, Culture and History, Jan 61: 62, 63–64
BÅGÉ, ETIENNE DE, Sep 61: 48, 57
BAGENAL, HOPE, Jul 62: 10
BAGHDAD, IRAQ, Abbasid Caliphate of, Sep 62: 75, 77, Nov 63: 26
BAGNANI, GILBERT, on classical revival of 18th century, quoted, Mar 62: 50
BAHRAM I, KING OF PERSIA, Jan 63: 51
BAHRAM GUR, garden of, May 59: cover, 3
BAHREIN ISLAND, Bronze Age road of, Jul 60: 86–87
BAHUR, INDIA, dance sculptures at, Sep 63: 72
BAILLIE, ISOBEL, Jan 60: 10
BAIRD, DAVID, Sep 60: 21
BAKER, CARLOS
 "Expanding Universe at Old Nassau, The," article by, Sep 59: 22–27, 118–19
 Friend in Power, Sep 60: 119
BAKER, FRED, Nov 62: 98, 99
BAKER, JOSEPHINE, Jan 61: 49
BAKER, NEWTON D., May 62: 8
BAKER, ROGER, in paintings by John Koch, Sep 60: 106, 108
BAKST, LEON, Jan 61: 27, 28
BAKUNIN, ALEXANDER, Sep 60: 134–35
"BALADINS, LES," painting by Picasso, Nov 61: 4; illus, Nov 61: 5
BALANCHINE, GEORGE, Sep 58: 60, Nov 59: 53, 54, 56, Jul 62: 10
 Interview with, Jan 61: 44–56
 Photographs of, Jan 61: 44–45, Sep 61: 16
BALBINUS, DECIMUS CAELIUS, ROMAN EMPEROR, Sep 63: 40
"BALCONY, THE," play, May 61: 50–51, Jul 61: 116, Nov 61: 99, Jan 62: 103, Sep 62: 34, Mar 63: 107
BALDICK, ROBERT, Pages from the Goncourt Journal, reviewed, Sep 62: 112–14
"BALD SOPRANO, THE," play, Nov 58: 63, Jan 61: 101, May 61: 89, 90, 91, Sep 62: 41
 Salome Jens in, Jan 62: 103
BALDWIN I, EMPEROR OF CONSTANTINOPLE (BALDWIN OF FLANDERS), Nov 63: 31
 In painting by Delacroix, Nov 63: 26–27
BALDWIN II, EMPEROR OF CONSTANTINOPLE, Nov 63: 31
BALDWIN II, KING OF JERUSALEM, Mar 61: 52
BALDWIN, JAMES, Jan 62: 8
 Alfred Kazin quoted on, Jul 62: 101, 102
BALDWIN, T. W., Jan 60: 92
BALI, INDONESIA, Mar 61: 23–24, 28, 31
BALKAN PENINSULA, Nov 63: 28, 31
"BALL," "happening" by Robert Whitman, Nov 62: 114
BALL, LUCILLE, May 63: 111
"BALLAD OF A SOLDIER," motion picture, Mar 62: 110–11
"BALLAD OF BABY DOE," opera, Jan 60: 14, 16, 122
"BALLAD OF THE SAD CAFÉ," by Carson McCullers, Sep 61: 79
BALLARD, KAYE, May 63: 46
BALLARD, LUCINDA, Jan 60: 51
BALLET
 Balanchine, George, Jan 61: 44–56
 At Bauhaus, Nov 61: 62, 71
 Denmark's Royal Ballet, Sep 60: 90–95
 Diaghilev company, Tyrone Guthrie quoted on, Jan 61: 27–28
 Equestrian, Nov 59: 3; illus, Nov 59: 2
 Kent, Allegra, Nov 59: 52–56
 In musical comedy, Sep 58: 60

San Francisco Ballet, Jan 59: 6
"BALLET BALLADS," television show, May 63: 49
"BALLETS AFRICAINS, LES," Jul 59: 49
BALLOONING, Sep 58: 114–28
BALTARD, VICTOR, May 63: 68
"BALTHAZAR," novel by Lawrence Durrell, Mar 60: 114, 117–18
 Excerpt from, Mar 60: 115
BALTIMORE, MD., Peabody Conservatory, and Ford Foundation's Humanities and the Arts program, Jan 62: 9
BALTIMORE, 6TH LORD (FREDERICK CALVERT), May 59: 62
BALZAC, HONORÉ DE, Jan 59: 103, May 61: 81, Jan 62: 97
 Adler, Edward, compared to, Sep 62: 65
 Aventures du Bon Roy Loys XI, Les, illustrations by André François for, May 59: 114–15
 Gambara, quoted, Jan 59: 124
 As idol of New Wave in French motion pictures, May 60: 51, 52
"BANBURY NOSE, THE," play, Nov 58: 137
BANCHIERI, ADRIANO, Nov 60: 89–90, 91
BANCROFT, ANNE, Nov 62: 108
BANCROFT, FREDERIC, Sep 63: 101
BANCROFT, MRS. THOMAS M., JR., Jul 60: 122
BANCROFT HISTORY AWARD, Jul 63: 68
"BAND WAGON, THE," musical, Sep 58: 59
BANGKOK, THAILAND, U.S. embassy building, Jan 60: 120
"BANG THE DRUM SLOWLY," book by Mark Harris, Jan 59: 19
BANHAM, REYNER, "The Newest Invasion of Europe," article by, Nov 60: 12–16, 124–25
BANISTER, JOHN, Nov 62: 43
BANKS
 Automation in, Sep 62: 120
 Your friendly fidvciary, Mar 61: 120–21
BANKS, JOSEPH, May 59: 129, Jul 59: 58, Sep 63: 42
BANQUETING HOUSE, of Whitehall Palace, London, Jul 61: 90, 91
"BAPTISM OF CHRIST," painting by Poussin, Mar 61: 89
"BARABBAS," motion picture, Mar 63: 109–11
"BARABBAS," novel by Pär Lagerkvist, Mar 63: 109–10
BARANTE, BARON DE (AMABLE GUILLAUME PROSPER BRUGIÈRE), Mar 59: 94
BARATTOLO, GENNARO, photograph of, Sep 63: 57
BARBARI, JACOPO DE', Sep 59: 131
BARBARIGO, AUGUSTINO, Jul 63: 50, 53, 57
BARBER, SAMUEL, Mar 61: 72
 On duo-pianists Arthur Gold and Robert Fizdale, quoted, Mar 61: 75
 Portrait of, Jan 60: 14
 Vanessa, Nov 58: 120, Jan 60: 15, 17, 122, 123
BARBERINI, FRANCESCO, CARDINAL, Mar 61: 79, Jul 63: 94
BARBERINI, PRINCESS, Nov 63: 63
BARBERINI VASE. See PORTLAND VASE
BARCELONA, SPAIN, Mar 59: 78, 126
 Church of Sagrada Familia, Sep 59: 7
 German pavilion of 1929, Sep 59: 18
 Park Güell seats, Nov 59: 111
BARDOT, BRIGITTE, May 59: 98, 99, May 60: 49, 52
BARENTS, WILLEM, Sep 58: 19
"BARGAINING IN THE ARAB WORLD," excerpt from The Silent Language, book by Edward T. Hall, May 59: 136
BARING, FRANCIS, Jul 63: 106
BARNARD, GEORGE GREY, Jul 59: 28
BARNES, ALBERT C., Jul 63: 22–23
 Photograph of, Jul 63: 22
BARNES, COURTLANDT D., JR., Sep 58: 134
BARNES, EDWARD W., The Rise of Christianity, Sep 63: 8–9
BARNETT, LINCOLN, "Who Is Behind the Assault on English?" article by, Jul 63: 33–48
BARNEY, NATALIE, Nov 61: 37
BARNSTABLE, MASS., Mar 60: 70
BARNUM, PHINEAS T., Jan 59: 25
BAROMETER, ANEROID, Pascal's statement of principle of, Jan 63: 100
BARONOVICH, VINCENT, Sep 60: 26
BAROQUE AGE, Jul 60: 33–64
 Architecture, Jul 60: 35, 42, 50
 Cherubim, Nov 60: 36–37 (illus)
 Cities, Jul 61: 52–53; Amsterdam, Jul 61: 58–59; squares and crescents in, Jul 61: 54–55
 Fountains, May 62: 13–15
 Handwriting, Sep 59: 127
 Influence of victory at Lepanto, Jul 63: 60
 Music, Mar 60: 76–77, Jul 60: 62, 64
 Mysticism, Jul 60: 38
 Ornamental cups, May 61: 2
 Painting, Jul 60: 38, 42, 50, 64

Philosophy, Jul 60: 36, 38
Poetry, Jul 60: 42, 50
"BAROQUE AGE, THE," article by Carl J. Friedrich, Jul 60: 33–64
BARR, ALFRED H., JR., May 59: 10, Nov 59: 121, Nov 60: 8
On Paul Klee, quoted, Nov 61: 65
BARR, DONALD, on J. D. Salinger, quoted, May 62: 101
BARR, RICHARD, on "absurd" plays, quoted, Sep 62: 40
BARRAS, PAUL FRANÇOIS JEAN NICOLAS DE, Mar 59: 94
BARRAULT, JEAN-LOUIS, Nov 60: 52, May 61: 93
Photographs of, Sep 61: 102–3, 108
"Why the French Need Shakespeare," article by, Sep 61: 102–9
BARRÈS, MAURICE, on funeral of Victor Hugo, quoted, Nov 59: 66–67
BARRIAS, LOUIS ERNEST, Mar 62: 99
BARRIE, J. M.
Shaw, G. B., quoted on, Nov 58: 134–35
Window in Thrums, A, quoted, Mar 63: 26–27
BARRINGTON, BIJOU, Nov 58: 138
BARRINGTON, PATRICK, "Platypus," quoted, Sep 58: 130–31
BARRYMORE, DIANA, Too Much, Too Soon, book about, Jul 60: 120
BARRYMORE, JOHN, Jul 60: 93
Photograph of, Sep 63: 78
BARRYMORE, 7TH EARL OF (RICHARD BARRY), Mar 62: 81–82, Nov 62: 23
BARSACQ, ANDRÉ, Nov 60: 52
BARSINE, wife of Alexander the Great, Mar 59: 38, 53
BARTH, JOHN, Jan 63: 37
Photograph of, Jan 63: 36
BARTH, KARL, Sep 63: 107
BARTHES, ROLAND, on Alain Robbe-Grillet, quoted, Jan 62: 100
BARTHOLOMEW, FREDDY, Sep 63: 77 (note)
BARTÓK, BÉLA, Jan 59: 125, Jan 61: 47–48, Nov 62: 46
BARZUN, JACQUES, Jan 60: 10, Jul 63: 41, 42 (note)
"Diller, a Dollar, a Very Expensive Scholar, A," article by, Sep 63: 60–63
Pleasures of Music, edited by, quoted, Jan 59: 124
Quoted: on ignorance of unlettered and of educated, Jul 63: 36; on university teaching situation, Sep 62: 16, 18–19
BASALDELLA, AFRO. See AFRO
BASEL, SWITZERLAND, Fastnacht, Mar 59: 84
BASIL I, BYZANTINE EMPEROR, Nov 63: 28
BASIL II BULGAROCTONOS, BYZANTINE EMPEROR, Nov 63: 28, 34
BASKERVILLE, JOHN, May 59: 92
BASSERMANN, ALBERT, Mar 62: 118–19
BASTILLE
Fall of, May 60: 124
Pleasures of, Jan 60: 83–88, 128
Storming of, Jan 60: 83, 128
Voltaire in, Mar 61: 117
BATAILLE, NICOLAS, May 61: 91
BATE, STANLEY, photograph of, May 60: 15
BATES, EDWARD, Jan 59: 25
BATES, ERNEST SUTHERLAND, Mar 61: 94
BATH, ENGLAND, Jul 61: 54–55
BATHS, TURKISH, of Near East, Sep 60: 125–26
BATHS OF ANCIENT ROME, May 60: 39–41
BATTEN, BARTON, DURSTINE & OSBORN, Nov 58: 33
"BATTLE OF LEPANTO," painting by Vincentino, Mar 63: 14
"BATTLE OF THE BARDS, THE," article by Donald Hall, Sep 61: 116–21
BATY, GASTON, Sep 61: 102
BAUDELAIRE, CHARLES PIERRE, May 63: 54
Kennedy, Mrs. John F., quoted on, Sep 61: 9
In painting by Manet, May 63: 74
Quoted: on art, Jul 61: 8; on childhood, Mar 59: 72, 74; on Delacroix, May 61: 74; on sensation, May 62: 105
BAUDIER, MICHEL, on Turkish court, quoted, May 59: 58, 59–60, 135
BAUER, RUDOLF, May 59: 10, 11
BAUHAUS, of Weimar and Dessau, Germany, Sep 59: 18, Nov 59: 48, Nov 61: 58–75
"BAUHAUS, THE," article by Wolf Von Eckardt, Nov 61: 58–75
BAULÉ TRIBE, of Africa, Mar 63: 41 (map), 46, 56
BAUM, VICKI, A Tale from Bali, Mar 61: 24, 31
BAVARIA, GERMANY
Castles of Ludwig II, Jan 61: 34–43
Prehistoric wheeled vehicles, Sep 58: 147
Witch mania, Nov 59: 61, 62
BAWDEN, EDWARD, painting by, May 62: 77
BAYER, HERBERT, Sep 58: 134, Nov 59: 48, Nov 61: 61, 71–72, 73, 74
Photographs of, Nov 61: 59, 74
On type styles, quoted, Nov 61: 69
Works by. See ILLUSTRATIONS INDEX

BAYON, TEMPLE OF, Jan 59: 62, 63, 64
"BAYONETS MENACING A FLOWER," mobile by Alexander Calder, Nov 62: 16
BAY PSALM BOOK, Nov 60: 97
BAYREUTH, GERMANY, opera at, Nov 58: 23–24, 27, Mar 59: 85, May 63: 40–45
BAZAINE, JEAN, Sep 62: 24
Stained-glass windows designed by, Sep 62: 25
BAZENTIN, LORD OF, Nov 58: 105
BAZIN, ANDRÉ, May 60: 51
BAZIOTES, WILLIAM, May 59: 11, Sep 60: 122
BEAKER PEOPLE, Jul 60: 90, 91
BEAN, G. E., Nov 58: 66
BEARD, CHARLES and MARY, Sep 63: 101
BEARDSLEY, AUBREY, Jul 60: 94
BEAT GENERATION
In American arts, Sep 58: 38–45, 134–35
Beatniks as enemies of language, Jul 63: 39
In literature, Jan 63: 74
Poetry of: Academics vs., Sep 61: 116–21; Auto-Beatnik, May 62: 96–99; Kazin, Alfred, quoted on, Jul 62: 101
Search for alienation by, Jan 60: 7
Zen Buddhism and, Jul 59: 71
BEATON, CECIL. See ILLUSTRATIONS INDEX
BEATTY, WARREN, Jan 62: 104
Photograph of, Jan 62: 105
BEAU BRUMMELL. See BRUMMELL, GEORGE BRYAN
BEAUDRIGUE, DAVID DE, Mar 61: 119
BEAUHARNAIS, HORTENSE DE, QUEEN OF HOLLAND, May 63: 54
BEAUHARNAIS, JOSÉPHINE DE, Nov 59: 86
Letter from Napoleon to, facsimile, Sep 59: 136
BEAUMANOIR, SIRE DE, Nov 58: 95
BEAUMONT THEATER. See VIVIAN BEAUMONT THEATER
BEAUPÈRE, JEAN, Mar 62: 91
"BEAU SERGE, LE," motion picture, May 60: 50, 52–53
"BEAUTIES," paintings by Peter Lely, Jul 63: 96
"BEAUTY AND THE BEAST," motion picture, Mar 61: 98
BEAUTY CULTURE, mechanization of, Nov 62: 115
BEAUVOIR, SIMONE DE, Jan 62: 111, 112
BEAUX, CECILIA, Jul 63: 18
BECK, JULIAN, and the Living Theatre, Mar 62: 106–9
BECKE, LOUIS, Jan 60: 125
BECKER, JACQUES, May 60: 51
BECKER, JOHN J., Jul 59: 20
"BECKET," play, Nov 60: 51, 52, 54, 127
BECKETT, SAMUEL, Sep 60: 112–16, Jan 61: 113, Jul 61: 116, Jan 62: 100, May 62: 112, Sep 62: 34, 35–36, 37, 41, Jan 63: 32
Endgame, Mar 63: 107
Ionesco, Eugène, quoted on, May 61: 91, 95
Waiting for Godot, Nov 58: 62, 63–64
BECKFORD, PETER, Nov 58: 52, Nov 59: 86
On foreign language problems, quoted, Nov 59: 84
BECKFORD, WILLIAM, Nov 61: 44
Fonthill Abbey, designed for, Mar 62: 62; illus, Mar 62: 36, Mar 63: 81
"BEDELIA," song, Mar 60: 28
BEDFORD, DUCHESS OF, 15th century, Mar 62: 91
BEDFORD, DUCHESS OF, 18th century, Nov 58: 46
BEDFORD, DUKE OF (JOHN OF LANCASTER), Nov 61: 97, Mar 62: 96
BEDFORD, 13TH DUKE OF (JOHN ROBERT RUSSELL), Jan 59: 59, 127
BEDFORD, DUKES OF, Nov 58: 50, 51
BEDMAR, MARQUIS OF, Nov 62: 36
BEDS THROUGH THE AGES, May 60: 129–36
BEEBE, LUCIUS, "Richesse Oblige," editorial by, reprinted from The Territorial Enterprise, Nov 58: 148
BEECHAM, THOMAS, Sep 59: 52, 55, Mar 62: 102–5
Brenner, Engelbert, quoted on, Jul 59: 17
Photograph of, Mar 62: 102
BEECHER, HENRY WARD, Jan 59: 25
BEECHEY, WILLIAM, Jul 63: 106
BEER, SAMUEL H., on university teaching situation, quoted, Sep 62: 17–18, 19
BEERBOHM, MAX, Jul 60: 96, May 61: 33–40, Jan 62: 52
On Beau Brummel, quoted, Mar 62: 63
Caricatures by, May 61: 34, 35, 36–37, 38–39
Self-caricature, May 61: 33
Zuleika Dobson, Sep 60: 119, May 61: 38
"BEER-BOTTLE ON THE PEDIMENT," article by Gilbert Highet, Jul 61: 116–18
BEETHOVEN, LUDWIG VAN, Sep 60: 121, May 61: 66, 70, 82, 84, Mar 62: 78, 81, 82
G Major Concerto (No. 4), Sep 61: 84, 85
Gould, Glenn, quoted on, Jan 62: 93
Music of, compared with tape recorder music, Jan 59: 124, 125
Stravinsky, Igor, quoted on, Sep 58: 84, 132
String quartets of, Nov 62: 44, 45, 46, 47

"BEFORE THE ARGO," article by Geoffrey Bibby, Jul 60: 84–91, 113
BEGOE, Etruscan deity, May 60: 62
BÉGON, MICHEL, May 60: 127
"BEGUM'S FORTUNE, THE," book by Jules Verne, Mar 63: 77–78
BEHAN, BRENDAN, Jan 61: 113–14
Hostage, The, Mar 61: 44–45
Quare Fellow, The, Mar 60: 120, 121
"BEHIND THE GOLDEN CURTAIN," article by Joseph Wechsberg, Nov 58: 23–27, 133
BEHRENS, PETER, Nov 60: 124, Nov 61: 61–62
BEHRMAN, S. N., Sep 58: 60, May 61: 56
BEIBARS, SULTAN OF TURKEY, Mar 61: 54
BEIDERBECKE, BIX, Jan 63: 75
BEIT-NUBA, PALESTINE, in Third Crusade, Jan 59: 130, 131
BEKKER, BALTHASAR, Nov 59: 62
BELAFONTE, HARRY, Mar 60: 128, May 63: 49
BELAIEV, M. P., Nov 62: 44
BELASCO, DAVID, Nov 58: 120
Box-stage used by, Jul 59: 44
BELDIBI, TURKEY, archaeological site, Sep 62: 8
BEL GEDDES, BARBARA, May 59: 55, Jul 59: 42
BEL GEDDES, NORMAN, Futurama City of, Jul 59: 5, 12
BELGIUM (see also BRUSSELS)
Fleisher, Leon, in, Jan 60: 76
Reaction to American abstract expressionism, Nov 59: 120
And Thirty Years' War, Nov 62: 33, 34, 38, 41
BELL, CLIVE, Jan 60: 107, Jan 61: 113
André Malraux compared to, Nov 58: 12, 115
BELL, HELEN, Mar 60: 13
BELL, VANESSA, Jan 60: 107
BELLA, STEFANO DELLA, Nov 59: 3
Drawing by, Nov 59: 2
BELLAMY, EDWARD, Looking Backward, Mar 63: 78
BELLANGER, MARGUERITE, May 63: 69
BELLANTE, ERNO, May 59: 104
BELLINI, GIOVANNI, Sep 61: 44, Mar 61: 80, 91
BELLOC, HILAIRE
Cautionary Verses, May 62: 103
On Oxford, quoted, Jan 63: 87
Verse by, quoted, Jul 61: 114
BELLOW, SAUL, Jan 62: 8
Articles on motion pictures by: "Adrift on a Sea of Gore," Mar 63: 109–11; "Art of Going it Alone, The," Sep 62: 108–10; "Buñuel's Unsparing Vision," Nov 62: 110–12; "Mass-produced Insight, The," Jan 63: 111–13
Kazin, Alfred, quoted on, Jul 62: 101, 102
Upper Depths, The, May 63: 14
"BELLS OF ST. MARY'S, THE," motion picture, Mar 60: 127
BELLUSCHI, PIETRO, Jan 60: 27, 119, Jul 62: 8, Jan 63: 13
Photograph of, Jul 62: 7
BELMONDO, JEAN-PAUL, Nov 61: 116, May 62: 81, Jan 63: 38
Photograph of, Nov 61: 117
BELMONT, AUGUST, Nov 58: 148
BELMONTE, JUAN, Jan 59: 133
BELOOF, ROBERT, Jan 59: 18
"BELOVED INFIDEL," book about Sheilah Graham, Jul 60: 120
BELVEDERE APOLLO, sculpture, Jan 62: 48; illus, Jan 62: 47
BELVEDERE TORSO, sculpture by Apollonius, Jan 62: 32; illus, Jan 62: 36
BEMBO, PIETRO, Jan 60: 68
BENAKIS, ALEXANDER, Nov 58: 76
BENCHLEY, ROBERT, Jul 62: 33, 34–36, 37, May 63: 46, Jul 63: 119
"Another Uncle Edith Christmas Story," quoted, Sep 58: 130
Caricature of, Jul 62: 32
BENDINER, ROBERT, "The Non-Teachers," article by, Sep 62: 14–19
BENEDICT XV, POPE, Mar 62: 98
BÉNÉDITE, GEORGES, Jul 60: 10
BENÉT, STEPHEN VINCENT, Mar 63: 28, 30
Devil and Daniel Webster, The, Jan 60: 122
Guggenheim Fellowship of, May 59: 9
John Brown's Body, May 59: 9, Sep 63: 101
Photograph of, May 59: 16
BENÉT, WILLIAM ROSE, Mar 63: 28, 30
BENEVOLI, ORAZIO, Jul 60: 64
"BEN-HUR," motion picture, May 61: 52, 53, 56–57, Mar 63: 109, 110
Paddy Chayefsky quoted on, Sep 60: 56
BENIN, NIGERIA, Mar 63: 41 (map)
Sculpture of, Mar 63: 46, 49, 51, 58 (illus); auctioned at Sotheby's, Nov 62: 59
BENNETT, ALAN, Mar 63: 109
BENNETT, ARNOLD, May 61: 35, Sep 63: 98
BENNETT, JAMES GORDON, Jan 59: 24

On S.S. *Great Western*, quoted, Jan 59: 41
BENNIGSEN, LEVIN A. P., Sep 63: 29, 31
BENNION, PEGGY, Nov 60: 116
BENOIS, NADIA. See USTINOV, NADIA BENOIS
BENOIST, ANDRÉ, Sep 59: 89
BENOIT, FERNAND, quoted, Nov 58: 77
BENTHAM, JEREMY
  Childhood of, May 60: 34, 35, 37
  Portrait of, May 60: 32
BENTLEY, ERIC, May 62: 35
  Adaptation of *A Man's a Man*, Mar 63: 107
  On melodramatic art, quoted, May 63: 106
BENTLEY, THOMAS
  As member of Josiah Wedgwood's group, May 59: 90–96, 128–30
  Portrait of, May 59: 90
BENTON, THOMAS HART, Jul 60: 114, Jul 62: 19
BENUZZI, FELICE, Sep 58: 137
BERANEK, LEO, Jul 62: 10
BÉRARD, CHRISTIAN, Sep 62: 111
BERBERS
  In Moslem Spain, Sep 62: 87, 88
  In Sicily, Sep 61: 28
BERCHEM, NICOLAES PIETERSZ, Jul 63: 106
BERCKHEYDE, GERRIT, painting by, Jul 61: 58
BERDYAEV, NICOLAS, on utopias, quoted. Mar 63: 73
BERENGARIA, QUEEN OF ENGLAND, Jan 59: 87
BERENSON, BERNARD, Mar 61: 22
  As advisor on Gardner collection, Jul 59: 28–32
  On Gardner, Isabella Stewart, quoted, Jul 59: 134
  Photographs of, Jul 59: 28, 29
BERG, ALBAN, Nov 58: 25, 26
  Stravinsky, Igor, quoted on, Sep 58: 132
  Wozzeck, Jan 60: 12–13; Thomas Beecham quoted on, Mar 62: 103
BERGER, JEAN-JACQUES, May 63: 64
BERGER, YVES, Jul 63: 74
BERGHOF, HERBERT, Jan 62: 103
BERGMAN, INGMAR, Nov 62: 110, Mar 62: 98, Mar 63: 35
  "Why I Make Movies," article by, Sep 60: 4–9
BERGMAN, INGRID, Sep 63: 80
BERGUES, LORD OF, Sep 58: 105
BERING, VITUS, Sep 59: 80
BERKELEY, CALIF., Christian Science Church, Jan 59: 10
BERKELEY, GEORGE, on America, quoted, May 61: 10
BERKELEY, R. G., Nov 62: 65
"BERKELEY IN TIME OF PLAGUE," poem by Jack Spicer, quoted, Jan 59: 19
BERLIN, GERMANY
  Airlift Memorial, May 61: 42; illus, May 61: 45
  Kleine Freiheit, Nov 58: 62
  Musical life of 1920's, Sep 61: 84
  State opera, Nov 58: 23–24, 133
  Tall buildings of West Berlin, Nov 60: 16
BERLIN, IRVING, Sep 58: 61
BERLINER ENSEMBLE, May 62: 35, 40
BERLIOZ, HECTOR, Sep 59: 53, May 61: 82–83, Sep 61: 105, May 63: 109, 110
  Portrait of, May 61: 82
BERMAN, EUGENE, Nov 58: 120
BERMAN, LEVI, Jan 59: 112, 121
BERNADOTTE, JEAN, Nov 58: 142
BERNANOS, GEORGES, Mar 62: 99
BERNARD, M., Nov 58: 142
BERNARD, PAUL, photograph of, Nov 62: 42
BERNARD DE CLUNY, Nov 63: 47
BERNARDI, THEODORE, Jan 59: 22
BERNARD OF CLAIRVAUX, SAINT, on church buildings, quoted, Sep 61: 57, Jan 62: 24
BERNAYS, EDWARD L., Jul 60: 121, Nov 60: 117
BERNHARD OF BREYDENBACH, Mar 60: 85–86, 89
  Peregrinatio in Terram Sanctam, woodcuts from, Mar 60: 86; illus, Mar 60: 81–89
BERNHARDT, SARAH, Jan 61: 27, May 61: 125
  Portraits of, May 60: 135, Jan 61: 28, Sep 61: 106–7
BERNIER, FRANÇOIS, Jul 59: 53
BERNINI, GIOVANNI LORENZO, Jul 60: 38, Sep 60: 69, Jul 61: 90, Sep 61: 74, 77, Jan 62: 43, 45, May 62: 12, 14, Jul 63: 93, 106
  On Poussin, quoted, Mar 61: 80, 91
  Works by. See ILLUSTRATIONS INDEX
BERNOULLI, DANIEL, Sep 59: 80
BERNSTEIN, LEONARD, Sep 58: 144, Jan 60: 11, Jul 60: 122, Jul 61: 98, Jan 62: 9, Jul 62: 30
  Age of Anxiety, Jan 60: 79
  As music director of New York Philharmonic, Jul 59: 16–23
  Photographs of, Jul 59: 16, 20–21, Jan 60: 9
  On television, Mar 60: 5, 126
BERNSTEIN, MAURICE, Jul 63: 86, 89
"BERNSTEIN SUITE, A," article by Henry Anatole Grunwald, Jul 59: 16–23

BEROSUS, on fish-god, quoted, Jan 60: 131
BERRY, DUC DE (JEAN DE FRANCE), Sep 60: 60–61, Nov 61: 97
  Book of Hours of, May 61: 113; illus from, Sep 60: 63
BERRYER, NICOLAS-RENÉ, Jan 60: 88
BERRYMAN, JOHN, Sep 61: 117
BERTELLI, FERRANDO, engraving by, Jul 63: 54–55
BERTIN, LOUIS-FRANÇOIS, portrait by Ingres, Jan 59: 95; illus, Jan 59: 95
BERTOIA, HARRY, Sep 59: 18
  Screen designed by, Sep 59: 13
BERTONOV, JEHOSHUA, Jan 61: 33
BERTRAM, COLIN, on polar exploration, quoted, Sep 58: 138
BESBORODKO, COUNT, Sep 60: 129
BESOYAN, RICK, Sep 60: 87
  Photograph of, Sep 60: 86
BESSUS, PRINCE OF BACTRIA, Mar 59: 40, 47
BEST, MARSHALL, Jan 62: 14
BESTIARY, MODERN, Jul 62: 120–28
"BEST YEARS OF OUR LIVES, THE," motion picture, May 62: 8
BETHEL, ME., Laboratory in Group Development, Nov 58: 32, 33
BÉTHUNE, MAXIMILIEN DE. See SULLY, DUC DE
"BETONGLAS," Sep 62: 24
"BETWEEN MEALS," book by A. J. Liebling, May 63: 21
BEVAN, ANEURIN, in painting by Feliks Topolski, Nov 60: 131
BEVAN, EDWYN, quoted, Sep 63: 6
"BEVERLY HILLBILLIES," television show, Mar 63: 114
BEVINGTON, HELEN, *When Found, Make a Verse of,* Sep 61: 115
"BEYOND THE FRINGE," revue, Mar 63: 108–9
"BE YOUR AGE," play, Sep 60: 88
BIALIK, CHAIM, Jan 61: 32–33
BIANCHI, MARTHA, Jul 61: 100
BIBBY, GEOFFREY, "Before the Argo," article by, Jul 60: 84–91, 113
BIBLE (see also GOSPELS)
  Attitude toward nature in Old Testament, Mar 60: 13
  Codex Sinaiticus, Nov 62: 94; illus, Nov 62: 82
  Codex Vaticanus, Jan 62: 27, Nov 62: 82
  As divining rod in archaeology, Nov 59: 4–10, 118–19
  Genesis, quoted, Sep 58: 66
  Illustrations from ancient paintings and artifacts, Nov 59: 11–19
  Messengers, or angels, of, Nov 60: 28–29
  Nazarene Gospel, The, by Robert Graves, Jan 62: 54
  New English version of New Testament, Mar 61: 94–97, Jul 63: 40
  Old Testament paintings of Shalom Moskovitz, Jul 61: 120–28
  Proverbs, quoted, Jan 59: 47
  Septuagint, Nov 62: 78
  Solomon's Song of Songs, and Sumerian love songs, Jul 63: 108–9
  Translations of Jerome, Erasmus and Luther, May 62: 92
"BIBLE AS DIVINING ROD, THE," article by Nelson Glueck, Nov 59: 4–10, 118–19
"BIBLE IS GIVEN NEW SPEECH, THE," article by Gilbert Highet, Mar 61: 94–97
BICKHAM, GEORGE, Sep 59: 127
BICYCLES, in Italy, Nov 61: 125
"BICYCLE THIEF, THE," motion picture, May 59: 99, Mar 61: 98, 100
BIDDLE, ANTHONY J. DREXEL, in group photograph, Jul 63: 17
BIDDLE, ANTHONY J. DREXEL, JR., in group photograph, Jul 63: 16
BIDDLE, CORDELIA, *My Philadelphia Father,* Jul 63: 17
BIDDLE, EDWARD, in group photograph, Jul 63: 17
BIDDLE, FRANCIS, in group photograph, Jul 63: 17
BIDDLE, GEORGE, Jul 63: 18
  On Philadelphia, quoted, Jul 63: 18
BIDDLE, MARGARET THOMPSON, Sep 61: 14
BIDDLE, NICHOLAS (1786–1844), Jul 63: 16–17
BIDDLE, NICHOLAS, JR., photograph of, Jul 63: 16
BIDDLE, WILLIAM, Jul 63: 16
BIDDLE FAMILY, of Philadelphia, Jul 63: 9, 17, 25
  Group photograph of, Jul 63: 16–17
BIEBER, MARGARET, on Laocoön group, quoted, May 59: 104
BIENEFELD, HEINZ, Sep 62: 24
  Stained-glass wall designed by, Sep 62: 30–31
"BIG DEAL, THE," musical, Jan 62: 70
"BIG DEAL, THE," play, Sep 60: 54, 56
"BIG DEAL ON MADONNA STREET," motion picture, Jan 63: 38
BIGELOW, WILLIAM STURGIS, Jul 59: 133
BIGGIN, GEORGE, Sep 58: 118–19
BIGGS, E. POWER

"King of Instruments Returns, The," article by, Mar 60: 72–80
  Photographs of, Mar 60: 78
BIG SUR, CALIF., Jan 59: 7, 18
BIHZAD, Persian miniaturist, Jan 63: 67
BILLBOARD INDUSTRY, May 61: 4, 5, 18
BILLBOARDS, of U.S. and U.S.S.R. compared, Jul 62: 118–19
BILLINGS, GLADYS RICE, May 60: 27
BILLINGSLEY, MARTIN, Sep 59: 127
BING, RUDOLPH, Nov 58: 118, 120, Sep 59: 51, 53, Mar 61: 72, Sep 61: 83, Jan 62: 13
  Attitude toward American singers, Nov 61: 78, 80
BINGHAM, ANNE WILLING (MRS. WILLIAM), portrait of, Jul 63: 9
BINGHAM, MILLICENT TODD, on Emily Dickinson, quoted, Jul 61: 100, 102, 104, 105
BIOGRAPHY
  Pulitzer Prize in, Jul 63: 71, 72
  Of Shaw, G. B., by Hesketh Pearson, writing of, Nov 58: 18–21, 134–37
BIOLOGY
  Effect of mechanistic theory on, Jul 61: 8
  Population increase and earth use, Sep 58: 48–55
"BIRD," sculptures by Constantin Brancusi, Mar 60: 108
BIRD, ISABELLA, Sep 58: 11–12
BIRD, J. MALCOLM, Jan 59: 108, 109
"BIRDMAN OF ALCATRAZ," motion picture, Mar 63: 35
"BIRD OF PARADISE, A," play, Jan 60: 125
"BIRDS FROM MY HOMELAND," woodcut book by Antonio Frasconi, Mar 61: 123; illus from, Mar 61: 126–27
BIRMINGHAM, ENGLAND, Philadelphia compared to, Jul 63: 13
BIRMINGHAM, MICH., office of Eero Saarinen at, Jul 60: 77
BIRTH CONTROL. See POPULATION CONTROL
"BIRTHDAY PARTY, THE," play, Jan 63: 31
"BIRTH OF AN ART FORM," photographs, Jan 59: 144
"BIRTH OF A NATION, THE," motion picture, Mar 60: 127
"BIRTH OF VENUS," painting by Alexandre Cabanel, Mar 60: 57
BISCHOFF, ELMER, Jan 59: 13, 14, Jul 60: 16, 114–16, Jul 62: 24, Sep 63: 96
  Drawing of, Jul 60: 115
  Works by. See ILLUSTRATIONS INDEX
BISHOP, MORRIS, "Pascal," article by, with photographs by Erich Lessing, Jan 63: 94–104
"BISHOP OF LIMPOPOLAND, THE," skit by Peter Ustinov, Nov 58: 85
BISMARCK, OTTO EDUARD LEOPOLD VON, PRINCE, Sep 59: 126, Sep 62: 21, May 63: 73
BITTER, KARL, Sep 60: 127
  Sculpture by, Sep 60: 103
"BITTER LEMONS," poems by Lawrence Durrell, Mar 60: 114
BIUMO, PANZA DI, Nov 59: 120
BIZET, GEORGES, Mar 62: 75
BLACK ALI, May 59: 60
"BLACKBOARD JUNGLE," motion picture, May 59: 101
BLACKBURN, HENRY, *Academy Notes,* quoted, May 62: 73
BLACKBURN, JACK, Jan 59: 134
BLACKBURN, ROBERT, Nov 60: 116
"BLACKCOCK," painting by Edwin Landseer, Mar 60: 58; illus, Mar 60: 68
BLACK DEATH, aftermath of, in England, Mar 61: 65
"BLACKLISTING, REPORT ON," by John Cogley, Mar 60: 48
BLACK MOUNTAIN COLLEGE, as poetry center, Sep 61: 117, 119, 121
BLACKMUR, R. P., photograph of, Sep 59: 24
"BLACK ORPHEUS," motion picture, May 60: 50, 53–54, 55, Nov 62: 109
"BLACK OXEN," novel by Gertrude Atherton, quoted, Jul 62: 37
"BLACKS, THE," play, Nov 61: 98, 99–102, Sep 62: 34, 111
BLACKSELL, J. E., Jan 63: 26
"BLACK SPIRAL," sculpture by Alexander Calder, Nov 62: 16
BLAKE, PETER, May 63: 17
  Photograph of, May 63: 16–17
  "Ugly America, The," article by, May 61: 4–19
BLAKE, WILLIAM, May 61: 72, Sep 61: 119, May 62: 60–61, Mar 63: 67, 69, Aug 63: 8
  Works by. See ILLUSTRATIONS INDEX
BLAMONT, HENRI DE, Nov 58: 105
BLANCA, PRINCESS, OF ENGLAND, May 63: 99
BLANCH, LESLEY, "Where Nothing Succeeds Like

Excess," article by, Sep 60: 129–36
BLANCHARD, JEAN-PIERRE, Sep 58: 118, 119–20
BLANCHARD, MADELEINE-SOPHIE, Sep 58: 120
BLANKENBURG, HEINZ, photograph of, Nov 61: 78
BLASHFIELD, EDWIN, Sep 60: 102, 127
BLATCHLEY, JOHN, Jan 63: 26
BLAU, HERBERT, Jan 59: 22
BLEGEN, CARL W., Jan 61: 77, 94
BLENHEIM, BATTLE OF, Sep 61: 71, 73
BLENHEIM PALACE, Nov 58: 51, 52, Sep 61: 68–77
BLIGH, WILLIAM
    And mutiny on H.M.S. *Bounty*, Sep 63: 42–48
    Portrait of, Sep 63: 48
BLINDER, MAOUM, Jul 60: 74
BLISS, ANTHONY A., Nov 58: 118
BLISS, ARTHUR, May 62: 61
BLISS, CORNELIUS N., Nov 58: 118
BLISS, LESLIE E., Nov 60: 100, 101
"BLITHEDALE ROMANCE, THE," novel by Nathaniel
    Hawthorne, Mar 63: 77
BLITZSTEIN, MARC, Jan 62: 13
    Cradle Will Rock, The, Jul 63: 87, 90
    Regina, Jan 60: 123
BLIXEN, BARONESS. See DINESEN, ISAK
BLOCH, BERNARD, on phoneme and morpheme, quoted,
    Jul 63: 45
BLOCH, ERNEST, Jan 59: 21, Jul 59: 21
BLOCH, RAYMOND, "In Search of the Etruscans," article
    by, May 60: 56–79
BLOCK, HERBERT (HERBLOCK)
    On Osborn, Robert, quoted, May 60: 18
    "Split-level living," cartoon, Jul 60: 67
BLOCK, PAUL, JR., Sep 58: 62–63
"BLOK" GROUP, May 61: 21–22
BLOMBERG, BARBARA, Jul 63: 50
BLOND, NEVILLE, Jan 63: 26
BLOOD, THOMAS, May 63: 101
BLOOM, CLAIRE, May 61: 55
BLOOM, ROBERT, Jan 62: 14
"BLOOMER GIRL," musical, Sep 58: 60
BLOOMFIELD, CONN., Connecticut General Life Insur-
    ance Company building, Sep 58: 91, May 62: 16, May
    63: 14
BLOOMFIELD, LEONARD, Jul 63: 44, 45, 46, 47
BLOOMFIELD HILLS, MICH., Cranbrook Academy of
    Art, Jul 60: 78
BLOOMGARDEN, KERMIT, May 63: 10
BLOOMSBURY GROUP, Jan 60: 107
"BLOSSOM TIME," musical, Sep 58: 57
"BLOW YOUR OWN TRUMPET," play, Nov 58: 137
BLOY, LÉON, on Georges Rouault, quoted, Nov 62: 48
BLÜCHER, PRINCE VON, Mar 61: 32
"BLUE DENIM," play, Nov 58: 64, Jan 59: 138
"BLUE LAGOON, THE," novel by Henry de Vere Stac-
    poole, Jan 60: 125
"BLUE MUSEUM, THE," article by C. W. Ceram and
    Peter Lyon, Nov 58: 66–77
BLUM, LÉON, Nov 59: 68
BLUME, PETER, May 59: 10, May 60: 25, Jul 62: 15
    Painting by, Mar 59: 11
    Photographs of, May 59: 16, May 60: 25, Jul 61: 74
    Tasso's Oak, painted by, Jul 61: 70–75
"BLUME'S OAK," article by Robert Cowley, Jul 61: 70–
    75
BLUNDEN, EDMUND, Jan 60: 108, Jan 62: 51
BLUNK, J. B., Jan 59: 14
BLUNT, WILFRID SCAWEN, quoted
    On Burton, Richard Francis, Jul 63: 112
    On tulip mania, May 59: 41
BLYTH, R. H., *Zen in English Literature*, quoted, Jul 59:
    126–27
BOABDIL EL CHICO, likenesses of, Sep 62: 92
BOAR, as source of ivory, May 60: 91
BOAS, FRANZ, Jul 63: 44
BOAS, GEORGE, on Greeks, quoted, Mar 62: 68
BOATWRIGHT, HELEN, Jan 62: 14
BOB AND RAY, Jan 63: 114
"BOB HOPE SHOW, THE," cost of, Jul 62: 94–95
BOB JONES UNIVERSITY, Jan 59: 6
BOCCA, GEOFFREY, "They Kept the Old Flag Flying,"
    article by, Sep 63: 74–81
BOCCACCIO, GIOVANNI, Nov 62: 93–94
    Portrait of, Nov 62: 87
BOCCIONE, UMBERTO, sculpture by, Nov 62: 4
BOCHUM, GERMANY
    Christ Church, Sep 62: 28
    Theatre at, Jul 59: 48
BOCK, RICHARD, Sep 60: 99
BÖCKLIN, ARNOLD, Jan 60: 130
    Painting by, Jan 60: 132
BODENHEIM, MAXWELL, Mar 63: 28
BODHIDHARMA, Jul 59: 71, 72
    Japanese folk tales concerning, Sep 62: 2
    Portrait of, Jul 59: 70

BODIN, JEAN, and witch mania, Nov 59: 60, 63
BOE, GUNNAR, Nov 63: 61
BOERS, vs. N'debele people, Nov 60: 65
BOETH, RICHARD, "On Stage: Carol Burnett," article
    by, Sep 61: 80–81
BOETHIUS, ANCIUS MANLIUS SEVERINUS, in
    Renaissance curriculum, Jan 60: 62
BOGAN, LOUISE, Mar 63: 31, Jul 63: 72
BOGART, HUMPHREY, Nov 61: 116
BOGULYUBOV, E., Jan 62: 120
BOHEMIA
    Destruction of Protestantism in, in 1620's, Mar 60: 101
    Prehistoric wheeled vehicles in, Sep 58: 147
    Royal regalia of, May 63: 94
    And Thirty Years' War, Nov 62: 33–41
BOHM, DOMINIKUS, Mar 59: 121
BOHM, KARL, Nov 58: 25
BOHNEN, MICHAEL, Sep 59: 57
BOHROD, AARON, Jul 62: 15
    Painting by, Jul 62: 18
BOILEAU-DESPRÉAUX, NICOLAS, May 61: 61
    On Seine River, quoted, Jul 62: 56
BOÏTO, ARRIGO, May 63: 42
BOJADOR, CAPE, SPANISH SAHARA, Portuguese ex-
    ploration of coast southward from, Nov 60: 76–83
BOLGER, RAY, Sep 58: 60
BOLÍVAR, SIMÓN
    Humboldt, Alexander von, and, Jul 59: 68
    Portrait of, Jul 59: 62
BOLLINGEN FOUNDATION, Sep 63: 85
BOLLINGEN PRIZE IN POETRY, Jul 63: 68, 69, 70,
    72–73
BOLSHEVISM, Jan 59: 121
BOLSHOI BALLET, Allegra Kent quoted on, Nov 59: 53
BOLT, ROBERT, Jul 62: 110
    Man for All Seasons, A, May 62: 110–11
BOLTIN, LEE, "A Pride of Chessmen," photographs by,
    Jan 62: 121–28
BON, OTTAVIANO, on Turkey, quoted, May 59: 58–59,
    60, 134
BONAPARTE, JOSEPH, KING OF SPAIN, May 63: 95
BONAPARTE, LOUIS NAPOLEON. See NAPOLEON
    III
BONAPARTE, MATHILDE, PRINCESSE, Nov 61: 36,
    May 63: 70
    Painting of, Nov 61: 37
BONAPARTE, NAPOLEON. See NAPOLEON I
BONAVENTURA, Mar 63: 5
BOND, SUDIE, Jul 62: 94
BONHEUR, ROSA, Mar 60: 57, Sep 62: 21
BONHOEFFER, DIETRICH, Sep 63: 105–6
BONIFACE III, COUNT OF MONTFERRAT, Nov 63: 31
BONIFACE, SAINT, on witches, quoted, Nov 59: 57
"BONJOUR TRISTESSE," motion picture, May 62: 81
BONNARD, PIERRE, Nov 60: 104, 113, Mar 62: 14–16,
    25–27, May 62: 78, Jul 62: 65
    Paintings by. See ILLUSTRATIONS INDEX
    Portraits of, Mar 62: 14, 27
    Rivers, Larry, quoted on, Sep 59: 98
BONNER, EUGENE, on Metropolitan Opera House,
    quoted, Nov 58: 119
BONPLAND, AIMÉ, Jul 59: 61–62, 67, 68
    Portrait of, Jul 59: 62
BONSAQUET, BERNARD, on art, quoted, Nov 58: 116
BOOK COLLECTING
    Forgeries affecting, Mar 59: 105, 107–9
    Of Gardner, Isabella Stewart, Jul 59: 29
    Rosenbach, A. S. W., and his activities in, Nov 60: 96–
    101
BOOK OF HOURS, of Etienne Chevalier, Nov 61: 88–97
BOOK OF HOURS ("LES TRÉS RICHES HEURES"),
    of Jean, Duc de Berry, Sep 60: 60–61, May 61:
    113; illus from, Sep 60: 63
"BOOK OF JOB, THE," production by Orlin and Irene
    Corey, Jan 63: 88
"BOOK OF KELLS," Sep 59: 125–26
"BOOK OF MANY SUNS, THE," woodcut book by
    Antonio Frasconi, Mar 61: 123; illus from, Mar 61:
    128
"BOOK OF TOURNEYS, THE." See "LIVRE DES
    TOURNOIS, LE"
BOOKS
    Auctions of, at Sotheby's, Nov 62: 61–62, 66
    Current, critical discussions of: "Beer-bottle on the Pedi-
    ment," Jan 61: 116–18; "Bible Is Given New Speech,
    The," Mar 61: 94–97; "Diary from the Depths, A," Nov
    62: 108–10; "Dreamer of Light and Dark," Jan 63: 109–
    11; "Greetings from Goethe's Land," Mar 63: 111–13;
    "Henry Miller's Stream of Self-consciousness," Nov 61:
    104–5; "History by Another Name," Sep 62: 112–14;
    "Ladies Who Tell All, but All," Jan 62: 111–12; "Life
    Behind the Ivy," Sep 60: 117–19; "Liszt and Chopin,"
    May 63: 109–10; "Only Yesterday: The Third Reich,"
    Nov 60: 119–21; "Our Man in Purgatory," May 61:

116–17; "Paris at Five O'Clock," May 62: 113–15;
    "Poor Winnie in Pooh-Latin," Jul 61: 112–15; "To the
    Sound of Hollow Laughter," Jul 62: 89–91; "Uncom-
    mon Thoughts in a Common Place," Sep 61: 114–15
    Microlibraries, Sep 62: 42–47
    Survival of, Nov 62: 74–95
    Woodcut books of Antonio Frasconi, Mar 61: 122–28
"BOOKS AND BOOK-COLLECTORS," book by John
    Carter, Mar 59: 109 (note)
"BOOR, THE," opera, Jan 60: 123
BORDONI, FAUSTINA, Sep 59: 51
BORGHESE, G. A., Sep 58: 102
BORGIA, LUCREZIA, Mar 63: 27
BORGIA, RODRIGO. See ALEXANDER VI, POPE
BORGLUM, GUTZON, Sep 61: 13
    Isamu Noguchi quoted on, Mar 60: 107
BORGNINE, ERNEST, Jul 62: 49
BORIE, ADOLPHE, Jul 63: 18
BORNEO
    Moorehead, Alan, in, Sep 60: 12
    Twining, Edward Francis, in, May 63: 92–93
BORODIN, ALEKSANDR P., Nov 62: 44
BORROMINI, FRANCESCO, Jul 60: 38
    Church designed by, Jul 60: 51
"BORSTAL BOY," book by Brendan Behan, Jan 61: 114
BORY, JEAN-LOUIS, Jul 63: 74
BORY, JEAN-MARC, May 60: 53
BOSCH, HIERONYMUS, Jan 59: 44, 132, 133, Nov 60:
    31, May 61: 113, Jan 62: 79
    Paintings by, Jan 62: 78, Mar 63: 72
BOSCO, PHILIP, Nov 60: 118
BOSQUEZ, DEMAS, Jan 60: 131
BOSSUET, JACQUES BÉNIGNE, Nov 59: 61, 62
BOSTON, MASS.
    City Hall design, Jan 63: 10–15
    Gardner, Isabella Stewart, and her museum, Jul 59: 26–
    40, 133–34
    Irish in, Jul 59: 124
    Philadelphia compared with, Jul 63: 8, 12–13
    Silent Traveller quoted on, Nov 59: 130, 136
    Street furniture, Nov 59: 107
"BOSTON CHOOSES THE FUTURE," article by Eric
    Larrabee, Jan 63: 10–15
BOSTON MUSEUM OF FINE ARTS, Jul 59: 29
    Japanese painting collection, May 60: 114
BOSTON POPS ORCHESTRA, Sep 59: 123
BOSTON SYMPHONY ORCHESTRA, Jul 59: 19, 28
    Time Cycle performance, Jan 63: 78 (note)
BOSWELL, JAMES, Mar 61: 118, May 61: 61
    On Grand Tour, Nov 59: 94, 95
BOTH, JAN, Jul 63: 106
BOTHWELL, EARL OF (JAMES HEPBURN), Jul 63:
    29–30
BOTKIN, HENRY, portrait of, with painting by, Jul 61:
    25
BOTT, FRANCIS, stained-glass window designed by, Sep
    62: 29
BOTTICELLI, SANDRO, Sep 58: 94, 95, 142
    Gardner Museum collection, Jul 59: 30
    Paintings by. See ILLUSTRATIONS INDEX
    Venus of, Nov 58: 114; illus, Sep 58: 94
BOTVINNIK, MIKHAIL, Jan 62: 118
    Photograph of, Jan 62: 117
BOUCHER, FRANÇOIS, Mar 62: 50, 63, 68
    Foreshadowed by Van Dyck, Jul 63: 96
    Painting by, Sep 63: 92
BOUCICAULT, DION, Nov 58: 135
BOUDIN, EUGÈNE LOUIS, Jul 62: 66
BOUGUEREAU, ADOLPHE WILLIAM, Mar 60: 53,
    Jul 62: 18–19
    Painting by, Mar 60: 61
BOUILLON, GODEFROY DE, Mar 61: 53
BOULDER, COLO., Jul 62: 114
BOULEZ, PIERRE, Jan 59: 53, Jan 63: 77
    Photograph of, Jan 59: 53
BOULLÉE, ETIENNE, Mar 62: 35
    Cenotaph designed by, Mar 62: 35
BOULTON, MATTHEW
    As member of Josiah Wedgwood's group, May 59: 91–96,
    128–30
    Portrait of, May 59: 91
"BOUND EAST FOR CARDIFF," play, Mar 60: 40, Jul
    61: 13
"BOUNTY," H.M.S., mutiny on, and aftermath, Sep 63:
    42–48
BOURBONS, role in Sicily, Sep 61: 38
BOURGET, MRS. PAUL, Jul 59: 133
BOURNE, RANDOLPH, Jul 62: 99
BOURNE, RUSSELL, "Church with a Twist," article by,
    Nov 62: 70–73
BOURNONVILLE, ANTOINE, Sep 60: 94
BOURNONVILLE, AUGUST, Sep 60: 91, 94
BOURSIN, MARIA. See MELIGNY, MARTHE DE
BOVIDIAN PEOPLES, May 59: 82, 83

BOWDLER, HENRIETTA, Sep 62: 69
BOWDLER, JANE, Sep 62: 69
BOWDLER, JOHN, *Reform or Ruin*, Sep 62: 69
BOWDLER, THOMAS, Sep 62: 68–71
BOWDOIN COLLEGE, visits of literary celebrities to, Nov 60: 66, 68
BOWER, EDWARD, Jul 61: 93
BOWERS, H. R., Sep 58: 8, 12, 138
BOWLES, CHARLES, Jul 61: 101, 104
BOWLES, JANE, *In the Summer House*, Mar 60: 119
BOWLES, MARY (MRS. SAMUEL), Jul 61: 101, 104
BOWLES, PAUL, Mar 61: 22, 75
BOWLES, SAMUEL, and Emily Dickinson, Jul 61: 100–5
Portrait of, Jul 61: 105
BOWLES, SAMUEL, JR., Jul 61: 104
"BOWLING GOES BOURGEOIS," article by Russell Lynes, Mar 63: 89–95
BOWLING PROPRIETORS' ASSOCIATION OF AMERICA, Mar 63: 92
BOWRA, C. M., "Homer's Age of Heroes," article by, Jan 61: 73–99
BOWRA, MAURICE, Jul 61: 113
Greek translation by, quoted, Jul 61: 114
BOWYER, ROBERT, Nov 62: 94
BOXER UPRISING, Sep 60: 12
"BOY AND GOOSE," sculpture, Henry Moore quoted on, Nov 60: 114
BOYCOTT, CHARLES CUNNINGHAM, May 60: 126–27
BOYD, STEPHEN, Sep 60: 56, May 61: 53
BOYER, CHARLES, May 63: 110–11
"BOY IN A RED WAISTCOAT," painting by Cézanne, Nov 62: 64
BOYLE, EDWARD, Jan 63: 86
BOYLE, KAY, on MacDowell Colony, quoted, Mar 63: 32
BRADBURY, MALCOLM, *Eating People Is Wrong*, Sep 60: 119
BRADBURY, RAY, *Fahrenheit 451*, Mar 63: 79
BRADY, "DIAMOND JIM," Nov 58: 148
BRADY, MATHEW B., Jan 59: 103, Mar 60: 126
BRAHMS, JOHANNES, Sep 61: 86, 87
Balanchine, George, quoted on, Jan 61: 47
Chamber music of, Nov 62: 46
German Requiem, Thomas Beecham quoted on, Mar 62: 103
BRAIDWOOD, ROBERT J., Sep 62: 5, 6, 7, 8
BRAINE, JOHN, *Room at the Top*, motion picture based on, May 62: 116
"BRAINSTORMING," Nov 58: 33
BRAKE, BRIAN, photographs by
"China of the Chinese," Sep 62: 48–56
Dance of India, Sep 63: 64–67, 69–71, 73
At San Men Dam, Jan 61: 4–9, 12–13
BRAKHAGE, STAN, Nov 62: 97
BRAMANTE, Jan 62: 32, 41, 43
BRANCUSI, CONSTANTIN, May 63: 91
Moore, Henry, quoted on, Nov 60: 115
Noguchi, Isamu, quoted on, Mar 60: 106, 107–8
"BRAND," play, Jan 62: 106, 108
BRAND, OSCAR, Sep 62: 66
BRANDEIS, LOUIS D., debate on right to privacy, Jul 60: 122
BRANDEIS UNIVERSITY CREATIVE ARTS AWARD, Jul 63: 72
BRANDENBURG, GERMANY, Peter the Great at court of, Sep 59: 66, 74
BRANDO, MARLON, Sep 58: 38, 42–44, Nov 61: 115, Nov 62: 107
In *Mutiny on the Bounty*, Sep 63: 42, 46
Photographs of, Sep 58: 38, Sep 63: 42
BRANDON, MARY, Jul 62: 37
BRANDT, M., teapot designed by, Nov 61: 71
BRAQUE, GEORGES, Jan 59: 132
On portrait of Somerset Maugham by Edouard MacAvoy, quoted, Jan 59: 107
Wyeth, Andrew, quoted on, Sep 61: 100
BRASILIA, BRAZIL, Sep 59: 20, Nov 59: 112, Mar 61: 36
BRASSEUR, PIERRE, Mar 62: 119
Portrait of, Mar 62: 118
BRATBY, JOHN, painting by, May 62: 76
BRATTLE, ROBERT, Nov 59: 63
BRAUN, KARL, photograph of, May 63: 40
"BRAVE NEW WORLD," novel by Aldous Huxley, Jul 59: 111, Mar 63: 73, 79, Nov 63: 104–5, 108
BRAZIL (see also BRASILIA; RIO DE JANEIRO)
Child of the Dark, book by Carolina Maria de Jesus, Nov 62: 109–10
BREASTED, JAMES H., Jul 63: 86
"BREATHLESS," motion picture, Nov 61: 116, May 62: 81
BRECHT, BERTOLT, Nov 58: 62, Nov 59: 56, Mar 60: 43, Mar 61: 44, 47 (illus), Jul 61: 116, May 62: 34–41
Good Woman of Setzuan, The, Jan 63: 29

Humor of, Mar 63: 107
Ionesco, Eugène, quoted on, May 61: 93, 97
In the Jungle of Cities, Mar 62: 108
Mother Courage, Mar 60: 121
Portrait of, May 62: 34
"BRECHT ON BRECHT," program of readings, May 62: 35
BREDA, NETHERLANDS, Sep 58: 19
BRÉE, GERMAINE
On Camus' *The Plague*, quoted, Nov 59: 71
"Innocent Amusements of Jean Anouilh, The," article by, Nov 60: 50–55, 126–27
BREER, ROBERT, Nov 62: 97
BREITENFELD, BATTLE OF, Nov 62: 38
BREMONT, balloonist, Sep 58: 114
BRENAN, GERALD
On *Don Quixote*, quoted, Nov 61: 113
"When Islam Ruled Iberia," article by, Sep 62: 72–93
BRENANS, lieutenant of Camel Corps, May 59: 71
BRENCHLEY, JULIUS, Jul 63: 114
BRENNAN, LIL, Mar 60: 27
BRENNER, ENGELBERT, on conductors of New York Philharmonic, quoted, Jul 59: 17
BRENTANO, GEORGES, Nov 61: 88
BRETEL, JACQUES, Nov 58: 105
BRETEUIL, EMILIE DE (MARQUISE DU CHÂTELET), Mar 61: 117–18
BRETON, ANDRÉ, Nov 60: 126
Ionesco, Eugène, quoted on, May 61: 95
Manifesto of Surrealism, Mar 59: 78
BREUER, HANS, photograph of, May 63: 42
BREUER, MARCEL, Mar 59: 122–23, Sep 59: 18, 19, Jan 60: 119, Nov 61: 61, 70, 72 73, 74, Jul 62: 8
House designed by, Nov 61: 74
Photographs of, Nov 61: 59, 74
BREWSTER, KINGMAN, JR., on research and teaching, quoted, Sep 62: 17
BRIALY, JEAN CLAUDE, May 60: 50
BRIAND, ARISTIDE, Mar 63: 6
BRICE, FANNIE, Sep 58: 58
Photograph of, Sep 58: 58
BRICKLEY, CHARLIE, Jul 62: 34
BRIDGEHAMPTON, N.Y., May 63: 7 (map), 8, 17, 18
"BRIDGE ON THE RIVER KWAI, THE," motion picture, Jan 59: 139, Mar 60: 128, Jul 62: 109
BRIDGES
At Clifton, England, Jan 59: 36–37
Khaju, at Isfahan, May 61: 24–32
At Maidenhead, England, Jan 59: 38
Of Maillart, Robert, Mar 59: 21
Peruvian cord, Jul 59: 66
Risorgimento, in Rome, Mar 59: 20–21
Royal Albert, Jan 59: 39–40
Of Seine River, Jul 62: 56
BRIDGES, ROBERT, Max Beerbohm quoted on, May 61: 40
BRIDGEWATER, CONN., May 60: 13 (map), 27
BRIDGMAN, PERCY, Mar 62: 73
"BRIEF ENCOUNTER," motion picture, Jul 62: 109, May 63: 111
BRIENNE, DUC DE, Cardinal Mazarin's farewell to his paintings described by, Nov 61: 82
"BRIGADOON," musical, Sep 58: 60, 143, May 61: 103
BRIGGS, ERNEST, Jan 59: 13
BRIGHTMAN, THOMAS, Mar 60: 101, 102
BRIGHTON, ENGLAND
Hippodrome Theatre, Jul 59: 115, 118
Royal Pavilion, Mar 62: 35 (illus), Nov 62: 20–31
BRIL, PAUL, Mar 61: 92
BRILL, REGINALD, painting by, May 62: 77
BRILLAT-SAVARIN, ANTHELME, May 61: 125, 126
"BRILLIANCE IN THE BUSH, A," article by Mary Cable with photographs by Pete Turner, Nov 60: 56–65
BRINDLEY, JAMES, as member of Josiah Wedgwood's group, May 59: 92, 94, 129
BRISSY, TESTU, Sep 58: 120
BRISTOL, ENGLAND, church of St. Mary Redcliffe, May 60: 36, 38
BRISTOL, 4TH EARL OF (FREDERICK AUGUSTUS HERVEY), Jul 59: 60–61, Nov 63: 74
BRITAIN (see also ENGLAND; GREAT BRITAIN)
Roman baths, May 60: 41
War chariots of Celts, Sep 58: 149
BRITISH & AMERICAN STEAM NAVIGATION COMPANY, Jul 59: 40
BRITISH COLONY OF HOLLYWOOD, Sep 63: 74–81
BRITISH MUSEUM, ancient books owned by, Nov 62: 82, 83 (illus), 94
"BRITISH QUEEN," S.S., Jan 59: 40
BRITISH ROYAL NAVY, hoax on, Jan 61: 66–68, 72
BRITTEN, BENJAMIN, Jan 60: 12, Nov 62: 46
BRITTON, THOMAS, Nov 62: 43
BROCA, PHILIPPE DE, Jan 62: 109–10
Photograph of, Jan 62: 109

BROCKHURST, GERALD, Jan 59: 99
BRODERSON, ROBERT, Jul 62: 22, 25
Painting by, Jul 62: 22
BRODIE, FAWN M., "The Hidden, the Unknowable, the Unthinkable," article by, Jul 63: 110–17
BRODIE, GANDY, Sep 59: 98
BRODKEY, HAROLD, Jan 62: 14
BROGAN, DENIS, May 60: 6
On impact of America, quoted, May 60: 7
BROMFIELD, LOUIS, on Algonquin Round Table, quoted, Jul 62: 36
BROMYARD, JOHN, on woman's adornment, quoted, Nov 59: 116
BRONOWSKI, J., and BRUCE MAZLISH, *The Western Intellectual Tradition*, excerpt from, May 62: 89–95
BRONTË, DUKES OF, Sep 61: 38
BRONZE AGE, commerce and travel during, Jul 60: 84–91, 113
BROOK, ALEXANDER, Jan 59: 101, Jul 62: 15, 17, May 63: 24
Paintings by, Jan 59: 101, Jul 62: 17
Photograph of, May 63: 24–25
BROOK, CLIVE, Sep 63: 79
Photographs of, Sep 63: 76
BROOK, MRS. CLIVE, photograph of, Sep 63: 76
BROOK, PETER, Nov 61: 116
BROOKE, RUPERT, Jan 60: 125
BROOK FARM, Mar 63: 77
BROOKS, CLEANTH, on poetry, quoted, Jul 59: 108
BROOKS, PAUL, "Man's Way with the Wilderness," article by, Mar 60: 12–16
BROOKS, VAN WYCK, May 60: 27, Jul 63: 70
Photograph of, May 60: 26
BROOM, ROBERT, Mar 62: 9
BROTHERS, JOYCE, Jul 60: 5–6
"BROTHERS KARAMAZOV, THE," novel by Dostoevsky, Jan 62: 62
Quoted, May 62: 102
BROUGHAM, HENRY, Mar 59: 92, 95
BROUGHTON, JAMES, Jan 59: 18
"BROUHAHA," play, Jan 61: 101
BROUN, HEYWOOD, Jul 62: 37, 39
Caricature of, Jul 62: 41
BROWER, BROCK, "On Stage: Matt Turney," article by, Nov 62: 68–69
BROWER, CHARLES H., Mar 62: 113
BROWN, HARRISON, "The Future of Machine Civilization," article by, Jan 59: 92–94, 128–29
BROWN, J. G., Sep 60: 102
BROWN, JOHN MASON
Excerpts from biography of Robert Sherwood by, May 62: 4–9, Jul 62: 32–41
On Ustinov, Peter, quoted, Nov 58: 82
BROWN, LANCELOT ("CAPABILITY"), Nov 58, 46, May 59: 31, 47, Sep 61: 76, 77, Nov 63: 74
Portrait of, May 59: 46
BROWNE, BYRON, portrait of, with painting by, Jul 61: 24
BROWNE, EDWARD G., on Persian literature, quoted, Jan 63: 53
BROWNE, E. MARTIN, on *The Book of Job*, quoted, Jan 63: 88
BROWNE, ROSCOE LEE, Nov 61: 100
BROWNING, COLLEEN, Jul 62: 25
Painting by, Jul 62: 24
BROWNING, ELIZABETH BARRETT, Jul 61: 101
FitzGerald, Edward, quoted on death of, May 63: 82
Sonnets from the Portuguese, forged edition, Mar 59: 107–9
On Venice, quoted, Mar 63: 15
BROWNING, JOHN, Jan 60: 74, 79, 81
Portrait of, Jan 60: 79
BROWNING, ROBERT, Jul 61: 101, May 63: 81–82
In painting by William P. Frith, May 62: 62
Portrait of, May 63: 82
"BROWNING VERSION, THE," television play, Mar 63: 35
BRUCE, JAMES, Mar 63: 53
BRUCE, NIGEL, Sep 63: 76, 77, 78, 80
Photograph of, Sep 63: 79
BRUCKNER, ANTON, Nov 62: 47
BRUEGEL, JAN, Jul 63: 96
BRUEGEL, PIETER THE ELDER, Jan 62: 79
Caravel from painting by, Sep 58: 3; illus, Sep 58: 2
Dulle Griet, Jan 59: 44–49
Tower of Babel, Sep 63: 11; illus, Sep 63: 10–11
Wedding Dance, Sep 60: 121
BRUENING, HEINRICH, May 62: 8
BRUGES, BELGIUM
College of Europe, Mar 63: 7
Tournament of 1392, Nov 58: 96
BRUHN, ERIK, Sep 60: 94
Photograph of, Sep 60: 95
BRUMMELL, GEORGE BRYAN (BEAU BRUMMELL),

Mar 62: 63, Nov 62: 22, 23

BRUNEL, ISAMBARD KINGDOM, Jan 59: 32–43, 136
Portrait of, Jan 59: 32
BRUNEL, MARC ISAMBARD, Jan 59: 34–35
BRUNELLESCHI, FILIPPO, Nov 58: 41, Jan 60: 66
BRUNI, LEONARDO, Jan 60: 64
BRUNSWICK CORPORATION, Mar 63: 92, 94
BRUSSELS, BELGIUM
American abstract expressionism in, Nov 59: 120
Centre Rogier, Nov 60: 16
International Exposition of 1958: *Book of Job* production, Jan 63: 88; U.S. Pavilion, Jan 60: 120; *Whirling Ear* construction, Nov 62: 16
J.B. production at, Jan 60: 50–51
Joust staged in, Nov 58: 107
U.S. embassy building, Jan 60: 25
BRUSTEIN, ROBERT, "The Cult of Unthink," article by, Sep 58: 38–45, 134–35
BRUTUS, MARCUS JUNIUS, Nov 58: 111, Sep 63: 35
BRYAN, WILLIAM JENNINGS, Washington, D.C., statue of, Sep 61: 13
BRYANT, JACOB, Jan 61: 91
BRYANT, WILLIAM CULLEN, on entering a wood, quoted, May 61: 12
BRYCE, JAMES (LORD BRYCE), *The American Commonwealth,* May 59: 23
BRYNNER, YUL, in *The Magnificent Seven,* May 61: 114, 115
BRZOZOWSKI, TADEUSZ, May 61: 22
BUCCI, MARC, Jan 60: 15, 123
BUCCLEUCH, DUKES OF, Nov 58: 50, Nov 59: 77
BUCHAN, JOHN, May 62: 8
Pilgrim's Way, Sep 61: 5
BUCHANAN, BESSIE A., Nov 61: 118–19
BUCHHOLZ, HORST, May 61: 114, 115
BUCHMAN, FRANK, Jan 63: 86
BÜCHNER, GEORG, *Wozzeck,* Jan 60: 12–13
BUCHWALD, ART, remark of Gregory Corso to, quoted, Jul 60: 72
BUCKINGHAM, 1ST DUKE OF (GEORGE VILLIERS), Sep 59: 120, Jul 61: 80, 89, 90, 91, 94, Jul 63: 93–94
BUCKINGHAM PALACE, collection of paintings, Jul 63: 105, 107
BUCKLAND, FRANK, Jan 63: 85
BUCKLEY, WALTER, *Modern Sociological Theory,* quoted, Mar 59: 135
"BUDDENBROOKS," novel by Thomas Mann, Jan 62: 62
BUDDHA. See GAUTAMA BUDDHA
BUDDHISM (see also ZEN BUDDHISM)
In Cambodia, Jan 59: 62, 63, 64
Kyoto, Mar 61: 27
Temple gardens, May 59: 50
Toynbee, Arnold J., quoted on, Jan 61: 63, 64, 65
BUHL, HERMANN, Sep 58: 8
"BUILDING A CHARACTER," book by Constantin Stanislavsky, Nov 62: 106–7
BULGARINI FAMILY, of Italy, May 63: 36
BULL. See WINGED BULL
BULLFIGHTING, Jul 60: 128
Drawings by John Rombola, Jul 60: 129–36
BULLION, CLAUDE DE, Jul 63: 82
BULLITT, STIMSON, "The Future American Class System," article excerpted from *To Be a Politician,* May 59: 20–23
BULLOCK, HUGH, Jul 63: 70 (note)
BÜLOW, COSIMA VON (COSIMA LISZT) Jan 61: 41, May 61: 84
BÜLOW, HANS VON, Jan 61: 41
BULTMANN, RUDOLPH, Sep 63: 8, 106, 107
Photograph of, Sep 63: 8
BUNDY, McGEORGE, Sep 61: 10
BUNNAGE, AVIS, photograph of, May 61: 50–51
BUNSHAFT, GORDON, Nov 60: 8, 9, May 63: 14
Photographs of, Jul 62: 7, May 63: 14
BUÑUEL, LUIS, Nov 62: 97, 110–12, Mar 63: 113
"BUÑUEL'S UNSPARING VISION," article by Saul Bellow, Nov 62: 110–12
BURBANK, CALIF., bowling establishment in, Mar 63: 93
BURCHFIELD, CHARLES, Sep 58: 113
BURCKHARDT, JACOB, on Baroque architecture, quoted, Jul 60: 35
BURCKHARDT, JOHANN, Jul 62: 29
BURDICK, EUGENE, Jan 59: 19
BURGER, BERTHA, Sep 59: 100
BURGESS, GELETT, limerick by, quoted, Sep 58: 130
"BURGESS HILL SCHOOL," illustrated feature, Sep 62: 105–7
BURGHLEY, Nov 58: 41
BURGKMAIR, HANS, woodcut by, Mar 60: 75
BURGUNDY, FRANCE, wine cellar tours, Mar 59: 83
BURGUNDY, DUKE OF (JEAN SANS PEUR), Mar 62: 91

BURGUNDY, DUKE OF (PHILIP THE GOOD), Mar 62: 89
BURGUNDY, DUKES OF, tombs of, at Dijon, Sep 58: 62
BURIAL CUSTOMS
Of Etruscans, May 60: 64, 74
Paleolithic, Jul 61: 35
Passage graves, Jul 60: 87, 90
Wheeled vehicles in, Sep 58: 146–47
BURKE, EDMUND, May 60: 99, 100, 101, 124, May 62: 62
BURKHARDT, FREDERICK, on university teaching situation, quoted, Sep 62: 17
BURLIN, PAUL, photograph of, Mar 63: 32
BURLINGTON HOUSE, in London, Nov 62: 59, 78
BURNE-JONES, EDWARD, painting by, Mar 60: 56
BURNET, GILBERT, BISHOP OF SALISBURY, Jan 60: 115, Mar 60: 100
BURNET, THOMAS, *Theory of the Earth,* quoted, Mar 60: 14
BURNETT, CAROL, Sep 61: 80
Photograph of, Sep 61: 81
BURNEY, CHARLES, Mar 61: 118
BURNEY, FANNY, Nov 62: 21
BURNHAM, DANIEL H., Jan 60: 23, May 63: 73
Plan for Chicago world's fair of 1893, May 60: 80–81, 87
BURNS, JAMES McGREGOR, on John F. Kennedy, quoted, Nov 63: 69
BURNS, ROBERT, Sep 61: 114, May 63: 82, 85
BURNS and McDONNELL, Jul 60: 121
"BURNT-OUT CASE, A," novel by Graham Greene, reviewed, May 61: 116–17
BURRI, ALBERTO, and new "art form," photographs, Jan 59: 144
BURROUGHS, WILLIAM, Sep 58: 40, Jul 63: 39–40
BURSA, TURKEY, Sep 60: 126
BURT, NATHANIEL, "Philadelphia Plain & Fancy," article drawn from *The Perennial Philadelphians,* Jul 63: 4–27
BURT, STRUTHERS, Jul 63: 7
BURTON, CATHERINE, Jul 63: 111
BURTON, DECIMUS, Mar 62: 36
Building constructed by, Mar 62: 36
BURTON, EDWARD, Jul 63: 111
BURTON, JOSEPH NETTERVILLE, Jul 63: 111–12
BURTON, MARTHA BAKER, Jul 63: 111–12
BURTON, RICHARD, May 61: 55, 113, Jan 63: 86, Sep 63: 75
BURTON, RICHARD FRANCIS, Jul 63: 110–17
On Africans, quoted, Mar 63: 40
Portraits of, Jul 63: 111, 114, 115, 117
BURTON, MRS. RICHARD FRANCIS (ISABEL ARUNDELL), Jul 63: 112, 113, 114, 115, 116, 117
Portraits of, Jul 63: 114, 115
BUSA, PETER, portrait of, with painting by, Jul 61: 25
BUSBECQ, AUGIER GHISLAIN DE, on Turkey, quoted, Sep 58: 46, 47
BUSCH, ADOLF, Sep 61: 84–85, 87
Photograph of, Sep 61: 84
BUSCH, FRITZ, Sep 61: 84
BUSCH, HERMANN, Sep 61: 84, 85
Photograph of, Sep 61: 84
BUSCH, IRENE (MRS. RUDOLF SERKIN), Sep 61: 84, 86–87
BUSCH-REISINGER MUSEUM, in Cambridge, Mass., organ at, Mar 60: 80
BUSH, VANNEVAR, May 62: 9
BUSH-BROWN, ALBERT, "Architect's Hero: Louis Kahn," article by, Sep 62: 57–63
BUSHMEN, of Kalahari desert, Mar 63: 40
BUSINESS and INDUSTRY
Contributions of Josiah Wedgwood, May 59: 89, 129.
Coolidge, Calvin, quoted on business, Sep 60: 38
Personal ethics in, Mar 63: 60–61
Regulation of, Mar 59: 6
Research and, Mar 63: 60
Supermarkets, Mar 59: 110–11
BUSINESSMAN, and art, Sep 60: 36
BUSONI, FERRUCCIO, Jul 59: 32, 134, Jan 60: 81, Sep 61: 84
"BUS STOP," motion picture, May 59: 100
BUSSY-RABUTIN, COMTE DE (ROGER DE RABUTIN), Nov 61: 33
"BUSTER KEATON'S WALK," play, Sep 62: 41
BUTE, 3D EARL OF (JOHN STUART), Jul 63: 105
BUTLER, FANNY KEMBLE
Portrait of, Mar 59: 90
On Smith, Sydney, quoted, Mar 59: 90
BUTLER, HOWARD CROSBY, Sep 63: 86
BUTLER, JOHN, *Portrait of Billie,* May 63: 49
BUTLER, NICHOLAS MURRAY, Sep 60: 119, Mar 63: 27
BUTLER, SAMUEL
Erewhon, Mar 63: 78, Nov 63: 104
Quoted, Nov 61: 113; on cheating, Mar 59: 105

BUTOR, MICHEL, Jan 62: 100–1
Portrait of, Jan 62: 100
BUTTERFIELD, HERBERT, quoted, Mar 59: 10
"BUTTERFIELD 8," motion picture, Sep 61: 110, 112, Jan 63: 112
BUTTERWICK, J. C., Nov 62: 65
BUXTEHUDE, DIETRICH, Mar 60: 74
BUXTON, ANTHONY, Jan 61: 68
"BY LOVE POSSESSED," novel by James Gould Cozzens, Jul 62: 102
BYNG, JOHN, Mar 61: 119
BYNNER, WITTER
Drawing of, May 60: 46
And Spectric poetry hoax, May 60: 42–48
BYOIR, CARL, Jul 60: 121
BYRES, JAMES, Nov 59: 95, Nov 63: 63
BYRON, GEORGE GORDON, BARON, Sep 59: 30–31, Jan 60: 31, Mar 63: 65, May 63: 84–85
Don Juan, Jan 62: 61
And Kean, Edmund, Mar 62: 116
Portraits of, Mar 59: 90, May 61: 60, May 63: 84
Quoted: on gamblers, May 60: 98; on George IV, May 60: 124; on Homer, Jan 61: 91; on St. Peter's, Rome, Nov 59: 96; on Smith, Sydney, Mar 59: 90; on Venice, Sep 58: 50
And romantic revolt, May 61: 60–61, 62, 65, 66, 70, 74
"BY VENICE POSSESSED," article by James Morris with portfolio of photographs by Alexander Liberman, Mar 63: 14–25
BYZANTINE ART, Nov 63: 25, 28, 31, 33
André Malraux quoted on, Nov 58: 15–16
BYZANTINE EMPIRE, Nov 63: 4–34
Sardis under, Sep 63: 89
Sicily under, Sep 61: 26, 28
"BYZANTINE EMPRESS," painting by Larry Rivers, Sep 59: 100; illus, Sep 59: 97
BYZANTINE INSTITUTE OF AMERICA, Washington, D.C., Nov 63: 6, 28
BYZANTIUM, town, Nov 63: 9
"BYZANTIUM: THE OTHER HALF OF THE WORLD," article by Philip Sherrard, Nov 63: 4–34

C

CABANEL, ALEXANDRE, Jul 62: 18–19
Birth of Venus, Mar 60: 57
CABARETS, Jan 62: 66–71
CABET, ÉTIENNE, *Journey to Icaria,* Mar 63: 76
"CABINET OF DR. CALIGARI, THE," motion picture, Jan 63: 111
"CABIRIA," motion picture, May 59: 99, Mar 61: 98, May 61: 54
CABLE, MARY, articles by
"Brilliance in the Bush, A," Nov 60: 56–65
"Emperor's Monumental Folly, The," May 63: 32–39
"Grand Seraglio, The," May 59: 56–63, 131–35
"House That Is More Than a Home, The," Sep 61: 68–77
"Ludwig's Dream Castles," Jan 61: 34–43
CACCINI, GIULIO, Jul 60: 42
CACOYANNIS, MICHAEL, May 61: 57
CADAMOSTO, ALVISE DA, on caravels, quoted, Nov 60: 83
CADWALADER FAMILY, of Philadelphia, Jul 63: 9, 17
CADY, JOSIAH CLEAVELAND, Nov 58: 28, 117, 118
CAESAR, GAIUS JULIUS, Sep 58: 140, Nov 58: 110–11, Mar 60: 113, May 60: 126, Nov 62: 78, 88, Mar 63: 99, Sep 63: 35, 89
Ban against wheeled traffic in Rome, Jul 61: 45
On Celtic chariots, quoted, Sep 58: 149
And enslavement of captives, May 62: 45, 46–47
Memorandum to Robert Moses from, Mar 59: 26–27
In southern Gaul, Jul 59: 95
CAESAR, SID, Jan 61: 123, May 63: 46
CAESAREA FESTIVAL, Jul 62: 30
CAESARIUS OF HEISTERBACH, Nov 58: 106
CAGE, JOHN, Nov 58: 91, Jan 59: 55, 125, Jul 59: 71, Sep 60: 31, 122, Mar 61: 75, Mar 62: 107, Jan 63: 77
Photograph of, Jan 59: 55
"CAGE, THE," ballet, Nov 59: 56
CAGNY, PERCEVAL DE, Mar 62: 90
"CAHIERS DU CINÉMA, LES," journal, May 60: 51
CAHILL, JAMES, "The Chinese Imperial Art Treasure," article by, Jan 61: 14–24
CAILLAVET, MME, Nov 61: 37
CAILLEBOTTE, GUSTAVE, in painting by Renoir, Jul 62: 70
CAIRO, EGYPT, Friar Felix Fabri at, Mar 60: 90, 91
CAJATI, ENZIO, photograph of, Sep 63: 52
CALAS, DONAT, Mar 61: 119
CALAS, JEAN, Mar 61: 114, 119
"CALCULATED RISK," play, May 63: 106–7
CALCULATING MACHINE, invented by Pascal, Jan 63:

97, 99; illus Jan 63: 95
CALDER, ALEXANDER, Sep 59: 18, Nov 59: 121, May 60: 18, Nov 62: 10–17
  Photographs of, Nov 62: 11, 14, 17
  Works by. See ILLUSTRATIONS INDEX
CALDER, ALEXANDER MILNE, Nov 62: 12
CALDER, A. STIRLING, Nov 62: 12
CALDER, RITCHIE, on scientists, quoted, Jul 61: 7
"CALDER EN CAMPAGNE," article by Jean Davidson, Nov 62: 10–17
CALDERÓN DE LA BARCA, PEDRO, Jul 60: 38, 42, 50, 64, Nov 60: 126
CALDWELL, BARRY, photographs of, Jul 61: 106–9
CALDWELL, BETTY, Sep 59: 122
CALDWELL, ERSKINE, Jan 59: 18, May 59: 100
  Satirized by "Compass" players, Jan 62: 68
CALDWELL, ZOE, Nov 63: 37
CALEF, ROBERT, Nov 59: 63
CALIFORNIA
  Billboards in, May 61: 5
  Derivation of name, Nov 61: 110
  Educational frontier in, Mar 60: 70, 71
  Hotel del Coronado, Jan 61: 104, 109
  Huntington Hartford Foundation, Mar 63: 27, 32
  Suburban developments in, May 61: 19
CALIFORNIA, UNIVERSITY OF, Jan 59: 7, 14, 19
  Music at, Jan 59: 21, 22
  Teaching situation, Sep 62: 15, 17
  Writers at, Jan 59: 19
CALIFORNIA AT LOS ANGELES, UNIVERSITY OF, Theatre Group, Jan 63: 106
"CALIFORNIAN," journal, Jan 59: 7
CALIFORNIA SCHOOL OF FINE ARTS, Jan 59: 7, 13, Jul 60: 16
"CALIGULA," play by Albert Camus, Nov 59: 70, Jul 60: 94
CALIGULA, ROMAN EMPEROR, coinage in reign of, Sep 63: 3, 39
CALIXTUS III, POPE, Mar 62: 94
CALLAS, MARIA MENEGHINI, Sep 59: 51, 53, 56
  At Metropolitan Opera House, Nov 58: 118, 120
  Portrait of, Sep 59: 50
  Price, Leontyne, quoted on, Mar 61: 72
CALLIGRAPHY. See HANDWRITING
CALLISTHENES, Mar 59: 33, 44
"CALL ME BY MY RIGHTFUL NAME," play, Jul 61: 118
"CALL ME MADAM," musical, Nov 58: 65
CALLOT, JACQUES
  Prints by. See ILLUSTRATIONS INDEX
  Temptation of St. Anthony, The, Sep 58: 130, Nov 60: 31; illus, Nov 60: 44–45
CALVÉ, EMMA, Sep 59: 53, 54
CALVIN, JOHN, on witches, quoted, Nov 59: 59
CALVINISM
  In Dutch Republic, Sep 58: 20–21, 22, 26
  And witch mania, Nov 59: 59–60, 62–63
CAMARGUE, THE, Jul 59: 97
CAMBODIA
  Angkor, Jan 59: 60–81
  Malraux, André, in, Nov 58: 6
CAMBRAI, FRANCE, tournament at, Nov 58: 105–6
CAMBRIDGE, MASS., Saarinen buildings and their environment, Sep 60: 38
CAMBRIDGE DRAMA FESTIVAL, *Macbeth* at, Mar 60: 121
CAMBYSES I, KING OF PERSIA, Jan 63: 43
CAMDEN, HARRIET PARKER, Oklahoma song, quoted, Nov 61: 119
"CAMELOT," article by William K. Zinsser, May 61: 102–13
"CAMERA THREE," television production, Mar 60: 126
CAMERON, NIGEL, articles by, with photographs by Brian Brake
  "Eternal Dance of India, The," Sep 63: 64–73
  "Secrets of San Men, The," Jan 61: 4–13, 124
CAMPANELLA, TOMMASO, *The City of the Sun,* Mar 63: 76
CAMPANIA, ITALY
  Art of 1st century A.D., Jul 60: 114–15, 116
  Burial and discovery of Pompeii and Herculaneum, Mar 62: 42–69
CAMPBELL, DOUGLAS, Nov 63: 37–38, 40
CAMPBELL, GEORGE, *Philosophy of Rhetoric,* Jul 63: 35
CAMPBELL, STELLA PATRICK, G. B. Shaw and, Nov 58: 136–37
CAMPBELL, THOMAS, Mar 59: 92, May 63: 82–83
CAMUS, ALBERT, Nov 59: 69–72, May 60: 53–54, Jan 62: 97, 112
  Caligula, Jul 60: 94
  On Don Juan, quoted, Jan 62: 59
  Ionesco, Eugène, quoted on, May 61: 93
  Portraits of, Nov 59: 70, May 60: 53
CANADAY, JOHN

On abstract expressionism, quoted, Nov 59: 121
  Articles by: "Back to the Nude," Sep 63: 90–96; "Floating Rocks and Flaming Tubas," Jan 62: 76–87; "From Salon to Cellar—and Back?" Mar 60: 52–69; "Gargoyles for the Machine Age," Mar 61: 104–13; "Pavilions on the Prairie," Nov 61: 42–47
CANALETTO, ANTONIO, Nov 59: 96, Jul 63: 92, 105
  Paintings by, Nov 59: 74, Jul 63: 104
CANCAN, Mark Twain quoted on, May 63: 70
"CAN-CAN," musical, Sep 58: 60 (illus), May 63: 13
CANDACE, ETHIOPIAN QUEEN, Mar 63: 57
CANDAULES, KING OF LYDIA, Sep 63: 84
CANDELA, FÉLIX, Mar 59: 123, Sep 59: 19
  Buildings designed by, Mar 59: 25, Sep 59: 16
CANDELL, VICTOR, Jul 61: 13–14, 20–21
  Portrait of, with painting by, Jul 61: 21
"CANDIDATES, THE," motion picture, Nov 62: 97
"CANDIDE," book by Voltaire, Mar 61: 116
"CANDIDE," musical, Jul 59: 22
CANFIELD, CURT, Jan 60: 50
"CAN MAN KEEP UP WITH HISTORY?" article excerpted from *The Torch of Life,* book by René Dubos, Nov 62: 4–9
CANNON, JACK, Nov 60: 116
CANNON, W. B., Jan 59: 110
CANOVA, ANTONIO, Sep 59: 49
CANROBERT, FRANÇOIS CERTAIN, May 63: 73
CANTERBURY, ARCHBISHOP OF. See FISHER, GEOFFREY FRANCIS; LAUD, WILLIAM; RAMSEY, MICHAEL
"CAN THIS DRUG ENLARGE MAN'S MIND?" article by Gerald Heard, May 63: 28–31, 114–15
CANTOR, ARTHUR, Sep 60: 55, May 63: 10
CANTOR, EDDIE, Sep 58: 58
CANTRIL, HADLEY, *The Invasion from Mars,* Jul 63: 88
CAOURSIN, GUILLAUME, Mar 61: 49
CAPA, ROBERT, photograph by, May 60: 4
CAPABLANCA, JOSÉ R., Jan 62: 116, 117, 118, 119, 120
  Photograph of, Jan 62: 115
CAPE COD, MASS., Provincetown, Jul 61: 10–29
CAPEHART, HOMER, on slum clearance, quoted, Jul 59: 7
ČAPEK, KAREL, *R. U. R.,* Mar 63: 78
CAPLOW, THEODORE, and REECE J. McGEE, *The Academic Marketplace,* quoted, Sep 62: 19
CAPOTE, TRUMAN
  Grass Harp, The, Mar 60: 120
  Other Voices, Other Rooms, Mar 59: 118
CAPRI, ITALY, Mar 61: 22, 24
"CAPTAIN STORMFIELD'S VISIT TO HEAVEN," story by Mark Twain, May 59: 126
CARACALLA, ROMAN EMPEROR, Mar 60: 113
  Baths of, May 60: 39
  Coin portraits of, Sep 63: 39; illus, Sep 63: 37
CARÀCAS, VENEZUELA, shopping center, "Helicoid of the Tarpeian Rock," Jan 62: 94
CARAUSIUS, MARCUS AURELIUS, Sep 63: 40
CARAVAGGIO, MICHELANGELO DA, Mar 61: 80, Jul 61: 90, 95, Jul 63: 93, 94
  Painting by, Jul 60: 46
CARAVEL, in painting by Pieter Bruegel, Sep 58: 3; illus, Sep 58: 2
CARAVELS, Nov 60: 83
CARCASSONNE, FRANCE, Jul 61: 49–51
CARDANO, GIROLAMO, on witchcraft, quoted, Nov 59: 59
CARDIGAN, EARL OF (THOMAS BRUDENELL), May 60: 128
CARDINALE, CLAUDIA, Jan 63: 38
  Photograph of, Jan 63: 39
"CARDINAL MAZARIN'S FAREWELL TO HIS PAINTINGS," as described by Duc de Brienne, Nov 61: 82
"CARDINAL'S FIRST TALE, THE," story by Isak Dinesen, Sep 59: 112
CARDOZO, NANCY, May 60: 24
"CARDS OF IDENTITY," play, Jan 63: 27, 29
CARDUS, NEVILLE, "The Never Repressible Beecham," article by, Mar 62: 102–5
"CARE AND FEEDING OF ARTISTS, THE," article by Herbert Kubly, Mar 63: 26–33
CARÊME, MARIE-ANTOINE, May 61: 122, 126, Nov 62: 29, 30
"CARETAKER, THE," play, May 62: 112, Sep 62: 34, 35, 36, 41, Jan 63: 31, 32
CAREY, ANN, Mar 62: 13
CAREY, HENRY, Mar 62: 13
CARIANS, pre-Greek people, Mar 63: 99
CARLISLE, ANTHONY, May 62: 61–62
CARLISLE, 3D EARL OF (CHARLES HOWARD), Sep 61: 73
CARLTON HOUSE, London, Nov 62: 23, 24, Jul 63: 105, 106

CARLYLE, THOMAS
  Portrait of, Mar 59: 90
  Quoted: on art, Nov 58: 116; on Smith, Sydney, Mar 59: 90
CARMEL, CALIF., Jan 59: 7
"CARMEN JONES," motion picture, Mar 60: 128, Nov 60: 86, May 63: 49
CARMER, CARL, at MacDowell Colony, Mar 63: 29
CARMICHAEL, ELIZABETH. See NABOKOV, IVAN, co-author
"CARMINA BURANA," cantata by Carl Orff, May 63: 49
"CARNAVAL," ballet, Jan 61: 27
CARNÉ, MARCEL, May 60: 51, Mar 61: 98, Sep 61: 110
  Portrait of, May 60: 55
CARNEGIE, ANDREW, Jul 60: 69
CARNEGIE HALL, New York City, Jul 62: 6
CARNEY, ART, May 63: 46
CARNEY, ROBERT B., Mar 60: 50
CAROLINE OF BRUNSWICK, QUEEN OF ENGLAND, Sep 59: 3, Nov 62: 24, 29
"CAROUSEL," musical, Sep 58: 57, 60, 61, 143
CARPACCIO, VITTORE, painting by, Sep 63: 18–19
CARPETS, PERSIAN, Jan 63: 51, 72; illus, May 59: 44, Jan 60: 110–12, Jan 63: 70–71
CARPI, SCIBEC DE, Sep 60: 64
CARPZOV, BENEDICT, and witch mania, Nov 59: 60
CARRACCI, ANNIBALE, Jul 63: 94
CARRACCI, ANTONIO MARZIALE, painting by, Nov 61: 83
CARRÈRE, JOHN MERVEN, Jan 61: 104
  Building designed by, Jan 61: 106–7
CARRINGTON, HEREWARD, Jan 59: 108, 109
CARRINGTON, RICHARD, "The Natural History of the Mermaid," article by, Jan 60: 129–36
CARROLL, DIAHANN, Nov 60: 86
  Photograph of, Nov 60: 87
CARROLL, JOHN B., on language, quoted, Jul 63: 47
CARROLL, LEWIS
  Alice's Adventures in Wonderland, ms. of, Nov 60: 97
  Greek and Latin translations of verses by, Jul 61: 113, 114, 115
  "Jabberwocky," Sep 58: 129–30
  At Oxford, Jan 63: 85
  Through the Looking Glass, quoted on words, Jul 63: 34
CARROLL, MADELEINE, Sep 63: 77 (note), 80
CARSON, RALPH M., on advertisers' use of English, quoted, Jul 63: 36
CARSTAIRS, JOSEPH, Sep 59: 128
CARTEAUX, VIRGINIA, Nov 62: 98, 99
CARTER, ELLIOTT, Jan 62: 9
CARTER, JOHN, Mar 59: 107–8, 109 (note)
CARTER, MORRIS, on Isabella Stewart Gardner, quoted, Jul 59: 30, 31, 134
CARTERET, PHILIP, Sep 63: 46
CARTHAGE
  Etruscan alliance with, May 60: 73
  Invasions of Sicily by, Sep 61: 23, 24, 26, 28–29
  As setting for screen epics, May 61: 53–54
"CARTHAGE IN FLAMES," motion picture, May 61: 53–54
CARTOON, definition of, May 59: 121
"CARTOUCHE," motion picture, Jan 63: 38
CARUSO, ENRICO, at Metropolitan Opera House, Nov 58: 120
CARVER COURT, Coatesville, Pa., Sep 62: 58
CARVING, of ivory, May 60: 89, 94, 120–21
CASALS, PABLO, Jul 60: 127, Sep 61: 84, 86, 87
  Photograph of, Sep 61: 86
CASANOVA, GIOVANNI JACOPO, Jan 62: 60
CASCA, PUBLIUS SERVILIUS, on Romans, quoted, May 60: 40
CASE, FRANK, Jul 62: 36
  Caricature of, Jul 62: 41
"CASE FOR REPERTORY, THE," article by Robert Hatch, Jan 63: 106–9
CASELLA, ALFREDO, Nov 62: 46
"CASE OF COEXISTENCE, A: CHRISTENDOM AND THE TURKS," article by H. R. Trevor-Roper, Sep 58: 46–47
CASERTA, ITALY, palace at, May 62: 15, 21
CASEY, BEN, television character, Sep 62: 115
CASSATT, MARY, May 60: 103, Sep 60: 102, Jul 63: 18
CASSAVETES, JOHN, Sep 58: 43, Mar 61: 16, 19
  Photograph of, Mar 61: 16
CASSEL, JEAN-PIERRE, Jan 62: 110
CASSILIS, EARL OF, Nov 58: 107
CASSIUS, CAIUS, Nov 58: 111
CASSIUS SEVERUS, Sep 62: 88
CASSIVELAUNUS, Sep 58: 149
CASSON, HUGH, Nov 60: 125
CASSON, LIONEL, photograph of, May 59: 17
CASTAGNO, ANDREA DEL, painting by, Nov 62: 87
CASTELLANI, RENATO, Mar 61: 98
CASTELMORON, MME DE, Nov 61: 34

CASTIGLIONE, BALDASSARE, Jan 60: 68, 73
  Colonna, Vittoria, quoted on, Jan 60: 65
  Courtier, The (Il Cortigiano), Mar 59: 38, Sep 59: 120, Jan 60: 65, 68; excerpt from, Jan 60: 73
  Portraits of, Jan 60: 65, Nov 61: 83
CASTIGLIONE, COUNTESS, May 63: 69–70
  Portraits of, May 63: 64, 65
CASTLE HOWARD, Sep 61: 73
"CASTLE OF THE PYRENEES," painting by René Magritte, Jan 62: 77–78; illus, Jan 62: 76
CASTRO, FIDEL, effects of regime seen during filming of *Our Man in Havana*, Nov 59: 31, 125
CASTROL HOUSE, London, Nov 60: 124, 125; illus, Nov 60: 14
ÇATAL HÜYÜK, TURKEY, neolithic site, Sep 62: 7 (map), 8
  Sculptures, Nov 63: 66–67
  Wall paintings, Sep 62: 10–13
"CATALOGUE, THE," book of drawings by Saul Steinberg, May 63: 13
CATANIA, ITALY, Sep 61: 34
"CATCHER IN THE RYE, THE," novel by J. D. Salinger, May 62: 101–2, 106, 107
  Excerpts from, May 62: 102
CATCOTT, GEORGE, May 60: 38
CATE, DOUGLAS, on French literary prizes, quoted, Jul 63: 74
CATER, DOUGLASS
  "Kennedy Look in the Arts, The," article by, Sep 61: 4–17
  On newspaper readers, quoted, Mar 60: 50
CATHCART, CHARLES, Nov 58: 53
CATHER, WILLA, Sep 62: 94, Mar 63: 28, 33
  Photograph of, Mar 63: 30
CATHERINE II, EMPRESS OF RUSSIA (CATHERINE THE GREAT), Sep 60: 130, 135 (illus), Mar 61: 118, Jul 61: 95, Sep 63: 30–31
  Imperial crown of, May 63: 96
"CATO," play, Mar 62: 56
"CAT ON A HOT TIN ROOF," play, May 59: 55, Jul 59: 42
CATS, JACOB, Sep 58: 24, 26
CATTANEO, SIMONETTA. See VESPUCCI, SIMONETTA
CATTELL, J. McKEEN, May 60: 33
CATTLE, value in Africa, Mar 63: 52
CATULLUS, survival of works by, Nov 62: 76, 80, 89
"CAUCASIAN CHALK CIRCLE, THE," play, Jan 62: 66, May 62: 35, 40, 41
CAUCHON, PIERRE, BISHOP OF BEAUVAIS, Mar 62: 92, 93–94, 97
  In illumination from *The Vigils of Charles VII*, Mar 62: 96
"CAUTIONARY VERSES," book by Hilaire Belloc, May 62: 103
CAVAFY, CONSTANTINE, Mar 60: 114
CAVAIGNAC, LOUIS EUGÈNE, Nov 63: 103–4
"CAVALCADE," motion picture, May 59: 99
CAVALCANTI, ALBERTO, May 62: 106
"CAVALLERIA RUSTICANA," opera, Mar 60: 119
CAVANAUGH, EDWARD F., Mar 60: 120
CAVAZZI, GIOVANNI-ANTONIO, on African dancing, quoted, Mar 63: 40
"CAVE-DWELLING CARVERS OF 5,000 YEARS AGO," article by Jean Perrot, Jan 62: 72–75
CAVE DWELLINGS, Jul 61: 34–35
CAVENDISH, HENRY, Sep 58: 116
"CAVE OF TIBERIUS, THE," article by Robert Emmett Ginna, May 59: 102–7, 122–24
CAVE PAINTINGS
  At Lascaux, Jul 61: 34, Sep 62: 11, 12
  Of Palermo and Levanzo, Sep 61: 23
  Of Tassili plateau in Sahara, May 59: 70–83, Sep 62: 11, 12, Mar 63: 43
CAVOUR, CAMILLO BENSO DI, COUNT, May 63: 70
CAYLUS, COMTE DE (ANNE CLAUDE PHILIPPE DE TUBIÈRES), Mar 62: 55
"CBS REPORTS," television program, Sep 61: 113, Jul 62: 95
CECIL, DAVID, "The Man Who Never Stopped Playing," article by, May 61: 33–40
CELA, CAMILO JOSÉ, Mar 59: 74, 126
CELEBES, INDONESIA, Mar 61: 22–23
CÉLINE, LOUIS-FERDINAND, Alfred Kazin quoted on, Jul 62: 100
CELLER, EMANUEL, Sep 61: 17
CELLINI, BENVENUTO, Sep 60: 62
  Bust of Bindo Altoviti by, Jul 59: 30
CELLINI, RENATO, Jan 62: 10–11
CELTS, wheeled vehicles of, Sep 58: 149, 150–51
CEMETERIES, PALEOLITHIC, Jul 61: 34–35
"CENCI, THE," play, Mar 62: 116
CENSORSHIP
  Bowdler, Thomas, and his version of Shakespeare, Sep 62: 68–71
  Communications satellites and, Jan 62: 20–21

And loss of ancient books, Nov 62: 88–89
CENTAURO-TRITONS, Jan 60: 134
"CENTIPEDE," sculpture by Noguchi, Mar 60: 106, 108, 112; illus, Mar 60: 107
CENTRAL RAILROAD OF NEW JERSEY, Jul 59: 6
CENTURY 21 EXPOSITION, May 62: 16
CERAM, C. W., and PETER LYON, "The Blue Museum," article by, Nov 58: 66–77
CERF, BENNETT, Jul 60: 122
CERVANTES SAAVEDRA, MIGUEL DE
  At Battle of Lepanto, Nov 61: 111, 112, Jul 63: 50, 58, 60
  Don Quixote de la Mancha, Sep 59: 114
  Portrait of, Nov 61: 107
  Two Spains of *Don Quixote*, Nov 61: 106–13
CÉSAR (CÉSAR BALDACCINI), Mar 63: 104
  Sculpture by, Mar 61: 106–7, 110–11
CEUTA, MOROCCO, Portuguese conquest of, Nov 60: 74, 76
CEYLON, Mar 61: 33
  Home of Paul Bowles in, Mar 61: 22
  National Dancers of, Sep 60: 106–9
CÉZANNE, PAUL, Jan 59: 103, Nov 59: 121, Mar 60: 53, 58, Jul 60: 115, Sep 60: 121, Mar 62: 25, Jul 62: 54, Nov 62: 57
  Boy in a Red Waistcoat, Nov 62: 64
  Influence of Poussin on, Mar 61: 78, 92
  Malraux, André, quoted on, Nov 58: 116
  Moore, Henry, quoted on, Nov 60: 114
  Paintings by. See ILLUSTRATIONS INDEX
CHABROL, CLAUDE, May 60: 50, 52–53, Sep 61: 110, Jan 62: 109
  Portrait of, May 60: 52
CHADDS FORD, PA., home of Andrew Wyeth, Sep 61: 88, 98
CHADWICK, GEORGE, *Melpomene*, Jul 59: 20
CHADWICK, LYNN, sculpture by, Mar 61: 106
CHAERONEA, BATTLE OF, Mar 59: 32
CHAGALL, MARC, Sep 62: 24
  Stained-glass windows designed by, Sep 62: cover, 3, 26–27
"CHAIRS, THE," play, May 61: 91, 93, Jul 61: 116, Sep 62: 36, 39, 40
CHALGRIN, JEAN FRANÇOIS THÉRÈSE, Mar 62: 62
CHALIAPIN, FEODOR, Sep 59: 57
CHÂLONS, BATTLE OF, May 63: 79
CHÂLONS, COUNT OF, in tournament with Edward I of England, Nov 58: 95
CHAMBERLAIN, HOUSTON STEWART, May 63: 41
CHAMBERLAIN, JOHN, sculpture by, Mar 61: 112
CHAMBERLAIN, JOHN R., Jan 60: 7
CHAMBERLAIN, NEVILLE, Mar 62: 29
CHAMBERLIN, WILLIAM HENRY, on *Time Cycle* performance by Boston Symphony Orchestra, quoted, Jan 63: 78 (note)
CHAMBER MUSIC PLAYERS, Sep 61: 87
CHAMBERS, ERNEST, "A Word from Our Sponsors," miniature satirical revue by, Jul 61: 77
CHAMBERS, MARY (MRS. EDMUND KEAN), Mar 62: 114–15, 116
CHAMBERS, WILLIAM, May 59: 47
CHAMBLESS, EDGAR, Jan 62: 94
CHAMFORT, SÉBASTIEN R. N., on love, quoted, Sep 61: 112
CHAMPAGNE, COUNTESS OF, May 60: 31, Jan 62: 57
CHAMPAIGNE, PHILIPPE DE, Jul 60: 38, 50
  Painting by, Jul 60: 40
CHAMS, of Annam, Jan 59: 74
CHANCE, as principle of artistic creation, Sep 60: 30–32, 121–24, Mar 61: 45–46, Jan 63: 77
"CHANCE MEETING ON THE AMERICAN ROAD, A," article by Oliver Jensen, Nov 58: 36–37
CHAND, DIP, painting by, Sep 60: 18
CHANDIGARH, INDIA, Nov 59: 112, Mar 61: 36
  Le Corbusier buildings, Sep 59: 18, Jan 60: 119
CHANDLER, RICHARD, NICHOLAS REVETT and WILLIAM PARS, *Antiquities of Ionia*, Mar 62: 55
CHANDLESS, WILLIAM, Jul 63: 114
CHANDOS, DUKE OF, Nov 58: 56
CHANEL OF PARIS, Mar 63: 94
CHANEY, LON, Nov 58: 133
"CHANGE OF AIR, A," short story by Ivan Gold, Mar 59: 118
"CHANGE OF HEART, A," novel by Michel Butor, Jan 62: 100–1
CHANNEL ISLANDS, ENGLAND, Mar 61: 32
CHANNELS (see also CRITIC'S VIEW: CHANNELS), articles by Stephen White
  "Abolish the Armchair Athlete," Nov 62: 112–13
  "Hershey Bar, The: Is Advertising Really Necessary?" May 63: 112–13
  "Suds in Your Eye," Jan 63: 113–14
  "21-inch Smokescreen, The," Mar 63: 113–14
  "Two Cheers for Mediocrity," Sep 62: 114–15
CHANNING, CAROL, May 63: 46

CHANNING, WILLIAM ELLERY (1818–1901), Mar 63: 77
CHANTELOU, PAUL FRÉART DE, Mar 61: 80, 90, 92
CHAO KAN, Jan 61: 25
  Painting by, Jan 61: 23
CHAO YEN, Jan 61: 3, 16
  Painting by, Jan 61: cover, 3
CHAPLIN, CHARLES S., May 59: 121, Jan 60: 96, Nov 61: 115, May 62: 38, Nov 62: 110, Mar 63: 15, May 63: 46, Sep 63: 75
  Tyrone Guthrie quoted on, Jan 61: 27
CHAPMAN, GEORGE, "On first looking into Chapman's Homer," by Keats, quoted, Jan 61: 91
CHAPMAN, JOHN JAY, May 60: 46
CHAPPELL FAMILY, of New London, Conn., Mar 60: 31
CHAPU, HENRI MICHEL ANTOINE, Mar 62: 97
CHARDIN, JEAN BAPTISTE SIMÉON, André Malraux quoted on, Nov 58: 116, 117
CHARDIN, TEILHARD DE, Sep 63: 109
  Photograph of, Sep 63: 8
CHARDOGNE, FERRI DE, Nov 58: 105
CHARGE OF THE LIGHT BRIGADE, May 60: 128
CHARIOTS, Sep 58: 147–49
  Chinese, found near San Men Dam, Jan 61: 124
  Egyptian, Nov 59: 18–19
  Homeric and Mycenaean, Jan 61: 81, 85
  In Sahara rock paintings, May 59: 83
CHARLEMAGNE, May 59: 44, Mar 60: 76, Jan 62: 26, Mar 63: 4, May 63: 96
  Handwriting of, Sep 59: 129
  Handwriting reform of, Sep 59: 126
  Portrait of, Sep 59: 129
CHARLEMONT, EDUARD, Mar 60: 58
  Painting by, Mar 60: 69
CHARLES, ARCHDUKE OF AUSTRIA, portrait of, Jul 63: 95
CHARLES V, HOLY ROMAN EMPEROR, Sep 60: 61, Mar 61: 65, May 62: 95, Jul 63: 50, Sep 63: 30
  Portrait of, Nov 61: 108; by Titian, Jul 61: 89, 94, 95, Jul 63: 94; illus, Jul 61: 83
  Sicily under, Sep 61: 34
  Spain under, Nov 61: 109, 110, 112
CHARLES I, KING OF ENGLAND, Sep 59: 120, Nov 59: 62, Mar 60: 103, Jan 63: 9, May 63: 102
  Death warrant of, facsimile, Sep 59: 133
  As patron of arts, Jul 61: 78–95, Jul 63: 92, 93–96
  Portraits of, Sep 59: 28, 133, Jul 61: 78, 93, Jul 63: 94
  Van Dyck portrait sold, Sep 61: 77
CHARLES II, KING OF ENGLAND, Mar 60: 100, 125, May 60: 98, Jul 61: 94, Sep 62: 114, May 63: 101, Jul 63: 93, 96
CHARLES V, KING OF FRANCE, Sep 60: 60
CHARLES VI, KING OF FRANCE, Mar 62: 89, 91
CHARLES VII, KING OF FRANCE, Sep 60: 61
  In illumination from *The Vigils of Charles VII*, Mar 62: 94
  Joan of Arc and, Mar 62: 89–95, 97
  As patron of Jean Fouquet, Nov 61: 88, 97
CHARLES VIII, KING OF FRANCE, Sep 60: 62
CHARLES III, KING OF NAPLES, Mar 62: 50, May 62: 15
CHARLES XII, KING OF SWEDEN, Sep 59: 79
CHARLES, J. A. C., Sep 58: 116, 117
CHARLES MOVIE THEATRE, New York City, Nov 62: 96–99
CHARLES OF ANJOU, Sep 61: 32, 37
CHARLES THE BOLD, DUKE OF BURGUNDY, Sep 58: 63, May 63: 94–95
"CHARLEY WEAVER'S LETTERS FROM MAMMA," book by Cliff Arquette, Jul 60: 121
CHARLOTTE, PRINCESS OF WALES AND OF SAXE-COBURG, Sep 59: 2, 3
CHARLOTTE SOPHIA, QUEEN OF ENGLAND, Jul 63: 105
  Portrait of, Jul 63: 95
CHARMATZ, WILLIAM, drawings by, Sep 62: 116–19
CHARMIDES, Jul 60: 103
CHARTRES CATHEDRAL, Sep 59: 5–6, 18
  André Malraux quoted on, Nov 58: 112–13
CHASE, RICHARD, Jul 61: 100, 104
CHASE, STUART, Jul 60: 66, 67, 68
CHASE MANHATTAN BANK, Mar 61: 120–21
  Art program of, Nov 60: 4–11
  Automation in, Sep 62: 120
  Building of, Nov 60: 16
CHASTEL, ANDRÉ, on American abstract expressionism, quoted, Nov 59: 120–21
CHASTELARD, PIERRE DE BOSCOSEL DE, Jul 63: 29
CHATEAUBRIAND, FRANÇOIS-RENÉ DE, May 61: 60, 61, 66, 67, 70, Mar 63: 76
  Portraits of, Nov 58: 89, May 61: 67
  Récamier, Mme, and, Nov 58: 86, 146
CHÂTEAU DE REUX, Normandy, France, stained-glass window in chapel of, Sep 62: 29

CHÂTEAUNEUF, ABBÉ DE (FRANÇOIS DE CASTA-GNÈRES), May 60: 35
CHÂTEAUNEUF, MARQUIS DE (PIERRE-ANTOINE DE CASTAGNÈRES), Mar 61: 116
CHÂTELET, MARQUISE DU (ÉMILIE DE BRETEUIL), Mar 61: 117–18
CHATHAM, 1ST EARL OF. See PITT, WILLIAM THE ELDER
CHATHAM, 2D EARL OF. See PITT, JOHN
CHATSWORTH, Nov 58: 50, 52, 56, Jan 59: 59
CHATTERJEE, SOUMITRA, Jan 61: 115
CHATTERTON, THOMAS
    Childhood of, May 60: 33, 34, 35–36, 37, 38
    Portrait of, May 60: 33
CHAUCER, GEOFFREY
    Attitude toward nature, Mar 60: 14
    Romaunt of the Rose, translation by, quoted, May 59: 41
CHAUNCEY, HENRY, Sep 59: 25
    Photograph of, Sep 59: 27
CHAUVENCY, FRANCE, tournament at, Nov 58: 105
CHAUVIN, NICOLAS, May 60: 128
CHAYEFSKY, PADDY
    Drawing of, Sep 60: 52–53
    Interview with, Sep 60: 49–56
"CHEATERS, THE," motion picture, Sep 61: 110
CHEKE, MARCUS, "Her Revenge," story by, Mar 59: 129–32
CHEKHOV, ANTON, Jul 59: 48, Mar 61: 43, Nov 62: 108
    Anouilh, Jean, quoted on, Nov 60: 126
    Mirsky, Prince, quoted on, Mar 62: 110
    Three Sisters, The, Tyrone Guthrie Theatre production, Nov 63: 38, 39–40, 41
CHELMSFORD, ENGLAND, holocaust of witches in, Nov 59: 61
CHEMICAL BANK & TRUST COMPANY, Mar 61: 121
CHEMICAL CORN EXCHANGE BANK, Mar 61: 121
CHEMISTRY
    Development of, Nov 63: 108
    Einstein quoted on, Mar 62: 74
    Ghana claim to origin of, Jan 63: 117
CHEN-CHI CHANG, Jul 59: 127
CHERRY-GARRARD, APSLEY, Sep 58: 8, 12, 138
    On Robert Falcon Scott, quoted, Sep 58: 9
CHERRY LANE THEATRE, New York City, Mar 60: 98
CHESS, Jan 62: 114–28
    And Cold War strategy, Nov 63: 61–62
    First description in European tongue, Sep 62: 83
    Spread of, Jan 63: 51, 58
CHESTER COUNTY, PA., home of Andrew Wyeth in, Sep 61: 88, 98
CHESTERTON, G. K.
    Beerbohm, Max, quoted on, May 61: 40
    Influence on C. S. Lewis, May 59: 66
CHEVALIER, ETIENNE, Book of Hours of, Nov 61: 88–97
CHEVALIER, MAURICE, Mar 60: 128
CHEVREUL, MARIE-EUGÈNE, picture interview with, Mar 59: 68–69
"CHEVY CHASE," ballad, Nov 63: 43, 44
CHEW, BENJAMIN, Jul 63: 14
CHEW, SAMUEL, portrait of, Jul 63: 14
CHIANCIANO, ITALY, hall at spa of, Mar 59: 22–23, 122
CHIANG YEE
    Silent Traveller, The, excerpts and paintings from, Nov 59: 129–36
    Sketch of, Nov 59: 129
CHICAGO, ILL.
    Bowling alley, suburban, Mar 63: 93
    "Compass, The," cabaret, Jan 62: 68, 70
    Disfiguring of, May 61: 4, 5
    Goodman Memorial Theatre, Jan 62: 13
    Loss of motion picture theatres, Mar 60: 127
    Playwrights company, Jan 62: 66, 68, Jul 62: 49
    State Street lighting, Nov 59: 107, 110
    Tribune Tower competition, Nov 60: 16, Jan 63: 12
    Wright, Frank Lloyd, in, Sep 60: 98–103, 127–28
CHICAGO, UNIVERSITY OF
    Hutchins, Robert, at, Sep 58: 102
    Saarinen, Eero, quoted on quadrangle of, Jul 60: 82
    Teaching situation at, Sep 62: 15
CHICAGO ART INSTITUTE, in 1896–1906, Sep 60: 102
CHICAGO SYMPHONY ORCHESTRA, Jul 59: 19
CHICAGO WORLD'S FAIR OF 1893. See WORLD'S COLUMBIAN EXPOSITION
"CHICKEN SOUP WITH BARLEY," play, Jul 61: 117
CHIDAMBARAM, INDIA. Shiva Nataraja sculpture at, Sep 63: 68, 72; illus, Sep 63: 64
"CHIEN ANDALOU, LE," motion picture, Nov 62: 97, 110, 111
CHIGI, PRICE LUDOVICO, portrait of, Mar 61: 69
CHILDE, V. GORDON. See JOPE, E. M., co-author
"CHILDE HAROLD'S PILGRIMAGE," poem by Byron, May 61: 60, 62–63, 65, 67
"CHILD GOD," print by Hodaka Yoshida, May 60: 113, 114; illus, May 60: 111
CHILDHOOD
    American children of today, Mar 62: 40–41
    Beaudelaire quoted on, Mar 59: 72, 74
    Cult of child, and its debunking, May 62: 102–3
    Of genius, May 60: 32–38
    IQ of American children, Mar 62: 74
    La Fontaine quoted on, Mar 59: 72
    On Plains Frontier, of Wallace Stegner, Sep 62: 94–95
"CHILDHOOD PATTERN OF GENIUS, THE," article by Harold G. McCurdy, May 60: 32–38
"CHILD OF THE DARK," book by Carolina Maria de Jesus, reviewed, Nov 62: 109–10
"CHILD OF THE FAR FRONTIER," article excerpted from Wolf Willow, book by Wallace Stegner, Sep 62: 94–95
"CHILDREN OF DARKNESS," play, Mar 60: 121
"CHILDREN OF SÁNCHEZ," book by Oscar Lewis, Nov 62: 110
CHILDREN'S BOOKS, of C. S. Lewis, May 59: 66, 127
"CHILDREN'S HOUR, THE," play, Sep 60: 51
CHILDS, MARQUIS W., "The World of Walter Paepcke," article by, Sep 58: 96–103, 133–34
CHIMBORAZO, peak in Ecuador, exploration of by Alexander von Humboldt, Jul 59: 62, 63, 64–65
CHINA
    Archaeological rescue project above San Men Dam, Jan 61: 4–13, 124
    Boxer Uprising, Sep 60: 12
    Early wheeled vehicles in, Sep 58: 147, 151
    Floating sages of, Nov 60: 32
    Gardens of, May 59: 25, 29–30
    Influence on early African cultures, Mar 63: 57, 58
    Photographs by Brian Brake, Sep 62: 48–56
    White man as pictured by artists of, Sep 60: 12, 13, 28
"CHINA OF THE CHINESE," portfolio of photographs by Brian Brake, Sep 62: 48–56
CHINESE ART
    Attitude toward nature in, Mar 60: 13
    Imperial treasure, Jan 61: 14–25
    Ivory carving, May 60: 94, 120
"CHINESE CHRISTIAN," painting by Godfrey Kneller, Jul 63: 96
"CHINESE IMPERIAL ART TREASURE, THE," article by James Cahill, Jan 61: 14–25
CHINY, COUNT OF. See LOOZ, LOUIS DE
"CHIPS WITH EVERYTHING," play, Jan 63: 26–27 (illus), 32
CHIUSI, ITALY, May 60: 77
CHIVALRY
    Arthurian legend, versions of James Knowles and Thomas Malory, May 60: 115–18
    Courtly love, Jan 62: 57–58
    Courts of Love, May 60: 30, 31
    Lichtenstein, Ulrich von, as example, Sep 59: 113–17
    Tournaments in development of, Nov 58: 92–107
    Two Spains of Don Quixote, Nov 61: 106–13
CHMIELNICKI, BOGDAN, Mar 60: 103
CHOATE, JOSEPH H., May 60: 13
CHOISEUL, DUC DE, Nov 61: 35
CHOLA DANCE FIGURES, Sep 63: 68, 72
CHOLMONDELEY, LORD, Sep 59: 128
CHOMSKY, NOAM, quoted, Jul 63: 45, 46
CHOPIN, FRÉDÉRIC FRANÇOIS, Mar 61: 75, May 61: 81
    Barcarolle manuscript, Sep 61: 86
    Frédéric Chopin by Franz Liszt, translated by Edward N. Waters, reviewed, May 63: 109–10
    Portrait of, May 61: 81
CHOSROES. See KHOSRAU
CHOU PERIOD, in China, Jan 61: 11, 124
CHOU TA-KWAN, on Angkor, quoted, Jan 59: 71, 74, 75
"CHRIST CARRYING THE CROSS," painting attributed to Giorgione, Jul 59: 31
CHRISTIAN, EDWARD, defense of Bounty mutineers, Sep 63: 43, 44, 45, 46
CHRISTIAN, FLETCHER, and mutiny on H.M.S. Bounty, Sep 63: 42–48
CHRISTIAN, LINDA, Jul 60: 120
    Portrait of, Jul 60: 7
CHRISTIAN ART. See under ART
CHRISTIAN CHURCH
    In Middle Ages, Jul 59: 130–31
    Millenary doctrine and philo-Semitism of 17th century, Mar 60: 101–3, 124–25
    Mysticism of Baroque age, Jul 60: 38
    Schism between Orthodox Church and Rome, Nov 63: 31
    And witchcraft cult, Nov 59: 57–63
CHRISTIANITY
    In ancient Rome, Jul 61: 45 (illus)
    In Byzantine Empire, Nov 63: 9, 11, 12, 15, 20, 23, 25;
    icon schism, Nov 63: 22, 26, 28
    Honest to God, by John A. T. Robinson, excerpt from and comments on, Sep 63: 4–9, 104–7
    Vs. Islam in Battle of Lepanto, Jul 63: 49–61
    In motion picture epics of classical world, May 61: 52, 53, 55, 56
    Toynbee, Arnold J., quoted on, Jan 61: 63–65
"CHRISTIANITY WITHOUT RELIGION," Sep 63: 105–6, 107
CHRISTIANOPOLIS, Mar 63: 75–76
"CHRISTIAN REGISTER," on Spectra, quoted, May 60: 43
"CHRISTIAN SPACEMAN, THE—C. S. LEWIS," article by Edmund Fuller, May 63: 64–67, 125–27
CHRISTINA, QUEEN OF SWEDEN, Jul 61: 94
    And messianic year of 1666, Mar 60: 125
"CHRISTINA'S WORLD," painting by Andrew Wyeth, Sep 61: 98, 100
"CHRIST IN THE UNIVERSE," poem by Alice Meynell, quoted, Jan 59: 122
"CHRISTMAS GIFT SUGGESTIONS," by Oliver Jensen, Nov 58: 140–41
CHRISTOFF, BORIS, Sep 59: 57
"CHRISTOPHER AND ME," motion picture, Mar 61: 17
CHRYSEROS, FLAVIUS, Mar 63: 98
CHRYSLER, WALTER P., JR., Jul 61: 16
CHRYSLER ART MUSEUM, in Provincetown, Mass., Jul 61: 16
CHURCH, FREDERICK, painting by (with Jervis McEntee and G. P. A. Healy), illus, Nov 59: 101
CHURCH, THOMAS, Jan 59: 8
CHURCHES and SYNAGOGUES (see also ILLUSTRATIONS INDEX)
    Berkeley, Calif., Christian Science, Jan 59: 10
    In Brazil: Church of Saint Francis at Pampulha, Sep 59: 20
    Byzantium-influenced, Nov 63: 28
    Collegeville, Minn., at St. John's University Abbey, Mar 59: 123
    Creve Coeur, Mo., at Priory of St. Mary and St. Louis, Mar 59: 123
    Of Dutch Republic, Sep 58: 20–21
    Elkins Park, Pa., Beth Sholom, Sep 59: 19
    In England: of St. Mary Redcliffe, Bristol, May 60: 36, 38; Saint Paul's, London, Jul 60: 50
    In France: Chartres Cathedral, Sep 59: 5–6, 18; at Le Couvent Sainte-Marie de la Tourette, Mar 61: 40; Matisse chapel. Vence, Mar 61: 39; St. Lazare Cathedral, Autun, sculptures of, Sep 61: 46–57; Saint-Trophime, Arles, Jul 59: 90, 132; Shrine of the Virgin, Ronchamp, Sep 59: 9, Mar 61: 39
    In Italy: Gesù, Rome, Jul 60: 38; at Palermo, Sep 61: 30, 32; St. Mark's, Venice, Nov 63: 9; St. Peter's, Rome, Jan 62: 22–32, 41–45, 48–49; San Giorgio Maggiore, Venice, Mar 63: 15; Sant' Agnese, Rome, Jul 60: 38; Santa Maria degli Angeli, Rome, May 60: 39; Sistine Chapel, Vatican, Jul 60: 50; Syracuse cathedral, Nov 60: 29, Sep 61: 22, 23, 26
    Jerusalem, Church of the Holy Sepulcher, Mar 60: 84, 85
    On Mount Sinai: Chapel of the Bush, Mar 60: 90; Saint Catherine's, Mar 60: 89, Nov 63: 25
    Nervi, Pier, influence on church design, Mar 59: 123
    New York City, Cathedral of St. John the Divine, Jan 63: 12
    Oak Park, Ill., Unity Temple, Sep 59: 6
    Rochester, N.Y., First Unitarian, Sep 62: 60, 62
    Rowayton, Conn., House of Worship, Nov 62: 70–73
    Stained-glass revival in, Sep 62: cover, 3, 22–32
    Stamford, Conn., First Presbyterian, Sep 59: 19
    In Turkey: Church of the Chora (Kariye Çami mosque), Istanbul, Nov 63: 31; Hagia Sophia, Istanbul, Nov 63: 9, 11, 12, 15, 25, 34; at Sardis, Sep 63: 89
CHURCHILL, HENRIETTA (DUCHESS OF MARLBOROUGH), Sep 61: 76
CHURCHILL, JOHN. See MARLBOROUGH, 1ST DUKE OF
CHURCHILL, RANDOLPH, Jul 60: 122
    Photograph of, Jul 60: 6
CHURCHILL, LADY RANDOLPH, photograph of, Sep 61: 77
CHURCHILL, WINSTON S., Nov 60: 21, 23, 119, May 62: 59, Mar 63: 14, Jul 63: 48, Sep 63: 101
    At age 15, portrait, Nov 60: 25
    On Europe, quoted, Mar 63: 4
    Marlborough, His Life and Times, quoted, Sep 61: 70, 77
    Painting by, May 62: 76
    In painting by Feliks Topolski, Nov 60: 132–33, 134, 135
    Portraits of, Jan 59: 103, 105; illus, Jan 59: 103
    World Crisis, quoted, Jan 59: 121
"CHURCH WITH A TWIST," article by Russell Bourne, Nov 62: 70–73
CIARDI, JOHN, Jan 62: 14
    On Jean Anouilh, quoted, Nov 60: 52
CICERO, MARCUS TULLIUS

Attitude toward nature, Mar 60: 13
Invention of shorthand by slave of, Jan 63: 116, 117
Quoted: on Caesar's second expedition to Britain, May 62: 46–47; on gestures, Mar 61: 89
In Renaissance curriculum, Jan 60: 62, Sep 63: 97
Survival of works by, Nov 62: 77, 89–90, 93
"CID, EL," motion picture, Mar 63: 109
CID, EL, statue of, Sep 62: 88
"CID, LE," play, Jul 60: 50
CIGARS and CIGARETTES, advertising of, Nov 59: 114–15, 117, Sep 60: 120, Mar 63: 113–14
CIMABUE, GIOVANNI, Jan 59: 103
CIMMERIANS, Sep 63: 85
CINCINNATI, UNIVERSITY OF, work at site of Troy, Jan 61: 77, 94
CINEMASCOPE, Mar 60: 128
"CIRCA 1400" EXHIBITION, Mar 63: 8
"CIRCLE IN THE SQUARE," article by Robert Hatch, Mar 60: 94–99, 119–21
CIRCLISM, in painting, Sep 61: 66–67
CITIES (see also CITY PLANNING; URBAN RENEWAL)
Death and Life of Great American Cities, The, book by Jane Jacobs, Jul 62: 50
Effect of population growth on, Sep 58: 50, 53, 54
Medieval and Renaissance, Sep 59: 28–29, 121
Origins, transformations, and prospects of: Amsterdam, Jul 61: 58–59; baroque city, Jul 61: 52–53; cemetery and cave, Jul 61: 34–35; Coketown, Jul 61: 60–61; earliest cities, Jul 61: 40–41; future of the city, Jul 61: 64–65; Greek polis, Jul 61: 42–43; kings, role of, Jul 61: 38–39; medieval town, Jul 61: 48–51; neolithic village, Jul 61: 36–37; Rome, Jul 61: 44–47; square and crescent, Jul 61: 54–55; suburbia, Jul 61: 62–63; Venice, Jul 61: 56–57
Street furniture, Nov 59: 105–12
Streets of Italy, Nov 61: 121–28
U.S.: disfigurement of, May 61: 4, 5, 18, 19; political bosses of, Jul 61: 68
Of U.S. and U.S.S.R. compared, Jul 62: 113–18
"CITIZEN HEARST," biography by W. A. Swanberg, Jul 63: 71
"CITIZEN KANE," motion picture, May 60: 51, Jul 63: 89, 90
"CITY IN HISTORY, THE," book by Lewis Mumford, pictorial treatment of, with excerpts from, Jul 61: 32–65
CITY LIGHTS, bookstore in San Francisco, Jan 59: 19
"CITY LIGHTS," motion picture, Nov 62: 110
"CITY OF GOD, THE," work by Saint Augustine, Nov 62: 81
"CITY OF THE SAINTS, THE," book by Richard Francis Burton, Jul 63: 110, 115
"CITY OF THE SUN, THE," book by Tommaso Campanella, Mar 63: 76
CITY PLANNING (see also URBAN RENEWAL), May 61: 19
American vs. French under Napoleon III, May 63: 52, 53–54, 66–67, 72, 74, 105
Amsterdam, Netherlands, Sep 58: 20
In ancient cities of Asia Minor, Sep 63: 89
Avant-garde designs, Mar 62: 35, 39
Theories of, Jul 59: 4–15
World's Fair plan of Victor Gruen, May 60: 80–87
CIVIC CONCERT SERVICE, INC., Sep 59: 88
CIVIC REPERTORY COMPANY, of New York, Jan 63: 107, 108
CLAIR, RENÉ, May 60: 51, May 61: 90, 95
CLAIRON, MLLE (CLAIRE JOSÈPHE LÉRIS), Mar 61: 118
CLAPHAM, JOHN HAROLD, Sep 63: 101
CLARENDON, 1ST EARL OF (EDWARD HYDE), Jul 61: 94
"CLARISSA HARLOWE," novel by Samuel Richardson, Mar 59: 118; Jan 62: 60–61, 63–64
CLARK, BARRETT, Mar 60: 33
CLARK, BOBBY, Sep 58: 58, 60
Photograph of, Sep 58: 58
CLARK, CHARLES W., Nov 60: 98
CLARK, ELEANOR, Rome and a Villa, quoted, May 63: 34
CLARK, JOSEPH SILL, JR., Sep 61: 17, Sep 62: 62, Jul 63: 9, 26
CLARK, KENNETH, May 62: 61
On painting of the nude, quoted, Jul 60: 116, Mar 62: 63
CLARK, ORVILLE, Sep 59: 91
CLARK, WALTER VAN TILBURG, Jan 59: 19
CLARKE, ARTHUR C., articles by
"In the Light of the Sun," Nov 63: 48–55
"Social Consequences of the Communications Satellites, The," Sep 62: 16–21
"Space and the Spirit of Man," Jan 59: 26–31, 122–23
"Tyranny of Time, The," Jul 62: 80–88
CLARKE, CHARLES COWDEN, Jan 61: 91
CLARKE, MARY (MME MOHL), Nov 61: 35
CLARKE, SHIRLEY, Mar 61: 16

Photograph of, Mar 61: 17
CLARKE, T. H., Nov 62: 59, 66
CLARKSON, CHRISTOPHER, May 63: 17
CLASSES IN AMERICA
Cultural class war, Jan 60: 4–11
Future class system, May 59: 20–23
Warner, W. Lloyd, quoted on, Nov 59: 22–23, 24
CLASSICAL REVIVAL OF 18TH CENTURY, Mar 62: 50, 55–56, 61–69
CLASSICAL TRADITION, rout of, in education, Nov 60: 17–24, Sep 63: 97–98
CLASSICAL WORLD, film epics based on, May 61: 52–57
CLASSICISM
Poussin as example of, Mar 61: 79, 89–90
Romanticism vs., May 61: 60
CLAUDE. See LORRAIN, CLAUDE
CLAUDEL, PAUL, Nov 59: 67, 68
CLAUDIUS I, ROMAN EMPEROR, coin portraits of, Sep 63: 38; illus, Sep 63: 33, 36
CLAUSEWITZ, KARL VON, Nov 63: 62
On strategy, quoted, Mar 59: 33
CLAY, GRADY, "Metropolis Regained," article by, Jul 59: 4–15
CLAY, HENRY, on America, quoted, May 61: 14
"CLEA," novel by Lawrence Durrell, Mar 60: 114, 117–18
Excerpt from, Mar 60: 117
"CLEAN AND DECENT," book by Lawrence Wright, excerpt from, May 60: 39–41
"CLEARING HOUSE, THE," magazine, quoted on teacher's role, Nov 58: 32
"CLEARING IN THE WOODS, THE," play, Nov 58: 64
"CLÉLIE," novel by Magdeleine de Scudéry, Jan 62: 58
CLEMENS, SAMUEL L. See TWAIN, MARK
CLEMENT IV, POPE, Jan 63: 8
CLEMENT V, POPE, Mar 61: 62
CLEMENT VII, POPE, Sep 58: 95
CLEMENT VIII, POPE, Jul 61: 70, Jan 62: 41
CLEON, Jan 60: 44, 45
CLEOPATRA, Nov 62: 78
CLERE, THOMAS, requiem for, quoted, Mar 63: 88
CLERICI, FABRIZIO, paintings by, Sep 63: 18, 26
CLEVELAND, OHIO, Longwood Village "exedra," Nov 59: 109–10
CLEVELAND, GROVER, Sep 59: 24
CLEVELAND, HARLAN, Sep 61: 13
On "overseasmanship," quoted, May 60: 9
CLEVELAND MUSEUM OF ART, Mourners of Dijon at, Sep 58: 62–63
CLEVELAND PLAY HOUSE, Jan 62: 9, Jan 63: 107
CLEVES, DUKE OF, and Thirty Years' War, Nov 62: 35, 37
CLIBURN, VAN, Jan 60: 6, 74, 79, 81
Portrait of, Jan 60: 80
CLIFTON, ENGLAND, Avon River bridge, Jan 59: 36–37
"CLIMAX," television show, Mar 63: 35
CLINT, GEORGE, Mar 63: 69
CLITUS, Mar 59: 52
CLIVE, ROBERT, BARON, May 63: 3
CLOAR, CARROLL, Nov 58: 78
Paintings by. See ILLUSTRATIONS INDEX
CLOISTERS, THE, New York City, Jul 59: 28
CLOSTERMAN, JOHN, painting by, Sep 61: 68
CLOTHIER FAMILY, of Philadelphia, Jul 63: 22
CLOTHING
Advertising of, Nov 59: 113–14, 115, 116–17
Effect of classical revival of 18th century, Mar 62: 63
"CLOUDS," play by Aristophanes, Jul 60: 117
"CLOUDS ON THE HORIZON"
". . . and Clearing Skies," illustrated feature, Nov 62: 114–17
Illustrated feature edited by Oliver Jensen, Mar 59: 133–35
"Who's Underdeveloped?" article by Oliver Jensen, Jan 63: 116–17
CLOUÉ, chef to Duke of Newcastle, Nov 58: 56
CLOUET, JEAN, portrait of Francis I by, Sep 60: 61; illus, Sep 60: 70
CLOUTIER, SUZANNE. See USTINOV, SUZANNE CLOUTIER
CLOVIS, KING OF THE FRANKS, quoted on Crucifixion, Jul 59: 131
"CLOWN JEWELS," revue, Jan 61: 122–23
CLUBS and GROUPS
Athenaeums of Boston and Philadelphia compared, Jul 63: 12–13
Bloomsbury Group, Jan 60: 107
Confrontation group of Warsaw painters, May 61: 22
Cracow group of Polish artists, May 61: 22
Dr. Johnson's circle, May 59: 92
Gentlemen's club as oasis of privacy, Jul 60: 122
Groupe de Recherches de Musique Concrète, Jan 59: 54
Jockey Club, Paris, May 63: 69
Lichfield Group, May 59: 92
Lunar Society, May 59: 92, 94, 128–30

Midland group of Josiah Wedgwood, May 59: 88–97, 128–30
Nabis, Mar 62: 15, 16
Philadelphia Club, Jul 63: 5
Society of Dilettanti, Mar 62: 55
CLUNY, GENEVIÈVE, Jan 62: 109
CLUNY MUSEUM, Mourners of Dijon at, Sep 58: 62–63
CLURMAN, HAROLD, Mar 60: 119, Jan 61: 32, Jan 62: 14, Nov 62: 106
COACH, vehicle, Sep 58: 150–51
COAST GUARD, U.S., swimming pool at Alameda, Calif., Jan 60: 121
COATESVILLE, PA., Carver Court, Sep 62: 58
COBB, LEE J., Sep 58: 44
COBBETT, WALTER WILLSON, Nov 62: 44
COBBETT, WILLIAM, on London, quoted, Jul 59: 11
COCHIN, CHARLES NICOLAS, Mar 62: 55
COCKER, E., calligraphic drawing by, Nov 63: 53
COCKERELL, CHARLES ROBERT, and Aegina marbles, Sep 59: 30–32, 49
COCKERELL, S. P., Nov 62: 24
"COCKTAIL PARTY, THE," play, Nov 58: 62, Jan 60: 6
COCTEAU, JEAN, Mar 61: 98, Mar 62: 107
On conformism and nonconformism, quoted, Nov 60: 4
Ionesco, Eugène, quoted on, May 61: 95
CODEX SINAITICUS, Nov 62: 94; illus, Nov 62: 82
COE, FRED, Sep 60: 50, 51, May 63: 10
COEUR, JACQUES, Nov 61: 97
"COFFEE," painting by Richard Diebenkorn, Jul 60: 116; illus, Jul 60: 19
COGHLAN, CHARLES F., Mar 62: 119
Portrait of, Mar 62: 118
COGLEY, JOHN, Report on Blacklisting, Mar 60: 48
COHAN, GEORGE M., on Algonquin Round Table, quoted, Jul 62: 38
COINAGE
Invention of, Sep 63: 82
Of Roman Empire, Sep 63: 33–41
COKE, THOMAS (EARL OF LEICESTER), house of, Nov 58: 44–45
COKETOWN, Jul 61: 60–61
COLBERT, JEAN BAPTISTE, Nov 59: 61, Sep 60: 67, 69, Jul 63: 82–83
COLE, HORACE DE VERE, hoaxes by, Jan 61: 66–68, 71, 72
COLE, THOMAS, paintings by, Jul 61: 32, Sep 63: 20–21
COLE, WILLIAM, "The Wacky World of Tomi Ungerer," article by, Jan 61: 128–36
COLEMAN, ORNETTE, May 61: 100
COLERIDGE, SAMUEL TAYLOR, May 61: 65, 68, May 63: 115
Childhood of, May 60: 33, 34, 35, 38
Portraits of, May 60: 32, May 61: 61
Quoted: on creative imagination, Jul 59: 108; on Kean, Edmund, Mar 62: 116
And story of Fletcher Christian, Sep 63: 47–48
COLET, JOHN, May 62: 91, 93
COLETTE (SIDONIE GABRIELLE CLAUDINE COLETTE), on Jean Anouilh, quoted, Nov 60: 51
COLF, HOWARD, Jan 63: 78, 80
Photograph of, Jan 63: 81
COLLAGES, of Antonio Gaudi, Mar 59: 126
COLLECTING, trends in, Nov 62: 59–60, 66
"COLLECTION, THE," play, May 63: 107
"COLLEGE ENGLISH," journal, quoted on English grammar in 1960's, May 60: 119
COLLEGE ENTRANCE EXAMINATION BOARD, Sep 59: 25
"COLLEGE HUMOR," magazine, Jul 63: 118
COLLEGE LIFE, novels of, Sep 60: 117–19
COLLEGES and UNIVERSITIES (see also by name)
"Address from the Class of 1944 to the Class of 1963, An," article by Henry Anatole Grunwald, May 63: 86–89
Architectural revolution at Yale, May 59: 84–87
In Dutch Republic, Sep 58: 23
Non-teaching professors, Sep 62: 14–19
Research and its economics, Sep 63: 60–63
COLLEGEVILLE, MINN., church at St. John's University Abbey, Mar 59: 123
COLLIER, CONSTANCE, May 61: 34
COLLINGWOOD, R. G., Sep 63: 99
COLLINS, CHARLES (HUTCH), Mar 60: 27
COLLINS, JANET, May 63: 49
COLLINS, JOAN, Sep 63: 80
COLLINS, JOHN F., Jan 63: 12
COLLINS, LeROY, and television advertising of cigarettes, Mar 63: 113–14
COLLINS, WILLIAM, on Royal Academy, quoted, May 62: 63
COLMAN, RONALD, Sep 63: 75–76, 77, 78, 79
Photographs of, Sep 63: 76, 78
COLOGNE, GERMANY
Carnival time, Mar 59: 84

Church of St. Mary the Queen, Sep 62: 24; illus, Sep 62: 30–31
Opera House, Nov 58: 118
COLOMA, CARLOS, Nov 62: 40–41
COLOMAN, KING OF HUNGARY, Nov 59: 57
COLOMBIA, Alexander von Humboldt in, Jul 59: 62
COLONNA, MARC ANTONIO, Jul 63: 50, 53, 57
COLONNA, VITTORIA, Jan 60: 68
On Baldassare Castiglione, quoted, Jan 60: 65
COLUM, MARY, Mar 63: 28, 29
COLUM, PADRAIC, Mar 63: 28
COLUMBIA BROADCASTING SYSTEM, May 61: 103
COLUMBIA UNIVERSITY
Architecture of, May 59: 87
And Beat Generation, Sep 61: 116
And Lincoln Center for the Performing Arts, Jul 62: 7
Loubat Prize, Jul 63: 68
Teachers College, Mar 60: 70, Jul 63: 38, 42, 43
COLUMBO, IGNAZIO, engraving by, Jul 63: 2, 3
COLUMBUS, CHRISTOPHER, quoted, Sep 62: 116
"COMBAT," underground French newspaper, Nov 59: 70
COMBAT OF THE THIRTY, Nov 58: 95, 105
"COMBATTIMENTO DI TANCREDI E CLORINDA, IL," composition by Claudio Monteverdi, Jan 59: 125
COMDEN, BETTY, Jan 62: 66, 68
"COME BACK, AFRICA," motion picture, Mar 61: 15, 19
"COME, GIRLS, ART CAN BE FUN!" excerpt from *A Modern Demonology,* by Frank Getlein, Sep 61: 64–65
COMENIUS, JOHN AMOS, Mar 60: 101
"COME OVER AND SEE FOR YOURSELF," illustrated feature, Sep 62: 116–19
"COMES A DAY," play, Jul 60: 93
COMIC BOOKS, Jul 63; 35–36
"COMIC CHARACTERS OF SHAKESPEARE," book by John Palmer, quoted on Shylock, Jan 60: 92
"COMIC HISTORY OF ENGLAND, THE," book by Gilbert Abbott à Beckett and John Leech, Mar 60: 129
Etchings from, Mar 60: 129–36
"COMING FLOOD OF PHARAOH'S TEMPLES, THE," article, Jul 60: 8–10
"COMING GENERATION OF GENIUS, THE," article by John Rader Platt, Mar 62: 70–75
"COMING OF THE WHITE MAN, THE," article by Alan Moorehead, Sep 60: 10–14
"COMING TALENT CASTS ITS SHADOW BEFORE, A," article by Robert Hatch, Jul 62: 91–94
COMITO, sister of Theodora, Nov 63: 10
"COMMEDIA DELL' ARTE," Jan 62: 68
As source for Shylock, Jan 60: 92–96
COMMERCE
Bargaining in Arab world, May 59: 136
Of Bronze Age, Jul 60: 84–91, 113
Of Dutch Republic, Sep 58: 19–20, 22–23
Of Etruscans, May 60: 64, 73
COMMISSION ON THE FREEDOM OF THE PRESS, Mar 60: 49
COMMITTEE TO DEFEND AMERICA BY AIDING THE ALLIES, May 62: 6
COMMODUS, LUCIUS AELIUS AURELIUS, coin portraits of, Sep 63: 39; illus, Sep 63: 39
COMMON MAN, Mar 59: 128
In Age of Leisure, Nov 63: 105–9
COMMON MARKET. See EUROPEAN ECONOMIC COMMUNITY
"COMMONPLACE BOOK," by Charles P. Curtis, Jul 61: 112, Sep 61: 115
COMMONPLACE BOOKS, Sep 61: 114–15
COMMUNICATIONS
Mass media and imaginary audience, Mar 60: 46–51
Social consequences of communications satellites, Jan 62: 16–21
Total, Nov 62: 105
COMMUNICATIONS THEORY, Mar 60: 48–49
COMMUNISM
In America: Bertolt Brecht, May 62: 39–40
French men of letters and, Nov 59: 71–72
Shaw, G. B., quoted on, Nov 58: 20, 134
In World War I aftermath, Jan 59: 115, 117, 121
COMMUNITY CONCERTS, INC., in Topeka, Kans., Sep 59: 88–91, 122, 123
COMMUTER TRAIN, as oasis of privacy, Jul 60: 122
COMO, PERRY, Jul 61: 97
COMPANIONSHIP, as motivation in adventure, Sep 58: 12
"COMPASS, THE," Chicago cabaret, Jan 62: 68, 70
"COMPLETE MUSICIAN, THE," article by Irving Kolodin, Sep 61: 82–87
"COMPOSERS ON MUSIC," book edited by Sam Morgenstern, May 63: 109
COMPTON, ARTHUR H., May 59: 5, 9
Photograph of, May 59: 16
COMPTON, HENRY, BISHOP OF LONDON, Jan 60: 114, 116

"COMPULSION," motion picture, Jul 63: 91
COMPUTERS
Calculating machine invented by Pascal, Jan 63: 97, 99; illus, Jan 63: 95
Electronic, use in banks, Sep 62: 120
COMSTOCK, DANIEL, Jan 59: 109
COMTE, AUGUSTE, Jan 59: 30, May 63: 89
CONCINI, CONCINO, Sep 60: 67
CONCORD, MASS., Silent Traveller quoted on, Nov 59: 131
CONCRETE, in architecture, Mar 59: 19–24, 121–24
CONDÉ, PRINCE DE (LOUIS II), Jul 63: 80
CONDER, NEVILLE (Nov 60: 125
CONDORCET, MARQUIS DE, Mar 61: 118
"CONFIRMATION, THE," painting by Poussin, Mar 61: 91
CONFRONTATION GROUP, of Warsaw painters, May 61: 22
CONFUCIUS, on language and government, quoted, Jul 63: 48
CONGDON, WILLIAM, Jul 62: 25
Painting by, Jul 62: 25
CONGRESS, U.S.
And Bollingen Prize in Poetry, Jul 63: 73
Inquiries into advertising language, Jul 63: 36
IQ of, Mar 62: 73–74
Merit of Representatives, May 59: 23
CONGREVE, WILLIAM, *The Way of the World,* Sep 62: 111
CONNECTICUT GENERAL LIFE INSURANCE COMPANY, headquarters of, Sep 58: 91, May 62: 16, May 63: 14
"CONNECTION, THE," motion picture, Mar 61: 16
"CONNECTION, THE," play, Mar 61: 44–45, Mar 62: 106–7, 109
CONNELL, LEIGH, Mar 60: 96, 120–21
CONNELLY, MARC, Jul 62: 37, 39, 40, Jul 63: 69
Caricature of, Jul 62: 41
CONNOLLY, CYRIL, Nov 59: 32
"CONQUESTS OF DR. ROSENBACH, THE," article excerpted from *Rosenbach: A Biography,* by Edwin Wolf 2nd and John F. Fleming, Nov 60: 96–101
CONRAD, JOSEPH, Jan 60: 125, Mar 60: 127
As caricatured by Max Beerbohm, May 61: 38
Outcast of the Islands, An, Mar 61: 22–23
CONRAD HOHENSTAUFEN, Nov 63: 31
CONRAD OF MONTFERRAT, Jan 59: 88, 130
CONSERVATION
Beginnings of, Mar 60: 15, 16
Population increase and, Sep 58: 50, 52
CONSTABLE, JOHN, May 60: 104, May 61: 66, 68, 74, May 62: 70–71, Mar 63: 70, Jul 63: 92, 106
Paintings by, May 61: 69, May 62: 70–71
On Poussin, quoted, Mar 61: 78
CONSTANCE, daughter of Roger II of Sicily, Sep 61: 32
CONSTANS II, BYZANTINE EMPEROR, Nov 63: 26
CONSTANTINE V, BYZANTINE EMPEROR (COPRONYMUS), Mar 60: 76, Nov 63: 26
CONSTANTINE VII, BYZANTINE EMPEROR (PORPHYROGENITUS), Sep 62: 78–79, Nov 63: 28, 34
CONSTANTINE XI, BYZANTINE EMPEROR (DRAGASES PALAEOLOGUS), Nov 63: 34
CONSTANTINE I, ROMAN EMPEROR (CONSTANTINE THE GREAT), Jan 62: 23, 26, Sep 63: 89, Nov 63: 6, 9, 11
At Arles, Jul 59: 130
Coin portraits of, Sep 63: 41; illus, Sep 63: 40, 41
Donation of, Jan 62: 30, May 62: 90
Library founded by, Nov 62: 78
Sculpture of, Mar 59: 4
CONSTANTINOPLE, Sep 58: 46, Nov 63: 9, 11–15, 26, 31
Fall of, Nov 63: 32, 34
Imperial library, Nov 62: 78
CONSTANTIUS I, ROMAN EMPEROR, medallion portrait of, Sep 63: 40; illus, Sep 63: 37
CONSTANTIUS II, ROMAN EMPEROR, Sep 63: 41, Nov 63: 9
"CONSTELLATIONS," sculptures by Alexander Calder, Nov 62: 16
"CONSTRUCTIONS," show at Museum of Modern Art, New York City, Mar 62: 107
CONSTRUCTIVISM, in painting, Nov 61: 69
"CONSUL, THE," opera, Jan 60: 122
CONTAINER CORPORATION OF AMERICA, Sep 58: 98, 102, 103
CONTARINI, AUGUSTINE, Mar 60: 83
"CONTEMPORARIES," book by Alfred Kazin, Jul 62: 98, 100
"CONTES BARBARES," painting by Paul Gauguin, Jan 60: 32; illus, Jan 60: 33
CONTI, NICCOLÒ DE', Sep 63: 68
CONTI, PRINCE DE, salon of, Nov 61: 33 (illus)
CONTINENTAL SYSTEM, of Napoleon I, Sep 63: 30, 32
"CONTINUOUS ON RED," painting by Alexander Liber-

man, Sep 61: 66–67
"CONVERSATIONS WITH ARTISTS," book by Selden Rodman, quoted, Mar 59: 135
"CONVERSATIONS WITH STRAVINSKY," book by Igor Stravinsky and Robert Craft, excerpts from, Sep 58: 82–84, 132
CONWAY, CURT, Sep 60: 50
CONWAY, HENRY, Mar 61: 116
CONYNGHAM, LADY, Nov 62: 29, Jul 63: 106
COOK, GEORGE CRAM, Jul 61: 13
COOK, JAMES, Jan 60: 30
In Australia, Sep 60: 11
COOK, JEAN, photograph of, Nov 61: 79
COOK, PETER, Mar 63: 109
COOKE, GEORGE FREDERICK, Mar 62: 116
COOLE, TREE OF. See "TREE OF COOLE, THE"
COOLIDGE, CALVIN, on business, quoted, Sep 60: 38
COOLIDGE, ELIZABETH SPRAGUE, Jan 61: 47, Nov 62: 44
COOLIDGE, THOMAS JEFFERSON, Jul 59: 29
COOMBS, PHILIP, Sep 61: 10
COON, MILDRED McKEE. See McKEE, MILDRED
COON RAPIDS, IOWA, Khrushchev visit to, Mar 60: 51
COOPER, GLADYS, Sep 63: 80
COOPER, JACKIE, Sep 62: 114
COOPER, JAMES FENIMORE, Mar 60: 15, Jan 62: 64
On Italian carriages, quoted, Nov 61: 125
COOPER, JOSEPH, on cowslip cream, quoted, May 59: 41
COOPER, MELVILLE, Sep 63: 77
COOPER, PETER, painting by, Jul 63: 6–7
COPEAU, JACQUES, Sep 61: 102
COPENHAGEN, DENMARK, May 61: 4
SAS building, Nov 60: 16
Tivoli Gardens street signs, Nov 59: 108
COPERNICUS, NICOLAUS, Jan 59: 30
COPLAND, AARON, May 59: 5, Jul 59: 20, Sep 61: 10, Jul 62: 104, Mar 63: 28, 31
Photographs of, May 59: 16, Mar 63: 30
Piano *Variations,* Igor Stravinsky quoted on, Sep 58: 132
COPLEY, JOHN SINGLETON, Sep 60: 34
COPPER, location of, in Promised Land, Nov 59: 9–10
COPPER, CITY OF, discovery of Biblical site, Nov 59: 9–10
COPPERPLATE SCRIPT, Sep 59: 127–28
COPPET, SWITZERLAND, home of Mme de Staël at, Nov 58: 86, 143
COQUELIN, May 61: 125
CORBETT, EDWARD, Jan 59: 13
CORBETT, MARIO, Jan 59: 8
CORBUSIER. See LE CORBUSIER
"CORBUSIER'S CLOISTER," article by Cranston Jones, Mar 61: 34–41
CORCORAN, KEVIN, Sep 60: 117
CORCORAN, W. W., Jul 59: 31
CORCORAN GALLERY OF ART, Washington, D.C., Jul 61: 75
CORCYRA (CORFU), GREECE, in Peloponnesian War, Jan 60: 44, 45
CÓRDOBA, SPAIN
Great Mosque, Sep 62: 75, 78
Under Moslem rule, Sep 62: 77–79, 82, 87
Plaza de las Flores, May 59: 49
COREY, ORLIN and IRENE
Book of Job, The, and other productions by, Jan 63: 88–91
Photograph of, Jan 63: 88
CORFU, GREECE (see also CORCYRA)
Turkish attack of 1571, Jul 63: 53
"CORINNE," novel by Mme de Staël, Nov 58: 88, 143
CORINTH, GREECE, meeting of Diogenes and Alexander, Mar 63: 10–13
CORINTH, LEAGUE OF, Mar 59: 32–33, 47
CORMAN, CID, publisher of *Origin,* Sep 61: 117, 121
CORNEILLE, PIERRE, Jul 60: 42, 50, 60, Jul 63: 83
Portrait of, Jul 60: 39
CORNELL, KATHARINE, Nov 60: 52, Jul 63: 86
CORNELL UNIVERSITY, Sardis expedition, Sep 63: 85, 86, 88–89
CORN EXCHANGE BANK, Mar 61: 121
"CORNHILL MAGAZINE," Jan 60: 108
CORNING MUSEUM OF GLASS, Sep 63: 85
"CORNISHMAN," train, Jan 59: 39
CORNWALL, CONN., May 60: 13, 21
COROMANDEL COAST, INDIA, Mar 61: 22
CORONADO, HOTEL DEL, near San Diego, Calif., Jan 61: 104, 109
"CORONATION OF POPPEA, THE," opera, Jul 60: 42
COROT, JEAN-BAPTISTE CAMILLE, Jul 60: 115, 116, Jul 62: 65–66, May 63: 70
Influence of Poussin on, Mar 61: 78, 91, 93
Painting by, Jul 62: 72–73
CORREGGIO, Jul 61: 89, 90, 94, 95, Jul 63: 94
Painting by, Nov 61: 82

CORSARO, FRANK, Nov 62: 108
CORSO, GREGORY, Sep 61: 116, 119, 120, Jan 63: 74
  "Death," quoted, Sep 61: 120
  Photograph of, Mar 61: 14–15
  Remark to Art Buchwald, quoted, Jul 60: 72
CORTES, HERNANDO
  Encounter with Montezuma, Nov 63: 92–96
  Portrayed in Codices, Sep 60: 24, 25
CORTIER, French captain, 1909, May 59: 71
CORTONA, PIETRO DA, Mar 61: 80
CORTOT, ALFRED, Jan 60: 81
CORWIN, NORMAN, The Rivalry, Jan 63: 88
COSENZA, LUIGI, Nov 59: 50
"COSÌ FAN TUTTE," opera, Nov 58: 120
COSIMO, PIERO DI, Sep 58: 142
  Painting by, Sep 58: 93
"COSMOPOLITAN," magazine, advertising in, Nov 59: 114
"COSMOS," system of nature by Alexander von Humboldt, Jul 59: 57, 59, 128
COSTA, LORENZO, painting by, Jan 60: 67
COSTA, LÚCIO, Sep 59: 20, Nov 60: 16, Mar 61: 36
COSTER, SAMUEL, Sep 58: 26
COT, PIERRE AUGUSTE, painting by, Mar 60: cover, 3, 60
COTSWORTH, STAATS, Jan 62: 106
COTTANCIN, PAUL, Mar 59: 20, 121
COTTEN, JOSEPH, May 63: 107
COTTERILL, ERICA, Nov 58: 135–36
COTTON, ROBERT BRUCE, Nov 62: 94
COUDENHOVE-KALERGI, ROBERT, Mar 63: 6
COULANGES, MARQUIS and MARQUISE DE, Nov 61: 34
COUNCIL FOR BASIC EDUCATION, excerpts from Bulletin of, Mar 60: 70–71
COUNCIL OF EUROPE. See EUROPE, COUNCIL OF
COUNTER REFORMATION, witchcraft cult during, Nov 59: 59–60
"COUNT OF MONTE CRISTO, THE," motion picture, Mar 60: 38, 40
"COUNT OF MONTE CRISTO, THE," play, James O'Neill in, Mar 60: 27
"COUNTRY WIFE, THE," play, Jan 63: 29
COUPLAND, R., on David Livingstone, quoted, Sep 58: 136
COURBET, GUSTAVE, Nov 59: 121, Mar 61: 78, 93, May 63: 54, 70
  Painting by, May 61: 82
COURCELLES, THOMAS DE, Mar 62: 94
COURCY, FRÉDÉRIC DE, Mar 62: 118
"COURIER," satellite, Jan 62: 18
COURTENAY, BAUDOUIN DE, Jul 63: 44
"COURTIER, THE" ("IL CORTIGIANO"), dialogue by Baldassare Castiglione, Mar 59: 38, Sep 59: 120, Jan 60: 65, 68
  Excerpt from, Jan 60: 73
COURTLY LOVE, May 60: 31, Jan 62: 57–58
  Ulrich von Lichtenstein as exponent of, Sep 59: 113–17
COURTS OF LOVE, May 60: 30, 31
"COUSINS, THE," motion picture, May 60: 50, 52–53, Sep 61: 110, May 63: 111
COUSTEAU, JACQUES-YVES, Sep 58: 11, Nov 58: 71, 73
  Photograph of, Sep 58: 11
COUTURIER, M.-A., Sep 62: 24
  Stained-glass window designed by, Sep 62: 32
COUVENT SAINTE-MARIE DE LA TOURETTE, LE, Eveux-sur-Arbresle, France, Mar 61: 34–41
COVENT GARDEN, London, Nov 58: 23–24, 26–27, 117
COWARD, NOËL, Nov 59: 31, Sep 63: 75
  Look After Lulu, Jan 61: 101, Jan 63: 29, 33 (illus)
COWLES, GARDNER, May 60: 24
COWLES, JOHN, May 60: 24
COWLES, RUSSELL, May 60: 24
  Photograph of, May 60: 24
COWLEY, actor of Shakespeare's day, Jan 60: 92
COWLEY, MALCOLM, Jan 59: 82, May 60: 22, 25, Jul 61: 75
  Photograph of, May 60: 22
  Roppel, Earl, hoax, May 60: 48
  "Ten Authors in Pursuit of One Subject," article by, Mar 59: 14–17, 117–19
COWLEY, ROBERT, "Blume's Oak," article by, Jul 61: 70–75
COWSLIP CREAM, recipe for, May 59: 41
COX, ALDERMAN, Mar 62: 116
COX, CATHARINE M., May 60: 33
COX, KENYON, Sep 60: 100, 102
COX, WALLY, May 63: 46
COXE, WILLIAM, Nov 59: 77
COXHEAD, ERNEST, Jan 59: 10
COZENS, JOHN ROBERT, Nov 59: 86
COZZENS, JAMES GOULD, Mar 59: 112, Sep 59: 118, Jul 63: 70

Alfred Kazin quoted on, Jul 62: 102
CRACOW GROUP, of Polish artists, May 61: 22
"CRADLE SONG, THE," play, Mar 60: 98
"CRADLE WILL ROCK, THE," play, Jul 63: 87, 90
CRAFT, ROBERT, and IGOR STRAVINSKY, Conversations with Stravinsky, excerpts from, Sep 58: 82–84, 132
CRAFTS
  In San Francisco Bay Region, Jan 59: 14
  In Scandinavia, exemplified by Tapio and Rut Bryk Wirkkala, Jul 60: 78
CRAIG, GORDON, Sep 62: 110, 112
CRAM, RALPH ADAMS, Jan 63: 12
CRANACH, LUCAS THE ELDER, Jul 63: 107
  Painting by, Sep 63: 92
CRANBROOK ACADEMY OF ART, Bloomfield Hills, Mich., Jul 60: 78
CRANDON, LE ROI GODDARD, Jan 59: 108–11
CRANDON, MRS, LE ROI GODDARD, Jan 59: 108–11
CRANE, DAVID A., on American cities, quoted, Jul 59: 7, 10
CRANE, HART, Jul 61: 75, Sep 61: 117
"CRANES ARE FLYING, THE," motion picture, Mar 62: 110, 112
  Reviewed, Nov 60: 122
CRATINUS, Nov 62: 76
CRAVEN, 2D EARL OF, Nov 58: 107
CRAWFORD, CHERYL, Jan 62: 103, Nov 62: 106, 108
CRAWFORD, F. MARION, Jul 59: 32
"CRAWLING ARNOLD," play by Jules Feiffer, Nov 61: 49–56
"CRAZY GANG, THE," English vaudeville comics, Jan 61: 122–23
"CREATIVE MAN AT WORK, THE," article by Stephen White, Mar 62: 112–13
CREATIVE PROCESS, May 63: 114–15
"CREATURES OF THE IRISH TWILIGHT," article by John Montague with portfolio of drawings by Morris Graves, Jul 60: 105–12
CREDIT CARDS, May 62: 118–19
CRÉDIT MOBILIER, French, May 63: 63–64
CREEVEY, THOMAS, on Lord Egremont, quoted, Mar 63: 68
CREHAN, HUBERT, on Georges Mathieu, quoted, Sep 60: 122
CRESQUES, ABRAHAM, Nov 60: 83
  Map by, Mar 63: 45
CRET, PAUL, Sep 62: 58
CRETE, GREECE, Sep 60: 125
  In Byzantine Empire, Nov 63: 28
  Turkish conquest of, Jul 63: 60
CRETE, ANCIENT, May 59: 83, Jan 61: 77
CREVE COEUR, MO., church at Priory of St. Mary and St. Louis, Mar 59: 123
CRÈVECOEUR, HECTOR ST. JEAN DE, Nov 59: 21
CRICKET, sport, Nov 58: 53 (illus), Sep 63: 77, 80
"CRICTOR," book by Tomi Ungerer, Jan 61: 128
CRIME, as product of prosperity, Nov 63: 106
"CRIME AND PUNISHMENT," play, Nov 58: 138
"CRIME OF GIOVANNI VENTURI, THE," book by Howard Shaw, Nov 60: 85
"CRISIS IN THE HUMANITIES," series of articles by J. H. Plumb
  "Sorry State of History, The," Sep 63: 97–100; comment on, by Allan Nevins, Sep 63: 101
CRISP, DONALD, Sep 63: 77
CRISTALDI, FRANCO, Jan 63: 38
CRITIAS, Jul 60: 103
CRITICISM
  Jargon of, Jul 63: 38–39
  Musical, Igor Stravinsky quoted on, Sep 58: 132
  Shaw, G. B., and the critics, Nov 58: 136
CRITIC'S VIEW: ADVERTISING, articles by Stephen White
  "Glass That Wasn't There, The," Nov 60: 123
  "No Deposit, No Return," May 61: 118
  "Sad End of the Word 'Fabulous,' The," Jan 61: 119
  "Today's Temple of Talent," Mar 61: 101
  "Uses of Adversity, The," Sep 60: 120
  "Would You Want Your Sister to Marry Rosser Reeves?" Jul 61: 118–19
CRITIC'S VIEW: BOOKS. See BOOKS. Current, critical discussions of
CRITIC'S VIEW: CHANNELS, articles by Stephen White
  "Creative Man at Work, The," Mar 62: 112–13
  "Television Culture in Round Numbers," Jul 62: 94–95
  "Whatever Became of Money?" May 62: 118–19
  "Who Put the Alphabet into the Soup?" Jan 62: 112–13
CRITIC'S VIEW: MOVIES. See "MOVIES"
CRITIC'S VIEW: RADIO, article by Stephen White
  "O for the Days of Amos 'n' Andy!" Nov 61: 102–3
CRITIC'S VIEW: TELEVISION, article by Stephen White
  "Culture in the Wee Hours," Sep 61: 113–14

CRITIC'S VIEW: THEATRE. See THEATRE, Current, articles by Robert Hatch on
CRITOBULUS, on Turkish conquest of Constantinople, quoted, Nov 63: 32
CRIVELLI, CARLO, Jul 59: 30
  Paintings by, Jul 59: 32–33, Sep 63: 14
CROCE, BENEDETTO, on history, quoted, Sep 63: 99
CROCKER, TEMPLETON, Nov 60: 98
CROESUS, KING OF LYDIA, Sep 63: 83–84, 85, 87, 88
CROLY, HERBERT, and Spectric poets, May 60: 46
CROMWELL, JOHN, Sep 60: 55
CROMWELL, OLIVER, Jul 61: 93, 94
  And philo-Semitism of 17th century, Mar 60: 100, 101, 102, 124–25
  Portraits of, Sep 59: 29, Mar 60: 103, Jul 61: 93
  Regicide signature of, Sep 59: 133
  Vs. witchcraft mania, Nov 59: 58
CRONYN, HUME, Nov 63: 37, 40, 41
CROSBIE, RICHARD, Sep 58: 118
CROSBY, BING, Mar 60: 126
CROSLAND, ANTHONY, on crime, quoted, Nov 63: 106
CROSSMAN, R. H. S., on postwar Europe's problem, quoted, Jan 62: 7
"CROSSROADS OF THE JAVA SEA," book by Hendrik de Leeuw, quoted, Mar 61: 28
CROUSE, RUSSEL, Jul 62: 37
CROWNINSHIELD, FRANK, Jul 62: 33–34, 35
  Caricature of, Jul 62: 32
CROWN JEWELS OF EUROPE, May 63: 92–104
CROWN OF THORNS, material of, Mar 60: 90–91
CROWN ZELLERBACH BUILDING, San Francisco, Jan 59: 11
"CRUCIBLE, THE," play, Jan 63: 27, 88
CRUIKSHANK, G. R., sketches by, Mar 62: 114, 115
"CRUISE OF THE SNARK, THE," book by Jack London, Jan 60: 125
CRUSADES
  In Constantinople and Byzantine lands, Nov 62: 78, Nov 63: 31
  First, Jan 59: 87, Mar 61: 51, Nov 63: 31
  Knights of the Temple and Knights of St. John's Hospital during, Mar 61: 48, 51–56, 60
  Richard I and Saladin, Jan 59: 86–91, 130–31
"CRY DAWN IN DARK BABYLON," play, Jan 63: 88
"CRY OF THE PEACOCK," play, Nov 60: 126, 127
CRYPTOGRAPHY, and world's most mysterious manuscript, Jan 63: 4–9
"CRYSTAL AGE, A," romance by W. H. Hudson, Mar 63: 77
CRYSTAL PALACE, London, waterworks of, May 62: 15
CTESIPHON, ancient city in Iraq, Jan 63: 51, 58 (map)
CUBA (see also HAVANA)
  Studies of Alexander von Humboldt, Jul 59: 67–68
CUEVAS, GEORGE DE, MARQUIS, photograph of, Jul 60: 7
CULLEN, GORDON, on Britain's "Subtopia," quoted, Jul 59: 7
"CULT OF UNTHINK, THE," article by Robert Brustein, Sep 58: 38–45, 134–35
"CULTURAL CLASS WAR, THE," article by Eric Larrabee, Jan 60: 4–11
CULTURE
  Map of, from The Silent Language, by Edward T. Hall, Mar 60: 123
  Mass vs. class, Jan 60: 4–11
"CULTURE AND HISTORY," book by Philip Bagby, Jan 61: 62, 63–64
"CULTURE IN THE WEE HOURS," article by Stephen White, Sep 61: 113–14
"CULTURE OF THE NON-HOTEL, THE," article by Joseph Morgenstern, Mar 63: 115–17
CUMBERLAND, DUKE OF (HENRY FREDERICK), Nov 62: 22
CUMMINGS, E. E., Jan 62: 8, Jul 63: 70
  Alfred Kazin quoted on, Jul 62: 101
CUMMINGS, ROBERT, Sep 63: 76
CUNARD, LADY, Mar 62: 102
"CUPID AND PSYCHE," painting by Van Dyck, Jul 63: 96; illus, Jul 63: 95
CUPIDS, in art, Nov 60: 30
CURIE, EVE (MRS. HENRY LABOUISSE), Sep 61: 10
"CURLY-HEADED KID, THE," television show, Jan 62: 104
"CURMUDGEON, THE." See "DYSKOLOS, THE"
CURRIE, FINLAY, Sep 60: 56
CURTAIN WALLS, in architecture, Nov 61: 62
CURTICE, HARLOW, May 59: 20
CURTIN, PHYLLIS, Nov 61: 80, Jan 62: 9, 14
  Photograph of, Nov 61: 79
CURTIS, CHARLES P., Sep 61: 115
  Commonplace Book, Jul 61: 112
CURTIS, GARNISS, Mar 62: 10
CURTIS INSTITUTE OF MUSIC, Sep 61: 83
CURTIUS RUFUS, QUINTUS, on Alexander the Great,

quoted, Mar 59: 41–46, 51, 58
CURZON, GEORGE NATHANIEL, BARON, Jan 63: 72
CUSHING, HARVEY, Nov 60: 99
CUVILLIES, FRANÇOIS DE, May 59: 32
CUYP, AELBERT, Sept 58: 26, Jul 63: 106
CUZZONI, FRANCESCA, Sep 59: 51
CYBELE (or KYBELE), cult of, Jul 61: 37, Sep 63: 84, 87
"CYBERNETICS," book by Norbert Wiener, Mar 60: 49
CYNICISM, of Diogenes, Mar 63: 11
CYPRESS HILLS, SASKATCHEWAN, childhood of Wallace Stegner in, Sep 62: 94–95
CYPRUS, GREECE
Conquered by Turks, Jul 63: 50, 53
Knights of St. John on, Mar 61: 60
Richard I of England and, Jan 59: 87, 130, 131
CYRUS, prefect of Theodosius II, Nov 63: 11
CYRUS, KING OF PERSIA, Jan 63: 42, 43, 44, 72, Sep 63: 83, 84
CZARTORYSKI, PRINCE, Sep 63: 31

D

DADAISTS, May 61: 95
DAGON, Babylonian god, Jan 60: 131, 134
DAGUERRE, LOUIS JACQUES MANDE, Jan 59: 103
DAGWOOD, cartoon character, Jul 60: 5
DAGWORTH, SIR NICHOLAS, Nov 58: 93
DAHL, ANDRÉ, Jeanne d'Arc Revint, Mar 62: 97
DAILEY, GARDNER, Jan 59: 8
DAKIKI, Persian poet, Jan 63: 53
DALBERG-ACTON, JOHN EMERICH EDWARD (LORD ACTON), Mar 59: 6, 7, 8, 10
Portrait of, Mar 59: 7
On universal history, quoted, Mar 62: 99
DALE, CHESTER, Jan 59: 105, Nov 61: 9
Portrait by Salvador Dali, Jan 59: 98
DALI, SALVADOR, Mar 59: 126, Jan 62: 78–79, Nov 62: 97
Works by, Jan 59: 98, Nov 61: 113
DALLAM, Englishman sent by Elizabeth I to Ottoman court, May 59: 132, 134
DALLAS, TEX.
Museum of Fine Arts, Sep 58: 113
Texas Instruments plant, Mar 59: 123
DALLAS–FORT WORTH BOWLING PROPRIETORS' ASSOCIATION, on boom in bowling, quoted, Mar 63: 95
"DALLE DE VERRE," stained-glass technique, Sep 62: 24
DALMAU, art dealer, Mar 59: 74
DALY, JAMES, in J.B., Jan 60: 53
DALZA, JOANAMBROSIA, Nov 60: 91
DAMATO, TONY, on MacDowell Colony, quoted, Mar 63: 32
"DAMNED, THE," motion picture, Mar 63: 36
"DAMN YANKEES!" musical, May 63: 13
DAMON, S. FOSTER, May 60: 48
DANA, CHARLES A., Jan 59: 25
On Brook Farm, quoted, Mar 63: 77
DANCE (see also BALLET)
In Africa, Jul 59: 49–55; Giovanni-Antonio Cavazzi quoted on, Mar 63: 40
Of Angkor, Jan 59: 63
Balinese, Mar 61: cover, 3, 23–24, 28, 31
Cancan, Mark Twain quoted on, May 63: 70
Ceylon's National Dancers, Sep 59: 106–9
De Lavallade, Carmen, May 63: 48–49
Education in, as part of Grand Tour, Nov 59: 90, 98–99
Etruscan, May 60: 59, 78
Of India, Sep 63: 64–73
Of Nikolais, Alwin, Nov 58: 90–91
On the Sound, motion picture, Nov 62: 98
In San Francisco Bay Region, Jan 59: 22–23
Turney, Matt, Nov 62: 68–69, 98
DANCE, GEORGE THE YOUNGER, Nov 63: 74
"DANCERS OF CEYLON," illustrated feature, Sep 59: 106–9
DANDRIDGE, DOROTHY, Mar 60: 128
"DANGER," television show, Sep 60: 51
"DANGERS OF NONCONFORMISM, THE," excerpts from article by Morris Freedman published in The American Scholar, Mar 59: 112
DANHAUSER, JOSEPH, painting by, May 61: 84–85
"DANIEL, THE PLAY OF," Nov 60: 89, 92–95
DANIEL AND FLORENCE GUGGENHEIM FOUNDATION, May 59: 7, 8, 11
DANIEL GUGGENHEIM FUND FOR THE PROMOTION OF AERONAUTICS, May 59: 7, 8
DANILOVA, ALEXANDRA, Jan 61: 49 (note)
D'ANNUNZIO, GABRIELE, May 61: 54

Sketch of, Sep 58: 83
Stravinsky, Igor, quoted on, Sep 58: 83
DANRY, JEAN (HENRI MASERS DE LATUDE), Jan 60: 86–87, 88, 128
Portrait of, Jan 60: 82
"DANSEUSES À LA BARRE," painting by Degas, Nov 61: 6
DANTE ALIGHIERI, Mar 60: 14, Jan 61: 117
Demons and angels of, Nov 60: 31, 32
Inferno, Jan 59: 46
Influence on Edward Adler, Sep 62: 65
Portrait of, Nov 60: 18
"DAPHNIS ET CHLOÉ," composition by Maurice Ravel, Jan 59: 125
DA PONTE, LORENZO, Jan 62: 60, May 63: 42
DARIUS I, KING OF PERSIA, Jan 63: 43, 44
DARIUS III, KING OF PERSIA, Mar 59: 38–40, 47
"DARK AT THE TOP OF THE STAIRS, THE," play, Nov 58: 64, Jan 59: 138
"DARK OF THE MOON," musical, Mar 60: 95
"DARK SIDE OF THE MOON, THE," anonymous recollections, Nov 60: 121
DARNLEY, HENRY STEWART, Jul 63: 31–32
DARRACH, HENRY B., "The New Wave," article by, May 60: 49–55
DART, RAYMOND, Mar 62: 9
DARUMA. See BODHIDHARMA
DARWIN, CHARLES, May 59: 130, Jul 60: 30, Mar 62: 9, 73
On Aristotle, quoted, Jul 61: 8
Chevreul, Marie-Eugène, quoted on, Mar 59: 69
Influence of Alexander von Humboldt on, Jul 59: 128
Portrait of, Jul 59: 62
In South Seas, Jan 60: 31
DARWIN, ERASMUS, Nov 63: 64
On ballooning, quoted, Sep 58: 117
As member of Josiah Wedgwood's group, May 59: 91–96, 128–30
Portrait medallion of, May 59: 91
DARWIN, ROBERT WARING, May 59, 130
DASBURG, ANDREW, Jan 62: 8
DASSIN, JULES, May 61: 57, 97
DAUBIGNY, CHARLES FRANÇOIS, Jul 62: 64
DAUDET, ALPHONSE, Nov 61: 36
On stage realism, quoted, Sep 62: 113
DAUMIER, HONORÉ, Mar 60: 57, Jul 62: 59, 61, May 63: 70
Drawings by. See ILLUSTRATIONS INDEX
DAVENPORT, MARY, photograph of, Nov 61: 79
DAVID, JACQUES-LOUIS, Mar 61: 114, May 61: 66, Mar 62: 35, 63, Jul 62: 18
Paintings by, Jul 60: 100–1, Sep 60: cover, 3
DAVID, PAUL, Nov 58: 146
DAVIDMAN, JOY, May 59: 66
DAVID SARNOFF RESEARCH CENTER, Sep 59: 25–26, 119
DAVIDSON, BASIL, "Africa: The Face Behind the Mask," article by, Mar 63: 38–59
Comment on, Mar 63: 105–6
DAVIDSON, BRUCE, "New Face of Britain, The," photographs by, with comment by Alan Pryce-Jones, Nov 61: 14–31
DAVIDSON, JEAN, "Calder en Campagne," article by, Nov 62: 10–17
DAVIDSON, MARSHALL B., articles by
"Enigmatic Islands of Paul Gauguin, The," Jan 60: 32
"Illumination of Jean Fouquet, The," Nov 61: 88–97
"Monuments for Our Times," May 61: 41–49
"People's Palaces, The," Jan 61: 102–12
DAVIDSON, MORRIS, portrait of, with painting by, Jul 61: 24
DAVIES, ROBERTSON, on Tyrone Guthrie, quoted, Nov 63: 36
DA VINCI. See VINCI
DAVIS, BETTE, Sep 62: 112
DAVIS, DONALD, in Krapp's Last Tape, Sep 60: 114–15
Photograph of, Sep 60: 112
DAVIS, ELMER, on 1948 Presidential election, quoted, Mar 60: 49
DAVIS, EMMETT, Jul 60: 121
DAVIS, MILES, May 61: 100, Jan 63: 75
Portrait of, May 61: 101
DAVIS, PAUL, and EDWARD SOREL, "A Modern Bestiary," portfolio by, Jul 62: 120–28
DAVIS, RICHARD HARDING, Jul 63: 118
DAVIS, ROY, in painting by John Koch, Sep 60: 107
DAVY, GLORIA, photograph of, Nov 61: 81
DAWN, MARPESSA, May 60: 54
"DAWN OF THE 'HIGH MODERN,' THE," article by Allan Temko, Sep 59: 4–21
DAWSON, CHRISTOPHER, on religion and history, quoted, Jan 61: 59, 64
DAY, HOLMAN, Joan of Arc of the North Woods, Mar 62: 98

DAY, J. EDWARD, Sep 61: 10
DAY, THOMAS
As member of Josiah Wedgwood's group, May 59: 90–96, 128–30
Portrait of, May 59: 90
"DAY OF THE GOD, THE," painting by Gauguin, Jan 60: 32; illus, Jan 60: 38–39
"DAY THE GOD CAME BACK, THE," article by J. H. Elliott, Nov 63: 92–96
"DEAD OF NIGHT," motion picture, May 62: 106
DEAN, JAMES, Sep 58: 38, 42–43
Photograph of, Sep 58: 42
"DEATH AND LIFE OF GREAT AMERICAN CITIES, THE," book by Jane Jacobs, Jul 62: 50, May 63: 52
"DEATH OF A MAN," book by Lael Tucker Wertenbaker, Jul 60: 120, Jan 62: 111–12
"DEATH OF A SALESMAN," play, at Tyrone Guthrie Theatre, Nov 63: 38, 41
"DEATH OF BESSIE SMITH, THE," play, Jul 61: 116–17, Sep 61: 79, Mar 63: 108
"DEATH OF SARDANAPALUS, THE," painting by Delacroix, May 61: 74; illus, May 61: 76–77
"DEATH OF SATAN, THE," play, Jan 62: 65, Jan 63: 27
DEAVER, JOHN D., Nov 60: 101
DE BECK, BILLY, quoted, Sep 62: 108
DEBUCOURT, PHILIBERT LOUIS, painting by, Nov 59: 80–81
DEBUSSY, CLAUDE, May 63: 109
String quartet of, Nov 62: 46
"DEBUT OF THE PICTURE INTERVIEW, THE," illustrated feature, Mar 59: 68–69
DECIUS, ROMAN EMPEROR, Sep 63: 40
Coin portrait of, Sep 63: 36
DECLARATION OF INDEPENDENCE, AMERICAN, script of, Sep 59: 127
"DECLINE AND FALL OF THE ROMAN EMPIRE," history by Edward Gibbon, quoted, Mar 59: 12
"DECLINE OF THE WEST," book by Oswald Spengler, Mar 59: 11
DE CRITZ, EMMANUEL, Jul 61: 94
DECROUX, ETIENNE, May 62: 81
DEE, JOEY, Jul 62: 49
"DEEP ATTACHMENT," print by Gen Yamaguchi, May 60: 113, 114; illus, May 60: 108
DEEP RIVER, CONN., May 60: 94
"DEER PARK, THE," novel by Norman Mailer, May 62: 55
DE FEO, JAY, Jan 59: 14
DEFFAND, MARQUISE DU, Nov 61: 34–35
DEFOE, DANIEL, on Blenheim Palace, quoted, Sep 61: 70
DEGAS, EDGAR, May 60: 103, Nov 61: 6, Mar 62: 25, May 63: 70, Sep 63: 96
Painting by, Sep 60: 78
Quoted: on Bonnard, Pierre, Mar 62: 16, 26; on Poussin, Mar 61: 78
DE GAULLE, CHARLES, Nov 59: 66, Nov 60: 119, Jul 63: 48
And European unity, Mar 63: 4, 7
Ionesco, Eugène, quoted on, May 61: 93
And Joan of Arc cult, Mar 62: 99
DE HAAN, MEYER, Jan 60: 32
DE JONG, MEVROUW, Nov 59: 120
DEKKER, THOMAS, The Shoemaker's Holiday, Jul 63: 87
DE KOONING, WILLEM, Sep 58: 109, 110, Nov 59: 120, 121, Mar 62: 107, Jul 62: 14, Jan 63: 16
Paintings by, Sep 58: 108, Jul 62: 14
Photograph of, Sep 58: 108
Rivers, Larry, quoted on, Sep 59: 98, 100
DELACROIX, EUGÈNE, Nov 59: 121, Mar 60: 55, May 60: 104, Sep 60: 81, Nov 60: 128, May 61: 66, 74
Portrait of, May 61: 74
Quoted: on photography, Jan 59: 96; on Poussin, Mar 61: 78
Works by. See ILLUSTRATIONS INDEX
DE LA MARE, WALTER, Jan 60: 108, Mar 63: 86, 87
DELANCEY, CHARLES, Jan 63: 78, 80
Photograph of, Jan 63: 81
DELANEY, SHELAGH, Mar 61: 102, 103, May 61: 51
DELANO, AMASA, Sep 63: 47
DE LA PUENTE, JOAQUIN, Nov 59: 120
DE LA TOUR, GEORGES, painting by, Sep 60: 70
DE LA TOUR, QUENTIN, painting by, Sep 60: 74
DELAUNAY, R., painting by, Nov 63: 54
DE LAURENTIIS, DINO, and motion picture Barabbas, Mar 63: 109–11
DE LAVALLADE, CARMEN, May 63: 49
Photograph of, May 63: 48
DE LEEUW, HENDRIK, on Bali, quoted, Mar 61: 28
DELHI, INDIA, May 62: 84–87
Red Fort, Mar 61: 21, May 62: 15
U.S. Embassy, Sep 58: 89, Jan 60: 119, May 62: 16
World Agricultural Fair, American Exhibit, Jan 60: 121

DE LIAGRE, ALFRED, JR., Jan 60: 51, 55
  Photograph of, May 63: 4–5
DELLO JOIO, NORMAN, Jan 60: 15, 123, Jan 62: 9, 10, 14
  Photographs of, Jan 62: 5, Mar 63: 30
DELMONICO'S, New York City, Nov 58: 119
DE L'ORME, PHILIBERT, Sep 60: 62: 65–66
DELOS, GREECE, May 62: 46
"DELPHINE," novel by Mme de Staël, Nov 58: 89, 142
DELVAUX, PAUL, Jan 62: 81–82
  Painting by, Jan 62: 81, Sep 63: 94–95
DEMANGEL, R., quoted, Nov 58: 73
DEMARATUS OF CORINTH, Mar 59: 40, 47
"DE MATERIA MEDICA," herbal by Dioscorides, Jan 63: 8
  Quoted, Nov 62: 104
DEMETER, bronze found in Aegean, Nov 58: 66; illus, Nov 58: 67
DEMETER OF ELEUSIS, Jan 61: 61
"DEMETRIUS AND THE GLADIATOR," motion picture, May 63: 49
DEMIDOV, PRINCE, Nov 61: 36
DE MILLE, AGNES, on television, Mar 60: 5, 126
DE MILLE, CECIL B., May 61: 52
DEMING, W. EDWARD, Nov 63: 61
DEMOCRACY
  Assault on correct English related to, Jul 63: 46–48
  Vs. classical tradition, Nov 60: 21–22
  In India, May 62: 85–87
  Socrates vs., Jul 60: 103
"DEMOCRACY IN AMERICA," book by Alexis de Tocqueville, quoted, Nov 62: 112
DE MORGAN, WILLIAM, May 62: 78
DEMOSTHENES
  On Philip II of Macedon, quoted, Mar 59: 30
  In Renaissance curriculum, Jan 60: 62
  Survival of speeches of, Nov 62: 76, 88
DEMPSEY, DAVID, "The Literary Prize Game," article by, Jul 63: 68–75
DENHAM, REGINALD, Sep 60: 88
DENIS, LÉON, Mar 62: 99
DENIS, LOUISE MIGNOT, Mar 61: 118
DENIS, MAURICE, Mar 62: 15
DENMARK (see also COPENHAGEN)
  Bronze Age in, Jul 60: 113
  Peter the Great and, Sep 59: 79
  Royal Danish Ballet, Sep 60: 90–95
"DENMARK'S ROYAL BALLET," article by Walter Terry, Sep 60: 90–95
DENNEY, REUEL, on news, quoted, Mar 60: 51
DENNIS, GEORGE, Sep 63: 86
DENNIS, NIGEL, Jan 63: 27, 29, 32
DENNIS, RICHARD, Nov 63: 43
DENNY, REGINALD, Sep 63: 75, 77, 79
  Photographs of, Sep 63: 77, 78
DENNY, WILLIAM, Jan 59: 21
DENVER, COLO.
  Englishman's impressions of, Jul 62: 115
  Zeckendorf Plaza, Nov 59: 111–12
"DEPARTURE OF REGULUS," painting by Benjamin West, Jul 63: 105; illus, Jul 63: 95
DEPTFORD, ENGLAND, Peter the Great in, Sep 59: 74
DE QUINCEY, THOMAS, Mar 62: 97
DERAIN, ANDRÉ, Jul 62: 65
DERCETO, Semitic goddess, Jan 60: 134
DERMOÛT, MARIA, on Dutch East Indies, quoted, Mar 61: 22
DE ROCHEMONT, LOUIS, Mar 61: 98
DESCARTES, RENÉ, Sep 58: 23–24, Jul 60: 38, Mar 61: 91, Jul 61: 8, Sep 61: 103; May 63: 115
  Portrait of, Jul 60: 39
"DESCRIPTION OF FORMOSA," book by George Psalmanazar, Jan 60: 115, 116
DESCRIPTIVE LINGUISTICS. See STRUCTURAL LINGUISTICS
"DESERTS," tape recorder composition by Edgard Varèse, Jan 59: 53
DESFONTAINES, ABBÉ, Mar 61: 119
DE SICA, VITTORIO, May 59: 99
"DESIRE UNDER THE ELMS," play, May 63: 107
"DESPERATE HOURS, THE," novel, play, and movie, May 63: 106
DES PRÉS, JOSQUIN, Nov 60: 90
DESSAU, GERMANY, Bauhaus, Nov 61: 61, 69, 72–74
D'ESTE. See ESTE
DETERMINISM, May 63: 89
DETROIT, MICH.
  Automotive industry, Jul 60: 69
  Eastland and Northland shopping centers, Nov 59: 108
DETROIT GAS COMPANY BUILDING, May 62: 16
DETROIT "NEWS," on Spectra, quoted, May 60: 44
DE VANE, WILLIAM C., on university teaching situation, quoted, Sep 62: 17
DEVERIA, ACHILLE, etching by, May 61: 83

DEVI, RUKMINI, Sep 63: 68, 70
"DEVIL AND DANIEL WEBSTER, THE," opera, Jan 60: 122
DEVINE, GEORGE, Mar 61: 103
  And English Stage Company, Jan 63: 26–33
  Photograph of, Jan 63: 28
DEVONSHIRE, DUCHESS OF (GEORGIANA CAVENDISH), May 60: 99
DEVONSHIRE, 11TH DUKE OF (ANDREW R. B. CAVENDISH), Jan 59: 59, May 62: 61
DEVONSHIRE, DUKES OF, Nov 58: 50
DeVOTO, BERNARD, Jan 60: 7
DEWEY, JOHN, Nov 58: 32, May 63: 89, Jul 63: 42, 75
DEWEY, THOMAS E., Mar 60: 49, Jul 61: 66
DEWHURST, COLLEEN, Jul 60: 94, Nov 60: 116, May 63: 107
  Portrait of, Jul 60: 95
DEXTER, JOHN, Jan 63: 26
DE ZOETE, BERYL, on Balinese dance, quoted, Mar 61: 23
DHARMA BUMS, Jul 59: 71
DIAGHILEV, SERGEI PAVLOVICH, Jan 61: 46
  Kennedy, Mrs. John F., quoted on, Sep 61: 9
  Sketch of, Sep 58: 132
  Stravinsky, Igor, quoted on, Sep 58: 83
DIAGHILEV BALLET COMPANY, Jan 61: 27–28
"DIALOGUES OF THE CARMELITES," opera, Mar 61: 72
DIAMANT, BERNARD, Mar 62: 87
DIANA OF EPHESUS, Sep 58: 85–87, 141
DIANE DE POITIERS, Sep 60: 64, 65
"DIARY FROM THE DEPTHS, A," article by Gilbert Highet, Nov 62: 108–10
"DIARY OF ANNE FRANK, THE," play, Nov 58: 63
DÍAZ, PORFIRIO, May 59: 6
DICKENS, CHARLES, Mar 59: 125, May 62: 73, Jul 62: 18
  Little Dorrit, quoted, Sep 58: 131
  Pickwick Papers, copy in H. B. Smith's "Sentimental Library," Nov 60: 97
  Portrait of, Mar 59: 90
  Portrayal of Americans by, May 60: 5
  Quoted: on Mormon emigrants, Jan 61: 31–32; on St. Peter's, Rome, Jan 62: 24; on Smith, Sydney, Mar 59: 90
  Real David Copperfield, The, book by Robert Graves, Jan 62: 54
  Salinger, J. D., compared to, May 62: 101, 103, 104
  Wilder, Thornton, quoted on, Jan 61: 31–32
DICKINSON, AUSTIN, Jul 61: 103, 104
DICKINSON, EDWIN, Jul 61: 28
  Portrait of, Jul 61: 29
DICKINSON, EMILY, Jul 61: 100–5
  Portrait of, Jul 61: 100
DICKINSON, LAVINIA, Jul 61: 103, 104
DICKINSON, SUSAN (MRS. AUSTIN), Jul 61: 104
DICKSEE, FRANK, May 62: 78
  Painting by, May 62: 74
"DICK VAN DYKE SHOW," on television, Sep 62: 115
DICTIONARIES, and English language, Jul 63: 34
DIDEROT, DENIS, Sep 60: 72, Mar 61: 116
  And South Seas dream, Jan 60: 30–31
DIEBENKORN, RICHARD, Sep 58: 113, Jan 59: 13–14, Jul 60: 16, 114–16, Jul 62: 24, Sep 63: 96
  Portraits of, Jan 59: 15, Jul 60: 115
  Works by: See ILLUSTRATIONS INDEX
DIETRICH, MARLENE, Jan 59: 99
DIETZ, HOWARD, Jul 62: 37
DIGENES AKRITAS, Nov 63: 33
DIGGES, DUDLEY, photograph of, Sep 63: 79
DIJON, FRANCE, missing mourners of, Sep 58: 62–63
"DILLAR, A DOLLAR, A VERY EXPENSIVE SCHOLAR, A," article by Jacques Barzun, Sep 63: 60–63
DILLON, DOUGLAS, Sep 61: 10, 14
  Photograph of, Sep 61: 12
DILWORTH, RICHARDSON, Sep 62: 62, Jul 63: 26
DINE, JIM, Jan 63: 25
  Painting by, Jan 63: 22
DINESEN, ISAK, Sep 59: 110–12
  Portrait of, Sep 59: 110
"DINING ROOM ON THE GARDEN," painting by Pierre Bonnard, Mar 62: 16; illus, Mar 62: 18–19
"DINNER AT EIGHT," motion picture, quoted, Sep 63: 96
"DINNER AT EIGHT," play, Nov 63: 41
"DINNER PARTY, THE," novel by Claude Mauriac, May 62: 113–14, 115
  Excerpts from, May 62: 114
DINOSAUR NATIONAL MONUMENT, building at, Jan 60: 121
DIOCLETIAN, ROMAN EMPEROR, Sep 61: 30, Nov 62: 88, 90, Sep 63: 40–41, Nov 63: 6
  Baths of, May 60: 39

Coin portrait of, Sep 63: 37
DIODORUS SICULUS, on Tyrrhenians, quoted, May 60: 74
DIOGENES, encounter with Alexander, Mar 63: 10–13
DIOGENES OF OENOANDA, Nov 62: 90
DIONYSIUS I, TYRANT OF SYRACUSE, Sep 61: 24
DIONYSIUS II, TYRANT OF SYRACUSE, Sep 61: 24
DIONYSIUS OF HALICARNASSUS, on Etruscans, quoted, May 60: 61
DIONYSUS, in Lydia, Sep 63: 84, 89
DIOR, CHRISTIAN, on fashion, quoted, Mar 59: 66
DIOSCORIDES, PEDANIUS, Nov 62: 104, Jan 63: 8
DIPLOMACY, memorandum from Prince Metternich to John Foster Dulles, Sep 58: 36–37
DIPTYCHS, in ancient Rome, May 60: 121
"DISAPPEARANCE OF DON JUAN, THE," article by Henry Anatole Grunwald, Jan 62: 56–65
DISC JOCKEYS, Jan 63: 138–39
"DISCOBOLUS," sculpture, Henry Moore quoted on, Nov 60: 114
"DISCOVERING A STONE AGE MUSEUM," excerpts from book by Henri Lhote, May 59: 72, 81–83
"DISENCHANTED, THE," play, Jan 62: 103
DISHER, M. WILLSON, on melodrama, quoted, May 63: 106
DISNEY, WALT
  Pollyanna and Toby Tyler, reviewed, Sep 60: 116–17
  Treasure Island, May 62: 116
DISRAELI, BENJAMIN
  Endymion, Nov 58: 107
  Portrait of, Mar 59: 90
  Quoted: on means and leisure, Sep 60: 34; on Smith, Sydney, Mar 59: 90
DIVAN, council of Ottoman Empire, May 59: 131
DIVING, UNDERSEA, Sep 58: 11, 12, 135
  Archaeological discoveries made during, Nov 58: 66–77
  History of, Nov 58: 70–71
DIVO, ANDREA, Jan 61: 117
"DIVORCE COURT," television program, Jul 60: 6
DIXON, BUDD, Jan 59: 14
DOBELL, WILLIAM, Sep 62: 97
DOBSON, THOMAS, Mar 62: 36
  Building designed by, Mar 62: 36–37
DOBSON, WILLIAM, Jul 61: 92
"DR. FAUSTUS," play, WPA production, Jul 63: 87
"DOCTOR'S DILEMMA, THE," play, Nov 58: 136
DOCUMENTARIES, on television, Sep 62: 115
DODDS, HAROLD, Sep 59: 118
DODGSON, CHARLES LUTWIDGE. See CARROLL, LEWIS
DODSON, OWEN, May 62: 82
DOGGETT, THOMAS, Jan 60: 92
DOGON PEOPLE, of Africa, Mar 63: 41 (map), 44
DOHNÁNYI, ERNST VON (ERNÖ), Jan 61: 72, Nov 62: 46
DOLAN, JOHN, Mar 60: 30–31
"DOLCE VIA, LA," article by James Marston Fitch, Nov 61: 120–28
"DOLCE VITA, LA," motion picture, Sep 61: 110–11, 112, Nov 62: 111
DOLCI, DANILO, Outlaws, quoted, Sep 61: 43
"DOLL'S HOUSE, A," play, Jan 62: 108, Mar 63: 108
DOME, significance in Byzantine architecture, Nov 63: 12, 15, 20
DOMENICHINO, IL (DOMENICO ZAMPIERI), Mar 61: 80
"DOMENICO GNOLI'S WORLD OF FANTASY," article by Niccolo Tucci, Jul 59: 135–36
DOMITIAN, ROMAN EMPEROR
  Coin portraits of, Sep 63: 38; illus, Sep 63: 37
  Juvenal quoted on, Jan 61: 72
"DOM JUAN," play, Jan 62: 59–60
DONAT, ROBERT, photograph of, Sep 63: 79
"DONATION OF CONSTANTINE," Jan 61: 30–31, May 62: 90
"DON GIOVANNI," opera, Nov 58: 120, Jan 60: 10–11, Jan 62: 60, May 63: 45
  Quoted, Jan 62: 57
DON JOHN OF AUSTRIA. See JOHN OF AUSTRIA
"DON JUAN," play, Jan 63: 27
"DON JUAN," poem by Byron, Jan 62: 61
"DON JUAN IN HELL," play, Jul 59: 48
"DON JUAN TENORIO," play, Jan 62: 60
DONLEAVY, J. P.
  Ginger Man, The, Mar 59: 17
  Photograph of, Mar 59: 15
DONNE, JOHN, Sep 58: 24, Jul 60: 42, 58
  "Devotion," quoted, Jul 60: 58
  Portrait of, Jul 60: 58
  Quoted: on human intellect, Mar 62: 5; on Nature, Mar 62: 11; on nature and miracle, Jul 60: 26, 27, 32
  Use of words by, Mar 63: 87, 88
DONOHUE, H. E. F., "After-Dark Satire Goes to Town," article by, Jan 62: 66–71

"DON PASQUALE," opera, Nov 58: 117

"DON QUIXOTE," composition by Richard Strauss, Jan 59: 125

DON QUIXOTE DE LA MANCHA, memorandum to Francisco Franco from, Jul 59: 24–25

"DON QUIXOTE DE LA MANCHA," novel by Cervantes, Sep 59: 114, Nov 61: 106–13

"DON'T CALL ME; I WON'T CALL YOU EITHER," letter from John Keats with answers from *Horizon* editors, Jan 63: 118–19

DOOLITTLE, JAMES, May 59: 8

DOORT, ABRAHAM VAN DER, Jul 61: 80

"DORADE III," Rouen-Paris steamer, Jul 62: 59

DORDOGNE, FRANCE, limestone caves of, Jul 61: 35

DORÉ, GUSTAVE, Jan 59: 44
Engravings by, Jul 61: 61, Nov 61: 110

DORFLES, GILLO, Nov 60: 125

DORFMAN, ANIA, in painting by John Koch, Sep 60: 106

DORIA, GIOVANNI ANDREA, Jul 63: 50, 57, 58

"DORMITION OF THE VIRGIN," painting by Mantegna, Jul 61: 95; illus, Jul 61: 81

DORSEY, THOMAS F., Mar 60: 35

DOS PASSOS, JOHN, Jul 61: 13, Jul 63: 71, 75
Alfred Kazin quoted on, Jul 62: 102

DOSTOEVSKY, FĒDOR, Sep 60: 129, 135, May 61: 81, Jan 62: 62
Brothers Karamazov, The, quoted, May 62: 102
Gambler, The, Nov 63: 62
Interest of Akira Kurosawa in, Jul 62: 45, 47
Stravinsky, Igor, quoted on, Sep 58: 82

"DOSTOEVSKY WITH A JAPANESE CAMERA," article by Donald Richie, Jul 62: 42–47

DOTREMONT, PHILIPPE, Nov 59: 120

DOUAI, FRANCE, Maison d'Europe, Mar 63: 7

DOUBLER. See H'DOUBLER

DOUCET, JACQUES, Mar 59: 70

DOUGLAS, JACK, *My Brother Was an Only Child,* Jul 60: 121

DOUGLAS, KIRK, Nov 58: 139, May 61: 53, 57

DOUGLAS, NORMAN, Mar 61: 22

DOUGLAS, PAUL H., photograph of, May 59: 17

DOW, ALDEN, house designed by, May 62: 30–31

DOWLING, EDDIE, Jan 61: 31

"DOWN AND OUT IN PARIS AND LONDON," book by George Orwell, Nov 62: 110

DOYLE, ARTHUR CONAN, Jan 59: 108, 110, Mar 62: 99
Sherlock Holmes on detection, quoted, Mar 59: 107

D'OYLY CARTE, RICHARD, May 61: 125

DOZY, REINHART, *Spanish Islam,* Sep 62: 87

DRAGONS, Eastern and Western conceptions, Nov 60: 31

DRAGUT, Barbary pirate, Mar 61: 61, 63

DRAKE, ALFRED
Photograph of, Mar 62: 12
Production of *Kean,* Mar 62: 117–18, 119

DRAKE, JOHN, "Obeying the Law," photographs by, Nov 63: 110–12

DRAMA. See THEATRE

DRAMA CRITICS' AWARD, 1958, Sep 58: 144

"DRAMATIC IMAGINATION, THE," book by Robert Edmond Jones, quoted, Jul 59: 48

DRAPER, WILLIAM, Jan 59: 99
Painting by, Jan 59: 104

DRAWING
Beerbohm, Max, caricatures by, May 61: 33–40
Feiffer, Jules, Nov 61: 48–57
Flora, Paul, Sep 59: 92–93, May 60: 120–23
François, André, May 59: 108–21
Gnoli, Domenico, Jul 59: 135–44
Graves, Morris, Jul 60: 105–12
Hoffnung, Gerard, cartoons by, Jul 62: 104–7
Julian, Philippe, "At Home Through the Ages," Mar 63: 80–83
Krahn, Fernando, "The Epic of Man," Sep 63: 108–12
Mariotti, Marcello, "A Theory of the Coiffured Lasses," Mar 63: 118–19
Myers, Lou, philosophical primer, Jul 61: 110–11
Osborn, Robert, Sep 60: 41–48; "Sight That Music Makes," album, May 62: 120–28
Reps, Paul, Zen telegrams, Jan 60: 46–47
Rombola, John: bullfight portfolio, Jul 60: 129–36; impressions of New York, May 63: 116–20
Searle, Ronald, "Paris Preserved," Mar 62: 120–28
Siné, Maurice, suggestions for swimming attire, May 62: 108–9
Soederlund, Peter, "Letters from Denmark," Jul 63: 120
Thaler, Michael, "history of art," Jan 61: 120–21
Ungerer, Tomi, Jan 61: 128–36

"DRAWING ROOM, PETWORTH," painting by Turner, Mar 63: 70

"DREADNOUGHT," H.M.S., hoax on, Jan 61: 66–68, 72

"DREAMER OF LIGHT AND DARK," article by Gilbert Highet, Jan 63: 109–11

"DREAM OF REASON, THE," article by René Dubos,

Jul 61: 4–9

"DREAM OF THE SOUTH SEAS, THE," article by James Ramsey Ullman, Jan 60: 28–31, 124–27

"DREAM PLAY," play, Sep 60: 8

DREAMS
Dinesen, Isak, quoted on, Sep 59: 112
Of Jung, Carl, Jan 63: 109–10

DREISER, THEODORE, Jul 63: 75
Sister Carrie, Jan 62: 63

"DRESSED TO THE NINES," revue, Jul 61: 76–77

DRESSELHUYS, LORRAINE MANVILLE, photograph of, Jul 60: 7

DRESSLER, MARIE, Sep 63: 96

DRIOTON, ÉTIENNE, "Abu Simbel: The Seal on the Gate of Egypt," article by, Jul 60: 10–15, 124–25

DRUGS
Japanese use of tranquilizers, Mar 61: 6
Mood- and consciousness-changing, May 63: 28–31, 114–15

"DRUNKEN ANGEL," motion picture, Jul 62: 42, 45

DRURY, ALLEN, *Advise and Consent,* and motion picture based on, May 62: 116–18

DRYDEN, JOHN, Jul 61: 113
On English language, quoted, Jul 63: 34

DRYSDALE, GEORGE RUSSELL, Sep 62: 97

"DU," magazine, Mar 60: 43

DUANE, MORRIS, portrait of, Jul 63: 24

DUANE FAMILY, of Philadelphia, Jul 63: 9

DUBLIN, IRELAND
U.S. embassy building design, Jan 60: 119–20
Welles, Orson, at Gate Theatre, Jul 63: 86

DuBOIS, GUY PÈNE, Nov 62: 15

DUBOIS, PAUL, Mar 62: 97

DUBOIS, PIERRE, Mar 63: 6

DUBOS, RENÉ, articles by
"Can Man Keep Up with History?" excerpt from *The Torch of Life,* book by, Nov 62: 4–9
"Dream of Reason, The," Jul 61: 4–9

DUBUFFET, JEAN, Nov 59: 120, May 61: 90, 95
Sculpture by, Mar 61: 110

DUBUISSON, French confidence man, Jan 60: 85

DU CAMP, MAXIME, on temples at Abu Simbel, quoted, Jul 60: 8

DUCCIO DI BUONINSEGNA, Jul 63: 107
Paintings by, Nov 60: 44, Jul 63: 97

DUCHAMP, MARCEL, May 59: 10, May 61: 90, 95, Nov 62: 15
Painting by, Mar 60: 56, Sep 63: 90

DUCHARTRE, PIERRE LOUIS, on Pantalone, quoted, Jan 60: 93

DUCHÊNE, French landscape architect, Sep 61: 77

"DUCHESS OF MILAN," portrait by Holbein, Jul 63: 92

DUCIS, JEAN FRANÇOIS, portrait of, Sep 61: 104

DUDENSING, VALENTINE, Nov 61: 12

DUDLEY, JOHN STUART, Nov 62: 108

DUDLEY, MARY, Sep 59: 91, 122

"DUEL AFTER THE MASQUERADE," painting by Jean Léon Gérôme, Mar 60: 57; illus, Mar 60: 68

"DUE NOTTI CON CLEOPATRA," motion picture, May 61: 54

DUERRENMATT, FRIEDRICH (HEINRICH DÜRENMATT), Sep 59: 92, Mar 61: 47, May 61: 95
The Visit, Nov 58: 63, 65

DUFALLO, RICHARD, Jan 63: 78, 80
Photograph of, Jan 63: 81

DUFAY, GUILLAUME, Nov 60: 90

DUFFY, EDMUND, Jul 62: 37

DUFY, RAOUL, Jul 62: 66

DUGGAN, ALFRED, "Richard and Saladin," article by, Jan 59: 86–91, 130–31

DUGONG, as source of mermaid legend, Jan 60: 135

DU GUESCLIN, BERTRAND, Nov 58: 93

DU HOUSSET, MADAME, Mar 61: 89

DU JARDIN, KAREL, Jul 63: 106

"DULCY," play, Jul 62: 40

"DULLE GRIET," painting by Pieter Bruegel the Elder, Jan 59: 44, 46–47; illus, Jan 59: 45, 48–49

DULLES, JOHN FOSTER
Memorandum to, from Metternich, Sep 58: 36–37
Publicity attending last illness, Jul 60: 120

DULLES INTERNATIONAL AIRPORT, Washington, D.C., Jul 60: 77, 123

DULLIN, CHARLES, Sep 61: 102

DUMAS, ALEXANDRE (PÈRE)
Kean, Mar 62: 13, 117–19
In painting by Joseph Danhauser, May 61: 84–85

DUMAS, FRÉDÉRIC, Nov 58: 71

DU MAURIER, DAPHNE, *The Little Photographer,* television version, Mar 63: 35

"DUMBWAITER, THE," play, Jan 63: 31, May 63: 107

DUMONT, MARGARET, Sep 62: 41

DUMUZI-INANNA CULT, Jul 63: 108–9

DUNCAN, DAVID DOUGLAS
Photograph by, Nov 61: 13

"Picasso's Lady," article and photographs by, Jan 60: 97–105
Picasso's Picassos, Nov 61: 7

DUNCAN, ISADORA, Jan 62: 111
George Balanchine quoted on, Jan 61: 47

DUNCAN, ROBERT, Sep 61: 121

DUNCAN, RONALD, Jan 63: 26, 27
The Death of Satan, Jan 62: 65

"DUNCIAD," poem by Alexander Pope, quoted, Nov 59: 90

DUNDEE, SCOTLAND, in 1841, Jul 59: 10

DUNNOCK, MILDRED, May 63: 108

DUNOIS, COMTE DE (BASTARD OF ORLÉANS), Mar 62: 92

DU NOÜY, PIERRE LECOMTE. See LECOMTE DU NOÜY, PIERRE

DUNOYER, OLYMPE, Mar 61: 116

DUNSANY, LORD, visit to Bowdoin College, Nov 60: 66, 68

DUNSTON, BERNARD, painting by, May 62: 77

DUPANLOUP, FELIX ANTOINE PHILIBERT, BISHOP OF ORLÉANS, Mar 62: 98

DU PONT, HENRY FRANCIS, Sep 61: 13

DU PUY, RAYMOND, Mar 61: 56

DUQUETTE, TONY, May 61: 104, 113
Costume designs by, May 61: 105–12

DURANTE, JIMMY, Sep 58: 58

DURAS, MARGUERITE, Nov 61: 116, Jan 62: 100, 101, 110
Portrait of, Jan 62: 101

DUREIN, FRANK, Sep 59: 91

DÜRENMATT, HEINRICH. See DUERRENMATT, FRIEDRICH

DÜRER, ALBRECHT, Sep 59: 126, 131, Jul 61: 80, 90, 94, 95, Jul 63: 93, 94
Chandelier design by, Jan 60: 132
Handwriting of, Sep 59: 131
Portrait of, Sep 59: 131
Woodcut by, Nov 63: 52

DURHAM, ANDERSON & FREED, church designed by, Nov 62: 72

DURRELL, LAWRENCE, Nov 61: 105, May 62: 55, 115
Alexandrians of, Mar 60: 113–18

DURUY, VICTOR, May 63: 54

DÜSSELDORF, GERMANY, Mar 59: 84
Skyscrapers in, Nov 60: 16, 124, 125

DUTCH EAST INDIA COMPANY, Sep 58: 19–20, 25

DUTCH REPUBLIC, Golden Age of, Sep 58: 14–35

DUTCH WEST INDIA COMPANY, Sep 58: 20

DU TEMPLE, RAYMOND, Sep 60: 60, 61, 67

DUTILLEUL, ROGER, Nov 61: 9

DUTTON, E. P., & CO., INC., Jul 61: 112

DUVEEN, JOSEPH, Jul 59: 31, Sep 60: 37, Nov 60: 99, 101

DUVIVIER, JULIEN, May 60: 51

DVOŘÁK, ANTON, Nov 62: 46, 47
Stabat Mater, Thomas Beecham quoted on, Mar 62: 103

DYAKS, visit of Alan Moorehead to, Sep 60: 12

"DYBBUK, THE," play, Jan 61: 32–33

DYER, LEE, Sep 59: 122

DYER-BENNET, RICHARD, May 60: 17
Photograph of, May 60: 16

DYMAXION HOUSE, Mar 60: 108

DYMLING, CARL ANDERS, Sep 60: 9

"DYSKOLOS, THE," of Menander, Jul 59: 78–79
Translation by Gilbert Highet, Jul 59: 80–88

E

EADFRITH, Nov 62: 94

EAKINS, THOMAS, Sep 58: 113, May 59; 121, Sep 60: 102, Jul 63: 18, Sep 63: 96
Paintings by. See ILLUSTRATIONS INDEX

EALING, ENGLAND, theatre at, Jul 59: 48

EAMES, CHARLES, Nov 61: 73

EAMES, EMMA, Jul 59: 32

"EARLY BIRD," motion picture, Nov 62: 98

EARTH
Resources of, and future of machine civilization, Jan 59: 92–94, 128–29
Use of, man's challenge, Sep 58: 48–55

EAST, JAMES, Sep 62: 107
Photograph of, Sep 62: 107

EASTBOURNE TERRACE, London, Nov 60: 124, 125; illus, Nov 60: 14

"EASTERN ART GOES WESTERN, AN," article by James A. Michener, May 60: 102–14

EASTERNERS, American, Jul 59: 123–25

EAST HAMPTON, N.Y., May 63: 5, 7 (map), 9, 10, 14, 22

EAST INDIA COMPANY, opposition of Charles James Fox to, May 60: 99, 101

EAST INDIES
Dutch in, in 17th century, Sep 58: 19–20, 25
Island "paradises" of, Mar 61: 22–23, 23–24, 28, 31
And Thirty Years' War, Nov 62: 41
EASTLAKE, CHARLES LOCK, May 62: 64, 73
Painting by, May 62: 74
EASTLAKE, ELIZABETH, May 62: 64, 73
EASTMAN, MAX, Jul 63: 70
"EATING PEOPLE IS WRONG," novel by Malcolm Bradbury, Sep 60: 119
EBERHARDT, RICHARD, Jul 63: 72
EBLE, KENNETH E., on university professor, quoted, Sep 62: 15
"ECCE HOMO," painting by Titian, Jul 63: 94
ECCLESIUS, ARCHBISHOP, Mar 59: 13
"ECHECS AMOUREUX, LES"
Illus from, Nov 58: 14, 15
Malraux, André, quoted on, Nov 58: 114
"ECHO," satellite, Jan 62: 17–18
ECKHART, JOHANNES, quoted, Jan 63: 111
ECKSTINE, BILLY, May 61: 100
"ECLIPSE, THE," motion picture, May 63: 112
"ÉCOLE DES FEMMES, L'," play, Sep 62: 111
ECONOMICS
Abundance vs. scarcity, Jul 60: 65–72
Art and the economy, Sep 60: 33–40
Future American class system, May 59: 20–23
Of research, Sep 63: 60–63
"ECONOMY OF ABUNDANCE, THE," book by Stuart Chase, Jul 60: 66, 67, 68
ECUADOR, Alexander von Humboldt in, Jul 59: 62, 67
EDDINGTON, ARTHUR STANLEY, Jan 59: 28
EDDY, NELSON, Nov 58: 58
EDESSA, during Crusades, Jan 59: 87
"EDGE OF THE CITY," motion picture, Sep 58: 43, May 59: 101
EDGEWORTH, RICHARD LOVELL
As member of Josiah Wedgwood's group, May 59: 91–96, 128–30
Portrait of, May 59: 91
EDINBURGH, SCOTLAND, Silent Traveller quoted on, Nov 59: 134
EDINBURGH INTERNATIONAL FESTIVAL, theatre established by Tyrone Guthrie, Nov 63: 36
"EDINBURGH REVIEW," periodical, Mar 59: 92–93, 95
On translations of *Arabian Nights' Entertainments*, quoted, Jul 63: 117
EDMAN, IRWIN, on amateur sociologists, quoted, Nov 59: 23
EDO. See TOKYO
EDUCATION
In Age of Leisure, Nov 63: 106, 109
Burgess Hill School, Sep 62: 105–7
Classical tradition and its rout, Nov 60: 17–24, Sep 63: 97–98
In Dutch Republic, Sep 58: 23
In England before 1700, Nov 59: 75
English, teaching of, Jul 63: 41–48
English grammar in 1960's, May 60: 119
And European unity, Mar 63: 7–8
Frontier deculturation, Sep 62: 94–95
Genius and, May 60: 34–38
Grand Seraglio, school of, May 59: 58–59
Grand Tour of 18th and 19th centuries as part of, Nov 59: 76–77, 86–87, 90, 94–96
History, teaching of, Sep 63: 97–100
IQ of teachers and pupils, Mar 62: 74
In Japan, Mar 61: 7, 8
Jargon of, Jul 63: 38–39
Memorandum from Jonathan Swift to Cliff Robinson, Nov 59: 64–65
Nonconformist ideology in, Mar 59: 112
Non-teaching college professors, Sep 62: 14–19
Progressive, excerpts from *Bulletin* of Council for Basic Education, Mar 60: 70–71
Of Renaissance Man, Jan 60: 57–68
Research and its economics, Sep 63: 60–63
In Russia under Peter the Great and successors, Sep 59: 80, 84
Togetherness cult and, Nov 58: 32–33, 146
Of women, in Renaissance, Jan 60: 62, 64
EDUCATIONAL TESTING SERVICE, Sep 59: 25
"EDUCATION OF RENAISSANCE MAN, THE," article by Iris Origo, Jan 60: 57–73
"EDUCATION SENTIMENTALE, L'," novel by Flaubert, Jul 62: 59
EDWARD I, KING OF ENGLAND, Nov 58: 95, May 63: 94
EDWARD II, KING OF ENGLAND, Mar 61: 62
EDWARD III, KING OF ENGLAND, Nov 58: 105
EDWARD IV, KING OF ENGLAND, portrait of, Jul 63: 95
EDWARD VI, KING OF ENGLAND, Jul 63: 92, 93
Handwriting of, Sep 59: 130
Portrait of, Sep 59: 130

EDWARD VII, KING OF ENGLAND, May 61: 120, Jul 63: 107
On Philadelphia, quoted, Jul 63: 17
As Prince of Wales, photograph, Sep 61: 77
EDWARD, KING OF PORTUGAL, Nov 60: 73–74
EDWARDS, HILTON, Jul 63: 86
EDWARDS, J. H., and W. W. VASSE, *Annotated Index to the Cantos of Ezra Pound,* Jan 61: 116–18
EDWARDS, JONATHAN, attitude toward nature, Mar 60: 15
EDWARDS, RALPH, photograph of, Jan 60: 9
EGAN, RICHARD, May 61: 57
EGLINTON, 13TH EARL OF (ARCHIBALD WILLIAM MONTGOMERIE), Nov 58: 107
EGREMONT, 2D EARL OF (CHARLES WYNDHAM), Mar 63: 65, 69
EGREMONT, 3D EARL OF (GEORGE O'BRIEN WYNDHAM), Nov 58: 56
As patron of artists, Mar 63: 62–71
Portrait of, Mar 63: 65
EGYPT (see also ALEXANDRIA)
Byzantine control lost, Nov 63: 26
Fabri, Felix, in, Mar 60: 90, 91
"EGYPT," S.S., bullion salvaged from, Nov 58: 77
EGYPT, ANCIENT
Achaeans and, Jan 61: 80–81
Art of, André Malraux quoted on, Nov 58: 12–13, 15
Conquest by Alexander the Great, Mar 59: 40
And early Negro cultures of Africa, Mar 63: 57–58
Evidence of Egyptian culture in Sahara rock paintings, May 59: 82
Gardens of, May 59: 25–26
Melting pot of, Nov 59: 14
Monuments threatened by Aswan Dam, Jul 60: 8–15, 124–25
Portraiture in, Jan 59: 99
Sundials and clocks in, Jul 62: 86
Tomb paintings that illustrate Bible passages, Nov 59: cover, 3, 14–19
Wheeled vehicles in, Sep 58: 147, 148
"EGYPTIAN, THE," motion picture, Nov 58: 138
EICHLER, JOSEPH, Jan 59: 10
"EIGHT RIDERS IN SPRING," painting by Chao Yen, Jan 61: 3, 16; illus, Jan 61: cover
"EINE FESTE BURG," hymn by Martin Luther, Sep 58: 46
EINSTEIN, ALBERT, Sep 59: 19, 118, Nov 60: 21, 24, Jul 63: 75
IQ of, Mar 62: 72
Quoted: on chance, Sep 60: 124; on chemistry, Mar 62: 74
Relativity theory, Jul 62: 86
EISELEY, LOREN, articles by
"Nature, Man, and Miracle," excerpt from *The Firmament of Time,* Jul 60: 25–32
"Time of Man, The," Mar 62: 4–11
EISENHART, LUTHER, Sep 59: 118
EISENHOWER, DWIGHT D., Nov 60: 121, 122, Jul 61: 66, 68, Sep 61: 9, 14, Jan 62: 17, Nov 62: 18, Mar 63: 107, Nov 63: 58, 59
On billboards, quoted, May 61: 18
Choices for Khrushchev's sight-seeing, May 60: 5
"People-to-People" program, Nov 58: 147
And poetry, Jul 63: 70
Publicity attending illness, Jul 60: 120
Time cover by Andrew Wyeth, Sep 61: 100
ELAGABALUS, ROMAN EMPEROR, Sep 63: 39
ELAM, position of women in, Nov 62: 104
EL CID. See CID
ELEANOR OF AQUITAINE, memorandum to Abigail van Buren and Ann Landers from, May 60: 30–31
ELEANOR OF BRITTANY, Jan 59: 130
ELECTORAL COLLEGE, U.S., Jul 61: 69
ELECTRONIC BANKING, Sep 62: 120
ELECTRONIC MUSIC, Jan 59: 50–55, 124–27, Jan 63: 78
"ELECTRONIC STUDY II," tape recorder composition by Karlheinz Stockhausen, Jan 59: 51
"ELEMENTS OF STYLE, THE," book by William Strunk, Jr., revised by E. B. White, Jul 63: 40
ELEPHANT
As source of ivory, May 60: 90–91, 93–94
Use in war, May 63: 3
"ELEPHANT OF PARIS, THE," excerpt from book by Clay Lancaster, Mar 59: 136
ELGAR, EDWARD, Mar 62: 103–4
ELGIN, 7TH EARL OF (THOMAS BRUCE), Sep 59: 30, 49
ELGIN MARBLES, Sep 59: 30, 31
Vs. Aegina marbles, Sep 59: 49
ELIE, RUDOLPH, on Isabella Stewart Gardner, quoted, Jul 59: 134
"ELIEZER AND REBECCA," painting by Poussin, Mar 61: 89, 92
ELIOT, CHARLES WILLIAM, Sep 60: 119

ELIOT, GEORGE, Mar 61: 32, Mar 63: 14
ELIOT, T. S., Sep 59: 27, 118, Nov 60: 68, Jul 61: 112, 113, Sep 61: 117, 118, 121, May 62: 61, Nov 63: 44
Cocktail Party, The, Nov 58: 62, Jan 60: 6
Influence of, Jul 63: 39
"Love Song of J. Alfred Prufrock, The," quoted, Sep 61: 117
"Mr. Eliot Revisits the Waste Land," poem by W. H. Armstrong, Jan 63: 92–93
"Mr. Eliot's Sunday Morning Service," quoted, Sep 61: 118
Murder in the Cathedral, Nov 60: 52, 127, Jan 63: 88
Playwriting of, Jan 60: 50, 56
Quoted: on art, Jan 62: 12; on New English Bible, Jul 63: 40; on poetry, Jul 59: 108
Sweeney Agonistes, Jan 63: 32
Travesty on, by Edward Adler, Sep 62: 65
"Waste Land, The": influence in Japan, Mar 61: 11; *Marquise Went Out at Five* compared to, May 62: 115; quoted, Sep 61: 117
ELISABETH, QUEEN OF BELGIUM, Jan 60: 76
ELIZABETH, COUNTESS OF SHREWSBURY, Nov 58: 40–41
ELIZABETH, EMPRESS OF AUSTRIA, Jan 61: 35, 42
ELIZABETH I, QUEEN OF ENGLAND, Sep 59: 29, Sep 61: 73, Jul 63: 29, 30, 32
Gifts to Ottoman court, Sep 58: 142, May 59: 131–32, 134
Handwriting of, Sep 59: 127, 132
Portrait of, Sep 59: 132
Tudor portrait, Jul 63: 93; illus, Jul 63: 95
ELIZABETH II, QUEEN OF ENGLAND, Jan 61: 122, Jan 63: 38
Coronation of, painted by Feliks Topolski, Nov 60: 128–36
Paintings in collection of, Jul 63: 92–107
Portrait of, Jul 63: 93
ELIZABETH PETROVNA, EMPRESS OF RUSSIA, Sep 59: 80, Sep 60: 130, 134 (illus)
ELKINS, WILLIAM M., Nov 60: 97, 98
ELKINS PARK, PA., Beth Sholom Synagogue, Sep 59: 19
ELLE, FERDINAND, Mar 61: 79
ELLIOTT, GEORGE P., Jan 59: 18
Parktilden Village, Mar 59: 17, 119
Photograph of, Mar 59: 16
ELLIOTT, J. H., "Great Confrontations V: Cortes and Montezuma," article by, Nov 63: 92–96
ELLIS, HAVELOCK, quoted
On biographies, May 60: 33
On Renaissance movement toward nature, Mar 60: 14
ELLISON, RALPH, Alfred Kazin quoted on, Jul 62: 102
ELMAN, MISCHA, Sep 59: 55
ELOTH, JUDEA, Nov 59: 118
ELSOM, CECIL, Eastbourne Terrace, designed by, Nov 60: 124, 125; illus, Nov 60: 14
ELUARD, PAUL, Mar 59: 78
ELWES, SIMON, Jan 59: 96
Painting by, Jan 59: 104–5
ELYMIANS, Sep 61: 23, 24
"EMBEZZLED HEAVEN," book by Franz Werfel, quoted on St. Peter's, Rome, Jan 62: 48
EMERSON, FAYE, Jan 63: 106
EMERSON, RALPH WALDO, May 61: 66, Jul 63: 114
And Brook Farm, Mar 63: 77
Portrait of, May 61: 66
Quoted: on law in natural world, Jul 60: 26, 29; on music, Jan 59: 21; on nature, Jan 61: 104; on stars, Jan 59: 28; on village play space, Jul 61: 62
EMIG, DONALD W., Nov 62: 72–73
EMMONS, DONN, Jan 59: 22
"EMOTION AND MEANING IN MUSIC," book by Leonard Meyer, quoted, Jul 59: 107–8
"EMPEROR," locomotive, Jan 59: 39
"EMPEROR AND GALILEAN," play, Jan 62: 108
"EMPEROR MING-HUANG'S JOURNEY TO SHU, THE," Chinese painting, Jan 61: 16; illus, Jan 61: 18
"EMPEROR'S MONUMENTAL FOLLY, THE," article by Mary Cable, May 63: 32–39
"EMPTY CANVAS, THE," novel by Alberto Moravia, May 62: 55
"EMPTY CHAIR, THE," play, Nov 58: 137
"ENCODE ME, MY SWEET ENCODABLE YOU," article by William K. Zinsser, Sep 62: 120
"ENDEAVOUR," ship of James Cook, Sep 60: 11
"ENDGAME," play, Sep 60: 113, 114, Jul 61: 116, Sep 62: 34–35 (illus), 36, 37, 38–39 (illus), Mar 63: 107
"ENDLESS COLUMN," sculptures by Constantin Brancusi, Mar 60: 108
"END OF SUMMER," play Sep 58: 60
"END OF THE ROAD, THE," novel by John Barth, Jan 63: 37
ENDORSEMENTS, INC., Jul 60: 122
"ENDYMION," novel by Benjamin Disraeli, Nov 58: 107
"ENEMY OF THE PEOPLE, AN," play, Jan 62: 108
"ENFANTS DU PARADIS, LES," motion picture, Mar 61: 98, Mar 62: 119, May 63: 111

ENGEL, HARRY, portrait of, with painting by, Jul 61: 25
ENGEL, MORRIS, Mar 59: 96, Mar 61: 19, Sep 62: 108–10
ENGHIEN, DUC D', Sep 63: 30, 31
ENGINEERING
   In ancient Rome, Jul 61: 45
   And architecture, Sep 59: 19
   Brunel, Isambard Kingdom, Jan 59: 32–43, 136
   Nervi, Pier Luigi, Mar 59: 18–25, 121–24
   Roman achievements at Arles, Jul 59: 129, 130
   Water tunnel dug by Hezekiah, Nov 59: 5–6
ENGLAND (see also BRITAIN; GREAT BRITAIN)
   Blenheim Palace, Sep 61: 68–77
   Burgess Hill School, Sep 62: 105–7
   Charles I as patron of arts and as king, Jul 61: 78–95
   Comic History of, etchings from, Mar 60: 129–36
   Education, classics in, Nov 60: 20
   Egremont, 3d Earl of, as patron of artists, Mar 63: 63–71
   Gardens of, May 59: 31, 46–47
   Grand Tour as form of education, Nov 59: 73–99, 102–4
   Handwriting in, Sep 59: 127–28
   Jews, readmission of, Mar 60: 100–1, 124–25
   Joan of Arc and the Hundred Years' War, Mar 62: 89–95
   Knights of St. John, Mar 61: 62, 65, 68–70
   Literary prizes, Jul 63: 73
   Millenarism and philo-Semitism of 17th century, Mar 60: 102, 103, 124–25
   Noble houses of 18th century, Nov 58: 38–61
   Oxford University, Jan 63: 82–87
   Peter the Great in, Sep 59: 74
   Philadelphia compared to, Jul 63: 8, 13
   Poker-playing in, Nov 63: 57, 59
   Theatres of, Jul 59: 44, 46, 48
   And Thirty Years' War, Nov 62: 33, 38–39, 40, 41
   Witch mania, Nov 59: 58–63
"ENGLAND MADE ME," novel by Graham Greene, May 61: 117
ENGLE, PAUL
   Homage to William Carlos Williams by, Mar 59: 60–61
   Photograph of, Mar 59: 61
"ENGLISH GRAMMAR IN THE 1960's," article by Ralph B. Long, passages from, May 60: 119
ENGLISH LANGUAGE
   Assault on, Jul 63: 33–48
   Grammar in 1960's, May 60: 119
   Names surviving as common nouns, May 60: 126–28
   Ustinov, Peter, quoted on, Nov 58: 139
ENGLISH STAGE COMPANY, Jan 63: 26–33
ENGRAVING, effect on handwriting, Sep 59: 127
"ENIGMATIC ISLANDS OF PAUL GAUGUIN, THE," article by Marshall B. Davidson, Jan 60: 32
"ENIGMATIC URN, THE," article by Neil McKendrick, Nov 63: 63–65
ENLIGHTENMENT, THE (AGE OF REASON)
   Attitude toward Joan of Arc during, Mar 62: 95–96
   End of witch mania during, Nov 59: 61–63
   As fourth period of unity in Europe, Mar 63: 5
   Religion in, May 61: 64
   Utopias of, Mar 63: 73, 76
   Voltaire's role, Mar 61: 114–19
ENNIUS, QUINTUS, Nov 62: 80
"ENQUIRY INTO THE NATURE OF CERTAIN NINETEENTH CENTURY PAMPHLETS, AN," book by John Carter and Graham Pollard, Mar 59: 107–8
ENSOR, JAMES, May 59: 121, Jan 62: 80–81
   Painting by, Jan 62: 79
"ENTERTAINER, THE," motion picture, Mar 63: 36
"ENTERTAINER, THE," play, Nov 58: 62, Jan 61: 30, Jan 63: 32, 33
ENTHOVEN, ALAIN, Sep 61: 13
"ENTOMBMENT, THE," painting by Poussin, Mar 61: 90; illus, Mar 61: 88
"ENTRY E," novel by Richard Frede, Mar 59: 16–17, 118
"EPHEBOS OF ANTIKYTHERA," Nov 58: 72
EPHESUS, Sep 58: 85–87, 140–42, Mar 59: 30, Sep 63: 89
EPHRON, PHOEBE and HENRY, *Take Her, She's Mine,* Mar 63: 108
"EPIC OF MAN, THE," drawings by Fernando Krahn, Sep 63: 108–12
EPICURUS
   Aphorism by, quoted, Sep 61: 115
   Survival of works by, Nov 62: 90
EPIDAURUS, GREECE, amphitheatre in, Jul 59: 45
EPISCOPALIANS, influence in Philadelphia, Jul 63: 5, 12, 25
"EPISODES," ballet, Nov 59: 56
EPPING, FRANC, photograph of, May 60: 15
EPSTEIN, ALVIN, Jan 62: 9, 14
EPSTEIN, JACOB, May 62: 60
ERASMUS, DESIDERIUS, Sep 59: 29, May 62: 89–95
   Portrait by Holbein, Jul 61: 95, Jul 63: 93, 94, 96; illus, May 62: 88

ERECH (URUK), BABYLONIA, Jul 61: 41, Jul 63: 108
   Fish-god of, Jan 60: 131
"EREWHON," novel by Samuel Butler, Mar 63: 78, Nov 63: 104
ERFURT, GERMANY, meeting of Napoleon and Alexander I at Congress of, Sep 63: 32
ERIGENA, JOHN SCOT, Nov 62: 80
ERIM, KENAN T., Mar 63: 98
ERLACH, FISCHER VON, church designed by, Jul 60: 53
"ERMINE, THE," play, Nov 60: 52, 54, 55
"ERNEST HEMINGWAY ON THE ART OF WRITING," interview by George Plimpton, Jan 59: 82–85, 132–35
ERNST, JIMMY, May 59: 11
ERNST, MAX, May 59: 11
   Painting by, May 59: 18
ERNST, MORRIS, on income in United States, quoted, Nov 63: 105
EROS, progressive conceptions of, Nov 60: 28, 30
"ERRAND FROM MY HEART—, THE," article by Winfield Townley Scott, Jul 61: 100–5
ERROL, LEON, Sep 58: 58
ERSKINE, JOHN (1509–1591), Jul 63: 32
   In painting by W. P. Frith, Jul 63: 28–29
ERSKINE, JOHN (1879–1951), Mar 63: 27
   On Emily Dickinson, quoted, Jul 61: 104
ERTEGUN, AHMET, Nov 60: 86
ESARHADDON, KING OF ASSYRIA, sixty-two curses of, Sep 59: 103–5
ESCAPISM
   In adventure, Sep 58: 12, 135–37
   In cult of unthink, Sep 58: 41, 42
   In science and historical fiction, May 61: 53
   Search for paradise, Mar 61: 20–33
   South Seas dream, Jan 60: 28–31, 124–27
   Of utopian communities, Mar 63: 77
ESCH, PERRINE D', Nov 58: 105
ESCHER, MAURITS, lithograph by, Sep 63: 22
ESCOBAR, MARISOL
   And her mannequins, Mar 63: 102–4
   Photograph of, Mar 63: 103
ESCOFFIER, GEORGES AUGUSTE, May 61: 120–28
   Portrait of, May 61: 120
"ESCOFFIER, GOD OF THE GASTRONOMES," article by Bernard Frizell, May 61: 120–28
ESHERICK, JOSEPH, Jan 59: 8
ESHNUNNA, Sumerian city, Jul 61: 41
ESKIMO ART, and stonecut by Natsivaar, Mar 63: 120
ESOTERIC RECORDS, Nov 60: 90–91
ESSEX, 2D EARL OF (ROBERT DEVEREUX), Nov 61: 110
ESSLIN, MARTIN, Sep 62: 35
   On Bertolt Brecht, quoted, Mar 61: 44
ESTE, BEATRICE D', Jan 60: 66
ESTE, IPPOLITO II D', CARDINAL, May 62: 18, May 63: 35
ESTE, ISABELLA D', Jan 60: 66
   "Allegory" painted for, Jan 60: 67
ESTE, LIONELLO D', Jan 60: 64
ESTERHÁZY, NIKOLAUS I, Mar 62: 77, 78, 80, Nov 62: 44
ESTERHÁZY, NIKOLAUS II, Mar 62: 80
ESTIENNE, HENRI, Mar 61: 94
ESTIVET, JEAN D', Mar 62: 94
"ETERNAL CITY," painting by Peter Blume, Jul 61: 75
"ETERNAL DANCE OF INDIA, THE," article by Nigel Cameron with photographs by Brian Brake, Sep 63: 64–73
ETHELDREDA, SAINT, May 60: 127–28
ETIQUETTE
   Endorsements, Jul 60: 122
   Grand Tour as education in, Nov 59: 77, 90, 98–99
   Self-advertising, Jul 60: 121–22
ETON COLLEGE, Charles James Fox at, May 60: 98
"ETRUSCAN PLACES," book by D. H. Lawrence, quoted, May 60: 58, 59
ETRUSCANS
   Ancient writers quoted on, May 60: 74
   Arts, May 60: 74–79
   Expansion and decline, May 60: 64, 73–74
   Ivory used by, May 60: 121
   Language, May 60: 63–64
   Lydians and, Sep 63: 86
   Origins, May 60: 60–62
   Religion, May 60: 62–63
   Tombs and tomb paintings, May 60: 59–60, 64, 74–78
ETTING, EMLEN, painting by, Jul 63: 9
ETTING, MRS. EMLEN, portrait of, Jul 63: 9
"ETUDE AUX CHEMINS DE FER," tape recorder composition by Pierre Schaeffer, Jan 59: 54
EUGENE, PRINCE OF SAVOY, Mar 62: 50
EUGENICS, positive, for man, Nov 62: 7–9
EUGÉNIE, EMPRESS OF FRANCE, Sep 60: 81, Nov 61:

36, May 63: 54, 71
   Memorandum to Jacqueline Bouvier Kennedy from, Sep 62: 20–21
   In painting by Tissier, Sep 60: 68
EUGENIUS IV, POPE, Jan 60: 59, Jan 62: 26
"EULA II," painting by Larry Rivers, Sep 59: 100; illus, Sep 59: 99
EULER, LEONHARD, Sep 59: 80
EUNUS, Sep 61: 26
"EUPHUES," romance by John Lyly, John Barth quoted on, Jan 63: 37
EUPOLIS, Nov 62: 76
EURATOM TREATY, Mar 63: 8
EUREKA STOCKADE, Sep 62: 98
EURIC, KING OF THE VISIGOTHS, Jul 59: 130
"EURIDICE," opera, Jul 60: 42
EURIPIDES
   Bacchantes, Sep 63: 84
   On gods, quoted, Nov 58: 14
   In Renaissance curriculum, Jan 60: 62
   Survival of works by, Nov 62: 80, 93
EUROPE, fifth period of unity in, Mar 63: 4–9
EUROPE, COLLEGE OF, Mar 63: 7
EUROPE, COUNCIL OF, exhibition "Circa 1400" organized by, Mar 63: 8
EUROPE, UNIVERSITY OF, Mar 63: 7–8
EUROPEAN COAL AND STEEL COMMUNITY, Mar 63: 7
EUROPEAN ECONOMIC COMMUNITY (COMMON MARKET), Mar 63: 7–9
"EUROPEAN GUIDE TO TEACHING, THE," pamphlet, Mar 63: 7
"EUROPE IN ANGUISH," portfolio of political posters, Jan 59: 112–21
"EUROPE'S BRIEF FLOOD TIDE OF PHILO-SEMITISM," article by H. R. Trevor-Roper, Mar 60: 100–3, 124–25
EUSEBIUS OF CAESAREA, on Pool of Gibeon, quoted, Nov 59: 8
EUWE, MAX, Jan 62: 116, 118
EVANS, ARTHUR, Jan 61: 77
EVANS, BERGEN, on New English Bible, quoted, Jul 63: 40
EVANS, EDITH, Jan 61: 30–31, Jul 62: 104
   Photograph of, Jan 61: 31
EVANS, GIL, May 61: 100
EVANS, RICHARD, Nov 62: 98
EVE. See ADAM and EVE
EVELYN, JOHN, quoted
   On basilica in Venice, Mar 63: 15
   On Rotterdam picture market, Sep 58: 28
   On Tuileries garden, Sep 60: 69
EVENDEN, J. F., Mar 62: 10
"EVENINGS AT THE BRIDGE," article by Terence O'Donnell, May 61: 24–32
EVERGOOD, PHILIP, Sep 58: 110
   Painting by, Sep 58: 111
EVEUX-SUR-ARBRESLE, FRANCE, Couvent Sainte-Marie de la Tourette, Mar 61: 34–41
EVLIYA EFFENDI, May 59: 131
EVOLUTION
   Of man, Mar 62: 8; in Africa, Mar 63: 43; effect of agriculture on, Sep 62: 5
   Man and his weapons instinct, Nov 61: 38–41
   Man's need to adapt himself to changing world, Nov 62: 5–9
   Man's role in, Sep 58: 48–55
EWALD, JOHANNES, Sep 59: 112
EWELL, TOM, Nov 62: 107
EXCHANGE STUDENTS, Mar 63: 8
EXEDRAE, Nov 59: 109–10
"EXILE AND THE KINGDOM," book of short stories by Albert Camus, Nov 59: 71
EXISTENTIALISM, Mar 63: 9
   Ionesco, Eugène, quoted on, May 61: 93
   J.B. and, Jan 60: 56
"EXODUS," motion picture, May 62: 116
"EXPANDING UNIVERSE AT OLD NASSAU, THE," article by Carlos Baker, Sep 59: 22–27, 118–19
"EXPLAINERS, THE," revue, Jan 62: 70
"EXPLAINERS, THE," satire by Jules Feiffer, Nov 61: 48, 57
"EXPLODING METROPOLIS, THE," book by Jane Jacobs, William H. Whyte, Jr., and others, Jul 59: 7
EXPLORATION (see also ANTARCTIC EXPEDITIONS; ARCTIC EXPEDITIONS)
   Of Burton, Richard Francis, Jul 63: 110–17
   Dutch, Sep 58: 19
   Prehistoric, Jul 60: 84–91, 113
   Of South Seas, Jan 60: 30
   Of Spanish America by Alexander von Humboldt, Jul 59: 62–67
   Of west coast of Africa south of Cape Bojador, Nov 60: 76–83

"EXTERMINATING ANGEL, THE," motion picture, Nov 62: 110

"EXTRAORDINARY DISLOCATION, AN," motion picture, Nov 62: 97

EYCK, HUBERT VAN, painting by, Sep 63: 7

EYCK, JAN VAN, Nov 58: 114, Sep 60: 72
  Paintings by, Nov 58: 17, Jul 61: 48

EYE, and sun's radiations, Nov 63: 51–52, 54

EZION-GEBER, ISRAEL, Biblical city, Nov 59: 10, 118, 119

"EZRA POUND," book by Charles Norman, Jan 61: 116, 119

F

FABIANI, fashion designer, Mar 63: 94

FABRI, FELIX, pilgrimage to Holy Land and Mount Sinai, Mar 60: 81–93

"FABULOUS," use of, in advertising, Jan 61: 119

"FABULOUS VISITOR FROM FORMOSA, A," article by Bradford Smith, Jan 60: 113–18

"FACE IN THE CROWD, A," motion picture, Sep 60: 88

FACTS FORUM, Mar 60: 48

"FACTS OF LIFE, THE," motion picture, May 63: 111

FAGG, BERNARD, Mar 63: 53

FAGUS WORKS, near Alfeld, Germany, Nov 61: 62

"FAHRENHEIT 451," book by Ray Bradbury, Mar 63: 79

FAÏENCE BEADS, Bronze Age trade in, Jul 60: 90

FAIRBANKS, DOUGLAS, JR., Sep 63: 76
  Photograph of, Sep 63: 80

FAIRBROTHER, NAN, "Gardens Since Eden," article by, May 59: 24–31

FALKENSTEIN, CLAIRE, Jan 59: 14
  Portrait of, with construction, Jan 59: 14

"FALL, THE," novel by Albert Camus, Nov 59: 71

"FALLEN IDOL, THE," motion picture, Nov 59: 126, Mar 61: 98

"FALL OF THE CITY, THE," radio play, Jan 60: 54

"FALSTAFF," opera, May 63: 42

"FALSTAFF," Shakespearean character, Jan 60: 96

FAMAGUSTA, CYPRUS, conquered by Turks, Jul 63: 53

FAMILY
  In Age of Leisure, Nov 63: 106–7
  Togetherness cult and revolt against, Nov 58: 30–33, 146–47

"FAMILY ALBUM," of Bertha F. Beasely (introduction by Oliver Jensen), Nov 58: 121–32

"FAMILY OF SALTIMBANQUES, THE," painting by Picasso, Nov 61: 9; illus, Nov 61: 8

"FAMILY SHAKESPEARE, THE," edited by Thomas Bowdler, Sep 62: 68–71

"FAMILY THEATER," advertising posters of, Nov 58: 30

FAMOUS PLAYERS FILM COMPANY, Mar 60: 38

"FANFARE," ballet, Sep 60: 94

FAN K'UAN, Jan 61: 16
  Painting by, Jan 61: 19

"FANNY," musical, Sep 58: 60

"FANNY HILL," novel, May 62: 55

"FANTASY IN SPACE," tape recorder composition by Otto Luening, Jan 59: 54

FANTIN-LATOUR, HENRI, in painting by Manet, May 63: 74

FARADAY, MICHAEL, Jul 61: 7

FARAN, JAMES J., JR., "How to Buy a Tuba," article by, Nov 63: 97–99

FARBER, MANNY, "Movies Aren't Movies Any More," quoted, Jan 63: 111

"FAR COUNTRY, A," play, Jan 62: 103

"FAREWELL TO ARMS," novel by Ernest Hemingway, Jan 59: 84

FARGUE, LÉON-PAUL, on Seine River, quoted, Jul 62: 60

FARINGTON, JOSEPH, on Lord Egremont, quoted, Mar 63: 65

"FARM, THE," painting by Joan Miró, Mar 59: 76; illus, Mar 59: 73

"FARM AT LAEKEN, THE," painting by Rubens, Jul 63: 106; illus, Jul 63: 98–99

FARMER, and art, Sep 60: 36

FARNSWORTH, DANA L., warning against mind-distorting drugs issued by, May 63: 115

"FAR OUT ON LONG ISLAND," article by William K. Zinsser with photographs by Hans Namuth, May 63: 4–27

FARRAR, DAVID, May 61: 57

FARRAR, GERALDINE, Sep 59: 51–52
  Farewell performance, Nov 58: 120

FARRELL, JAMES T., Jul 63: 71, 75

FARWELL, ARTHUR, May 60: 48

FASHION
  For bowlers, Mar 63: 94

Classical revival of 18th century, Mar 62: 55–56, 61–69

Common Market and, Mar 63: 8

Cycles of, Mar 59: 62–67, 113–17

Empire style, origin of, Nov 58: 87

In hairdressing, Mar 63: 118–19

Memorandum from Empress Eugénie to Jacqueline Bouvier Kennedy, "On Setting the Style of an Age," Sep 62: 20–21

Togetherness theme in, Nov 58: 31

In U.S.S.R., changes in, Nov 62: 116–17

FAST, HOWARD, May 61: 57

FAULKNER, WILLIAM, May 59: 100, Sep 59: 118, 124, Jan 62: 64, 97, Jul 63: 70, 71, 75
  Kazin, Alfred, quoted on, Jul 62: 99, 100, 101, 102
  Motion pictures based on stories by, Sep 60: 88
  Old Man, television version, Mar 63: 35

FAUQUEZ, ARTHUR, Reynard the Fox, Jan 63: 88, 90

"FAUST," opera, Nov 58: 119

FAUSTINA THE ELDER, coin portraits of, Sep 63: 39; illus, Sep 63: 38

FAUSTINA THE YOUNGER, Nov 63: 64
  Coin portraits of, Sep 63: 39; illus, Sep 63: 38

FAUSTINUS, May 59: 123

FAVI, TOMMASO, photograph of, Sep 63: 54

FAWCETT, explorer, disappeared 1925, Sep 58: 135

FEDDEN, ROBERT, on Krak of the Knights, quoted, Mar 61: 54

FEDE FAMILY, of Italy, May 63: 35

FEDER, MRS. EDGAR, in painting by John Koch, Sep 60: 106

FEDERAL HIGHWAYS PROGRAM, and billboards, May 61: 5, 18

FEDERAL HOUSING ADMINISTRATION, May 61: 5, 19

FEDERAL THEATRE PROJECT, Orson Welles and, Jul 63: 87

FEDERAL TRADE COMMISSION, and TV commercials, Nov 60: 123

FEDOR III, CZAR OF RUSSIA, Sep 59: 62, 66

FEIBLEMAN, PETER, Tiger, Tiger, Burning Bright, May 63: 107–8

FEIFFER, JULES, Nov 61: 48, 57
  Crawling Arnold, play by, Nov 61: 49–56
  Drawings by, Nov 61: 49, 51, 52, 54

FEININGER, LYONEL, Sep 59: 18, Nov 61: 60, 61, 64
  Painting by, Nov 61: 66
  Photograph of, Nov 61: 59

FELGENHAUER, PAUL, Mar 60: 101, 102

FELIPE DE JESÚS, SAINT, Nov 61: 111

FELLINI, FEDERICO, May 59: 99, May 60: 51, Mar 61: 98, 100, Nov 62: 110, 111
  La Dolce Vita, Sep 61: 110–11, Nov 61: 8

"FELLINI-8½," motion picture, Jan 63: 38

FELTRE, VITTORINO DA. See VITTORINO DA FELTRE

FENCING, education in, as part of Grand Tour, Nov 59: 90, 98–99

FENELLOSA, ERNEST, May 60: 114

FENTON, CHARLES A., on university teaching situation, quoted, Sep 62: 17

FENWAY COURT (ISABELLA STEWART GARDNER MUSEUM), Jul 59: 26–40, 133–34

FERBER, EDNA, Jul 62: 37, Jul 63: 43
  Caricature of, Jul 62: 41

FERDINAND II, HOLY ROMAN EMPEROR, Nov 62: 35, 36, 37

FERDINAND III, KING OF CASTILE AND LEÓN, Sep 62: 88

FERDINAND V, KING OF CASTILE AND LEÓN, bronze relief of, Sep 62: 92

FERGUSSON, FRANCIS, The King and the Duke, Mar 60: 98, 120

FERGUSSON, ROBERT, May 63: 85

FERLINGHETTI, LAWRENCE, Jan 59: 19, Sep 61: 119, Jul 63: 70

FERRARA, ITALY, Renaissance court at, Jan 60: 64, 66

FERRARIS, GALILEO, Nov 59: 47

FERRIS, JAMES, Jan 59: 11, Mar 59: 123
  Photograph of, Jan 59: 8

FERRO-CEMENTO, Mar 59: 21, 122–24

FERRY, JULES, on Baron Haussmann, quoted, May 63: 63, 74

FERTILITY CULT, revealed in Çatal Hüyük sculptures, Nov 63: 66–67

FESCH, JOSEPH, CARDINAL, Nov 60: 99, Jan 62: 48

FESTIVALS
  At ancient sites, Jul 62: 27–31
  European, to be avoided, Mar 59: 83, 84–85
  San Francisco Art Festival, Jan 59: 6

FESTSPIELHAUS, Bayreuth, Nov 58: 23–24, 27

"FÊTE CHAMPÊTRE," painting attributed to Giorgione, Jul 61: 95; illus, Jul 61: 84–85

FETI. See FETTI

FETTER, EVERETT, Sep 59: 91

FETTI, DOMENICO, Jul 61: 90, Jul 63: 94

FEUCHTWANGER, LION, May 62: 39

FEUDALISM, in Latin Kingdom of Jerusalem, Mar 61: 60, 65

FEUERMANN, EMANUEL, Sep 61: 83

FEYNMAN, RICHARD P., quoted, Sep 62: 42

FICHANDLER, ZELDA, Jan 62: 13

FICINO, MARSILIO, on Federigo da Montefeltro, quoted, Jan 60: 73

FICKE, ARTHUR DAVISON
  Drawing of, May 60: 46
  And Spectric poetry hoax, May 60: 42–48

"FIDELIO," opera, Nov 58: 24–25

FIEDLER, ARTHUR, Sep 59: 123

FIEDLER, LESLIE
  On Clarissa Harlowe, quoted, Jan 62: 60
  Eye of Innocence, The, quoted, May 62: 102–3

FIELD, CYRUS, Nov 58: 119

FIELD, SHIRLEY ANNE, Mar 63: 36
  Photograph of, Mar 63: 37

FIELDS, W. C., Sep 58: 58
  Photograph of, Sep 58: 58

"FIFTH EUROPE, THE," article by Edgar Ansel Mowrer, Mar 63: 4–9

FIFTH MONARCHISTS, Mar 60: 124, 125

"FIFTH NEED OF MAN, THE," article by John Rader Platt, Jul 59: 106–11

"FIGHTING COCK, THE," play, Nov 60: 51, 52, 126

FIGINI, LUIGI, Nov 59: 50

"FIGURE IN THE CARPET, THE," ballet, Jan 61: 49

"FIGURES TO THE FORE," article by Eleanor C. Munro, Jul 60: 16–24, 114–16

FIJI, Jan 60: 127, May 60: 121

FILARETE, ANTONIO, Nov 61: 88, Jan 62: 26

FILDES, LUKE, The Widower, May 62: 73

FILELFO, FRANCESCO, Jan 60: 62, 66

FILLMORE, ABIGAIL (MRS. MILLARD), Sep 61: 9

"FILM CULTURE," magazine, quoted on New York film movement, Mar 61: 19

FINE, IRVING, Mar 63: 29

FINE, REUBEN, Jan 62: 116

FINLAND
  Designers Tapio and Rut Bryk Wirkkala, Jul 63: 62–67
  Peter the Great and, Sep 59: 80

FINLEY, M. I., articles by
  "Old World's Peculiar Institution, The," May 62: 42–49
  "Thucydides' War," Jan 60: 41–45
  "Was Socrates Guilty as Charged?" Jul 60: 100–4, 117
  —— and D. MACK SMITH, "Sicily," article by, Sep 61: 20–45

"FINNEGANS WAKE," book by James Joyce, Jul 63: 39

FINNEY, ALBERT, Mar 63: 36

FIORENTINO, Il Pecorone, Jan 60: 92, 96

FIRDAUSI, Jan 63: 62, 67, 72
  In Persian miniature, Jan 63: 62

"FIRE," novel by George R. Stewart, Jan 59: 19

FIRE ESCAPES, photographs by John Drake, Nov 63: 110–12

"FIRMAMENT OF TIME, THE," book by Loren Eiseley, excerpt from, Jul 60: 25–32

"FIRST LOVE," play, Jul 62: 49

FIRST NATIONAL CITY BANK OF NEW YORK, Mar 61: 121

FIRUZKOH, archaeological site, Nov 59: 43

FISCHER, BOBBY, Jan 62: 117, 118, 119, 120
  Photograph of, Jan 62: 118

FISCHER, EDWIN, Jan 60: 81

"FISH," sculpture by Constantin Brancusi, Mar 60: 108

FISHER, GEOFFREY FRANCIS, ARCHBISHOP OF CANTERBURY, Sep 63: 9

FITCH, JAMES MARSTON, articles by
  "Avant-Garde or Blind Alley?" Mar 62: 30–39
  "Dolce Via, La," Nov 61: 120–28
  "Frank Lloyd Wright's War on the Fine Arts," Sep 60: 96–103, 127–28

FITTON, JAMES, painting by, May 62: 76

FITTS, DUDLEY, Jan 63: 29, Jul 63: 72

FITZGERALD, EDWARD, on death of Elizabeth Barrett Browning, quoted, May 63: 82

FITZGERALD, F. SCOTT, Jul 63: 75
  Kazin, Alfred, quoted on, Jul 62: 100, 102
  Salinger, J. D., compared to, May 62: 101

FITZHERBERT, MARIA ANNE (MRS, FITZHERBERT), May 60: 124, Nov 62: 22–23, 24
  Caricatures of, Nov 62: 22

FITZPATRICK, RICHARD, May 60: 124

"FIVE-DAY LOVER, THE," motion picture, Jan 62: 110

FIZDALE, ROBERT, Mar 61: 75, May 63: 14, 18
  Portrait of, Mar 61: 74

FLADE, DIETRICH, Nov 59: 60

FLAGLER, HENRY M., Jan 61: 104

FLAGSTAD, KIRSTEN, Nov 58: 120, Sep 59: 52, May 63: 42

FLAHERTY, ROBERT, Mar 61: 17, 98

FLANAGAN, BUD, Jan 61: 122–23

FLANAGAN, WILLIAM, Sep 61: 79

"FLASH AND FILIGREE," novel by Terry Southern, Mar 59: 17, 117, 118

FLATIRON BUILDING, New York City, Nov 60: 125

FLAUBERT, GUSTAVE, May 61: 53, 81, Nov 61: 36, May 63: 54

    Anecdote told by, Sep 62: 113

    Education sentimentale, Jul 62: 59

    Madame Bovary, Jan 62: 62, 64

    On Turkish baths, quoted, Sep 60: 125

FLAXMAN, JOHN, Mar 62: 61, Mar 63: 69

"FLEDERMAUS, DIE," opera, Nov 58: 120

FLEISCHER, RICHARD, and motion picture *Barabbas,* Mar 63: 109–11

FLEISHER, LEON, Jan 60: 74, 76, 81, Jan 62: 5, 9

    Portrait of, Jan 60: 76

FLEMING, JOHN F. See WOLF, EDWIN 2ND, co-author

FLEMISH ART, André Malraux quoted on, Nov 58: 114

FLENTROP, D. A., Mar 60: 80

FLESCH, CARL, Sep 61: 84

FLETCHER, JOHN GOULD, Mar 63: 30

    On Spectric poets, quoted, May 60: 43

FLETCHER, ROBERT, costumes by, Nov 60: 92–93, 95

FLEUR, ABBÉ, Jan 60: 85

FLEXNER, ABRAHAM, Jan 62: 13–14

FLICKER, THEODORE J. (TED), Jan 62: 66, 70

    Photographs of, Jan 62: 69

"FLOATING OPERA, THE," novel by John Barth, Jan 63: 37

"FLOATING ROCKS AND FLAMING TUBAS," article by John Canaday, Jan 62: 76–87

FLOOD LEGEND, and origin of mermaid legend, Jan 60: 131

FLORA, PAUL, Sep 59: 92

    Drawings by, Sep 59: 92–93, May 60: 120–23

FLORENCE, ITALY

    Laurentian library, Nov 62: 94; illus, Nov 62: 88

    Market days in, Nov 61: 122

    Stadium designed by Pier Nervi, Mar 59: 24

    Suburbs of, Jul 61: 62

    University of Europe, Mar 63: 8

FLORENTINUS, on slavery, quoted, May 62: 44

FLORENVILLE, AGNES DE, Nov 58: 105

FLORIDA, resort hotels of, Jan 61: 102–4, 106–7, 108–9

FLORIDA SOUTHERN COLLEGE, Sep 59: 8

"FLOURISH OF STRUMPETS, A," photographs by Milton H. Greene, May 61: 50–51

"FLOWERING OF SAN FRANCISCO, THE," article by Allan Temko, Jan 59: 4–23

"FLOWERING PEACH, THE," play, Sep 60: 51

FLOYD, CARLISLE, Jan 60: 122, Jan 62: 14

    Portrait of, Jan 60: 15

"FLYING DUTCHMAN," train, Jan 59: 39

"FLYING HIGH," musical, Sep 58: 59

FLYNN, ERROL, photograph of, Sep 63: 81

FOCUS, PROJECT, Sep 59: 27

FOGG MUSEUM OF ART, Cambridge, Mass., Jul 59: 28

FOKINE, MICHEL, Sep 60: 94

    Les Sylphides, Jan 61: 27

"FOLD-IN" WRITING, Jul 63: 39–40

FOLEY, EDWARD, Sep 61: 5

FOLGER, HENRY C., Nov 60: 98

FOLGER, MAYHEW, Sep 63: 47

FOLK MUSIC, Joan Baez, singer of, Sep 62: 66–67

"FOLLOW THROUGH," musical, Sep 58: 59

FONDA, HENRY, May 61: 117

    In *Advise and Consent,* May 62: 117–18

    On Ustinov, Peter, quoted, Nov 58: 139

FONTAINE, JOAN, Sep 63: 80

FONTAINE, PIERRE, Sep 60: 81

FONTAINEBLEAU, PALACE OF, Sep 60: 62

FONTAINEBLEAU HOTEL, Miami Beach, Jan 61: 102–3

FONTANA, DOMENICO, May 59: 32

    Portrait of, May 59: 32

FONTANNE, LYNN (MRS. ALFRED LUNT), Jan 61: 31, Jul 62: 40, Nov 62: 107

    Caricature of, Jul 62: 32

    In *The Visit,* Nov 58: 62–63, 65

FONTEYN, MARGOT, Sep 60: 94

FONTHILL ABBEY, Mar 62: 36, 62

FOOD and DRINK

    Advertising of, Nov 59: 114, 116; by airlines, Jan 62: 113; alcoholic beverages, Sep 60: 120

    Apology for gluttons, Jan 63: 34–35

    In Bastille, Jan 60: 86–87

    And Common Market, Mar 63: 8

    Cowslip cream recipe, May 59: 41

    And culture of non-hotel, Mar 63: 115–17

    Escoffier, May 61: 120–28

    In Europe, Mar 59: 85, 120

    In France during Franco-Prussian War, May 61: 125, 127, Sep 62: 113

    In Moslem Spain, Sep 62: 77–78, 82

    In noble houses of 18th century England, Nov 58: 56–57

    Of Ottoman sultans, May 59: 134

    Prince Regent's banquets at Brighton, May 61: 122, Nov 62: 29–30

    Supermarket food, Mar 59: 110–11

    Tea ceremony of Japan, Jul 59: 126

    Vegetarianism, G. B. Shaw quoted on, Nov 58: 135

    Wine, Sep 58: 104–7, 145; in ancient Egypt, Nov 59: 14

FOOD PRODUCTION, population increase vs., Sep 58: 50, 51

"FOOLS ARE PASSING THROUGH," play, Mar 61: 47

FOOTE, HORTON, Sep 60: 51

"FOOTNOTE TO HISTORY, A," book by Robert Louis Stevenson, Jan 60: 124

FOPPA, VINCENZO, painting by, Jan 60: 57

FORAIN, JEAN-LOUIS, May 62: 78

FORBES, SCOTT, Jan 63: 106

"FORBIDDEN PLANET," motion picture, Jan 59: 126

"FORCE DE L'AGE, LA," memoir by Simone de Beauvoir, Jan 62: 112

FORD, GLENN, "Glenn Ford March" of Ronny Graham, Nov 60: 85

FORD, HENRY

    "Chance Meeting on the American Road, A," by Oliver Jensen, Nov 58: 36–37

    Guggenheims compared with, May 59: 5

    Quoted: on art, Sep 60: 36; on building a motor car, May 61: 6; on history, Mar 59: 5

FORD, HENRY II

    "Chance Meeting on the American Road, A," by Oliver Jensen, Nov 58: 36–37

    Estate of, May 63: 14; illus, May 63: 15

    On Fund for the Republic, quoted, Jan 62: 4

FORD, O'NEIL, Mar 59: 123

FORD FOUNDATION, Jul 63: 69

    And creative arts, Jan 62: 4–15

    Grand opera grants, Jan 60: 14

    Repertory theatre grants, Jan 63: 106

FORD MOTOR COMPANY, television advertising of, Mar 63: 114

"FORD MOVES IN ON THE ARTS," article by Martin Mayer, Jan 62: 4–15

FOREIGN AID, May 60: 6–7, 9

FOREIGN TRADE, balance of payments and industrial design, Sep 60: 39

FOREMAN, CARL, May 63: 10

FORESTER, C. S., Jan 59: 18

FORESTS, of American Colonies, Mar 60: 14–15

FORGERY, in art and book publishing, Mar 59: 105–9

FORMOSA, fabulous visitor (George Psalmanazar) from, Jan 60: 113–18

FORREST, GEORGE, Mar 62: 119

FORRESTAL RESEARCH CENTER. See JAMES FORRESTAL RESEARCH CENTER

FORRESTER, MAUREEN, Mar 62: 87

    Photograph of, Mar 62: 86

FORSTER, E. M., Jan 59: 134, Jan 60: 107

    On culture, quoted, Sep 60: 37

FORSTER, GEORG, Jul 59: 58

"FORSYTE SAGA, THE," series of novels by John Galsworthy, Jan 62: 62

FORT ROTTERDAM, Makassar, Indonesia, Mar 61: 23

FORT ST. ANGELO, Malta, Mar 61: 63

FORT ST. ELMO, Malta, Mar 61: 61, 63

"FORTUNE," periodical, Jul 60: 69

    On Groupthink, quoted, Nov 58: 33

    MacLeish, Archibald, as editor of, Jan 60: 53, 55

FORT WORTH, TEX., city planning in, Jul 59: 9, 13

"FOR WHOM THE BELL TOLLS," novel by Ernest Hemingway, Jan 59: 134, Jan 62: 64

    Television version, Mar 60: 4

FOSS, LUKAS, Jan 62: 9, 13, Mar 63: 29

    On Bernstein, Leonard, quoted, Jul 59: 23

    Improvisation Chamber Ensemble, of, Jan 63: 76–81, 105

    Photographs of, Jan 63: 76, 81

FOSSE, BOB, May 63: 13

FOSTER, BENJAMIN, Sep 59: 124

FOSTER, JOHN, and Aegina marbles, Sep 59: 30–32, 49

FOSTER, STEPHEN, home of, Nov 58: 36

FOUCHE, JOSEPH, Nov 58: 142

    Portrait of, Nov 58: 88

FOUNTAINS, May 62: 12–29

    Of Hadrian's Villa, May 63: 36, 37

    In Renaissance, May 59: 29, 32

FOUNTENAY, Jesuit priest, Jan 60: 115–16

FOUQUET, JEAN, May 61: 113, Nov 61: 88, 97

    Paintings by, Nov 61: 89–96

    Portrait of, Nov 61: 88

FOUQUET, NICOLAS

    Portrait of, Jul 63: 76

    And Vaux-le-Vicomte, May 62: 14, Jul 63: 76–83

"400 BLOWS, THE," motion picture, May 60: 50, 53, Sep 60: 53, Mar 61: 19

FOURIER, CHARLES, Mar 63: 76–77

"FOUR MEN," painting by David Park, Jul 60: 115; illus, Jul 60: 20–21

FOX, CAROLINE, May 60: 98

FOX, CHARLES JAMES, Mar 59: 92, May 60: 96–101, 124–25, Mar 61: 118, Nov 62: 22, Mar 63: 65

    Portrait of, May 60: 97

FOX, HENRY (1ST BARON HOLLAND), May 60: 96, 98, 100

FOX, HENRY RICHARD VASSALL. See HOLLAND, 3D BARON

FOX, STEPHEN, May 60: 96

F. P. A. See ADAMS, FRANKLIN PIERCE

FRA ANGELICO. See ANGELICO

FRAGONARD, JEAN HONORÉ, Mar 62: 50, 63

    Drawing by, in White House, Sep 61: 13–14; illus, Sep 61: 6

    Paintings by, Nov 59: 85, Sep 60: 75

FRANCE (see also MARSEILLES; PARIS)

    Angevin invasion of Sicily, Sep 61: 32, 34, 37

    Arles, Jul 59: 90–105, 129–32

    Carcassonne, Jul 61: 49–51

    Cave paintings at Lascaux, Jul 61: 34, Sep 62: 11, 12

    Caves of Dordogne, Jul 61: 35

    Churches. See under CHURCHES and SYNAGOGUES

    Couvent Sainte-Marie de la Tourette, Mar 61: 34–41

    Crown jewels, May 63: 96

    Front Lopulaire hoax, Jan 61: 71

    Gardens of, in Renaissance, May 59: 29, 32

    And Grand Tour of 18th and 19th centuries, Nov 59: 76–86

    Joan of Arc and successive judgments upon her, Mar 62: 88–99

    Literary prizes, Jul 63: 73–74

    Motion pictures, new wave in, May 60: 49–55, Mar 61: 13, 19

    Motion picture version of, May 59: 98–99

    And movement toward European unity, Mar 63: 6–7

    Novel, revolution in, Jan 62: 96–101

    Painting in: and "New American Painting," Nov 59: 120–21; salon art, Mar 60: 54–58

    Peter the Great and, Sep 59: 80

    Revolution of 1830, May 61: 85

    Seine River, Jul 62: 52–79

    Theatre of, Jul 59: 46

    And Thirty Years' War, Nov 62: 33–41

    Witch mania, Nov 59: 58, 60, 61, 62, 63

    World War I aftermath, Jan 59: 112, 121

    Writer as conscience of, Nov 59: 66–72

FRANCE, ANATOLE, Nov 61: 37

    Quoted: on Joan of Arc, Mar 62: 96; on Seine River, Jul 62: 53, 60; on writing, Jul 63: 40

FRANCESCA, PIERO DELLA, Jan 59: 103, Jul 59: 30, Jan 60: 68, Nov 61: 4

    Paintings by, Jan 60: 69–72

FRANCESCATTI, ZINO, May 60: 17

    Photograph of, May 60: 17

FRANCESCO DI GIORGIO, Jan 60: 68

FRANCIA, J. G. R., Jul 59: 68

FRANCINE, FRANÇOIS and PIERRE DE, May 62: 14

FRANCIS II, HOLY ROMAN EMPEROR, Sep 63: 30

FRANCIS I, KING OF FRANCE, Sep 60: 61–62

    Portrait by Clouet, Sep 60: 61; illus, Sep 60: 70

FRANCIS, CLARENCE, Jul 62: 4

FRANCIS, PHILIP, May 60: 101, 125

FRANCIS, SAM, Jan 59: 13, Nov 59: 41, 120

    Painting by, Nov 59: 33

    At work, photograph of, Nov 59: 32

FRANCIS OF ASSISI, fresco drawing by Cimabue, Jan 59: 103

FRANCK, CÉSAR, Mar 60: 80

FRANCO, FRANCISCO

    Memorandum to, from Don Quixote, Jul 59: 24–25

    Valley of the Fallen, The, May 61: 42, 47

FRANÇOIS, ALESSANDRO, May 60: 72

FRANÇOIS, ANDRÉ, May 59: 109–12, 121

    Photograph of, May 59: 112

    Works by, May 59: 108–11, 113–20

FRANCO-PRUSSIAN WAR, food in France during, May 61: 125, 127, Sep 62: 113

FRANK, ANNE, Mar 62: 75

    Diary of, play, Nov 58: 63

FRANK, FRITZ, Nov 59: 10

FRANK, GEROLD, Jul 60: 120

FRANK, ROBERT, Mar 61: 14

    Photograph of, Mar 61: 15

FRANKEL, JEAN, Nov 61: 98

FRANKENBERG, ABRAHAM VON, Mar 60: 101, 102

FRANKENBERG, LLOYD, Jul 62: 21

FRANKENHEIMER, JOHN, Jan 62: 104, Mar 63: 35

    Photograph of, Mar 63: 34

FRANKENSTEIN, ALFRED, "And Now the Atonal Ad Lib," article by, Jan 63: 76–81, 105

FRANKFURTER, ALFRED, "Picasso and His Public," article by, Nov 61: 4–13

FRANKLIN, BENJAMIN
Attitude toward nature, Mar 60: 15
On ballooning, quoted, Sep 58: 116, 118
As friend of Josiah Wedgwood, May 59: 91, 94, 129
Handwriting of, Sep 59: 127, 135
Letter to David Hartley, 1782, facsimile, Sep 59: 135
And Philadelphia, Jul 63: 5, 9, 14, 25, 26
Portraits of, May 59: 91, Sep 59: 135
"FRANK LLOYD WRIGHT'S WAR ON THE FINE ARTS," article by James Marston Fitch, Sep 60: 96–103, 127–28
"FRANNY AND ZOOEY," stories by J. D. Salinger, May 62: 100, 101, 103–5, 107
Excerpts from, May 62: 104
FRASCONI, ANTONIO, Mar 61: 122–24
Photograph of, May 59: 16
Self-portrait, Mar 61: 122
Woodcuts by. See ILLUSTRATIONS INDEX
FRASCONI, PABLO, Mar 61: 123, 124
Portrait of, Mar 61: 122
"FRAUENDIENST," autobiography of Ulrich von Lichtenstein, Sep 59: 114
FREDE, RICHARD
Entry E, Mar 59: 16–17, 118
Photograph of, Mar 59: 15
"FRÉDÉRIC CHOPIN BY FRANZ LISZT," book, translated by Edward N. Waters, reviewed, May 63: 109–10
FREDERICK III, ELECTOR OF SAXONY, May 62: 94
FREDERICK, EMPRESS OF PRUSSIA, Jul 59: 30
FREDERICK II, HOLY ROMAN EMPEROR, Sep 59: 125
In Sicily, Sep 61: 30, 32, 36
FREDERICK II, KING OF PRUSSIA (FREDERICK THE GREAT), Mar 60: 76, Nov 61: 4, 6, Mar 63: 5
Voltaire and, Mar 61: 115, 118
FREDERICK IV, PALATINE ELECTOR, Nov 62: 34, 37
FREDERICK, DUKE OF YORK. See YORK
FREDERICK, PAULINE, Jan 61: 27
FREDERICK HENRY, PRINCE OF ORANGE-NASSAU, Sep 58: 15, 19, 34
Portrait by Paulus van Hillegaert, Sep 58: 14
FREDERICK LOUIS, PRINCE OF WALES, as collector of paintings, Jul 63: 96, 105
FREDERICK WILLIAM II, KING OF PRUSSIA, Nov 62: 44
FREDERICK WILLIAM III, KING OF PRUSSIA, Sep 63: 29, 31, 32
FREDERICK WILLIAM IV, KING OF PRUSSIA, Jul 59: 68
Portrait of, Jul 59: 59
FREDERIK IX, KING OF DENMARK, Sep 60: 91
FREED, ALAN, Jan 59: 139
FREEDMAN, GERALD, Nov 60: 117
FREEDMAN, MORRIS, "The Dangers of Nonconformism," excerpts from article published in *The American Scholar,* Mar 59: 112
FREEDOM OF SPEECH
Commission on the Freedom of the Press, Mar 60: 49
And Hypodermic Theory of Communication, Mar 60: 49–50
FREEMAN, DOUGLAS SOUTHALL, photograph of, May 59: 17
FREER, CHARLES LANG, Sep 60: 37
FREIESLEBEN, KARL, Jul 59: 58
FRÉMIET, EMMANUEL, Mar 62: 97
FRENCH, DANIEL CHESTER, May 60: 17
FRENCH ACADEMY. See ACADÉMIE FRANÇAISE; ACADEMY OF FINE ARTS, INSTITUTE OF FRANCE
FRENCH LANGUAGE, Peter Ustinov quoted on, Nov 58: 139
FRENCH REVOLUTION
Attitude toward Joan of Arc during, Mar 62: 96, 97
British reactions to, May 60: 124–25; support by Josiah Wedgwood's group, May 59: 130
Louvre during, Sep 60: 72
Malta as refuge from, Mar 61: 68
Storming of Bastille, Jan 60: 83, 128
Voltaire and, Mar 61: 114–19
FRÉRET, NICOLAS, Etruscan hypothesis of, May 60: 60–61
FRESCOBALDI, GIROLAMO, Nov 60: 91
FRESNAY, PIERRE, Nov 60: 52
FREUD, SIGMUND, Jan 62: 97–98, 107, Mar 62: 73, Jan 63: 109–10, Sep 63: 101
Anticipated by Charles Fourier, Mar 63: 76
And Don Juan story, Jul 62: 64–65
Dramatizations of discoveries of, Sep 58: 60
Hollywood's Freudian "insight," Jan 63: 111–13
Memorandum to Norman Mailer, Tennessee Williams, Alberto Moravia, Jean Genet, et al., from, May 62: 54–55
On psychoanalysis, quoted, May 63: 115
Theory of, vs. cult of child, May 62: 102–3
Theory of God, Sep 63: 104

FREYSSINET, EUGÈNE, Mar 59: 21
FRICK, HENRY CLAY, Nov 58: 120, Jul 59: 28
FRICK MUSEUM, New York City, Jul 59: 28
FRIEDLAND, BATTLE OF, Sep 63: 29, 30, 31
FRIEDMAN, WILLIAM F., Jan 63: 9
FRIEDRICH, CARL J., "The Baroque Age," article by, Jul 60: 33–64
FRIEDRICH, CASPAR DAVID, May 61: 72
Painting by, May 61: 73
"FRIEND IN POWER," novel by Carlos Baker, Sep 60: 119
FRIES, CHARLES CARPENTER, Jul 63: 47
FRIML, RUDOLF, Sep 58: 57
Rose Marie compared to *Little Mary Sunshine,* Sep 60: 87
FRINK, ELISABETH, sculpture by, Mar 61: 111
FRISBIE, ROBERT DEAN, Jan 60: 126
FRITH, WILLIAM POWELL, May 62: 73, 78
Paintings by. See ILLUSTRATIONS INDEX
FRIZELL, BERNARD, articles by
"Escoffier, God of the Gastronomes," May 61: 120–28
"On Screen: Jean-Paul Belmondo," Nov 61: 116–17
FRIZELL, WILLIAM, Jul 61: 90
FROBEN, JOHANN, May 62: 92, 93
FROHMAN, DANIEL, Mar 60: 38
FROISSART, JEAN, on jousts, quoted, Nov 58: 93
"FROM 'BULLY!' TO 'VIGAH!'" article by Archie Robertson, Mar 63: 68–71
"FROM EDEN TO THE NIGHTMARE," article by Henry Anatole Grunwald, Mar 63: 72–79
"FROM HERE TO ETERNITY," novel by James Jones, Jul 62: 101–2
FROMM, ERICH, Jul 59: 71, 72
"FROM RED BANNERS TO BALLADS," article by Warren Miller, Mar 62: 110–12
"FROM SALON TO CELLAR—AND BACK?" article by John Canaday, Mar 60: 52–69
"FROM THE SECOND CITY," revue, Jan 62: 66–70
"FROM THE SHAPELY FORM TO A NEW ART FORM," article by D. M. Marshman, Jr., Sep 58: 56–61, 143–44
FRONTEIRA, PALACE OF, May 59: 49
FRONTIER
Deculturation of, Sep 62: 94–95
Plains. See PLAINS FRONTIER
"FRONT PAGE, THE," play, Sep 58: 60, Mar 61: 43
FROST, ROBERT, Nov 58: 34–35, Sep 61: 117, 121, Mar 63: 31, 32, Jul 63: 69–70, 75, Nov 63: 44
On divine purpose, quoted, Jan 60: 11
And Kennedy administration, Sep 61: 5, 10, 17
Photographs of, Nov 58: 34–35, Sep 61: 8
Travesty on, by Edward Adler, Sep 62: 65
Wyeth, Andrew, quoted on, Sep 61: 100
"FROST IN THE EVENING," article by Francis Russell, Nov 58: 34–35
FROUDE, JAMES ANTHONY, on history, quoted, Mar 59: 5
FRY, CHRISTOPHER, Nov 60: 52, May 61: 56
And motion picture *Barabbas,* Mar 63: 109–11
Sleep of Prisoners, A, Jan 63: 88
FRY, ELIZABETH, Mar 59: 94
FRY, MAXWELL, Nov 61: 70
FRYER, JOHN, journal of, and *Bounty* mutiny, Sep 63: 43, 44, 45
FUCHS, JOSEPH, Jan 62: 9
FUCHS, VIVIAN, Sep 58: 9
FUELS, Jan 59: 92–94, 128–29
FULANI PEOPLE, of Africa, Mar 63: 52
FULLARTON, WILLIAM, Sep 60: 19
FULLER, BUCKMINSTER, Sep 62: 58
Noguchi, Isamu, quoted on, Mar 60: 108, 112
Portrait sculpture of, Mar 60: 111
FULLER, EDMUND, May 60: 22
"Christian Spaceman, The—C. S. Lewis," article by, May 59: 64–67, 125–27
Photograph of, May 60: 22
FULLER, MARGARET, Jan 59: 25, Mar 63: 77
FULTON, ROBERT, Jul 62: 59
"FUME OF POPPIES, THE," novel by Jonathan Kozol, Mar 59: 14, 17, 117, 118
FUND FOR THE REPUBLIC, Jan 62: 4
Report on Blacklisting, Mar 60: 48
FURNAS, J. C., Jan 60: 126
"FURNISHED ROOM, THE," motion picture, Jan 63: 38
FURNITURE
Bauhaus influence on design, Nov 61: 71 (illus), 73
Fashion cycles in, Mar 59: 114–15
FURTSEVA, EKATERINA, photographs of, Nov 62: 116
FURTWAENGLER, WILHELM, Sep 61: 84–85, Mar 62: 104, May 63: 45
FUSELI, HENRY, May 61: 72, Mar 63: 69
Painting by, May 61: 72
FUTURAMA CITY, in New York World's Fair, Jul 59: 5, 12
"FUTURE, THE," poem by Matthew Arnold, quoted, Jul 62: 88

"FUTURE AMERICAN CLASS SYSTEM, THE," article by Stimson Bullitt, May 59: 20–23
"FUTURE AS HISTORY, THE," book by Robert L. Heilbroner, quoted, Jul 60: 70
"FUTURE OF MACHINE CIVILIZATION, THE," article by Harrison Brown, Jan 59: 92–94, 128–29

G

GABLE, CLARK, photograph of, Sep 63: 42
GABO, NAUM, Sep 59: 18–19
Construction designed by, Sep 59: 17
GABOR, DENNIS, "The Perils of Leisure," article by, Nov 63: 102–9
GABOR, ZSA ZSA, Jul 60: 120
GABRIEL, JACQUES ANGE, Sep 60: 72
GABRIELI, GIOVANNI, Nov 60: 91
GABURO, KENNETH, Jul 59: 21
GAETANI, COUNT, photograph of, Sep 63: 54
GAGARIN, YURI, photograph of, Nov 62: 116
GAINSBOROUGH, THOMAS, Jul 59: 28–29, May 62: 60, Mar 63: 69, Jul 63: 105
Paintings by. See ILLUSTRATIONS INDEX
GAISERIC, KING OF THE VANDALS, May 63: 77, 80
GALBA, SERVIUS SULPICIUS, ROMAN EMPEROR, coin portraits of, Sep 63: 38; illus, Sep 63: 37
GALBRAITH, JOHN KENNETH, Nov 59: 23, Jul 60: 66, 67, 71, Jul 62: 115, Nov 63: 61
Affluent Society, The, quoted, Nov 63: 103
"Muse and the Economy, The," article by, Sep 60: 33–40
Photograph of, May 59: 17
GALDÓS, PÉREZ, Nov 62: 111
GALEN, Nov 62: 104, Jan 63: 9, Nov 63: 64
GALEOTTI, VINCENZO, Nov 60: 94
GALILEO, Sep 58: 23, Nov 59: 62, Jan 62: 45
"GALILEO," play, May 62: 40–41
GALITZIN, NIKOLAI, Nov 62: 44
GALITZINE, PRINCESS, fashion designer, Mar 63: 94
GALLAGHER, BUELL, on university teaching situation, quoted, Sep 62: 17
GALLATIN, ALBERT, Jul 59: 69
GALLE, CEYLON, Mar 61: 33
GALLEASS, in Battle of Lepanto, Jul 63: 50, 52, 57, 58
"GALLIC LAUGHTER OF ANDRÉ FRANÇOIS, THE," article by Ben Shahn, May 59: 108–21
GALLIENUS, PUBLIUS, ROMAN EMPEROR, Sep 63: 40
Coin portrait of, Sep 63: 36
GALLIPOLI CAMPAIGN, paintings by Sidney Nolan, Sep 62: 102, 104; illus, Sep 62: 102–3
"GALLOWS HUMOR," play, Sep 62: 38–39 (illus)
GALLUP, GEORGE, Sep 59: 25, 118
Photograph of, Sep 59: 25
GALLUP POLL, Sep 59: 25, 118
GALLUS, TREBONIANUS, ROMAN EMPEROR, Sep 63: 40
GALOIS, ÉVARISTE, Mar 62: 75
GALSWORTHY, JOHN, Jul 63: 13, 75, Sep 63: 98
The Forsyte Saga, Jan 62: 62
GALTON, FRANCIS, *Hereditary Genius,* May 60: 33
GAM, RITA, Nov 63: 37
"GAMBARA," by Honoré de Balzac, quoted, Jan 59: 124
GAMBETTA, LÉON, Sep 58: 120
"GAMBLER, THE," book by Dostoevsky, Nov 63: 62
GAMBLING
In 18th-century England, May 60: 98
Man's need of novelty and, Jul 59: 110
GAMES and SPORTS. See SPORTS and GAMES
GAMES THEORY, Nov 63: 60–61
GANDHARA, INDIA, Mar 59: 57, 58
GANDY, J. M.
John Soane Museum, water color by, Nov 63: 76; illus, Nov 63: 72
Soane's church designs, drawing by, Nov 63: 75; illus, Nov 63: 78–79
GANEY, JOSEPH ("DOC"), Mar 60: 28, 32, 36
GANNETT, LEWIS, May 60: 21
Photograph of, May 60: 20
GANS, HERBERT, on Jane Jacobs, quoted, Jul 62: 50
GANYMEDES SEIZED BY EAGLE, sculpture, May 59: 122, 123, 124; illus, May 59: 103, 105
GARCIA, KING OF NAVARRE, Sep 62: 79
GARDEN, MARY, Sep 59: 52, 53, 56
GARDEN CITIES, Jul 59: 11–12
"GARDEN CITIES OF TOMORROW," book by Ebenezer Howard, Jul 59: 11
GARDEN CITY, Long Island, Jul 59: 12
GARDENS, May 59: 24–53
Of Blenheim Palace, Sep 61: 73–74, 76, 77
Of Grand Seraglio, May 59: 60
Japanese, May 59: 50–51, Jul 59: 126, May 60: 113–14, Sep 61: 60, 63

In Moslem Spain, May 59: 27, 48–49, Sep 62: 82
Of Oxford University, Jan 63: 86–87
Parks of England's 18th-century houses, Nov 58: 46, May 59: 46–47
Persian, May 59: 26, 27, 44–45, Jan 63: 72
Romantic revolt in garden design, May 61: 61
Thoughts on, quotations, May 59: 41
Of UNESCO headquarters in Paris, Mar 60: 110–11
At Vaux-le-Vicomte, Jul 63: 78–79, 80
"GARDENS SINCE EDEN," article by Nan Fairbrother, May 59: 24–53
GARDNER, HERB, *A Thousand Clowns*, Mar 63: 108
GARDNER, ISABELLA STEWART (MRS. JACK)
In group photograph, Jul 59: 31
And her palace of paintings, Jul 59: 26–40, 133–34
Portraits of, Jul 59: 27, 30
GARDNER, JOHN L., Jul 59: 28, 29, 32, 134
GARDNER, JULIA, Jul 59: 32
GARDNER, REGINALD, Sep 63: 77 (note)
GARDNER, RICHARD, Sep 61: 13
GARFIELD, JOHN, Sep 58: 44, Nov 62: 108
"GARGOYLES FOR THE MACHINE AGE," article by John Canaday, Mar 61: 104–13
GARIBALDI, GIUSEPPE, Sep 61: 37, 38, Mar 63: 14
Portraits of, Sep 61: 38, 39
GARMISCH-PARTENKIRCHEN, GERMANY, Mar 59: 120
GARNERAY, engraving by, May 61: 86–87
GARNERIN, ANDRÉ JACQUES, Sep 58: 120
GARNIER, CHARLES, May 63: 71
GARNIER, JEAN LOUIS CHARLES, Nov 58: 27
GARNIER, TONY, city design by, Mar 62: 39; illus, Mar 62: 38
"GARRICK GAIETIES, THE," musical, Sep 58: 59
GARROWAY, DAVE, Archibald MacLeish on TV show of, Jan 60: 51
GARSON, GREER, Mar 60: 126, Sep 63: 80
GARY, ROMAIN, Nov 59: 68
GAS, ILLUMINATING, invention of, effect on cities, Jul 61: 61
GASKELL, ELIZABETH C., Nov 61: 35
GASKILL, WILLIAM, Jan 63: 26, 29, 33
GASOLINE, advertising of, Jan 62: 113
GASSMAN, VITTORIO, Mar 62: 119, Jan 63: 38, Mar 63: 110
GATCH, LEE, Jan 62: 8
"GATE OF HELL," motion picture, May 59: 100
GATE OF THE EXECUTIONER, of Grand Seraglio, May 59: 60, 62, 131
GATES, FORREST, Sep 59: 123
GATE THEATRE, Dublin, Orson Welles at, Jul 63: 86
GATTI-CASAZZA, GIULIO, Nov 58: 118, 120, Sep 59: 52, 57, Nov 61: 80
GAUDI, ANTONIO, Mar 59: 126, Sep 59: 7, Nov 59: 111, Mar 62: 39
Buildings designed by. See ILLUSTRATIONS INDEX
GAUGAMELA. See ARBELA, BATTLE OF
GAUGUIN, PAUL, Nov 59: 121, Sep 60: 34, 102, Mar 61: 22, 91, Mar 62: 15
Paintings and woodcuts by. See ILLUSTRATIONS INDEX
In South Seas, Jan 60: 32, 124
GAUL, southern Rhone River region, Jul 59: 90–98, 129–32
GAUSS, KARL FRIEDRICH, Mar 62: 73
GAUTAMA BUDDHA (SIDDHARTHA GAUTAMA), Jul 59: 74, 76
In art, Mar 59: 57, 58
GAUTIER, THÉOPHILE, May 61: 83, Nov 61: 36
In painting by Manet, May 63: 75
Quoted: on Seine River, Jul 62: 60; on Turkish baths, Sep 60: 125
GAVIN, JAMES, Sep 61: 10
GAYLORD FARM SANATORIUM, Mar 60: 40
GAY-LUSSAC, JOSEPH LOUIS, Sep 58: 114
GAZA, THEODORE, Jan 60: 62
GAZZARA, BEN, Sep 58: 42, Nov 62: 107
GAZZO, MICHAEL V., Jan 62: 68
"G. B. S.: A FULL LENGTH PORTRAIT," book by Hesketh Pearson, writing of, Nov 58: 18–21, 134–37
GEIGER, DON, Jan 59: 18
GEIRINGER, ROBERT, Nov 60: 116
GEISMAR, MAXWELL, on J. D. Salinger, quoted, May 62: 100, 101, 105
GELB, ARTHUR and BARBARA, *The Life of Eugene O'Neill*, excerpts from, Mar 60: 25–40
GELB, JAN, portrait of, with painting by, Jul 61: 26
GELBER, JACK, Sep 62: 37
Apple, The, Mar 62: 109
Connection, The, Mar 61: 16, 44–45, Mar 62: 106–7, 109
GELLER, ESTHER, Mar 63: 29
GELON, TYRANT OF SYRACUSE, Sep 61: 22, 23
GÉMIER, FERMIN, Sep 61: 102
GENÉE, ADELINE, Sep 60: 94, May 62: 61

"GENERAL DELLA ROVERE," motion picture, reviewed, Mar 61: 99–100
GENERAL GRANT STYLE, in Federal architecture, Jan 60: 22
GENERAL MOTORS CORPORATION, May 59: 20, May 63: 112
Futurama City of, Jul 59: 5, 12
GENERAL MOTORS TECHNICAL CENTER, Warren, Mich., Jul 60: 82, May 62: 16
GENERAL OUTDOOR ADVERTISING COMPANY, Nov 58: 30
GENERAL SERVICES ADMINSTRATION, Jan 60: 119, 120
"GENERATION OF VIPERS," book by Philip Wylie, quoted, Mar 59: 134
"GENESIS," portfolio of photographs, Sep 58: 64–81
GENET, JEAN, Jan 61: 113, Jul 61: 116, Nov 61: 98–102, Mar 62: 107, Sep 62: 34, 37, Mar 63: 109
Balcony, The, May 61: 50–51, Mar 63: 107
Ionesco, Eugène, quoted on, May 61: 95
Memorandum from Sigmund Freud to, May 62: 54–55
GENETICS, and man's need to adapt himself to changing world, Nov 62: 5–9
GENEVA, SWITZERLAND
Hôtel du Rhône, Mar 63: 117
Witch trials in, Nov 59: 59, 61
GENGHIS KHAN, Jan 63: 67
GENIUS
Childhood pattern of, May 60: 32–38
Coming generation of, Mar 62: 70–75
Creative process in, May 63: 114–15
GENNARO, DON, photograph of, Sep 63: 55
GENOA, and Battle of Lepanto, Jul 63: 50, 57
GENOVESE, VITO, Sep 61: 44
GENSERIC. See GAISERIC
GENTILESCHI, ORAZIO, Jul 61: 90
Painting by, Nov 61: 83
"GENTLE PEOPLE, THE," play, Nov 62: 106
GEOFFRIN, MARIE THÉRÈSE, Nov 59: 81, Nov 61: 32
GEOLOGY
Contributions of Alexander von Humboldt, Jul 59: 62–67
"Neptunists" vs. "Vulcanists," Jul 59: 59, 67
GEORGE, EMIR OF ANTIOCH, Sep 61: 28
GEORGE I, KING OF ENGLAND, Sep 61: 76, Jul 63: 96
GEORGE II, KING OF ENGLAND, Jul 63: 96
GEORGE III, KING OF ENGLAND, Nov 58: 39, May 60: 101, Mar 61: 119, Nov 62: 22, 24
As collector of paintings, Jul 63: 96, 105
As historical topic, Sep 63: 98
And mermaid legend, Jan 60: 130
Portraits of, Mar 59: 90, Jul 63: 94
Quoted: on Blenheim Palace, Sep 61: 70; on Smith, Sydney, Mar 59: 90
And Royal Academy, May 62: 59, 60, 62–63
GEORGE IV, KING OF ENGLAND
And Brighton Pavilion, Nov 62: 20–31
Caricatures of, Nov 62: 22, 23
As collector of paintings, Jul 63: 92, 96, 105–7
Portraits of, Mar 59: 90, Jul 63: 94
As Prince of Wales, May 60: 100, 101, 124
On Smith, Sydney, quoted, Mar 59: 90
GEORGE V, KING OF ENGLAND, Sep 59: 3, May 61: 120, 123, Jul 61: 94, Mar 63: 65
GEORGE VI, KING OF ENGLAND, visit with Queen Elizabeth at Roosevelt home, Sep 63: 77 (note)
GEORGE, SAINT, reliquary of, May 59: 2, 3
GEORGE, HENRY, Jan 59: 7
GEORGE OF TREBIZOND, Jan 60: 62
"GEORGIAN POETRY," anthology, Jan 60: 108
Quoted, Jan 60: 109 (note)
GERARD, FRANÇOIS PASCAL, portrait of Mme de Staël by, Nov 58: 88; illus, Nov 58: 86
GERARD, ROLF, Nov 58: 120
GERARD OF CREMONA, Sep 62: 80, 92
GERARD THE BLESSED, Mar 61: 51, 56
GERBAULT, ALAIN, Sep 58: 8, Jan 60: 126
GERBIER, BALTHASAR, Jul 61: 89
GÉRICAULT, THÉODORE, May 61: 66
Painting by, Sep 60: 70
GERICKE, WILHELM, Jul 59: 28
GERMANICUS CAESAR, Sep 63: 3
GERMANY (see also BERLIN; DÜSSELDORF)
American abstract expressionism in, Nov 59: 120
Castles of Ludwig II of Bavaria, Jan 61: 34–43
Crowns of, May 63: 94, 96; illus, May 63: 97, 99
Destruction of Protestantism in 1620's, Mar 60: 101
Effects of Grand Tour on, Nov 59: 94
Handwriting and printing styles, Sep 59: 126
Ivory, use in, May 60: 92
Köpenick hoax by Wilhelm Voigt, Jan 61: 68–71, 72
Literary prizes, Jul 63: 73
Organ (musical instrument) in, Mar 60: 74, 76
Postwar playhouses, Jul 59: 48

Rise and Fall of the Third Reich, reviewed, Nov 60: 119–21
And Russia under Peter the Great and successors, Sep 59: 80
Teutonic types, photographs by August Sander, Mar 60: 41–45
And Thirty Years' War, Nov 62: 33–41
And trend toward European unity, Mar 63: 8–9
Witch mania, Nov 59: 58–62
World War I aftermath, Jan 59: 117, 119, 121
GÉRÔME, JEAN LÉON, Mar 60: 53, 56–57
Paintings by, Mar 60: 52, 68
"GERONTIUS, DREAM OF," composition by Elgar, Thomas Beecham and George Moore quoted on, Mar 62: 103
GERSHWIN, GEORGE, Sep 58: 61, Jan 61: 49, May 61: 38, 113
Compared with Leonard Bernstein, Jul 59: 22
GERSHWIN, IRA, Jan 61: 49
"GERSHWIN YEARS, THE," television show, May 63: 49
GETLEIN, FRANK
"Art Against the Grain," article by, Jul 62: 12–25
Modern Demonology, A, excerpts from, Jul 61: 66–69, Sep 61: 64–65
GETTY, J. PAUL, Nov 62: 65–66
GEVA, TAMARA, Jan 61: 49 (note)
GEYL, PIETER, on Dutch Republic, quoted, Sep 58: 22
GEYRE, TURKEY, Mar 63: 97, 100
GHALIB, Moslem general, Sep 62: 82
GHANA, Mar 63: 56, 105
Ancient kingdom of, Mar 63: 41 (map), 44
Claims by, to various inventions, Jan 63: 116–17
GHIBERTI, LORENZO, detail from doors by, Nov 60: 48–49
GHIRLANDAIO, DOMENICO, Sep 58: 94, 142
Adoration of the Magi, Nov 60: 30; illus, Nov 60: 26–27
GHISELIN, BREWSTER, Jan 62: 14
GHISTELLES, LORD OF, Nov 58: 96
GHOR, minaret of Jham, Nov 59: 42–43
"GHOSTS," play, Jan 62: 106, 107
GIACOMETTI, ALBERTO, May 62: 59
On Miró, Joan, quoted, Mar 59: 72
Noguchi, Isamu, quoted on, Mar 60: 112
GIANNINI, VITTORIO, Jan 60: 15, 122–23, Jan 62: 10
Portrait of, Jan 60: 15
"GIANT," motion picture, Sep 58: 43, May 59: 100
"GIANT OF MARATHON, THE," motion picture, May 61: 57
GIBBON, EDWARD
Grand Tour of, Nov 59: 86, 95
Quoted: on Byzantine Empire, Nov 63: 4, 6; on Church Fathers, Nov 59: 58; on Fox, Charles James, May 60: 99, 100; on Hadrian, May 63: 33; on history, Nov 60: 119; on progress, Mar 59: 12; on second century, Sep 63: 40; on traveler's qualifications, Nov 59: 84
Toynbee, Arnold J., quoted on, Jan 61: 60–61
GIBBONS, GRINLING, Sep 61: 69, 74, Mar 63: 69
Carvings by, Sep 61: 71, Mar 63: 64
GIBEON, POOL OF, Nov 59: 6, 8–9
GIBNEY, FRANK, "The 'Nothing' Plays and How They Have Grown on Us," article by, Nov 58: 62–65
GIBSON, BOB, Sep 62: 66
GIBSON, CHARLES DANA, Jul 63: 118
GIBSON, HARRY, Nov 60: 85
GIBSON, WALKER, on beatniks, quoted, Jul 63: 39
GIBSON GIRL, Jul 63: 118, 119
GIBSON MAN, Jul 63: 118
GIDE, ANDRÉ, Nov 59: 66, 68, Mar 61: 98, Jan 62: 97
GIEDION, SIGFRIED, on Bauhaus, quoted, Nov 61: 65
GIELGUD, JOHN, Nov 58: 138, Mar 63: 35
Dinesen, Isak, quoted on, Sep 59: 111
Guthrie, Tyrone, quoted on, Jan 61: 28–29
Portrait of, Jan 61: 30
GIEROWSKI, STEFAN, May 61: 22
Painting by, May 61: 23
"GIGI," motion picture, May 61: 104, 113
GIGLI, BENIAMINO, Sep 59: 53
"GIGSTERS, THE," motion picture, Mar 63: 36
GILBERT, HENRY, Jul 59: 20
GILBERT, W. S., and ARTHUR SULLIVAN, Mar 63: 107
H.M.S. Pinafore, Jan 61: 72
"GIL BLAS," novel by Lesage, Jul 62: 59
GILCHRIST, ANNE, Jul 61: 103
GILDER, RICHARD WATSON, Sep 61: 117
GIL EANNES (GILIANES), Nov 60: 83
GILLESPIE, DIZZY, May 61: 100
GILLMORE, MARGALO, Jul 62: 37
GILMAN, RICHARD, "Total Revolution in the Novel," article by, Jan 62: 96–101
GILMORE, VOIT, Sep 62: 116
GILSON, ETIENNE, on Christian art, quoted, Nov 58: 115
"GINGER MAN, THE," novel by J. P. Donleavy, Mar 59: 17

GINNA, ROBERT EMMETT, articles by
"Allegra Kent," Nov 59: 52–56
"Cave of Tiberius, The," May 59: 102–7, 122–24
"On Screen": Remick, Lee, Sep 60: 88–89; Seberg, Jean, May 62: 80–81; York, Susannah, Nov 61: 114–15
"Our Man in Havana," Nov 59: 26–31, 122–26
"Tree of Coole, The," Mar 59: 86–89
GINSBERG, ALLEN, Sep 58: 40, 41–42, Jan 59: 19, Sep 61: 116, 119, 121, May 62: 55, Jan 63: 74
Photographs of, Sep 58: 41, Mar 61: 14–15
GIOCOSA, LA, school of Vittorino da Feltre, Jan 60: 59–68
GIORGIONE, IL, Jul 59: 31, Jul 61: 94, 95, Jul 63: 96
Influence on Poussin, Mar 61: 80, 92
Painting attributed to, Jul 61: 84–85
GIOTTO, André Malraux quoted on, Nov 58: 113–14
GIOVANNI and NICCOLÒ, painting by, Jan 62: 32; illus, Jan 62: 35
GIOVANNI DA FIESOLE. See ANGELICO, FRA
GIRARD, ALEXANDER, painting by, Nov 63: 53
GIRAUDOUX, JEAN, Nov 59: 68, Nov 60: 54, 55, Mar 63: 109
"GIRL BEFORE A MIRROR," painting by Picasso, Nov 61: 12
"GIRL IN A FUR WRAP," painting by Titian, Jul 61: 89, 95, Jul 63: 94; illus, Jul 61: 82
"GIRL OF THE GOLDEN WEST," opera, Nov 58: 120
"GIRL ON THE VIA FLAMINIA, THE," play, Mar 60: 98, 120
"GIRL WADING," painting by Elmer Bischoff, Jul 60: 115; illus, Jul 60: 24
"GIRL WITH A MANDOLIN, THE," painting by Picasso, Nov 61: 10
"GIRL WITH THE SUITCASE, THE," motion picture, Jan 63: 38
GIRODET-TRIOSON (ANNE LOUIS GIRODET DE ROUCY), paintings by, May 61: 67
GIROLAMO DA TREVISO, Jul 63: 92
Painting attributed to, Jul 63: 95
GISH, LILLIAN, on Eugene O'Neill, quoted, Mar 60: 37
"GISLEBERTUS HOC FECIT," article by Fernand Auberjonois, with portfolio of sculptures, Sep 61: 46–57
"GISLEBERTUS: SCULPTEUR D'AUTUN," monograph by Denis Grivot and George Zarnecki, Sep 61: 48
GIULIANO, Italian brigand, Sep 61: 44
GIUSTINIANI, commander of *Capitano* at Lepanto, Jul 63: 58
"GIVING NEW LIFE TO OLD MUSIC," article by Richard Murphy, Nov 60: 88–95
GLACIER NATIONAL PARK HOTEL, Jan 61: 112
GLADIATORS, May 62: 47, 49
"GLADIATORS, THE," novel by Arthur Koestler, May 61: 57
GLADSTONE, HERBERT JOHN, in painting by William P. Frith, May 62: 62
"GLAD TIDINGS OF ISRAEL, THE," book by Paul Felgenhauer, Mar 60: 102
GLANVILL, JOSEPH, Nov 59: 60
GLARNER, FRITZ, painting by, Nov 60: 4
GLASGOW, ELLEN, Jul 63: 71
GLASPELL, SUSAN, Jul 61: 13
GLASS (see also STAINED GLASS)
Designs of Tapio Wirkkala, Jul 63: 63–64
Television advertising of, Nov 60: 123
"GLASS MENAGERIE, THE," play, Jan 61: 31, May 61: 99, May 63: 10
"GLASS THAT WASN'T THERE, THE," article by Stephen White, Nov 60: 123
GLAZUNOV, ALEKSANDR K., Nov 62: 44
"GLEANINGS IN BUDDHA-FIELDS," book by Lafcadio Hearn, quoted, Mar 61: 27
GLEASON, MADELINE, Jan 59: 18
GLENN, CARROLL, Jan 62: 14
"GLENN GOULD," interview by Bernard Asbell, Jan 62: 88–93
"GLIMPSES OF UNFAMILIAR JAPAN," book by Lafcadio Hearn, quoted, Mar 59: 133
"GLORIFICATION OF WAR," sculpture by Karl Bitter, Sep 60: 127; illus, Sep 60: 103
"GLORY OF AN ISLE OF GREECE, THE," article by Geoffrey Grigson, Sep 59: 30–32, 49
GLUCK, CHRISTOPH W., *Orpheus and Eurydice,* Jan 61: 56
GLUECK, NELSON, "The Bible as Divining Rod," article by, Nov 59: 4–10, 118–19
GLUSKER, IRWIN
Introduction to "A Modern Bestiary," portfolio by Edward Sorel and Paul Davis, Jul 62: 120
"What Next in Art?" article by, Jan 63: 16–25
GLUTTONS, APOLOGY FOR, Jan 63: 34–35
GNOLI, DOMENICO, Jul 59: 135–36
Drawings by. See ILLUSTRATIONS INDEX
GOBEL, GEORGE, Sep 61: 80

"GOD AND THE BISHOP OF WOOLWICH," excerpt from *Honest to God,* book by John A. T. Robinson, Sep 63: 4–7, 104–6
GODARD, JEAN-LUC, Nov 61: 116, Jan 62: 109
GODDARD, ROBERT, May 59: 8
GODDEN, RUMER, *The Greengage Summer,* motion picture based on, Nov 61: 115
"GODDESS, THE," motion picture, Sep 60: 49, 55, 56
GODFREY, ARTHUR, Jul 60: 120
GODOLPHIN, SIDNEY (1ST EARL), Sep 61: 73, 74, 75
GODOWSKY, LEOPOLD, Sep 59: 55
Photograph of, Nov 62: 42
"GODS IN ART, THE," article by Henry Anatole Grunwald, Nov 58: 4–17, 112–17
GODWIN, FRANCIS, *The Man in the Moone,* Mar 63: 76
GODWIN, MARY, Nov 60: 97
GOELET, OGDEN, Nov 58: 119
GOES, HUGO VAN DER, Jul 63: 94
Painting by, Jul 63: 95
GOETHE, JOHANN WOLFGANG VON, Nov 58: 143, May 59: 104, Sep 59: 124, Jul 60: 50, Mar 61: 115, 116, Mar 62: 61, Nov 63: 107
Beecham, Thomas, quoted on, Mar 62: 103
Bicentennial celebration at Aspen, Colo., Sep 58: 102
Childhood of, May 60: 34, 37, 38
Humboldt, Alexander von, and, Jul 59: 57, 59, 67
Portraits of, May 60: 32, May 61: 61
Quoted: on Aegina marbles, Sep 59: 49; on landscape, Mar 61: 92; on Lorrain, Claude, Jul 60: 42; on portraiture, Jan 59: 105
And romantic revolt, May 61: 61, 64, 65, 66, 70
Sorrows of Young Werther, Jan 62: 62
At Weimar, lithograph, Jul 59: 58
GOFF, BRUCE, and his "pavilions on the prairie," Nov 61: 42–47
GOGARTY, OLIVER ST. JOHN, Mar 59: 88
On the English, quoted, Nov 58: 85
GOGH. See VAN GOGH.
GOHEEN, ROBERT F., photograph of, Sep 59: 24
"GOING BROKE ON $10,000 A YEAR," article in *Harper's Magazine,* Nov 59: 128
GOLD
Achaemenid goldsmiths, Jan 63: 53; Marlik goldsmiths as forerunners of, Nov 62: 104
In early African cultures, Mar 63: 56, 58
Etruscan goldsmiths, May 60: 77
Of Lydia, Sep 63: 85
Mines of Ophir, Nov 59: 119
Mycenaean goldsmiths, Jan 61: 86
GOLD, ARTHUR, Mar 61: 75, May 63: 14, 18
Portrait of, Mar 61: 74
GOLD, HERBERT, Jan 62: 10
Alfred Kazin quoted on, Jul 62: 102
GOLD, IVAN, *A Change of Air,* Mar 59: 118
GOLD, NAUGHTON &, Jan 61: 122–23
GOLDBERG, MRS. ARTHUR, Sep 61: 10
Portrait of, with paintings by, Sep 61: 11
GOLDBERG, VICKI, "Mondrian Is a Paper Napkin," article by, May 63: 90–91
"GOLDBERG VARIATIONS," by Johann Sebastian Bach, Glenn Gould quoted on, Jan 62: 89
GOLD COAST, of Africa, Mar 63: 56, 105
"GOLD EAGLE GUY," play, Nov 62: 106
"GOLDEN AGE OF THE DUTCH REPUBLIC, THE," article by C. V. Wedgwood, Sep 58: 14–35
"GOLDEN ASS, THE," romance by Apuleius, Nov 62: 87, 89 (illus), 91, 94
"GOLDEN BOY," play, Jan 61: 32, Mar 61: 43, Nov 62: 106
"GOLDEN ERA," journal, Jan 59: 7
GOLDEN HORN, May 59: 58, Nov 63: 9, 32
"GOLDEN SARDIS," article by George M. A. Hanfmann, Sep 63: 82–89
GOLDHURST, WILLIAM, "Martinet or Martyr," article by, Sep 63: 42–48
"GOLD OF NAPLES," motion picture, May 59: 99, Mar 61: 100
GOLDONI, CARLO, *Servant of Two Masters,* Mar 61: 47
GOLDSCHMIDT, JAKOB, Nov 62: 64
GOLDSMITH, H. H., Jul 60: 75
GOLDSMITH, MYRON, Jan 59: 11, Mar 59: 123
Portrait of, Jan 59: 8
GOLDSMITH, OLIVER, Jul 59: 47
Quoted: on Bath, Jul 61: 55; on Johnson, Samuel, Jul 61: 115
GOLDWATER, BARRY M., Arizona home of, Sep 63: 103
GOLDWYN, SAMUEL, Jan 61: 49, Sep 63: 78
"GOLDWYN FOLLIES, THE," motion picture, Jan 61: 49
GOLLINS, MELVIN AND WARD, Castrol House, designed by, Nov 60: 124, 125; illus, Nov 60: 14
GOLOBEFF, MME, Sep 58: 83
GOLUB, LEON, painting by, Nov 60: 4

GOMBRICH, ERNST, Sep 58: 134
GONCHAROV, IVAN, Sep 60: 129
GONCOURT, EDMOND and JULES, *Pages from the Goncourt Journal,* edited by Robert Baldick, reviewed, Sep 62: 112–14
GONCOURT PRIZE, Jul 63: 73–74, 75
GONDOMAR, COUNT OF, Nov 62: 39, 40, 41
"GONE WITH THE WIND," novel by Margaret Mitchell, Mar 62: 71
GONNE, MAUD, on William Butler Yeats, quoted, Nov 60: 66
GONZAGA, CARLO, Jan 60: 60, 64, 66
GONZAGA, CECILIA, Jan 60: 62, 64
GONZAGA, ELISABETTA, Jan 60: 66, 68
Portrait of, Jan 60: 65
GONZAGA, FEDERIGO, Jan 60: 64
In family portrait, Jan 60: 58
GONZAGA, FRANCESCO, Jan 60: 66
GONZAGA, GIANFRANCESCO (MARQUIS OF MANTUA), Jan 60: 59–60
In family portrait, Jan 60: 58
GONZAGA, GIANLUCIDO, Jan 60: 62
GONZAGA, LUDOVICO (MARQUIS OF MANTUA), Jan 60: 60, 64, 66
And his family, portrait, Jan 60: 58–59
GONZAGA, MARGHERITA, Jan 60: 62, 64
GONZAGA FAMILY (DUKES OF MANTUA), Jul 61: 90, 95, Jul 63: 94
GONZALES, JULIO, Sep 59: 96
GOOCH, DANIEL, Jan 59: 39, 136
"GOODBYE AGAIN," motion picture, May 62: 116
"GOOD HOUSEKEEPING," magazine, Jan 63: 114
"GOOD-HUMOURED LADIES, THE," ballet, Jan 61: 27
GOODMAN, PAUL, *Utopian Essays and Practical Proposals,* Mar 63: 79
GOODMAN, PERCIVAL, on open competition in architectural design, quoted, Jan 63: 11, 15
GOODMAN, THEODORE, Sep 60: 50
"GOOD NEWS," musical, Sep 58: 59
GOODNOUGH, ROBERT, painting by, Nov 60: 4
"GOOD SOLDIER SCHWEIK, THE," opera, Jan 60: 123
"GOOD WOMAN OF SETZUAN, THE," play, Mar 61: 47 (illus), Jan 63: 29
GORDON, ARTHUR E., Nov 58: 108
GORDON, CAROLINE, Jul 61: 75
GORDON, DAVID, Jan 62: 70
GORDON, KERMIT, Sep 61: 13
GORDON, PATRICK, Sep 59: 66
GORDON, RUTH, Jul 62: 37
GORDONI, VIRGINIA, photographs of, Nov 61: 79, 81
GORELIK, MORDECAI, Jan 62: 14
"GORGIAS," dialogue of Plato, quoted, Jan 63: 9
GORKY, MAXIM
Lower Depths, The: motion picture based on, Jul 62: 43–44; quoted, Nov 62: 110
Mother, The, adaptation by Bertolt Brecht, May 62: 37
Quoted: on his father, Mar 62: 111–12; on Tolstoy, May 62: 51
GORTYN, CODE OF, Nov 62: 90
GOSPELS
Coptic, discovered in 1945, Nov 62: 93
Early manuscript books of, André Malraux quoted on, Nov 58: 16
Lindisfarne, Nov 62: 94; illus, Nov 62: 74
Of Saint John, earliest known fragment of, Nov 62: 82
Of Saint Mark, format of, Nov 62: 86
GOSSE, EDMUND, Mar 59: 107
GOTHIC ARCHITECTURE, Clive Bell quoted on, Nov 58: 115
GOTHIC ART
Dijon tombs of Dukes of Burgundy, Sep 58: 62
Malraux, André, quoted on, Nov 58: 112–13
GOTHIC STYLE, in handwriting, Sep 59: 126, 127, 129
GOTHS, May 63: 78, Nov 63: 11
"GÖTTERDÄMMERUNG," opera, May 63: 41, 42, 45
GOTTLIEB, ADOLPH, Sep 58: 44, 110, Mar 59: 135, May 59: 11, Nov 59: 41, Jan 63: 16
Painting by, Nov 59: 39
Photograph of, Mar 59: 135
GOTTSCHALK, LAURA RIDING. See RIDING, LAURA
GOUJON, JEAN, Sep 60: 62, 64, 65
GOULD, GEORGE, Jul 61: 104
GOULD, GLENN, Jan 60: 74, 81
Interview with, Jan 62: 88–93
Photographs of, Jan 60: 75, Jan 62: 88, 92, 93
GOULD, JAY, Nov 58: 119
GOUNOD, CHARLES FRANÇOIS, *Redemption,* Thomas Beecham quoted on, Mar 62: 103
GOVE, PHILIP B., Jul 63: 41
GOVERNMENT
Jargon of, Jul 63: 37
And literary awards, Jul 63: 72–73

Power in, theories, Mar 59: 10
Research and, Sep 63: 60
United States: buildings of, Jan 60: 18–27, 119–21; and culture, Sep 61: 4–17; effects of Togetherness cult, Nov 58: 147
GOWER, JOHN, quoted, Sep 59: 23
GOWHAR SHAD, Jan 63: 67
GOYA, FRANCISCO JOSÉ DE, May 59: 121, Jul 61: 5, Nov 61: 12
Works by. See ILLUSTRATIONS INDEX
GOYEN, JAN VAN, Sep 58: 26, Sep 60: 34
GOZZOLI, BENOZZO, Jul 63: 107
Paintings by, Nov 60: cover, 3, Jul 63: 95
GRACE, W. G., Sep 63: 77
GRACQ, JULIEN, Jul 63: 74
On literary heroes, quoted, Nov 59: 72
GRAESNER, GEORG WILHELM, painting by, Jul 63: 51
GRAF, HERBERT, Nov 61: 80
Photograph of, Nov 61: 79
GRAFFIGNY, FRANÇOISE, Mar 61: 117
GRAFFMAN, GARY, Jan 60: 74, 76
Portrait of, Jan 60: 76
GRAHAM, BILLY (WILLIAM F.), Sep 63: 8
GRAHAM, MARTHA, Mar 60: 105, 112, Jan 62: 103, Nov 62: 68
Episodes, choreography by, Nov 59: 56
Influence on stagecraft of José Quintero, Mar 60: 119, 120
GRAHAM, RONNY, Nov 60: 85
Photograph of, Nov 60: 84
GRAHAM, SHEILA, Sep 63: 79, 80
Beloved Infidel, book about, Jul 60: 120
GRAHN, LUCILE, Sep 60: 94
GRANADA, SPAIN, Sep 62: 92
GRAND HOTEL, Mackinac Island, Jan 61: 104, 108
GRAND HOTEL, Monte Carlo, May 61: 125
GRAND OPERA
American operas, contemporary, Jan 60: 12–17, 122–23
American singers abroad, Nov 61: 76–81
In Baroque age, Jul 60: 42
Ford Foundation aid to, Jan 62: 10–11, 13
"Her Revenge," short story by Marcus Cheke, Mar 59: 129–32
Li Shao Ch'uan as Monkey King in Journey to the West, Sep 62: 48, 54
Metropolitan. See METROPOLITAN OPERA
Moffo, Anna, Jul 61: 96–97
Price, Leontyne, Mar 61: 72–73
Prima donnas, past and present, Sep 59: 50–57
San Francisco Opera House, Jan 59: 6
Wagnerian, new look in Valhalla, May 63: 40–45
World's opera houses, Nov 58: 23–27, 133
"GRAND SERAGLIO, THE," article by Mary Cable, May 59: 56–63, 131–35
GRAND TOUR, Nov 59: 73–104, Mar 62: 55, 56, Nov 63: 63
"GRAND TOUR, THE," article by J. H. Plumb, Nov 59: 73–104
GRANGER, STEWART, Sep 63: 79, 80
GRANT, CARY, Sep 63: 75, 78
Photograph of, Sep 63: 80
Reed, Carol, quoted on, Nov 59: 122
GRANT, JANE, Jul 62: 37
GRANT, MICHAEL, "The High Art of Portraiture on Roman Coins," article by, Sep 63: 33–41
GRANVILLE, J. J., cartoon by, May 61: 83
"GRAPES OF WRATH, THE," motion picture, May 59: 101
"GRAPHIS," magazine, quoted on Tomi Ungerer, Jan 61: 128
GRASS, GÜNTER, The Tin Drum, Jul 63: 73
Reviewed, Mar 63: 111–13
GRAU, SHIRLEY ANN
Hard Blue Sky, The, Mar 59: 14, 118
Photograph of, Mar 59: 16
GRAVES, MORRIS, Jul 59: 71, Jul 60: 105
Works by. See ILLUSTRATIONS INDEX
GRAVES, ROBERT, Mar 61: 22, Jan 62: 50–55, Jul 63: 73
Articles by: "Poet in a Valley of Dry Bones, The," Mar 63: 84–88; "Poetry's False Face," Nov 63: 42–47; "Pretense on Parnassus," May 63: 81–85
Portraits of, Jan 62: 50, 53
——— and ALAN HODGE, The Reader Over Your Shoulder, quoted on "Whitehallese," Jul 63: 37 (note)
GRAY, EDDIE, Jan 61: 122–23
GRAY, THOMAS, Mar 62: 56
Letter from Rheims, quoted, Nov 59: 84
GRAY'S INN, London, Jul 61: 54
GREAT BARRINGTON, MASS., May 60: 13 (map), 17, 19
Bowling establishments of, Mar 63: 89, 95
"GREAT BOOKS," Sep 58: 103
GREAT BRITAIN (see also BRITAIN; ENGLAND)
American abstract expressionism in, Nov 59: 32, 41, 121

City planning in, Jul 59: 7, 11
Coronation of Elizabeth II as painted by Topolski, Nov 60: 128–36
Crown jewels of, May 63: 94; illus, May 63: 100–1
Egremont, 3d Earl, as patron of arts, Mar 63: 62–71
Fox, Charles James, May 60: 96–101, 124–25
George IV and Brighton Pavilion, Nov 62: 20–31
Hoax aboard H.M.S. Dreadnought, Jan 61: 66–68, 72
Ivory, use in, May 60: 94
Motion picture version of, May 59: 99
In Napoleonic Wars, Sep 63: 30, 31, 32
New face of, Nov 61: 14–31
Occupation of Sicily, Sep 61: 38
Royal Academy of Arts, May 62: 56–79
Royal collection of paintings, Jul 63: 92–107
World War I aftermath, Jan 59: 119, 121
"GREAT BRITAIN," locomotive, Jan 59: 39
"GREAT BRITAIN," S.S., Jan 59: 42, 136
GREAT CONFRONTATIONS, series of articles
  I. "Diogenes and Alexander," by Gilbert Highet, Mar 63: 10–13
  II. "Leo the Great and Attila the Hun," by C. V. Wedgwood, May 63: 76–80
  III. "Mary, Queen of Scots, and John Knox," by H. R. Trevor-Roper, Jul 63: 28–32
  IV. "Napoleon and Alexander," by J. Christopher Herold, Sep 63: 28–32
  V. "Cortes and Montezuma," by J. H. Elliott, Nov 63: 92–96
"GREAT EASTERN," S.S., Jan 59: 42–43, 136
"GREAT ENGINEER, THE: ISAMBARD KINGDOM BRUNEL," article by L. T. C. Rolt, Jan 59: 32–43, 136
"GREATEST OF COURTLY LOVERS, THE," excerpt from The Natural History of Love, by Morton M. Hunt, Sep 59: 113–17
"GREATEST WIT IN ENGLAND, THE," article by Hesketh Pearson, Mar 59: 90–95, 124–25
"GREAT EXPECTATIONS," motion picture, Mar 61: 98, Jul 62: 109
"GREAT GATSBY, THE," novel by F. Scott Fitzgerald, May 62: 101, Jul 62: 102
"GREAT GOD BROWN, THE," play, Mar 60: 29
"GREAT IDEAS OF WESTERN MAN," discussion of, at Aspen, Colo., Sep 58: 103, 133, 134
"GREAT ILLUSION, THE," book by Norman Angell, Mar 63: 6
"GREATNESS IN THE THEATER," article by Tyrone Guthrie, Jan 61: 26–33
GREAT NORTHERN WAR, Sep 59: 79–80
GREAT PACKINGTON, ENGLAND, Handel organ at, Mar 60: 73
"GREAT SEA BATTLES," book by Oliver Warner, article adapted from, Jul 63: 49–61
"GREAT WESTERN," locomotive, Jan 59: 39
"GREAT WESTERN," S.S., Jan 59: 40–42
GREAT WESTERN RAILWAY, Jan 59: 34, 37–40
GRECO, EMILIO, Nov 59: 46
Monument designed by, Nov 59: 47
GREECE (see also CRETE; RHODES)
Athens Festival, Jul 62: 30
Lemnos as possible stopping-place of Etruscans, May 60: 62
GREECE, ANCIENT
Aegina marbles, Sep 59: 30–49
Alexander the Great influenced by, Mar 59: 32, 47
Art of, André Malraux quoted on, Nov 58: 13–15
Attitude toward nature in, Mar 60: 13
Barberini vase. See Portland vase, below
Bronze statues found at Piraeus, Mar 60: 6–11
Diogenes' encounter with Alexander the Great, Mar 63: 10–13
Epidaurus, amphitheatre at, Jul 59: 45
Etruscans and, May 60: 73, 77
Homeric Age, historic light on, Jan 61: 73–99
Ivory sculpture of, May 60: 120–21
Jury system in, Jul 60: 100–1
Peloponnesian War, Jul 60: 102; Thucydides' account, Jan 60: 41–45
Persian wars, Jan 63: 49, 50
Philosophy of, in relation to modern science, Jul 61: 5–6, 7, 8, 9
Polis, Jul 61: 42–43
Portland vase, Nov 63: 63–65
Portraiture in, Jan 59: 99
Religion of, Jul 60: 103; André Malraux quoted on, Nov 58: 14–15
As setting for screen epics, May 61: 53, 55, 57
Settlements by: on Rhone River, Jul 59: 92, 93, 95; in Sicily, Sep 61: 22, 23–24
Slavery in, May 62: 42–49
Socrates, guilt or innocence of, Jul 60: 100–4, 117
Spartan ideal, alterations in, Mar 59: 133
Wheeled vehicles in, Sep 58: 149–50, 151
Winged deities of, Nov 60: 27–30
"GREECE AND ROME," magazine, Jul 61: 113

GREEK FIRE, Nov 63: 24, 26
GREEK LANGUAGE
In Renaissance curriculum, Jan 60: 62
Translations from English into, Jul 61: 112–13, 114, 115
"GREEK MYTHS, THE," book by Robert Graves, Jan 62: 54
GREEK REVIVAL, in Federal architecture, Jan 60: 22
GREELEY, HORACE, Jul 63: 114
Memorandum to John Hay Whitney from, Jan 59: 24–25
GREEN, ADOLPH, Jan 62: 66, 68
GREEN, HENRY, Nov 58: 64
GREEN, JOHN R., on Oxford, quoted, Jan 63: 83
GREEN, MARTIN, on J. D. Salinger, quoted, May 62: 107
GREEN, PETER, "The Movies Make Hay with the Classic World," article by, May 61: 52–57
GREEN, TIMOTHY, "Topolski's Coronation," article by, Nov 60: 128–36
GREENBELT, MD., Jul 59: 11
GREENBELT TOWNS, Jul 59: 11–12
GREENBERG, CLEMENT, Sep 59: 97, Jan 60: 7
GREENBERG, NOAH
Photographs of, Nov 60: 89, 90
Revival of early music by, Nov 60: 88–95
GREENBROOK, N.J., Jul 59: 12
GREENE, GRAHAM, Nov 58: 65, Jan 59: 135, May 61: 116–17, Jul 63: 73
Our Man in Havana, motion picture based on, Nov 59: 26–31, 122–26
Quiet American, The, May 60: 8
GREENE, MILTON H., "A Flourish of Strumpets," photographs by, May 61: 50–51
GREENE, RICHARD, Sep 63: 77, 78, 80
GREENFIELD, ALBERT, Jul 63: 26
"GREENGAGE SUMMER, THE," novel by Rumer Godden, motion picture based on, Nov 61: 115
GREENHAM, PETER, painting by, May 62: 77
GREEN SEA OF DARKNESS, Nov 60: 78
GREENSLET, FERRIS, and CHARLES P. CURTIS, The Practical Cogitator, Sep 61: 115
GREENWICH, ENGLAND, Queen's House, Jul 61: 90
"GREENWICH VILLAGE FOLLIES," musical, Sep 58: 59
GREGOROVIUS, on St. Peter's, Rome, quoted, Jan 62: 27
GREGORY I, POPE (GREGORY THE GREAT), on pictures and images, quoted, Jan 62: 24
GREGORY VII, POPE, Sep 59: 129, May 63: 97
GREGORY, ANDRÉ, May 63: 10
GREGORY, AUGUSTA (LADY GREGORY), Jul 59: 134
House of Coole, Mar 59: 86–89
GREGORY, ROBERT, Mar 59: 88
GREGORY, WILLIAM HENRY, Mar 59: 87
GRENFELL, BERNARD P., Nov 62: 82, 93
GRENVILLE, RICHARD TEMPLE. See TEMPLE, 1ST EARL
GREVENIUS, HERBERT, Sep 60: 8
GREVILLE, CHARLES, Mar 62: 61
On Lord Egremont and Petworth House, quoted, Mar 63: 67–68
GREY, CHARLES (2D EARL), Mar 59: 95, May 60: 125
Portrait of, Mar 59: 90
On Smith, Sydney, quoted, Mar 59: 90
GREY, JANE, Sep 59: 127
GRIAULE, MARCEL, on mentality of black peoples, quoted, Mar 63: 44
GRIEG, EDVARD, Glenn Gould quoted on, Jan 62: 91
GRIFFITH, D. W., Mar 60: 127, May 61: 52
GRIFFITH, THOMAS, "Those Strange Americans Across the Hudson," essay reprinted from The Waist-High Culture, Jul 59: 121–25
GRIFFO, superintendent of antiquities for Agrigento, quoted on Temple of Zeus, Sep 61: 23
GRIGSON, GEOFFREY, "The Glory of an Isle of Greece," article by, Sep 59: 30–32, 49
GRILLER, SIDNEY, Jan 59: 21
GRILLER QUARTET, Jan 59: 21, 22
GRIMKÉ, SARAH MOORE, Mar 62: 98
GRIS, JUAN, Jan 59: 132
GRISAILLE, in stained-glass windows, Sep 62: 24
"GRISLY FOLK, THE," story by H. G. Wells, Jul 62: 84
GRIST, RERI, photographs of, Nov 61: 79, 81
GRISWOLD, A. WHITNEY, May 59: 86
On group thinking, quoted, Nov 58: 33
GRISWOLD, ERWIN N., on applicants to Harvard Law School, quoted, Jul 63: 41
GRIVOT, DENIS, and sculptures of St. Lazare Cathedral at Autun, France, Sep 61: 46–48, 57
GRIZZARD, GEORGE, May 62: 118, Nov 63: 37, 39, 41
GROCYN, WILLIAM, May 62: 91
GROHMANN, WILL, quoted
On American abstract expressionists, Nov 59: 120
On Klee, Paul, Nov 61: 65
GRONAU, CARMEN, Nov 62: 65
GRONCHI, GIOVANNI, Jan 63: 38
GROPIUS, WALTER, May 59: 84, Sep 59: 18, Nov 59:

48, Jan 60: 21, 23, Nov 60: 16, Mar 62: 32, 33, 39, Jan 63: 11, 12
Automobile designed by, Nov 61: 71
Building designed by (in collaboration), Nov 61: 72
As director of Bauhaus, Nov 61: 60–74
Photographs of, Nov 61: 59, 73
GROS, ANTOINE-JEAN, May 61: 70, 74
Painting by, May 61: 70
GROSS, CHAIM, portrait of, with sculpture by, Jul 61: 26
GROSS, ROBERT, Jan 59: 21
GROSS, SAMUEL, in painting by Thomas Eakins, Jul 63: 20
GROSSER, MAURICE, in paintings by John Koch, Sep 60: 106, 108
GROSSETESTE, ROBERT, Nov 62: 80
GROSSMITH, GEORGE, Jan 59: 56
GROSZ, GEORGE, May 59: 109, Mar 60: 43
GROTIUS, HUGO, Sep 58: 15, 24
Childhood of, May 60: 34, 35
On Holy Roman Empire, quoted, Jul 60: 64
Portraits of, Sep 58: 33, May 60: 32
GROUP DYNAMICS, in education, Nov 58: 32
GROUPE DE RECHERCHES DE MUSIQUE CONCRÈTE, Jan 59: 54
GROUPS. See CLUBS and GROUPS
GROUP THEATRE, Sep 58: 44, Nov 62: 106
Tyrone Guthrie quoted on, Jan 61: 32
GROUPTHINK, Nov 58: 33, 147
"GROWING UP IN NEW GUINEA," book by Margaret Mead, May 60: 122
GRUEN, JOHN, May 63: 14, 18
GRUEN, VICTOR, Jul 59: 9, Nov 59: 108
Photograph of, May 60: 84
Plan for 1964 World's Fair, May 60: 80–87
GRUNWALD, CONSTANTIN DE, "Peter and the West," article by, Sep 59: 58–85
GRUNWALD, HENRY ANATOLE, articles by
"Address from the Class of 1944 to the Class of 1963, An," May 63: 86–89
"Bernstein Suite, A," Jul 59: 16–23
"Disappearance of Don Juan, The," Jan 62: 56–65
"From Eden to the Nightmare," Mar 63: 72–79
"Gods in Art, The," Nov 58: 4–17, 112–17
"'He Touches Something Deep in Us . . . ,'" May 62: 100–7
GRÜTERS, HUGO, Sep 61: 87
GRUTHUYSE, LORD OF. See JEAN DE BRUGES
GUARDI, FRANCESCO, paintings by, Nov 59: 88–89, Jul 61: cover, 3
"GUARD OF HONOR," novel by James Gould Cozzens, Jul 62: 102
"GUARDSMAN, THE," play, Tyrone Guthrie quoted on, Jan 61: 31
GUARINO OF VERONA, Jan 60: 62
GUDDEN, BERNHARD VON, Jan 61: 127
GUERMONPREZ, TRUDE, Jan 59: 14
"GUERNICA," painting by Picasso, Sep 60: 121, Nov 61: 8, 12
GUERNSEY, ENGLAND, Mar 61: 32
GUERRERO, JOSÉ, painting by, Nov 60: 5
GUESCLIN, BERTRAND DU. See DU GUESCLIN, BERTRAND
GUEST, MRS. WINSTON, Jul 60: 122
Photograph of, Jul 60: 7
GUGGENHEIM, BENJAMIN, May 59: 6, 7
GUGGENHEIM, DANIEL, May 59: 5, 7, 8
GUGGENHEIM, HARRY, May 59: 5, 8, 11
GUGGENHEIM, IRENE (MRS. SOLOMON R.), May 59: 11
GUGGENHEIM, ISAAC, May 59: 6, 7
GUGGENHEIM, MEYER, May 59: 5–7
And his sons, photograph of, May 59: 6–7
GUGGENHEIM, MURRY, May 59: 6, 7
GUGGENHEIM, OLGA HIRSCH (MRS. SIMON), May 59: 5, 7, 10, 11, 12–13
Photograph of, May 59: 13
GUGGENHEIM, PEGGY, May 59: 5, 6, 10–11, 18–19
Photograph of, May 59: 18
GUGGENHEIM, SIMON, May 59: 5, 7, 8–10
GUGGENHEIM, SOLOMON R., May 59: 5, 7, 10–11, 14–15
On Kandinsky, quoted, Jul 62: 19
Photographs of, May 59: 7, 15
GUGGENHEIM, WILLIAM, May 59: 7, 10
GUGGENHEIM FAMILY, May 59: 4–19
GUGGENHEIM FELLOWSHIPS, May 59: 8–10, 11, 18–19
GUGGENHEIM FOUNDATIONS. See DANIEL AND FLORENCE GUGGENHEIM FOUNDATION; JOHN SIMON GUGGENHEIM MEMORIAL FOUNDATION; MURRY AND LEONIE GUGGENHEIM FOUNDATION; SOLOMON R. GUGGENHEIM FOUNDATION
GUGGENHEIM FUNDS. See DANIEL GUGGENHEIM FUND FOR THE PROMOTION OF AERONAUTICS;

MUSEUM OF MODERN ART, Collection of Olga Hirsch (Mrs. Simon) Guggenheim
GUGGENHEIM JEUNE, May 59: 10–11
GUGGENHEIM MUSEUMS and GALLERIES. See ART OF THIS CENTURY; GUGGENHEIM JEUNE; PALAZZO VENIER DEI LEONI; SOLOMON R. GUGGENHEIM MUSEUM
"GUIDE MICHELIN," on Baron Haussmann and Paris, quoted, May 63: 51
GUILD, LESLIE, Sep 59: 91, 122
GUILDFORD, HENRY, portrait by Holbein, Jul 63: 96; illus, Jul 63: cover, 3
GUIMARD, HECTOR, Nov 59: 111
GUINEVERE, versions of James Knowles and Thomas Malory, May 60: 116–17
GUINNESS, ALEC, May 59: 99, Nov 59: 31, 122, 124–25, Jan 61: 101, Mar 61: 98, Nov 61: 115, Jul 62: 109
GUISCARD, ROBERT, Sep 61: 36
GUISE, CARDINAL OF, Jul 63: 29, 31
GUISE, DUKE OF, Jul 63: 29, 31
GUITRY, LUCIEN, Mar 62: 118
GULLIKSEN, HAROLD, photograph of, Sep 59: 25
GUMBEL, E. J., Nov 63: 61
GUNEYA, NITTAWALA MULYAKDESSALAGE, Sep 59: 107
GUNN, HOMER, photograph of, May 60: 15
GUNN, MARTHA, Nov 62: 22
GUSTAD, JOHN W., on evaluation of college teaching, quoted, Sep 62: 19
GUSTAVUS II, KING OF SWEDEN (GUSTAVUS ADOLPHUS), Mar 60: 101, Nov 62: 36, 38
Portrait of, Jul 60: 39
On Russians, quoted, Sep 59: 60
GUSTAVUS III, KING OF SWEDEN, Sep 58: 118
Letter from Mme de Staël to, quoted, Mar 62: 64
GUSTAVUS ADOLPHUS. See GUSTAVUS II
GUSTON, PHILIP, Sep 58: 110, Nov 59: 41
Painting by, Nov 59: 34
GUTENBERG, JOHANN, Sep 59: 126
GUTENBERG BIBLE, Nov 60: 97
GUTHEIM, FREDERICK, quoted
On governmental buildings, Jan 60: 120
On World's Fair plan of Victor Gruen, May 60: 81
GUTHMAN, EDWIN, Sep 61: 10
GUTHRIE, TYRONE, Jul 59: 45, Sep 60: 54, 55, 56, Nov 60: 116, Jan 63: 108
"Greatness in the Theater," article by, Jan 61: 26–33
Photographs of, Jan 61: 26, Nov 63: 35
Staging of The Merchant of Venice, Jan 60: 91
And Tyrone Guthrie Theatre, Minneapolis, Sep 63: 106, Nov 63: 35–41
GUTTUSO, RENATO, copy of painting by, Sep 61: 37
GUTWILLIG, ROBERT, "On Screen: Shirley Anne Field," article by, Mar 63: 36–37
GUY DE LUSIGNAN, Jan 59: 88, 130
GUYS, CONSTANTIN, painting by, May 63: 68
"GUYS AND DOLLS," musical, Sep 58: 57, 60, 143, Mar 61: 101
GUZMÁN, GASPAR DE. See OLIVARES
GWENN, EDMUND, Sep 63: 77
GWINNETT, BUTTON, Nov 60: 97
GWYNNE, EDWARD, Nov 60: 98
GYGES, KING OF LYDIA, Sep 63: 84, 85
"GYPSY," musical, Jul 61: 98

H

HAAKON, PAUL, Sep 60: 94
HAAS, ERNST, photographs of Angkor by, Jan 59: 64–80
HAAS, WILLY, on Wieland Wagner, quoted, May 63: 44
HABIMA, The Dybbuk produced by, Jan 61: 32–33
HACILAR, TURKEY, archaeological site, Sep 62: 7 (map), 8, Nov 62: 104
HACKETT, BUDDY, May 63: 46
HADAMARD, JACQUES, The Psychology of Invention in the Mathematical Field, quoted, May 63: 114
HADASSAH-HEBREW UNIVERSITY MEDICAL CENTER, Jerusalem, stained-glass windows of synagogue, Sep 62: 24; illus, Sep 62: cover, 3, 26–27
HADRIAN, ROMAN EMPEROR, Sep 58: 140, Jan 62: 45, May 62: 3, Mar 63: 4
Coin portraits of, Sep 63: 38; illus, Sep 63: 36
Sculptured head of, May 63: 35
Villa built by, May 63: 32–39; art objects from, Nov 59: 102
"HADRIAN'S MEMOIRS," book by Marguerite Yourcenar, quoted, May 63: 35
HAFIZ, SHAMS UD-DIN MOHAMMED, May 61: 30, Jan 63: 67
HAGEN, UTA, Jan 62: 14
HAGERTY, JAMES, Mar 60: 50, Jul 60: 120

HAGESANDROS, May 59: 104, 124
HAGIA SOPHIA, Istanbul, Nov 63: 9, 11, 12, 15, 25, 34
HAGUE, THE, NETHERLANDS, U.S. government building, Jan 60: 119
HAGUE TRIBUNAL, THE, Mar 63: 6
HAIDAR ALI, Sep 60: 20
HAIGH, KENNETH, Jul 60: 94
"HAIRY APE, THE," play, Mar 60: 32
HAKAM I, AL-, EMIR OF CÓRDOBA, Sep 62: 77
HAKAM II, AL-, CALIPH OF CÓRDOBA, Sep 62: 79, 82
HALDANE, J. B. S., Jan 59: 28
On the Universe, quoted, Jul 62: 88
HALE, MATTHEW, and witch mania, Nov 59: 60
HALE, ROBERT BEVERLY, Nov 60: 8–9
HALE, RUTH, Jul 62: 37
HALE, WILLIAM HARLAN, articles by
"In Revolt Against Togetherness," Nov 58: 30–33, 146–47
"Ladies Who Tell All, but All," Jan 62: 111–12
"Memorandum from Adolph Hitler to Professor A. J. P. Taylor," Mar 62: 28–29
"Memorandum from Don Quixote de la Mancha to Generalissimo Francisco Franco," Jul 59: 24–25
"Memorandum from Eugénie, Empress of the French, to Jacqueline Bouvier Kennedy," Sep 62: 20–21
"Memorandum from Ex-Secretary of State Thomas Jefferson to Secretary of State Dean Rusk," Jul 61: 30–31
"Memorandum from François-Marie Arouet de Voltaire to the Spacemen," Sep 61: 18–19
"Memorandum from H. L. Mencken to the President-Elect," Nov 60: 70–71
"Memorandum from Horace Greeley to John Hay Whitney," Jan 59: 24–25
"Memorandum from Jonathan Swift to Cliff Robinson," Nov 59: 64–65
"Memorandum from Prince Klemens von Metternich to John Foster Dulles," Mar 58: 36–37
"Memorandum from Sigmund Freud to Norman Mailer, Tennessee Williams, Alberto Moravia, Jean Genet, et al.," May 62: 54–55
"Memorandum to the President from the Secretary of Arts and Leisure," Nov 62: 18–19
"Minister's Fatal Showplace, The," Jul 63: 76–83
"Out of the Gargoyles and into the Future," May 59: 84–87
"—To me, it sounds like Newspeak," Mar 61: 97
HALES, ROBERT, Mar 61: 65
HALICARNASSUS, mausoleum at, May 59: 122
HALL, DONALD, Jan 62: 14
"Battle of the Bards, The," article by, Sep 61: 116–21
Interviews by: "Archibald MacLeish: On Being a Poet in the Theater," Jan 60: 48–56; "Henry Moore," Nov 60: 102–4, 113–15
HALL, EDWARD T., The Silent Language, Mar 60: 122–23
"Bargaining in the Arab World," excerpt from, May 59: 136
HALL, JAMES NORMAN (see also NORDHOFF, CHARLES, co-author), Jan 60: 126
HALL, ROBERT A., JR., on language, quoted, Jul 63: 43, 47
HALL, WILLIS, The Long and the Short and the Tall, Jan 63: 32–33
HALLE, KAY, Sep 61: 5
HALLERSTEIN, HALLER VON, and Aegina marbles, Sep 59: 30–32, 49
HALLEY, EDMUND, Jan 60: 117, May 62: 60
HALLIDAY, E. M., "The Man Who Cleaned Up Shakespeare," article by, Sep 62: 68–71
HALLIDIE BUILDING, San Francisco, Jan 59: 11
HALPRIN, ANN, Jan 59: 22
Photograph of, Jan 59: 23
HALPRIN, LAWRENCE, Jan 59: 22
HALS, FRANS, Sep 58: 15, 21, Jul 60: 38, Sep 60: 34, Nov 62: 65
Painting by, Sep 58: 31
HALSMAN, PHILIPPE, Jump Book, Jul 60: 120
HAMBURG, GERMANY
Messianic year of 1666, Mar 60: 125
Reeperbahn, Mar 59: 83, 84
HAMILCAR, Sep 61: 23
HAMILTON, EMMA (LADY HAMILTON), Mar 59: 65, Nov 59: 96, Mar 62: 55, 61, 114
Portraits of, Nov 59: 95, Mar 62: 69
HAMILTON, JERALD, May 59: 122
Photograph of, Sep 59: 88
HAMILTON, WILLIAM, Nov 59: 96, Mar 62: 55, 56, 61
And Portland vase, Nov 63: 63–64
Portraits of, Nov 59: 94, Mar 62: 62, Nov 63: 63
"HAMLET," play by Shakespeare, Sep 63: 104
Ambiguities of, Sep 62: 33, 36
Bowdlerized version, Sep 62: 71
Guthrie, Tyrone, quoted on performance of John Gielgud in, Jan 61: 28–29
Humor in, Mar 63: 106

Motion picture based on, Jul 63: 85
Quoted, May 59: 41
Tyrone Guthrie Theatre production, Nov 63: 38–39, 40, 41
HAMMAMS, Sep 60: 125–26
HAMMAREN, TORSTEN, Sep 60: 8
HAMMARSKJÖLD, DAG, Jul 63: 75
HAMMERSTEIN, OSCAR I, Sep 59: 52, 53
HAMMERSTEIN, OSCAR II, May 61: 103
HAMMETT, DASHIELL, May 61: 116
HAMMOND, EDWARD C., Mar 60: 30–31
HAMMOND, PHILIP C., Jul 62: 29
HAMPDEN, JOHN, Jul 61: 92
HAMPTON COURT PALACE, Jul 61: 90
HANBURY, WILLIAM, on gardening, quoted, May 59: 31
HANCOCK, JOHN, contemporary theatre director, Mar 63: 107
HANCOCK LIFE INSURANCE BUILDING, San Francisco, Jan 59: 11
HAND, LEARNED, Jul 60: 120, May 61: 104
HANDEL, GEORGE FREDERICK, Jul 60: 64
And prima donnas, Sep 59: 51
Recording of organ music of, Mar 60: 73
HANDICRAFTS. See CRAFTS
HANDWRITING
Art of, Sep 59: 124–28
Portfolio of historic manuscripts, Sep 59: 129–36
HANDWRITING FOUNDATION, Sep 59: 124
HANFMANN, GEORGE M. A., "Golden Sardis," article by, Sep 63: 82–89
HANGARS
Designed by Freyssinet, Eugène, Mar 59: 21
Designed by Nervi, Pier Luigi, Mar 59: 18–19, 24, 121
HANGER, GEORGE, portrait of, Nov 62: 22
HANGÖ-UDDE, BATTLE OF, Sep 59: 80
HANISCH, ARTHUR, Sep 58: 89, 91
Portrait of, Sep 58: 88
HANISH, Californian, founder of Mazdaznan, Nov 61: 68
HANLEY, GERALD, Mar 61: 32
HANNA, LEONARD C., Sep 58: 62, 63
HANNIBAL, Sep 58: 140
HANOVER, crown jewels of, May 63: 96
HANOVER PARK, N. J., Mar 60: 71
"HAN PALACE, THE," Chinese painting of 12th century, Jan 61: 25; illus, Jan 61: 20
HANSEATIC LEAGUE, fear of Russia, Sep 59: 60
HANSEN, WINIFRED, Sep 59: 91
HANSLICK, EDUARD, on Adelina Patti, quoted, Sep 59: 54
HAPGOOD, secretary to Henry E. Huntington, Nov 60: 99, 100
HAPGOOD, HUTCHINS, Jul 61: 13
"HAPPENING," as art form, Nov 62: 114
"HAPPY DAYS," play, Sep 62: 36, 38–39 (illus), 41
"HAPPY HAVEN, THE," play, Jul 62: 91, 93–94, Jan 63: 31, 32, 33
HAPSBURGS
Role in Sicily, Sep 61: 38
And Thirty Years' War, Nov 62: 33–41
HARALD, PRINCE OF NORWAY, Jan 63: 86
HARAR, SOMALILAND, penetration by Richard Francis Burton, Jul 63: 112–13
HARBOR SPRINGS, MICH., Mar 60: 70
"HARD BLUE SKY, THE," novel by Shirley Ann Grau, Mar 59: 14, 118
"HARD-EDGE" PAINTING, Jan 63: 19, 25
HARDERWIJK, UNIVERSITY OF, Sep 58: 23
HARDING, WARREN G., Jul 63: 119
HARDWICKE, CEDRIC, Sep 63: 77, 80
HARDWICK HALL, Nov 58: 41, 50
HARDY, THOMAS, Mar 63: 87, Nov 63: 44
HARDY, MRS. THOMAS, Jul 63: 75
HARDYNG, JOHN, on tournaments, quoted, Nov 58: 105
"HARE AND JAYS," painting by Ts'ui Po, Jan 61: 16, 25; illus, Jan 61: 17
HAREM OF GRAND SERAGLIO, May 59: 132, 134–35
HAREWOOD, 7TH EARL OF (GEORGE H. H. LASCELLES), Jan 63: 26
HARKNESS, EDWARD STEPHEN, Mar 60: 30–31
"HARLEQUIN'S FAMILY, THE," painting by Picasso, Nov 61: 9
HARLOW, GEORGE HENRY, Mar 63: 69
HARLOW, JEAN, Sep 63: 96
HARMON, LILY, portrait of, with painting by, Jul 61: 25
HARNACK, ADOLF VON, Sep 63: 107
HARRIET MONROE POETRY AWARD, Jul 63: 72
HARRIMAN, MARGARET CASE, The Vicious Circle, quoted, Jul 62: 37
HARRIMAN, W. AVERELL, Sep 61: 10
Portrait of, Sep 61: 15
HARRINGTON, JAMES, Oceana, Mar 63: 76
HARRIS, BARBARA, Jan 62: 66
Photographs of, Jan 62: 67
HARRIS, FRANK, biography of G. B. Shaw by, Nov 58: 137

HARRIS, JULIE, Nov 60: 52, May 61: 99
HARRIS, MARK, Jan 59: 19, Jan 62: 10
Photograph of, Mar 63: 29
HARRIS, ROY, Jul 59: 20, Mar 63: 28
HARRISON, FREDERIC, on present-day world, quoted, Jan 60: 127
HARRISON, JAY S., articles by
"On Stage: Gold and Fizdale," Mar 61: 74–75
"On Stage: Maureen Forrester," Mar 62: 86–87
HARRISON, LOU, Mar 61: 72
HARRISON, REX, Sep 58: 61, Nov 58: 82, Nov 60: 52, Sep 63: 79, 80
Photograph of, Sep 58: 59
Reed, Carol, quoted on, Nov 59: 122
HARRISON, WALLACE K., Nov 58: 28, 117, 118, 120, Sep 59: 19, Jul 62: 4, 6, 7, 8, 9, 10, Sep 62: 24
Building designed by, Sep 59: 20, 21
Letter on William Zeckendorf from, Jan 63: 115
Photograph of, Jul 62: 7
HARRISON & ABRAMOVITZ, Nov 58: 28, Mar 59, 123
Building designed by, Mar 59: 25
HART, MOSS, Sep 58: 59, 60, Nov 60: 55, May 61: 103, Jul 62: 39
On George S. Kaufman, quoted, Jul 62: 40
HARTE, BRET, Jan 59: 7
HARTFIELD, JOSEPH, Jul 62: 5
HARTFORD, CONN., Mutual Insurance Company building, Sep 59: 19
HARTFORD, HUNTINGTON, JR., Jul 63: 70 (note)
HARTIGAN, GRACE, Sep 58: 44, Sep 59: 102, Nov 59: 41, Mar 62: 107
Painting by, Nov 59: 40
HARTLEY, DAVID, letter from Benjamin Franklin to, facsimile, Sep 59: 135
HARTLIB, SAMUEL, Mar 60: 101
HARTNOLL, PHYLLIS, on Charles Macklin as Shylock, quoted, Jan 60: 92
HART SCHAFFNER & MARX, book awards given by, Jul 63: 68
"HARVARD LAW REVIEW," on right to privacy, quoted, Jul 60: 122
HARVARD UNIVERSITY
Busch-Reisinger Museum organ, Mar 60: 80
Graduate Center architecture, Sep 59: 18
Investigation of "Margery," Jan 59: 108, 109, 110
Sardis expedition, Sep 63: 85, 86, 88–89
Teaching situation at, Sep 62: 16, 18
Warning to students against mind-distorting drugs, May 63: 115
Yale vs., in architecture, May 59: 84–87
"HARVEY," play, Mar 60: 127
HARVEY, ALEXANDER, on art in America, quoted, Sep 60: 40
HARVEY, LAURENCE, Jan 63: 112
HARVEY, WILLIAM, May 63: 115
On Francis Bacon, quoted, Jul 61: 6
HASANLU, IRAN, golden bowl of, Nov 62: 102
HASEGAWA, SABRO, Jul 59: 126
HASHIMOTO, OKIIE, May 60: 113–14
Print by, May 60: 110
HASKELL, HARRY G., JR., Sep 58: 109
HASS, HANS, Sep 58: 11
HASTINGS, MICHAEL, Jan 63: 32
HASTINGS, THOMAS, Jan 61: 104
Building designed by, Jul 63: 106–7
HASTINGS, WARREN, May 60: 101
HATANO, ISOKO and ICHIRO, Mother and Son, Nov 62: 109
HATCH, ROBERT, articles by (see also THEATRE, Current, articles by Robert Hatch on)
"Adult Prodigy," Jul 63: 84–91
"At the Tip of Cape Cod," Jul 61: 10–29
"Circle in the Square," May 59: 49, 99, 119–21
"Tyrone Guthrie: The Artist As Man of the Theatre," Nov 63: 35–41
"HATFUL OF RAIN, A," play and motion picture, May 59: 101, Jan 62: 68
HATHAWAY, SYBIL, Mar 61: 33
HATSHEPSUT, QUEEN OF EGYPT, temple-tomb of, Jul 60: 87
HATTIN, SYRIA, Jan 59: 88, 90
HAUSER, ARNOLD, on Renaissance artists, quoted, Sep 60: 34
HAUSSMANN, GEORGES EUGÈNE, BARON, Sep 60: 81, Nov 60: 13
In painting by Adolphe Yvon, May 63: 50
Rebuilding of Paris by, May 63: 50–75, 105
HAVANA, CUBA
Filming of Our Man in Havana, Nov 59: 27–31, 122–26
U.S. embassy building, Jan 60: 25, 27
HAVOC, JUNE, Nov 62: 108
"Old Vaudevillians, Where Are You Now?" article by, Jul 59: 112–20
Photographs of, Jul 59: 112, 113, 119

HAWAII, in South Seas dream, Jan 60: 125, 127
HAWKINS, JACK, May 61: 56
HAWTHORNDEN PRIZE, Jul 63: 73
HAWTHORNE, CHARLES W., Jul 61: 13, 16, 25, 28
In group photograph, Jul 61: 12
HAWTHORNE, JO, Jul 61: 16
HAWTHORNE, NATHANIEL, May 60: 13
And Brook Farm, Mar 63: 77
House of the Seven Gables, quoted, May 61: 42
Scarlet Letter, The, Mar 59: 15
HAY, ELIJAH (MARJORIE ALLEN SEIFFERT), May 60: 43, 47
HAY, JOHN, Jan 59: 24, 25
HAYDEN, MELISSA, Nov 59: 54
HAYDN, JOSEPH
Chamber music of, Nov 62: 44, 45, 46
Gould, Glenn, quoted on, Jan 62: 91
Renaissance of, Mar 52: 76–83
"HAYDN: A PRESENCE MORE BRILLIANT THAN EVER," article by Joseph Wechsberg, Mar 62: 76–83
HAYDON, BENJAMIN ROBERT, Mar 63: 69, Jul 63: 106
Autobiography, quoted, Mar 63: 63, 65, 66, 68
HAYES, ALFRED, The Girl on the Via Flaminia, Mar 60: 98, 120
HAYES, CATHERINE, Jan 59: 7
HAYES, HELEN, Nov 60: 52, Mar 62: 107
HAYES, JOSEPH, Calculated Risk, May 63: 106–7
HAYES, PETER LIND, May 63: 46
HAYES, RUTHERFORD, B., desk presented by Queen Victoria to, Sep 61: 13
"HAY WAIN," painting by Constable, May 61: 74
HAYWORTH, RITA, Jul 63: 86
Photograph of, Jul 63: 89
HAZLITT, WILLIAM, quoted
On Kean, Edmund, Mar 62: 115–16, 117
On Last Judgment of Michelangelo, Jan 62: 41
On Poussin, Mar 61: 93
On Royal Academy, May 62: 63–64
HAZOR, GALILEE, archaeological work at site of, Nov 59: 10, 118, 119
H'DOUBLER, MARGARET, Nov 62: 68
HEADDRESSES, drawings by Marcello Mariotti, Mar 63: 118–19
HEALD, HENRY, Jan 62: 13
HEALTH, concept of, in contemporary civilization, Nov 62: 6–7
HEALTH, EDUCATION, AND WELFARE, DEPARTMENT OF, Mar 60: 70
HEALY, G. P. A., painting by (with Frederick Church and Jervis McEntee), Nov 59: 101
HEARD, GERALD, "Can This Drug Enlarge Man's Mind?" article by, May 63: 28–31, 114–15
HEARN, LAFCADIO, Mar 61: 22
Glimpses of Unfamiliar Japan, quoted, Mar 59: 133
On Kyoto, quoted, Mar 61: 27
HEARST, WILLIAM RANDOLPH
Citizen Hearst, book by W. A. Swanberg, Jul 63: 71
And motion picture Citizen Kane, Jul 63: 89, 90
"HEARTBREAK HOUSE," play, Jul 63: 87
HECHT, BEN, on Algonquin Round Table, quoted, Jul 62: 38
"HEDDA GABLER," play, Jan 62: 106
Anne Meacham in, May 61: 99
"HEDGEROW ANIMAL," drawing by Morris Graves, Jul 60: 105; illus, Jul 60: 105
HEDIN, SVEN, Sep 58: 8, 138
HEGEL, GEORG WILHELM FRIEDRICH, Sep 61: 115
Quoted: on Dutch genre painting, Sep 58: 31; on right and wrong, Mar 59: 10
HEIDEGGER, MARTIN, Jul 59: 72
HEIDELBERG, GERMANY, Mar 59: 85
HEIFETZ, JASCHA, Sep 59: 55, Jan 60: 76, Jan 61: 49
HEILBRONER, ROBERT L., The Future as History, quoted, Jul 60: 70
HEIM, FRANÇOIS JOSEPH, painting by, Mar 60: 54–55
HEINE, HEINRICH
Beecham, Thomas, quoted on, Mar 62: 103
Quoted: on Chopin and George Sand, May 61: 81; on existence, Sep 60: 113
HELD, JOHN, JR., Jul 63: 118–19
Cartoons by, Jul 63: 118, 119
HELENA, SAINT, Nov 63: 11
HELICOID OF THE TARPEIAN ROCK, Jan 62: 94
HELIOGABALUS. See ELAGABALUS
HELLENISTIC AGE, Mar 59: 58
The Dyskolos, of Menander, Jul 59: 78–79; translation by Gilbert Highet, Jul 59: 80–88
HELLENISTIC ART, Nov 63: 25
HELLER, ERICH, Alfred Kazin quoted on, Jul 62: 103
HELLEU, PAUL, on Pierre Bonnard, quoted, Mar 62: 26
HELLMAN, LILLIAN, Nov 60: 52
Influence on Paddy Chayefsky, Sep 60: 51
Little Foxes, The, Jan 60: 123, Jan 63: 112

HELLMUTH, OBATA, & KASSABAUM, Mar 59: 123, Jan 60: 120

HEM, FRANCE, stained-glass wall in chapel at, Sep 62: 24; illus, Sep 62: 28

HEMANS, FELICIA, Jan 59: 59

HEMINGWAY, ERNEST, Sep 59: 124, Mar 60: 127, Jul 60: 122, Jan 62: 64, May 62: 35, Jul 63: 71, 75, Nov 63: 109
On art of writing, interview, Jan 59: 82–85, 132–35
Miró painting owned by, Mar 59: 76; illus, Mar 59: 73
Portraits of, Jan 59: 82, 85
Quoted by Archibald MacLeish, Jan 60: 55
Wertenbaker, Lael Tucker, compared to, Jan 62: 111

HÉNAULT, CHARLES, Nov 61: 34, 35

HENDERSON, ARCHIBALD, biography of George Bernard Shaw by, as altered by Max Beerbohm, May 61: 38, 40

HENDERSON, W. J., on Geraldine Farrar, quoted, Sep 59: 51–52

HENDY, PHILIP, on Isabella Stewart Gardner collection, quoted, Jul 59: 27, 28, 31

HENEGHAN, JIM, Sep 63: 79

HENNEBIQUE, FRANÇOIS, Mar 59: 20–21, 24

"HENNESEY," television show, Sep 62: 114–15

HENRI DE LAON, Nov 58: 105

HENRIETTA ANNE, DUCHESSE D'ORLÉANS, Jul 63: 80

HENRIETTA MARIA, QUEEN OF ENGLAND, Jul 61: 89, 91, 92

"HENRY IV," play by Shakespeare, Bowdlerized version, Sep 62: 71

"HENRY V," play by Shakespeare, Sep 60: 61
Bowdlerized version, Sep 62: 70
New York Shakespeare Festival production, Nov 60: 117–18

"HENRY VI," play by Shakespeare, Mar 62: 95

HENRY, COUNT OF CHAMPAGNE, Jan 59: 130

HENRY III, COUNT OF LUXEMBOURG, at tournament of Chauvency, Nov 58: 105

HENRY IV, HOLY ROMAN EMPEROR, May 63: 97
Vs. Gregory VII, Sep 59: 128
Handwriting of, Sep 59: 128
Portrait of, Sep 59: 129

HENRY VI, HOLY ROMAN EMPEROR, in Sicily, Sep 61: 30, 32

HENRY IV, KING OF ENGLAND, Nov 60: 74

HENRY V, KING OF ENGLAND, Nov 60: 74, May 63: 94

HENRY VII, KING OF ENGLAND, Jul 61: 80, 90

HENRY VIII, KING OF ENGLAND, Sep 59: 29, Mar 61: 65, May 62: 92, 95, May 63: 94
Castles built by, May 60: 3
As collector of paintings, Jul 63: 92–93
And fashion, Mar 59: 66
Handwriting of, Sep 59: 130
Portraits of, Sep 59: 130, Jul 63: 94

HENRY II, KING OF FRANCE, Sep 60: 64
Death of, Nov 58: 106

HENRY III, KING OF FRANCE, Jul 62: 56

HENRY IV, KING OF FRANCE (HENRY OF NAVARRE), Sep 60: 66, 69, Nov 62: 35

HENRY, PRINCE, OF ENGLAND, Jul 61: 80

HENRY, PIERRE, Jan 59: 54

HENRY FREDERICK, DUKE OF CUMBERLAND. See CUMBERLAND

"HENRY MILLER'S STREAM OF SELF-CONSCIOUSNESS," article by Gilbert Highet, Nov 61: 104–5

HENRY OF FLANDERS, Nov 63: 31

HENRY THE LION, Jan 59: 88

HENRY THE NAVIGATOR, PRINCE OF PORTUGAL, May 60: 90, Nov 60: 72–83
Portrait of, Nov 60: 72

HENSCHE, HENRY, Jul 61: 13, 18, 25
Portrait of, with painting by, Jul 61: 24

HENTRICH AND PETSCHNIGG, Phoenix-Rheinrohr building, designed by, Nov 60: 124, 125; illus. Nov 60: 14

HEPBURN, KATHARINE, Sep 60: 88, Jul 61: 98, Jul 62: 109

HEPHAESTION, Mar 59: 38, 39, 52

HERACLITUS, aphorism by, quoted, Sep 61: 115

HERACLIUS, BYZANTINE EMPEROR, Nov 63: 26

HERAKLION, GREECE, Sep 60: 125

HERBERT, GEORGE, quotation from, on Milton Academy shield, May 62: 7

HERBERT, VICTOR, Sep 58: 57

HERBERT FAMILY. See PEMBROKE, EARLS OF

HERBLOCK. See BLOCK, HERBERT

HERBODEAU, EUGÈNE, May 61: 126

HERCULANEUM, Nov 59: 87, 96
Burial and discovery of, Mar 62: 42–69

HERCULES, at Arles, Jul 59: 90, 92, 132

"HERCULES UNCHAINED," motion picture, May 61: 53, 54–55

"HEREDITARY GENIUS," book by Francis Galton, May 60: 33

HERGESHEIMER, JOSEPH, Andrew Wyeth quoted on, Sep 61: 100

HERLIHY, JAMES LEO, Nov 58: 64

HERM, ENGLAND, Mar 61: 32

HERMES, ALICE, May 62: 81

HERMITAGE MUSEUM, in Leningrad, Sep 59: 83, Jan 60: 112

HERMOLAUS, Mar 59: 44, 58

"HERNANI," play, May 61: 82, 83

HERODOTUS, Jan 60: 42–43, 45
Influence on Charles James Fox, May 60: 99
Known world of, Jul 60: 85
Quoted: on Africa, Nov 60: 77; on Croesus and the Lydians, Sep 63: 83–84, 85, 86, 88; on Etruscans, May 60: 61; on Leonidas, Mar 59: 133; on pomegranate used as symbol, Nov 62: 104; on slave trade, May 62: 48–49
In Renaissance curriculum, Jan 60: 62
Survival of works by, Nov 62: 78

"HEROES AND ORATORS," novel by Robert Phelps, Mar 59: 17, 119

HEROLD, J. CHRISTOPHER, Sep 63: 98
Articles by: "Great Confrontations IV: Napoleon and Alexander," Sep 63: 28–32; "Pleasures of the Bastille, The," Jan 60: 82–88, 128

HEROSTRATUS, Sep 58: 87

"HER REVENGE," story by Marcus Cheke, Mar 59: 129–32

HERRIGEL, EUGENE, Zen in the Art of Archery, Jul 59: 75

HERRING, PENDLETON, on university teaching situation, quoted, Sep 62: 17

HERRIOT, ÉDOUARD, Nov 59: 68

HERSEY, JOHN, The War Lover, motion picture version, Mar 63: 36

HERSH, BURTON, "The Man in the Ironic Mask," article by, May 62: 34–41

HERSHEY CHOCOLATE CORPORATION, May 63: 113

HERTER, CHRISTIAN, Jul 60: 120

HERTFORD, LADY, Nov 62: 29

HERVEY, FREDERICK AUGUSTUS. See BRISTOL, 4TH EARL OF

HERZEN, ALEXANDER, Sep 60: 134–35

HERZFELD, ERNST, Iran in the Ancient East, quoted, Nov 62: 104

HESIOD, on earliest history, quoted, Jul 60: 86

HESSE, FRITZ, Nov 61: 72

HESYCHIUS, May 60: 64

"HE TAUGHT US TO BE FREE," article excerpted from The Age of Reason, book by Harold Nicolson, Mar 61: 114–19

"'HE TOUCHES SOMETHING DEEP IN US . . . ,'" article by Henry Anatole Grunwald, May 62: 100–7

"HE WHO GETS SLAPPED," opera, Jan 60: 123

HEYDEN, JAN VAN DER, Jul 63: 106

HEYER, HAROLD, Mar 60: 38

"HEY, LET'S TWIST," motion picture, Jul 62: 49

HEYN, PIET, Sep 58: 15, 20, 21
Bust of, Sep 58: 20

HEYWARD, DOROTHY, Mar 63: 28

HEYWARD, DuBOSE, Mar 63: 28

HEYWOOD, PETER, Sep 63: 45, 47, 48

HEYWOOD, THOMAS, Jan 60: 92

HEZEKIAH, KING OF JUDAH, water tunnel dug by, Nov 59: 5–6

HIALEAH, FLA., Mar 60: 71

"HIBERNATION, 1954," drawing by Morris Graves, Jul 60: 105; illus, Jul 60: 110–11

HICKEL, KARL ANTON, painting by, May 60: 97

HICKEY, WILLIAM, Sep 62: 114

HICKS, G. E., May 62: 73

HICKS-BEACH, MICHAEL, Mar 59: 92

"HIDDEN, THE UNKNOWABLE, THE UNTHINKABLE, THE," article by Fawn M. Brodie, Jul 63: 110–17

"HIDDEN PERSUADERS, THE," book by Vance Packard, Nov 58: 147

HIGGINS, MARGUERITE, Jul 60: 120

HIGGINSON, HENRY L., Jul 59: 133

HIGGINSON, THOMAS WENTWORTH, Jul 61: 101, 102, 104

"HIGH ART OF PORTRAITURE ON ROMAN COINS, THE," article by Michael Grant, Sep 63: 33–41

"HIGHBROW, LOWBROW, MIDDLEBROW," magazine article by Russell Lynes, Nov 59: 24

HIGHET, GILBERT, May 63: 22
Articles by: "Alexandrians of Lawrence Durrell, The," Mar 60: 113–18; "Art of the Hoax, The," Jan 61: 66–72; "Great Confrontations I: Diogenes and Alexander," Mar 63: 10–13; "Iconography of Heavenly Beings, An," Nov 60: 26–49; "Love Among the Romans," Nov 58:

108–11; "Memorandum from Lucius Annaeus Seneca to Tennessee Williams," May 59: 54–55; "Mystery of Mad Maggie, The," Jan 59: 44–49; "Sense and Nonsense," Sep 58: 129–31; "Their Names Are Writ in Webster," May 60: 126–28; "Try 'Massachusetts' on Your Piano," Nov 61: 118–19; "When Forgery Becomes a Fine Art," Mar 59: 105–9; "Wondrous Survival of Records, The," Nov 62: 74–95, comment on, Nov 62: 105
"Books," critical discussions: "Beer-bottle on the Pediment," Jan 61: 116–18; "Bible Is Given New Speech, The," Mar 61: 94–97; "Diary from the Depths, A," Nov 62: 108–10; "Dreamer of Light and Dark," Jan 63: 109–11; "Greetings from Goethe's Land," Mar 63: 111–13; "Henry Miller's Stream of Self-consciousness," Nov 61: 104–5; "History by Another Name," Sep 62: 112–14; "Life Behind the Ivy," Sep 60: 117–19; "Liszt and Chopin," May 63: 109–10; "Only Yesterday: The Third Reich," Nov 60: 119–21; "Our Man in Purgatory," May 61: 116–17; "Paris at Five O'Clock," May 62: 113–15; "Poor Winnie in Pooh-Latin," Jul 61: 112–15; "To the Sound of Hollow Laughter," Jul 62: 89–91; "Uncommon Thoughts in a Common Place," Sep 61: 114–15
Dyskolos, The, comedy by Menander, translated by, Jul 59: 80–88
Photograph of, May 63: 23

"HIGH SCHOOL CONFIDENTIAL," motion picture, Jan 59: 137

"HIGH SPIRITS IN THE TWENTIES," excerpt from biography of Robert Sherwood by John Mason Brown, Jul 62: 32–41

HIGHWAYS. See ROADS and HIGHWAYS

HILDRETH, RICHARD, Sep 63: 101

HILL, DAVID OCTAVIUS, Jan 59: 103

HILL, GEORGE WASHINGTON, Jul 61: 118, Mar 63: 114

HILL, JAMES J., Jul 61: 107

HILL, JEROME, Jul 61: 107
"How to Build a Sand Castle," article by, Jul 61: 108–9
Photograph of, Jul 61: 107

HILL, ROGER, Jul 63: 86

HILL, ROWLAND, Jan 59: 142

HILLARY, RICHARD, Sep 58: 10

HILLER, LEJAREN A., Jan 63: 78

HILLMAN, SERRELL, "Peter Ustinov," article by, Nov 58: 82–85, 137–39

HILLMER, JACK, Jan 59: 10
House designed by, Jan 59: 11

"HILLS LIKE WHITE ELEPHANTS," story by Ernest Hemingway, Jan 59: 134

HILTON HOTELS, Mar 61: 116–17
In Istanbul, Sep 60: 125, 126

HINDEMITH, PAUL, Mar 60: 80, Nov 61: 70, 71, Nov 62: 46, 47, Jan 63: 78
George Balanchine quoted on, Jan 61: 48

HINDENBERG, PAUL VON, handwriting of, Sep 59: 127

HINDUISM, Jan 61: 62–63
Attitude toward nature in, Mar 60: 13
In Cambodia, Jan 59: 62, 63, 81

HINDU TRILOGY, motion pictures, Jan 61: 115, Mar 61: 98

"HINDU TRILOGY, THE," article by Jean Stafford, Jan 61: 115

HINGLE, PAT, in J.B., Jan 60: 49, 53
Drawing of, Jan 60: 54

HINKSON, MARY, Nov 62: 68, 98

HIPPOCRENE, FOUNTAIN OF, May 62: 12

HIPPOPOTAMUS, as source of ivory, May 60: 91, 94

HIRATSUKA, UN' ICHI, print by, May 60: 113

HIROHITO, EMPEROR OF JAPAN, Jul 63: 73
Portrait of, May 60: 7

HIROSHIGE, ICHIRYUSAI, May 60: 103, 104, 114
Print by, May 60: 102

HIROSHIMA, JAPAN
Children's Library, Sep 61: 63
Peace Center, Sep 61: 60
Peace Memorial, Sep 61: 58, 60
Peace Park bridges, Mar 60: 111

"HIROSHIMA, MON AMOUR," motion picture, May 60: 50, 54–55; Mar 61: 58; Jan 62: 101
Reviewed, Nov 60: 121–22

HISHAM I, EMIR OF CÓRDOBA, Sep 62: 75

HISHAM II, CALIPH OF CÓRDOBA, Sep 62: 82

"HISTORIAN'S STRUGGLE WITH RELIGION, THE," article excerpted from Reconsiderations, book by Arnold Toynbee, Jan 61: 57–65

HISTORICAL FICTION, May 61: 53

HISTORICAL WRITING
Judgments upon Joan of Arc, Mar 62: 88–99
Misuses of the past, Mar 59: 4–13, 128
Prizes for, Jul 63: 68
Religion and, Jan 61: 57–65

35

Sorry state of, Sep 63: 97–101
Thucydides, Jan 60: 41–45
HISTORY
    End of, Nov 63: 107–8
    Gibbon, Edward, quoted on, Nov 60: 119
    Goncourt *Journal* as, Sep 62: 113–14
    And Plains frontier, Sep 62: 95
    Ranke, Leopold von, quoted on, Sep 62: 114
HISTORY, STUDY OF, in Renaissance curriculum, Jan 60: 62
"HISTORY BY ANOTHER NAME," article by Gilbert Highet, Sep 62: 112–14
"HISTORY OF ART, A," drawings by Michael Thaler, Jan 61: 120–21
"HISTORY OF CHRISTIANITY UNDER THE EMPIRE," book by Henry Hart Milman, Mar 59: 94
"HISTORY OF SANDFORD AND MERTON, THE," book by Thomas Day, May 59: 92
"HISTORY OF TECHNOLOGY, A," edited by Charles Singer and others, excerpts from, Sep 58: 146–51
"HISTORY OF THE CROWN JEWELS OF EUROPE, A," book by Edward Francis Twining, May 63: 92–96
"HISTORY TODAY," periodical, Jan 60: 108
HITCH, CHARLES J., Sep 61: 10
HITCHCOCK, ALFRED, Jan 63: 112
HITCHCOCK, HENRY-RUSSELL, Nov 63: 76
HITLER, ADOLF, Sep 59: 126, Jul 61: 66, Nov 61: 9, Nov 62: 41, Mar 63: 14
    Memorandum to Professor A. J. P. Taylor from, Mar 62: 28–29
    Rise and Fall of the Third Reich, The, reviewed, Nov 60: 119–21
HITTITES, Nov 59: 119, Jul 60: 14, 124, Sep 63: 84–85
    Achaeans and, Jan 61: 80–81
    Use of wheeled vehicles in war, Sep 58: 148–49
HITTORFF, JACQUES-IGNACE, May 63: 66
"H.M.S. PINAFORE," comic opera, Jan 61: 72
HOAXES
    Art of, Jan 61: 66–72
    Spectral poets of Pittsburgh, May 60: 42–48
"HOAXES," book by Curtis MacDougall, Jan 61: 72
HOBBEMA, MEINDERT, Jul 63: 106
HOBBES, THOMAS, Jul 60: 38
    Portrait of, Jul 60: 39
HOBSON, A. R. A., Nov 62: 66
HOCKEY, Yale University rink, May 59: 84–87
HODGE, ALAN. See GRAVES, ROBERT, co-author
HOFFMAN, MIRIAM, Jan 59: 14
HOFFMANN, BANESH, on multiple-choice tests, quoted, Jul 63: 43
HOFFNUNG, GERARD, Jul 62: 104, 107
    Cartoons by, Jul 62: 104–7
HOFHAIMER, PAUL, picture of, Mar 60: 75
HOFMANN, ALBERT, May 63: 29
HOFMANN, HANS, Sep 59: 96, 97, Nov 59: 121, Jul 61: 13, 16, Mar 63: 103
    Portrait of, with painting by, Jul 61: 17
HOFMANN, JOSEF, Sep 61: 83
HOFMANNSTHAL, HUGO VON, Nov 58: 25, Nov 61: 9, May 63: 42
HOG, as source of ivory, May 60: 92
HOGARTH, MARY, Nov 60: 97
HOGARTH, WILLIAM, Jul 60: 116, May 62: 60
    Engravings in John Soane Museum, Nov 63: 76; illus, Nov 63: 81
HOHENSTAUFEN, HOUSE OF, rule in Sicily, Sep 61: 24–25 (map), 30, 36
HOIBY, LEE, Jan 60: 123
HOKINSON, HELEN, Mar 60: 14
HOKUSAI, KATSUSHUKA, May 60: 104, 114
HOLBEIN, HANS THE YOUNGER, Jul 61: 90, 95, May 62: 92, Jul 63: 92–93, 94, 96
    Drawings and paintings by. See ILLUSTRATIONS INDEX
HOLDEN, CHARLES, Nov 60: 13
HOLDEN, WILLIAM, Nov 59: 126
HOLDER, GEOFFREY, May 63: 49
HOLFORD, GEORGE, sale of Shakespeareana by, Nov 60: 100–1
HOLFORD, ROBERT STAYNER, Shakespeare collection of, Nov 60: 100–1
HOLKHAM HALL, Nov 58: 45
HOLLAND. See NETHERLANDS
HOLLAND, 1ST BARON. See FOX, HENRY
HOLLAND, 3D BARON (HENRY RICHARD VASSALL FOX), Mar 59: 82, 93, 94, 125
HOLLAND, HENRY, Nov 62: 21, 23, 30, Nov 63: 74
    On George IV, quoted, Nov 62: 22–23
HOLLAND, JOHN, Nov 58: 106
HOLLAND, LADY (ELIZABETH VASSALL FOX), Mar 59: 93, 125
HOLLAND, PHILEMON, Jan 60: 134
HOLLAND HOUSE, Mar 59: 92, 125
HOLLIDAY, BILLIE, Jan 63: 75, May 63: 49
HOLLIDAY, JUDY, Jan 62: 66, 68

HOLLYWOOD, CALIF.
    British colony of, Sep 63: 74–81
    Ustinov, Peter, quoted on, Nov 58: 138
HOLMES, OLIVER WENDELL (1809–1894), May 60: 13
    And Isabella Stewart Gardner, Jul 59: 28, 133–34
HOLMES, SHERLOCK, IQ of, Mar 62: 72
HOLY ALLIANCE, Mar 63: 5
"HOLY FAMILY, THE," painting by Poussin, Mar 61: 90; illus, Mar 61: 91
HOLY LAND (see also PALESTINE)
    Military Orders in, Mar 61: 48–53, 56, 60, 70
    In Third Crusade, Jan 59: 85–91, 130–31
HOLY LEAGUE, and Battle of Lepanto, Jul 63: 50
HOLY ROMAN EMPIRE
    As second period of unity in Europe, Mar 63: 4–5
    Sicily under, Sep 61: 30, 32, 36
    Struggle with Ottoman Empire, Jul 63: 52, 60
"HOMAGE TO CÉZANNE," painting by Maurice Denis, Mar 62: 15
"HOME FROM THE HILL," novel by William Humphrey, Mar 59: 14, 117
HOME FURNISHINGS. See HOUSE FURNISHINGS
HOMER, Jan 60: 45, Sep 63: 97
    Age of, Jan 61: 73–99
    Attitude toward nature, Mar 60: 13
    Early manuscripts of works by, Nov 62: 78; illus, Nov 62: 84–85
    Known world of, Jul 60: 85
    Odyssey, use of: by Ezra Pound, Jan 61: 116, 117–18; by James Joyce, Jan 61: 116
    In Renaissance curriculum, Jan 60: 62
    Sculptured head of, Jan 61: 76
    Travelers to world of, quoted, Jan 61: 91
    On wild swans, quoted, Sep 58: 87, 140
HOMER, WINSLOW, Sep 58: 113, Sep 60: 34, 102
    Painting by, May 63: cover, 3
"HOMER'S AGE OF HEROES," article by C. M. Bowra, Jan 61: 73–99
"HOMMES DE LA DANSE, LES," book, photographs by Michel Huet from, Jul 59: 49–55
HOMPESCH, FERDINAND VON, Mar 61: 68
HONDIUS, GERRIT, portrait of, with painting by, Jul 61: 25
HONEGGER, ARTHUR, Mar 62: 99, Nov 62: 46
"HONEST TO GOD," book by John A. T. Robinson
    Comment on, by Douglas Auchincloss, Sep 63: 8–9
    Excerpt from, Sep 63: 4–7, 104–6
    Reply to, by Archbishop of Canterbury, Sep 63: 107
HONORIUS, ROMAN EMPEROR, quoted on Arles, Jul 59: 130
"HONOURABLE PICNIC, THE," quoted, Mar 61: 10
HONTHORST, GERARD VAN, Jul 61: 90
HOOCH, PIETER DE, Sep 58: 28, Jul 63: 106
HOOD, RAYMOND, Jan 63: 12
HOOFT, PIETER CORNELISZOON, Sep 58: 26
HOOVER, HERBERT, Mar 63: 107
    Quoted: on American system, Mar 59: 6; on depression, Sep 63: 101
    As Scarcity man, Jul 60: 68
HOPE, BOB, May 63: 111
"HOPE OF ISRAEL, THE," book by Menasseh ben Israel, Mar 60: 103
HOPKINS, BARBARA, Nov 59: 126
HOPKINS, GERARD MANLEY, Sep 61: 119
HOPKINS, MARK, Jan 59: 7
HOPKINS, MATTHEW, Nov 59: 61
HOPKINS INSTITUTE OF ART, Jan 59: 7
HOPKINSON, EDWARD, JR., portrait of, Jul 63: 4
HOPPER, EDWARD, Sep 58: 113, Jul 62: 15
    Paintings by, Sep 58: 113, Jul 61: 11
    Portrait of, Jul 61: 10
HOPPER, HEDDA, Jul 63: 89
HOPPNER, JOHN, Mar 63: 69, Jul 63: 106
HORACE, Sep 58: 130
    Quoted: on Greece, May 62: 44; on his poetry, May 59: 11; on nature, Sep 63: 107
    In Renaissance curriculum, Jan 60: 62
    Survival of works by, Nov 62: 76, 89
HORAN, ROBERT, Jan 59: 18, 19
"HORIZON," English magazine, quoted on American painting, Nov 59: 32, 41
HORN, CAPE, Sep 58: 19
HORNER, FRANCIS, Mar 59: 92
HORNEY, KAREN, Jul 59: 72
HOROWITZ, VLADIMIR, Jan 60: 76, Sep 61: 84, 85
"HORRIBLE," book by Tomi Ungerer, Jan 61: 128, 130
HORROCKS, BRIAN, portrait of, May 62: 77
HORSE
    Ancient harness for, Sep 58: 149
    Earliest use as draft animal, Sep 58: 147–48
HORSEMANSHIP, education in, as part of Grand Tour, Nov 59: 90, 98–99
HORSE RACING, among Etruscans, May 60: 78

HORSLEY, JOHN, Jan 59: 33
HORTA, VICTOR, Mar 62: 39
    Building designed by, Mar 62: 38–39
HORTENSE, QUEEN OF HOLLAND, May 63: 54
HORUS, FOLLOWERS OF, Mar 63: 57
HOSPITALLERS. See KNIGHTS OF ST. JOHN
HOSPITAL OF ST. JOHN OF JERUSALEM, MOST VENERABLE ORDER OF, Mar 61: 70
"HOSTAGE, THE," play, Mar 61: 44–45, May 61: 51
    Reviewed, Jan 61: 113–14
HOSTILIAN, Sep 63: 40
HOTCHNER, A. E., Jan 62: 103
HOTELS, culture of non-hotel, Mar 63: 115–17
"HOT-TEMPERED HIGH C, THE," article by Joseph Wechsberg, Sep 59: 50–57
HOUDETOT, MME D', Mar 61: 117
HOUDINI, HARRY (EHRICH WEISS), Jan 59: 108, 109
    Photograph of, Jul 59: 116
HOUET, LAURENS, painting by, Sep 60: 66–67
HOUGHTON, ARTHUR A., JR., Jul 62: 4, 6–7, 9
    Portrait of, Jul 62: 8
HOUGHTON HALL, Nov 58: 42, 46, 52
HOULIHAN (or HOOLIGAN), PATRICK, May 60: 128
"HOUSATONIC, THE," photographs by Hans Namuth, May 60: 10–29
HOUSE FURNISHINGS
    Advertising of, Nov 59: 113, 116
    Bauhaus influence on, Nov 61: 71, 72, 73
    Designs by Isamu Noguchi, Mar 60: 105
HOUSEHOLD APPLIANCES, fashion cycles in design of, Mar 59: 115
HOUSEMAN, JOHN, Jan 63: 106, Jul 63: 87
"HOUSE OF CONNELLY, THE," play, Nov 62: 106
"HOUSE OF EXILE, THE," book by Nora Waln, Nov 63: 107
"HOUSE OF FLOWERS," musical, Nov 60: 86, May 63: 49
"HOUSE OF MIRTH, THE," novel by Edith Wharton, Mar 59: 15
"HOUSE OF REGRETS," play, Nov 58: 82, 85, 137
HOUSE OF THE VETTII, Mar 62: 45
"HOUSE ON 92ND STREET, THE," motion picture, Mar 61: 98
"HOUSE THAT IS MORE THAN A HOME, THE," article by Mary Cable, Sep 61: 68–77
HOUSING (see also ARCHITECTURE, Domestic)
    Developments, cartoon, Sep 58: 53
    In Paris as rebuilt by Haussmann, May 63: 56, 67
    In U.S. and U.S.S.R. compared, Jul 62: 113–15
HOUSMAN, A. E., Jul 61: 113
    Quoted, Nov 61: 104, Jul 63: 73
HOUSTON, TEX., May 61: 18
    Alley Theatre, Jan 62: 9, 13
HOUTMAN, CORNELIS DE, Sep 58: 19, 25
HOVEDEN, ROGER OF. See ROGER OF HOVEDEN
HOVHANESS, ALAN, Nov 58: 91
HOWARD, physician of Baltimore, Md., *c.* 1800, Nov 59: 86
HOWARD, shoemaker's daughter, Brighton, England, *c.* 1848, May 63: 58
HOWARD, EBENEZER, Jul 59: 11
HOWARD, HENRY (EARL OF SURREY), Mar 63: 88
HOWARD, JOHN, May 59: 129
HOWARD, JOHN GALEN, Jan 59: 10
HOWARD, LESLIE, Sep 63: 76
    Photographs of, Sep 63: 77, 78
HOWARD, ROBERT, Jan 59: 14
HOWARD, THOMAS (1ST EARL OF SUFFOLK), house built by, Nov 58: 41 (illus), 51
HOWARD, TREVOR, May 63: 111, Sep 63: 42
HOWARD JOHNSON CHAIN, Mar 63: 117
"HOW CAN MAN GET ALONG WITHOUT WAR?" excerpt from *African Genesis,* book by Robert Ardrey, Nov 61: 38–41
HOWE, GEORGE, Sep 62: 58
HOWE, IRVING, Jan 60: 7
HOWE, JULIA WARD, Jul 59: 32
HOWE, RICHARD, EARL, Mar 62: 82
HOWELL, JAMES, on Venice, quoted, Mar 63: 15
HOWELLS, WILLIAM DEAN, Alfred Kazin quoted on, Jul 62: 99, 100
"HOWL," poem by Allen Ginsberg, Sep 58: 38, 41, 42, Jan 59: 19, Sep 61: 116
    Quoted and satirized, Sep 61: 119, 121
"HOW THEY LIVE AND DIE IN NAPLES," photographs by Herbert List with text by Vittorio de Sica, Sep 63: 49–59
"HOW TO BUY A TUBA," article by James J. Faran, Jr., Nov 63: 97–99
"HOW TO MAKE THE ROUND TABLE SQUARE," article by Kenneth R. Morgan, May 60: 115–18
"HOW TO SHOOT DUCKS, HOW TO CATCH TROUT," book by Robert Osborn, Sep 60: 43
HOYLE, FRED, Jan 59: 123

HSÜAN TSANG, on India, quoted, Sep 63: 68
HUBER, JOHANN, painting by, Mar 61: 119
"HUCKLEBERRY FINN," novel by Mark Twain
Characterization of "Jim," Jan 60: 96
Compared to *The Catcher in the Rye,* May 62: 101, 102, 103
Hemingway, Ernest, quoted on, Jan 59: 133
King and the Duke, The, play based on, Mar 60: 98, 120
Quoted, Sep 59: 27
HUDNUT, JOSEPH, on Washington Monument, quoted, Jan 60: 21–22
HUDSON, HENRY, Sep 58: 19
Mermaid-sighting by, Jan 60: 131
HUDSON, W. H., Sep 63: 100
Crystal Age, A, Mar 63: 77
"HUDSON REVIEW, THE," Sep 61: 119
On "Beat" poetry, quoted, Sep 61: 121
HUERTA, JEAN DE LA, Sep 58: 62
HUET, MICHEL, "Where the Dance Enacts Daily Life," photographs by, from *Les Hommes de la Danse,* Jul 59: 49–55
HUET, PIERRE DANIEL, Nov 61: 33, 34
HUGHES, RICHARD, Jan 60: 108
HUGHES, ROBERT, Mar 61: 100
HUGHES, THOMAS, Sep 61: 13
HUGH-JONES, SIRIOL, "The Lord and the Regalia," article by, May 63: 92–96
HUGO, VICTOR, Nov 59: 66–67, 68, Mar 61: 32, May 61: 65, 70, 82, 83, Sep 62: 20, Mar 63: 7
In painting by Joseph Danhauser, May 61: 84–85
Portrait of, May 61: 83
On regime of Napoleon III, quoted, Sep 62: 113
Seine River anecdote told by, Jul 62: 61, 64
HUGUENOTS, Mar 60: 101
HUGUES II, DUKE OF BURGUNDY, Sep 61: 48, 57
"HUIS CLOS." See "NO EXIT"
HULAGU KHAN, Jan 63: 67
HULTBERG, JOHN, Jan 59: 13
"HUMAN CONDITION II, THE," painting by René Magritte, Jan 62: 82; illus, Jan 62: 87
"HUMAN DESTINY," book by Pierre Lecomte du Noüy, Jan 59: 28
HUMANISM
Erasmus as symbol of, May 62: 89–95
Vs. witch mania, Nov 59: 59
HUMANITIES, CRISIS IN. See "CRISIS IN THE HUMANITIES"
HUMBERT I, KING OF ITALY, Nov 58: 107
HUMBOLDT, ALEXANDER VON, Jul 59: 56–69, 128
Paintings from sketches by, Jul 59: 60–61, 63–66
Portraits of, Jul 59: 56, 69
HUMBOLDT, WILHELM VON, Jul 59: 57–58
HUME, BENITA, Sep 63: 76
HUME, DAVID, attitude toward Joan of Arc, Mar 62: 95, 96
HUME, TOBIAS, Nov 60: 94
HUMOR
Of contemporary playwrights, Mar 63: 106–9
Of English vaudeville, vs. American stage humor, Jan 61: 122–23
Of François, André, May 59: 108–21
Hall, Edward T., quoted on jokes, Mar 60: 123
Hoax, art of, Jan 61: 66–72
Man's need of novelty and, Jul 59: 108–9
Sense and nonsense, Sep 58: 129–31
HUMPHREY, WILLIAM
Home from the Hill, Mar 59: 14, 117
Photograph of, Mar 59: 15
HUMPHREY OF TORON, Jan 59: 88, 89–90, 91
HUMPHRIES, ROLFE, Nov 58: 108
"HUMPTY DUMPTY," sculpture by Isamu Noguchi, Mar 60: 108
HUNDRED YEARS' WAR
France during, Nov 61: 88, 97
Joan of Arc's career in, Mar 62: 89–95
HUNGARY
Crown jewels of, May 63: 94, 95
Kocsi carts, Sep 58: 150
Messianic year of 1666, Mar 60: 125
Poker-playing in, Nov 63: 57, 58
Sovereign Order of Malta, Mar 61: 70
Struggle with Ottoman Empire, Jul 63: 52, 60
Witch mania, Nov 59: 58, 59
World War I aftermath, Jan 59: 121
"HUNGRY I, THE," San Francisco cabaret, Jan 62: 66, 68
HUNS, Attila and Leo the Great, May 63: 76–80
HUNT, ALBERT W., May 62: 8
HUNT, A. S., Nov 62: 93
HUNT, H. L., Mar 60: 48
HUNT, HOLMAN, May 62: 64, 73, 78
HUNT, LEIGH, on William Charles Macready and Edmund Kean, quoted, Mar 62: 117
HUNT, MORTON M., articles by

Excerpt from *The Natural History of Love,* Sep 59: 113–17
"Love According to Madison Avenue," Nov 59: 113–17
"Memorandum from Eleanor of Aquitaine to Abigail van Buren and Ann Landers," May 60: 30–31
HUNTER, IAN, Sep 63: 77, 80
HUNTER, JEAN, Sep 59: 123
HUNTER, RENNA, Sep 59: 123
HUNTER, SAM, Nov 59: 120
HUNTER, TAB, Jan 59: 139
"HUNT FOR HEROES, THE," article by Robert Hatch, May 62: 110–12
"HUNTING OF THE SNARK," verses by Lewis Carroll, Jul 61: 113
Quoted, Jul 61: 114; in Latin, Jul 61: 114
HUNTINGTON, ANNA HYATT, Mar 62: 97, 98
HUNTINGTON, HENRY E., Jul 59: 28–29, Nov 60: 98, 99–100, 101
HUNTINGTON HARTFORD FOUNDATION, Mar 63: 27, 32, Jul 63: 70
HUNTLEY, G. P., Jan 59: 56
HURD, PETER, Sep 61: 97
HUROK, SOL, Jan 61: 49
HURST, DAVID, Jan 61: 101
Portrait of, Jan 61: 100
HURST, FANNIE, *Back Street,* motion picture version, May 63: 110–11
HUSSEIN BAYQARA, Jan 63: 67
HUSSEY, TACITUS, Iowa song, quoted, Nov 61: 119
"HUSTLER, THE," motion picture, Jan 62: 112
HUSTON, JOHN, Mar 60: 5, Nov 61: 115, Jul 63: 90
HUTCHINS, ROBERT M., Sep 58: 98, 102, Mar 60: 49, Jan 62: 4
Photograph of, Sep 58: 99
HUTTON, JAMES, Jul 60: 30
HUXLEY, ALDOUS, Jan 60: 6, Jul 61: 5, May 63: 28, Jul 63: 13, 70
After Many a Summer Dies the Swan, quoted, Jan 60: 11
Brave New World, Jul 59: 111, Mar 63: 73, 79, Nov 63: 104–5, 108
Island, Nov 63: 108, 109
Quoted: on armies, May 60: 123; on Baroque art, Jul 60: 42; on solitude, Sep 58: 53; on speed, Jan 62: 18; on utopias, Mar 63: 73–74, 78
HUXLEY, JULIAN
On God, quoted, Sep 63: 9
"Man's Challenge: The Use of the Earth," article by, Sep 58: 48–55
In painting by Feliks Topolski, Nov 60: 131
HUXLEY, THOMAS HENRY
In painting by W. P. Frith, May 62: 62
In South Seas, Jan 60: 31
HUXTABLE, ADA LOUISE, articles by
"Out of a Fair, a City," May 60: 80–87
"Street Furniture," Nov 59: 105–12
"Water: The Wine of Architecture," May 62: 10–33
HUYGENS, CONSTANTIJN, Sep 58: 24, 26
Portrait of, Sep 58: 33
HUYSMANS, JORIS-KARL, Jul 62: 90
HYDE, JAMES HAZEN, Nov 58: 73, Jul 63: 77
HYDRAULUS, Mar 60: 74
HYPERBOLUS, Jan 60: 44
HYPODERMIC THEORY OF COMMUNICATION, Mar 60: 49

I

IANELLI, ALFONSO, Sep 60: 128
"IA ORANA MARIA," painting by Paul Gauguin, Jan 60: 32; illus, Jan 60: 40
IBERIA, Moslem rule in, Sep 62: 72–93
IBN AL-ARABI, Sep 62: 88
IBN-HAWQAL, on Palermo, quoted, Sep 61: 28
IBN-HAZM, Sep 62: 87
IBN-JUBAIR, on Palermo, quoted, Sep 61: 30
IBN TUFAIL, Sep 62: 88
IBNU SA'ID, Moorish historian, quoted, Sep 62: 87
IBRAHIM, OTTOMAN SULTAN, May 59: 131
IBSEN, HENRIK, Jul 59: 48, Jul 61: 116, Nov 63: 41
Caricatures of, Jan 62: 107
Hedda Gabler, with Anne Meacham, May 61: 99
Persistence of Ibsenism, Jan 62: 106–8
"ICARIA, JOURNEY TO," romance by Étienne Cabet, Mar 63: 76
"ICELANDER, THE," poet, Jan 60: 108–9
"ICEMAN COMETH, THE," play, Jan 59: 22, Mar 60: 32, Sep 62: 111
At Circle in the Square, Mar 60: 98, 120, 121
ICHTHYOCENTAURS, Jan 60: 134
ICONOCLAST, origin of word, Nov 63: 22

"ICONOGRAPHY OF HEAVENLY BEINGS, AN," article by Gilbert Highet, Nov 60: 26–49
ICONS, in Byzantine Empire, Nov 63: 22, 26, 28
IDAHO, state song, quoted, Nov 61: 119
"IDIOT, THE," motion picture, Jul 62: 42
"IDIOT'S DELIGHT," play, Jul 62: 40
IDLEWILD AIRPORT. See NEW YORK INTERNATIONAL AIRPORT
IDRI-MI, KING OF ALALAKH, life story of, Nov 62: 90; illus, Nov 62: 79
IDRISI, AL-
Map by, Sep 62: 80–81
On Palermo, quoted, Sep 61: 30
IFE, NIGERIA, Mar 63: 41 (map), 44, 46, 53
Art objects from, illus, Mar 63: 47, 51
IGNATIUS OF LOYOLA, Nov 61: 109
"I HAIL THEE, MARY," painting. See "IA ORANA MARIA"
"I HEAR AMERICA SINGING—ABROAD," article by Winthrop Sargeant, Nov 61: 76–81
IHERING, HERBERT, on Bertolt Brecht, quoted, May 62: 36
"IKIRU," motion picture, Jul 62: 45–46
"I KNOW WHERE I'M GOING," motion picture, Mar 61: 98
ILE DE LA CITÉ, Paris, May 63: 52–53, 64
"ILIAD, THE"
Historical light on, Jan 61: 73–79, 94
Sculptural representations of heroes of, in Cave of Tiberius, May 59: 122–24
ILIFFE. See WYNDHAM, "MRS."
"I'LL CRY TOMORROW," book about Lillian Roth, Jul 60: 120
ILLINOIS, UNIVERSITY OF, projected assembly hall, Mar 59: 123
ILLINOIS STATE NORMAL UNIVERSITY, Mar 60: 71
ILLUMINATED MANUSCRIPTS, André Malraux quoted on, Nov 58: 16
"ILLUMINATION OF JEAN FOUQUET, THE," article by Marshall B. Davidson, Nov 61: 88–97
"I MADE A FOOL OF MYSELF OVER JOHN FOSTER DULLES," song, Sep 61: 80
"IMAGE OF THE WHITE MAN IN THE ART OF OTHER RACES, THE," portfolio assembled and described by John Maass, Sep 60: 15–29
"IMAGINARY AUDIENCE, THE," article by Eric Larrabee, Mar 60: 46–51
"IMAGINARY INVALID, THE," play by Molière, May 62: 51
IMAGINARY MUSEUM, Nov 58: 8, 115, 117
IMBRIE, ANDREW, Jan 59: 21
IMMACULATE HEART TRIO, photograph of, Nov 62: 47
"IMMORTAL HUSBAND, THE," play, May 61: 99
IMPERIAL HOTEL, Tokyo, Sep 59: 8
IMPRESSIONISTS, of painting, Sep 58: 113, Jul 62: 65
IMPROVISATION, as aesthetic principle, Sep 60: 31
In cabaret and revue satire, Jan 62: 66–71
In music, Jan 63: 76–81
In theatre, Mar 61: 45
"IMPROVISATION, OR THE SHEPHERD'S CHAMELEON," play by Eugène Ionesco, May 61: 95
Excerpt from, May 61: 92, 94, 96
IMPROVISATION CHAMBER ENSEMBLE, Jan 63: 76–81, 105
"I'M TALKING ABOUT JERUSALEM," play, Jul 61: 117
"IN AND OUT BOOK," Nov 59: 22
INANNA, new treasures found in temple dedicated to, Nov 61: 84–87
INCOME TAX, Sep 61: 17, Nov 62: 118, 119
"INDEPENDENT SIX, THE," May 60: 15
INDIA
Alexander the Great in, Mar 59: 45–46, 55–56
Apsarases of, Nov 60: 30–31
Babur quoted on, Mar 61: 31–32
Bronze Age trade of, Jul 60: 86–87
Burton, Richard Francis, in, Jul 63: 110–12
Chandigarh, Mar 61: 36
Coromandel Coast, Mar 61: 22
Dance of, Sep 63: 64–73
Delhi, May 62: 84–87; Red Fort at, Mar 61: 21
Fox, Charles J., vs. British imperialism in, May 60: 99, 101
Gardens of, May 59: 27, 31, 44
Kashmir, Mar 61: 31, 32
Racial relations before and after mutiny of 1857, Sep 60: 12–13
White man as portrayed by artists of, Sep 60: 12, 13–14, 19–21
INDIANS, AMERICAN
Ivory used by, May 60: 121
Languages of: their study in relation to Structural Linguistics and teaching of English, Jul 63: 34, 44

Of Mexico, Alexander von Humboldt quoted on, Jul 59: 67

Montezuma's encounter with Cortes, Nov 63: 92–96

Shinnecocks, May 63: 8

White man as portrayed by, Sep 60: 26–27

"INDIFFERENT SHEPHERD, THE," play, Nov 58: 137–38

INDIVIDUALISM
Business pressures against, Mar 59: 6, 128
Federal tax laws vs., Nov 62: 118–19
As legacy of romantic revolt, May 61: 64, 65, 66, 72
Nonconformism, dangers of, Mar 59: 112
Revolt against Togetherness, Nov 58: 30–33, 146–47
In Scarcity and in Abundance economies, Jul 60: 71–72

INDONESIA, island "paradises" of, Mar 61: 22–23, 23–24, 28, 31

INDUSTRIAL ACCIDENTS, role of Knights of St. John, Mar 61: 70

INDUSTRIAL CIVILIZATION
Future of, Jan 59: 92–94, 128–29
Leisure in, Nov 63: 102–9
As spread by United States, May 60: 6–9, 122–23

INDUSTRIAL DESIGN
Bauhaus and its influence, Nov 61: 58–75
In Finland: Tapio and Rut Bryk Wirkkala, Jul 63: 62–67
In United States, Sep 60: 38–40

INDUSTRIAL REVOLUTION
Effect on cities, Jul 61: 61
Escape motif following, May 61: 52, 53
In India, May 62: 84–85
Schism between science and philosophy in, Jul 61: 9

INDUSTRY (see also BUSINESS and INDUSTRY)
In urban centers, Venice as model for, Jul 61: 57

"INFERNO," poem by Dante, Jan 59: 46

INFORMATION THEORY, Jul 59: 107

INFRARED RAYS, Nov 63: 50

"IN FRONT OF THE WINDOW," painting by Pierre Bonnard, Mar 62: 16; illus, Mar 62: 17

INGE, WILLIAM, Jan 62: 104, Nov 62: 108
The Dark at the Top of the Stairs, Nov 58: 64

INGERSOLL, R. STURGIS, Jul 63: 23
Portrait of, Jul 63: 23

INGRES, JEAN AUGUSTE DOMINIQUE, Jan 59: 95, May 61: 66, Mar 62: 63
Paintings by. See ILLUSTRATIONS INDEX
Self-portrait, Sep 60: 70

"INHERIT THE WIND," play, Nov 58: 63

INLAND STEEL COMPANY, Sep 58: 110

"INMOST LEAF, THE," book by Alfred Kazin, Jul 62: 98, 100

INNES, WILLIAM, Jan 60: 114, 117

INNOCENT III, POPE, Nov 58: 106

INNOCENT IV, POPE, Nov 58: 106

INNOCENT VIII, POPE, Jan 62: 31, 32
And witch mania, Nov 59: 59

INNOCENT X, POPE, Jan 62: 45

"INNOCENT AMUSEMENTS OF JEAN ANOUILH, THE," article by Germaine Brée, Nov 60: 50–55, 126–27

"INNOCENT EYE OF A MAN OF GALILEE, THE," paintings by Shalom Moskovitz, Jul 61: 120–28

"IN PRINT," articles on American authors
Adler, Edward, Sep 62: 64–65
Barth, John, Jan 63: 36–37
Jacobs, Jane, Jul 62: 50–51
Updike, John, Mar 62: 84–85

INQUISITION
History of, by H. C. Lea, Nov 59: 59, 62
Witch mania developed by, Nov 59: 59–63

"IN REVOLT AGAINST TOGETHERNESS," article by William Harlan Hale, Nov 58: 30–33, 146–47

"IN SEARCH OF PARADISE," article by Santha Rama Rau, Mar 61: 20–33

"IN SEARCH OF SHYLOCK," article by Walter Kerr, Jan 60: 89–96

"IN SEARCH OF THE ETRUSCANS," article by Raymond Bloch, May 60: 56–79

INSTITUTE FOR ADVANCED STUDY, Sep 59: 25

INSTITUTE FOR DEFENSE ANALYSES, Princeton, N.J., Sep 59: 27

INSTITUTE FOR INTERNATIONAL SOCIAL RESEARCH, Sep 59: 25

INSTITUTE OF ENVIRONMENTAL ENGINEERS, Sep 59: 25

INSURANCE COMPANIES OF PHILADELPHIA, Jul 63: 25

INTELLIGENCE QUOTIENT
And coming generation of genius, Mar 62: 72–75
In industrial civilization, Nov 63: 104
Of twenty geniuses, May 60: 32, 33

INTERIOR DECORATION
Art and, May 63: 90–91
"At Home Through the Ages," drawings by Philippe Julian, Mar 63: 80–83

INTERNATIONAL BUSINESS MACHINES CORPORATION, Sep 58: 110

INTERNATIONAL COUNCIL OF THE MUSEUM OF MODERN ART, Sep 58: 113

INTERNATIONAL EXPOSITION OF ART, SCIENCE, INDUSTRY AND MANUFACTURE, May 60: 80

INTERNATIONAL GEOPHYSICAL YEAR, Nov 63: 53

INTERNATIONALISM
Europe's fifth period of unity, Mar 63: 4–9
Roosevelt, Theodore, and, Nov 63: 71

INTERVIEWS. See "ARTIST SPEAKS FOR HIMSELF, THE"

"IN THE GLOW OF THE PERFECT PATRON," article by Peter Quennell, Mar 63: 62–71

"IN THE JUNGLE OF CITIES," play, Mar 62: 108, May 62: 35

"IN THE LIGHT OF THE SUN," article by Arthur C. Clarke, Nov 63: 48–55

"IN THE SEVEN WOODS," poems by William Butler Yeats, Mar 59: 87–88

"IN THE SOUTH SEAS," book by Robert Louis Stevenson, Jan 60: 124

"IN THE SUMMER HOUSE," play, Mar 60: 119

"IN THE WORLD'S ATTIC," book by Henrietta Sands Merrick, quoted, Mar 61: 31

"INTOLERANCE," motion picture, May 61: 52

"INTRODUCTION TO THE SITWELLS, AN," article by Peter Quennell, Jan 60: 108–9

"INVASION FROM MARS, THE," book by Hadley Cantril, Jul 63: 88

"INVENTION," tape recorder composition by Otto Luening, Jan 59: 54

INVERNESS, CALIF., Jan 59: 7

IONESCO, EUGÈNE, Jul 61: 116, Sep 62: 34, 35, 36, 37, 39, 40, 41, May 63: 108
Bald Soprano, The, Nov 58: 63, Jan 61: 101, Jan 62: 103
Improvisation, or The Shepherd's Chameleon, excerpt from, May 61: 92, 94, 96
Interview with, May 61: 89–91, 93, 95, 97
Jack, Jan 61: 101
Portrait of, May 61: 94
Rhinoceros, May 62: 51, 112, Mar 63: 107

"IONISATION," musical composition by Edgard Varèse, Sep 58: 132

IOWA
Khrushchev visit to Coon Rapids, Mar 60: 51
State song, quoted, Nov 61: 119

IQ. See INTELLIGENCE QUOTIENT

IRAN (see also ISFAHAN; PERSIA)
Marlik Tepe and its gold treasure, Nov 62: 100–4
Tepe Sarab, Sep 62: 4, 7 (map)

"IRAN IN THE ANCIENT EAST," book by Ernst Herzfeld, quoted, Nov 62: 102

IRAQ (see also MESOPOTAMIA)
Archaeological discoveries near Kirkuk, Sep 62: 4–9

IRELAND
House of Coole, Mar 59: 86–89
Monastery manuscripts, Sep 59: 125–26
Rural buses, Mar 59: 120

IRENE, BYZANTINE EMPRESS, Nov 63: 26

IRIS, SAMUEL, Jul 62: 49

IRISH LAND LEAGUE, May 60: 127

"IRMA LA DOUCE," musical, May 61: 51

IRON AGE
In Africa, Mar 63: 41 (map), 43–44, 53, 57, 58
Beginning of, Jul 60: 113

IRON CURTAIN
In Russia, Sep 59: 60, 62
Of Turkish Empire, Sep 58: 46

"IRON DUKE," locomotive, Jan 59: 39

IRVING, TEX., May 61: 19

IRVING, HENRY, Jul 59: 28

IRVING, JULES, Jan 59: 22

IRVING, WASHINGTON, Nov 59: 100
On Moslems leaving Granada, quoted, Sep 62: 92
Portrait of, Nov 59: 100

ISAACSON, LEONARD M., Jan 63: 78

ISABELLA, ARCHDUCHESS OF AUSTRIA, Jul 61: 90

ISABELLA I, QUEEN OF CASTILE, in bronze relief, Sep 62: 92

ISABELLA, QUEEN OF JERUSALEM, Jan 59: 88, 89–90, 130

ISABELLA OF BAVARIA, Mar 62: 89, 91

ISABEY, JEAN BAPTISTE, portrait of Mme de Staël by, Nov 58: 88

"ISAK DINESEN: MASTER TELLER OF TALES," article by Jean Stafford, Sep 59: 110–12

ISFAHAN, IRAN, Mar 61: 28, May 61: 24–32, Jan 63: 59 (map), 69, 72

ISHERWOOD, CHRISTOPHER. See AUDEN, W. H., co-author

ISIDORE THE MILESIAN, Nov 63: 12

ISIS, island and temple of, at Philae, Egypt, Jul 60: 10

"IS IT TRUE WHAT THE MOVIES SAY ABOUT

...," article by William K. Zinsser, May 59: 98–101

ISLAM (see also MOSLEMS)
Christian Military Orders vs., Mar 61: 51–65
Malikite school of theology, Sep 62: 75–76
In Persia, Jan 63: 52 (chart), 53, 69
Rule of, in Iberia, Sep 62: 72–93
Toynbee, Arnold J., quoted on, Jan 61: 63

"ISLAND," novel by Aldous Huxley, Mar 63: 79, Nov 63: 108, 109

"ISLAND GOD, THE," opera, Jan 60: 15

"IS OXFORD OUT OF THIS WORLD?" article by James Morris, Jan 63: 82–87

ISRAEL
Archaeological sites of Mallaha and Mount Carmel, Sep 62: 7 (map), 8
Caesarea festival, Jul 62: 30
Cave-dwellers of Safadi and Abu Matar, and their ivory figurines, Jan 62: 72–75
Chagall windows at Jerusalem medical center, Sep 62: 24; illus, Sep 62: cover, 3, 26–27
Extent of ancient kingdom, Nov 59: 118
Missing Ten Tribes of. See TEN LOST TRIBES OF ISRAEL

ISSUS, BATTLE OF, Mar 59: 34, 38

ISTANBUL, TURKEY, Sep 60: 125–26
Museum of Grand Seraglio, May 59: 56, 131

ISTOMIN, EUGENE, Jan 60: 74, 76, 81, Sep 61: 85, 86, Jul 62: 30
Portrait of, Jan 60: 77

ITALY (see also cities of, by name)
Architectural designs of Pier Luigi Nervi, Mar 59: 18–25, 121–24
And Battle of Lepanto, Jul 63: 50, 58
Byzantine legacy, Nov 63: 33–34
Capri, Mar 61: 22, 24
Churches. See under CHURCHES and SYNAGOGUES
Cities of, drawings by Domenico Gnoli, Jul 59: 135–44
Domestic architecture, Nov 58: 41
Etruscans in, May 60: 56–79
Fountains of, May 62: 12, 13–14, 15, 18–23
Gardens of, in Renaissance, May 59: 28–29, 32
In Grand Tour of 18th and 19th centuries, Nov 59: 86, 87, 94–96
Hadrian's Villa, May 63: 32–39; art objects from, Nov 59: 102
Herculaneum, Nov 59: 87, 96, Mar 62: 42–69
Literary prizes, Jul 63: 73
Motion pictures from, May 59: 99
Napoleon III and campaign of 1859, May 63: 63
Olivetti enterprises, Nov 59: 45–51, 127
Organ (musical instrument) in, Mar 60: 74
Pasta's influence, Jan 63: 34–35
Pompeii, Nov 59: 87, 96, Mar 62: 42–69; baths of, May 60: 39, 40–41
Sicily as province of, Sep 61: 38, 44
Streets of, Nov 61: 121–28
And Thirty Years' War, Nov 62: 33–41
Witch mania in, Nov 59: 62

"IT COULD BE YOU," television program, Jul 60: 6

"ITINERARIUM REGIS RICARDI," English chronicle, Jan 59: 130

ITTEN, JOHANNES, Nov 61: 64, 68
Photograph of, Nov 61: 62

ITURBI, JOSÉ, Jan 60: 10

IVAN III, GRAND DUKE OF RUSSIA, Nov 63: 34

IVAN IV, CZAR OF RUSSIA (IVAN THE TERRIBLE), Sep 60: 130, May 63: 102
In painting by Repin, Sep 60: 131

IVAN V, CZAR OF RUSSIA, Sep 59: 62, 66

"IVANHOE," novel by Walter Scott, Nov 58: 107

IVES, BEATRICE, Jul 63: 86

IVES, BURL, Nov 59: 31, 122, 124, 125

IVES, CHARLES, Jul 59: 20

"I VITELLONI," motion picture, May 59: 99, Mar 61: 98

IVORY, man's passion for and use of, May 60: 88–95, 120–21

IVORYTON, CONN., May 60: 94

IVREA, ITALY, Olivetti company in, Nov 59: 46–47, 50, 51, 127

"I WAS A TEEN-AGE FRANKENSTEIN," motion picture, Jan 59: 137

J

"JABBERWOCKY," poem by Lewis Carroll, Sep 58: 129–30, Jul 61: 113
Quoted, Jul 61: 115; in Greek, Jul 61: 115

"JACK," play, Jan 61: 101, May 61: 91, 97, Jul 61: 116

"JACKASS, THE," play, Mar 61: 47

JACKSON, ANDREW, Jul 63: 17

JACKSON, ANNE, May 63: 10
Photograph of, May 63: 11

JACKSON, C. D., Jul 62: 4, 5, 6, 11
Portrait of, Jul 62: 8
JACKSON, MAHALIA, Jan 60: 10
JACOBS, JANE, Jul 62: 50
On city-redevelopment projects, quoted, Jul 59: 7, May 63: 52
Photograph of, Jul 62: 51
JACOBSEN, ARNE, Nov 60: 16
JACOBSEN, JOSEPHINE, on J. D. Salinger, quoted, May 62: 101
JACOBS-HAVENITH, L., Jan 59: 47
JACOB'S PILLOW, May 60: 15
JACOPI, GIULIO, work in Cave of Tiberius, May 59: 102–7, 122–24
JACOPONI DA TODI, May 63: 29
JACQUEMARD, SIMONNE, Jul 63: 74
JACQUES DE VERONA, sketch by, Mar 60: 91
JAFFA
As port of entry for pilgrims to Holy Land, Mar 60: 84, 85
In Third Crusade, Jan 59: 90–91, 130–31
JAFFÉ, ANIELE, Memories, Dreams, Reflections, reviewed, Jan 63: 109–11
JAIME OF MAJORCA, Nov 60: 83
JAINISM, Jan 61: 63
JAKARTA, INDONESIA, trade fair at, May 60: 8
JALAL-UD-DIN-RUMI, May 61: 30, Jan 63: 67
JAMES I, KING OF ENGLAND, Sep 59: 132, Jul 61: 80, Nov 62: 38–39
British royal collection in time of, Jul 63: 93
Quoted: on Audley End, Nov 58: 41; on Oxford, Jan 63: 86
And witch mania, Nov 59: 60
JAMES II, KING OF ENGLAND, as collector of paintings, Jul 63: 96
JAMES III, KING OF SCOTLAND, and his son, in painting by Hugo van der Goes, Jul 63: 95
JAMES, SAINT, Nov 61: 111
Moslem raid on shrine of, Sep 62: 82
JAMES, CHARLES, May 63: 22
JAMES, CLIFTON, Jan 61: 71–72
JAMES, HENRY, Mar 59: 17, Jan 60: 7, Mar 60: 127, May 60: 13, Jan 62: 64
Gardner, Isabella Stewart, and, Jul 59: 27, 29
"Portrait" of, by Max Beerbohm, May 61: 36
Portrait of a Lady, play from, Mar 60: 120
Quoted: on American way, May 60: 7; on Capri, Mar 61: 24; on curiosity concerning the poet, Jul 61: 105; on Hugo, Nov 59: 68; on Renaissance fountains, May 59: 32
JAMES, JOHN, May 62: 14, 15
JAMES, WILLIAM, Jan 60: 7, May 63: 28, 114, Nov 63: 104
"Moral Equivalent of War, The," quoted, Nov 63: 106
On solitude, quoted, Sep 58: 12
JAMES FORRESTAL RESEARCH CENTER, Sep 59: 26, 119
JAMI, Jan 63: 67
JANIS, SIDNEY, Nov 59: 121
JANISSARIES, May 59: 60, 62, 63, 131
JANK, CHRISTIAN, Jan 61: 42
JANNINGS, EMIL, Jan 61: 27
JANSENISM
Pascal and, Jan 63: 100, 102
Voltaire's attitude toward, Mar 61: 115, May 61: 64
JAPAN
Airline advertisement for, Mar 59: 133
Architecture of Kenzo Tange, Sep 61: 58–63
Gardens of, May 59: 31, 50–51, Jul 59: 126
Imperial Poetry Contest, Jul 63: 73
Kyoto, Mar 61: 27
Lotus and the Robot, The, book by Arthur Koestler, excerpt from, Mar 61: 4–11
Motion pictures from, May 59: 99–100
White man as pictured by artists of, Sep 60: 12, 13, 14–17, 28
Zen Buddhism, Jul 59: 70–77, 126–27
JAPANESE ART
Influence on Frank Lloyd Wright, Sep 60: 127
Painting, May 60: 114
Wood block prints, revolution in, May 60: 102–14
JARMO, IRAQ, archaeological site, Sep 62: 7 (map), 8
JARRELL, RANDALL, Jul 63: 72
On Eisenhower administration and the arts, quoted, Sep 61: 9
Pictures from an Institution, Sep 60: 118–19
JARRY, ALFRED, May 61: 89
JASON, myth of, in Cave of Tiberius sculpture, May 59: 123
JAUREGUI, JUAN DE, painting attributed to, Nov 61: 107
JAVITS, JACOB, Jul 61: 68, Sep 61: 17, Nov 62: 18, Jul 63: 73
JAY, JOHN, Nov 60: 20–21

Portrait of, Nov 60: 22
JAYAVARMAN II, KING OF CAMBODIA, Jan 59: 62
JAYAVARMAN VII, KING OF CAMBODIA, Jan 59: 81
JAZZ
Davis, Miles, May 61: 100–1
Impression of, drawing by Bob Gill, Jan 63: 120
Improvisation in, Jan 63: 77, 79
Musician as artist of tradition, Jan 63: 74–75
As popular art, Jan 60: 10
Stravinsky, Igor, quoted on, Sep 58: 132
"JAZZ DANCE," motion picture, Mar 61: 17
"JAZZ ON A SUMMER'S DAY," motion picture, Mar 61: 18–19
"J.B.," play, Jul 59: 42, 44, Jan 60: 49–56, May 62: 82, Jan 63: 88
"JEALOUSY," novel by Alain Robbe-Grillet, Jan 62: 99, 100
"JEAN CHRISTOPHE," novel by Romain Rolland, Mar 63: 6
JEAN DE BRUGES (LORD OF GRUTHUYSE), Nov 58: 96
In tournament, painting, Nov 58: cover, 3
"JEANNE D'ARC REVINT," novel by André Dahl, Mar 62: 97
JEANNE DES ARMOISES, Mar 62: 93
JEAN SANS PEUR, DUKE OF BURGUNDY, Mar 62: 91
JEBBA, NIGERIA, Tsoede bronzes found at, Mar 63: 51
"JEDERMANN," play, Tyrone Guthrie quoted on, Jan 61: 32
JEFFERIES, RICHARD, May 61: 53
JEFFERS, ROBINSON, Jan 59: 16, Jul 63: 70
Medea, Mar 60: 119
Portrait of, Jan 59: 19
JEFFERSON, THOMAS, Jul 60: 42, Nov 60: 20, Sep 61: 13
On cities, quoted, Jul 59: 11
Humboldt, Alexander von, and, Jul 59: 62, 69
Influence on American architecture, Jan 60: 22
Memorandum to Dean Rusk from, Jul 61: 30–31
Portraits of, Nov 60: 23, Jul 61: 30
JEFFERSON MEMORIAL, Washington, D.C., Eero Saarinen quoted on, Jul 60: 79, 82
JEFFERSON NATIONAL EXPANSION MEMORIAL, St. Louis, Mo., Jul 60: 79, 82
JEFFREY, FRANCIS, Mar 59: 92, 93, 95
JEFFRIES, JOHN, Sep 58: 119
JEHANGIR, EMPEROR OF HINDUSTAN, Mar 61: 31, 32
JELLICOE, ANN, Jan 63: 32
Photograph of, Jan 63: 31
JENA, BATTLE OF, Sep 63: 30, 31
JENKINS, CLAUDE, Jan 63: 85
JENKINS, JOHN, Nov 62: 43
JENKINS, KATHLEEN, Mar 60: 32
JENKINS, THOMAS, Nov 59: 95
JENNINGS, C. ROBERT, articles by
"On Screen: John Frankenheimer," Mar 63: 34–35
"On Stage: Salome Jens," Jan 62: 102–3
JENS, ARNETTE, Jan 62: 103
Photograph of, May 61: 50
JENS, ARNOLD JOHN, Jan 62: 103
JENS, SALOME, Jan 62: 103
Photograph of, Jan 62: 102
JENS, SALOMEA SZUJEWSKI, Jan 62: 103
JENSEN, GEORG, Jul 63: 63
JENSEN, OLIVER, articles and features by
"Amateurs All," Jul 62: 96–97
"Chance Meeting on the American Road," Nov 58: 36–37
"Christmas Gift Suggestions," Nov 58: 140–41
"Clouds on the Horizon," Mar 59: 133–35
Introduction to "Family Album" of Bertha F. Beasely, Nov 58: 122
"On the Horizon: The forward look and a backward glance," Sep 58: 152
"Proposal of Marriage, A," Jan 60: 106–7
"Sand Castle, The," Jul 61: 106–7
"See Manhattan While It Lasts: A Walking Tour," with drawings by John Rombola, May 63: 116–20
"Sociologists at Work," Mar 60: 122–23
"Trojan Horseless Carriage, The," Jul 60: 118–19
"Who's Underdeveloped?" Jan 63: 116–17
"Your Friendly Fidvciary," Mar 61: 120–21
"JEREMIAH," symphony by Leonard Bernstein, Jul 59: 22
JERICHO, archaeological work at site of, Sep 62: 7 (map), 8
JERITZA, MARIA, Sep 59: 53, 56–57
JEROME, SAINT, Mar 61: 94, May 62: 92
Portrait of, Nov 62: cover, 3
In Renaissance curriculum, Jan 60: 62
JERSEY, ENGLAND, Mar 61: 32
JERUSALEM
Chagall windows at medical center synagogue, Sep 62: 24; illus, Sep 62: cover, 3, 26–27
Knights of St. John and Knights of the Temple in, Mar 61:

51–52
Pilgrimage of Friar Felix Fabri to, Mar 60: 81–85, 90–91
St. John's Hospital, Mar 61: 48, 51, 52, 56, 70
Siege of, in First Crusade, Jan 59: 87, Mar 61: 51, 53
Third Crusade, Jan 59: 86–91, 130–31
Turkish capture of, Nov 63: 31
JERUSALEM, LATIN KINGDOM OF. See LATIN KINGDOM OF JERUSALEM
"JERUSALEM THE GOLDEN," hymn, Nov 63: 47
JESSE, F. TENNYSON, May 61: 116
"JESSICA," painting by Turner, Mar 63: 70
JESUITS, Nov 62: 36, 39
Vs. Jansenism, Jan 63: 100, 102
JESUS, early portrayals of, Nov 60: 29
JESUS, CAROLINA MARIA DE, Child of the Dark, reviewed, Nov 62: 109–10
JEWELL, EDWARD ALDEN, on Museum of Non-Objective Art, quoted, May 59: 10
"JEW OF MALTA, THE," play, Jan 60: 90, 92, 96
JEWS (see also JUDAISM)
God's messengers sent to, Nov 60: 28
Humboldt, Alexander von, and, Jul 59: 57–58, 128
Ivory, use by, May 60: 120
Joan of Arc and, Mar 62: 97
Philo-Semitism and millenarism of 17th century, Mar 60: 100–3, 124–25
Shylock, interpretations of, Jan 60: 89–96
Status in America, May 59: 22–23
Torah ceremony, Nov 62: 76
JHAM, LOST MINARET OF, Nov 59: 42–43
JHELUM RIVER, INDIA, Mar 61: 31
JOAD, C. E. M., on work, quoted, Nov 63: 104
JOAN, QUEEN OF SICILY, Jan 59: 91, 130
JOAN OF ARC, Nov 61: 97, Jul 62: 59
In illuminations from The Vigils of Charles VII, Mar 62: 90, 91, 94, 95, 96, 99
Judgments on and attitudes toward, Mar 62: 88–99
Portraits of, Mar 62: 88, 97
Voltaire's La Pucelle, concerning, Mar 61: 115, 118
"JOAN OF ARC OF THE NORTH WOODS," book by Holman Day, Mar 62: 98
"JOAN OF ARC WAS ON HER OWN WHEN SHE WAS QUITE A CHILD," song by Jerome Kern, Mar 62: 98
"JOAN OF ARKANSAS," song, Mar 62: 98
"JOAN OF LORRAINE," play, Mar 62: 98
JOB, plays about. See "J.B."; "BOOK OF JOB, THE"
JOHANSEN, JOHN, design for U.S. embassy building at Dublin, Jan 60: 119–20
JOHN, KING OF ENGLAND, Jan 59: 87, 90, 130, May 63: 94
JOHN II, KING OF FRANCE, Sep 60: 60
JOHN I, KING OF PORTUGAL, Nov 60: 73–74
JOHN IV, KING OF PORTUGAL, Mar 60: 102, 125
JOHN, SAINT
Robinson, John A. T., quoted on, Sep 63: 6
On Sardis, quoted, Sep 63: 86, 87
Tomb of, Sep 58: 141
JOHN, AUGUSTUS, Jan 59: 105, Mar 59: 88, May 62: 78
In painting by Feliks Topolski, Nov 60: 131
Self-portrait, May 62: 79
JOHN, ERROL, Jan 63: 32
JOHN, WILLIAM GOSCOMBE, sculpture by, May 62: 74
"JOHN BROWN'S BODY," poem by Stephen Vincent Benét, May 59: 9, Sep 63: 101
"JOHN BULL'S OTHER ISLAND," play, Nov 58: 136
"JOHN GABRIEL BORKMAN," play, Jan 62: 108
"JOHNNY JOHNSON," play, Nov 62: 106
JOHN OF AUSTRIA
And Battle of Lepanto, Nov 61: 110, 111, Jul 63: 49–61
Portrait of, Jul 63: 52
JOHN OF LANCASTER (DUKE OF BEDFORD), Mar 62: 96
JOHN VIII PALAEOLOGUS, BYZANTINE EMPEROR, Nov 63: 31
JOHNS, JASPER, May 61: 119, Jan 63: 25
Painting by, Jan 63: 19
Sculpture by, May 61: 119
JOHN SIMON GUGGENHEIM MEMORIAL FOUNDATION, May 59: 7, 8–10, 11, 16–17, Jan 62: 11, 12
JOHN III SOBIESKI, KING OF POLAND, Jul 63: 60
JOHNSON, BEN, painting by, Sep 63: 93
JOHNSON, CELIA, May 63: 111
JOHNSON, EDWARD, Nov 61: 78, 80
JOHNSON, GERALD W., Jan 60: 7
JOHNSON, HAROLD, Miles Davis quoted on, May 61: 100
JOHNSON, HJALMAR, Sep 58: 133
JOHNSON, JOHN and MABEL, Nov 60: 86
JOHNSON, JOHN G., Jul 63: 22
JOHNSON, LAURENCE A., Mar 60: 47–48
JOHNSON, LYNDON, Sep 61: 5

JOHNSON, OWEN, *Stover at Yale*, Sep 60: 119
JOHNSON, PHILIP, Sep 58: 110, Jan 59: 11, May 59: 86, 87, Sep 59: 6, May 62: 16, Jul 62: 8, 9, 10, 11
Building designed by, with Mies van der Rohe, Nov 61: 73
Home of, Nov 58: 33
Photograph of, Jul 62: 7
JOHNSON, SAMUEL (DR. JOHNSON), May 59: 129, Nov 59: 86, 87, May 61: 61, May 62: 60, Nov 63: 43
Dictionary compiled by, Jul 63: 34; quoted on chess, Jan 62: 114
Goldsmith, Oliver, quoted on, Jul 61: 115
Literary circle of, May 59: 92
At Oxford, Jan 63: 85, 87
Quoted: on ballooning, Sep 58: 117, 118; on *Don Quixote*, Nov 61: 108; on Lord Scarsdale's house, Nov 58: 47; on patrons, May 59: 9; on Psalmanazar, George, Jan 60: 118; on writing, Jul 63: 40
JOHNSON, THOMAS H., Jul 61: 100, 102 (note)
JOHNSON & JOHNSON, television commercial for, Mar 61: 101
JOHNSONVILLE, TENN., steam-electric plant at, Jan 60: 120
JOHNSTON, EDWARD, Sep 59: 128
JOHN THE BAPTIST, in painting by Flemish master, Sep 60: 58
JOHN THE FEARLESS, Sep 58: 63
"JOKER, THE," motion picture, Jan 62: 110
JOLLAIN, NICOLAS RENÉ, drawing by, Nov 62: 91
JŌMON, Japanese culture, Sep 61: 60, 63
JONES, CRANSTON, articles by
"Corbusier's Cloister," Mar 61: 34–41
"Making Something New of Tradition," Sep 61: 58–63
JONES, HARRY W., on teachers in government, quoted, Sep 62: 18, 19
JONES, INIGO, Nov 58: 41, 59, Jul 59: 46, Jul 61: 80, 90, 91
Building designed by, Jul 61: 90–91, 95
JONES, JAMES, Alfred Kazin quoted on, Jul 62: 101–2
JONES, MARVIN, Sep 61: 14
JONES, MERVYN, "Where Kursk and Kansas Meet," article by, Jul 62: 112–19
JONES, ROBERT, Nov 59: 90
JONES, ROBERT EDMOND, Jul 61: 13, Mar 62: 107
Dramatic Imagination, The, quoted, Jul 59: 48
JONGKIND, JOHAN BARTHOLD, Jul 62: 66
JONGLEURS, THE, drama group, Jan 63: 88
JONSON, BEN, Jan 60: 92
Volpone, Nov 63: 41
JOPE, E. M., and V. GORDON CHILDE, "A Short History of Wheeled Vehicles," excerpts from *A History of Technology*, Sep 58: 146–51
JORDA, ENRIQUE, Jan 59: 22
JORDAENS, JACOB, Jul 61: 90, Jul 63: 93
JORDAN
Discovery of Pool of Gibeon, Nov 59: 6, 8–9
Filming of *Lawrence of Arabia*, Jul 62: 108–11
Petra, Jul 62: 26–29, Sep 62: 7 (map), 8
JOS, NIGERIA, museum at, Mar 63: 53
JOSEPH (ÉMINENCE GRISE), French monk, Jul 60: 38
JOSEPH II, EMPEROR OF AUSTRIA, Mar 61: 118
JOSEPHINE, EMPRESS OF FRANCE. See BEAUHARNAIS, JOSÉPHINE DE
JOSEPH OF COPERTINE, SAINT, Nov 60: 31
JOSEPHS, DEVEREUX, Jul 62: 4, 7
JOUBERT, PETRUS, Nov 60: 65
JOURNALISM
Mass media and imaginary audience, Mar 60: 46–51
Memorandum, Horace Greeley to John Hay Whitney, Jan 59: 24–25
As popular art, Jan 60: 10
JOURNALS, LEARNED, Sep 62: 19
"JOURNEY TO ICARIA," romance by Étienne Cabet, Mar 63: 76
JOUSTING, Nov 58: 106
JOUVET, LOUIS, Nov 60: 54, Sep 62: 111
JOWETT, BENJAMIN, Jan 63: 86
JOYCE, JAMES, Mar 60: 25, Sep 61: 121, Jan 62: 97, Jan 63: 75, Mar 63: 112
Beckett, Samuel, and, Sep 60: 114
Hemingway, Ernest, quoted on, Jan 59: 132
Influence of: on Adler, Edward, Sep 62: 65; on present-day writers, Jul 63: 39–40
Jung, Carl G., quoted on, Nov 61: 105
Portrait of the Artist as a Young Man, quoted, Sep 60: 121
Ulysses, Jan 61: 116, Jan 62: 64; *Marquise Went Out at Five* compared to, May 62: 115; quoted, Sep 58: 131; *Ulysses in Nighttown*, play based on, May 62: 51
JUAN OF CARDONA, Jul 63: 58
JUÁREZ, BENITO, Jul 59: 67
JUDAISM, Jan 61: 62–63
"JUDGE AND THE HANGMAN, THE," novel by Friedrich Duerrenmatt, Mar 61: 47
"JUDGMENT OF SOLOMON, THE," painting by Pous-

sin, Mar 61: 80, 89; illus. Mar 61: 92–93
"JUDGMENTS OF JOAN, THE," article by Charles Wayland Lightbody, Mar 62: 88–99
JUILLARD SCHOOL OF MUSIC, and Lincoln Center for the Performing Arts, Jul 62: 7
JUKEBOXES, Jan 59: 138, 139
"JULES FEIFFER'S WICKED EYE AND EAR," article by Russell Lynes, Nov 61: 48, 57
JULIA DOMNA, Sep 63: 39
Coin portrait of, Sep 63: 38
JULIA MAESA, Sep 63: 39
Coin portrait of, Sep 63: 39
JULIAN, PHILIPPE, "At Home Through the Ages," drawings by, Mar 63: 80–83
JULIENNE, JEAN DE, Nov 61: 6
JULIUS II, POPE, Jan 62: 26, 31, 32, 41, May 63: 80
In painting by Melozzo da Forlì, Jan 62: 44
"JULIUS CAESAR," play by Shakespeare
American Shakespeare Festival production, 1955, Sep 62: 110
Mercury Theatre production, Jul 63: 87, 90
"JUMP BOOK," by Philippe Halsman, Jul 60: 120
JUNG, CARL GUSTAV
Memories, Dreams, Reflections, reviewed, Jan 63: 109–11
Quoted: on Joyce, James, Nov 61: 105; on psychic epidemics, Nov 60: 121; on Zen Buddhism, Jul 59: 73, 126
JUNGFRAUJOCH, Mar 59: 83–84
JUNGK, ROBERT, on Americans, quoted, May 60: 8
JUNK SCULPTURE, Mar 61: 104–13
Marisol's mannequins, Mar 63: 102–4
"JUNO AND THE PAYCOCK," play, quoted, Jan 62: 68
JURADE, Sep 58: 104–6
JURY SYSTEM, in Socrates' Greece, Jul 60: 100–1
"JUST ASSASSINS, THE," book by Albert Camus, Nov 59: 70–71
JUSTIN I, BYZANTINE EMPEROR, Nov 63: 11
"JUSTINE," novel by Lawrence Durrell, Mar 60: 114, 116, 117
Excerpt from, Mar 60: 114
JUSTINIAN, BYZANTINE EMPEROR, Mar 60: 89, Sep 61: 26, Nov 63: 10–12, 15, 25–26
Mosaic portraits of, Nov 63: cover, 3, 16–17
JUSTINIAN CODE, Nov 63: 12
On slavery, May 62: 44
"JUST ONE OF THOSE THINGS," song by Cole Porter, Jan 61: 119
JUSTUS VAN GHENT, Jan 60: 68, Jul 63: 107
JUVENAL, Jan 61: 72, Jul 61: 45
In Renaissance curriculum, Jan 60: 62

K

"KABBALA," Mar 60: 125
KABOTIE, FRED, Sep 58: 103
KABUKI, Jul 59: 126
KABUL, AFGHANISTAN, Mar 61: 31–32
"KADDISH," book by Allen Ginsberg, Sep 61: 119
KADESH, BATTLE OF, Jul 60: 14, 124
KAFKA, FRANZ, Jan 62: 97
Quoted by J. D. Salinger, Mar 61: 46
Shopping with ghost of, Mar 59: 110–11
Trial, The, motion picture based on, Jul 63: 85, 89, 90, 91
KAGAWA, JAPAN, prefectural hall, Sep 61: 58
KAHN, FLORENCE, May 61: 34
KAHN, HERMAN, Nov 63: 61
KAHN, LOUIS, Sep 62: 57–63, Jan 63: 14
Buildings designed by. See ILLUSTRATIONS INDEX
Photograph of, Sep 62: 59
KAHN, OTTO H., Nov 58: 118
KAHN & JACOBS, Sep 59: 19
Building designed by, Sep 59: 10–11
KAHNWEILER, DANIEL-HENRY, Nov 61: 8–9, May 62: 78
KAILA, EINO, Sep 60: 9
KAISER, GEORG, Mar 62: 99
KAISER FRIEDRICH MUSEUM, Berlin, Jul 59: 28
KALAMAZOO, MICH., Upjohn Company administration center, May 62: 16
KALI, Hindu goddess, Jul 61: 37
KALLEN, HORACE M., and Spectric poets, May 60: 47
KALLMANN, GERHARD M.
And design for Boston City Hall, Jan 63: 10–15
Photograph of, Jan 63: 11
KAMIHIRA, BEN, Jul 62: 23, 25
Painting by, Jul 62: 23
KANDINSKY, VASILY, May 59: 15, Sep 59: 18, Nov 59: 48, May 60: 113, Nov 61: 61, 64, 65, 68, 73
Guggenheim, Solomon, quoted on, Jul 62: 19
Paintings by. See ILLUSTRATIONS INDEX
Photograph of, Nov 61: 59
Wright, Frank Lloyd, quoted on, Sep 60: 128

KANE, ART, "Rapallo's Reflections," photographs by, Jul 60: 96–99
KANIN, GARSON, Nov 58: 120, Sep 60: 50, Jan 62: 111
KANO TANYU, Jul 59: 77, 126
Painting by, Jul 59: 74–75
KANSAS, cultural development in Topeka, Sep 59: 86–91, 122–23
"KANSAS CITY STAR," Ernest Hemingway on, Jan 59: 132, 134
KANT, IMMANUEL, on talent in Arcady, quoted, Nov 63: 109
KANTOR, TADEUSZ, May 61: 22
Painting by, May 61: 20
Portrait of, May 61: 22
KAO-TSUNG, EMPEROR OF CHINA, Jan 61: 15, 25
KAPLAN, JOE, portrait of, with painting by, Jul 61: 25
KAPP, ISA, on J. D. Salinger, quoted, May 62: 101
KARAJAN, HERBERT VON, Nov 58: 25, Mar 61: 72, May 63: 43
KARAMZIN, NIKOLAI, on Peter the Great, quoted, Sep 59: 84
KARAS, ANTON, Nov 59: 126
KARIM SHAHIR, IRAQ, archaeological site, Sep 62: 7, 8
"KARL," painting by Andrew Wyeth, Sep 61: 97; illus, Sep 61: 89
KARLOFF, BORIS, Sep 63: 77, 80
Photograph of, Sep 63: 77
KARNS, ROSCOE, Sep 62: 114
KARO, GEORGE, Nov 58: 72, 76
KARSH, YOUSUF, May 61: 103
Photograph by, Jan 59: 103
KASH, EUGENE, Mar 62: 87
KASHMIR, INDIA, Mar 61: 31, 32
KASPER, JOHN, Jan 59: 135
KATAVOLOS, WILLIAM, city design by, Sep 63: 25
KATIMS, MILTON, Jan 62: 14
KATSURA PALACE, near Kyoto, Japan, Sep 61: 63
KATZENBACH, NICHOLAS deB., Sep 61: 13
KAUFFMANN, ANGELICA, Mar 63: 69
KAUFFMANN, STANLEY, "The Trail of the Splendid Gypsy," article by, Mar 62: 12–13, 114–19
KAUFMAN, BEATRICE, Jul 62: 37
KAUFMAN, GEORGE S., Jul 62: 37, 38, 39–40
Caricature of, Jul 62: 41
On satire, quoted, Sep 58: 58
KAVADH I, KING OF PERSIA, Jan 63: 52
KAY, HERSHY, Nov 59: 56
KAY, MONTE, Nov 60: 86
KAYE, DANNY, Sep 58: 58, Jan 61: 123
KAZAN, ELIA, Mar 60: 119, Sep 60: 51, 88, Jan 62: 103, 104, Nov 62: 106, 108, Jan 63: 106, 108, 109
As director of *J.B.*, Jan 60: 49, 50, 51–53
Use of stage, Jul 59: 42, 44
KAZIN, ALFRED
Interview with, Jul 62: 98–103
Photograph of, May 59: 17
On Salinger, J. D., quoted, May 62: 100, 103, 104
KAZIS, NICOLAS, Sep 62: 24
Wall of church designed by, Sep 62: 22
KEABLE, ROBERT, Jan 60: 125
"KEAN," motion picture, Mar 62: 119
"KEAN," musical, Mar 62: 117–18, 119
KEAN, CHARLES, Mar 62: 114–15, 117
KEAN, EDMUND, Mar 62: 12–13, 114–19
Portrait of, Mar 62: 13
KEAN, EDMUND, SR., Mar 62: 13, 114
KEAN, MOSES, Mar 62: 114
KEARNS, CARROLL, Sep 61: 14
KEATON, BUSTER, Nov 61: 73
KEATS, JOHN, American writer, articles by
"Don't Call Me; I Won't Call You Either," Jan 63: 118–19
"Long Form, Short Shrift," Nov 62: 118–19
"Shopping with Kafka," Mar 59: 110–11
KEATS, JOHN, English poet, Nov 60: 97, May 61: 58, 65, Mar 62: 75, 116, May 63: 85
"Ode on a Grecian Urn," Mar 62: 68
"On First Looking into Chapman's Homer," quoted, Jan 61: 91
Portrait of, May 61: 64
Quoted: on claret, Sep 58: 145; on mechanical man-eating tiger, Sep 60: 21; on use of words, Mar 63: 88
KEBLE, JOHN, Jan 63: 86
KEIR, JAMES, as member of Josiah Wedgwood's group, May 59: 92, 128–30
KEISER, DAVID, Jul 59: 18, 19, Jul 62: 4
KEITH, ARTHUR, quoted, Nov 63: 107
KEITH, WILLIAM, Jan 59: 7
KELLOGG-BRIAND PACT, Mar 63: 6
KELLY, ELLSWORTH, Jan 63: 25
Painting by, Jan 63: 20
KELLY, FANNY, Nov 60: 97
KELLY, GENE, Sep 58: 60, Nov 58: 138
KELLY, GERALD, May 62: 59
Portraits of Somerset Maugham by, Jan 59: 106; illus, Jan

59: 106
KELLY, GRACE, Jul 63: 5, 22
KELLY, JAMES, Jan 59: 14
KELLY, JOHN B., Jul 63: 26
KELLY, NED, Sep 62: 98–99, 100
  Paintings of, by Sidney Nolan, Sep 62: 100; illus, Sep 62: 100, 101
KEMAL ATATURK, MUSTAFA, Sep 58: 142
KEMBLE, JOHN PHILIP, Mar 62: 117
KEMP, THOMAS, Nov 62: 23
KEMP, WILLIAM, Jan 60: 92
KEMPTON, MURRAY, "The Artist in Our Time," article by, Jan 63: 73–75
  Comment on, Jan 63: 105
KENDALL, GEORGE, Mar 63: 30, 32
KENNAN, GEORGE F., Sep 59: 118, May 60: 9, 122
KENNEDY, CHARLES WILLIAM, Sep 59: 118
KENNEDY, JACQUELINE BOUVIER (MRS. JOHN FITZGERALD), Sep 61: 9, Nov 63: 68, 69
  Memorandum from Empress Eugénie to, Sep 62: 20–21
  At National Gallery with André Malraux, Jan 63: 73
  Photograph of, Sep 61: 16
KENNEDY, JOHN FITZGERALD
  Influence of President and Mrs. Kennedy in the arts, Sep 61: 4–17, Mar 63: 27
  Photographs of, Sep 61: 6, Nov 63: 68–69, 70, 71
  Roosevelt, Theodore, compared with, Nov 63: 68–71
  Virginia house of, Sep 63: 102
KENNEDY, JOSEPH P., Jul 62: 9
"KENNEDY LOOK IN THE ARTS, THE," article by Douglass Cater, Sep 61: 4–17
KENNERLEY, MITCHELL, and Spectric poets, May 60: 42, 46
KENT, CONN., May 60: 13 (map), 22
KENT, ADALINE, Jan 59: 14
  Sculpture by, Jan 59: 12
KENT, ALLEGRA, Nov 59: 52–56
  Photographs of, Nov 59: 52–53, 55
KENT, DUCHESS OF (VICTORIA MARY LOUISA), Jul 63: 107
KENT, WILLIAM, Nov 58: 46, 51, 52, May 59: 47
  Houses designed by, Nov 58: 42, 44–45, 51, 58–59
  Portraits of, Nov 58: 60, May 59: 46
KENTFIELD, CALVIN, Jan 59: 18
KENTUCKY, Corey production of The Book of Job at Pine Mountain State Park, Jan 63: 88
KEPLER, JOHANNES, portrait of, Jul 60: 39
KERAK, Jan 59: 89–90
KERN, JEROME, Sep 58: 61
  "Joan of Arc Was on Her Own When She Was Quite a Child," Mar 62: 98
  Show Boat, Jan 60: 14
KERNS, ROBERT, photograph of, Nov 61: 79
KEROUAC, JACK, Sep 58: 38, 39–42, Jan 59: 6, 19, Jul 59: 71, Mar 61: 14, Sep 61: 116, 119, May 62: 55, Jan 63: 74
  On the Road, quoted, Jul 63: 39
  Photograph of, Sep 58: 40
KERR, DEBORAH, Sep 63: 80
KERR, JEAN, Mary, Mary, Mar 63: 108
KERR, ROBERT (EARL OF ANCRAM), Jul 61: 90, Jul 63: 94
KERR, WALTER
  Articles by: "In Search of Shylock," Jan 60: 89–96; "Making a Cult of Confusion," Sep 62: 33–41; "Theatre Breaks Out of Belasco's Box, The," Sep 59: 41–48; "Theatre of Form and Anti-Form, The," Mar 61: 42–47; "What Good Is Television," Mar 60: 4–5, 126–28; "What Will the Robin Do Then, Poor Thing?" Mar 62: 40–41
  Quoted: on Beatty, Warren, Jan 62: 104; on Hurst, David, Jan 61: 101; on Lampert, Zohra, Jul 62: 49; on "Theatre of Chance," Sep 60: 124
KERR, WILLIAM, "Counting Sheep," quoted, Jan 60: 109 (note)
KETCHUM, MILO, Mar 59: 123
KEW GARDENS, Syon Vista, May 59: 47
"KEY, THE," motion picture, Nov 59: 126
KEYNES, JOHN MAYNARD, Jan 60: 107, Jan 61: 113, Nov 63: 106
KHAFAJE, Sumerian city, Jul 61: 41
KHAJU BRIDGE, Isfahan, Iran, May 61: 24–32
KHALAF, carving by, Sep 62: 74
KHIRBET NAHAS, Wadi Araba, identification with Biblical City of Copper, Nov 59: 10
KHMERS, of Cambodia, Jan 59: 62–63, 64, 71–75, 81
KHORSABAD, ASSYRIA, Jul 61: 38, 41
KHOSRAU I (CHOSROES), KING OF PERSIA, Jan 63: 51
  Cup of, Jan 63: 56
  Winter Carpet of, May 59: 44
KHOSRAU II, KING OF PERSIA, Sep 63: 89, Nov 63: 26
  Pictured in Persian miniature, Jan 63: 66
KHRUSHCHEV, NIKITA S., Mar 61: 32, Jul 62: 113

"Amateurs All," by Oliver Jensen, Jul 62: 96–97
Ionesco, Eugène, quoted on, May 61: 93
Reporting of visit to United States, Mar 60: 50–51
KHUDOVEKOV SISTERS, photograph of, Nov 62: 117
KIDDELL, A. J. B., Nov 62: 65, 66
KIEPURA, JAN, Sep 59: 57
KIERKEGAARD, SÖREN AABYE, Mar 61: 46, May 61: 64, 66
  On maturity, quoted, Jul 60: 32
KIERZKOWSKI, BRONISLAW, May 61: 22
  Painting by, May 61: 23
KIESLER, FREDERICK, Jan 62: 10
KIESWETTER, ERNEST C., Sep 59: 89, 90–91
  Photograph of, Sep 59: 89
KIEV, U.S.S.R., Englishman's impressions of, Jul 62: 113, 118–19
KIEV, GRAND DUCHY OF, Sep 59: 62
KILGALLEN, DOROTHY, portrait of, Jan 60: 9
"KILLER, THE," play, May 61: 91
"KILLERS, THE," story by Ernest Hemingway, Jan 59: 133
KILLIGREW, THOMAS, Jul 63: 105
KILLMAYER, WILHELM, Mar 61: 72
KILRAIN, JAKE, Mar 60: 30
KIMBALL, FISKE, Jul 63: 23
KING, A. HYATT, on chamber music, quoted, Nov 62: 43, 46–47
KING, CLARENCE, Jan 59: 7
KING, ELLEN, West Virginia hymn, quoted, Nov 61: 119
"KING AND I, THE," musical, Sep 58: 60, 143
"KING AND THE DUKE, THE," play, Mar 60: 98, 120
"KING ARTHUR AND HIS KNIGHTS," book by James Knowles, May 60: 115–18
"KING CREOLE," motion picture, Jan 59: 137–38
KINGDOM, SOPHIA, Jan 59: 34
KINGDOM OF THE TWO SICILIES, Sep 61: 38
"KING LEAR," play by Shakespeare, Jul 60: 50, Sep 62: 33
  Guthrie, Tyrone, quoted on Laurence Olivier in, Jan 61: 29
  Hemingway, Ernest, quoted on, Jan 59: 133
"KING OF INSTRUMENTS RETURNS, THE," article by E. Power Biggs, Mar 60: 72–80
"KING OF KINGS," motion picture, Sep 63: 77
KINGS, role of, in development of cities, Jul 61: 38–39
KINGSLEY, SIDNEY, May 61: 116
KINGSPORT, TENN., Jul 59: 11
"KING STEPS OUT, THE," motion picture, Sep 59: 55
KINSEY, ALFRED C., Nov 59: 23
KINTNER, EARL W., Nov 60: 123
KIPLING, RUDYARD, May 63: 82, 83–84
  Caricature of, by Max Beerbohm, May 61: 38; illus, May 61: 37
  Portrait of, May 63: 83
KIP'S BAY PLAZA, New York City, Jan 63: 115
KIRCHER, ATHANASIUS, Jan 63: 6–7
KIRCHNER, LEON, Jan 59: 21, 22, Jan 62: 5, 9, 14
  Photograph of, Jan 59: 21
KIRKPATRICK, WILLIAM, Sep 62: 20
KIRKUK, IRAQ, archaeological discoveries near, Sep 62: 4–9
KIRSTEIN, LINCOLN, Nov 60: 94, Jan 61: 46, Jul 62: 6, 7, 10–11
  On Lowry, W. McNeil, quoted, Jan 62: 13
  Portrait of, Jul 62: 9
KISSINGER, HENRY A., Nov 63: 61
"KISS ME KATE," musical, Sep 58: 60, 61, 143
KIST, GERRIT, Sep 59: 74
"KITTY FOYLE," novel by Christopher Morley, Jul 63: 5
KIUSEM, mother of Murad IV, May 59: 63, 131
KLEE, FELIX, Nov 61: 70
KLEE, LILY, Nov 61: 70
KLEE, PAUL, Mar 59: 72, May 59: 15, 121, Sep 59: 18, Nov 59: 48, Nov 61: 61, 64–65, 70–71, 74, May 63: 91
  Paintings by, Nov 61: cover, 3, 65
  Photograph of, Nov 61: 59
KLEINE FREIHEIT, DIE, Nov 58: 62
KLEIST, HEINRICH VON, Mar 59: 72
KLINE, FRANZ, Sep 58: 38, 44, Nov 59: 120, Jul 61: 18, Mar 62: 107, Jul 62: 13, Jan 63: 16
  Photograph of, Jul 61: 18
  Wyeth, Andrew, quoted on, Sep 61: 100
KLING, VINCENT, Nov 60: 21
KLOPFER, MR. and MRS. R. C., Sep 59: 123
"KNACK, THE," play, Jan 63: 31, 32
KNATHS, KARL, Jul 61: 18
  Portrait of, with painting by, Jul 61: 19
KNEE, GINA, May 63: 24
KNELLER, GODFREY, Jul 63: 96
  Paintings by, Sep 61: 72
"KNICK-KNACK PEDDLER, THE," painting by Li Sung, Jan 61: 25; illus, Jan 61: 21
KNIGHT, I. M., Nov 62: 45
KNIGHT, LAURA, May 62: 59
KNIGHTHOOD

Tournaments, Nov 58: 92–107
Training for, Nov 58: 94–95
KNIGHTS OF MALTA (see also KNIGHTS OF ST. JOHN), Mar 61: 65–70, Jul 63: 50
KNIGHTS OF RHODES (see also KNIGHTS OF ST. JOHN), Mar 61: 62, 65
KNIGHTS OF ST. JOHN, Mar 61: 48–71
"KNIGHTS OF THE MALTESE CROSS, THE," article by Edith Simon, Mar 61: 48–71
KNIGHTS OF THE TEMPLE, Mar 61: 48, 51–52, 56, 60, 62
KNISH, ANNE (ARTHUR DAVISON FICKE), May 60: 42–48
KNOEDLER, M., AND COMPANY, Sep 61: 88
KNOSSOS, CRETE, Jan 61: 77, 81
KNOWLES, EDWARD F., and design for Boston City Hall, Jan 63: 10–15
KNOWLES, JAMES, King Arthur and His Knights, book by, May 60: 115–18
KNOWLES, JOHN, "All-Out in the Desert," article by, Jul 62: 108–11
KNOX, JOHN
  And Mary, Queen of Scots, Jul 63: 28–32
  In painting by W. P. Frith, Jul 63: 28–29
KNOX, NERVO &, Jan 61: 122–23
KNOX, RONALD, Mar 61: 95–96, Jul 61: 113, May 63: 88
  In Three Tongues, quoted, Jul 61: 115
KOBE, JAPAN, U.S. consulate building, Jan 60: 120
KOBZDEJ, ALEKSANDER, May 61: 22
KOCH, DORA ZASLAVSKY (MRS. JOHN), Sep 60: 105, 111
  In paintings by John Koch, Sep 60: 104, 107, 108, 109, 110
KOCH, JOHN, Sep 60: 105, 111
  Paintings by. See ILLUSTRATIONS INDEX
  Self-portraits, Sep 60: 106, 110
KOCH, KENNETH, Sep 61: 119
  "Fresh Air," quoted, Sep 61: 119
KODÁLY, ZOLTÁN, Nov 62: 46
KOESTLER, ARTHUR
  On continuity and change, quoted, Mar 63: 9
  Gladiators, The, May 61: 57
  Lotus and the Robot, The, excerpt from, Mar 61: 4–11
KOIKE, SHINJI, on Kenzo Tange, quoted, Sep 61: 58
KOKOSCHKA, OSKAR, May 59: 121, May 60: 113
  Poster by, Jan 59: 117
KOLB, PETER, on elephant hunting, quotation and illustration, May 60: 91
KOLBE, GEORG, Sep 59: 18
  Statue by, Sep 59: 12
KOLODIN, IRVING
  "Complete Musician, The," article by, Sep 61: 82–87
  On Metropolitan Opera House, quoted, Nov 58: 117
KONARAK, SUN TEMPLE OF, Sep 63: 68
KONDOS, DEMETRIOS, Nov 58: 72
KONINCK, PHILIPS DE, Sep 58: 26
KONINGSBERGER, HANS, articles by
  "Love in Another Country (Where They Order It Better)," May 63: 110–12
  "Not by the Book," May 62: 116–18
KOOK, EDWARD F., Jul 59: 48
KOPIT, ARTHUR L., Oh Dad, Poor Dad, Mamma's Hung You in the Closet and I'm Feelin' So Sad, Sep 62: 34–35 (illus), 37, Mar 63: 107
KORAN, quoted, May 59: 59, 63, 135
KORDA, ALEXANDER, Nov 58: 138, Nov 62: 59
KORE OF EUTHYDIKOS, sculpture, Nov 58: 13; illus, Nov 58: 6
KORNBLUTH, C. M. See POHL, FREDERIK, co-author
"KOUROS," sculpture by Isamu Noguchi, Mar 60: 108; illus, Mar 60: 107
KOUROS OF MILO, sculpture, Nov 58: 14; illus, Nov 58: 7
KOUSSEVITZKY, SERGE, Thomas Beecham quoted on, Mar 62: 104
KOVACS, ERNIE, Nov 59: 31, 122, 124, 125
KOZOL, JONATHAN
  Fume of Poppies, The, Mar 59: 14, 17, 117, 118
  Photograph of, Mar 59: 15
KRACHMALNICK, SAMUEL, photographs of, Nov 61: 79, 81
KRAHN, FERNANDO, "The Epic of Man," drawings by, Sep 63: 108–12
KRAKEN, Nov 58: 70
KRAK OF THE KNIGHTS, Mar 61: 52, 54
KRAMAR, VINCENT, Nov 61: 9
KRAMER, SAMUEL NOAH, "O Ye Daughters of Sumer!" article by, Jul 63: 108–9
"KRAPP'S LAST TAPE," play, Sep 60: 112–16, Jul 61: 117, Sep 62: 34, 38–39 (illus), 41, 111
KRASKER, ROBERT, May 61: 55
KRASNER, LEE, May 63: 9, 22
  Photograph of, May 63: 22
KRAUS, H. P., Jan 63: 5

KREISLER, FRITZ, Sep 61: 84, May 63: 109
KREMLIN, Moscow, Sep 59: 62, Nov 63: 34
KRENEK, ERNST, Igor Stravinsky quoted on, Sep 58: 132
KRESS, SAMUEL H., Jan 59: 105
KREUGER, IVAR, Jan 61: 72, May 61: 117
KREYMBORG, ALFRED, Mar 63: 28, 29
  And Spectric poets, May 60: 43, 44, 47, 48
KRONENBERGER, LOUIS, "Whatever Became of Personal Ethics?" article by, Mar 63: 60–61
KROPOTKIN, PETER, Mar 63: 113
KROSNEY, HERBERT, Nov 62: 98, 99
KROYT, BORIS, photograph of, Nov 62: 44
KRUSZEWSKI, NIKOLAI, Jul 63: 44
KRUTCH, JOSEPH WOOD, quoted
  On teaching of English, Jul 63: 47
  On wilderness, Mar 60: 16
KUBIK, GAIL, Mar 63: 30
KUBITSCHEK, JUSCELINO, May 60: 54
KUBLY, HERBERT, "The Care and Feeding of Artists," article by, Mar 63: 26–33
KUBRICK, STANLEY, May 61: 57
KUH, KATHERINE, "An Interview with Isamu Noguchi," article by, Mar 60: 104–12
KUHLMAN, WALTER, Jan 59: 13, 14
KUMP, ERNEST J., Jan 59: 10, Jan 60: 121
  Building designed by, Jan 60: 24
KUN, BÉLA, Jan 59: 121
K'UNG TE-CH'ENG, Jan 61: 16
KUNITZ, STANLEY, Sep 61: 117, Mar 63: 30
KUO STATE CEMETERY, at Shang Ts'un Ling, China, Jan 61: 11, 124
KURASHIKI, JAPAN, city hall, Sep 61: 63
KURKA, ROBERT, Jan 60: 123
KUROSAWA, AKIRA, Jul 62: 42–47
  Photograph of, Jul 62: 42
  Seven Samurai, May 61: 114–15
KURZ, SELMA, Sep 59: 56
KUSHITE STATE, of Africa, Mar 63: 53, 57, 58
KWAMMU, EMPEROR OF JAPAN, Mar 61: 27
KYBELE. See CYBELE
KYD, THOMAS, Jan 60: 92
KYOTO, JAPAN, Mar 61: 27
  Temple garden, May 59: 50

L

LA BARRE, CHEVALIER DE, Mar 61: 119
LA BEAUMELLE, Jan 60: 86, 88
LABIENUS, TITUS, Nov 62: 88
LABOR
  In Age of Leisure, Nov 63: 104–5
  Contributions of Josiah Wedgwood, May 59: 89, 129
  Domestic, in England, 16th to 20th centuries, Nov 58: 51
  Status in America, May 59: 21–22
LABOUISSE, MRS. HENRY (EVE CURIE), Sep 61: 10
LACLOS, PIERRE CHODERLOS DE, May 60: 53 (note)
LACOURIÈRE, ROGER, Nov 62: 57
LADE, JOHN, Nov 62: 23
LADE, LETTY, Nov 62: 23
"LADIES' HOME JOURNAL, THE," Jan 63: 114
"LADY AND THE PAINTER, THE," novel by Eleanor Palffy, Jul 59: 29–30
"LADY CHATTERLEY'S LOVER," novel by D. H. Lawrence, Nov 61: 105, Jan 62: 63
"LADY FROM SHANGHAI, THE," motion picture, Jul 63: 90
"LADY IN THE DARK," musical, Sep 58: 60, Nov 58: 64
"LADY WITH A FAN," painting by Rembrandt, Jul 63: 106; illus, Jul 63: 101
LA FARGE, GRANT, Jan 63: 12
LA FARGE, JOHN, in South Seas, Jan 60: 125
LA FAYETTE, COMTESSE DE, Nov 61: 33–34, Jul 63: 81
LAFAYETTE, MARQUIS DE, May 61: 85
LA FONTAINE, JEAN DE, Nov 61: 34, Jul 63: 77, 80, 83
  On childhood, quoted, Mar 59: 72
LAGERKVIST, PÄR, Barabbas, and motion picture based on, Mar 63: 109–11
LaGUARDIA, FIORELLO, Jul 62: 4
LAGUERRE, LOUIS, Mar 63: 69
LA HARPE, FRÉDÉRIC CÉSAR DE, Sep 63: 31
LA HARPE, JEAN FRANÇOIS DE, Mar 61: 118
LAHR, BERT, Sep 58: 58, 59, Jan 60: 96
  Photographs of, Sep 58: 58, Nov 58: 64
  On Waiting for Godot, quoted, Nov 58: 62
LAKELAND, FLA., Florida Southern College buildings, Sep 59: 8
LALLEMAND, GEORGES, Mar 61: 79
LALLI, interpreting song to Shiva, photographs, Sep 63: 70–71

LALLY, THOMAS ARTHUR DE, Mar 61: 119
LALLY-TOLLENDAL, TROPHIME GÉRARD DE, Mar 61: 119
LAMARTINE, ALPHONSE DE, May 61: 65, Mar 62: 97
  Portrait of, May 61: 65
LAMB, CAROLINE, on Byron, quoted, May 63: 85
LAMB, CHARLES, Nov 58: 107
  On trying to be witty, quoted, Jul 62: 37
  Works by, in H. B. Smith's "Sentimental Library," Nov 60: 97
LAMB, HENRY, paintings by, Jan 60: 106, May 62: 77
LAMB, WILLIAM (2D VISCOUNT MELBOURNE), Mar 63: 65
  On George III, quoted, Jul 63: 105
LAMBERT, GERARD B., Sep 59: 24
LAMBERT, MME DE, Nov 61: 34
LAMI, LOUIS EUGÈNE, painting by, May 63: 69
LAMONT, ROSETTE, "The Outrageous Ionesco," interview by, May 61: 89–91, 93, 95, 97
LAMONT, MRS. THOMAS W., Jul 63: 70 (note)
LA MONTAINE, JOHN, Mar 63: 33
  Photograph of, Mar 63: 30
LAMOUR, DOROTHY, Jan 60: 125
LAMPEDUSA, GIULIO DI, Sep 61: 40
  Portrait of, Sep 61: 40
LAMPEDUSA, GIUSEPPE DI, The Leopard, Sep 61: 40
  Motion picture based on, Jan 62: 104, Jan 63: 38
  Quoted, Sep 61: 40, Jan 63: 38
LAMPERT, ZOHRA, Jul 62: 49
  Photograph of, Jul 62: 48
LANA, FATHER, Sep 58: 114
LANCASTER, BURT, Jan 63: 38, Mar 63: 35
LANCASTER, CLAY, Architectural Follies in America, excerpt from, Mar 59: 136
LANCASTER, DUKE OF, Nov 58: 106
LANCELOT, versions of James Knowles and Thomas Malory, May 60: 116–18
LANCÔME, FRED, photograph of, May 60: 15
LANCRET, NICOLAS, Nov 61: 4, 6
LANDERS, ANN, memorandum to, from Eleanor of Aquitaine, May 60: 30–31
LANDIR, HELMUT, stained-glass windows designed by, Sep 62: 28
LANDO, PETER DE, Mar 60: 83
LANDON, ALFRED M., May 59: 10, Sep 59: 123
  Photograph of, Sep 59: 90
LANDON, MARGARET FLEMING (MRS. ALFRED M.), Sep 59: 123
  Photograph of, Sep 59: 91
LANDOR, WALTER SAVAGE, Mar 62: 97
LANDRUM, CHARLEY, Jul 60: 122
"LANDSCAPE OF ANCIENT ROME," painting by Poussin, Mar 61: 91
"LANDSCAPE WITH POLYPHEMUS," painting by Poussin, Mar 61: 89, 93; illus, Mar 61: 86–87
"LANDSCAPE WITH SAINT GEORGE," painting by Rubens, Jul 61: 91, Jul 63: 106
LANDSEER, EDWIN, Mar 60: 57, 58, May 62: 73, Jul 63: 107
  Paintings by. See ILLUSTRATIONS INDEX
LANDUYT, OCTAVE, Jan 62: 82
  Painting by, Jan 62: 79
"LAND WITHOUT BREAD," motion picture, Nov 62: 110, 111
LANE, HARRY, photograph of, May 60: 15
LANFRANCHI, MARIO, Jul 61: 97
LANG, ANDREW, Mar 62: 99
LANG, JOHN, letter from Erasmus to, quoted, May 62: 93, 94
LANGFORD, SAMUEL, Mar 62: 105
LANGFUS, ANNA, Jul 63: 74
LANGHANS, CARL GOTTHARD, Nov 62: 44
LANGHORST, FRED, Jan 59: 8
LANGLOIS, HENRI, May 60: 51
LANGNER, LAWRENCE, May 60: 28
  Photograph of, May 60: 29
LANGSTROTHER, JOHN, Mar 61: 65
LANGUAGE (see also ENGLISH LANGUAGE)
  Communications satellites and, Jan 62: 20
  Japanese, Mar 61: 9–10
  Lydian, Sep 63: 86
  Mother tongues of human race, percentages, Jan 62: 20
  Persian, sound of, Jan 63: 67
  Spanish, origin of, Sep 62: 79
  Sumer's language of love, Jul 63: 108
  Translations from English into classical languages, Jul 61: 112–13; examples, Jul 61: 114–15
  Winnie ille Pu, reviewed, Jul 61: 112–15
LANGUAGE STUDY
  On Grand Tour, Nov 59: 90
  In Renaissance curriculum, Jan 60: 62
LANIÈRE, NICOLAS, Jul 61: 89, 94
LANSBURY, ANGELA, Mar 61: 103, May 61: 51

LANSDALE, NELSON, articles by
  "La Vie Bohème on Central Park West," Sep 60: 104–11
  "Mrs. Gardner's Palace of Paintings," Jul 59: 26–32, 133–34
  "Out of the Old Met, the New," Nov 58: 28–29, 117–20
LANSDOWNE, MARQUESS OF
  Portrait of, Mar 59: 90
  On Smith, Sydney, quoted, Mar 59: 90
LANSNER, KERMIT, "Olivetti: A Man and a Style," article by, Nov 59: 44–51, 127
LANZA, MARIO, Jul 61: 97
LAOCOÖN GROUP, Sperlonga and Vatican versions, May 59: 104, 123, 124
LAO-TSE, aphorism by, quoted, Sep 61: 115
"LA PERLA," painting by Raphael, Jul 61: 94
LAPIDUS, MORRIS, building designed by, Jan 61: 102–3
LAPLACE, PIERRE SIMON DE, Jul 60: 30
"LARK, THE," play, Nov 60: 51, 52, 54, Mar 62: 99
LARKIN, PETER, Jan 62: 14
LA ROCHEFOUCAULD, DUC DE, Nov 61: 33, 34
LARRABEE, ERIC, articles by
  "After Abundance, What?" Jul 60: 65–72
  "Boston Chooses the Future," Jan 63: 10–15
  "Cultural Class War, The," Jan 60: 4–11
  "Imaginary Audience, The," Mar 60: 46–51
  "In Print: Jane Jacobs," Jul 62: 50–51
  "Memorandum from Julius Caesar to Robert Moses," Mar 59: 26–27
  "Our Face to the World," May 60: 4–9, 122–23
  "Wreck of the Status System, The," Nov 59: 20–25, 128
"LARRY RIVERS: 'WHY I PAINT AS I DO,'" interview by Frank O'Hara, Sep 59: 94–102
LA SCALA, Milan, Nov 58: 23–24, 118, Jul 59: 18
LASCAUX, FRANCE, cave paintings, Jul 61: 34, Sep 62: 11, 12
LASKER, EDWARD, The Adventure of Chess, quoted, Jan 62: 115
LASKER, EMANUEL, Jan 62: 116, 117, 118, 119, 120
  Photograph of, Jan 62: 114
LASKI, HAROLD, Jul 63: 13
LASSO, ORLANDO DI, Nov 60: 90
LASSWELL, HAROLD, Mar 60: 48
"LAST ANGRY MAN," motion picture, Nov 58: 139
"LAST DAYS OF POMPEII, THE," motion picture, May 61: 54
"LAST JUDGMENT, THE," painting by Michelangelo, Jan 62: 41
  Henry Moore quoted on, Nov 60: 113
"LAST OF THE MOHICANS, THE," novel by James Fenimore Cooper, Mar 60: 15
"LA STRADA," motion picture, May 59: 99, May 60: 51, Mar 61: 98
"LAST SUPPER," painting by Leonardo da Vinci, Sep 60: 121
"LAST TYCOON, THE," novel by F. Scott Fitzgerald, May 62: 101
"'LAST UNIVERSAL MAN, THE,'" article by H. R. Trevor-Roper, Jul 59: 56–69, 128
LATIMER, FREDERICK B., Mar 60: 33–34, 37
LATIN AMERICA, Alexander von Humboldt in, Jul 59: 62–68, 128
LATIN KINGDOM OF JERUSALEM, Jan 59: 87–88, 131, Mar 61: 51–52, 54, 56, 60
LATIN LANGUAGE
  In Renaissance curriculum, Jan 60: 62
  Translation of Winnie-the-Pooh and other English writings into, Jul 61: 112–15
LATOUCHE, JOHN, Jan 60: 122
LATUDE. See DANRY, JEAN
LAUD, WILLIAM, ARCHBISHOP OF CANTERBURY, Sep 59: 120, 121, Nov 59: 62, Mar 60: 101
LAUDER, GEORGE, Jan 60: 113–14
"LAUGH NOW, PAY LATER," article by Robert Hatch, Mar 63: 106–9
LAUGHTON, CHARLES, Jan 61: 27, May 61: 53, Nov 61: 115, May 62: 40, Sep 63: 42, 77 (note), 78, 80
  Photographs of, May 62: 116, Sep 62: 42
LAUGIER, PIERRE, Nov 63: 75
LAUNAY, DE. See STAAL DE LAUNAY
LAURANA, LUCIANO DA, Jan 60: 66
LAURENCE, WILLIAM, L., May 62: 9
LAURENCIN, MARIE, portrait of Somerset Maugham by, Jan 59: 106; illus, Jan 59: 106
LAURENS, HENRY, Sep 59: 135
"LAURENTIC," S.S., bullion salvaged from, Nov 58: 77
LAURENTIIS. See DE LAURENTIIS
LAURENTS, ARTHUR, Jul 61: 98
  The Clearing in the Woods, Nov 58: 64
LA VALETTE, JEAN DE, Mar 61: 61, 65
"LAVENDER HILL MOB, THE," motion picture, Mar 61: 98
"LA VIE BOHÈME ON CENTRAL PARK WEST," article by Nelson Lansdale, Sep 60: 104–11

LAVROVSKY, LEONID, Jan 61: 56
LAW
Code of Gortyn, Nov 62: 90
International, Hugo Grotius and, Sep 58: 24
Jury system in Socrates' Greece, Jul 60: 100–1
Justinian Code, Nov 63: 12; on slavery, May 62: 44
Roman, inheritance case, Nov 58: 110
LAW, WILLIAM, *Serious Call to a Devout and Holy Life,* Jan 60: 117
LAWLER, RAY, Sep 62: 97
LAWRENCE, SAINT, in painting by Fra Angelico, Jan 62: 32, 40
LAWRENCE, A. LOWELL, May 62: 8
LAWRENCE, D. H., Nov 58: 31, Jan 60: 108, May 62: 55, Sep 63: 100
Etruscan Places, quoted, May 60: 58, 59
Lady Chatterley's Lover, Nov 61: 105, Jan 62: 63
Quoted: on America, Sep 62: 94–95; on Venice, Mar 63: 15
In Tuscany, May 60: 59
LAWRENCE, GERTRUDE, Sep 58: 59, 60
LAWRENCE, THOMAS, Jul 59: 30, May 62: 63–64, Jul 63: 106
Paintings by, May 62: 65, Jul 63: 95
Portrait of John Soane by, Nov 63: 75–76; illus, Nov 63: 75
LAWRENCE, THOMAS EDWARD (T. E.), May 61: 117, Jan 63: 87
As portrayed in *Ross,* May 62: 111–12
"LAWRENCE OF ARABIA," motion picture, filming of, Jul 62: 108–11
LAWSON, HENRY, Sep 62: 97
LAYE, EVELYN, Sep 63: 77 (note)
"LAZARILLO DE TORMES," motion picture, Nov 62: 111
LEA, H. C., research on witch mania, Nov 59: 59, 62
LEACOCK, RICHARD, Mar 61: 17
Photograph of, Mar 61: 17
LEADVILLE, COLO., Guggenheim silver mines at, May 59: 6
LEAGUE OF NATIONS, Mar 63: 6
Competition for palace of, Jan 63: 12
Ideas of Theodore Roosevelt on, Nov 63: 71
"LEAGUE OF YOUTH, THE," play, Jan 62: 108
LEAKEY, L. S. B., Mar 62: 9, 10
LEAN, DAVID, Mar 60: 128, Mar 61: 98
As director of *Lawrence of Arabia,* Jul 62: 109–11
LEAR, EDWARD, Mar 61: 22, Nov 63: 101
Limerick by, quoted, Sep 58: 130
LÉAUD, JEAN-PIERRE, May 60: 53
LEAVIS, F. R., Sep 63: 98, 99, 100
LEBANON, Baalbek Festival, Jul 62: 30
LEBENSTEIN, JAN, May 61: 22
Painting by, May 61: 23
LE BLOND, JEAN-BAPTISTE, May 62: 15
LE BRUN, CHARLES, Mar 61: 89, 90, Jul 63: 79, 81, 82, 83
Portrait of, Jul 63: 81
Works by. See ILLUSTRATIONS INDEX
LEBRUN, RICO, Jul 62: 15
Painting by, Jul 62: 15
LECKY, WILLIAM, on Byzantine Empire, quoted, Nov 63: 4
LeCLERCQ, TANAQUIL, Nov 59: 54, Jan 61: 49 (note)
LECOMTE DU NOÜY, PIERRE, Jan 59: 28
LE CORBUSIER (see also ILLUSTRATIONS INDEX), Jan 59: 8, 11, May 59: 113, Sep 59: 6, 8–9, 18, 20, Nov 61: 61–62, 70, Jan 62: 94, Mar 62: 32, 33, 39, Jan 63: 12, 14
Buildings at Chandigarh, India, Jan 60: 119
Couvent Sainte-Marie de la Tourette, Mar 61: 34–41
And European skyscrapers, Nov 60: 16, 125
Influence on Kenzo Tange, Sep 61: 60, 63
Saarinen, Eero, quoted on, Jul 60: 82
On Venice, quoted, Mar 63: 16
LEDA AND THE SWAN, series of paintings by Sidney Nolan, Sep 62: 100, 102; illus, Sep 62: 102
LEDOUX, CLAUDE-NICOLAS, community designed by, Mar 62: 35; illus, Mar 62: 34
LEE, MASS., May 60: 13 (map), 15
LEE, ALWYN, Sep 62: 104
LEE, GEORGE, May 62: 9
LEECH, JOHN, etchings by. See ILLUSTRATIONS INDEX
LEECH, MARGARET, Jul 62: 37
LEEDS, ENGLAND, Jul 61: 61
LEEMPUT, REMIGIUS VAN, Jul 63: 93
LEEUWENHOEK, ANTON VAN, Sep 58: 23
Portrait of, Sep 58: 33
LEFORT, FRANÇOIS, Sep 59: 66
LEFUEL, HECTOR MARTIN, Sep 60: 81, May 63: 68
LE GALLIENNE, EVA, Jan 63: 106, 107, 108
"LEGEND OF LOVERS," play, Nov 60: 54, 127
LÉGER, FERNAND, Sep 62: 24
Stained-glass window designed by, Sep 62: 25

LE HAVRE, FRANCE, stained-glass window in Dominican chapel, Sep 62: 32
LEHMANN, LOTTE, Sep 59: 56–57
LE HON, COUNTESS, May 63: 54
LEIBNIZ, GOTTFRIED WILHELM VON
Childhood of, May 60: 34–35, 37
Portrait of, May 60: 32
LEICESTER, EARL OF. See COKE, THOMAS
LEIGH, VIVIEN, Sep 63: 77 (note), 80
LEIGH FERMOR, PATRICK, "An Apology for Gluttons," article by, Jan 63: 34–35
LEIGHTON, FREDERICK, BARON, May 62: 78
LEIPZIG, GERMANY, Mozart in, Mar 60: 74
LEISURE
Distribution of, in America, May 59: 22
Memorandum to the President from the Secretary of Arts and Leisure, Nov 62: 18–19
Perils of, Nov 63: 102–9
LEITCH, DAVID, on J. D. Salinger, quoted, May 62: 100, 104
LELY, PETER, Jul 61: 93, Jul 63: 96
LE MAISTRE, JEAN, Mar 62: 92, 94
LEMAÎTRE, FRÉDÉRICK, Mar 62: 118
LEMERCIER, JACQUES, Sep 60: 67
LEMME, DOMMENICO, photograph of, Sep 63: 56
LEMNOS, GREECE, as possible stopping-place of Etruscans, May 60: 62
LE MOITURIER, ANTOINE, Sep 58: 62
LEMONNIER, ANICET-CHARLES-GABRIEL, painting by, Nov 59: 81
LENARD, ALEXANDER, *Winnie ille Pu,* reviewed, Jul 61: 112–15
L'ENCLOS, NINON DE, Mar 61: 116
LENIN, NIKOLAI, Nov 63: 62
LENINGRAD, U.S.S.R., Hermitage Museum, Sep 59: 83, Jan 60: 112
LENNOX, KINCAID, Nov 62: 65–66
LE NÔTRE, ANDRÉ, May 59: 28, 29, 32, Sep 60: 69, May 62: 14, Jul 63: 78, 80, 82, 83
Portrait of, May 59: 32
LENOX, JAMES, Nov 58: 148
LENYA, LOTTE
On Brecht, Bertolt, quoted, May 62: 39–40
Photograph of, May 62: 34
LEO III, BYZANTINE EMPEROR, Nov 63: 26
LEO V, BYZANTINE EMPEROR, Nov 63: 22
LEO VI, BYZANTINE EMPEROR, Nov 63: 22
LEO I, POPE (LEO THE GREAT), encounter with Attila, May 63: 76–80
LEO III, POPE, Jan 62: 26
LEO X, POPE, Jan 62: 41, 43, 45, May 63: 80
LEO XIII, POPE, Jan 62: 45
LEOCHARES, May 59: 122
LEONARDO. See VINCI, LEONARDO DA
LEONBRUNO, MIMMO, photograph of, Sep 63: 52
LEONIDAS
Herodotus quoted on, Mar 59: 133
Statue of, Mar 59: 133
LEONIDAS, EVANGELOS, Nov 58: 73
"LEOPARD, THE," novel by Giuseppe di Lampedusa, Sep 61: 40
Motion picture based on, Jan 62: 104, Jan 63: 38
Quoted, Sep 61: 40, Jan 63: 38
LEOPARDI, GIACOMO
Childhood of, May 60: 34, 35, 37
Portrait of, May 60: 32
LEOPOLD I, HOLY ROMAN EMPEROR, Sep 59: 74
LEOPOLD WILHELM, ARCHDUKE OF AUSTRIA, Jul 61: 94, 95
LEPANTO, BATTLE OF, Nov 61: 110, Jul 63: 49–61
Cervantes at, Nov 61: 111, 112, Jul 63: 50, 58, 60
LEPIDUS, MARCUS AEMILIUS, Nov 58: 111
LE QUEUX, WILLIAM, May 61: 117
LERCHE, CHARLES O., "Contrasting Strategic Styles in the Cold War," quoted, Nov 63: 62
LERICI, CARLO M., May 60: 59–60
LERMA, DUKE OF, Sep 59: 120, Nov 62: 38
LERMAN, LEO, in painting by John Koch, Sep 60: 106–7
LERNER, ALAN JAY, and FREDERICK LOEWE, *Camelot,* May 61: 102–13
LERNER, CARL, Mar 61: 15
LERNER, MAX, on 1948 Presidential election, quoted, Mar 60: 49
LE ROY, JULIEN-DAVID, *Les Ruines des plus beaux monuments de la Grèce,* Mar 62: 55
LESAGE, ALAIN RENÉ, *Gil Blas,* Jul 62: 59
LES ALISCAMPS CEMETERY, Arles, France, Jul 59: 131
LESCAZE, WILLIAM, Sep 59: 8, Sep 62: 58
LESCOT, PIERRE, Sep 60: 62, 65, 66, 67
LESLIE, AL, Jan 63: 25
Painting by, Jan 63: 21
LESLIE, CHARLES ROBERT, Mar 63: 69, Jul 63: 18
LESPINASSE, JULIE DE, Nov 61: 35

Portrait of, Nov 61: 35
LESSING, DORIS, Jan 63: 32
LESSING, ERICH, "Pascal," photographs by, with article by Morris Bishop, Jan 63: 94–104
LESSING, GOTTHOLD EPHRAIM, May 59: 104
"LESSON, THE," play, May 61: 91, 97
Quoted, Sep 62: 35
LE SUEUR, HUBERT, Jul 61: 90
LETCHWORTH, ENGLAND, Jul 59: 11
LE TOURNEUR, PIERRE, Sep 61: 103 (illus)
"LETTER FROM ITALY, A," poem by Joseph Addison, Nov 63: 43–44
"LETTERS FROM DENMARK," drawings by Peter Soederlund, Jul 63: 120
"LETTRES DE CACHET," Jan 60: 85–86
LEVAILLANT, MAURICE, "Napoleon and the Femmes Fatales," article based on *The Passionate Exiles,* book by, Nov 58: 86–89, 142–46
LE VAU, LOUIS, Sep 60: 67, Jul 63: 78, 80, 82, 83
LEVEQUE, GIL, Nov 62: 98
LEVER HOUSE, New York City, Sep 60: 39, Nov 60: 16, May 63: 14
LEVERSON, ADA, Jan 60: 109
LEVERTOV, DENISE, Sep 61: 120
"An Ignorant Person," quoted, Sep 61: 120
LEVIATHAN, Nov 58: 70
LEVIN, MEYER, on Shakespeare Workshop of Joseph Papp, quoted, Nov 60: 117
LEVINE, JACK, Sep 58: 109, 110, 113, Jul 62: 15, 16
Paintings by, Sep 58: 113, Jul 62: 16
Photographs of, Sep 58: 111, May 59: 16
LEVITATION, Nov 60: 31–32
LEVITTOWN, May 60: 5
LEVITZKY, chess player, Jan 62: 116
LEVY, REUBEN, translation of *A Mirror for Princes,* quoted, Jan 63: 60
LEWIS, C. S., Jan 59: 122, May 59: 64–69, 125–27, Sep 63: 7
Portrait of, May 59: 65
Quoted: on advent of romantic love, Jan 62: 57; on verbicide, Jul 63: 37
LEWIS, G., on Dundee, Scotland, quoted, Jul 59: 10
LEWIS, JERRY, Jan 61: 123
LEWIS, JOHN, May 61: 100
LEWIS, OSCAR, *Children of Sánchez,* Nov 62: 110
LEWIS, ROBERT, Mar 60: 119, Nov 62: 106, 107
LEWIS, ROBERT Q., Sep 60: 51
LEWIS, SINCLAIR, Jul 61: 13, Jul 63: 68–69
LEWIS, WYNDHAM, Jan 60: 109
LEYSTER, JUDITH, Sep 58: 26
LHEVINNE, ROSINA, Jan 60: 79, 81
LHOTE, HENRI
"Discovering a Stone Age Museum," excerpts from book by, May 59: 72, 81–83
Photograph of, May 59: 81
LIADOV, ANATOLI K., Nov 62: 44
"LIAISONS DANGEREUSES, LES," motion picture, May 60: 53 (note), Sep 61: 110, May 62: 55
LIANCOURT, DUC DE, Jul 63: 96
LIBBEY-OWENS-FORD, TV commercials of, Nov 60: 123
LIBBY, WILLARD FRANK, photograph of, May 59: 16
LIBERACE, Jan 61: 122
LIBERALISM
In American politics, Jul 61: 66, 68
Personal ethics and, Mar 63: 60–61
LIBERMAN, ALEXANDER
And Circlism, Sep 61: 66–67
"Stones of Venice, The," portfolio of photographs by, Mar 63: 16–24
LIBERTY, Lord Acton's theories, Mar 59: 6, 7
LIBRARIES (see also LIBRARY OF CONGRESS)
At Alexandria, Egypt, Nov 62: 78
At Constantinople, Nov 62: 78
Electronic, Jan 62: 19
Laurentian, in Florence, Nov 62: 94; illus, Nov 62: 88
Of Matthias Corvinus of Hungary, Nov 62: 3, 78
Microlibraries, Sep 62: 42–47, Nov 62: 83
In Moslem Spain, Sep 62: 79, 82, 87
Of Vatican, Jan 62: 27, 31
LIBRARY OF CONGRESS
Award of Bollingen Prize in Poetry, Jul 63: 72–73
Kennedy administration proposals concerning, Sep 61: 14
LIBYA, ANCIENT, May 59: 82, 83
LICHFIELD GROUP, May 59: 92
LICHTENSTEIN, ROY, Jan 63: 25
LICHTENSTEIN, ULRICH VON, Sep 59: 113–17
LICINIUS, ROMAN EMPEROR, Nov 63: 6
"LIEBESTOD," song from *Tristan und Isolde,* Sep 60: 121, May 63: 42, 45
LIEBLING, A. J., May 63: 21
Photograph of, May 63: 21
"LIE DOWN IN DARKNESS," novel by William Styron, May 60: 28
LIEVEN, PRINCESS DE, on music room of Brighton

Pavilion, quoted, Nov 62: 30
"LIFE," magazine (1883–1936), John Held, Jr., and, Jul 63: 118–19
"LIFE," magazine (1936–   ), Jul 61: 66
  Advertising in, Nov 59: 116–17
  Nonconformism of, Mar 59: 112
"LIFE BEHIND THE IVY," article by Gilbert Highet, Sep 60: 117–19
LIFE EXPECTANCY, Jan 59: 94
"LIFELINE UNLIMITED," television program, Sep 61: 113
"LIFE OF EUGENE O'NEILL, THE," book by Arthur and Barbara Gelb, excerpts from, Mar 60: 25–40
"LIFE OF SAMUEL JOHNSON, THE," television play, Nov 58: 82–83
"LIFE ON THE EDUCATIONAL FRONTIER," excerpts from *Bulletin* of Council for Basic Education, Mar 60: 70–71
"LIFTING THE FEDERAL FAÇADE," article by Allan Temko, Jan 60: 18–27, 119–21
LIGHTBODY, CHARLES WAYLAND, "The Judgments of Joan," article by, Mar 62: 88–99
"LIGHTNING," locomotive, Jan 59: 39
LIGORIO, PIRRO, May 63: 35
LIGURIANS, Jul 59: 92–93
LILLIE, BEATRICE, Sep 58: 61
  Photograph of, Sep 58: 58
"LILY WHITE BOYS, THE," musical, Jan 63: 33
LIMERICKS, Sep 58: 130, Nov 63: 100–1
LINACRE, THOMAS, May 62: 91
LINCOLN, ABRAHAM, Mar 60: 16, May 61: 42
  Meet Mr. Lincoln, television production, Mar 60: 126
  And Southern vote, Jul 61: 68
LINCOLN CENTER FOR THE PERFORMING ARTS, New York City, Jul 62: 4–11
  And Actors Studio, Nov 62: 108
  Fountain proposed for, May 62: 16
  Opera house, Nov 58: 28–29, 117–20
  Repertory theatre building, Jul 59: 48
  Vivian Beaumont Theater, Jan 63: 106, 109
LINCOLN MEMORIAL, Washington, D.C., Eero Saarinen quoted on, Jul 60: 79
LINDBERGH, CHARLES A., Sep 58: 10–11, May 59: 5, 8
  Photograph of, Sep 58: 10
LINDFORS, VIVECA, Sep 62: 109–10
LINDSAY, CATHERINE, photograph of, Mar 63: 26
LINDSTROM, ROY, photograph of, May 60: 15
LINEAR B SCRIPT, Jan 61: 77, 81, 98
LINGUET, SIMON NICOLAS HENRI, Jan 60: 86
LINGUISTIC SCIENCE, MODERN. See STRUCTURAL LINGUISTICS
LINNAEUS, CAROLUS, Nov 58: 70
"LION HUNT, THE," painting by Delacroix, May 61: 74; illus, May 61: 78–79
LIONNI, LEO, "exedra" designed by, Nov 59: 109–10
"LION OF SPARTA, THE," motion picture, May 61: 57
LIPCHITZ, JACQUES, Sep 62: 24
LIPKIN, SEYMOUR, Jan 60: 74, 79, 81, Jan 62: 14
  Portrait of, Jan 60: 78
LIPPMANN, WALTER, May 60: 9, 122, Sep 61: 5
  Portrait of, Jan 60: 9
  Quoted: on abundance, Jul 60: 67; on 1948 Presidential election, Mar 60: 49
LIPPOLD, RICHARD, Mar 62: 107
  Construction by, Sep 59: 12
  Painting by, Nov 63: 55
LIPS, JULIUS E., on first appearance of white man in tribal territory, quoted, Sep 60: 11–12
LIPSET, SEYMOUR M., on Vance Packard, quoted, Nov 59: 22
LIPSKY, ELEAZAR, *The Scientists*, Sep 60: 118
LISBON, PORTUGAL
  Earthquake of 1755, Mar 61: 115–16
  Palace of Fronteira garden, May 59: 49
LIST, HERBERT, "How They Live and Die in Naples," photographs by, with text by Vittorio de Sica, Sep 63: 49–59
"LISTENER, THE," magazine, quoted on Jackson Pollock, Sep 60: 121–22
"LISTENING TO THE WIND IN THE PINES," painting by Ma Lin, Jan 61: 25; illus, Jan 61: 22
LI SUNG, Jan 61: 25
  Painting by, Jan 61: 21
LISZT, COSIMA. SEE BÜLOW, COSIMA VON
LISZT, FRANZ, Mar 61: 75, May 61: 84, Mar 63: 27
  Frédéric Chopin by Franz Liszt, reviewed, May 63: 109–10
  In painting by Joseph Danhauser, May 61: 85
  As pianist, Jan 60: 74, 81
  On Sand, George, quoted, May 61: 81
"LITERARY PRIZE GAME, THE," article by David Dempsey, Jul 63: 68–75
LITERATURE (see also AMERICAN LITERATURE; BOOKS; POETRY)
  Ability in, and inbreeding, Mar 62: 75

Beat movement in, Jan 63: 74
Beerbohm, Max, May 61: 33–40
Bowdler, Thomas, Sep 62: 68–71
Byzantine, Nov 63: 33
Dinesen, Isak, Sep 59: 110–12
Don Juan and his disappearance, Jan 62: 56–65
Durrell, Lawrence, Alexandrians of, Mar 60: 113–18
Dutch, of 17th century, Sep 58: 24, 26
And 18th-century neoclassicism, Mar 62: 68
Escapism, in science and historical fiction, May 61: 53
France, writer as conscience of, Nov 59: 66–72
From Freud, Sigmund, memorandum to Norman Mailer, Tennessee Williams, Alberto Moravia, Jean Genet, et al., May 62: 54–55
Iliad and *Odyssey*, historical light on, Jan 61: 73–99
Irish, commemorated by Tree of Coole, Mar 59: 86–89
Joan of Arc in, Mar 62: 97–99
Lewis, C. S., May 59: 64–67, 125–27
Mass culture and, Jan 60: 5, 7, 11
Midland group of Josiah Wedgwood, May 59: 88–97, 128–30
Modern child's taste in, Mar 62: 40–41
"Most mysterious manuscript," Jan 63: 4–9
Motion pictures vs., Sep 60: 7–8
Nature in, Mar 60: 13–16
Nouveau roman, Jan 62: 96–101
Persian, Jan 63: 53, 67
Plays and playwrights. See under THEATRE
Realism in, May 59: 66–67
Romantic revolt, May 61: 58–68, 83
Sitwells, introduction to, Jan 60: 108–9
Smith, Sydney, Mar 59: 90–95, 124–25
Two Spains of *Don Quixote*, Nov 61: 106–13
Utopias and anti-utopias, Mar 63: 72–79
Wodehouse, P. G., and his world, Jan 59: 56–59, 127
Woolf, Virginia, and Lytton Strachey, Jan 60: 106–7
Zen in English Literature, by R. H. Blyth, quoted, Jul 59: 126–27
LITTELL, PHILIP, and Spectric poets, May 60: 46
"LITTLE DORRIT," novel by Charles Dickens, quoted, Sep 58: 131
"LITTLE EYOLF," play, Jan 62: 108
"LITTLE FLIGHT MUSIC, A," article by William K. Zinsser, Mar 62: 100–1
"LITTLE FOXES, THE," play, Jan 60: 123, Jan 63: 112
"LITTLE FUGITIVE, THE," motion picture, Mar 61: 19, Sep 62: 108, 109
"LITTLE LORD FAUNTLEROY," novel by Frances H. Burnett, Mar 63: 107
"LITTLE MARY SUNSHINE," musical, Sep 60: 87
"LITTLE PHOTOGRAPHER, THE," television play, Mar 63: 35
"LITTLE SHOW," musical, Sep 58: 59
LITTLEWOOD, JOAN, Jan 61: 114, Mar 61: 44–45, 103
"LIVE LIKE PIGS," play, Jul 62: 91, 92, 93, 94, Jan 63: 32
LIVIA, EMPRESS OF ROME
  Garden room of, May 59: 27
  Mosaic pavement from villa of, Jul 59: 27, 30
"LIVING ART AND THE PEOPLE'S CHOICE," article, Sep 58: 108–13
"LIVING ROOM, THE," play, Nov 58: 62
LIVINGSTONE, DAVID, Sep 58: 10, 135–36
LIVING THEATRE, THE, Mar 61: 44–46, Mar 62: 106–9, May 62: 35, Sep 62: 111, Jan 63: 107
  "Theatre of Chance" of, Sep 60: 124
"LIVRE DES TOURNOIS, LE," Nov 58: 96
  Illus from, Nov 58: cover, 3, 92–104
LIVY
  On divers, quoted, Nov 58: 71
  In Renaissance curriculum, Jan 60: 62, 68
  Survival of Roman history written by, Nov 62: 76
LLOYD, ARTHUR, "Marriage to a Mermaid," song by, Jan 60: 130
LLOYD, WILLIAM, Nov 63: 64
LOBDELL, FRANK, Jan 59: 13, 14
LOBKOWITZ, JOSEF FRANZ MAXIMILIAN, Nov 62: 44
LODGE, OLIVER, Jan 59: 110
LODGE, THOMAS, *Rosalynde*, Nov 60: 98
LOEFFLER, CHARLES MARTIN, Jul 59: 133
LOESSER, ARTHUR, on Franz Liszt, quoted, Jan 60: 74, 81
LOEWE, FREDERICK, and **ALAN JAY LERNER,** *Camelot*, May 61: 102–13
LOEW'S HOTELS, Jul 63: 115–16
LOGAN, JOSHUA, May 59: 100, Jan 62: 104, May 63: 108
LOGICAL POSITIVISM, Mar 63: 9, May 63: 89
"LOHENGRIN," opera, May 63: 41, 45
  Thomas Beecham quoted on, Mar 62: 103
LOIRE, GABRIEL, Sep 62: 24
LOKESVARA, Jan 59: 62, 64
"LOLITA," novel by Vladimir Nabokov, Jul 62: 90, 91

Motion picture based on, May 63: 112
LOLLOBRIGIDA, GINA, May 59: 99, Mar 61: 99, Sep 63: 80
LOMBART, PIERRE, engravings by, Jul 61: 93
LONDON, ENGLAND
  Banqueting House, Jul 61: 90, 91
  Carlton House, Nov 62: 23, 24
  Covent Garden, Nov 58: 23–24, 26–27, 117
  Of Fox, Charles James, May 60: 98
  Louis Napoleon influenced by, May 63: 58
  Messianic year of 1666 in, Mar 60: 125
  Palladium, Jan 61: 122
  Regent's Park, Nov 62: 29
  Royal Court Theatre, and English Stage Company productions, Jan 63: 26–33
  Royal Festival Hall, Nov 58: 118
  St. Paul's Cathedral, Jul 60: 50
  Savoy Hotel, May 61: 125–26
  Sotheby & Co., Nov 62: 58–67
  Squares of, Jul 61: 54
  Street furniture, Nov 59: 111
  Tall buildings of, Nov 60: 13, 16, 124–25
  Time-Life Building, Eero Saarinen quoted on, Jul 60: 79
  U.S. embassy building, Jan 60: 119, 120, Jul 60: 79
  Water consumption, May 60: 39
LONDON, GEORGE, photograph of, May 63: 44
LONDON, JACK
  Impersonated on television, Mar 63: 35
  In South Seas, Jan 60: 125
LONDON INSTITUTE OF CONTEMPORARY ARTS, Nov 59: 41
"LONDON SHAKESPEARE, THE," by John Munro, quoted on Shylock, Jan 60: 92
"LONELY CROWD, THE," book by David Riesman, quoted, Jul 60: 69, 71
LONG, EARL, on highways, quoted, Jul 60: 71
LONG, RALPH B., on English grammar in 1960's, quoted, May 60: 119
"LONG AND THE SHORT AND THE TALL, THE," play, Jan 63: 32–33
"LONG DAY'S JOURNEY INTO NIGHT," play, Nov 58: 63
  New London, Conn., background of, Mar 60: 25–40
LONGFELLOW, HENRY WADSWORTH, Nov 59: 100
  "My Lost Youth," quoted, May 61: 8
  In painting of Arch of Titus, Nov 59: 101
"LONG FORM, SHORT SHRIFT," article by John Keats, Nov 62: 118–19
LONGGOOD, WILLIAM, on Puritans and bowling, quoted, Mar 63: 93
"LONG, HOT SUMMER, THE," motion picture, Sep 60: 88, Jul 63: 91
LONG ISLAND, N.Y.
  Eastern end of, May 63: 4–27
  Syosset Lanes style show for bowlers, Mar 63: 94
LONGLEAT, Nov 58: 41
"LONG WATCH, THE," play, May 61: 99
"LOOK," magazine, Jul 60: 120
"LOOK AFTER LULU," play, Jan 61: 101, Jan 63: 29, 33 (illus)
"LOOK BACK IN ANGER," play, Nov 58: 62, Jan 63: 27–29, 33 (illus)
"LOOK HOMEWARD, ANGEL," play, Nov 58: 63, 64, Jan 59: 138
"LOOKING BACKWARD," novel by Edward Bellamy, Mar 63: 78
"LOOK-SAY" READING SYSTEM, Jul 63: 42
"LOOK: WE'VE COME THROUGH," play, Jul 62: 49
LOOZ, GÉRARD DE, Nov 58: 105
LOOZ, LOUIS DE, COUNT OF CHINY, Nov 58: 105
LOP, FERDINAND, Jan 61: 71
LOPE DE VEGA. See VEGA
LOPEZ, RUY, Jan 60: 90, 96, Jan 62: 117
LOPOKOVA, LYDIA, Jan 61: 27
LORD, OTIS P., Jul 61: 100, 102, 104, 105
  Portrait of, Jul 61: 103
"LORD AND THE REGALIA, THE," article by Siriol Hugh-Jones, May 63: 92–96
"LORD OF THE ISLES," locomotive, Jan 59: 39
LOREN, SOPHIA, May 59: 99, Nov 59: 126, Mar 61: 99, May 61: 54, Sep 63: 80
LORENZO THE MAGNIFICENT. See MEDICI, LORENZO DE
LORRAIN, CLAUDE, Jul 60: 42, 50, Mar 61: 91, 93, Mar 62: 55, Jul 63: 96, 106
  Painting by, Jul 60: 47
LORRAINE, witchcraft mania in, Nov 59: 58, 60, 61, 62
LOS ANGELES, CALIF.
  Billboards in, May 61: 5
  Mass culture in, Jan 60: 6
  Street furniture, Nov 59: 108
  Suburban areas of, May 61: 19, Jul 61: 63
"LOSS OF INNOCENCE," motion picture, Nov 61: 115

"LOSS OF ROSES, A," play, Jan 62: 104
"LOST MINARET OF JHAM, THE," illustrated feature, Nov 59: 42–43
LOTHIAN, 11TH MARQUIS OF (PHILIP HENRY KERR), Sep 63: 77, 78
LOTI, PIERRE
On Delhi palace, quoted, Mar 61: 21
In South Seas, Jan 60: 125
"LOTUS AND THE ROBOT, THE," book by Arthur Koestler, excerpt from, Mar 61: 4–11
LOUIS VII, KING OF FRANCE, Nov 63: 31
LOUIS IX, KING OF FRANCE (SAINT LOUIS), Sep 60: 60
In painting by Flemish master, Sep 60: 58
LOUIS XI, KING OF FRANCE, May 63: 94
As patron of Jean Fouquet, Nov 61: 88, 97
LOUIS XIII, KING OF FRANCE, Jul 60: 38, Sep 60: 67, Mar 61: 90, Jul 61: 89, 90, Jul 63: 82
Portrait of, Sep 60: 66
LOUIS XIV, KING OF FRANCE, Jul 60: 64, Sep 60: 67, 69, Mar 61: 68, 90, May 61: 126, Jul 61: 94, Nov 61: 34, Jan 63: 102
Bastille in reign of, Jan 60: 85–86, 87
Court of, Nov 59: 76–77; festivals at, Jul 60: 60–61
Cult of bed during reign of, May 60: 129
Fouquet, Nicolas, Vaux-le-Vicomte, and, May 62: 14, Jul 63: 76–83
Gardens of, May 59: 29, 32
Influence on Ludwig II of Bavaria, Jan 61: 35, 42, 125, 126–27
Portrait of, Jul 63: 77
LOUIS XV, KING OF FRANCE, Mar 61: 118, 119, Mar 63: 5, May 63: 102
Gifts to Ottoman court, May 59: 131
And Peter the Great, Sep 59: 80
LOUIS XVI, KING OF FRANCE, Sep 60: 72
Edict on ballooning, Sep 58: 117
LOUIS XVIII, KING OF FRANCE, Jul 62: 56
LOUIS, MORRIS, Jan 63: 25
LOUIS DE BRUGES, Nov 58: 3
LOUISE, QUEEN OF PRUSSIA, May 63: 96, Sep 63: 31, 32
LOUISIANA, Shreveport theatre of Orlin and Irene Corey, Jan 63: 88
"LOUISIANA STORY," motion picture, Mar 61: 17, 98
LOUIS NAPOLEON. See NAPOLEON III
LOUIS PHILIPPE, KING OF FRANCE, Nov 61: 36, May 61: 85, May 63: 57
LOUIS SEIZE STYLE, Mar 62: 61, 64
LOUVAIN, UNIVERSITY OF, Erasmus at, May 62: 94
LOUVRE, Paris, Jul 59: 28, May 63: 67–68
History and architecture of, Sep 60: 57–69, 72, 81–85
Ladies of, paintings, Sep 60: 72–80
Mourners of Dijon at, Sep 58: 62–63
Paintings from collection of Charles I of England owned by, Jul 61: 95
Treasures of, Sep 60: 70–71
"LOUVRE, THE," article by Allan Temko, Sep 60: 57–69, 72, 81
LOVE
In advertising, Nov 59: 113–17
Counselling on, memorandum from Eleanor of Aquitaine to Abigail van Buren and Ann Landers, May 60: 30–31
Courtly, of Middle Ages, Sep 59: 113–17, Jan 62: 57–58
In novels of Lawrence Durrell, May 63: 115–16
Songs from ancient Sumer, Jul 63: 108–9
"LOVE ACCORDING TO MADISON AVENUE," article by Morton M. Hunt, Nov 59: 113–17
"LOVE AMONG THE ROMANS," article by Gilbert Highet, Nov 58: 108–11
"LOVE GAME, THE," motion picture, Jan 62: 109–10
"LOVE OF FOUR COLONELS, THE," play, Nov 58: 82, 83, 138
"LOVERS, THE," motion picture, May 60: 50, 53, Sep 61: 110
"LOVERS AND LOLLIPOPS," motion picture, Mar 61: 19, Sep 62: 108–9
"LOVES OF THE PLANTS, THE," poems by Erasmus Darwin, quoted, Sep 58: 117
"LOVE SONG OF J. ALFRED PRUFROCK, THE," poem by T. S. Eliot, quoted, Sep 61: 117
LOW, DAVID, Jan 61: 72
"LOW & INSIDE," book by Robert Osborn, Sep 60: 43
LOWELL, AMY, Sep 61: 117
And Spectric poets, May 60: 43, 48
LOWELL, FRANCIS, *Joan of Arc,* Mar 62: 98, 99
LOWELL, JAMES RUSSELL, Jul 59: 133
LOWELL, ROBERT, Sep 61: 117, 118, Jan 62: 10, Jul 63: 72
"Children of Light," quoted, Sep 61: 118
Translation of Heine by, quoted, Sep 60: 113
"LOWER DEPTHS, THE," motion picture, Jul 62: 43–44
"LOWER DEPTHS, THE," play, Nov 62: 110

LOWES, JOHN LIVINGSTON, *The Road to Xanadu,* cited, May 63: 115, Sep 63: 48
LOWRY, LEROY, in painting by John Koch, Sep 60: 107
LOWRY, L. S., painting by, May 62: 76
LOWRY, W. McNEIL
As director of Humanities and Arts program of Ford Foundation, Jan 62: 7–14
Photograph of, Jan 62: 4
"LOW SPEED," tape recorder composition by Otto Luening, Jan 59: 54
LSD. See LYSERGIC ACID DIETHYLAMIDE
LUBELL, SAMUEL, Nov 59: 23
LÜBKE, WILHELM, May 63: 68
LUCAN
On Phocaean diver, quoted, Nov 58: 71
In Renaissance curriculum, Jan 60: 62
LUCE, CLARE BOOTHE, Jul 60: 120
LUCIAN, quoted
On paintings, Mar 61: 91; of marriage of Roxane and Alexander, Mar 59: 55
On Semitic moon-goddess, Jan 60: 134
LUCIANO, LUCKY, Sep 61: 44
LUCILIUS, GAIUS, Nov 62: 80
LUCKMAN, CHARLES, Jul 60: 121
"LUCKY JIM," novel by Kingsley Amis, Sep 60: 119
LUCRETIUS
On mountains, quoted, Mar 60: 13
Survival of works by, Nov 62: 76, 80
LUCULLUS, Sep 58: 140
LUDLOW, FRITZ HUGH, Jul 63: 114
LUDWIG I, KING OF BAVARIA, Jan 61: 37–38
And Aegina marbles, Sep 59: 30–32, 49
LUDWIG II, KING OF BAVARIA, Nov 61: 4
And his castles, Jan 61: 34–43
In painting by Wenig, Jan 61: 37
LUDWIG III, PALATINE ELECTOR, May 63: 99
"LUDWIG'S DREAM CASTLES," article by Mary Cable, Jan 61: 34–43
LUENING, OTTO, Jan 59: 54, Sep 60: 32
Photograph of, Jan 59: 52
LUFTHANSA, advertising by, Jan 62: 113
LUKACS, JOHN, "Poker and American Character," article by, Nov 63: 56–62
LUKE, SAINT, John A. T. Robinson quoted on, Sep 63: 5
LULLY, JEAN BAPTISTE, May 59: 29, Jul 60: 50, Sep 60: 69, Nov 62: 80, 91, Jul 63: 77, 81
"LULU," opera, Igor Stravinsky quoted on, Sep 58: 132
LUMET, SIDNEY, Sep 60: 51, Mar 63: 35
LUNARDI, VINCENT, Sep 58: 5, 118–19
LUNAR SOCIETY, May 59: 92, 94, 128–30
"LUNCH HOUR, THE," motion picture, Mar 63: 36
LUNGSHAN CULTURE, of China, Jan 61: 11
LUNNING PRIZE, Jul 63: 63
LUNT, ALFRED, Nov 58: 120, Jan 61: 31, Jul 62: 40, Nov 62: 107
Caricature of, Jul 62: 32
In *The Visit,* Nov 58: 62–63, 65
LUPINO, IDA, Sep 63: 80
LURÇAT, JEAN, Sep 62: 24
LUSIERI, GIOVANNI BATTISTA, on Aegina marbles, quoted, Sep 59: 49
LUSIGNAN. See GUY DE LUSIGNAN
"LUST FOR LIFE," biography by Irving Stone, Jan 63: 75
LUTF ULLAH, SHEIK, Jan 63: 72
LUTHER, MARTIN, Sep 58: 46
Vs. Erasmus, May 62: 90, 91, 93–95
And witchcraft, Nov 59: 58, 59
LUTTRELL, HENRY, Nov 59: 92, 95
LÜTZEN, BATTLE OF, Nov 62: 38
LUVISI, LEE, Sep 61: 87
LUXEMBOURG, European school in, Mar 63: 7
LUXEMBOURG, COUNT OF, Nov 58: 105
LYCON, Jul 60: 100, 102, 117
LYDIA
As place of origin of Etruscans, May 60: 61–62
Sardis, Sep 63: 82–89
LYLY, JOHN, *Euphues,* John Barth quoted on, Jan 63: 37
LYNCH, CHARLES (JUDGE LYNCH), May 60: 126
LYNES, RUSSELL, Nov 59: 23, 24, May 60: 19
Articles by: "Bowling Goes Bourgeois," Mar 63: 89–95; "Jules Feiffer's Wicked Eye and Ear," Nov 61: 48, 57; "Osborn's Americans," Sep 60: 41–43
On government aid to artists, quoted, Mar 63: 27
Photograph of, May 60: 19
Surfeit of Honey, A, quoted, Jul 60: 67
Tastemakers, The, quoted, Mar 59: 113, 114
LYON, PETER (see also CERAM, C. W., co-author), articles by
"Adventurous Angels, The," May 59: 4–19
"Artful Banker, The," Nov 60: 4–11
"When Man First Left the Earth," Sep 58: 114–28
LYSERGIC ACID DIETHYLAMIDE, May 63: 28–31, 114–15

LYSIPPUS
Malraux, André, quoted on, Nov 58: 15
Portraits of Alexander by, Jan 59: 99
Sculpture by, Nov 58: 7
"LYSISTRATA," play by Aristophanes, Jan 63: 29
LYTTELTON, THOMAS (2D BARON), on gardens at Stowe, quoted, May 59: 47

M

MAASS, JOHN
"Image of the White Man in the Art of Other Races, The," portfolio assembled and described by, Sep 60: 15–29
"Stately Mansions of the Imagination, The," article by, with portfolio of paintings and designs, Sep 63: 10–27
MABUSE, JAN, Jul 63: 93
MacAGY, DOUGLAS, Jan 59: 13
"MACARONIS," May 60: 98
MacARTHUR, DOUGLAS, Nov 60: 122
Portrait of, May 60: 7
MacARTHUR, JAMES, Mar 63: 35
MACAULAY, THOMAS BABINGTON, Mar 59: 125
Childhood of, May 60: 34, 35
Portraits of, Mar 59: 90, May 60: 32
Quoted: on Peter the Great, Sep 59: 66; on Pitt, William the Younger, May 60: 37; on Smith, Sydney, Mar 59: 90
MacAVOY, EDOUARD, portrait of Somerset Maugham by, Jan 59: 107; illus, Jan 59: 106
"MACBETH," play by Shakespeare, Mar 60: 121
All-Negro production, Jul 63: 87
Humor in, Mar 63: 106
Motion pictures based on: Japanese, Jul 62: 44; production of Orson Welles, Jul 63: 85, 90
Quoted, Mar 63: 88
"McCALL'S," magazine, Jan 63: 114
Story of Zsa Zsa Gabor bought by, Jul 60: 120
Togetherness campaign of, Nov 58: 30–31, 147
MACCARI, Italian artist, May 59: 109
McCARTHY, FRANCIS JOSEPH, Jan 59: 8
McCARTHY, JOSEPH, Nov 63: 69
Peter Ustinov quoted on, Nov 58: 139
McCARTHY, MARY, Sep 60: 118, Jul 63: 39
Quoted: on gadgets, Jul 60: 71; on present-day journalism, Mar 60: 51; on Salinger, J. D., May 62: 100–1
McCARTHYISM, May 62: 9
McCHESNEY, ROBERT, Jan 59: 13, 14
McCLOY, JOHN J., Jul 60: 120
McCLURE, MICHAEL, Sep 58: 40, 42
McCONNELL, FREDERIC, Jan 63: 107
McCORMACK, JOHN, Sep 59: 52
McCORMICK, HAROLD, Sep 60: 102
McCORMICK, MRS. HAROLD, Sep 60: 102
McCOY, WILLIAM, Sep 63: 48
McCRACKEN, JAMES, Nov 61: 80
Photographs of, Nov 61: 77, 79, 81
McCULLERS, CARSON, *Ballad of the Sad Café,* Sep 61: 79
McCURDY, HAROLD G., "The Childhood Pattern of Genius," article by, May 60: 32–38
MACDONALD, DWIGHT
As critic of mass culture, Jan 60: 6, 7
On teaching of English, quoted, Jul 63: 41
MACDONALD, GEORGE, *Phantastes,* May 59: 66
MacDONALD, JEANETTE, Sep 58: 58
McDONALD, JOHN, *Strategy in Poker, Business, and War,* Nov 63: 57 (note), 58–59, 61
MacDOUGALL, CURTIS, *Hoaxes,* Jan 61: 72
McDOUGALL, WILLIAM, Jan 59: 109
MacDOWELL, EDWARD, Jul 59: 20, Mar 63: 27–28
Bust of, Mar 63: 31
McDOWELL, HARRIS B., JR., Sep 61: 17
MacDOWELL, MARIAN NEVINS (MRS. EDWARD)
And MacDowell Colony, Mar 63: 26–33
Photograph of, Mar 63: 31
MacDOWELL COLONY, Mar 63: 26–33
MACEDONIA, Alexander the Great of, May 59: 28–59
McENTEE, JERVIS, painting by (with Frederick Church and G. P. A. Healy). Nov 59: 101
McGAHEY, JEAN, Jan 59: 18
McGEE, REECE J. See CAPLOW, THEODORE, co-author
McGHEE, GEORGE C., Sep 61: 13
McGINLEY, ARTHUR, Mar 60: 27, 28, 35–36, 39
McGINLEY, EVELYN ESSEX, Mar 60: 27, 30
McGINLEY, JOHN, Mar 60: 27, 29
MacGRATH, LEUEEN, Jan 62: 106
MACHIAVELLI, NICOLÒ, May 62: 89, 95
MACHINE CIVILIZATION. See INDUSTRIAL CIVILIZATION
McHUGH, VINCENT, Jan 59: 18
MacINNES, HELEN, May 63: 22

Photograph of, May 63: 23
MacIVER, LOREN, Jul 62: 15, 21
  Painting by, Jul 62: 21
McKAIN, BRUCE, portrait of, with painting by, Jul 61: 25
MACKAY, CLARENCE, Sep 58: 63
McKEE, ALEXANDER, *H.M.S. Bounty,* Sep 63: 42, 45 (note), 47
McKEE, MILDRED, Sep 59: 89–90, 122
  Photograph of, Sep 59: 88
McKENDRICK, NEIL, articles by
  "Enigmatic Urn, The," Nov 63: 63–65
  "Pompeii," Mar 62: 42–69
  "Wedgwood and His Friends," May 59: 88–97, 128–30
McKENNA, SIOBHAN, Mar 60: 121
MACKENZIE, COMPTON, Mar 61: 32
MACKENZIE, HENRY, May 63: 82
McKIM, CHARLES, May 63: 73
McKIM, MEAD, AND WHITE, Jan 60: 23, Jan 63: 11
MACKINAC ISLAND, MICH., Grand Hotel, Jan 61: 104, 108
McKINNELL, NOEL MICHAEL
  And design for Boston City Hall, Jan 63: 10–15
  Photograph of, Jan 63: 11
MACKINTOSH, JAMES, Mar 59: 92
MACKLIN, CHARLES, Jan 60: 92
  Portrait of, Jan 60: 90
McKNIGHT, NANCY, Nov 62: 68
McLAGLEN, VICTOR, photograph of, Sep 63: 80
MacLAINE, SHIRLEY, Jan 62: 104
MacLEISH, ARCHIBALD, Jan 59: 134, Jul 63: 69, 70, 72
  Drawing of, Jan 60: 48
  Interview with, on being a poet in the theatre, Jan 60: 48–56
  J.B., Jan 60: 49–56, May 62: 82, Jan 63: 88
  Panic, Jul 63: 87
MacLENNAN, HUGH, "The Rout of the Classical Tradition," article by, Nov 60: 17–24
MACLEOD, GEORGE, Sep 63: 106
McLIAM, JOHN, Nov 60: 116
MACLISE, DANIEL, painting by, Sep 59: 72–73
MacLOW, JACKSON, *The Marrying Maiden,* Sep 60: 124, Mar 61: 45–46
McMEIN, NEYSA, Jul 62: 37
MACMILLAN, HAROLD, photograph of, May 62: 58
MacMONNIES, FREDERICK WILLIAM, Sep 60: 100, 127
McNALLY, JAMES B., Nov 60: 117
McNAMARA, ROBERT, Sep 61: 10
McNAUGHTON, JOHN, Sep 61: 13
McNEIL, CLAUDIA, May 63: 108
McPEAK, WILLIAM, Jan 62: 7
McQUADE, LAWRENCE, Sep 61: 13
McQUEEN, STEVE, May 61: 114, 115, Mar 63: 36
MACREADY, WILLIAM CHARLES, Mar 62: 117
MACY'S STORES, Togetherness campaign, Nov 58: 31
"MADAME BOVARY," novel by Flaubert, Jan 62: 62, 64
MADDOW, BEN, Mar 61: 14
"MADEMOISELLE," magazine, advertising in, Nov 59: 113, 115
"MADEMOISELLE COLOMBE," play, Nov 60: 127
MADERNA, CARLO, Jan 62: 43
MADINAT AL-ZAHIRA, Sep 62: 82, 87
MADINAT AL-ZAHRA, Sep 62: 78, 87
MADISON, DOLLEY, Sep 61: 9, 14
  Washington, D.C., home of, Sep 61: 14
"MAD MAGGIE." See "DULLE GRIET"
"MADNESS AT MONK'S PLACE, THE," Jul 61: 76–77
"MADONNA AND CHILD," painting by Raphael, Nov 60: 30
"MADONNA OF CHANCELLOR ROLIN," painting by Jan van Eyck, Sep 60: 72
"MADONNA WITH RABBIT," painting by Titian, Jul 61: 95; illus, Jul 61: 86
"MAD PROFESSOR, THE," novel by Hermann Sudermann, Sep 60: 119
MADRID, SPAIN
  American abstract expressionism in, Nov 59: 120
  Hilton Hotel, Mar 63: 117
  U.S. embassy building, Jan 60: 25, 27
  Zarzuela Hippodrome, Sep 59: 19
MAECENAS, GAIUS, May 59: 11
MAEKAWA, KUNIO, Jul 61: 60
MAFIA, Sep 61: 32, 38, 44
MAGAZINES, mass media and imaginary audience, Mar 60: 46–51
MAGELLAN, FERDINAND, Jan 60: 30
MAGENTA, BATTLE OF, May 63: 63
MAGGS BROTHERS, Nov 60: 99
MAGIC REALISM, in painting, Sep 58: 109, 113
MAGNANI, ANNA, Mar 61: 99
MAGNENTIUS, FLAVIUS POPILIUS, ROMAN EMPEROR, Sep 63: 41

"MAGNIFICENT AMBERSONS, THE," motion picture, Jul 63: 90
"MAGNIFICENT SEVEN, THE," motion picture, Jul 62: 46
  Reviewed, May 61: 114–15
MAGNOL, PIERRE, May 60: 127
"MAGOO, MR.," Nov 60: 122
"MAGPIE'S NEST IN A LONDON MANSION," article by Peter Quennell, Nov 63: 72–83
MAGRITTE, RENÉ, Jan 62: 77–79, 81, 82
  Paintings by. See ILLUSTRATIONS INDEX
MAGUIRE'S OPERA HOUSE, San Francisco, Jan 59: 6
"MAHABHARATA," Hindu epic, Jan 59: 63
MAHAN, EDDIE, Jul 62: 34
MAHARAJ, BRIJMOHAN, photograph of, Sep 63: 66
MAHDIA, TUNISIA, underwater archaeological discoveries at, Nov 58: 73
MAHLER, ALMA (MRS. GUSTAV), Nov 61: 61
MAHLER, GUSTAV, Nov 58: 25, Jul 59: 18, 21, May 63: 43
  Balanchine, George, quoted on, Jan 61: 47
  Stravinsky, Igor, quoted on, Sep 58: 82
MAHMUD II, SULTAN OF TURKEY, May 59: 60, 62
MAHMUD OF GHAZNI, Jan 63: 67
  In Persian miniature, Jan 63: 62
MAI, ANGELO, Nov 62: 77, 84, 89–90
"MAIDS, THE," play, Nov 61: 99
MAIL. See POST OFFICE
MAILER, NORMAN K., Jul 61: 13, Jul 63: 69
  Advertisements for Myself, Jul 60: 120
  On alienation of artist, quoted, Jan 60: 7
  Kazin, Alfred, quoted on, Jul 62: 101, 102
  Memorandum from Sigmund Freud to, May 62: 54–55
MAILLART, ROBERT, Mar 59: 21, 24, Sep 59: 6
MAIMONIDES, Sep 62: 88
MAINE, state song, quoted, Nov 61: 119
MAINE, DUC DU, Nov 61: 34
MAINE, DUCHESSE DU, Mar 61: 116, 118
"MAIN LINE, THE," of Pennsylvania Railroad, Jul 63: 7–8, 24
MAINTENON, MARQUISE DE (FRANÇOISE D'AUBIGNÉ), Sep 59: 80
MAINZ, GERMANY, Mar 59: 84
MAISON D'EUROPE, Douai, France, Mar 63: 7
"MAJOR BARBARA," play, Nov 58: 136, Jan 63: 88, May 63: 10
MAJORCA, SPAIN, Mar 61: 22
  Home of Robert Graves on, Jan 62: 53, 55
MAKASSAR, INDONESIA, Mar 61: 22–23
"MAKING A CULT OF CONFUSION," article by Walter Kerr, Sep 62: 33–41
"MAKING OF A MASTER, THE," article by Theodore H. White, Jul 60: 73–75, 126–27
"MAKING SOMETHING NEW OF TRADITION," article by Cranston Jones, Sep 61: 58–63
MALAMUD, BERNARD, Jan 62: 8
  Alfred Kazin quoted on, Jul 62: 101, 102
MALASPINA, ALEJANDRO, Jul 59: 62
MALATESTA, BATTISTA, Jan 60: 64
MALEBRANCHE, NICOLAS DE, quoted, Mar 61: 92
MALEVICH, KASIMIR, Nov 59: 121, May 61: 21, Nov 61: 69
MALIBRAN, MARIA, Sep 59: 55, 56
MA LIN, Jan 61: 25
  Painting by, Jan 61: 22
MALINA, JUDITH, Sep 60: 124
  And The Living Theatre, Mar 62: 106–9
MALIPIERO, FRANCESCO, Nov 62: 46
MALLAHA, ISRAEL, archaeological site, Sep 62: 7 (map), 8
MALLE, LOUIS, May 60: 53, 55, Sep 61: 110, Jan 62: 109
  Portrait of, May 60: 51
MALLORY, GEORGE, on mountain climbing, quoted, Sep 58: 7
MALLOWAN, M. E. L., Sep 59: 103
"MALONE DIES," novel by Samuel Beckett, Sep 60: 113
MALORY, THOMAS, *Morte d'Arthur,* May 59: 126, May 60: 115–18
MALRAUX, ANDRÉ, Jul 59: 129, Nov 59: 68, 72, May 60: 55, Jan 62: 97, May 62: 81
  Ionesco, Eugène, quoted on, May 61: 93
  Man's Fate, Jul 63: 75
  Metamorphosis of the Gods, discussed, Nov 58: 4–17, 112–17
  Quoted: on arts of delectation, Jan 63: 113; on Gislebertus, Sep 61: 48; on paintings in National Gallery of Art, Jan 63: 73
MALTA, Knights of St. John on, Mar 61: 61, 63–69, Jul 63: 50
MALTA, SOVEREIGN ORDER OF, Mar 61: 70
MALTHUS, THOMAS ROBERT, Mar 59: 95
MAMAEA, Nov 63: 63
MAMEROT, SEBASTIEN, painting by, Mar 61: 53
MAMMOTH, as source of ivory, May 60: 93, 121

MAN, SCIENCE OF. See ANTHROPOLOGY
"MAN AND SUPERMAN," play, Nov 58: 136
MANASSEH BEN ISRAEL. See MENASSEH BEN ISRAEL
MANATEE, as source of mermaid legend, Jan 60: 135
"MANCHURIAN CANDIDATE, THE," motion picture, Mar 63: 35
MANDANE, mother of Cyrus the Great, Jan 63: 43
"MANDARINS, THE," novel by Simone de Beauvoir, Jan 62: 111
MANDEL, LORING, May 62: 117
MANDER, CAREL VAN, Jan 59: 44, 47
MANESSIER, ALFRED, Sep 62: 24
  Stained-glass wall designed by, Sep 62: 28
MANET, ÉDOUARD, Jan 59: 103, Nov 59: 121, Mar 60: 54, 57, May 60: 103, Jul 62: 64, 72, Nov 62: 64, May 63: 70, Sep 63: 96
  Paintings by, Sep 60: 76–77, May 63: 74–76
MANET, EUGÈNE, in painting by Édouard Manet, May 63: 75
MANEY, RICHARD, May 61: 103
"MAN FOR ALL SEASONS, A," play, May 62: 110–11, Sep 62: 111
MANFREDI, BARTOLOMEO, Jan 60: 66
MANGANO, SILVANA, May 59: 99, Mar 61: 100
  In *Barabbas,* Mar 63: 110
MANHEIM, RALPH, *The Tin Drum,* translated by, reviewed, Mar 63: 111–13
"MANHUNT," television show, Sep 60: 51
MANI and MANICHAEISM, Jan 61: 63, May 61: 117, Jan 63: 52, 58, 59, 67
"MANIFESTO OF SURREALISM," by André Breton, Mar 59: 78
"MAN IN MODERN FICTION," book by Edmund Fuller, quoted, May 60: 22
"MAN IN THE IRONIC MASK, THE," article by Burton Hersh, May 62: 34–41
"MAN IN THE MOONE, THE," romance by Francis Godwin, Mar 63: 76
MANKOWITZ, WOLF, on Wedgwood copy of Portland vase, quoted, Nov 63: 64
MANLY, JOHN M., Jan 63: 6
MANN, DELBERT, Sep 60: 51
MANN, HORACE, in painting by Zoffany, Nov 59: 92–93
MANN, THEODORE, Mar 60: 95, 96, 120–21
  Photograph of, Mar 60: 94
MANN, THOMAS, Sep 59: 118, Nov 60: 119, May 62: 39, 40, Mar 63: 6, 25
  Buddenbrooks, Jan 62: 62
MANNA, Mar 60: 89
"MANNA," painting by Poussin, Mar 61: 89
MANNERS. See ETIQUETTE
MANNES, MARYA, May 63: 17
  Photograph of, May 63: 16
MANNESMANN BUILDING, Düsseldorf, Nov 60: 124, 125; illus, Nov 60: 12–13
MANNHEIM, GERMANY, theatre at, Jul 59: 48
"MANON," opera, Thomas Beecham quoted on, Mar 62: 103
"MAN OUT OF SEASON, A," excerpt from *The Western Intellectual Tradition,* book by J. Bronowski and Bruce Mazlish, May 62: 88–95
"MAN'S A MAN, A," play, Mar 63: 107
"MAN'S CHALLENGE: THE USE OF THE EARTH," article by Julian Huxley, Sep 58: 48–55
"MAN'S FATE," novel by André Malraux, Jul 63: 75
MANSFIELD, JAYNE, Nov 62: 113
"MAN'S FIRST MURALS," article by James Mellaart, Sep 62: 10–13
"MAN'S FIRST REVOLUTION," article by John Pfeiffer, Sep 62: 4–9
MANSO, LEO, Jul 61: 13–14, 20–21
  Portrait of, with painting by, Jul 61: 20
MANSOURI, LOTFI, photograph of, Nov 61: 79
MANSUR-AL. See ALMANZOR
"MAN'S WAY WITH THE WILDERNESS," article by Paul Brooks, Mar 60: 12–16
MANTEGNA, ANDREA, Jul 59: 29, Jan 60: 66, Jul 61: 90, 94, 95, Jan 62: 31, Jul 63: 94
  Paintings by. See ILLUSTRATIONS INDEX
MANTUA, ITALY
  Renaissance court at, Jan 60: 64, 66
  School of Vittorino da Feltre (La Giocosa), Jan 60: 59–68
MANTUA, DUKES OF. See GONZAGA FAMILY
MANUFACTURERS TRUST COMPANY
  Art program of, Nov 60: 4, 8
  Building in New York City, Sep 59: 18
MANULIS, MARTIN, Mar 63: 35
MANUS, of Admiralty Islands, Americanization of, May 60: 122–23
MANUTIUS, ALDUS, Sep 59: 126
MANUWAI, RAPHAEL, May 60: 123
"MAN WHO CLEANED UP SHAKESPEARE, THE," article by E. M. Halliday, Sep 62: 68–71

"MAN WHO 'DESTROYED' PARIS, THE," article by Wolf Von Eckardt, May 63: 50–75
Comment on, May 63: 105
"MAN WHO NEVER STOPPED PLAYING, THE," article by David Cecil, May 61: 33–40
"MAN WITH THE GOLDEN ARM, THE," motion picture, May 62: 117
MAN WITH THE IRON MASK, Jan 60: 85
"MANY LOVES," dramatic sketches by William Carlos Williams, Mar 62: 106, 107
MANZIKERT, BATTLE OF, Nov 63: 28, 31
MANZONI, ALESSANDRO, May 61: 70
MAPLESON, JAMES H., Nov 58: 119
On Adelina Patti, quoted, Sep 59: 54
MAPOGA, N'debele chief, Nov 60: 65
MAPS. See ILLUSTRATIONS INDEX
MAPUNGUBWE, archaeological site in northern Transvaal, Mar 63: 41 (map), 58
MAQQARI, AL-, *History of the Mohammedan Dynasties in Spain,* quoted, Sep 62: 87
MARANTZ, IRVING, portrait of, with painting by, Jul 61: 24
"MARATHON BOY," statue, Nov 58: 73, 76; illus, Nov 58: 74
MARBLE, FANNY and HARRY, Jul 59: 114–15
MARCA-RELLI, CONRAD, painting by, Nov 60: 8
MARCEL, ETIENNE, Sep 60: 60
MARCELLINUS, AMMIANUS, Jan 60: 41
MARCH, FREDRIC, May 61: 55
MARCHAL, HENRI, on Angkor, quoted, Jan 59: 81
MARCHIOLY. See MATTIOLI
MARCI, JOANNES MARCUS, Jan 63: 6–7
MARCIANA, Sep 63: 39
MARCKS, GERHARD, Nov 61: 61, 64
MARCUS, MARCIA, Jan 63: 25
Painting by, Jan 63: 18
MARCUS AURELIUS, May 63: 38, Nov 63: 64
Coinage during reign of, Sep 63: 38, 39; illus, Sep 63: 36, 39
MAREN, ROGER, on accident as principle of composition, quoted, Sep 60: 32
"MARGERY" (MRS. LE ROI GODDARD CRANDON), Jan 59: 108–11
MARGHERITA OF SAVOY, Nov 58: 107
MARGO, BORIS, portrait of, with painting by, Jul 61: 27
MARI, Mesopotamian city, Jul 61: 39
MARIA AMALIA, QUEEN OF NAPLES, Mar 62: 50
Portrait of, Mar 62: 50
MARIA CAROLINA, QUEEN OF NAPLES, Mar 62: 56
"MARIAGE DE LOTI, LE," novel by Pierre Loti, Jan 60: 125
"MARIA GOLOVIN," opera, Jan 60: 15, 17, 122
MARICQ, ANDRÉ, Nov 59: 43
MARIE, QUEEN OF BAVARIA, Jan 61: 37, 38–39
MARIE ANTOINETTE, QUEEN OF FRANCE, Mar 62: 35
And classical revival, Mar 62: 61, 64, 68
Fox, Charles James, quoted on execution of, May 60: 124
Jewels of, May 63: 96
MARIEMONT, OHIO, Jul 59: 11
MARIGNY, MARQUIS DE, Sep 60: 72
MARILLAC, MICHEL, Sep 59: 121
MARINA, Indian interpreter for Cortes, Nov 63: 95–96
MARINATOS, SPYRIDON, Nov 62: 93
MARINO, GIOVANNI BATTISTA, Mar 61: 79, 80
MARINO, JOSEPH, Jan 62: 106
MARIOTTI, MARCELLO, "A Theory of the Coiffured Lasses," drawings by, Mar 63: 118–19
"MARISOL'S MANNEQUINS," illustrated feature, Mar 63: 102–4
MARITAIN, JACQUES, Sep 59: 118, Nov 59: 68, Mar 62: 99
Photograph of, Sep 59: 26
On Rouault, Georges, quoted, Nov 62: 48, 57
MARIUS, GAIUS, May 62: 45, 46
MARK, SAINT, format of gospel by, Nov 62: 86
MARK ANTONY (MARCUS ANTONIUS), Nov 58: 111, Sep 63: 35
At Ephesus, Sep 58: 140
And library at Alexandria, Nov 62: 78
MARKELIUS, SVEN, Jul 62: 8
MARKET PSYCHOLOGY INC., Jul 61: 118
MARKHAM, EDWIN, Jul 63: 69
MARKOVA, ALICIA, Jan 61: 46
MARKS, HENRY STACY, painting by, May 62: 74
MARKS, PERCY, Jul 63: 118
MARLBORO CIGARETTES, advertising by, Jan 62: 113
MARLBORO COLLEGE, Sep 61: 83, 87
MARLBOROUGH, 1ST DUCHESS OF (SARA), Sep 61: 70–76
Portrait of, Sep 61: 72
MARLBOROUGH, DUCHESS OF (CONSUELO VANDERBILT), Sep 61: 77
Photograph of, Sep 61: 77

MARLBOROUGH, DUCHESS OF (LILLIAN WARREN), Sep 61: 77
MARLBOROUGH, 1ST DUKE OF (JOHN CHURCHILL), Sep 61: 69–77
Portrait of, Sep 61: 68
MARLBOROUGH, 3D DUKE OF (CHARLES SPENCER), Sep 61: 76
MARLBOROUGH, 4TH DUKE OF (GEORGE SPENCER), Sep 61: 76
MARLBOROUGH, 7TH DUKE OF, Sep 61: 77
MARLBOROUGH, 8TH DUKE OF, Sep 61: 77
MARLBOROUGH, 9TH DUKE OF, Sep 61: 77
On Blenheim Palace, quoted, Sep 61: 70
Photograph of, Sep 61: 77
MARLBOROUGH, 10TH DUKE OF, Sep 61: 69
MARLIK, IRAN, archaeological site, Nov 62: 100–4
MARLOW, WILLIAM, painting by, Sep 63: 19
MARLOWE, CHRISTOPHER, *The Jew of Malta,* Jan 60: 90, 92, 96
MARMONTEL, JEAN FRANÇOIS, Jan 60: 88
MARMSTEDT, LORENS, Sep 60: 8
MARNOCK, chamber-boy to Mary, Queen of Scots, Jul 63: 32
MARQUAND, J. P., on Algonquin Round Table, quoted, Jul 62: 38
MARQUESAS ISLANDS, Gauguin in, Jan 60: 32, 124
"MARQUISE WENT OUT AT FIVE, THE," novel by Claude Mauriac, May 62: 113, 114–15
MARRIAGE, as seen by advertisers, Nov 59: 116–17
"MARRIAGE OF THE VIRGIN, THE," illumination by Jean Fouquet, Nov 61: 97; illus, Nov 61: 90
MARRIAGE STELE, of Ramses II, Jul 60: 124
"MARRYING MAIDEN, THE," play, Sep 60: 124, Mar 61: 45–46
MARS, planet, Jan 59: 29, Nov 63: 52
MARSCHAK, JACOB, Nov 63: 61
MARSEILLES, FRANCE, May 61: 4
Apartment house designed by Le Corbusier, Nov 60: 125, Mar 61: 36
Early history of, Jul 59: 92, 93, 95
MARSH, FELICIA MEYER (MRS. REGINALD), in painting by John Koch, Sep 60: 107
MARSHALL, ALFRED, *Principles of Economics,* quoted, Sep 60: 35
MARSHALL, ARMINA, May 60: 28
MARSHALL, FRANK JAMES, Jan 62: 116, 119
Photograph of, Jan 62: 114
MARSHALL, GEORGE C., May 62: 8
MARSHALL, HERBERT, Sep 63: 77, 78, 79
Photograph of, Sep 63: 76
MARSHALL, THURGOOD, Nov 60: 86
MARSHALL ISLANDS, Jan 60: 127
MARSHMAN, D. M., JR., "From the Shapely Form to a New Art Form," article by, Sep 58: 56–61, 143–44
MARSICANO, NICHOLAS, painting by, Sep 63: 92
MARTEL, CHARLES, Sep 62: 74–75
"MARTEREAU," novel by Nathalie Sarraute, Jan 62: 97, 98
MARTIAL, quoted, Jul 61: 112
On Pompeii, Mar 62: 44
On Vesuvius, Mar 62: 43, 45
MARTIN, MR. and MRS. BRADLEY, Nov 58: 148, Jul 63: 77
MARTIN, JEROME, "Mitosis by Martin," cartoons by, Nov 62: 120
MARTIN, THEODORE, on Queen Victoria, quoted, May 61: 40
MARTIN, VICTOR, Jul 59: 79
MARTINEAU, HARRIET, on Americans, quoted, Nov 59: 22
"MARTINET OR MARTYR," article by William Goldhurst, Sep 63: 42–48
MARTINI, SIMONE, *Madonna and Child with Four Saints,* Jul 59: 30
"MARTY," television play and motion picture, May 59: 101, Sep 60: 49, 51, 54, 56
MARTYN, EDWARD, Mar 59: 87
"MARTYRDOM OF SAINT APOLLONIA, THE," illumination by Jean Fouquet, Nov 61: 97; illus, Nov 61: 94
MARVELL, ANDREW, quoted, Mar 61: 93
On mountains, Mar 60: 14
MARX, GROUCHO, Sep 62: 41
MARX, KARL, Jan 59: 25, Mar 59: 9, 10, 12, Jul 62: 18, Mar 63: 76, 79, May 63: 54
On art, quoted, Sep 60: 38
Portrait of, Mar 59: 9
MARX, LOUIS, May 61: 102
MARX BROTHERS, May 61: 91
And "absurd" plays, Sep 62: 41
MARXISM
And chess, Nov 63: 62
And idea of progress, Sep 63: 99–100

MacLeish, Archibald, quoted on, Jan 60: 53–54
MARY, DOWAGER QUEEN OF ENGLAND, May 63: 96
MARY I, QUEEN OF ENGLAND (MARY TUDOR), May 63: 95, Jul 63: 30
MARY, QUEEN OF SCOTS (MARY STUART)
Confrontation by John Knox, Jul 63: 28–32
In painting by W. P. Frith, Jul 63: 28–29
"MARY, MARY," play, Mar 63: 108
MARY OF LORRAINE, Jul 63: 29
MARY STUART. See MARY, QUEEN OF SCOTS
MASEFIELD, JOHN, Nov 60: 68, Jan 62: 52
MASERS DE LATUDE, HENRI. See DANRY, JEAN
MASHAM, favorite of Queen Anne, Sep 61: 75
MASINA, GIULIETTA, Mar 61: 98
MASON, JAMES, May 63: 112, Sep 63: 75, 79, 80
MASSACHUSETTS (see also BOSTON)
"Try *Massachusetts* on Your Piano," Nov 61: 118–19
MASSACHUSETTS INSTITUTE OF TECHNOLOGY, Sep 62: 18
Auditorium designed by Eero Saarinen, Jul 60: 82
"MASSACRE AT SCIO," painting by Delacroix, May 61: 66, 74; illus, May 61: 74–75
MASSALIA, Jul 59: 92
MASS CULTURE
Vs. class culture, Jan 60: 4–11
Definition of, Jan 60: 5
"MASS CULTURE," magazine, Jan 60: 7
MASSENET, JULES, Jul 59: 134
Manon, Thomas Beecham quoted on, Mar 62: 103
"MASSES, THE," periodical, Mar 60: 33
MASSEY, RAYMOND, Jan 60: 49, 53
Drawing of, Jan 60: 52
MASSEY, VINCENT, May 62: 8
MASSINE, LÉONIDE, Jan 61: 47
On Joan Miró, quoted, Mar 59: 70
MASSINGER, PHILIP, *A New Way to Pay Old Debts,* Mar 62: 116
MASS MAN, Mar 59: 128
MASS MEDIA, and imaginary audience, Mar 60: 46–51
MASSON, ANDRÉ, Mar 59: 70, 74, 76, 78
"MASS-PRODUCED INSIGHT, THE," article by Saul Bellow, Jan 63: 111–13
"MASTER BUILDER, THE," play, Jan 62: 108
MASTERS, EDGAR LEE, Jul 63: 69
And Spectric poets, May 60: 43, 46
MATANZAS, BAY OF, Dutch destruction of Spanish fleet in, Sep 58: 20, 21
"MATERIA MEDICA." See "DE MATERIA MEDICA"
MATERNA, AMALIE, photograph of, May 63: 42
MATHEMATICS
As field of brilliance, Mar 62: 73, 75
Mnemonic for value of pi, Jul 61: 115
In Moslem Spain, Sep 62: 88
Pascal's contribution, Jan 63: 99
MATHER, COTTON, and witch mania, Nov 59: 63
MATHEWS, EDWARD J., May 63: 14
MATHIEU, GEORGES, Nov 60: 31, 122
Photograph of, with painting by, Sep 60: 30
MATIDIA, Sep 63: 39
MATILDA, daughter of Henry II of England, Jan 59: 88
MATISSE, HENRI, Jan 59: 13, 103, Mar 60: 58, Sep 60: 102, Nov 61: 8, 12, May 62: 78, Nov 62: 57, Sep 63: 96
Chapel at Vence, France, Mar 61: 39
Paintings by. See ILLUSTRATIONS INDEX
Photograph of, May 60: 134
MATT, LEONARD VON, photographs of Aegina marbles by, Sep 59: cover, 3, 33–48
MATTERHORN, PROJECT, Sep 59: 26, 27, 119
"MATTER OF LIFE AND DEATH, A," book by Virgilia Peterson, Jan 62: 111, 112
MATTHIAS, HOLY ROMAN EMPEROR, Nov 62: 36
MATTHIAS CORVINUS, KING OF HUNGARY, library of, Nov 62: 3, 78
MATTINGLY, GARRETT, "Navigator to the Modern Age," article by, Nov 60: 72–83
MATTIOLI, ERCOLE ANTONIO, Jan 60: 85
MATZENAUER, MARGARETE, photograph of, May 63: 40
MAUGHAM, SOMERSET, Mar 61: 43
"On Having My Portrait Painted," article by, Jan 59: 106–7
Painting collection auctioned at Sotheby's, Nov 62: 59, 64
Portraits of, Jan 59: 106–7
In South Seas, Jan 60: 125
Trio, motion picture based on, May 62: 116
MAUPASSANT, GUY DE
Bel-Ami, Jan 62: 62
Goncourt *Journal* quoted on, Sep 62: 113
On Seine River, quoted, Jul 62: 60, 61, 64
MAURIAC, CLAUDE, May 62: 113–15
On French literary prizes, quoted, Jul 63: 74
MAURIAC, FRANÇOIS, Nov 59: 68
On *Belmondisme,* quoted, Nov 61: 116

MAURICE OF LORRAINE, Mar 62: 50
MAURICE OF NASSAU, Sep 58: 19, 22
In painting by Adam van Breen, Sep 58: 16
MAURY, LUCIEN, on novel *Barabbas*, quoted, Mar 63: 109–10
MAXENTIUS, ROMAN EMPEROR, Nov 63: 6
"MAXIMES," book by La Rochefoucauld, Nov 61: 34
MAXIMIAN (MAXIMIANUS I), ROMAN EMPEROR, Jul 59: 130, Sep 61: 30
MAXIMILIAN, KING OF BAVARIA, Jan 61: 37, 38–39
MAXIMINUS I, ROMAN EMPEROR, coin portraits of, Sep 63: 40; illus, Sep 63: 37
MAXIMINUS II, ROMAN EMPEROR, coin portraits of, Sep 63: 41; illus, Sep 63: 37
MAXWELL, ELSA, photograph of, Jul 60: 7
MAXWELL, GAVIN, *The Ten Pains of Death*, quoted, Sep 61: 43
MAXWELL, JAMES CLERK, Jul 61: 7
MAXWELL HOUSE COFFEE, television commercial for, Mar 61: 101
MAY, ELAINE, Sep 61: 80, Jan 62: 66, 68, May 63: 91
MAYAKOVSKY, VLADIMIR, Jul 62: 100
MAYBECK, BERNARD, Jan 59: 8, 10, Jan 61: 107
Church designed by, Jan 59: 10
"MAYBE TUESDAY," play, Jul 62: 49
MAYER, BENA FRANK, photograph of, Mar 63: 28
MAYER, EDWIN JUSTUS, *Children of Darkness*, Mar 60: 121
MAYER, MARTIN
Articles by: "Ford Moves in on the Arts," Jan 62: 4–15; "New York's Monument to the Muses," Jul 62: 4–11
Schools, The, quoted, Jul 63: 43
MAYER, RALPH, photograph of, Mar 63: 28
MAYER, WHITTLESEY & GLASS, Nov 59: 109
MAYES, WENDELL, May 62: 116
MAYNIEL, JULIETTE, May 60: 50
MAYO, C. W., Jan 59: 99
Portrait of, Jan 59: 104
MAYS, DAVID, J., *Edmund Pendleton*, Jul 63: 72
MAZARIN, JULES, CARDINAL, Jul 60: 64, Sep 60: 67, Jul 61: 94, 95, Jul 63: 80, 82, 83
Farewell to his paintings by, Nov 61: 82–83
Portrait of, Nov 61: 83
MAZDAISM, Jan 61: 63
MAZDAKITE MOVEMENT, in Persia, Jan 63: 52
MAZDAZNAN, Nov 61: 68
MAZET, balloonist, Sep 58: 114
MAZET, JEAN CLAUDE, city design by, Jul 61: 64
MAZLISH, BRUCE. See BRONOWSKI, J., co-author
MAZZONI, SEBASTIANO, painting by, Jul 60: 43
"ME," painting by Larry Rivers, Sep 59: 95, 102; illus, Sep 59: 94
MEACHAM, ANNE, May 61: 99
Portrait of, May 61: 98
MEAD, MARGARET, Nov 59: 23
Growing Up in New Guinea, May 60: 122
Research among Manus of Admiralties, May 60: 123
MEALE, GAETANO (UMANO), Mar 63: 6
MEARA, ANNE, Nov 60: 116
"MEASURE FOR MEASURE," play by Shakespeare
Bowdlerized version, Sep 62: 70, 71
New York Shakespeare Festival production of, Nov 60: 117, 118
"MEASUREMENT OF MEANING, THE," book by Charles E. Osgood, Mar 60: 122
MECCA, ARABIA, penetration by Richard Francis Burton, Jul 63: 110, 112
MECHANISTIC THEORY OF LIFE, Jul 61: 8
MECKLENBURG-STRELITZ, GRAND DUCHESS OF, May 63: 96
MEDAWAR, P. B., on human genetics, quoted, Nov 62: 8
MEDE, JOSEPH, Mar 60: 102
"MEDEA," play, Tyrone Guthrie quoted on performance of Sybil Thorndike in, Jan 61: 30
"MEDEA," television production, Mar 60: 119
MEDES, Jan 63: 42–43, 49
MEDIA. See MASS MEDIA
MEDICI, GIULIANO DE', Sep 58: 94
MEDICI, LORENZO DE' (LORENZO THE MAGNIFICENT), Sep 58: 92, 94, 95
MEDICI, PIERO DE', Sep 58: 95
MEDICI FAMILY, garden of, May 59: 32, 34–35
MEDICINE, PRACTICE OF
Beginnings of organized medical services in war, Mar 61: 70
Darwin, Erasmus, as physician, May 59: 96
In Moslem Spain, Sep 62: 80, 89
MÉDICIS, CATHERINE DE, Sep 60: 64–66
MÉDICIS, MARIE DE, Sep 59: 120, 121, Sep 60: 66–67, Mar 61: 79, Jul 61: 89, Nov 62: 39
Paintings by Rubens on theme of, Jan 60: 132–33, Jul 60: 37
Portraits of, Sep 59: 28, Sep 60: 66
MEDINA, ARABIA, penetration by Richard Francis Burton, Jul 63: 110, 112

MEDITERRANEAN SEA, and Battle of Lepanto, Jul 63: 50
"MEDIUM, THE," opera, Jan 60: 15
MEE, CHARLES L., JR., articles by
"On Stage: Woody Allen," May 63: 46–47
"On Stage: Zohra Lampert," Jul 62: 48–49
"Where Talent Is Tried and Tested," Nov 62: 96–99
MEEGEREN, HANS VAN, Mar 59: 109
MEEHAN, THOMAS, "They All Add Up to Zero," article by, May 62: 50–53
MEEKER, RALPH, Sep 58: 42
MEERSCHAUM, May 60: 91
"MEET MR. LINCOLN," television production, Mar 60: 126
"MEGATANE RATING," Jan 62: 113
MEGIDDO, PALESTINE, Biblical city, Nov 59: 10, 118
"MEISTERSINGER, DIE," opera, Nov 58: 26, 27, May 63: 42, 44, 45
Thomas Beecham quoted on, Mar 62: 103
MEKAS, JONAS, Mar 61: 19
MELANCHTHON, PHILIPP
Childhood of, May 60: 34, 37, 38
Portrait of, May 60: 32
MELBA, NELLIE, Jul 59: 32, 134, Sep 59: 52–53, 56, Jan 61: 27, May 61: 121
Portraits of, Jan 61: 28, May 61: 124
MELBOURNE, LADY (ELIZABETH MILBANKE LAMB), Mar 63: 65
MELBOURNE, LORD. See LAMB, WILLIAM
MELCHIOR, LAURITZ, May 63: 42
MELETUS, Jul 60: 100, 102, 104, 117
MÉLIÈS, GEORGES, Nov 62: 97
MELIGNY, MARTHE DE (MRS. PIERRE BONNARD), Mar 62: 25, 27
MELLAART, JAMES, Sep 62: 5, 8, Nov 63: 66
"Man's First Murals," article by, Sep 62: 10–13
MELLO, BRENO, May 60: 54
MELLON, ANDREW, Nov 58: 53, 120, Jan 59: 105
MELLON, PAUL, May 59: 86, Jul 63: 70 (note), 72–73
"MELODRAMA ON BROADWAY: OUR SECRET LIVES ARE SHOWING," article by Robert Hatch, May 63: 106–8
MELOZZO DA FORLI, fresco by, Jan 62: 44
"MELPOMENE," composition by George Chadwick, Jul 59: 20
MELVILLE, HERMAN, May 60: 13, Sep 61: 116
Moby Dick, Mar 59: 17, Jan 62: 64
And South Seas, Jan 63: 31, 124
Typee, quoted, Mar 61: 27
MEMLING, HANS, painting by, Sep 63: 16–17
"MEMOIRS OF A DUTIFUL DAUGHTER," book by Simone de Beauvoir, Jan 62: 112
"MEMORANDUM, A: FROM ADOLF HITLER TO A. J. P. TAYLOR," article by William Harlan Hale, Mar 62: 28–29
"MEMORANDUM, A: FROM DON QUIXOTE DE LA MANCHA TO GENERALISSIMO FRANCISCO FRANCO," article by William Harlan Hale, Jul 59: 24–25
"MEMORANDUM, A: FROM ELEANOR OF AQUITAINE TO ABIGAIL VAN BUREN AND ANN LANDERS," article by Morton M. Hunt, May 60: 30–31
"MEMORANDUM, A: FROM EUGÉNIE, EMPRESS OF THE FRENCH, TO JACQUELINE BOUVIER KENNEDY," article by William Harlan Hale, Sep 62: 20–21
"MEMORANDUM, A: FROM EX-SECRETARY OF STATE THOMAS JEFFERSON TO SECRETARY OF STATE DEAN RUSK," article by William Harlan Hale, Jul 61: 30–31
"MEMORANDUM, A: FROM FRANÇOIS-MARIE AROUET DE VOLTAIRE TO THE SPACEMEN," article by William Harlan Hale, Sep 61: 18–19
"MEMORANDUM, A: FROM H. L. MENCKEN TO THE PRESIDENT-ELECT," article by William Harlan Hale, Nov 60: 70–71
"MEMORANDUM, A: FROM HORACE GREELEY TO JOHN HAY WHITNEY," article by William Harlan Hale, Jan 59: 24–25
"MEMORANDUM, A: FROM JONATHAN SWIFT TO CLIFF ROBINSON," article by William Harlan Hale, Nov 59: 64–65
"MEMORANDUM, A: FROM JULIUS CAESAR TO ROBERT MOSES," article by Eric Larrabee, Mar 59: 26–27
Comment on, May 63: 105
"MEMORANDUM, A: FROM LUCIUS ANNAEUS SENECA TO TENNESSEE WILLIAMS," article by Gilbert Highet, May 59: 54–55
"MEMORANDUM, A: FROM PRINCE KLEMENS VON METTERNICH TO JOHN FOSTER DULLES," article by William Harlan Hale, Sep 58: 36–37

"MEMORANDUM, A: FROM SIGMUND FREUD TO NORMAN MAILER, TENNESSEE WILLIAMS, ALBERTO MORAVIA, JEAN GENET, ET AL.," article by William Harlan Hale, May 62: 54–55
"MEMORANDUM, A: TO THE PRESIDENT FROM THE SECRETARY OF ARTS AND LEISURE," article by William Harlan Hale, Nov 62: 18–19
"MEMORIES, DREAMS, REFLECTIONS," book by Aniele Jaffé, with Carl Gustav Jung, reviewed, Jan 63: 109–11
MENANDER
Dyskolos, The, Jul 59: 78–79; translation by Gilbert Highet, Jul 59: 80–88
On guardian Genius, quoted, Nov 60: 29
Quintilian quoted on, Jul 59: 89
Sculpture of, Jul 59: 78, 89
"MEN AND EVENTS," book by H. R. Trevor-Roper, essay from, Sep 58: 46–47
MENASSEH BEN ISRAEL, Mar 60: 103, 124–25
Portrait of, Mar 60: 102
MENCKEN, H. L.
Memorandum to President-elect from, Nov 60: 70–71
Portrait of, Nov 60: 70
Quoted: on American South, Jan 60: 5; on artist, Sep 60: 35; on Lowell, Amy, May 60: 43
MENDELSOHN, ERICH, Sep 59: 19, Jan 60: 23
Tower designed by, Mar 62: 39
MENDELSSOHN, FANNY, Mar 61: 75
MENDELSSOHN, FELIX, Mar 61: 75
Gould, Glenn, quoted on, Jan 62: 92
New York Philharmonic and Italian Symphony of, Jul 59: 19
MENEKRATOUS, May 59: 122
MENELAUS WITH PATROCLUS, sculpture, May 59: 122, 123
MENGELBERG, WILLEM, Jul 59: 18
"MEN INTO MONUMENTS," gallery by Edward Sorel, Sep 61: 122–28
"MEN IN WHITE," play, Nov 62: 106
MENJOU, ADOLPHE, Sep 60: 116
"MEN LIKE GODS," book by H. G. Wells, Mar 63: 79
MENNINGER, KARL, Sep 59: 123
MENNINGER FOUNDATION, Sep 59: 90–91, 122, 123
"MENO," dialogue by Plato, Jul 60: 104
"MEN OF GOOD WILL," series of novels by Jules Romains, compared to *The Marquise Went Out at Five*, May 62: 115
MENOTTI, GIAN-CARLO, Jan 60: 14, 15, 122
Photographs of, May 59: 16, Jan 60: 15
MENUHIN, YEHUDI, May 62: 61
"MEN, WOMEN AND PIANOS," book by Arthur Loesser, quoted on Franz Liszt, Jul 62: 74, 81
"MERCHANT OF VENICE, THE," play by Shakespeare, role of Shylock in, Jan 60: 89–96
MERCIER, LOUIS SÉBASTIEN, *Tableau de Paris*, quoted, Jul 61: 52
MERCIER, PHILIPPE, Jul 63: 96
MERCK PHARMACEUTICAL LABORATORIES, Sep 59: 26
MERCOURI, MELINA, May 61: 97, Jan 63: 38
MERCURY THEATRE, THE, Jul 63: 87
MERCURY THEATRE OF THE AIR, THE, and Orson Welles' production of *The War of the Worlds*, Jul 63: 87–88
"MERE CHRISTIANITY," book by C. S. Lewis, May 59: 66
MEREDITH, GEORGE, as caricatured by Max Beerbohm, May 61: 38
MEREDITH, WILLIAM, Sep 61: 119, 121
MERES, FRANCIS, Jan 60: 91
MERIAN, MATTHEW, engraving by, Sep 60: 66
MÉRIMÉE, PROSPER, Sep 62: 20, 21
MERION, PA., Barnes collection of paintings, Jul 63: 22–23
MERMAID, NATURAL HISTORY OF, Jan 60: 129–36
MERMAN, ETHEL, Sep 58: 59
MERNEPTAH, KING OF EGYPT, Jan 61: 80
MEROË, ancient Nubian city, Mar 63: 41 (map), 43 (illus), 53, 57, 58
MERRIAM, ROBERT, Sep 61: 9
MERRICK, HENRIETTA SANDS, on Kashmir, quoted, Mar 61: 31
MERRILL, ELMER D., photograph of, May 59: 16
MERRITT, ARTHUR TILLMAN, on Leonard Bernstein, quoted, Jul 59: 21
"MERRY WIVES OF WINDSOR, THE," play by Shakespeare, quoted, Nov 62: 94
MERSON, ISOBEL, Sep 60: 88
MERTON, JOHN R., Jan 59: 99
Painting by, Jan 59: 96–97
MESCALINE, May 63: 29, 115
MESOPOTAMIA (see also IRAQ)
Cities of, Jul 61: 38–41, 62

Evidence of Bronze Age trade found in, Jul 60: 86–87
New treasures from Nippur, Nov 61: 84–87
Wheeled vehicles in, Sep 58: 146–48
MESSEMER, HANNES, Mar 61: 99
MESSIAEN, OLIVER, Jan 59: 54
MESSIANISM, millenary doctrine of 17th century, Mar 60: 100–3, 124–25
MESSINA, ITALY, Sep 61: 28
Gathering of ships before Battle of Lepanto, Jul 63: 52–53
METALLURGY (see also GOLD)
Etruscan, May 60: 64, 73, 77
Of Israelites, Nov 59: 9–10
"METAMORPHOSES." See "GOLDEN ASS, THE"
"METAMORPHOSIS OF THE GODS, THE," book by André Malraux, discussed, Nov 58: 4–17, 112–17
MÉTEZEAU, LOUIS, Sep 60: 66
METHOD ACTING, Nov 58: 139, Nov 62: 106–8
Chayefsky, Paddy, quoted on, Sep 60: 56
In *On the Waterfront,* Sep 58: 44
Remick, Lee, quoted on, Sep 60: 88
METHODIST TEMPERANCE BOARD, Nov 58: 147
METOCHITES, THEODORE, Nov 63: 28
On Byzantine mosaics, quoted, Nov 63: 31
Mosaic portrait of, Nov 63: 29
"METROPOLIS REGAINED," article by Grady Clay, Jul 59: 4–15
"METROPOLITAN MAGAZINE," Mar 60: 33
METROPOLITAN MUSEUM OF ART, New York City, Jul 59: 28, May 63: 91
Costume Institute, Mar 59: 66
METROPOLITAN OPERA, Jan 62: 13, Jan 63: 106, 107, 109
And American singers, Nov 61: 78, 80
And Lincoln Center for the Performing Arts, Jul 62: 5–6, 9, 10
Old and new opera house, Nov 58: 28–29, 117–20
Prima donnas of, Sep 59: 51–52, 53
Quality of performances, Nov 58: 23–24, 25–26
METROPOLITAN THEATRE, San Francisco, Jan 59: 6
METSU, GABRIEL, Jul 63: 106
METTERNICH, KLEMENS WENZEL NEPOMUK LOTHER VON
Memorandum to John Foster Dulles from, Sep 58: 36–37
In painting of Café Tortoni, May 63: 71
MEXICO
Conquest of, as pictured in Codices, Sep 60: 24–25
Montezuma and Cortes, Nov 63: 92–96
Studies of Alexander von Humboldt, Jul 59: 67, 68, 128
MEXICO, UNIVERSITY OF, campus buildings, Sep 59: 20
MEYER, ADOLF, Nov 61: 70
MEYER, HANNES, Nov 61: 74
MEYER, LEONARD B.
"Art by Accident," article by, Sep 60: 30–32, 121–24
Emotion and Meaning in Music, quoted, Jul 59: 107–8
MEYERS, SIDNEY, Mar 61: 14, 19
Photograph of, Mar 61: 14
MEYNELL, ALICE
Beerbohm, Max, quoted on, May 61: 40
"Christ in the Universe," quoted, Sep 59: 122
MIAMI BEACH, FLA., Jul 60: 69, Jan 61: 103
MICHAEL VIII PALAEOLOGUS, BYZANTINE EMPEROR, Nov 63: 31
MICHEL, SALLY, Jul 61: 28, Jul 62: 20
MICHELANGELO (see also in ILLUSTRATIONS INDEX), May 60: 39, Jul 60: 50, Sep 60: 34, 62, 64, 72, Sep 63: 35
As architect, Nov 58: 41, Mar 59: 124
Laocoön group studied by, May 59: 104, 124
Moore, Henry, quoted on, Nov 60: 103, 113, 114
Pietà, Sep 58: 95, Jan 62: 48
And portraiture, Jan 59: 95
Virgin and Child with Saint John, relief, May 62: 78
Work on St. Peter's, Rome, Jan 62: 25, 26, 31, 41, 43
MICHELET, JULES, interpretation of Joan of Arc, Mar 62: 97
MICHENER, JAMES A., Jan 60: 126
"An Eastern Art Goes Western," article by, May 60: 102–14
MICHIGAN, Grand Hotel, on Mackinac Island, Jan 61: 104, 108
MICHIGAN, UNIVERSITY OF, repertory theatre group, Jan 63: 106
MICKIEWICZ, ADAM, *Pan Tadeusz,* May 63: 110
MICKLE, SAMUEL, Sep 58: 120
MICROFILM BOOKS, and need for selection, Nov 62: 83
MICROSCOPIC PRINTING, and microlibraries, Sep 62: 42–47
"MIDAS TOUCH, THE," story by Frederik Pohl, Jul 60: 66, Mar 63: 79
MIDDLE AGES
Arles, France, during, Jul 59: 131–32
Arthurian legend, versions of James Knowles and Thomas Malory, May 60: 115–18
Attitude toward nature in, Mar 60: 13–14

Christian Church in, Jul 59: 130–31
Cities of, Sep 59: 28–29
Courtly love in, Sep 59: 113–17
Courts of love vs. modern love-counselling, May 60: 30–31
Gardens of, May 59: 27
Handwriting in, Sep 59: 125–26
Jews during, Mar 60: 100
Louvre during, Sep 60: 59–61
Military Orders of, Mar 61: 48–71
Richard I and Saladin, Jan 59: 86–91, 130–31
Street fountains of, May 62: 12
Suburbia in, Jul 61: 62
Survival of books during, Nov 62: 89–90
Theatre of, Jul 59: 46
Tournaments, Sep 58: 92–107
Towns of, Jul 61: 48–51
Wheeled vehicles in, Sep 58: 150–51
Witches and witchcraft during, Nov 59: 57, 59
MIDDLE EAST, bargaining in, May 59: 136
"MIDDLE OF THE NIGHT," play and motion picture, Sep 60: 49, 54, 56
MIDDLETON, CONYERS, Jan 63: 117
MIDDLETON, JOHN IZARD, Nov 59: 100
Painting by, Nov 59: 100
MIDDLE WEST, motion picture versions of, May 59: 100
MIDLAND GROUP OF JOSIAH WEDGWOOD, May 59: 88–97, 128–30
"'MIDRASH' THEORY," Sep 63: 8
MIDWAY GARDENS, Chicago, Sep 60: 99–100, 127–28
MIELZINER, JO, Jul 59: 42, 48
MIES VAN DER ROHE, LUDWIG, Sep 58: 110, Jan 59: 8, 11, Sep 59: 6–7, 18, Nov 59: 48, Jan 60: 21, 23, Sep 60: 39, Nov 60: 4, Mar 61: 36, Nov 61: 61–62, 73, 74, Mar 62: 32, 33, 39
Buildings designed by, Sep 59: 6, 12, Nov 61: 73
Photograph of, Nov 61: 73
Saarinen, Eero, quoted on, Jul 60: 82
MIFUNE, TOSHIRO, Jul 62: 46, 47
Photograph of, Jul 62: 45
MIGNARD, PIERRE, Nov 61: 34
MIGNOT, LOUISE, Mar 61: 118
"MIKADO, THE," operetta, influence on Rick Besoyan, Sep 60: 87
MILAN, ITALY
American abstract expressionism in, Nov 59: 120
La Scala, Nov 58: 23–24, 118
In Renaissance, Sep 60: 62
Renaissance court at, Jan 60: 66
Skyscrapers in, Nov 60: 16, 125; Pirelli building, Mar 59: 123
And Thirty Years' War, Nov 62: 33, 34–35, 36, 37
MILAN, JUDITH, "On Stage: Joan Baez," article by, Sep 62: 66–67
MILANO 2000, Utopian city, Nov 60: 16
MILANOV, ZINCA, Sep 59: 53
MILES, JOSEPHINE, quoted, Jan 59: 19
MILHAUD, DARIUS, Sep 58: 134, Jan 59: 21, Mar 61: 75, Nov 62: 46
Photograph of, Sep 58: 98
"MILK AND HONEY," musical, Nov 62: 68
"MILK TRAIN DOESN'T STOP HERE ANYMORE, THE," play, May 63: 108
MILL, JOHN STUART
Childhood of, May 60: 34, 37, 38
Portrait of, May 60: 32
MILLAIS, JOHN, May 62: 64, 73
MILLAND, RAY, Sep 63: 75
MILLAR, OLIVER, "The Queen's Pictures," article by, Jul 63: 92–107
MILLAY, EDNA ST. VINCENT, May 60: 46, 48
MILLENARY DOCTRINE, in 17th century, Mar 60: 101–3, 124–25
MILLENIUM, memorandum from H. L. Mencken to the President-elect regarding, Nov 60: 70–71
MILLER, ALICE DUER, Jul 62: 37
MILLER, ARTHUR, Nov 58: 139, Jul 59: 48, Jan 62: 14
On British theatre, quoted, Jan 63: 26
Chayefsky, Paddy, quoted on, Sep 60: 51
Crucible, The, Jan 63: 27, 88
Death of a Salesman, at Tyrone Guthrie Theatre, Nov 63: 38, 41
MILLER, DOROTHY, Nov 60: 8
MILLER, HENRY, Jan 59: 18, Nov 61: 104–5, Mar 62: 107, May 62: 55, Mar 63: 113
Photograph of, Jan 59: 17
Wisdom of the Heart, quoted, Jul 60: 72
MILLER, HERMAN, Nov 61: 73
MILLER, JOHN PERRY, on university teaching situation, quoted, Sep 62: 15
MILLER, JONATHAN, Mar 63: 109
MILLER, LEA, Jan 59: 14
Textile by, Jan 59: 4

MILLER, STANLEY, Jan 59: 28
MILLER, WARREN, articles by
"From Red Banners to Ballads," Mar 62: 110–12
"Jester of the New Wave," Jan 62: 109–10
"On Stage: Warren Beatty," Jan 62: 104–5
MILLES, CARL, fountain by, May 62: 28–29
MILLET, JEAN-FRANÇOIS, May 63: 70
MILLIKEN, WILLIAM M., Sep 58: 62
MILLS, C. WRIGHT, Nov 59: 23, 25, Sep 62: 16
MILLS, HAYLEY, Sep 60: 116–17
MILLS, JOHN, Nov 61: 115, May 62: 112
Photograph of, May 62: 111
MILLS COLLEGE, musicians at, Jan 59: 21
MILLSTEIN, GILBERT, articles by
"In Print: Edward Adler," Sep 62: 64–65
"On Stage": Besoyan, Rick, Sep 60: 86–87; Carroll, Diahann, Nov 60: 86–87; Davis, Miles, May 61: 100–1; Dewhurst, Colleen, Jul 60: 94–95; Graham, Ronny, Nov 60: 84–85; Meacham, Anne, May 61: 98–99; Scott, George C., Jul 60: 92–93
MILMAN, HENRY HART, *History of Christianity Under the Empire,* Mar 59: 94
MILNE, A. A., *Winnie-the-Pooh,* Latin version, reviewed, Jul 61: 112–15
MILO, TITUS ANNIUS PAPIANUS, Nov 58: 110
MILTNER, FRANZ, statue of Artemis discovered by, Sep 58: 85
MILTON, JOHN, Sep 59: 120, Jul 60: 38, 42, 64
Family records in handwriting of, Sep 59: 134
Paradise Lost, Jan 61: 117; Jul 61: 113; quoted, Sep 58: 81
Portraits of, Sep 59: 134, Jul 60: 39
Quoted: on Dagon, Jan 60: 131, 134; on mountains, Mar 60: 14
MILTON ACADEMY, addresses of Robert Sherwood at, May 62: 5–9
MINEO, SAL, Jan 59: 139
MINES and MINING
Copper and iron in Promised Land, Nov 59: 9–10
Guggenheim interests in, May 59: 6–7
Mines of Ophir, Nov 59: 119, Mar 63: 57 (illus)
MINIATURES
Monastery, André Malraux quoted on, Nov 58: 16
Persian, Jan 63: 57, 62, 67–69; illus, Jan 63: 61, 63–66
"MINISTER'S FATAL SHOWPLACE, THE," article by William Harlan Hale, Jul 63: 76–83
MINISTRY OF EDUCATION BUILDING, Rio de Janeiro, Nov 60: 16, 125
MINNEAPOLIS, MINN.
Southdale shopping center, Nov 59: 108
Tyrone Guthrie Theatre, Jan 63: 106, Nov 63: 35, 36–41
MINNEAPOLIS SOCIETY OF FINE ARTS, Jan 62: 11
MINNEAPOLIS SYMPHONY, Sep 58: 102
MINNESOTA DEPARTMENT OF HIGHWAYS, on roadside signs, quoted, May 61: 18
MINOW, NEWTON, Sep 61: 17, Jan 63: 92
Portrait of, Sep 61: 12
MIRABEAU, COMTE DE (HONORÉ RIQUETI)
Childhood of, May 60: 33, 34, 36, 38
On English countryside, quoted, Sep 58: 46–47
Portrait of, May 60: 32
MIRABEAU, MARQUIS DE (VICTOR RIQUETI), Jan 60: 85
"MIRACLES," book by C. S. Lewis, May 59: 66
MIRACULOUS, in natural world, Jul 60: 25–32
MIRANDOLA. See PICO DELLA MIRANDOLA
MIRÓ, JOAN, Mar 59: 70–81, 126–27, May 59: 15, Sep 59: 18
Photographs of, Mar 59: 71, 73, 75
Works by. See ILLUSTRATIONS INDEX
"MIRROR FOR PRINCES, A," Persian book of etiquette, excerpt from, Jan 63: 60
MIRSKY, PRINCE, *History of Russian Literature,* Mar 62: 110
"MISANTHROPE, THE," play, Sep 62: 33, 35, 41
"MISER, THE," play, Jan 60: 93, 96, Jan 63: 88
Tyrone Guthrie Theatre production, Nov 63: 38, 40, 41
"MISFITS, THE," motion picture, Jan 63: 112
"MISSING MOURNERS OF DIJON, THE," article by Fernand Auberjonois, Sep 58: 62–63
MISSISSIPPI
Roosevelt, Theodore, and, Nov 63: 70
State ode, quoted, Nov 61: 119
"MR. _____ BUILDS HIS DREAM HOUSE," illustrated feature, Sep 63: 102–3
"MR. ARKADIN," motion picture, Jul 63: 91
"MR. ELIOT'S SUNDAY MORNING SERVICE," poem by T. S. Eliot, quoted, Sep 61: 118
"MR. WRIGHT MAKES HIMSELF CLEAR," a recollection by Dennis Whelan, Sep 60: 128
"MRS. GARDNER'S PALACE OF PAINTINGS," article by Nelson Lansdale, Jul 59: 26–32, 133–34
"MRS. LANDON'S HARP," article by Bernard Asbell,

Sep 59: 86–91, 122–23

"MISUNDERSTANDING, THE," play, Nov 59: 70

"MISUSES OF THE PAST," article by Herbert J. Muller, Mar 59: 4–13, 128

MITCHELL, JOAN, Nov 59: 120

MITFORD, NANCY, Mar 59: 107, Mar 61: 117
"Rooms for Improvement," article by, Nov 61: 32–37

MITGANG, HERBERT, "On Screen: Claudia Cardinale," article by, Jan 63: 38–39

MITHRA CULT, in Persia, Jan 63: 58, 59

"MITOSIS BY MARTIN," cartoons, Nov 62: 120

MITROPOULOS, DIMITRI, Jan 59: 21, Jul 59: 18–19

MIZENER, ARTHUR, quoted
On Salinger, J. D., May 62: 104
On Scarlet Sister Mary, Jul 63: 71

MIZNER, WILSON, on 1920 election, quoted, May 59: 23

MOBILES, of Alexander Calder, Nov 62: 10–17

MOBILGAS, advertising of, Nov 62: 113

"MOBY DICK," novel by Herman Melville, Mar 59: 17, Jan 60: 124, Jan 62: 64

MOCENIGO, LUIGI, in painting by Georg Wilhelm Graesner, Jul 63: 51

"MODERATO CANTABILE," motion picture, Nov 61: 116

"MODERN BESTIARY, A," portfolio by Edward Sorel and Paul Davis, Jul 62: 120–28

"MODERN DEMONOLOGY, A," book by Frank Getlein, excerpts from, Jul 61: 66–69, Sep 61: 64–65

"MODERN SOCIOLOGICAL THEORY," book by Walter Buckley, quoted, Mar 59: 135

"MODERN UTOPIA, A," book by H. G. Wells, Mar 63: 78, Nov 63: 106

"MODIFICATION, LA," novel by Michel Butor, Jan 62: 100–1

MOE, HENRY ALLEN, May 59: 8–10, Jan 62: 12
Photograph of, May 59: 17

MOFFETT, ROSS, portrait of, with painting by, Jul 61: 24

MOFFO, ANNA, Jul 61: 97
Portrait of, Jul 61: 96

MOHAMMED, Nov 60: 32

MOHAMMED II, SULTAN OF TURKEY, May 59: 59, 134, Jul 59: 40, Nov 63: 31, 32, 34, Jul 63: 50
Portrait of, May 59: 61

MOHAMMED III, SULTAN OF TURKEY, May 59: 63

MOHAMMEDANISM. See ISLAM

MOHAMMEDANS. See ISLAM; MOSLEMS

MOHAMMED REZA PAHLAVI, SHAH OF IRAN, Jan 63: 42, 72
Photograph of, Jan 63: 43

MOHENJO-DARO, evidence of Bronze Age trade found at, Jul 60: 86–87

MOHL, MME (MARY CLARKE), Nov 61: 35

MOHOLY-NAGY, LÁSZLÓ, Nov 59: 48, Nov 61: 61, 64, 69, 74
Photograph of, Nov 61: 59
Works by, Nov 61: 64, 68

MOISEIWITSCH, TANYA, Jul 59: 45, Nov 63: 38

MOISEYEV, IGOR, Jan 61: 49

MOISEYEV, MRS. IGOR, Jan 61: 49, 56

MOISSI, ALEXANDER, Jan 61: 32

MOITESSIER, MME, portrait of, Mar 62: 66

MOLANDER, OLOF, Sep 60: 8

MOLIÈRE, May 59: 29, Jul 59: 46, Jan 60: 93, 96, Jul 60: 60, Sep 60: 69, Jul 61: 116
Contrasted with Shakespeare, Sep 61: 102, 105–6
Dom Juan, Jan 62: 59–60
École des Femmes, L', Sep 62: 111
Imaginary Invalid, The, May 62: 51
Misanthrope, The, Sep 62: 33, 35, 41
Miser, The, Jan 63: 88; Tyrone Guthrie Theatre production, Nov 63: 38, 40, 41
Patronage of Nicolas Fouquet, Jul 63: 77, 81–82, 83
Psyché, Nov 62: 91

MOLINA, TIRSO DE. See TIRSO DE MOLINA

MOLINOS, MIGUEL DE, Nov 61: 111

MOLLAN, MALCOLM, on Eugene O'Neill, quoted, Mar 60: 34

MÖLLENSTEDT, G., Sep 62: 42

"MOLLOY," novel by Samuel Beckett, Sep 60: 113

MOLMENTI, POMPEO, on Venice, quoted, Jul 61: 3

"MOMENT OF TRUTH," play, Nov 58: 82

"MOMENT OF TRUTH, THE," article by Stephen White, Jul 60: 128

"MOMISM"
In advertising, Mar 59: 134
In Ottoman court, May 59: 135

"MONA LISA," painting by Leonardo da Vinci, May 63: 91

MONASTICISM, significance in Byzantium, Nov 63: 23, 25

MONCADA, FRANCISCO DE. See OSUNA

MONCRIF, ABBÉ DE, Jan 60: 85

MONDRIAN, PIET, Sep 58: 110, Nov 62: 15, May 63: 91
Influence of Poussin on, Mar 61: 78, 91
Moore, Henry, quoted on, Nov 60: 114

"MONDRIAN IS A PAPER NAPKIN," article by Vicki Goldberg, May 63: 90–91

MONET, CLAUDE, May 60: 103, 113, Mar 61: 78, 93, Jul 62: 64, 65, 72, May 63: 70
Hemingway, Ernest, quoted on, Jan 59: 132
Paintings by, Jul 62: 72, 78–79
Sketch of, Sep 58: 132
Stravinsky, Igor, quoted on, Sep 58: 83–84

MONEY. See COINAGE

MONGOLS, invasions of Persia by, Jan 63: 52 (chart), 53, 60, 67

MONK, JULIUS, Jul 61: 77, Jan 62: 68
Photograph of, Jul 61: 76

MONK, THELONIUS, May 61: 100
Homage to, woodcut book by Antonio Frasconi, Mar 61: 123

"MONKEY, THE," story by Isak Dinesen, Sep 59: 111

MONNET, JEAN, Mar 63: 7

MONRO, JOHN U., warning against mind-distorting drugs issued by, May 63: 115

MONROE, HARRIET, Sep 61: 117
And Spectric poets, May 60: 43, 47–48

MONROE, JAMES, Sep 61: 13

MONROE, MARILYN, Jan 63: 112, Mar 63: 36

"MONSIEUR LE BARON HAS EATEN TOO MUCH," motion picture, Nov 62: 97

"MONSIEUR VERDOUX," motion picture, Nov 62: 110

MONSTRELET, ENGUERRAND DE, Mar 62: 91

MONTAGU, ASHLEY, portrait of, Jan 60: 9

MONTAGU, ELIZABETH ROBINSON, Sep 62: 69
On Adam decorations, quoted, Mar 62: 62

MONTAGU, GEORGE, letter from Horace Walpole to, quoted, Jul 63: 105

MONTAGUE, MARY WORTLEY, quoted
On Homeric scenes, Jan 61: 91
On Turkish court, May 59: 58, 62

MONTAGU, WILLIAM, Nov 58: 106

MONTAGUE, JOHN, "Creatures of the Irish Twilight," article by, Jul 60: 105

MONTAIGNE, MICHEL EYQUEM DE, quoted
On society and humanitarians, Nov 60: 22
On witch trials, Nov 59: 60

MONTANA
Glacier National Park Hotel, Jan 61: 112
State song, quoted, Nov 61: 119

MONTAUK HIGHWAY, May 63: 6–7

MONTE CARLO, MONACO, Mar 59: 85
Grand Hotel, May 61: 125

MONTE CASSINO, Boccaccio's visit to, Nov 62: 93–94

MONTEFELTRO, AGNESINA DA, Jan 60: 68

MONTEFELTRO, FEDERIGO DA, DUKE OF URBINO, Jan 59: 103, Sep 59: 126, Jan 60: 66, 68, Nov 61: 4
Ficino, Marsilio, quoted on, Jan 60: 73
Portraits of, Jan 60: 63, 69

MONTEFELTRO, GUIDOBALDO DA, DUKE OF URBINO, Jan 60: 66, 68, Jul 61: 80
Portraits of, Jan 60: 63, 65

MONTEREY, MASS., May 60: 13 (map), 15, 17

MONTESQUIEU, BARON DE, Mar 61: 115
On Don Quixote, quoted, Nov 61: 106

MONTESSORI, MARIA, Jul 63: 42

MONTEUX, PIERRE, Jan 59: 22
First performance of Sacre du Printemps, Sep 58: 83

MONTEVERDI, CLAUDIO, Jan 59: 125, Jul 60: 42, 64, Nov 60: 90
Portrait of, Jul 60: 39

MONTEZ, LOLA, Jan 61: 37–38

MONTEZUMA II, AZTEC EMPEROR, Sep 60: 25
Encounter with Cortes, Nov 63: 92–96

MONTFERRAT, ITALY, and Thirty Years' War, Nov 62: 35, 37

MONTGOLFIER, ETIENNE, Sep 58: 116–17

MONTGOLFIER, JOSEPH, Sep 58: 116

MONTGOMERY, BERNARD LAW, Sep 59: 124
Impersonation of, by Clifton, James, Jan 61: 71–72

MONTGOMERY, RUTH, Jul 60: 120

MONTMARTRE, Paris, as tourist trap, Mar 59: 83, 84

MONTMORENCY, MATHIEU DE, Nov 58: 145–46

MONTOYA, CARLOS, May 63: 21
Photograph of, May 63: 20

MONTPENSIER, MLLE, Nov 61: 33

"MONUMENTS FOR OUR TIMES," article by Marshall B. Davidson, May 61: 41–49

MONVILLE, MAZIÈRE DE, building designed by, Mar 62: 35; illus, Mar 62: 30, 31

"MOON FOR THE MISBEGOTTEN, A," play, Jan 62: 103
New London, Conn., background of, Mar 60: 26–40

"MOON IS BLUE, THE," motion picture, May 62: 117

MOORE, ARCHIE, Miles Davis quoted on, May 61: 100

MOORE, DOUGLAS, Jan 60: 14, 16, 122, Jan 62: 10, Mar 63: 28, 30
Portrait of, Jan 60: 14

MOORE, DUDLEY, Mar 63: 109

MOORE, GARRY, Mar 60: 47, Sep 61: 80, May 63: 46

MOORE, GEORGE, Mar 59: 87, 88
Quoted: on Elgar's Dream of Gerontius, Mar 62: 103; on Royal Academy, May 62: 78

MOORE, GRACE, Sep 59: 55, 57

MOORE, HENRY, Sep 59: 18
Interview with, Nov 60: 102–4, 113–15
Photograph of, Nov 60: 105
Works by. See ILLUSTRATIONS INDEX

MOORE, JOHN ROBERT, Jan 60: 93 (note)

MOORE, MARIANNE, Nov 58: 36, Jul 63: 69, 72

MOORE, ROBERT, Nov 62: 71, 72, 73

MOORE, ROSALIE, Jan 59: 18

MOORE, THOMAS, Mar 59: 92
Portrait of, Mar 59: 90
On Smith, Sydney, quoted, Mar 59: 90

MOORE, VICTOR, Sep 58: 58

MOOREHEAD, AGNES, Sep 60: 116

MOOREHEAD, ALAN
Articles by: "Artist from the Outback," Sep 62: 96–104; "Coming of the White Man, The," Sep 60: 10–14
On Burton, Richard Francis, quoted, Jul 63: 113

MOORE-TURNER, PERCY, Sep 58: 63

"MOORISH CHIEF," painting by Eduard Charlemont, Mar 60: 58; illus, Mar 60: 69

MOORS
Loss of Ceuta to Portuguese, Nov 60: 74, 76
In Spain. See SPAIN, Moslems in

MOOS, MALCOLM, Sep 61: 9

MORAES, DOM, Jan 63: 86

"MORAL EQUIVALENT OF WAR, THE," address by William James, quoted, Nov 63: 106

MORAVIA, ALBERTO, Jan 63: 38
Memorandum from Sigmund Freud to, May 62: 54–55

MORE, HANNAH, Sep 62: 69
On Holkham Hall, quoted, Nov 58: 45

MORE, HENRY, and witch mania, Nov 59: 60

MORE, THOMAS, Sep 59: 29, May 62: 89, 91, 92, 93
As portrayed in A Man for All Seasons, May 62: 110–11
Utopia, Mar 63: 74–75

MOREAU, GUSTAVE, Nov 62: 48

MOREAU, JEANNE, May 60: 50, 53

"MORE IN ANGER," book by Marya Mannes, May 63: 17

MOREL-FATIO, A., on Don Quixote, quoted, Nov 61: 106

MORELLET, ANDRÉ, Jan 60: 88

MORELLI, GIOVANNI, on his sister, quoted, Jan 60: 62, 64

MORELLI, MEA, Jan 60: 62, 64

MORELLY, Mar 63: 76

MOREUIL, FRANÇOIS, May 62: 81

MORGAN, EMANUEL (WITTER BYNNER), May 60: 42–48

MORGAN, FRANK, Sep 58: 59

MORGAN, FREDERICK, Jan 62: 14

MORGAN, GLADYS, Jul 59: 115
Photograph of, Jul 59: 114

MORGAN, J. P., Nov 58: 119, 120, 148, Mar 61: 120, 121, Nov 63: 69
Photograph of, Jul 60: 4

MORGAN, JULIA, Jan 59: 10

MORGAN, KENNETH R., "How to Make the Round Table Square," article by, May 60: 115–18

MORGAN, MAC, May 60: 17
Photograph of, May 60: 17

MORGAN LE FAY, versions of James Knowles and Thomas Malory, May 60: 118

MORGENSTERN, JOSEPH, "The Culture of the Non-Hotel," article by, Mar 63: 115–17

MORGENSTERN, OSKAR
Photograph of, Sep 59: 25
—— and JOHN VON NEUMANN, Theory of Games and Economic Behavior, Nov 63: 61

MORGENSTERN, SAM, Composers on Music, May 63: 109

MORGENTHAU, HANS J., Nov 63: 61

MÖRIKE, EDUARD, Sep 62: 42

MORISON, SAMUEL ELIOT, Jul 63: 73

MORISON, STANLEY, Sep 59: 128

MORLEY, CHRISTOPHER, Kitty Foyle, Jul 63: 5

MORLEY, GRACE McCANN, Jan 59: 13
Portrait of, Jan 59: 12

MORLEY, JOHN, on Voltaire, quoted, Mar 61: 119

MORMONS, studied by Richard Francis Burton, Jul 63: 110, 114–16, 117

MORNY, DUC DE, Nov 61: 36, May 63: 54, 57, 69
In painting of Café Tortoni, May 63: 71
Portrait of, May 63: 64

MORO, ANTONIO, portrait of Mary Tudor by, Jul 59: 30

MOROSOV, Russian businessman, Nov 61: 10

MORPHEME, Jul 63: 45

MORPHY, PAUL, Jan 62: 117–18

MORRIS, CARL, portrait of, Jan 62: 15

MORRIS, C. C., photograph of, Jul 63: 15

MORRIS, HILDA

On grants to artists, quoted, Jan 62: 13
Portrait of, Jan 62: 15
MORRIS, JAMES, articles by
"By Venice Possessed," Mar 63: 14–16, 25
"Is Oxford Out of This World?" Jan 63: 82–87
"Rome of Asia, The," May 62: 84–87
MORRIS, KYLE, painting by, Nov 60: 7
MORRIS, LLOYD, *The Young Idea*, book edited by, May 60: 44, 47
MORRIS, SAMUEL, Jul 63: 14
MORRIS, WILLIAM, May 61: 53, Mar 62: 36, 39
News from Nowhere, Mar 63: 77
MORRIS FAMILY, of Philadelphia, Jul 63: 25
MORRISON, ALFRED, autograph collection of, Nov 60: 97
MORRISON, COLIN, Nov 59: 95
MORRISON, HOBE, on *Camelot,* quoted, May 61: 113
MORRISON, JAMES, journal of, and *Bounty* mutiny, Sep 63: 43, 44, 45
MORROW, JO, Nov 59: 31, 124, 125
MORSE, WAYNE, Mar 60: 126, Jul 60: 120
"MORTE D'ARTHUR," by Thomas Malory, May 59: 126, May 60: 115–18
MORTIMER, JOHN, Mar 63: 36
MOSAICS
Christian, Nov 58: 15–16
Of Ravenna, Nov 63: 25
Sicilian, of Piazza Armerina, Sep 61: 26, 30
MOSCHELES, IGNAZ, Jan 62: 120
MOSCOW, U.S.S.R.
American abstract expressionism in, Nov 59: 121
Delhi compared to, May 62: 84, 85, 86–87
Early history of, Sep 59: 62
Englishman's impressions of, Jul 62: 113, 114, 116–17
As third Rome, Nov 63: 34
MOSCOW ART THEATRE, Nov 62: 106
MOSEL, TAD, Sep 60: 51
MOSES, ROBERT, Jul 62: 5–6, 8, 9, 10
Compared to Baron Haussmann, May 63: 52, 72, 105
Memorandum to, from Julius Caesar, Mar 59: 26–27; comment on, May 63: 105
On roadside signs, quoted, May 61: 18
Vs. Shakespeare Festival, Nov 60: 117
MOSKOVITZ, SHALOM, Jul 61: 120
Paintings by, Jul 61: 121–28
MOSLEMS
Attacks on Byzantine Empire, Nov 63: 26, 28, 34
At Battle of Lepanto, Jul 63: 49–61
Burton, Richard Francis, and, Jul 63: 112–13, 115–16
Christian Military Orders vs., Mar 61: 51–65
In Sicily, Sep 61: 28, 32, 34
MOSMENT, balloonist, Sep 58: 114
MOSQUES, PERSIAN, Jan 63: 57
MOSS, RICHARD, "A Pair of Designing Finns," article by, Jul 63: 62–67
MOSSBAUER, R. L., Jul 62: 86
MOSTEL, ZERO, May 62: 50–53
Photographs of, May 62: 50, 52–53
"MOST HAPPY FELLA, THE," musical, Sep 58: 60, Jan 60: 14
"MOST MYSTERIOUS MANUSCRIPT, THE," article by Alfred Werner, Jan 63: 4–9
"MOTAMOTION," motion picture, Nov 62: 98
MOTELS, in New York City, Mar 63: 115, 117
"MOTHER AND SON," book by Isoko and Ichiro Hatano, Nov 62: 109
"MOTHER COURAGE," play, Mar 60: 121
MOTHERHOOD, as seen by advertisers, Nov 59: 116–17
"MOTHER OF US ALL, THE," composition by Virgil Thomson, Jul 59: 20
MOTHERWELL, ROBERT, Sep 58: 44, May 59: 11, Nov 59: 41, Jan 63: 16
Painting by, Sep 59: 38
MOTION PICTURES (see also "MOVIES"; "ON SCREEN")
Bergman, Ingmar, "Why I Make Movies," article by, Sep 60: 4–9
British colony of Hollywood, Sep 63: 74–81
Charles Theatre, New York City, Nov 62: 96–99
Chayefsky, Paddy, interview with, Sep 60: 49–56
Cult of unthink in, Sep 58: 38, 42–44
Cultural Exchange Program, U.S. contribution to, Mar 62: 110 (note)
Decline of, Mar 60: 127–28
Electronic music in, Jan 59: 126
Epics based on classical antiquity, May 61: 52–57
Film libraries, May 60: 51
French, New Wave in, May 60: 49–55, Mar 61: 13, 19
"Funny movies," Jan 61: 123
Of Kurosawa, Akira, Jul 62: 42–47
Lawrence of Arabia, filming of, Jul 62: 108–11
"Little Flight Music, A," article by William K. Zinsser, Mar 62: 100–1
New wave in. See NEW WAVE IN MOTION PICTURES

In New York City: Charles Theatre, Nov 62: 96–99; new wave, Jul 62: 12–19
Nonconformist taste in, Mar 59: 112
Our Man in Havana, filming of, Nov 59: 26–31, 122–26
As popular art, Jan 60: 10
As representative of countries producing them, May 59: 98–101
Teen-age tyranny over, Jan 59: 137–39
On television, Mar 60: 127
Welles, Orson, career of, Jul 63: 88–91
MOTIVATIONAL RESEARCH, Nov 58: 146, 147
MOUHOT, HENRI, on Angkor Vat, quoted, Jan 59: 62
MOULINS, MASTER OF, painting by, Sep 60: 71
MOUNTAINEERING, Sep 58: 7, 11, 139
On Grand Tour, Nov 59: 86
In Renaissance, Mar 60: 14
MOUNTAIN HOUSE, on Lake Mohonk, N.Y., Jan 61: 104, 110–11
MOUNTBATTEN, 1ST EARL, Jan 61: 67
MOUNT CARMEL, ISRAEL, archaeological site, Sep 62: 7 (map), 8
"MOUNTOLIVE," novel by Lawrence Durrell, Mar 60: 114, 117, 118
Excerpt from, Mar 60: 116
MOUNT SAN ANTONIO COLLEGE, Mar 60: 71
MOUNT SINAI, pilgrimage of Friar Felix Fabri to, Mar 60: 81–93
"MOURNERS OF DIJON," Sep 58: 62–63
MOUSSORGSKY, MODEST
Piston, Walter, quoted on, Jul 59: 23
Sketch of, Sep 58: 83
Stravinsky, Igor, quoted on, Sep 58: 82
"MOVIES," articles on current motion pictures
"Adrift on a Sea of Gore," by Saul Bellow, May 63: 109–11
"Art of Going it Alone, The," by Saul Bellow, Sep 62: 108–10
"Buñel's Unsparing Vision," by Saul Bellow, Nov 62: 110–12
"From Red Banners to Ballads," by Warren Miller, Mar 62: 110–12
"Hindu Trilogy, The," by Jean Stafford, Jan 61: 115
"Jester of the New Wave," by Warren Miller, Jan 62: 109–10
"Love in Another Country (Where They Order It Better)," by Hans Koningsberger, May 63: 110–12
"Mass-produced Insight, The," by Saul Bellow, Jan 63: 111–13
"Neo-realismo Revisited," by Jean Stafford, Mar 61: 98–100
"Not by the Book," by Hans Koningsberger, May 62: 116–18
"Samurai, With Sword, Won't Travel," by Jean Stafford, May 61: 114–15
"Sour Truth About the Sweet Life, The," by John Simon, Sep 61: 110–12
"Three Orphans and Their Patron Saint," by Jean Stafford, Sep 62: 116–17
"War and Peace in Two Foreign Films," by Jean Stafford, Nov 60: 121–22
"MOVIES MAKE HAY WITH THE CLASSIC WORLD, THE," article by Peter Green, May 61: 52–57
MOWRER, EDGAR ANSEL, "The Fifth Europe," article by, Mar 63: 4–9
MOY, SEONG, portrait of, with painting by, Jul 61: 24
MOYSE, MARCEL, Sep 61: 87
MOZART, WOLFGANG AMADEUS, Jan 60: 10–11, Mar 62: 75, 81, Nov 63: 109
Balanchine, George, quoted on, Jan 61: 47, 48
Chamber music of, Nov 62: 43, 44, 45, 46, 47
Don Giovanni, Jan 60: 10–11, Jan 62: 60
G Minor Symphony, Jan 59: 125
Gould, Glenn, quoted on, Jan 62: 91
In group painting, Nov 61: 33
Operas of, Nov 58: 23, 24, 25
As organist, Mar 60: 74
Prague Symphony conducted by Thomas Beecham, Mar 62: 105
MOZHUKHIN, IVAN, Mar 62: 119
MUCHE, GEORG, Nov 61: 68, 72
Photograph of, Nov 61: 58
MUDARRA, ALONSO, Nov 60: 94
MUDEJAR STYLE, Sep 62: 75, 89
"MUDRAS," in dance of India, Sep 63: 70–71
MUIR, JOHN, Jan 59: 7, Mar 60: 15–16
MUKERJEE, RADHAKAMAL, on eternally dancing Shiva, quoted, Sep 63: 72
"MULBERRY BUSH, THE," play, Jan 63: 27
MULLER, HERBERT J.
On American culture, quoted, Jan 60: 7
"Misuses of the Past," article by, Mar 59: 4–13, 128
MULLER, HERMANN J., May 59: 9
Photograph of, May 59: 16
On positive genetics for man, quoted, Nov 62: 8

MÜLLER, ROBERT, sculpture by, Mar 61: 107, 108–9
MULLGARDT, LOUIS CHRISTIAN, Jan 59: 10
MULLIGAN, GERRY, May 61: 100
Photograph of, Mar 61: 18
"MULTIPLE ROBERT GRAVES, THE," article by Peter Quennell, Jan 62: 50–55
MUMFORD, LEWIS, Jan 60: 10
City in History, The, pictorial treatment of, with excerpts from, Jul 61: 32–65
Quoted: on architecture, Jan 60: 23; on Haussmann's rebuilding of Paris, May 63: 52, 64, 66, 74; on historic symbols, May 61: 42; on Kennedy inaugural, Sep 61: 5; on utopias, Mar 63: 76, 77
MUNCH, EDVARD, May 60: 113
MUNDT, ERNEST, Jan 59: 13
MUNICH, GERMANY
Glyptothek, and Aegina marbles, Sep 59: 30, 49
Oktoberfest, Mar 59: 83, 84
U.S. consulate building, Jan 60: 120
MUNRO, ELEANOR C., articles by
"Figures to the Fore," Jul 60: 16–24, 114–16
"Portraits in Our Time," Jan 59: 95–105
MUNRO, JOHN, on Shylock, quoted, Jan 60: 92
MUNRO, WILLIAM, mermaid-sighting by, Jan 60: 130, 135
MUNTHE, AXEL, Jul 61: 112
MURAD III, SULTAN OF TURKEY, May 59: 131–32, 134
MURAD IV, SULTAN OF TURKEY, May 59: 59, 60, 63, 131
MURASAKI, LADY, *The Tale of Genji,* Mar 61: 9
MURAT, VIOLETTE, Sep 58: 84
MURCH, WALTER, painting by, Nov 60: 9
MURCHISON, RODERICK, Jul 63: 114
"MURDER IN THE CATHEDRAL," play, Nov 60: 52, 127, Jan 63: 88
MURDOCK, ROLAND P., Sep 58: 113
MURILLO, BARTOLOMÉ, Jul 63: 96
MURPHY, DENNIS, Jan 59: 18
Photographs of, Jan 59: 17, Mar 59: 16
Sergeant, The, Mar 59: 118, 119
MURPHY, RICHARD, articles by
"Giving New Life to Old Music," Nov 60: 88–95
"In Print": Barth, John, Jan 63: 36–37; Updike, John, Mar 62: 84–85
"On Stage": De Lavallade, Carmen, May 63: 48–49; Moffo, Anna, Jul 61: 96–97; Price, Leontyne, Mar 61: 72–73
MURRAY, DON, May 62: 118
MURRAY, JOHN, Mar 59: 92, 95, 124
MURRAY, MARGARET, Mar 62: 99
MURRELL, BOB, Nov 59: 125
MURROW, EDWARD R., Mar 60: 126, Jul 60: 6
MURRY AND LEONIE GUGGENHEIM FOUNDATION, May 59: 6, 7
MUSA IBN NUSAIR, Sep 62: 74
MUSA MALI, KING OF GUINEA, picture of, on map, Mar 63: 45
MUSATTI, RICCARDO, Nov 59: 48, 49
MUSAWARAT-ES-SAFRA, ruins in Butana desert, Mar 63: 41 (map), 57
"MUSE AND THE ECONOMY, THE," article by John Kenneth Galbraith, Sep 60: 33–40
MUSEUM OF MODERN ART, New York City, Sep 58: 84, 89, Jul 62: 14, 24, Jan 63: 106
Collection of Olga Hirsch (Mrs. Simon) Guggenheim, May 59: 10, 11, 12–13
"Constructions" show, Mar 62: 107
"New American Art," traveling show of, Nov 59: 41, 120–21
New painters exhibit, 1959, Jan 63: 75
And street furniture, Nov 59: 107, 111
Sutton, Denys, quoted on, Nov 59: 32
Tape recorder music introduction at, Jan 59: 51–52, 126
MUSEUM OF NON-OBJECTIVE ART. See SOLOMON R. GUGGENHEIM MUSEUM
MUSEUMS, development of, Nov 63: 73
MUSEUM WITHOUT WALLS. See IMAGINARY MUSEUM
MUSIC (see also GRAND OPERA; JAZZ; SYMPHONY ORCHESTRAS)
Aleatory, Jan 63: 77, 78
American: society's attitude toward composer, Jan 63: 74–75; Stravinsky, Igor, quoted on, Sep 58: 132
American pianists, Jan 60: 74–81
Amram, David, May 62: 82–83
Andalusian, Sep 62: 77
At Aspen, Colo., Sep 58: 98, 99, 102, 134
Baez, Joan, Sep 62: 66–67
For ballet, George Balanchine quoted on, Jan 61: 46–48
In Baroque age, Jul 60: 62, 64
At Bauhaus, Nov 61: 62, 71
Beecham, Thomas, Mar 62: 102–5
Bernstein, Leonard, and New York Philharmonic, Jul 59: 16–23

Byzantine, Nov 63: 33

"Canned," captive audiences of, Mar 60: 5

Chamber music, Nov 62: 42–47; Improvisation Chamber Ensemble of Lukas Foss, Jan 63: 76–81

Chance as principle of creation in, Sep 60: 30–32, 121–24

Duo-pianists Arthur Gold and Robert Fizdale, Mar 61: 74–75

1812 Overture of Tchaikovsky hoax at Rochester, N.Y., Jan 61: 71

Emotion and Meaning in Music, by Leonard Meyer, quoted, Jul 59: 107–8

Etruscan, May 60: 59, 78

And European unity trend, Mar 63: 9

Festivals at ancient sites, Jul 62: 27–31

Ford Foundation aid to, Jan 62: 9, 12–13

Forrester, Maureen, Mar 62: 87

Gould, Glenn, Jan 62: 88–93

Haydn renaissance, Mar 62: 76–83

Instrumentation, Igor Stravinsky quoted on, Sep 58: 132

Instruments of medieval Italy, Jan 59: 2, 3

Mass culture and, Jan 60: 5–6, 10–11

Motion pictures and, Sep 60: 7–8

Musical mind and inbreeding, Mar 62: 75

Musical plays, development of, Sep 58: 56–61, 143–44

In noble houses of 18th-century England, Nov 58: 56

Organ, king of instruments, returns, Mar 60: 72–80

In Persian Empire, Jan 63: 51

Popular, cult of unthink in, Sep 58: 38, 43

Renaissance music, revival by Noah Greenberg and New York Pro Musica, Nov 60: 88–95

Romantic revolt, May 61: 66, 82–83, 84

In San Francisco Bay Region, Jan 59: 20–22

Serial technique, Sep 60: 32; total serialism, Jan 63: 77–78

Serkin, Rudolf, Sep 61: 82–87

Sex and the musical vocation, Mar 62: 71

Stern, Isaac, Jul 60: 73–75, 126–27

Stravinsky, Igor, conversational memoirs of, Sep 58: 82–84, 132

Summer festivals, Mar 59: 84–85

Tape recorder music, Jan 59: 50–55, 124–27

In Topeka, Kans., Sep 59: 86–91, 122–23

Tuba-buying, Nov 63: 97–99

Twelve-tone row, Jan 63: 77–78, 79, 80

"MUSICAL AMERICA," magazine, quoted on Topeka, Kans., Sep 59: 86

MUSICAL SHOWS, as root of contemporary grand opera, Jan 60: 14

"MUSIC BOX REVUE," musical, Sep 58: 59

"MUSIC LESSON, THE," painting by Vermeer, Jul 63: 105; illus, Jul 63: 100

"MUSIC MAN, THE," musical, Sep 58: 144, Jan 60: 14, Jan 63: 106

"MUSIC OF FRIENDS, THE," article by Joseph Wechsberg, Nov 62: 42–47

MUSIQUE CONCRÈTE, Jan 59: 52, 54

MUSSET, ALFRED DE, Nov 61: 36, May 61: 81, May 63: 57

Childhood of, May 60: 33, 34, 37

Portrait of, May 60: 32

Self-portrait, with George Sand, May 61: 81

MUSSOLINI, BENITO, Jan 59: 121, Sep 61: 44

Motion pictures made during regime of, May 61: 54

MUSTAFA I, SULTAN OF TURKEY, May 59: 63

MUTAMID, AL-, KING OF SEVILLE, Sep 62: 87

MUTUAL INSURANCE COMPANY BUILDING, Hartford, Conn., Sep 59: 19

"MY BROTHER WAS AN ONLY CHILD," book by Jack Douglas, Jul 60: 121

MYCENAEAN CIVILIZATION, as related to Homeric Age, Jan 61: 73–99

MYERS, LOU, "Philosophical Primer," drawings by, Jul 61: 110–11

"MY FAIR LADY," musical, Sep 58: 57, 60, 61, 143, 144, Mar 60: 127, May 61: 102, 113

"MY FRIEND HENRY MILLER," book by Alfred Perlès, quoted, Nov 61: 104

MYHERS, JOHN, Sep 62: 109

"MY LOST YOUTH," poem by Longfellow, quoted, May 61: 8

"MY NAME AND I," poem by Robert Graves, quoted, Jan 62: 53

"MY PHILADELPHIA FATHER," book by Cordelia Biddle, Jul 63: 17

MYRON, sculpture by, Jan 62: 47

"MYSTERY OF MAD MAGGIE, THE," article by Gilbert Highet, Jan 59: 44–49

MYSTICISM, Christian, of Baroque age, Jul 60: 38

"MYTH OF SISYPHUS, THE," book of essays by Albert Camus, Nov 59: 70

"MY UNINVITED COLLABORATOR: G. B. S.," article by Hesketh Pearson, Nov 58: 18–21, 134–37

"MY WORLD AND WHAT HAPPENED TO IT," article by P. G. Wodehouse, Jan 59: 56–59, 127

N

NAARDEN, NETHERLANDS, Jul 61: 53

NABIS, Mar 62: 15, 16

NABOKOV, IVAN, and ELIZABETH CARMICHAEL, "Balanchine," interview by, Jan 61: 44–56

NABOKOV, VLADIMIR

Pale Fire, reviewed, Jul 62: 89–91

Photograph of, May 59: 16

Pnin, Sep 60: 119

NADAR (FELIX TOURNACHON), Jan 59: 103

In picture interview with Marie-Eugène Chevreul, Mar 59: 68–69

NADIR SHAH, KING OF PERSIA, Jan 63: 72

NAGA, ancient Nubian city, Mar 63: 41 (map), 43 (illus)

NAGEL, ERNEST, Nov 63: 61

NAIRN, IAN, on Britain's "Subtopia," quoted, Jul 59: 7

NAJDORF, MIGUEL, Jan 62: 117

NAKAYAMA, TADASHI, May 60: 114

Print by, May 60: 112

"NAKED AND THE DEAD, THE," novel by Norman K. Mailer, Jul 62: 101

NAMES

Humboldt as place name in Americas, Jul 59: 67

Survival as common nouns, May 60: 126–28

NAMIER, LEWIS B., Sep 63: 99

NAMUTH, HANS, photographs by

Calder, Alexander, at home, Nov 62: 10–11, 14, 17

Far out on Long Island, May 63: 10–27

Housatonic Valley residents, May 60: 12–29

NAPIER, CHARLES, Jul 63: 110–11

NAPLES, ITALY, Mar 59: 120

Cinema Augusteo, Mar 59: 24

In classical revival of 18th century, Mar 62: 56, 61, 62

Domination of Sicily by, Sep 61: 38

Drawings by Domenico Gnoli, Jul 59: 135–41

Photographs by Herbert List with text by Vittorio de Sica, Sep 63: 49–59

Street life in, Nov 61: 122

And Thirty Years' War, Nov 62: 33, 35–36

NAPOLEON I, Sep 58: 120, Jul 62: 56, 59, May 63: 102

Attitude toward Joan of Arc, Mar 62: 96

Letter to Josephine, facsimile, Sep 59: 136

Louvre under, Sep 60: 72, 81

Mme de Staël, Mme Récamier, and, Nov 58: 86–89, 142–46

Malta seized by, Mar 61: 68

Meeting with Alexander I at Tilsit, Sep 63: 28–32

Nationalism stimulated by, Mar 63: 5

Portraits commissioned by George IV to commemorate overthrow of, Jul 63: 106

Portraits of, Nov 58: 88, Sep 59: 136, Sep 60: cover, 3, 68, May 61: 71

Quoted: on Alexander the Great, Mar 59: 30; on Chateaubriand, May 61: 67; on Square of St. Mark's, Venice, Jul 59: 15

And rebuilding of Paris, May 63: 54, 57, 58, 67

And romantic revolt, May 61: 70

Vignali collection of relics of, Nov 60: 99

NAPOLEON III (LOUIS NAPOLEON), Nov 58: 107, Mar 60: 57, Jul 61: 52, Nov 61: 36, Sep 62: 20, 21, 112–13

Louvre under, Sep 60: 81

In painting by Tissier, Sep 60: 68; by Yvon, May 63: 50

Rebuilding of Paris under, May 63: 50–75

Sale of Peregrina pearl by, May 63: 95

"NAPOLEON AND THE FEMMES FATALES," article by Maurice Levaillant, Nov 58: 86–89, 142–46

NAPOLEONIC WARS, balloons in, Sep 58: 120

NARAYAN, V. K., Nov 62: 109

NARNIA, CHRONICLES OF, by C. S. Lewis, May 59: 127

NARVA, BATTLE OF, Sep 59: 79

NARWHAL, as source of ivory, May 60: 91, 92–93

NARYSHKIN, PRINCESS, Sep 63: 31

NASH, JOHN (see also in ILLUSTRATIONS INDEX), Nov 62: 24, 29

NASH, OGDEN, on billboards, quoted, May 61: 5

NASSAU COUNTY, N.Y., May 61: 19

NASSUF PASHA, May 59: 59–60

NAST, CONDÉ, Jul 62: 33, 35

NATALIA NARYSHKIN, Sep 59: 66

NATIONAL BOOK AWARDS, Jul 63: 68, 69, 72

NATIONAL BROADCASTING COMPANY, vs. Philco Corporation, Sep 61: 113

NATIONAL COUNCIL OF TEACHERS OF ENGLISH, Jul 63: 41–42, 43

NATIONAL EDUCATION ASSOCIATION, Mar 60: 71

"Group Development" sessions, Nov 58: 33

NATIONAL GALLERY, London, Jul 59: 28, May 62: 78

NATIONAL GALLERY OF ART, Washington, D.C., Jul 59: 28

Kennedy, Mrs. J. F., quoted on, Sep 61: 9

Portraits of patrons, Jan 59: 105

NATIONAL INSTITUTE OF ARTS AND LETTERS, Jul 63: 68, 69, 70, 72

NATIONALISM

Joan of Arc as symbol of, Mar 62: 97

And trend toward unity in Europe, Mar 63: 5–6

NATIONAL PARK SYSTEM

Beginning of, Mar 60: 16

Buildings of, Jan 60: 121

"NATIONAL POLICE GAZETTE." See "POLICE GAZETTE"

NATIONAL REPERTORY THEATRE, Jan 63: 106

NATIONAL TRAINING LABORATORY IN GROUP DEVELOPMENT, Bethel, Me., Nov 58: 32, 33

NATSIVAAR, stonecut by, Mar 63: 120

"NATURAL HISTORY OF LOVE, THE," book by Morton M. Hunt, excerpt from, Sep 59: 113–17

"NATURAL HISTORY OF THE MERMAID, THE," article by Richard Carrington, Jan 60: 129–36

NATURAL RESOURCES, population increase vs., Sep 58: 50–52

NATURE

Emerson quoted on, Jan 61: 104

Man, miracle, and, Jul 60: 25–32

As refuge for privacy, Jul 60: 5

Wilderness, man's way with, Mar 60: 12–16

"NATURE, MAN, AND MIRACLE," article by Loren Eiseley, Jul 60: 25–32

"NATURE OF THE UNIVERSE, THE," book by Fred Hoyle, Jan 59: 123

NAUGHTON & GOLD, Jan 61: 122–23

"NAUGHTY MARIETTA," musical, Sep 58: 57

NAVARRETE, FERNÁNDEZ, Sep 59: 121

NAVIGATION

Henry the Navigator, Nov 60: 72–83

Venetian practices, Mar 60: 84

"NAVIGATOR TO THE MODERN AGE," article by Garrett Mattingly, Nov 60: 72–83

NAVY, U.S., Theodore Roosevelt and, Nov 63: 70

"NAZARENE GOSPEL, THE," book by Robert Graves, Jan 62: 54

"NAZARIN," motion picture, Nov 62: 110, 112

NAZIS, Jan 59: 121

N'DEBELE PEOPLE, Nov 60: 56–65

NEAGLE, JOHN, Jul 63: 18

NEALE, J. M., Nov 63: 47

NEARCHUS, Mar 59: 56

NECKER, JACQUES, Nov 58: 86, 87

Portrait of, Nov 58: 88

NEER, AART VAN DER, Sep 58: 26

NEFERTARI, QUEEN OF EGYPT, Jul 60: 14, 124

NEGAHBAN, EZAT O., and excavations at Marlik Tepe, Iran, Nov 62: 100–4

NEGROES, AMERICAN, interest in Africa, Mar 63: 105–6

NEHRU, JAWAHARLAL, on U.S. embassy building at New Delhi, quoted, Jan 60: 119

NEILLY, HELEN, May 60: 17

NELSON, HORATIO, Mar 62: 114, Sep 63: 42

"NENNELE," ketch, Mar 59: 122

NEOLITHIC VILLAGE, Jul 61: 36–37

"NEO-REALISMO REVISITED," article by Jean Stafford, Mar 61: 98–100

NERO, ROMAN EMPEROR, May 59: 55, May 63: 81, 85

Coin portraits of, Sep 63: 38; illus, Sep 63: 37

As organist, Mar 60: 74

NERVI, ANTONIO, Mar 59: 124

NERVI, PIER LUIGI, Jan 59: 11, Mar 59: 18–25, 121–24, Sep 59: 19, Nov 60: 125

Photograph of, Mar 59: 20

Structures designed by. See ILLUSTRATIONS INDEX

NERVO & KNOX, Jan 61: 122–23

NESKI, JULIAN, May 63: 17

NESTORIANISM, Jan 63: 52

NETHERLANDS (see also AMSTERDAM)

Arnhem monument, May 61: 42

Golden Age of Dutch Republic, Sep 58: 14–35

Naarden, Jul 61: 53

Organ (musical instrument) of, Mar 60: 74, 76, 80

Peter the Great in, Sep 59: 66, 74

Rotterdam's sculpture by Naum Gabo, Sep 59: 18–19

And Thirty Years' War, Nov 62: 33–41

Witch mania in, Nov 59: 62, 63

NETSCH, WALTER A., Jan 63: 13

NEUDÖRFFER, JOHANN, Sep 59: 127

NEUMANN, BALTHASAR, stairwell designed by, Jul 60: 56–57

NEUMANN, JOHN VON, Mar 62: 73

NEUTRA, RICHARD, Jan 60: 21

NEVELSON, LOUISE, Mar 63: 104

"NEVER ON SUNDAY," motion picture, May 61: 97

"NEVER REPRESSIBLE BEECHAM, THE," article by Neville Cardus, Mar 62: 102–5

NEVINS, ALLAN, Jan 60: 7

Comment by, on article by J. H. Plumb, Sep 63: 101

NEVINS, MARIAN. See MacDOWELL, MARIAN NEVINS

NEW AMERICAN PAINTING. See ABSTRACT EX-
PRESSIONISM

"'NEW AMERICAN PAINTING' CAPTURES
EUROPE," article by John Russell, Nov 59: 32, 41,
120–21

"NEW AMERICAN POETRY: 1945–1960," anthology,
Sep 61: 116–17

"NEW AMERICAN POET SPEAKS: THE WORKS
OF A. B.," May 62: 96–99

"NEW ATLANTIS, THE," treatise by Francis Bacon, Jul
61: 6, Mar 63: 75

NEWBOLD, WILLIAM R., and world's most mysterious
manuscript, Jan 63: 4–9

NEWBURYPORT, MASS., studies on, as "Yankee City,"
Nov 59: 22–23, 24

NEWCASTLE, DUKES OF, Nov 58: 50, 56–57

NEW DELHI. See DELHI

"NEW DIRECTIONS," annual publication, Sep 61: 117

NEW DRAMATISTS COMMITTEE, Jan 62: 11

NEW ENGLAND
Millenarism and philo-Semitism in, Mar 60: 102, 124–25
Witch mania in, Nov 59: 59–60, 62–63

NEW ENGLANDERS, Jul 59: 123–24

"NEWEST INVASION OF EUROPE, THE," article by
Reyner Banham, Nov 60: 12–16, 124–25

"NEW FACE OF BRITAIN, THE," photographs by
Bruce Davidson with comment by Alan Pryce-Jones, Nov
61: 14–31

"NEW FACES OF 1952," review, Nov 60: 85

"NEW GIRL IN TOWN," musical, Sep 58: 60, 143, May
63: 13

NEW HAMPSHIRE, MacDowell Colony, Mar 63: 26–33

NEWHART, BOB, Jan 62: 66, 68

NEWHOUSE, SEWALL, Mar 63: 77

NEW JERSEY
Greenbelt towns in, Jul 59: 11, 12
Ocean Grove, Jan 61: 104, 112

"NEW LIFE AMONG THE RUINS," illustrated feature,
Jul 62: 26–31

"NEW LIFE IN THE OLD OPERA HOUSE," article
by Winthrop Sargeant, Jan 60: 12–17, 122–23

NEW LONDON, CONN., youth of Eugene O'Neill in, Mar
60: 25–40

NEW LONDON "DAY," Mar 60: 27, 33

NEW LONDON "TELEGRAPH," Eugene O'Neill on,
Mar 60: 33–37, 40

"NEW LOOK IN VALHALLA, THE," article by Joseph
Wechsberg, May 63: 40–45

NEWMAN, BARNETT, Nov 59: 120

NEWMAN, JOHN HENRY, CARDINAL, Jan 63: 86
Quoted, Nov 58: 113

NEWMAN, PAUL, Sep 58: 42, Nov 62: 107, 108

"NEW MAPS OF HELL," book by Kingsley Amis,
quoted, Mar 63: 79

NEW MILFORD, CONN., May 60: 13 (map), 22, 24

"NEW MOON, THE," musical, Sep 58: 57

"NEW MUSIC MADE WITH A MACHINE, A," article
by David Randolph, Jan 59: 50–55, 124–27

NEW ORLEANS, LA., street furniture in, Nov 59: 107

NEW ORLEANS OPERA, Jan 62: 10–11

"NEW PHASES OF 1960," revue, Jan 62: 70

"NEW POETS OF ENGLAND AND AMERICA, THE,"
anthology, Sep 61: 116

NEWPORT, R.I.
Folk Festival of 1959, Sep 62: 66
Jazz on a Summer's Day, motion picture of jazz festival at,
Mar 61: 18–19

NEW REALISM, in painting, Jan 63: 25

"NEW REPUBLIC, THE," journal
Quoted on paintings bought by Chase Manhattan Bank, Nov
60: 10
And Spectric poets, May 60: 46

"NEWS FROM NOWHERE," romance by William Morris, Mar 63: 77

NEWSPAPERS (see also by name)
American, demons of, Jul 61: 69
Communications satellites and, Jan 62: 19
Mass media and imaginary audience, Mar 60: 46–51

NEWTON, CONN., May 60: 13 (map), 28

NEWTON, ISAAC, Jul 60: 30, Mar 62: 73, May 62: 60,
Jan 63: 97, May 63: 115, Sep 63: 101
Portrait of, Nov 60: 20

NEWTON, ROBERT, Sep 63: 79

"NEW TREASURES FROM SUMER'S HOLY CITY,"
illustrated feature, Nov 61: 84–87

"NEW WAVE, THE," article by Henry B. Darrach, May
60: 49–55

NEW WAVE IN MOTION PICTURES
In France, May 60: 49–55, Mar 61: 13, 19
Jester of: Philippe de Broca, Jan 62: 109–10
In New York, Mar 61: 12–19
Origin of, Sep 62: 108
Seberg, Jean, and, May 62: 81

"NEW WAY TO PAY OLD DEBTS, A," play, Edmund
Kean in, Mar 62: 116

"NEW WORLDS FOR OLD," book by Margaret Mead,
May 60: 123

NEW YORK
Long Island, eastern end, May 63: 4–27
Mountain House, on Lake Mohonk, Jan 61: 104, 110–11
Nassau County, May 61: 19
Proposed state song, Nov 61: 118–19
Syosset (L.I.) Lanes style show for bowlers, Mar 63: 94
Yaddo colony, at Saratoga, Mar 63: 27, 32

NEW YORK, N.Y.
Architecture of, Sep 60: 39; influence in Europe, Nov 60:
12–16, 124–25
Cathedral of St. John the Divine, Jan 63: 12
Channel 13, Jul 62: 94–95
Charles Movie Theatre, Nov 62: 96–99
City-planning: effects of, Jul 59: 5–6; and Moses, Robert,
May 63: 52, 67, 72, 105
Englishman's impressions of, Jul 62: 114, 116
Fort Tryon Park, Silent Traveller quoted on, Nov 59: 132
Hotels, recent, Mar 63: 115–17
Lincoln Center for the Performing Arts. See LINCOLN
CENTER FOR THE PERFORMING ARTS
Manufacturers Trust Company building, Sep 59: 18
Metropolitan Opera. See METROPOLITAN OPERA
Motels, Mar 63: 115, 117
Motion pictures produced in, Mar 61: 12–19
Motion picture versions of, May 59: 101
Museums. See by name
People of, Jul 59: 124–25
Philadelphia compared with, Jul 63: 7, 8, 12
Phoenix Theatre, Jan 62: 9
Photographed by Ruth Orkin, Mar 59: 96–104
As port city, May 61: 4
Save-the-West-Village campaign, Jul 62: 50
Seagram building, Sep 59: 6–7
"See Manhattan While It Lasts: A Walking Tour," text by
Oliver Jensen, drawings by John Rombola, May 63:
116–20
Shakespeare Festival, Nov 60: 116–18
Street furniture, Nov 59: 106, 107–8
Theatres, Jul 59: 41–42, 44, 48
Traffic situation, memorandum from Julius Caesar to Rob-
ert Moses on, Mar 59: 26–27; comment on, May 63: 105
Water consumption, May 60: 39–40
Whitman, Walt, quoted on, Jul 59: 5
Wright, Frank Lloyd, quoted on, Jul 59: 5, 10–11

"N.Y., N.Y.," motion picture, Mar 61: 12–13, 19

NEW YORK CITY BALLET, Nov 59: 54, 56, Jan 61: 44,
46, Sep 61: 9, Jan 63: 107, 108

NEW YORK CITY CENTER, Jul 62: 10
Opera at, Jan 60: 14, 122–23

"NEW YORKER, THE," magazine, Nov 58: 64, Jul 63:
70
Advertising in, Nov 58: 31, Mar 59: 112, Nov 59: 117,
Jan 61: 119
On New York City and Topeka, Kans., quoted, Sep 59: 86
"Profiles" of, Jul 60: 120
"Seymour, an Introduction," story by J. D. Salinger pub-
lished in, Jan 61: 42–43, 44, 46, May 62: 105–6, 107

NEW YORK "EVENING POST," Earl Roppel hoax ex-
posed in, May 60: 48

NEW YORK "HERALD," Jan 59: 24
Quoted: on Spectric poetry, May 60: 43; on S.S. Great
Western, Jan 59: 41

NEW YORK "HERALD-TRIBUNE," memorandum from
Horace Greeley to John Hay Whitney on acquisition of,
Jan 59: 24–25

NEW YORK INTERNATIONAL AIRPORT (IDLE-
WILD)
Architecture, Sep 59: 19
Mobile by Alexander Calder, Nov 62: 16
Street lighting, Nov 59: 106
TWA terminal, Jul 60: 82

NEW YORK "JOURNAL-AMERICAN," story on John
Foster Dulles' death, quoted, Jul 60: 120

NEW YORK PHILHARMONIC, Jan 59: 21, Jul 62: 30,
Jan 63: 106, 109
Beecham, Thomas, quoted on, Mar 62: 104
Bernstein, Leonard, as music director, Jul 59: 16–23
And Lincoln Center for the Performing Arts, Jul 62: 6, 8,
9, 10
Soviet tour, Jan 60: 11

"NEW YORK POST," on 1948 Presidential election,
quoted, Mar 60: 49

NEW YORK PRO MUSICA, Nov 60: 88–95

NEW YORK PUBLIC LIBRARY, and Lincoln Center for
the Performing Arts, Jul 62: 7

NEW YORK SCHOOL, of painting. See ABSTRACT EX-
PRESSIONISM

"NEW YORK'S MONUMENT TO THE MUSES," article by Martin Mayer, Jul 62: 4–11

"NEW YORK'S NEW WAVE OF MOVIE MAKERS,"
article by Elizabeth Sutherland, Mar 61: 12–19

NEW YORK STATE EDUCATION DEPARTMENT,
Mar 60: 71

NEW YORK STATE THEATRE, Jul 62: 8, 10–11

NEW YORK TELEPHONE COMPANY, unlisted sub-
scribers, Jul 60: 5

"NEW YORK TIMES, THE," Mar 59: 112, Mar 60: 50,
51, Jul 60: 67
Clothing advertisement in, Nov 59: 117
How to compete with, Jan 59: 24–25
Interview with William P. Orr, quoted, Jan 63: 113
J.B., review of, Jan 60: 49, 51
Letter from John Q. Academicus, quoted, Sep 62: 16
Quoted: on abstract expressionism, Nov 59: 121; on Broad-
way theatre, Jan 63: 106; on Cologne opera house, Nov
58: 118; on housing, Nov 58: 147; on Scott, George C.,
Jul 60: 93

NEW YORK "TRIBUNE," Jan 59: 24–25

NEW YORK UNIVERSITY
Excavations at Aphrodisias, Mar 63: 98–100
School of Aeronautics, May 59: 8

NEW YORK WORLD'S FAIR
Of 1939, Futurama City of, Jul 59: 5, 12
Projected for 1964, May 60: 80, 87

NEW YORK "WORLD-TELEGRAM," on Puritans and
bowling, quoted, Mar 63: 93

"NIAGARA," S.S., bullion salvaged from, Nov 58: 77

NIAGARA FALLS, English comment on, Mar 60: 13

NICCOLI, NICCOLÒ, Nov 62: 94

NICCOLÒ. See GIOVANNI and NICCOLÒ

"NICE AND ABSTRUSE GAME, A," article by Harold
C. Schonberg, with photographs by Lee Boltin, Jan 62:
114–28

NICHOLAS V, POPE, Jan 62: 27, 31

NICHOLS, MIKE, Jan 62: 66, 68, May 63: 91

NICHOLSON, MABEL, Jan 62: 52

NICHOLSON, NANCY (MRS. ROBERT GRAVES), Jan
62: 52–53

NICHOLSON, VIRGINIA, photograph of, Jul 63: 86

NICHOLSON, WILLIAM, Jan 62: 52, 53

NICKLAUS, JACK, Nov 62: 113

NICOLLE, V. J., painting by, Sep 60: 57

NICOLSON, HAROLD
Articles by: "He Taught Us to Be Free," excerpted from
The Age of Reason, book by, Mar 61: 114–19; "Roman-
tic Revolt, The," May 61: 58–88
On Europe during the Enlightenment, quoted, Mar 63: 5

NICOMEDES II, KING OF BITHYNIA, May 62: 46

NICOT, JEAN, May 60: 127

NIEBUHR, BARTHOLD GEORG
Childhood of, May 60: 34, 36, 37–38
Portrait of, May 60: 32

NIELSON, PETER, Sep 58: 103

NIEMEYER, OSCAR, Sep 59: 6, 20, Mar 61: 36
Buildings designed by, Sep 59: 9, 15

NIETZSCHE, FRIEDRICH WILHELM, May 61: 66,
Sep 63: 8
Quoted: on Greeks, May 62: 48; on Venice, Mar 63: 14

NIEUWERKERKE, COUNT DE, Nov 61: 36, May 63:
70

NIGERIA, early cultures of, Mar 63: 44, 46–51, 53–55,
57–58

"NIGHT AMERICA TREMBLED, THE," television
show, Jan 62: 104

"NIGHT AND FOG," motion picture, May 60: 54

"NIGHT AT PISA," painting by René Magritte, Jan 62:
82; illus, Jan 62: 86

"NIGHT BEAT," television program, Jul 60: 122

"NIGHT HEDGEROW ANIMAL," drawing by Morris
Graves, Jul 60: 105; illus, Jul 60: 112

"NIGHT LAND," sculpture by Isamu Noguchi, Mar 60:
108, 110; illus, Mar 60: 110

"NIGHT OF THE IGUANA, THE," play, Sep 62: 111–
12, May 63: 108

"NIGHT TRAIN," motion picture, Nov 59: 31

NIJINSKY, WASLAW, Igor Stravinsky quoted on, Sep 58:
83

NIKA RIOT, in Constantinople, Nov 63: 12

NIKE OF SAMOTHRACE, sculpture, May 59: 122

NIKOLAIS, ALWIN, and his dancers, Nov 58: 90–91

NILE RIVER
Ancient monuments near, threatened by Aswan Dam, Jul
60: 8–15, 124–25
Search by Richard Francis Burton for source of White
Nile, Jul 63: 110, 113–14

NILSSON, BIRGIT, Jul 61: 97, May 63: 42

NIMPTSCH, ULI, sculpture by, May 62: 77

NIMRUD, ASSYRIA, Sep 59: 103

NIMZOVITCH, ARON, Jan 62: 114
Photograph of, Jan 62: 114

"NINE MUSES, THE," painting by Tintoretto, Jul 61: 94

"NINETEEN EIGHTY-FOUR," book by George Orwell,
Jul 59: 111, Mar 63: 74, 79, Jul 63: 37

NINETEEN-TWENTIES
Algonquin Round Table, Jul 62: 36–41

Held, John, Jr., Jul 63: 118–19
Vanity Fair, magazine, Jul 62: 33–36
NINEVEH, ASSYRIA, Jul 61: 41
"NINTH WAVE, THE," novel by Eugene Burdick, Jan 59: 19
NIPPUR, Mesopotamian city, Jul 61: 40, Jul 63: 108
New treasures from, Nov 61: 84–87
NITZE, ELIZABETH. See PAEPCKE, ELIZABETH NITZE
NITZE, WILLIAM A., Sep 58: 102
NIVEN, DAVID, Nov 58: 137, Sep 63: 76, 77, 78
Photographs of, Sep 63: 76, 78, 79
NIVOLA, CONSTANTINO, Sep 59: 19, Nov 59: 48, May 63: 26
Photograph of, May 63: 26
Sculptured wall designed by, Sep 59: 14
NIXON, PATRICIA RYAN (MRS. RICHARD M.), Jan 60: 112
NIXON, RICHARD M., Jul 60: 120, Sep 61: 5
Photograph of, Jul 60: 4
NIZAM-UL-MULK, VIZIER OF PERSIA, Jan 63: 53
NIZZOLI, MARCELLO, Nov 59: 49
NKRUMAH, KWAME, Jan 63: 116, 117
NOBEL PRIZES
Awarded to Guggenheim Fellows, May 59: 9
In literature, Jul 63: 69, 74–75
NOBLE, RAY, Sep 63: 77 (note)
NOBLE, WILLIAM, Nov 58: 64
"NOBLE HOUSES OF EIGHTEENTH-CENTURY ENGLAND, THE," article by J. H. Plumb, Nov 58: 38–61
"NOBODADDY," play, Jan 60: 53
NOCERINO, GIOVANNI BATTISTA, Mar 62: 49–50
NOCK, ALBERT JAY, on reading, quoted, Nov 60: 24
"NO DEPOSIT, NO RETURN," article by Stephen White, May 61: 118
"NO EXIT" ("HUIS CLOS"), play, Jul 61: 117, Nov 62: 111, Mar 63: 107
NOGAROLA, ISOTTA and GINEVRA, Jan 60: 62
NOGUCHI, HIDEYO, Isamu Noguchi quoted on, Mar 60: 107
NOGUCHI, ISAMU, May 59: 5, Sep 59: 18, May 62: 16
Interview with, Mar 60: 104–12
Photographs of, May 59: 16, Mar 60: 105, 106
Works by. See ILLUSTRATIONS INDEX
NOH DRAMA, Jul 59: 126, 127
NOK CULTURE, of Africa, Mar 63: 41 (map), 46 (illus), 53, 57–58
NOLAN, LLOYD, Mar 63: 35
NOLAN, SIDNEY, Sep 63: 97–104
Paintings by. See ILLUSTRATIONS INDEX
Photograph of, Sep 62: 97
NOLAND, KENNETH, Jan 63: 25
Painting by, Jan 63: 17
NOLEN, JOHN, Jul 59: 11
"NOLI ME TANGERE," painting by Holbein, Jul 63: 96
"NOLI ME TANGERE," painting by Rembrandt, Jul 63: 106
NONCONFORMISM, dangers of, Mar 59: 112
"NON-TEACHERS, THE," article by Robert Bendiner, Sep 62: 14–19
NORDHOFF, CHARLES, Jan 60: 126
———— and JAMES NORMAN HALL, *Bounty* trilogy, novels by, Sep 63: 42, 48
Motion pictures based on, Sep 63: 42, 46
NORMAN, CHARLES, *Ezra Pound*, Jan 61: 116, 119
NORMANS, in Sicily, Sep 61: 22, 24–25 (map), 26, 28, 30, 32
NORRIS, TENN., Jul 59: 11
NORRIS, FRANK, Jan 59: 7, Jul 62: 18
NORRIS DAM, Jan 60: 23–24
NORTH, FREDERICK, 8TH BARON (LORD NORTH), May 60: 99, 100, 101, 124
NORTH AFRICA, Tassili rock paintings, May 59: 70–83, Sep 62: 11, 12, Mar 63: 43
NORTHCOTE, JAMES, Mar 63: 69
NORTH EGREMONT, MASS., May 60: 13 (map), 19
NORTHERN WAR. See GREAT NORTHERN WAR
NORTHUMBERLAND, 1ST DUKE OF (HUGH SIMPSON), Mar 62: 67
NORTHUMBERLAND, 9TH EARL OF (HENRY PERCY), Mar 63: 69
NORTHWEST ORIENT AIRLINES, Mar 60: 79
NORTON, CHARLES ELIOT, Isabella Stewart Gardner and, Jul 59: 29–30
NORTON, RICHARD, Jul 59: 29
NORWAY
Ocean-going fleets of Bronze Age, Jul 60: 91
Rock carvings of, Jul 60: 90
NORWICH, ENGLAND, exhibition of works collected during Grand Tours of 18th century, Nov 59: 95–96
"NO SIGN OF THE DOVE," play, Nov 58: 138
"NOT ABOUT NIGHTINGALES," play, May 59: 55
"NOT A PALACE BUT A PILL FACTORY," illustrated feature, Sep 58: 88–91

"NOT BY THE BOOK," article by Hans Koningsberger, May 62: 116–18
"NOTES FROM A DARK STREET," novel by Edward Adler, Sep 62: 65
"'NOTHING' PLAYS AND HOW THEY HAVE GROWN ON US, THE," article by Frank Gibney, Nov 58: 62–65
"NO T.O. FOR LOVE," musical, Sep 60: 50
NOVAK, KIM, Sep 60: 54
NOVAK, STEFAN, Jan 59: 14
Sculpture by, Jan 59: 4
NOVARINA, MAURICE, Sep 62: 24
Church designed by, Sep 62: 25
NOVELLI, ERMETE, Mar 62: 119
NOVELTY, as fifth need of man, Jul 59: 106–11
NOYCE, WILFRID
Photograph of, Sep 58: 8
"Why Men Seek Adventure," article by, Sep 58: 6–13, 135–39
NOYES, JOHN HUMPHREY, Mar 63: 77
"NOZZE DI FIGARO, LE," opera, Nov 58: 23, 25, May 63: 42
NUBIA, ancient monuments in, threatened by Aswan Dam, Jul 60: 8–15, 124–25
"NUDE, THE," book by Kenneth Clark, quoted, Jul 60: 116
"NUDE IN FRONT OF A MIRROR," painting by Pierre Bonnard, Mar 62: 25; illus, Mar 62: 23
"NUDE IN THE BATHTUB," painting by Pierre Bonnard, Mar 62: 25; illus, Mar 62: 20–21
"NULL-P," story by William Tenn, Mar 63: 79
NYS, DANIEL, Jul 61: 90

O

OAK PARK, ILL., Unity Temple, Sep 59: 8
OANNES, fish deity, Jan 60: 131
OATES, WHITNEY J., photograph of, Sep 59: 26
OBATA, GYO, Jan 60: 120
OBELISKS, Jan 60: 21–22
OBERLIN, RUSSELL, Nov 60: 91
OBERON, MERLE, photograph of, Sep 63: 76
"OBEYING THE LAW," photographs by John Drake, Nov 63: 110–12
"OBJECT NO 2," print by Koshiro Onchi, May 60: 113, 114; illus, May 60: 105
O'BRIEN, FREDERICK, Jan 60: 125
O'CASEY, SEAN, Mar 59: 88, Jan 60: 96, Mar 60: 126, Jul 63: 73
Juno and the Paycock, quoted, Jan 62: 68
"OCEANA," romance by James Harrington, Mar 63: 76
OCEAN GROVE, N.J., Jan 61: 104, 112
"OCEAN VIEW FROM WINDOW," painting by Richard Diebenkorn, Jul 60: 116; illus, Jul 60: 18
O'CONNOR, DONALD, Jan 61: 123
O'CONNOR, FLANNERY, Jan 62: 8
"OCTOPUS, THE," book by Frank Norris, Jan 59: 7
"ODD MAN OUT," motion picture, Nov 59: 31, Mar 61: 98
"ODDS AGAINST TOMORROW," play, May 63: 49
ODEGARD, PETER, on university teaching situation, quoted, Sep 62: 17, 19
"ODE ON A GRECIAN URN," poem by Keats, Mar 62: 68
ODETS, CLIFFORD, Sep 58: 44, Nov 58: 65, Jul 61: 117, Nov 62: 106
Golden Boy, Jan 61: 32, Mar 61: 43
Influence on Paddy Chayefsky, Sep 60: 51
ODETTA, Sep 62: 66
O'DONNELL, TERENCE, articles by
"Evenings at the Bridge," May 61: 24–32
"Twenty-Five Centuries of Persia," Jan 63: 40–72
ODYSSEUS-SCYLLA GROUP, sculpture in Cave of Tiberius, May 59: 123–24
"ODYSSEY, THE"
On garden of Alcinous, quoted, May 59: 41
Historical light on, Jan 61: 73–99
As inspiration of James Joyce and Ezra Pound, Jan 61: 116, 117–18
Interpretation of dream in, May 63: 31, 114
Lands of, Jan 61: 96
Sculptural representations of heroes of, in Cave of Tiberius, May 59: 123–24
"OEDIPUS," play by Sophocles, quoted, Nov 62: 118
OENSLAGER, DONALD, Jan 62: 14
Stage design for *J.B.,* Jan 60: 50, 51
OESTERLEN, DIETER, church designed by, Sep 62: 28
OETTINGEN-WALLERSTEIN, PRINCE, Jul 63: 107
OFFENBACH, JACQUES, May 63: 69, 70
In painting by Manet, May 63: 75
"OFFICIALESE," Jul 63: 37
"O FOR THE DAYS OF AMOS 'N' ANDY!" article by

Stephen White, Nov 61: 102–3
"OF STARS AND MEN," book by Harlow Shapley, quoted, Jan 59: 28, 123
"OF THEE I SING," musical, Sep 58: 59, Mar 63: 107
OGG, OSCAR, Sep 59: 128
O'GORMAN, JUAN, Sep 59: 20
Building designed by, Sep 59: 8
OGOTOMMELI, Dogon sage, Mar 63: 44
O'HARA, FRANK, Sep 61: 119
"Larry Rivers: 'Why I Paint As I Do,'" interview by, Sep 59: 94–102
O'HARA, GERRY, Nov 59: 123, 125–26
O'HARA, JOHN, Sep 59: 118, 119, Jan 62: 64, Jan 63: 37
O'HARA, MAUREEN, Nov 59: 31, 122, 124, 125
Photographs of, Nov 59: 30, Jul 60: 6
"OH DAD, POOR DAD, MAMMA'S HUNG YOU IN THE CLOSET AND I'M FEELIN' SO SAD," play, Sep 62: 34–35 (illus), 37, Mar 63: 107
"OH KAY," musical, Sep 58: 59
OKADA, EJIE, May 60: 54
O'KEEFFE, GEORGIA, Jul 62: 15
"OKLAHOMA," musical, Sep 58: 57, 59, 60, 143
Compared with *Ballad of Baby Doe,* Jan 60: 14
OKLAHOMA, state song, quoted, Nov 61: 119
OLDENBURG, CLAES, Jan 63: 25
"OLD MAN," television play, Mar 63: 35
"OLD MAN AND THE SEA, THE," novel by Ernest Hemingway, Jan 59: 134
OLDS, IRVING, Jul 62: 6, 7
OLDUVAI GORGE, archaeological discoveries in, Mar 62: 9, 10
"OLD VAUDEVILLIANS, WHERE ARE YOU NOW?" article by June Havoc, Jul 59: 112–20
"OLD WORLD'S PECULIAR INSTITUTION, THE," article by M. I. Finley, May 62: 42–49
OLGA, SAINT, Nov 63: 34
OLIVARES, COUNT-DUKE OF, Sep 59: 120, 121, Jul 60: 38, Nov 62: 38
Portraits of, Sep 59: 29, Jul 60: 41
OLIVER, KING, Jan 63: 75
OLIVETTI, ADRIANO, Nov 59: 44–51, 127
Portrait of, Nov 59: 44
OLIVETTI, CAMILLO, Nov 59: 46–48
"OLIVETTI: A MAN AND A STYLE," article by Kermit Lansner, Nov 59: 44–51, 127
OLIVIER, LAURENCE, Sep 58: 42, Nov 60: 51, Jan 63: 107, Mar 63: 36, Jul 63: 85, Sep 63: 77 (note), 78, 80
Barrault, Jean-Louis, quoted on, Sep 61: 109
Guthrie, Tyrone, quoted on, Jan 61: 29–30
Meacham, Anne, quoted on, May 61: 99
Photograph of, Jan 61: 30
OLLIVIER, MARIE, photograph of, Mar 62: 118
OLMSTED, FREDERICK LAW, Jul 59: 12, Mar 60: 16, May 63: 73
OLONNE, DUC D', Jan 60: 85
OLSZEWSKA, MARIA, Sep 59: 56–57
"OLVIDADOS, LOS," motion picture, Nov 62: 110
"OLYMPIA," painting by Édouard Manet, Mar 60: 54, 57
"OLYMPIAN SPRING," poem by Carl Spitteler, Jan 63: 111
OLYMPIAS, mother of Alexander the Great, Mar 59: 30, 32
OLYMPIC GAMES, 1960, stadiums designed for, Mar 59: 22–23, 122, 123–24
OMINUS, JEAN, Nov 58: 117
"OMNIBUS," television production, Mar 60: 5
"OMOO," story by Herman Melville, Jan 60: 124
ONAGERS, Sep 58: 147–48
"ON BEING UPSTAGED BY SCENERY," article by Robert Hatch, Sep 62: 110–12
"ONCE AND FUTURE KING, THE," novel by T. H. White, May 61: 103–4
"ONCE UPON A MATTRESS," musical, Sep 61: 80
ONCHI, KOSHIRO, May 60: 113, 114
Print by, May 60: 105
ONEIDA COMMUNITY, Mar 63: 77
O'NEILL, ELLA QUINLAN, mother of Eugene O'Neill, Mar 60: 26–40
Portrait of, Mar 60: 30
O'NEILL, EUGENE, Sep 58: 60, 143, Jan 63: 107, 108
Chayefsky, Paddy, quoted on, Sep 60: 56
Desire Under the Elms, May 63: 107
Iceman Cometh, The, Sep 62: 111; at Circle in the Square, Mar 60: 98, 120, 121
Long Day's Journey Into Night, Nov 58: 63
New London, Conn., youth of, Mar 60: 25–40
Portraits of, Mar 60: 26, 28, 34, 39
In Provincetown, Mass., Jul 61: 13, 16, 26
O'NEILL, JAMES, father of Eugene O'Neill, Mar 60: 26–40
Portraits of, Mar 60: 31, 34
O'NEILL, JAMIE, brother of Eugene O'Neill, Mar 60: 26–40
Portraits of, Mar 60: 34, 36
O'NEILL, KATHLEEN JENKINS, Mar 60: 32

"ONE-WAY PENDULUM," play, Jan 63: 31
"ON HAVING MY PORTRAIT PAINTED," article by Somerset Maugham, Jan 59: 106–7
"ON LITERATURE," book by Mme de Staël, Nov 58: 89
"ONLY A TRILLION," book by Isaac Asimov, Jan 59: 28
"ONLY YESTERDAY: THE THIRD REICH," article by Gilbert Highet, Nov 60: 119–21
"ON NATIVE GROUNDS," book by Alfred Kazin, Jul 62: 98, 99–100, 103
ONO, TADASHIGE, May 60: 113
Print by, May 60: 106
"ON SCREEN," articles on motion picture personalities
Belmondo, Jean-Paul, Nov 61: 116–17
Cardinale, Claudia, Jan 63: 38–39
Field, Shirley Ann, Mar 63: 36–37
Frankenheimer, John, Mar 63: 34–35
Remick, Lee, Sep 60: 88–89
Seberg, Jean, May 62: 80–81
York, Susannah, Nov 61: 114–15
"ON STAGE," articles on theatre personalities
Albee, Edward, Sep 61: 78–79
Allen, Woody, May 63: 46–47
Amram, David, May 62: 82–83
Baez, Joan, Sep 62: 66–67
Beatty, Warren, Jan 62: 104–5
Besoyan, Rick, Sep 60: 86–87
Burnett, Carol, Sep 61: 80–81
Carroll, Diahann, Nov 60: 86–87
Davis, Miles, May 61: 100–1
De Lavallade, Carmen, May 63: 48–49
Dewhurst, Colleen, Jul 60: 94–95
Fizdale, Robert, Mar 61: 74–75
Forrester, Maureen, Mar 62: 86–87
Gold, Arthur, Mar 61: 74–75
Graham, Ronny, Nov 60: 84–85
Hurst, David, Jan 61: 100–1
Jens, Salome, Jan 62: 102–3
Lampert, Zohra, Jul 62: 48–49
Meacham, Anne, May 61: 98–99
Moffo, Anna, Jul 61: 96–97
Price, Leontyne, Mar 61: 72–73
Sondheim, Stephen, Jul 61: 98–99
Turney, Matt, Nov 62: 68–69
"ON THE BOWERY," motion picture, Mar 61: 15, 19
"ON THE HORIZON," Nov 62: 105, Jan 63: 105, Mar 63: 105–6, May 63: 105
"ON THE HORIZON: THE FORWARD LOOK AND A BACKWARD GLANCE," article by Oliver Jensen, Sep 58: 152
"ON THE ROAD," novel by Jack Kerouac, Sep 58: 40, 42, Sep 61: 116, 119
Quoted, Jul 63: 39
"ON THE SOUND," motion picture, Nov 62: 98
"ON THE TOWN," musical, Sep 58: 60
Quoted, Nov 61: 118
"ON THE WATERFRONT," motion picture, Sep 58: 43, 44
"ON YOUR TOES," musical, Sep 58: 59–60
OPARIN, ALEKSANDR I., Jan 59: 28
"OPEN CITY," motion picture, May 59: 99, May 60: 51, Mar 61: 98, 99, 100
OPERA. See GRAND OPERA
OPERA CLUB, New York City, Nov 58: 120
"OPERA NEWS," magazine, on new Metropolitan Opera House, quoted, Nov 58: 118
OPERETTA, Sep 58: 57–58, 59
OPHIR, Nov 59: 119, Mar 63: 57 (illus)
"OPINION," television program, Sep 61: 113
OPINION RESEARCH CORPORATION, on "leadership elite for change," quoted, Nov 59: 21
OPPENHEIM, DAVID, May 63: 14, 18
Photograph of, May 63: 15
OPPENHEIMER, J. ROBERT, Jul 59: 111, Sep 59: 118, Jul 60: 120, Nov 60: 21, 24, May 62: 9
"OPTICAL ERUPTION IN DOWNTOWN NEW YORK, AN," illustrated feature, Nov 58: 90–91
ORANGE COUNTY, CALIF., May 61: 19
"O RARE HOFFNUNG," cartoons by Gerard Hoffnung, Jul 62: 104–7
ORCHESTRAS. See SYMPHONY ORCHESTRAS
"ORESTES, OR THE ART OF SMILING," story by Domenico Gnoli, Jul 60: 3
"ORFEO," opera, Jul 60: 42
ORFF, CARL, Carmina Burana, May 63: 49
ORGAN
In Baroque age, Jul 60: 64
Return of, Mar 60: 72–80
"ORGANIZATION MAN, THE," book by William H. Whyte, Jr., Nov 58: 147, Jul 59: 7, Jul 60: 68, 69
"ORIENTAL PALACE FOR AN ENGLISH KING, AN," article by J. H. Plumb, Nov 62: 20–31
"ORIGIN," magazine, Sep 61: 117, 121
"ORIGINS OF THE SECOND WORLD WAR, THE," book by A. J. P. Taylor, Mar 62: 28–29
ORIGO, IRIS, "The Education of Renaissance Man," arti-

cle by, Jan 60: 57–73
ORINOCO RIVER, exploration by Alexander von Humboldt, Jul 59: 62, 63
ORKIN, RUTH, Sep 62: 108
Photograph of, Mar 59: 96
Photographs of New York City by, Mar 59: 96–104
ORLANDI, FRANCESCO, Sep 58: 126
ORLANS, HAROLD, report on university teaching situation, quoted, Sep 62: 15, 16, 17
ORLÉANS, FRANCE, Joan of Arc and, Mar 62: 92, 93, 96
ORLÉANS, CHARLES D' (DUKE OF ORLÉANS), Mar 62: 89, 90
Portrait of Joan of Arc from manuscript by, Mar 62: 88
ORLÉANS, PHILIPPE D', Sep 59: 52
ORLOV, COUNTESS, Sep 60: 130
ORLOVSKY, PETER, Mar 61: 14, Sep 61: 119
ORLY, FRANCE, dirigible hangars, Mar 59: 21, 24
"ORNIFLE," play, Nov 60: 126
OROSIUS, PAULUS, on library at Alexandria, quoted, Nov 62: 78
"ORPHEUS AND EURYDICE," opera, Jan 61: 56
"ORPHEUS AND EURYDICE," painting by Poussin, Mar 61: 91, 92–93; illus, Mar 61: 82–83
"ORPHEUS DESCENDING," play, May 59: 55
ORR, WILLIAM P., on television, quoted, Jan 63: 113
ORRERY, May 59: 93
ORSINI, FELICE, May 63: 71
ORTEGA Y GASSET, JOSÉ, Sep 58: 102, Mar 63: 6
ORTMAN, GEORGE, Jan 63: 25
Painting by, Jan 63: 24
ORVIETO, ITALY, May 60: 77
ORWELL, GEORGE, Nov 62: 110, Nov 63: 106
On degradation of language, quoted, Jul 63: 37
Nineteen Eighty-Four, Jul 59: 111, Mar 63: 74, 79
OSBORN, ALEX F., Nov 58: 33
OSBORN, ROBERT, May 59: 109, May 60: 18, Sep 60: 41–43, Nov 61: 57
Drawings by, Sep 60: 41–48
Photograph of, May 60: 18
"Sight That Music Makes, The," album by, May 62: 120–28
OSBORNE, JOHN, Nov 58: 62, Jan 61: 113, Mar 61: 102, Jul 61: 116, Mar 63: 109
And English Stage Company, Jan 63: 26, 27–29, 32, 33
Entertainer, The, Jan 61: 30
In painting by Feliks Topolski, Nov 60: 131
Photograph of, Jan 63: 30
"OSBORN ON LEISURE," book by Robert Osborn, Sep 60: 43
"OSBORN'S AMERICANS," article by Russell Lynes, Sep 63: 41–43
OSBOURNE, LLOYD, Jan 60: 125
In group photograph, Jan 60: 31
OSGOOD, CHARLES E., The Measurement of Meaning, Mar 60: 122
OSGOOD, CHARLES GROSVENOR, Sep 59: 118
OSLO, NORWAY, U.S. embassy building, Jul 60: 79, May 62: 16
OSMAN II, SULTAN OF TURKEY, May 59: 63
OSTADE, ADRIAEN VAN, Jul 63: 106
OSTIA, ITALY, beach pavilion, Mar 59: 122
OSTROGOTHS, in Sicily, Sep 61: 24, 26
OSUNA, DUKE OF (FRANCISCO DE MONCADA), Nov 62: 35–36, 41
"OTHELLO," play by Shakespeare
Bowdlerized version, Sep 62: 68, 70, 71
Motion picture based on, Jul 63: 85, 90
OTHER-DIRECTED MAN, Sep 60: 32
"OTHERS," magazine, and Spectric poets, May 60: 43–44, 46–47
"OTHER VOICES, OTHER ROOMS," novel by Truman Capote, Mar 59: 118
"OTHO THE GREAT," play by Keats, Mar 62: 116
O'TOOL, PETER, Jul 62: 111
Photograph of, Jul 62: 108
OTTO I, HOLY ROMAN EMPEROR, May 63: 99
Embassy to Abd al-Rahman III, Sep 62: 78–79
OTTO, PRINCE OF BAVARIA, Jan 61: 37
OTTOMAN EMPIRE
Attack on Maltese islands, Mar 61: 61, 63–64, 65
Attacks on Rhodes, Mar 61: 56–59, 65
And Battle of Lepanto, Jul 63: 49–61
Coexistence with Christendom, Sep 58: 46–47
Grand Seraglio, May 59: 56–63, 131–35
Napoleon I and, Sep 63: 30, 32
OTTOMAN TURKS, conquest of Constantinople, Nov 63: 31, 32, 34
OUIDA (MARIE LOUISE DE LA RAMÉE), on Richard Francis Burton, quoted, Jul 63: 112, 116
"OUR BETTERS," play, Mar 61: 43
"OUR FACE TO THE WORLD," article by Eric Larrabee, May 60: 4–9, 122–23
"OUR LADY OF THE FLOWERS," book by Jean Genet, Nov 61: 98, 99, May 62: 115
"'OUR MAN IN HAVANA,'" article by Robert Emmett Ginna, Nov 59: 26–31, 122–26

"OUR MAN IN HAVANA," novel by Graham Greene, May 61: 117
Filming of motion picture based on, Nov 59: 26–31, 122–26
"OUR MAN IN PURGATORY," article by Gilbert Highet, May 61: 116–17
"OUR TOWN," play, May 59: 101, Mar 60: 98, 121, Mar 63: 30, 31
"OUTCAST OF THE ISLANDS, AN," novel by Joseph Conrad, Mar 61: 22–23
OUTER SPACE
Lewis, C. S., and, May 59: 64–67, 125–27
And spirit of man, Jan 59: 26–31, 122–23
Voltaire to the spacemen, memorandum, Sep 61: 18–19
"OUTLAWS," book by Danilo Dolci, quoted, Sep 61: 43
"OUT OF A FAIR, A CITY," article by Ada Louise Huxtable, May 60: 80–87
"OUT OF AFRICA," book by Isak Dinesen, Sep 59: 111–12
"OUT OF THE GARGOYLES AND INTO THE FUTURE," article by William Harlan Hale, May 59: 84–87
"OUT OF THE NIGHT," motion picture, Nov 62: 97–98
"OUT OF THE OLD MET, THE NEW," article by Nelson Lansdale, Nov 58: 28–29, 117–20
"OUT OF THE SILENT PLANET," novel by C. S. Lewis, Jan 59: 122, May 59: 64, 67, 125, 126–27
"OUTRAGEOUS IONESCO, THE," interview by Rosette Lamont, May 61: 89–91, 93, 95, 97
"OVERLAND MONTHLY," magazine, Jan 59: 7
"OVERRULED," play, Nov 58: 134–35
"OVERSEASMANSHIP," May 60: 9
OVID
Art of Love, Nov 58: 108
Fasti, quoted, Nov 63: 43
Portrait of, Nov 63: 44
In Renaissance curriculum, Jan 60: 62
OWEN, ALUN, Jan 63: 32
OWINGS, NATHANIEL A., Jan 60: 120
"OX-BOW INCIDENT, THE," novel by Walter Van Tilburg Clark, Jan 59: 19
"OXFORD COMPANION TO THE THEATRE, THE," on Charles Macklin as Shylock, quoted, Jan 60: 92
"OXFORD ENGLISH DICTIONARY," use of, by Robert Graves, Mar 63: 85, 86, 87
OXFORD GROUP, Jan 63: 86
OXFORD HISTORY OF ENGLISH LITERATURE, May 59: 66
OXFORD UNIVERSITY, ENGLAND, Jan 63: 82–87
Psalmanazar, George, at, Jan 60: 116
Silent Traveller quoted on, Nov 59: 133
OXYRHYNCHUS PAPYRI, Nov 62: 93
"O YE DAUGHTERS OF SUMER!" article by Samuel Noah Kramer, Jul 63: 108–9
OYO EMPIRE, Mar 63: 41 (map), 46, 53
"OZYMANDIAS OF EGYPT," poem by Shelley, quoted, Jul 60: 8

P

PAAR, JACK, Mar 60: 126, Jul 60: 6, 121
PACHECO, DUARTE, on Henry the Navigator, quoted, Nov 60: 76–77
PACHELBEL, JOHANN, Mar 60: 74
PACKARD, VANCE, Nov 58: 147, Nov 59: 21, 22, 24
PADEREWSKI, IGNACE JAN, Jul 59: 32, Jan 60: 81
PAEPCKE, ELIZABETH NITZE, Sep 58: 102
PAEPCKE, WALTER, Sep 58: 96–103, 133–34
Portrait of, Sep 58: 96–97
PAGANINI, NICOLÒ, in painting by Joseph Danhauser, May 61: 84–85
PAGE, EUPHEMIA, Sep 59: 88, 89, 91
PAGE, GERALDINE, Mar 60: 120, Jan 62: 14, Nov 62: 107, 108, Mar 63: 35
"PAGLIACCI," opera, Mar 60: 119
PAHLAVI LINE, shahs of Persia, Jan 62: 42, 52 (chart), 72
PAINE, ALBERT BIGELOW, Mar 62: 98
PAINTING (see also TOMB PAINTINGS)
American abstract expressionism: in Europe, Nov 59: 32, 41, 120–21; search for successor to, Jan 63: 16–25
And architecture, Sep 59: 18
Architecture as subject of, Sep 63: 10–27
"Art Against the Grain," article by Frank Getlein, Jul 62: 12–25
Artist in our time, Jan 63: 73–75, 105
Baroque, Jul 60: 38, 42, 50, 64; illus, Jul 60: 37, 40–41, 43–49
Bonnard, Pierre, Mar 62: 14–27
British royal collection, Jul 63: 92–107
Cardinal Mazarin's farewell to his paintings, Nov 61: 82–83
Çatal Hüyük wall paintings, Sep 62: 10–13

Chance as principle of creation in, Sep 60: 30–32, 121–24

Charles I of England as patron of, Jul 61: 78–95

Chase Manhattan Bank collection, Nov 60: 4–11

Chicago taste, 1890–1913, Sep 60: 102, 127

Chinese imperial art treasure, Jan 61: 14–25

Christian, André Malraux quoted on, Nov 58: 113–14

Circlism of Alexander Liberman, Sep 61: 66–67

Cloar, Carroll, Nov 58: 78–81

Dulle Griet (Mad Maggie), by Pieter Bruegel, interpretation of, Jan 59: 44–49

Dutch, of 17th century, Sep 58: 19–20, 26–35

Egyptian, André Malraux quoted on, Nov 58: 15

England's Royal Academy, May 62: 56–79

And European unity, Mar 63: 8, 9

Figure painting of Elmer Bischoff, David Park and Richard Diebenkorn, Jul 60: 16–24, 114–16

Ford Foundation aid to, Jan 62: 8–9, 12

Fouquet, Jean, Nov 61: 88–97

François, André, May 59: 108–21

French, of Second Empire, May 63: 70

Gardner (Isabella Stewart) collection, Jul 59: 26–40, 133–34

Gottlieb, Adolph, Mar 59: 135

International style, May 60: 113–14

Japanese, May 60: 114

Japanese prints: influence in Europe, May 60: 103–4; influence of European painters on, May 60: 104–14

Koch, John, Sep 60: 104–11

Magritte, René, and other Belgian painters, Jan 62: 76–87

Maugham, Somerset, portraits of, Jan 59: 106–7

Miró, Joan, Mar 59: 70–81, 126–27

Moskovitz, Shalom, primitive paintings of, Jul 61: 120–28

Mostel, Zero, May 62: 50–53

Nolan, Sidney, Sep 62: 96–104

Nude, return to, Sep 63: 90–96

People's choice, Sep 58: 108–13

Persian miniatures, Jan 63: 57, 62, 67–69; illus, Jan 63: 61–66

Philadelphia painters and collectors, Jul 63: 18–23

Picasso, Pablo and his public, Nov 61: 4–13; Roque, Jacqueline, and, Jan 60: 97–105

Portraiture, Jan 59: 95–105

Posters, political, painted in Europe after World War I, Jan 59: 112–21

Poussin, Nicolas, Mar 61: 76–93

In Provincetown, Mass., Jul 61: 10–29

Rivers, Larry, Sep 59: 94–102

Rock paintings of Sahara, May 59: 70–83, Sep 62: 11, 12, Mar 63: 43

Roman, of 1st century A.D., Jul 60: 114–15, 116

Romantic revolt, May 61: 66, 72, 74

Rouault, Georges, Nov 62: 48–57

Salon art, Mar 60: 52–69

In San Francisco Bay Region, Jan 59: 12–15

Sivard, Robert, Nov 63: 84–91

Topolski, Feliks, coronation murals by, Nov 60: 128–36

Unthink in, Sep 58: 38, 44–45, 134–35

Vatican masterpieces, Jan 62: 32, 41, 45, 48; illus, Jan 62: cover, 3, 30–31, 35, 37–40, 44

Vespucci, Simonetta, Renaissance ideal, Sep 58: 92–95, 142

Wyeth, Andrew, Sep 61: 88–101

Zen Buddhism and, Jul 59: 77, 126

"PAINT YOUR WAGON," musical, May 61: 103

"PAIR OF DESIGNING FINNS, A," article by Richard Moss, Jul 63: 62–67

"PAIR OF MODERN MASQUERS, A," illustrated feature, Jan 63: 88–91

"PAISAN," motion picture, May 59: 99, Mar 61: 98

"PAJAMA GAME," musical, Sep 58: 57, 60, 143

PALANCE, JACK, in *Barabbas*, Mar 63: 109, 110

PALATINATE, and Thirty Years' War, Nov 62: 34, 35, 37, 41

PALAZZO VENIER DEI LEONI, Venice, May 59: 5, 6, 11, 18

"PALEFACE AND REDSKIN," essay by Philip Rahv, Sep 61: 116

"PALE FIRE," novel by Vladimir Nabokov, reviewed, Jul 62: 89–91

PALERMO, ITALY, Sep 61: 28, 30, 32, 34, 38

Battle of Ammiraglio, Sep 61: 37

PALESTINE

Archaeological discoveries in, Nov 59: 4–10, 118–19

Moslem capture of, Nov 63: 26

Pilgrimage of Friar Felix Fabri to, Mar 60: 81–85

PALFFY, ELEANOR, on Isabella Stewart Gardner, quoted, Jul 59: 29–30, 134

PALIMPSEST, Nov 62: 89; illus, Nov 62: 77

PALISSY, BERNARD, May 62: 13

"PAL JOEY," musical, Sep 58: 60, 143

PALLADIO, ANDREA, Nov 58: 41, Jul 60: 42

PALLADIUM, London, Jan 61: 122

PALLADIUM, THEFT OF, sculpture, May 59: 122, 123, 124

PALLOY, PIERRE FRANÇOIS, drawing by, Jan 60: 84

PALM BEACH, FLA., resort hotels of, Jan 61: 104, 108–9

PALMER, A. N., and Palmer Method of handwriting, Sep 59: 128

PALMER, ARNOLD, Nov 62: 113

PALMER, EDGAR, Sep 59: 24

PALMER, JOHN, on Shylock, quoted, Jan 60: 92

PALMER, LILLI, Sep 63: 80

PALMER, MRS. POTTER, Sep 60: 102, 127

PALMERSTON, 3D VISCOUNT (HENRY JOHN TEMPLE), Nov 59: 86, Jul 62: 59

PALMOLIVE RAPID SHAVE, television commercial for, Nov 60: 123

"PALM-WINE DRINKARD, THE," book by Amos Tutuola, Nov 62: 109

PAMPULHA, BRAZIL, Church of Saint Francis, Sep 59: 20

PANAMA-PACIFIC EXPOSITION, 1915, Jan 59: 13

PANCOAST, ELLA (MRS. JOSEPH E. WIDENER), Jul 63: 22

"PANDORA," H.M.S., Sep 63: 45

PAN-EUROPEAN UNION, Mar 63: 6

"PANIC," play, Jan 60: 53–54, 55, Jul 63: 87

PANNINI, GIOVANNI PAOLO, paintings by. See ILLUSTRATIONS INDEX

PANOFSKY, ERWIN, Sep 59: 118

Photograph of, Sep 59: 26

PANTALONE, Jan 60: 92–96

PAOLOTTO, BROTHER, photograph of, Sep 63: 56–57

PAOLOZZI, EDUARDO, sculpture by, Mar 61: 105

PAPACY, status of medieval Military Orders and, Mar 61: 51–52, 62

PAPAL BULLS, Sep 59: 127

PAPAL STATES, and Battle of Lepanto, Jul 63: 50

PAPIAS, Mar 63: 98

PAPINI, GIOVANNI, on novel *Barabbas*, quoted, Mar 63: 109

PAPP, JOSEPH, Nov 60: 116–18, May 62: 82, Jan 63: 107, 108

PAPYRUS, as material for books, Nov 62: 83, 86, 89

"PARABLE OF DEATH," composition by Lukas Foss, Jan 63: 78

PARACELSUS, PHILIPPUS AUREOLUS, May 63: 115

PARADISE, SEARCH FOR, Mar 61: 20–33

"PARADISE LOST," poem by Milton, Jul 60: 38, Jan 61: 117, Jul 61: 113

Quoted, Sep 58: 81

"PARALLEL LIVES," biographies by Plutarch, Mar 59: 34

PARCHMENT, as material for books, Nov 62: 83, 86, 89

PARENTUCELLI, CARDINAL. See NICHOLAS V, POPE

PARIS, FRANCE

American abstract expressionism in, Nov 59: 120–21

As baroque city, Jul 61: 52–55

Haussmann's rebuilding of, May 63: 50–75, 105

International artists' city in, proposed, Mar 63: 8

Louvre, history and treasures of, Sep 60: 57–85

Metro street furniture, Nov 59: 111

Montmartre, Mar 59: 83, 84

Opèra (Théâtre National de l'Opèra), Nov 58: 24, 27, 133, May 63: 66–67

Place de Furstemberg, Silent Traveller quoted on, Nov 59: 135

Restaurant du Petit Moulin Rouge, May 61: 125

Role in Grand Tour of 18th and 19th centuries, Nov 59: 76–86

Seige of 1870–71, balloon in, Sep 58: 120

Seine River in, May 61: 4, Jul 62: 53, 56, 59–61

Skyscrapers projected for, Nov 60: 16

Théâtre des Nations Festival, and New York's Living Theatre, Mar 62: 107

UNESCO buildings, Mar 59: 122–23, Sep 59: 18; gardens, Mar 60: 110–11; monument by Alexander Calder, Nov 62: 16

U.S. embassy building, Jan 60: 25–26

What not to see in, Mar 59: 84

PARIS, UNIVERSITY OF, Mar 63: 5

Erasmus at, May 62: 90

Role in trial of Joan of Arc, Mar 62: 92

"PARIS BLUES," motion picture, Nov 60: 86

PARIS EXPOSITION OF 1937, Mercury Fountain at, Nov 62: 16

"PARIS NOT SO GAY," play, Nov 58: 139

"PARIS PRESERVED," portfolio of drawings by Ronald Searle, Mar 62: 120–28

"PARIS REVIEW, THE," magazine, Jan 59: 82

PARK, DAVID, Jan 59: 13, 14, Jul 60: 16, 114–16, Jul 62: 24, Sep 63: 96

Drawing of, Jul 60: 115

Works by. See ILLUSTRATIONS INDEX

PARK, MUNGO, Sep 58: 8, 135

PARKE-BERNET, auction gallery in New York City, Nov 62: 59, 64

PARKER, CHARLIE, Sep 59: 96, May 61: 100, Jan 63: 75

PARKER, DOROTHY, Jul 62: 33, 34, 35, 36, 37, 38

Caricature of, Jul 62: 32

PARKER, EDWIN, Jul 62: 35

PARKER, JOHN, Nov 59: 95

PARKINSON'S LAW, Nov 63: 104

"PARKTILDEN VILLAGE," novel by George P. Elliott, Mar 59: 17, 119

PARLIAMENT, English, under Charles I, Jul 61: 92, 93

"PARLIAMENT OF SAINTS," Mar 60: 124

PARMENIO, Mar 59: 30, 35, 40, 47, 52

PARMIGIANINO, Jul 61: 95, Jul 63: 94

PARR, CATHERINE, Sep 59: 132

PARRINGTON, VERNON L., Sep 63: 101

PARROTT, THOMAS MARC, Sep 59: 118

PARS, WILLIAM (see also CHANDLER, RICHARD), Nov 59: 86

"PARSIFAL," opera, Nov 58: 27, May 63: 41, 42, 44, 45

Thomas Beecham quoted on, Mar 62: 103

PARSONS, LOUELLA, Jul 63: 89, Sep 63: 79

PARSONS, TALCOTT, quoted, Mar 59: 135

PARTHENON MARBLES. See ELGIN MARBLES

PARTHIANS, Jan 63: 49, 52 (chart)

"PARTISAN REVIEW," magazine, Jan 60: 7

"PARTY AT CRANTON, THE," novel by John W. Aldridge, Sep 60: 119

PASADENA, CALIF., Stuart Company building, Sep 58: 88–91

PASARGADAE, ancient city in Iran, Jan 63: 42 (illus), 44, 59 (map)

"PASCAL," article by Morris Bishop with photographs by Erich Lessing, Jan 63: 94–104

PASCAL, BLAISE

Article on, with photographs commemorating, Jan 63: 94–104

Childhood of, May 60: 34, 35

Portraits of, May 60: 32, Jul 60: 39, Jan 63: 94

Quoted: on man and the natural, Jul 60: 27, 30, 32; on rivers, Jul 62: 56

PASCAL, GILBERTE, Jan 63: 100, 104

PASCAL, JACQUELINE, May 60: 35, Jan 63: 100, 104

"PASCALINE," Jan 63: 97, 99; illus, Jan 63: 95

"PASHA," locomotive, Jan 59: 39

PASSAGE GRAVES, Jul 60: 87, 90

"PASSENGER TO TEHERAN," book by Victoria Sackville-West, quoted, May 59: 41, Mar 61: 28

"PASSION," book of etchings and engravings by Georges Rouault, with text by André Suarès, Nov 62: 48, 57

"PASSION ACCORDING TO ROUAULT, THE," illustrated feature, Nov 62: 48–57

"PASSIONATE EXILES, THE," book by Maurice Levaillant, article based on, Nov 58: 86–89, 142–46

"PASSION FOR IVORY, A," article by Ivan T. Sanderson, May 60: 88–95, 120–21

PASTERNAK, BORIS L., Mar 63: 33, Jul 63: 75

PASTEUR, LOUIS, Jul 61: 7, May 63: 54

Chevreul, Marie-Eugène, quoted on, Mar 59: 68

IQ of, Mar 62: 72, 73

PATAGONIA, derivation of name, Nov 61: 110

'PATAPHYSICS, May 61: 89–90, 93, 95

PATAY, BATTLE OF, Mar 62: 92

PATCH, BLANCHE, Nov 58: 20

PATCH, THOMAS, Nov 59: 96

PATEL, PIERRE, painting by, Nov 59: 78–79

PATER, WALTER, satirized by Max Beerbohm, May 61: 38

"PATHER PANCHALI," motion picture, reviewed, Jan 61: 115

PATINHO, J., Sep 58: 114

PATON, JOSEPH NOËL, May 62: 64

PATRAS, GULF OF, Battle of Lepanto, Jul 63: 49–61

PATRICK, SAINT, Sep 59: 125

PATTERSON, REBECCA, on Emily Dickinson, quoted, Jul 61: 102, 103

PATTERSON, TOM, Jul 59: 45

PATTI, ADELINA, Sep 59: 54

PAUL I, CZAR OF RUSSIA, Sep 60: 131, Mar 61: 68, Sep 63: 31

PAUL, GRAND DUKE OF RUSSIA, Mar 62: 66

PAUL II, POPE, Jan 62: 45

PAUL III, POPE, Jan 62: 43

PAUL IV, POPE, Jan 62: 41

With Michelangelo, painting, Jan 62: 24

PAUL, SAINT, Mar 59: 54, Mar 63: 4

At Ephesus, Sep 58: 140

Opinion of Menander, Jul 59: 79

Robinson, John A. T., quoted on, Sep 63: 6

PAULHAN, JEAN, May 61: 91

PAULING, LINUS, May 59: 9, Mar 62: 73

Photograph of, May 59: 16

PAULINUS OF NOLA, Nov 60: 29

PAUL THE SILENTIARY, Nov 63: 33

On Hagia Sophia, quoted, Nov 63: 15

PAUSANIAS, quoted

On Aegina, Sep 59: 32

On carving recovered from Aegean Sea, Nov 58: 71

On ivory sculpture, May 60: 120
On Mycenae, Jan 61: 78
"PAVILIONS ON THE PRAIRIE," article by John Canaday, Nov 61: 42–47
PAVLOV, IVAN, Sep 63: 101
PAVLOVA, ANNA, on school of Imperial Ballet, quoted, Sep 63: 67
PAWNSHOP, decline of, Jul 60: 67
PAXSON, E. W., Nov 63: 61
PAXTON, JOSEPH, Mar 62: 36
Building designed by, Mar 62: 37
PAYNE, JOHN, translation of *Arabian Nights' Entertainments*, Jul 63: 116–17
PAYNE, ROBERT, *The Splendor of Persia*, quoted, Jan 63: 67
"PAY OR DIE," motion picture, Jul 62: 49
"PEACE AND WAR," painting by Rubens, Jul 61: 91
"PEACE GIMMICK, THE," musical, Jan 63: 88
PEACOCK, as symbol of Baroque, Jul 60: 38
PEACOCK, THOMAS LOVE, letter from Shelley to, quoted, May 63: 85
PEALE, CHARLES WILLSON, Jul 63: 18
Self-portrait, Jul 63: 19
PEALE, NORMAN VINCENT, Nov 58: 146
PEARSON, DREW, Jul 60: 6
PEARSON, HESKETH, articles by
"Greatest Wit in England, The," Mar 59: 90–95, 124–25
"My Uninvited Collaborator: G. B. S.," Nov 58: 18–21, 134–37
PEARY, ROBERT, Sep 58: 138
Portrait of, Sep 58: 13
PEASE, JAMES, photograph of, Nov 61: 81
PEASE, PETER, Sep 58: 10
PÊCHE MELBA, May 61: 121, 124
"PECORONE, IL," work by Fiorentino, Jan 60: 92, 96
PEEL, ROBERT, Nov 62: 30
"PEER GYNT," play, Jan 62: 108, Nov 62: 108
PEI, I. M., Nov 59: 111
Kip's Bay Plaza, designed by, Jan 63: 115
PELAYO, KING OF ASTURIAS, Sep 62: 75
PELHAM-HOLLES, THOMAS, DUKE OF NEWCASTLE, Nov 58: 50, 56–57
PELLISSON, PAUL, Jul 63: 82, 83
PELOPONNESIAN WAR, Jul 60: 102
Corruption of language during, Jul 63: 37
Thucydides' account of, Jan 60: 41–45
PEMBERTON, BROCK, Jul 62: 37
PEMBERTON, MURDOCK, Jul 62: 37
PEMBROKE, 3D EARL OF (WILLIAM HERBERT), Jul 63: 94, 96
PEMBROKE, 4TH EARL OF (PHILIP HERBERT), Jul 61: 90, Jul 63: 96
PEMBROKE, 8TH EARL OF (THOMAS HERBERT), Jan 60: 114, 116
PEMBROKE, 10TH EARL OF (HENRY HERBERT), Nov 59: 77, 87, Mar 62: 56
PEMBROKE, 11TH EARL OF (GEORGE AUGUSTUS HERBERT), Nov 59: 77
PENDLETON, EDMUND, biography of, by David J. Mays, Jul 63: 72
PENN, ARTHUR, Nov 62: 108
PENN, WILLIAM, Jul 63: 5, 14, 26
Attitude toward Russia, Sep 59: 60
PENNEBAKER, D. A., Mar 61: 17
PENNELL, JOSEPH, Nov 60: 97, Jul 63: 18
PENNSYLVANIA, UNIVERSITY OF
Richards Medical Research Building, Sep 62: 57, 59–60; illus, Mar 62: 31, Sep 62: 58, 62, 63
Sumerian expedition, Jul 63: 108
PENNSYLVANIA RAILROAD, Jul 63: 14
Main Line of, Jul 63: 7–8, 26
PENROE, JOHN, Sep 58: 105
PENROSE, BOIES, Jul 63: 26
PENROSE, ROLAND, Nov 61: 10
"PENSÉES," book by Pascal, Jan 63: 102, 103
PENZER, NORMAN M., on India report of Richard Francis Burton, quoted, Jul 63: 111
"PEOPLE'S PALACES, THE," article by Marshall B. Davidson, Jan 61: 102–12
PEPIN THE SHORT, Mar 60: 76
PEPPER FAMILY, of Philadelphia, Jul 63: 9
PEPSI-COLA, merchandising of, May 61: 118
PEPUSCH, JOHN CHRISTOPHER, Nov 58: 56
PEPYS, SAMUEL, Sep 62: 114
PERCIER, CHARLES, Sep 60: 81
PERCY, HENRY. See NORTHUMBERLAND, 9TH EARL OF
PEREIRA, I. RICE, Mar 62: 107
"PERELANDRA," novel by C. S. Lewis, Jan 59: 122, May 59: 64, 125, 127
Passage and illustration from, May 59: 68–69
PERELMAN, S. J., Jan 59: 139, May 63: 46
"PERENNIAL PHILADELPHIANS, THE," book by Nathaniel Burt, article drawn from, Jul 63: 4–27

PERETTI, PAOLO SAVELLI, garden of, May 59: 32, 34–35
PEREZ, JUANNITA, Sep 58: 114
"PERFECT BEAUTY, THE," article by Irving Stone, Sep 58: 92–95, 142
PERFUMES, advertising of, Nov 59: 115–16
PERGAMUM, altar to Zeus in, May 59: 122, 124
PERGOLESI, GIOVANNI BATTISTA, Jul 59: 21
PERI, JACOPO, Jul 60: 42
PERICLES
On Athens, quoted, Jul 60: 102
As presented by Thucydides, Jan 60: 42, 44, 45
"PERILS OF DRINK, THE," article by Raymond Postgate, Sep 58: 104–7, 145
"PERILS OF LEISURE, THE," article by Dennis Gabor, Nov 63: 102–9
"PERIOD OF ADJUSTMENT," play, May 63: 108
Reviewed, Mar 61: 102–3
PERKINS, ANTHONY, Jul 63: 91
PERKINS, HOLMES, Sep 62: 59
PERKINS, MAXWELL, Jul 61: 98
Ernest Hemingway quoted on, Jan 59: 132
PERKINS, WILLIAM, and witch mania, Nov 59: 59–60
"PERLA, LA," painting by Raphael, Jul 61: 94
PERLÈS, ALFRED, *My Friend Henry Miller*, quoted, Nov 61: 104
PERÓN, JUAN, Mar 59: 134
PERRAULT, CLAUDE, Sep 60: 69
PERRET, AUGUSTE, Nov 60: 16
PERRET-CARNOT, M., Sep 58: 63
PERRINS, C. W. DYSON, Nov 62: 66
PERROT, JEAN, Sep 62: 5, 8
"Cave-Dwelling Carvers of 5,000 Years Ago," article by, Jan 62: 72–75
PERRY, ARTHUR, B., May 62: 8
PERRY, MARSDEN J., Nov 60: 98
PERRY, MATTHEW, C., Mar 61: 8
PERSE, ST.-JOHN, Nov 59: 68
"PERSECUTION OF WITCHES, THE," article by H. R. Trevor-Roper, Nov 59: 57–63
PERSEPOLIS, IRAN, Jan 63: 44–49, 52, 59 (map)
Alexander the Great at, Mar 59: 40, 44, 47, 50, 53
PERSIA (see also IRAN; ISFAHAN)
Aesthetic life of the people May 61: 27–32
Architecture, Jan 63: 44, 51, 57
Art, Jan 63: 49, 51–52, 53, 72; miniatures, Jan 63: 57, 62, 67–69
Attacks on Byzantine Empire, Nov 63: 26
Conquest of, by Alexander the Great, Mar 59: 37–54
Dynasties: Achaemenid, Jan 63: 43–49, 58, Nov 63: 15; Safavid, Jan 63: 58, 69, 72; Sasanian, Jan 63: 49–52, 58; Timurid, Jan 63: 57, 58, 67, 68–69
Gardens of, May 59: 26, 27, 44–45
Government of Empire, Jan 63: 43
Literature, Jan 63: 53, 67
Lydia defeated by, Sep 63: 83–84, 88
Napoleon I and, Sep 63: 30
Religion, Jan 63: 43–44, 49, 51, 52–53, 58, 59, 69
Rulers, chart, Jan 63: 52
"PERSIANS," play by Aeschylus, quoted, Sep 63: 85
PERSIGNY, DUC DE, on Baron Haussmann, quoted, May 63: 51
"PERSISTENCE OF IBSENISM, THE," article by Robert Hatch, Jan 62: 106–8
"PERSONAL VALUES, THE," painting by René Magritte, Jan 62: 82; illus, Jan 62: 84
"PERSON TO PERSON," television program, Jul 60: 6
PERSSE, ISABELLA AUGUSTA. See GREGORY, AUGUSTA
PERU, Alexander von Humboldt in, Jul 59: 62
PERUGINO, IL, Jan 62: 31
PETALI, GULF OF, archaeological discovery in, Nov 58: 73
PETER, son of John I of Portugal, Nov 60: 73–74
PETER, APOSTLE, and St. Peter's Church, Rome, Jan 62: 23, 26, 29
PETER I, CZAR OF RUSSIA (PETER THE GREAT), Mar 60: 76, Sep 60: 129
And mermaid legend, Jan 60: 130–31
Portraits of, Sep 59: 58, 63, 67
And the West, Sep 59: 59–85
PETER III, KING OF ARAGON, Sep 61: 34, 37
PETER, HUGH, Mar 60: 102
"PETER AND THE WEST," article by Constantin de Grunwald, Sep 59: 58–85
PETERBOROUGH, N.H., MacDowell Colony, Mar 63: 26–33
PETERDI, GABOR, Jan 62: 12
PETERHOF, summer palace of Peter the Great, May 62: 15, 25
PETERKIN, JULIA, Mar 63: 30
Scarlet Sister Mary, Jul 63: 71
PETER OF EBOLI, *Carmen de Motibus Siculis*, Sep 61: 32
"PETER PLYMLEY'S LETTERS," book by Sydney Smith, Mar 59: 93

PETERS, ROBERTA, Sep 59: 122
Photographs of, Sep 59: 89, 90–91
PETERSON, GLADE, photographs of, Nov 61: 79, 81
PETERSON, VIRGILIA, *A Matter of Life and Death*, Jan 62: 111, 112
"PETER USTINOV," article by Serrell Hillman, Nov 58: 82–85, 137–39
PETRA, JORDAN, Jul 62: 26–29, Sep 62: 7 (map), 8
PETRARCH, May 62: 89
Quoted: on handwriting, Sep 59: 126; on his role in revival of learning, Jan 60: 73; on mountain climbing, Mar 60: 14
PETRI, EGON, Jan 59: 22
"PETRIFACTION," painting by Octave Landuyt, Jan 62: 82; illus, Jan 62: 79
PETRONIUS, GAIUS
Quoted, Nov 58: 109
Trimalchio's Dinner, Nov 62: 86, May 63: 81
"PETROUCHKA," ballet, Sep 60: 94
PETRYN, ANDREW, photograph of, Nov 62: 42
PETWORTH HOUSE, Mar 63: 62–71
"PEYTON PLACE," motion picture, May 59: 100–1
PFAU, BERNHARD, Nov 60: 124
PFEIFFER, JOHN, "Man's First Revolution," article by, Sep 62: 4–9
PFISTERER, HENRY, Sep 62: 58
PFITZNER, HANS, Nov 62: 46, May 63: 43
"PHANTASTES," book by George Macdonald, May 59: 66
"PHANTOM OF THE OPERA, THE," motion picture, Nov 58: 133
"PHASE 2," New York City cabaret, Jan 62: 66, 70, 71
PHELPS, ROBERT
Heroes and Orators, Mar 59: 17, 119
Photograph of, Mar 59: 16
PHIDIAS
And Elgin marbles, Sep 59: 31, 49
Parthenon Athena by, copies of, Nov 58: 76
PHILADELPHIA, PA., Jul 61: 61
Artists and collectors of, Jul 63: 18–23
Athenaeum, Jul 63: 12–13; literary award by, Jul 63: 68
Character of, Jul 63: 5–14
Insurance companies, Jul 63: 24–25
Old families, Jul 63: 16–17
Redevelopment of, Jul 63: 9, 26–27; plan of Louis Kahn for, Sep 62: 62
Richards Medical Research Building, Sep 62: 57, 59–60; illus, Mar 62: 31, Sep 62: 58, 62, 63
PHILADELPHIA CLUB, Jul 63: 5
"PHILADELPHIAN, THE," novel by Richard Powell, quoted, Jul 63: 17
PHILADELPHIA ORCHESTRA, THE, Jul 59: 19
"PHILADELPHIA PLAIN & FANCY," article by Nathaniel Burt, Jul 63: 4–27
PHILADELPHIA "PUBLIC LEDGER," on Spectric poets, quoted, May 63: 43
PHILADELPHIA SAVING FUND SOCIETY TOWER, Sep 62: 58
"PHILADELPHIA STORY, THE," play and motion picture, Jul 63: 5
PHILAE, EGYPT
Flooding of temples at, Jul 60: 8, 10
Temple of Isis, Jul 60: 10
PHILCO CORPORATION, vs. National Broadcasting Company, Sep 61: 113
PHILIDOR, FRANÇOIS ANDRÉ DANICAN, Jan 62: 117
PHILIP, DUKE OF EDINBURGH, Nov 60: 128
In painting by Feliks Topolski, Nov 60: 129, 135
PHILIP II, KING OF FRANCE (PHILIP AUGUSTUS), Jan 59: 87, 88, 90, Sep 60: 59–60
PHILIP IV, KING OF FRANCE, Sep 60: 60, Mar 61: 62
PHILIP II, KING OF MACEDON, Mar 59: 30, 32–33, May 62: 45
Coin portrait of, Mar 59: 31
PHILIP V, KING OF MACEDON, May 62: 45
PHILIP II, KING OF SPAIN, Sep 58: 18–19, Nov 61: 7, 110, 112, 113, Nov 62: 38, May 63: 95, Jul 63: 50, 52
In painting by Georg Wilhelm Graesner, Jul 63: 51
Portrait of, Nov 61: 108
PHILIP III, KING OF SPAIN, Sep 59: 121, Nov 61: 110, Nov 62: 38
Portrait of, Sep 59: 28
PHILIP IV, KING OF SPAIN, Sep 59: 120, Jul 61: 89, 94, Jul 63: 94
PHILIP V, KING OF SPAIN, May 63: 95
PHILIPE, GÉRARD, May 60: 53 (note)
PHILIP OF FLANDERS, Nov 58: 105
PHILIPPE, DUC D'ORLÉANS, Jul 63: 80
PHILIPPINE ISLANDS, Zamboanga, Mar 61: 23
PHILIPS, CHARLES, Jul 63: 96
PHILIP THE ARAB, ROMAN EMPEROR, Sep 63: 40
Coin portrait of, Sep 63: 37
PHILIP THE BOLD, Sep 58: 62
PHILIP THE GOOD, Sep 58: 63, Mar 62: 89

PHILISTINES, Nov 59: 119

PHILLIPS, J. B., Sep 63: 7

PHILLIPS, WENDELL, contemporary archaeologist, Nov 59: 119

PHILLIPS, WILLIAM, Jan 60: 7

PHILODEMUS, Mar 62: 44–45

PHILO-SEMITISM, of 17th century, Mar 60: 100–3, 124–25

PHILOSOPHY
African, Mar 63: 44, 106
Of Baroque age, Jul 60: 36, 38
Of class of 1944, May 63: 88–89
Cult of unthink, Sep 58: 38–45, 134–35
Diogenes and his encounter with Alexander, Mar 63: 10–13
In Japan, Mar 61: 11
In Moslem Spain, Sep 62: 88–89
Primer of, drawings by Lou Myers, Jul 61: 110–11
Romantic revolt in, May 61: 66
Science and, Jul 61: 4–9
Space and the spirit of man, Jan 59: 26–31, 122–23
Togetherness, revolt against, Nov 58: 30–33, 146–47
After World Wars I and II, Mar 63: 9
Zen Buddhism, Jul 59: 70–77, 126–27

PHILOTAS, Mar 59: 47

PHOCAS, BYZANTINE EMPEROR, Nov 63: 11

"PHOCION'S ASHES," painting by Poussin, Mar 61: 80

PHOENICIANS, May 60: 73
In Sicily, Sep 61: 23, 24
Use of ivory, May 60: 91–92, 120

PHOENIX, ARIZ., May 61: 19

PHOENIX-RHEINROHR BUILDING, Düsseldorf, Nov 60: 124, 125; illus, Nov 60: 14

PHOENIX THEATRE, New York City, Mar 60: 98

PHONEME, Jul 63: 44, 45

PHONOGRAPH RECORDS. See RECORDINGS

PHOTOGRAPHY
Of buried tombs, in archaeology, May 60: 59–60
Debut of picture interview, Mar 59: 68–69
Effect on portrait painting, Jan 59: 96, 103
Influence of Moholy-Nagy, Nov 61: 69

PHYSICS
IQ and, Mar 62: 72–73
Pascal's contribution, Jan 63: 99–100
Present status of, Nov 63: 108
Radiations and evolution of the sun, Nov 63: 48–55

PIA, EMILIA, Jan 60: 68

PIAZZA NAVONA, Rome, May 62: 12, 14

"PIAZZETTA, VENICE, THE," painting by Canaletto, Jul 63: 105; illus, Jul 63: 104

PICASSO, PABLO, Jan 59: 13, 103, 132, May 59: 121, Sep 59: 18, 96, Mar 60: 58, May 60: 113, Sep 60: 121, May 62: 59, 78, Nov 62: 57
Bonnard, Pierre, and, Mar 62: 25
And his public, Nov 61: 4–13
Moore, Henry, quoted on, Nov 60: 114
Photographs of, Nov 61: 13
Roque, Jacqueline, and, Jan 60: 97–105
Society's attitude toward, Jan 63: 74
Works by. See ILLUSTRATIONS INDEX
Wyeth, Andrew, quoted on, Sep 61: 100

"PICASSO AND HIS PUBLIC," article by Alfred Frankfurter, Nov 61: 4–13

"PICASSO'S LADY," article and photographs by David Douglas Duncan, Jan 60: 97–105

PICCAVER, ALFRED, Sep 59: 57

PICCOLOMINI, AENEAS SILVIUS, May 62: 89, 90

PICKFORD, MARY, Sep 60: 116

"PICNIC," motion picture, May 59: 100

PICO DELLA MIRANDOLA, Jan 60: 66

"PICTURE HISTORY OF PHOTOGRAPHY, THE," book by Peter Pollack, picture interview from, Mar 59: 68–69

"PICTURES FROM AN INSTITUTION," novel by Randall Jarrell, Sep 60: 118–19

PIDGEON, WALTER, May 62: 118

PIEL'S BEER, television advertising of, Jan 63: 114

PIEN WEN-CHIN, Jan 61: 25
Painting by, Jan 61: 24

"PIETÀ," illumination by Jean Fouquet, Nov 61: 97; illus, Nov 61: 96

"PIETÀ," sculpture by Michelangelo in St. Peter's, Rome, Jan 62: 48

"PIETÀ" (RONDANINI), sculpture by Michelangelo in Milan, Henry Moore quoted on, Nov 60: 114

PIGGOTT, REGINALD, Sep 59: 128

PIGNATELLI, ALPHONSE, Nov 58: 143

PIKE, JAMES A., Sep 63: 9, 105
Photograph of, Sep 63: 8

"PIKE COUNTY BALLADS," by John Hay, Jan 59: 25

PILA-GHALE, archaeological site in Iran, Nov 62: 101

PILÂTRE DE ROZIER, FRANÇOIS, Sep 58: 114, 117, 119
Portrait of, Sep 58: 125

PILGRIMS, at Provincetown, Mass., Jul 61: 13

"PILGRIM'S WAY," autobiography of John Buchan, Sep 61: 5

"PILGRIM TO THE HOLY MOUNT," article by H. F. M. Prescott, Mar 60: 81–93

"PILLARS OF SOCIETY, THE," play, Jan 62: 108

PILLSBURY, HARRY NELSON, Jan 62: 116, 119

PILSUDSKI, JOZEF, Jan 59: 115

PINDAR, Sep 61: 24, Nov 63: 43, 44
In Renaissance curriculum, Jan 60: 62
Sculpture of, Nov 63: 43
Survival of works by, Nov 62: 89, 93
On Syracuse, quoted, Sep 61: 26

PINERO, ARTHUR WING
Shaw, G. B., quoted on, Nov 58: 134–35
Trelawny of the "Wells," quoted, Mar 62: 117

PINKERT, REGINA, Sep 59: 53

PINKIE, BATTLE OF, Sep 59: 130

PINTER, HAROLD, Sep 62: 34, 37, 40, Jan 63: 26, 32, Mar 63: 109
Caretaker, The, Mar 62: 112, Sep 62: 34, 35, 36, 41, Jan 63: 31, 32
Collection, The, May 63: 107
Dumbwaiter, The, May 63: 107
Photograph of, Jan 63: 30

PINTORI, GIOVANNI, Nov 59: 48, 49
Designs by. See ILLUSTRATIONS INDEX

PINTURICCHIO (BERNARDINO BETTI), Jan 62: 32
Paintings by, Mar 61: 71, Jan 62: 32, 38

PIPER, DAVID, on Hans Holbein the Younger, quoted, Jul 63: 3

PIRACY, and slave trade, in ancient world, May 62: 46

PIRAEUS, GREECE
Bronze statues found in, Mar 60: 6–11
Marble reliefs found underwater in harbor, Nov 58: 76

PIRANDELLO, LUIGI, Sep 61: 44

PIRANESI, FRANCESCO, etching by, Mar 62: 63

PIRANESI, GIAMBATTISTA, Mar 62: 55, May 63: 35
Engravings by. See ILLUSTRATIONS INDEX

PIRELLI BUILDING, Milan, Nov 60: 125; illus, Nov 60: 15

PIRKHEIMER, BILIBALD, Sep 59: 131

PISANELLO, IL, medal by, Jan 60: 59

PISSARRO, CAMILLE, May 60: 103, 113, Jul 62: 64, 69
On Bonnard, Pierre, quoted, Mar 62: 16
Painting by, Jul 62: 68–69

PISTON, WALTER, Jul 59: 20
Quoted: on arts and the Kennedy administration, Sep 61: 5; on Moussorgsky and Leonard Bernstein, Jul 59: 23

PITCAIRN ISLAND, Sep 63: 46–48

PITOËFF, GEORGES, Nov 60: 52, Sep 61: 102
Photograph of, Sep 61: 109

PITOËFF, LUDMILLA, Sep 61: 102
Photograph of, Sep 61: 109

PITT, JOHN (2D EARL OF CHATHAM), Joseph Haydn quoted on, Mar 62: 82

PITT, WILLIAM THE ELDER (1ST EARL OF CHATHAM), May 60: 36, 100
Portrait of, Nov 60: 21

PITT, WILLIAM THE YOUNGER, Sep 58: 136
Childhood of, May 60: 33, 34, 36–37
And French Revolution, May 60: 124, 125
Portrait of, May 60: 32

PITTSBURGH AIRPORT, mobile in, by Alexander Calder, Nov 62: 16

PITTSBURGH POETS. See "SPECTRAL POETS OF PITTSBURGH, THE"

PIUS II, POPE, Jan 62: 27
On Hadrian's Villa, quoted, May 63: 35

PIUS IV, POPE, Jan 62: 48

PIUS V, POPE, Jul 63: 50, 52
In painting by George Wilhelm Graesner, Jul 63: 51
Portrait of, Jul 63: 59

PIUS VI, POPE, Jan 62: 45

PIUS IX, POPE, Jan 62: 48, Sep 63: 100

PIUS XI, POPE, Sep 58: 139, Jan 62: 45

PIUS XII, POPE, Jan 62: 29, Sep 63: 9 (note)
On space exploration, quoted, Jan 59: 123

PIZA, A. L. TOLEDO, mosaic by, Nov 63: 54

PLACE NAMES, Humboldt in the Americas, Jul 59: 67

PLACE PIGALLE, Paris, Mar 59: 84

"PLAGIARISM, THE," painting by René Magritte, Jan 62: 82; illus, Jan 62: 85

PLAGUE. See BLACK DEATH

"PLAGUE, THE," novel by Albert Camus, Nov 59: 70–71

PLAINS FRONTIER, childhood of Wallace Stegner on, Sep 62: 94–95

"PLANETARIUM, THE," novel by Nathalie Sarraute, Jan 62: 97, 98

PLATO, Mar 63: 12, 27, Sep 63: 97
Apology, Jul 60: 102, 103, 104
Gorgias, quoted, Jan 63: 9
Meno, Jul 60: 104
And modern science, Jul 61: 5–6, 9

Quoted: on barbarians, Mar 59: 47; on mind and body, Jan 60: 60; on music, Jan 60: 62; on restoration of democracy, Jul 60: 103
Republic, The, Mar 63: 74, 79
In Sicily, Sep 61: 24
Survival of works by, Nov 62: 76
Symposium, and violin serenade by Leonard Bernstein, Jul 59: 22

PLATT, CHARLES ADAMS, Sep 60: 102

PLATT, JOHN RADER
Articles by: "Coming Generation of Genius, The," Mar 62: 70–75; "Fifth Need of Man, The," Jul 59: 106–11; "Where Will the Books Go?" Sep 62: 42–47, comment on, Nov 62: 105
On need of science for poets, quoted, Jul 60: 71

"PLATYPUS," poem by Patrick Barrington, quoted, Sep 58: 130–31

PLAUTUS, TITUS MACCIUS, Nov 62: 80
In Renaissance curriculum, Jan 60: 62

"PLAYBOY," magazine, advertising in, Nov 59: 117

"PLAYBOY OF THE WESTERN WORLD, THE," play, Mar 59: 87

PLAYFAIR, GILES, on Edmund Kean, quoted, Mar 62: 13

PLAYHOUSE DANCE COMPANY, New York City, Nov 58: 90–91

"PLAYHOUSE 90," television show, Mar 63: 35

"PLAY OF DANIEL, THE," Nov 60: 89, 92–95

PLAYWRIGHTS COMPANY, of Chicago, Jan 62: 66, 68, Jul 62: 49

PLEASENCE, DONALD, May 62: 112
Photograph of, May 62: 111

"PLEASURES OF THE BASTILLE, THE," article by J. Christopher Herold, Jan 60: 82–88, 128

"PLEDGE, THE," novel by Friedrich Duerrenmatt, Mar 61: 47

PLESSIS-BELLIÈRE, MME DU, Jul 63: 83

PLIMPTON, GEORGE, Sep 59: 95 (note)
"Ernest Hemingway on the Art of Writing," interview by, Jan 59: 82–85, 132–35
——— and DONALD STEWART, "Andrew Wyeth," interview by, Sep 61: 88–101

PLINY THE ELDER, May 59: 27, Nov 62: 104
Quoted: on Ganymedes of Leochares, May 59: 122; on Laocoön sculpture, May 59: 104; 124; on mermaids, Jan 60: 134

PLINY THE YOUNGER, Sep 58: 140, Sep 62: 114
On eruption of Vesuvius, quoted, Mar 62: 45

PLISETSKAYA, MAYA, Nov 59: 56

PLOTINA, Sep 63: 39

PLOTINUS, May 63: 114

PLUMB, J. H.
Articles by: "Grand Tour, The," Nov 59: 73–104; "Noble Houses of Eighteenth-Century England, The," Nov 58: 38–61; "Oriental Palace for an English King, An," Nov 62: 20–31; "Sorry State of History, The," Sep 63: 97–100, comment on, by Allan Nevins, Sep 63: 101
On *Pêche Melba,* quoted, May 61: 124

PLUM ISLAND, MASS., Samuel Sewall quoted on, Mar 60: 15

PLUMMER, CHRISTOPHER, Jul 59: 42, Jan 60: 49, 53, Jul 60: 93
Drawing of, Jan 60: 51

PLUTARCH
On Alexander the Great, quoted, Mar 59: 38–39, 40, 50, Jan 61: 91, Nov 63: 15, 20
Opinion of Tiberius, May 59: 107
Parallel Lives, Mar 59: 34
In Renaissance curriculum, Jan 60: 62

"PNIN," novel by Vladimir Nabokov, Sep 60: 119, Jul 62: 90

PODHORETZ, NORMAN, on Beat Generation, quoted, Sep 61: 116

POE, EDGAR ALLAN, *The Face of Edgar Allan Poe,* woodcut book by Antonio Frasconi, Mar 61: 123

"POÈME ELECTRONIQUE," tape recorder composition by Edgard Varèse, Jan 59: 53

"POEM IN CYCLES AND BELLS, A," tape recorder composition by Otto Luening and Vladimir Ussachevsky, Jan 59: 54

"POET IN A VALLEY OF DRY BONES, THE," article by Robert Graves, Mar 63: 84–88

POETRY
Aiken, Conrad, limericks by, Nov 63: 100–1
Auto-Beatnik, May 62: 96–99
Baroque, Jul 60: 42, 50
Battle of the bards, Sep 61: 116–21
Cult of unthink in, Sep 58: 38–42
Dickinson, Emily, inspiration of her love poems, Jul 61: 100–5
Dutch, of 17th century, Sep 58: 24
"Free-write," Jul 63: 39
Frost, Robert, Nov 58: 34–35
Graves, Robert, Jan 62: 50–55
Greek and Latin that disappeared or survived, Nov 62: 76, 78, 80, 89

MacLeish, Archibald, on being a poet in the theatre, interview, Jan 60: 48–56
In Moslem Spain, Sep 62: 87–88
Oral, as exemplified in Homer, Jan 61: 76–77, 86, 93
Persian, May 61: 30, 32, Jan 63: 67
"Poet in a Valley of Dry Bones, The," article by Robert Graves, Mar 63: 84–88
"Poetry's False Face," article by Robert Graves, Nov 63: 42–47
Pound, Ezra, Jan 61: 116–18
"Pretense on Parnassus," article by Robert Graves, May 63: 81–85
Prize awarding and winning, Jul 63: 69–70, 72–73
Of San Francisco Bay Region, Jan 59: 16, 18–19
Spectra hoax, May 60: 42–48
Sumerian love songs, Jul 63: 108–9
Williams, William Carlos, homage to, by Paul Engle, Mar 59: 60–61
Women as poets, Mar 62: 71
Yeats, William Butler, Nov 60: 66–69
Zen Buddhism and, Jul 59: 126–27
Zen telegrams of Paul Reps, Jan 60: 46–47
"POETRY," magazine, Sep 61: 117
And Spectric poets, May 60: 43, 47–48
"POETRY'S FALSE FACE," article by Robert Graves, Nov 63: 42–47
POETRY SOCIETY OF AMERICA, Jul 63: 70
POHL, FREDERIK, "The Midas Touch," Jul 60: 66, Mar 63: 79
———— and C. M. KORNBLUTH, *The Space Merchants*, Mar 63: 79
POINCARÉ, JULES HENRI, May 63: 115
POIRET, PAUL, on fashion, quoted, Mar 59: 63, 116, 117
POITIERS, BATTLE OF, Sep 62: 74–75
"POKER AND AMERICAN CHARACTER," article by John Lukacs, Nov 63: 56–62
POLAND
Art in, May 61: 20–23
Peter the Great and, Sep 59: 74, 79, 80
Pogroms of mid-17th century, Mar 60: 103
Royal regalia of, May 63: 96
POLAR EXPLORATION. See ANTARCTIC EXPEDITIONS; ARCTIC EXPEDITIONS
"POLICE GAZETTE," drawings by Alexander Calder in, Nov 62: 15
POLIGNAC, MARIE-BLANCHE, COMTESSE DE, Nov 61: 37
POLITICS
Corruption of language by, Jul 63: 36–37
Demons of, liberal and reactionary, Jul 61: 66–69
Future American class system, May 59: 20–23
Romantic revolt in, May 61: 66, 85
POLIZIANO, ANGELO, Sep 58: 94, Jan 60: 62, 66
POLK, WILLIS, Jan 59: 10, 11
POLLACK, PETER, *The Picture History of Photography*, picture interview from, Mar 59: 68–69
POLLAIUOLO, ANTONIO, Sep 58: 142
POLLARD, GRAHAM, Mar 59: 107–8
POLLINI, GINO, Nov 59: 50
POLLOCK, JACKSON, Sep 58: 44, 110, 134, Jan 59: 13, May 59: 5, 11, Nov 59: 41, 120, 121, Sep 60: 31, 121–22, May 61: 21, Jul 62: 13, 19, 24, Jan 63: 16, Sep 63: 96
Long Island home of, May 63: 9, 22
Paintings by. See ILLUSTRATIONS INDEX
Rivers, Larry, quoted on, Sep 59: 100
Wyeth, Andrew, quoted on, Jul 61: 97, 100
POLL TAX, in England, Mar 61: 65
"POLLYANNA," motion picture, reviewed, Sep 60: 116–17
POLO, in Persia, Jan 63: 51, 58; illus, Jan 63: 63
POLO, MARCO, Sep 58: 8, May 59: 31
POLTAVA, BATTLE OF, Sep 59: 79
POLYBIUS, on army of Philip V, quoted, May 62: 45
POLYDOROS, May 59: 104, 124
POLYGAMY, studied by Richard Francis Burton, Jul 63: 114–16
POLZELLI, LUIGIA, Mar 62: 82
POMEGRANATE, significance in ancient cultures, Nov 62: 104
POMPADOUR, MARQUISE DE, Sep 60: 72, Mar 61: 118, 119, Mar 62: 68
Portrait of, Sep 60: 74
"POMPEII," article by Neil McKendrick, Mar 62: 42–69
POMPEII, ITALY, Nov 59: 87, 96, Mar 62: 42–69
Baths of, May 60: 39, 40–41
PONCE DE LEON HOTEL, Saint Augustine, Fla., Jan 61: 104, 106–7
PONS, LILY, Jul 60: 75
PONTE, LORENZO DA. See DA PONTE
PONTE AMMIRAGLIO, BATTLE OF, Sep 61: 37
PONTI, GIO, Mar 59: 123, Nov 60: 125
"POOL, THE," painting by Larry Rivers, Sep 59: 100
"POOR BITOS," play, Nov 60: 127

"POORHOUSE FAIR, THE," novel by John Updike, Mar 62: 84
"POOR WINNIE IN POOH-LATIN," article by Gilbert Highet, Jul 61: 112–15
"POP ART," Jan 63: 23, 25, Sep 63: 92, 96
POPE, ALEXANDER, May 61: 60, 61
Childhood of, May 60: 34, 36
Dunciad, quoted, Nov 59: 90
Epigram on Inigo Jones gate, Nov 58: 59
Letter from Lady Mary Wortley Montagu to, quoted, Jan 61: 91
Portrait of, May 60: 32
Quoted: on moon, Mar 60: 14; on Shylock of Charles Macklin, Jan 60: 92
POPE, ARTHUR UPHAM, on Persian art, quoted, Jan 63: 72
POPE, THOMAS, Jan 60: 92, 96
POPULATION CONTROL, Sep 58: 53
POPULATION INCREASE
Earth use and, Sep 58: 48–55
Technological advance and, Jan 59: 93, 128, 129
PORDEN, WILLIAM, Nov 62: 24
"PORGY AND BESS," motion picture, Nov 60: 86
"PORGY AND BESS," opera, Sep 58: 57, Mar 61: 72
PORNOGRAPHY, May 61: 54
PORPHYRY, Nov 62: 88
On Plotinus, quoted, May 63: 114
Portrait of, Sep 62: 79
PORTA, GIACOMO DELLA, church designed by (with Giacomo da Vignola), Jul 60: 52
PORTER, COLE, Sep 58: 61, Jan 59: 139
"Just One of Those Things," Jan 61: 119
PORTER, ELEANOR H., *Pollyanna*, motion picture based on, Sep 60: 116–17
PORTER, ENDYMION, Jul 61: 91
Portrait of, Jul 61: 88
PORTER, KATHERINE ANNE, Jan 62: 8
PORTINARI, CANDIDO, Sep 59: 20
PORTINARI, TOMMASSO, and his wife, in painting by Hans Memling, Sep 63: 16–17
PORTLAND, DUCHESS OF, Nov 63: 64
Portrait of, Nov 63: 63
PORTLAND, DUKE OF, Jan 59: 59
PORTLAND, 3D DUKE OF (WILLIAM HENRY CAVENDISH BENTINCK), Nov 63: 64
PORTLAND, FAIRFIELD, Jan 59: 105
PORTLAND VASE, Nov 59: 95, Nov 63: 63–65
"PORTRAIT OF A CAVALIER," painting by Franz Hals, Nov 62: 65
"PORTRAIT OF A LADY," play, Mar 60: 120
"PORTRAIT OF A MAN UNKNOWN," novel by Nathalie Sarraute, Jan 62: 97, 98
"PORTRAIT OF BILLIE," television show, May 63: 49
"PORTRAIT OF HIS FATHER," painting by Dürer, Jul 61: 94, Jul 63: 93
"PORTRAIT OF THE ARTIST AS A YOUNG MAN," book by James Joyce, quoted, Sep 60: 121
PORTRAITS, INCORPORATED, Jan 59: 96, 104
"PORTRAITS IN OUR TIME," article by Eleanor C. Munro, Jan 59: 95–105
PORTRAITURE, Jan 59: 95–105
In Baroque age, Jul 60: 50
In British royal collection, Jul 63: 92–93, 96, 105, 106, 107
Etruscan, May 60: 77
Koch, John, Sep 60: 111
On Roman coins, Sep 63: 33–41
PORT ROYAL CONVENT, Jan 63: 100, 102
PORTUGAL
In Africa, May 60: 90
Henry the Navigator, Nov 60: 72–83
Lisbon earthquake of 1755, Mar 61: 115–16
Millenary doctrine of 17th century in, Mar 60: 102–3, 125
Organ (musical instrument) in, Mar 60: 74
And Thirty Years' War, Nov 62: 41
PORTUGUESE IN AMERICA, in Provincetown, Mass., Jul 61: 13
PORUS, INDIAN RAJAH, Mar 59: 45, 46, 55
POSITIVISM, LOGICAL, Mar 63: 9, May 63: 89
POST, EMILY, quoted
On gentlemen's club, Jul 60: 122
On self-advertising, Jul 60: 121
POSTERS (see also in ILLUSTRATIONS INDEX)
Influence of Japanese prints on, May 60: 104
Of World War I aftermath, Jan 59: 112–21
POSTGATE, RAYMOND, "The Perils of Drink," article by, Sep 58: 104–7, 145
POST OFFICE, orbital, Jan 62: 19
POTEMKIN, GRIGORI, Sep 60: 130, 135 (illus)
POTSDAM OBSERVATORY, Sep 59: 19
POTTER, DAVID, Jul 60: 66
POTTER, MARY KNIGHT, on Raphael and Michelangelo, quoted, Jan 62: 41
POTTER, PAUL, Sep 58: 26
POTTER, SIMEON, on phoneme, quoted, Jul 63: 45

POTTER, STEPHEN, Nov 59: 23, 24
"POTTING SHED, THE," play, Nov 58: 62
POULENC, FRANCIS, Jan 60: 13, Mar 61: 75, Nov 62: 46
Dialogues of the Carmelites, Mar 61: 72
POUND, EZRA, May 60: 48, Jul 60: 96, Sep 61: 117, 121, Jul 63: 73, Nov 63: 44
Critical estimate of, by Gilbert Highet, Jan 61: 116–18
Hemingway, Ernest, quoted on, Jan 59: 132, 135
POUND, ROSCOE, on foundations, quoted, Jan 62: 13–14
POUSETTE-DART, RICHARD, May 59: 11
"POUSSIN," article by Pierre Schneider, Mar 61: 76–93
POUSSIN, GASPARD, Jul 63: 96
POUSSIN, NICOLAS, Nov 59: 95, Jul 60: 50, Mar 61: 76–80, 89–93, Mar 62: 55, Jul 62: 66, Jul 63: 79, 80
Paintings by. See ILLUSTRATIONS INDEX
On pleasures of intelligence, quoted, May 59: 29
Self-portrait, Mar 61: 78–79; illus, Mar 61: 78
POWER, in government, theories of, Mar 59: 10
POWER, E. J., Nov 59: 41, 120
POWER, TYRONE, Jul 60: 120
"POWER AND THE GLORY, THE," motion picture, May 61: 117
"POWER ELITE, THE," book by C. Wright Mills, Nov 59: 23, 25
POYNTER, EDWARD J., May 62: 78
POZZO, ANDREA, fresco by, Jul 60: 48–49
POZZO, CASSIANO DAL, Mar 61: 79, 80
POZZUOLI, ITALY, Olivetti factory, Nov 59: 50
"PRACTICAL COGITATOR, THE," book compiled by Charles P. Curtis and Ferris Greenslet, Sep 61: 115
PRADO MUSEUM, in Madrid, paintings from collection of Charles I of England owned by, Jul 61: 94–95
PRAETORIUS, EMIL, May 63: 43
PRAETORIUS, MICHAEL, organ described by, Mar 60: 75
PRAGMATISM, May 63: 88, 89
"PRAGUERIE," Mar 62: 90
PRAIRIE. See PLAINS FRONTIER
"PRAIRIE, THE," composition by Lukas Foss, Jan 63: 78
"PRAISE OF FOLLY, THE," book by Erasmus, May 62: 90, 92, 93, 95
PRANDTAUER, JAKOB, monastery designed by, Jul 60: 55
PRATT, BELINDA MARDEN, on polygamy, quoted, Jul 63: 115
PRAXITELES
Malraux, André, quoted on, Nov 58: 15
Sculpture by, Jan 62: 46
PREAH KHAN, CAMBODIA, Jan 59: 64
PREMINGER, OTTO, May 62: 81
Advise and Consent, motion picture produced by, May 62: 116–18
Portraits of, May 62: 116, 117
"PREMISE, THE," New York City cabaret, Jan 62: 69, 70
PRESCOTT, H. F. M., "Pilgrim to the Holy Mount," article by, Mar 60: 81–93
PRESCOTT, WILLIAM H., debt to Alexander von Humboldt, Jul 59: 128
PRESIDENT-ELECT, memorandum to, from H. L. Mencken, Nov 60: 70–71
PRESIDENT OF THE UNITED STATES, memorandum to, from Secretary of Arts and Leisure, Nov 62: 18–19
PRESLEY, ELVIS, Jan 59: 137–38, 139
Photograph of, Sep 58: 43
PRESS, FREEDOM OF. See FREEDOM OF SPEECH
PRESTER JOHN, search by Henry the Navigator for, Nov 60: 77
PRESTON, RICHARD, Nov 62: 97
PRESTON, STUART, Mar 61: 104
PRESTOPINO, ELIZABETH DAUBER and GREGORIO, photograph of, Mar 63: 28
"PRETENSE ON PARNASSUS," article by Robert Graves, May 63: 81–85
PREUILLY, GEOFFROY DE, Nov 58: 94
"PREVALENCE OF DEMONS, A," excerpts from *A Modern Demonology*, by Frank Getlein, Jul 61: 66–69
PRÉVERT, JACQUES, May 61: 95
PRICE, LEONTYNE, Mar 61: 72, Jul 61: 97
Portrait of, Mar 61: 73
PRICE, PETON, May 62: 81
"PRIDE OF CHESSMEN, A," photographs by Lee Boltin, Jan 62: 121–28
PRIESTLEY, JOSEPH, Jan 63: 97
As member of Josiah Wedgwood's group, May 59: 88–96, 128–30
Portrait medallion of, May 59: 90
Rudiments of English Grammar, The, Jul 63: 34–35
PRIETO, ANTONIO, Jan 59: 14
Ceramics by, Jan 59: 5
"PRIMER OF EZRA POUND, A," book by M. L. Rosenthal, Jan 61: 116
PRIMROSE, WILLIAM, Sep 58: 134
PRINCE, HAL, Jul 61: 98

PRINCE, WALTER FRANKLIN, Jan 59: 109
"PRINCE IGOR," ballet, Sep 60: 94
"PRINCE OF PATRONS, THE," article by C. V. Wedgwood, Jul 61: 78–95
"PRINCESSE DE CLÈVES, LA," novel by Mme de La Fayette, Nov 61: 34
PRINCETON THEOLOGICAL SEMINARY, Sep 59: 25
PRINCETON UNIVERSITY
   Architecture of, May 59: 87
   Expanding universe at, Sep 59: 22–27, 118–19
   "No-English" bulletin board, Jul 63: 36
PRINTING, Bauhaus influence on, Nov 61: 69
PRINT MAKING, woodcuts of Antonio Frasconi, Mar 61: 122–28
"PRISONNIÈRE, LA," painting by Paul Delvaux, Jan 62: 81–82; illus, Jan 62: 81
PRITCHARD, JAMES B., discovery of Pool of Gibeon, Nov 59: 6, 8–9
"PRIVACY LOST," article by William K. Zinsser, Jul 60: 4–7, 120–22
PRIZES, LITERARY, Jul 63: 68–75
PROBABILITY THEORIES, Nov 63: 61
"PROBLEM OF PAIN, THE," book by C. S. Lewis, May 59: 66
PROCOPIUS, quoted
   On Hagia Sophia, Nov 63: 15
   On Justinian and Theodora, Nov 63: 10
PROCTER & GAMBLE, Nov 60: 123, Jul 62: 95, May 63: 112
"PRODIGAL, THE," play, Mar 61: 46–47
"PROFILES IN COURAGE," book by John F. Kennedy, Sep 61: 5
PROGRESS
   Idea of, and study of history, Sep 63: 99–100
   Theories of, Mar 59: 6, 7, 8, 12, 128
PROJECT FOCUS, Sep 59: 27
PROJECT MATTERHORN, Sep 59: 26, 27, 119
"PROJECT 20," television production, Mar 60: 126
PROKOFIEV, SERGEI, May 63: 109
   Larry Rivers quoted on, Sep 59: 98
PRO MUSICA OF NEW YORK, Nov 60: 88–95
PROPAGANDA
   European political posters after World War I, Jan 59: 112–21
   Of Ramses II, Jul 60: 124–25
PROPERTIUS, SEXTUS, *Homage to,* by Ezra Pound, Jan 61: 116, 118
"PROPOSAL OF MARRIAGE, A," article by Oliver Jensen, Jan 60: 106–7
PROTAGORAS, Jul 60: 117
PROTAT, ADÈLE, Jul 62: 64
"PROTESTANT ETHIC," Jul 60: 68, 69, 70
PROTESTANTISM
   Defeats of 1620's, Mar 60: 101–2
   Knox, John, vs. Mary, Queen of Scots, Jul 63: 28–32
   And Thirty Years' War, Nov 62: 32–41
"PROTOCOLS OF THE ELDERS OF ZION," Jan 61: 72
PROUDHON, PIERRE-JOSEPH, May 63: 54
PROUST, MARCEL, Nov 60: 134, Jan 62: 97
   Guermantes Way, quoted, Jan 63: 74
   Influence on Lawrence Durrell, Mar 60: 114, 118
   Ionesco, Eugène, quoted on, May 61: 97
   Kazin, Alfred, quoted on, Jul 62: 10
   Remembrance of Things Past, quoted on Monet and Poussin, Mar 61: 78
   Sketch of, Sep 58: 84
   Stravinsky, Igor, quoted on, Sep 58: 84
PROVENCE, FRANCE, early history of, Jul 59: 90–98, 129–32
PROVIDENCE, R.I., May 61: 4
PROVINCETOWN, MASS., Jul 61: 10–29
   Rivers, Larry, in, Sep 59: 96
   When We Dead Awaken produced at, Jan 62: 106
PROVINCETOWN "ADVOCATE," Jul 61: 14
PROVINCETOWN ART ASSOCIATION, Jul 61: 14–15, 24–25
PROVINCETOWN PLAYERS, Jul 61: 13
PROVINCETOWN SYMPHONY, Jul 61: 16
"PROVINCIAL LETTERS," book by Pascal, Jan 63: 102
PRUDENTIAL INSURANCE COMPANY, May 63: 113
PRUSSIA
   As member of Holy Alliance, Mar 63: 5
   In Napoleonic Wars, Sep 63: 29, 30, 31, 32
   Peter the Great and, Sep 59: 66, 74, 80
PRUTZ, ROBERT, Mar 62: 99
PRYCE-JONES, ALAN, Jan 62: 7–8, 13
   "But cheerfulness keeps breaking in . . . ," comment by, Nov 61: 16–17
PRYDE, JAMES, Jan 62: 52
PRYNNE, WILLIAM, Jul 61: 92
PSALMANAZAR, GEORGE, Jan 60: 113–18
PSAMMON, Mar 59: 50
PSAMTIK II, KING OF EGYPT, Jul 60: 124
PSYCHIC PHENOMENA, "Margery," Jan 59: 108–11

"PSYCHO," motion picture, Jan 63: 112
PSYCHOANALYSIS
   Dinesen, Isak, quoted on, Sep 59: 112
   Dramatizations of, Sep 58: 60
   Freud, Sigmund, quoted on, May 63: 115
PSYCHOLOGY
   Childhood pattern of genius, May 60: 32–38
   Creative process in genius, May 63: 114–15
   Freudian, in Hollywood motion pictures, Jan 63: 111–13
   Group dynamics and Togetherness cult, Nov 58: 32–33, 146
   Lysergic acid diethylamide and other mood- and consciousness-changing drugs, May 63: 28–31, 114–15
   Novelty as fifth need of man, Jul 59: 106–11
"PSYCHOLOGY OF THE PERSONALITY," book by Eino Kaila, Sep 60: 9
PTAH, Egyptian god, Jul 61: 38
PTOLEMY I, KING OF EGYPT, library founded by, Nov 62: 78
PTOLEMY XII, KING OF EGYPT, Nov 62: 78
PTOLEMY, CLAUDIUS, Nov 60: 77
PUBLIC RELATIONS INDUSTRY, Mar 60: 48, Jul 60: 121–22
"PUBLIC SCHOOL VERSE," anthology, Jan 60: 108
PUBLISHING, forgeries in, Mar 59: 105, 107–9
PUCCINI, GIACOMO, Nov 58: 120, Jan 60: 12
PUGET, PIERRE, Mar 63: 69
PUGIN, AUGUSTUS WELBY, Mar 62: 36
   Buildings designed by, Mar 62: 37
P'U-I, EMPEROR OF CHINA, Jan 61: 15
PULITZER, JOSEPH, Jul 63: 71
PULITZER PRIZES
   Awarded to Guggenheim Fellows, May 59: 9–10
   In literature, Jul 63: 68–69, 70–72
   Winners among MacDowell colonists, Mar 63: 30
"PULL MY DAISY," motion picture, Mar 61: 14, 19
"PUNCH," magazine
   Cartoons from. See ILLUSTRATIONS INDEX
   Use of term cartoon by, May 59: 121
PUNT, LAND OF, Jul 60: 87
PURCELL, HENRY, Mar 60: 74
PURDOM, EDMUND, Sep 63: 79
PURDY, JAMES, Jan 62: 10
PURISM, in art, May 61: 21–22
PURITANISM
   In England, Sep 59: 120
   And nature, Mar 60: 15
   And witch mania, Nov 59: 59–60
PURITANS, under Charles I of England, Jul 61: 92, 93
"PURPLE PEOPLE EATER," tape recorder composition, Jan 59: 52
PUSHKIN, ALEXANDER, Sep 60: 130
   On St. Petersburg, quoted, Sep 59: 82
PUTENHAM, RICHARD, Nov 63: 42
PUTNEY, VT., Oneida Community, Mar 63: 77
P'U YI, MANCHU EMPEROR, May 60: 120
PUZZLES, English, Jul 61: 112
PYBUS, CATHERINE, Mar 59: 92
"PYGMALION," play, Sep 58: 144
"PYGMALION AND GALATEA," cartoon by Daumier, Mar 60: 57; illus, Mar 60: 53
"PYGMALION AND GALATEA," painting by Jean Léon Gérôme, Mar 60: 56–57; illus, Mar 60: 52
PYGMIES, of Congo, Mar 63: 40
PYNE, M. TAYLOR, Sep 59: 24
PYRAMIDS, Egyptian, André Malraux quoted on, Nov 58: 12–13

Q

QAJARS, of Persia, Jan 63: 52 (chart), 72
   In rock carving, Jan 63: 70–71
QUAKERS, influence in Philadelphia, Jul 63: 5, 6, 12, 13, 16
"QUARE FELLOW, THE," play, Mar 60: 120, 121, Jan 61: 114
QUARITCH, ALFRED, Nov 60: 99
QUARITCH, BERNARD, on invention of writing, quoted, Jan 63: 116–17
QUARTIMAX ROTATION OF THE CENTROID, Mar 60: 122
QUASIMODO, SALVATORE, Sep 61: 44, Jul 63: 74
QUAYLE, ANTHONY, Jan 62: 109
QUEEN ANN'S MANSIONS, London, Nov 60: 13
"QUEEN FOR A DAY," television program, Jul 60: 6
"QUEEN'S PICTURES, THE," article by Oliver Millar, Jul 63: 92–107
QUENEAU, RAYMOND, May 61: 90–91, 95
QUENNELL, PETER
   Articles by: "In the Glow of the Perfect Patron," Mar 63: 62–71; "Magpie's Nest in a London Mansion," Nov 63: 72–83; "Multiple Robert Graves, The," Jan 62: 50–55;

"Rampant Fox, The," May 60: 96–101, 124–25
   Portrait of, Jan 60: 109
   Sign of the Fish, The, excerpt from, Jan 60: 108–9
QUETZALCOATL, arrival of Cortes in Mexico interpreted as second coming of, Nov 63: 93–96
QUEVEDO, GARCÍA DE, Nov 62: 111
QUEVEDO Y VILLEGAS, FRANCISCO GÓMEZ DE, Sep 59: 120
QUICHERAT, JULES, Mar 62: 90, 93, 98
"QUIET AMERICAN, THE," novel by Graham Greene, May 60: 8, May 61: 117
"QUIET ONE, THE," motion picture, Mar 61: 14, 98
QUINN, ANTHONY, Nov 60: 51, Mar 61: 98, Jul 62: 109, 111
   In *Barabbas,* Mar 63: 109, 110
QUINTERO, JOSÉ, Mar 60: 95–96, 119–21, Jan 62: 104, Sep 62: 111, May 63: 107
   Photographs of, Mar 60: 95, 96–97
QUINTILIAN, quoted
   On Menander, Jul 59: 89
   On precision of language, Jul 63: 48
QUOGUE, N.Y., May 63: 6, 8
"QUO VADIS," motion picture, Nov 58: 82, 138, May 61: 53

R

"RABBIT, RUN," novel by John Updike, Mar 62: 84
RABELAIS, FRANÇOIS, Sep 58: 145, Sep 60: 62
   Lawyer's speech by, quoted, Sep 58: 131
RABIN, MICHAEL, Sep 59: 90, Jan 62: 9
RACHMANINOFF, SERGEI, May 63: 109
   On English conductors, quoted, Mar 62: 105
RACINE, JEAN BAPTISTE, Sep 61: 102, 103, 104, 105, Mar 62: 56, Jul 62: 54
   Quoted, Mar 61: 115
"RACOON," painting by Andrew Wyeth, Sep 61: 98
RADBURN, N.J., Jul 59: 7, 11
RADCLIFFE, REGGIE, Jul 59: 118
RADHAKRISHNAN, SARVEPALLI, May 63: 114
RADIANT CITY (also called UNITÉ D'HABITATION), in Marseilles, Nov 60: 125, Mar 61: 36
RADIO
   Communications satellites and, Jan 62: 16–21
   Decline of, Nov 61: 102–3
   And English language, Jul 63: 35
   FM commercials, Mar 59: 112
   Guthrie, Tyrone, in, Nov 63: 35, 36
   Mass media and imaginary audience, Mar 60: 46–51
   Teen-age tyranny over, Jan 59: 138–39
   Transistor radios in Japan, Mar 61: 6–7
   Welles, Orson, career of, Jul 63: 87–88
RADIO CORPORATION OF AMERICA (RCA)
   David Sarnoff Research Center, Sep 59: 25–26, 119
   Recording of *J.B.,* Jan 60: 52
   And world's most mysterious manuscript, Jan 63: 9
RADIO WAVES, Nov 63: 50–51, 53
RADZIWILL, ANTON, PRINCE, May 63: 110
RADZIWILL, PRINCESS, Nov 61: 36–37
RAHV, PHILIP, Sep 61: 116
RAILROADS
   Central of New Jersey, Jul 59: 6
   Effects on cities and towns, Jul 61: 61
   Gauges of, Brunel vs. Stephensons, Jan 59: 38–39
   Great Western of England, Jan 59: 34, 37–40
   Pennsylvania, and its Main Line, Jul 63: 7–8, 14, 26
   South Devon, Jan 59: 39
"RAISIN IN THE SUN," play, Sep 60: 54
"RAKE'S PROGRESS, THE," opera, Sep 58: 84, 132, Jan 60: 12
RAKOCZI, GEORGE, Mar 60: 101
RALEIGH, WALTER, Nov 62: 59
   On Dutch trade, quoted, Sep 58: 19
RAMA RAU, SANTHA, articles by
   "Angkor," Jan 59: 60–63, 81
   "In Search of Paradise," Mar 61: 20–33
RAMATAIA, KING OF MEDIA, Sep 59: 103
"RAMAYANA," Hindu epic, Jan 59: 63
RAMBALDONI, VITTORINO. See VITTORINO DA FELTRE
RAMBOUILLET, MARQUISE DE, Nov 61: 32
RAMEAU, JEAN PHILIPPE, Mar 61: 118
RAMÉE, MARIE LOUISE DE LA. See OUIDA
RAMPAL, JEAN-PIERRE, Jul 62: 30
"RAMPANT FOX, THE," article by Peter Quennell, May 60: 96–101, 124–25
RAMSAY, ALLAN, Jul 63: 105
RAMSES II, KING OF EGYPT, monuments built by, Jul 60: 8, 10, 14, 124–25
RAMSES III, KING OF EGYPT, Jan 61: 80
RAMSEY, MICHAEL, ARCHBISHOP OF CANTERBURY
   Photograph of, Sep 63: 107

Reply to *Honest to God*, book by John A. T. Robinson, Sep 63: 107

RAND, H. W., Jan 59: 110

RANDALL, CLARENCE, Sep 58: 134

RANDALL, TONY, Sep 61: 80

RANDOLPH, DAVID, "A New Music Made with a Machine," article by, Jan 59: 50–55, 124–27

RANK, J. ARTHUR, Sep 63: 79, 80

RANKE, LEOPOLD VON, Jan 62: 51
On historian's job, quoted, Sep 62: 114

RANSOM, JOHN CROWE, Sep 61: 117, Jan 62: 53

RANSON, PAUL, Mar 62: 15

RAPALLO, ITALY, Jul 60: 96
Reflections, portfolio of photographs, Jul 60: 96–99

"RAPE OF EUROPA," painting by Claude Lorrain, Jul 63: 106

RAPHAEL, Jan 60: 68, Jul 60: 36, 38, Sep 60: 34, Nov 60: 30, Mar 62: 50
Ansidei Madonna, sale of, Sep 61: 77
Influence on Poussin, Mar 61: 80
Painting of Leo I and Attila, May 63: 77, 80; illus, May 63: 76–77
Paintings by: collected by Charles I of England, Jul 61: 80, 89, 90, 94, 95, Jul 63: 94, 96; in Gardner Museum, Jul 59: 30, 35; in Vatican, Jan 62: 41, 43, 45, 48; reproduced, see ILLUSTRATIONS INDEX

RAPSON, RALPH, Jan 63: 13

RASHID-UD-DIN, VIZIER OF PERSIA, Jan 63: 53

"RASHOMON," motion picture, Jul 62: 42, 43

RASPONI, LANFRANCO, Jul 60: 121
Photograph of, Jul 60: 7

RASPUTIN, GRIGORI, portrait of, Sep 60: 130

RASUMOVSKY, ANDREAS (1752–1836), Nov 62: 44

RASUMOVSKY, ANDREAS, music critic of *Frankfurter Zeitung*, Nov 62: 44

RATHBONE, BASIL, Jan 59: 139, Sep 63: 76, 77, 80
Photographs of, Sep 63: 78, 79

RATHBONE, PERRY, Nov 60: 9

RATHENAU, WALTHER, quoted, Nov 63: 107

RATTI, ACHILLE. See PIUS XI, POPE

RATTIGAN, TERENCE
Ross, May 62: 111–12
Sleeping Prince, Jan 61: 30
On West End taste, quoted, Jan 63: 26

RATTNER, ABRAHAM, Jan 62: 8, Jul 62: 15
Painting by, Jul 62: 19

RAUBITSCHEK, ANTONY E., photograph of, Sep 59: 25

RAVEL, MAURICE, May 63: 109
Daphnis et Chloé, Jan 59: 125
Stravinsky, Igor, quoted on, Sep 58: 83
String quartet of, Nov 62: 46

RAVENNA MOSAICS, Nov 63: 25

RAY, ANDREW, Mar 61: 103

RAY, JAMES, Nov 60: 117–18

RAY, MAN, photograph by, Nov 61: 13

RAY, SATYAJIT, Jan 61: 115, Mar 61: 98

RAYMOND, ARCHBISHOP OF TOLEDO, Sep 62: 88–89

RAYMOND, HENRY, Jan 59: 24

RAYMOND, THOMAS, May 60: 43

RAYTINSKY, STANLEY, Mar 63: 91

REA, OLIVER, Nov 63: 36

REAAL, LAURENS, Sep 58: 26

REACTIONARIES, in American politics, Jul 61: 67, 69

READ, HERBERT, May 59: 10, 11

"READER OVER YOUR SHOULDER, THE," book by Robert Graves and Alan Hodge, quoted on "Whitehallese," Jul 63: 37 (note)

READING
"Look-say" method of teaching, Jul 63: 42
And microlibraries, Sep 62: 42–47

"REALITY IN ADVERTISING," book by Rosser Reeves, Jul 61: 119

"REASON WHY, THE," book by Mrs. Cecil Woodham-Smith, May 60: 128

REBAY, HILLA, May 59: 10–11

"REBEL, THE," philosophical work by Albert Camus, Nov 59: 71, 72

"REBEL WITHOUT A CAUSE," motion picture, Sep 58: 43, Jan 59: 139

REBUFFAT, GASTON, Sep 58: 11

RÉCAMIER, AMÉLIE, Nov 58: 146

RÉCAMIER, JACQUES-ROSE, Nov 58: 86–89, 142–46

RÉCAMIER, JEANNE FRANÇOISE JULIE ADE-LAIDE (JULIETTE), Nov 58: 86–89, 142–46
Portraits of, Nov 58: 87, 89

RECEVINTHUS, KING OF THE VISIGOTHS, May 63: 104

RECKORD, BARRY, Jan 63: 32

"RECONSIDERATIONS," book by Arnold J. Toynbee, article excerpted from, Jan 61: 57–65

RECORDINGS
By American pianists, Jan 60: 74, 76
Camelot album, May 61: 103

Of Handel's organ music, Mar 60: 73
Of Haydn's compositions, Mar 62: 77
By Improvisation Chamber Ensemble, Jan 63: 78
Of *J.B.,* Jan 60: 52
Renaissance music on, Nov 60: 90–91
Splicing, Glenn Gould quoted on, Jan 62: 90
Teen-agers' taste, Ahmet Ertegun quoted on, Nov 60: 86
Teen-age tyranny over, Jan 59: 138–39

"RECORD OF A LIVING BEING, THE," motion picture, Jul 62: 44–45

"RÉCRÉATION, LA," motion picture, May 62: 81

RED CROSS, association of Military Orders with, Mar 61: 70

"RED EYE OF LOVE, THE," play, Sep 62: 41

RED FORT, at Delhi, Mar 61: 21, May 62: 15, 84, 86

REDGRAVE, MICHAEL, Jan 61: 31, May 62: 106

REDGRAVE, RICHARD, Jul 63: 107

"REDHEAD," musical, May 63: 13

"RED, HOT AND BLUE," musical, Sep 58: 59

REECE, CARROL, Jan 62: 4

REED, CAROL, Mar 61: 98
As director of *Our Man in Havana,* Nov 59: 26–31, 122–26
Photographs of, Nov 59: 26–30

REED, JOHN, Mar 60: 33, Jul 61: 13

REEDY, WILLIAM MARION, and Spectric poets, May 60: 43, 46, 47

REEVES, ROSSER, *Reality in Advertising,* Jul 61: 119

REEVES, STEVE, May 61: 53, 54–55

REFORMATION
Knox, John, vs. Mary, Queen of Scots, Jul 63: 28–32
Witchcraft cult during, Nov 59: 59–60

"REFORM OR RUIN," pamphlet by John Bowdler, Sep 62: 69

REGENT'S PARK, London, Nov 62: 29

"REGINA," opera, Jan 60: 123

"REHEARSAL, THE," play, Nov 60: 126, 127

REICH, JOHN, Jan 62: 13

REICH, WILHELM, Sep 58: 42

REID, JOHN LYON, Jan 60: 21

REID, WHITELAW, Jan 59: 24, 25

REIMER, GEORG, portrait of, Mar 62: 118

REINACH, THEODORE, on underwater archaeological discoveries, quoted, Nov 58: 72

REINER, FRITZ, Jul 59: 19, Jan 62: 9

REINHARDT, AD, May 59: 11

REINHARDT, MAX, *Jedermann* produced by, Jan 61: 32

RÉJANE, Jul 63: 77
Colleen Dewhurst, compared, Jul 60: 94

RELATIVISM, May 63: 88, 89

RELATIVITY THEORY, Jul 62: 86

RELIGION (see also religions and sects by name)
African beliefs, Mar 63: 44, 106
American resort hotels influenced by, Jan 61: 104
In Angkor, Jan 59: 61–63, 81
In Dutch Republic, Sep 58: 22
Earliest known religious sculptures, Nov 63: 66–67
Etruscan, May 60: 62–63
Gods of Homer, Jan 61: 98
Greek, of Socrates' day, Jul 60: 103
Greene, Graham, as writer on, May 61: 117
Historian's struggle with, Jan 61: 57–65
In historical theory, Mar 59: 6, 13
In Japan, Mar 61: 8
Lewis, C. S., and, May 59: 64–67, 125–27
Mermaid in, Jan 60: 131, 134
Metamorphosis of the Gods, book by André Malraux, discussed, Nov 58: 4–17, 112–17
As motivation in adventure, Sep 58: 138–39
In Persia, Jan 63: 43–44, 49, 51, 52–53, 58, 59, 69
Prehistoric art and, May 59: 81
Role in development of cities, Jul 61: 35, 37, 38
Romantic revolt in, May 61: 61, 64, 65
Space and the spirit of man, Jan 59: 26–31, 122–23
Time and, Jul 62: 80
Togetherness cult in, Nov 58: 30, 146
Toleration in Moslem Spain, Sep 62: 74, 82
Voltaire's views on, Mar 61: 115

RELIGIOUS WARS, Sep 60: 64–65, 66, Jan 61: 58

REMBRANDT VAN RIJN, Sep 58: 15, 33–34, Mar 60: 124, Jul 60: 38, 50, Sep 60: 34, Nov 62: 65–66
Paintings by: in British Royal collection, Jul 61: 90, 94, Jul 63: 92, 93, 94, 106; in Gardner Museum, Jul 59: 29; reproduced, see ILLUSTRATIONS INDEX
Self-portrait, Sep 60: 70
Wyeth, Andrew, quoted on, Sep 61: 97, 100–1

"REMEMBRANCE OF THINGS PAST," novels by Marcel Proust, quoted on Monet and Poussin, Mar 61: 78

REMICK, LEE, Sep 60: 88
Photograph of, Sep 60: 89

REMY, JULES, Jul 63: 114

RÉMY, NICOLAS, and witch mania, Nov 59: 60, 63

RENAISSANCE
Attitude toward Joan of Arc in, Mar 62: 95

Attitude toward nature in, Mar 60: 14
Baroque vs., Jul 60: 35, 36, 64
Education at La Giocosa, Mantua, Jan 60: 57–68
Fountains of, May 62: 12–13
Gardens of, May 59: 27–29, 32–40, 49
Handwriting in, Sep 59: 126–27
Louvre during, Sep 60: 61–67
Music of, revived by Noah Greenberg, Nov 60: 88–95
Paintings of, in British royal collection, Jul 63: 92, 94, 96
Portrayal of angels during, Nov 60: 30
Sudden end of, Sep 59: 28–29, 120–21
As third period of unity in Europe, Mar 63: 5
Vespucci, Simonetta, ideal of, Sep 58: 92–95, 142
Witchcraft cult during, Nov 59: 59–63
Wright, Frank Lloyd, quoted on, Sep 60: 101

RENAN, JOSEPH ERNEST
Goncourt *Journal* quoted on, Sep 62: 113
On Persian religion, quoted, Jan 63: 43

RENATA THEATRE, New York City, Mar 60: 98

RENAUD, MADELEINE, Sep 61: 102

RENAULT, FRANCIS, Jul 59: 114

"RENÉ," novel by Chateaubriand, May 61: 60, 67

RENÉ, DUKE OF ANJOU, Nov 58: 96, 105

RENI, GUIDO, Jul 61: 90

RENNER, PAUL, Sep 59: 128

RENOIR, JEAN, May 60: 51, Sep 61: 110

RENOIR, PIERRE AUGUSTE, Mar 59: 105, Mar 60: 53, Nov 61: 12, Mar 62: 25, Jul 62: 64, 65
On female nude, quoted, Mar 62: 63
Paintings by. See ILLUSTRATIONS INDEX

REPIN, ILYA EFIMOVICH, paintings by, Sep 60: 131, 136

REPS, PAUL, "Zen Telegrams," drawings by, Jan 60: 46–47

REPTON, HUMPHREY, Nov 62: 24

"REPUBLIC, THE," dialogue by Plato, Mar 63: 74, 79

RESEARCH, economics of, Sep 63: 60–63

RESETTLEMENT ADMINISTRATION, Jul 59: 11–12

RESHEVSKY, SAMUEL, Jan 62: 117, 119–20
Photograph of, Jan 62: 118

RESNAIS, ALAIN, May 60: 54–55, Jan 62: 109, May 62: 81
Portrait of, May 60: 50

RESNIK, REGINA, photograph of, Nov 61: 79

"RESOLUTE," H.M.S., Presidential desk made from timbers of, Sep 61: 13

RESORT HOTELS, Jan 61: 102–12

"RESOUNDING TINKLE, A," play, Jan 63: 29, 31

"REST DURING THE FLIGHT INTO EGYPT," painting by Poussin, Mar 61: 90

RESTIF DE LA BRETONNE, Jul 62: 56

"RESTLESS HEART," play, Nov 60: 54

RESTON, JAMES B., Sep 58: 37, Mar 60: 50, 51, Jul 60: 67
On American language, quoted, Jul 63: 37

RESZKE, JEAN DE, Jul 59: 32

RETZ, CARDINAL DE, Nov 61: 34

REUBKE, JULIUS, Mar 60: 80

REUCHLIN, JOHANN, May 60: 37

"REUNION IN VIENNA," play, Jul 62: 36

REUTHER, WALTER P., Sep 58: 133
Photograph of, Sep 58: 99

REUWICH, ERHARD, woodcuts by, Mar 60: 81–89

"REVIEW," painting by William Beechey, Jul 63: 106

"REVOLT AGAINST THE WEST END," article by Irving Wardle, Jan 63: 26–33

"REVOLT OF THE MASSES, THE," book by Ortega y Gasset, Mar 63: 6

REVOLUTION, AMERICAN. See AMERICAN REVOLUTION

REVOLUTION, FRENCH. See FRENCH REVOLUTION

REXROTH, KENNETH, Sep 58: 40, Sep 61: 117, 119

REY, HENRI-FRANÇOIS, Jul 63: 74

"REYNARD THE FOX," play by Arthur Fauquez, Jan 63: 88, 90

REYNOLDS, CHARLIE, May 62: 9

REYNOLDS, JOSHUA, Nov 59: 96, Mar 63: 65, 69, Jul 63: 105, 106
Influence on Royal Academy, May 62: 60–62, 78
Painting by, Jul 63: 95
Quoted: on Blenheim Palace, Sep 61: 69–70; on Poussin, Mar 61: 90
Self-portraits, Nov 59: 95, May 62: 56

REYNOLDS, QUENTIN, Sep 63: 78

REYNOLDS METALS COMPANY BUILDING, in Detroit, May 62: 16

"RHAPSODIC VARIATIONS FOR TAPE RECORDER AND ORCHESTRA," composition by Otto Luening and Vladimir Ussachevsky, Jan 59: 54

RHEINBERGER, JOSEPH GABRIEL, Mar 60: 80

"RHEINGOLD, DAS," opera, Nov 58: 27, May 63: 40–45

RHINE, J. B., Jul 62: 88

"RHINOCEROS," play, May 61: 89, 91, 93, May 62: 51, 112, Sep 62: 34–35 (illus), 37, 41, Mar 63: 107, May 63: 10
RHODES, GREECE, Sep 60: 125
  Knights of St. John on, Mar 61: 56–59, 62, 65
  Sculpture from, in Cave of Tiberius, May 59: 104–7, 122–24
  Sieges of, Mar 61: 56–59, 65
RHODESIA. See SOUTHERN RHODESIA
RHODES SCHOLARS, in Kennedy administration, Sep 61: 13
RHONE RIVER, Jul 59: 90, 92, 97, 132
RIBART, CHARLES FRANÇOIS, Elephant of Paris designed by, Mar 59: 136
RIBERA, JOSÉ, Jul 63: 96
RIBICOFF, ABRAHAM, photograph of, Sep 61: 8
RICE, ELMER, Street Scene, Jan 60: 123
RICH, ALAN, "On Stage: David Amram," article by, May 62: 82–83
"RICHARD III," play by Shakespeare
  Chayefsky, Paddy, quoted on, Sep 60: 53
  Guthrie, Tyrone, quoted on Laurence Olivier in, Jan 61: 29–30
  Humor in, Mar 63: 106–7
RICHARD I, KING OF ENGLAND (RICHARD THE LION-HEARTED), Sep 60: 59, May 63: 94
  In painting by Solomon Alexander Hart, Jan 59: 86
  Saladin and, Jan 59: 86–91, 130–31
"RICHARD AND SALADIN," article by Alfred Duggan, Jan 59: 86–91, 130–31
RICHARD CLAY & SONS LTD., Mar 59: 107–8
RICHARDS MEDICAL RESEARCH BUILDING, Philadelphia, Sep 62: 57, 59–60; illus, Mar 62: 31, Sep 62: 58, 62, 63
RICHARDSON, HENRY HANDEL, Sep 62: 97
RICHARDSON, H. H., Jan 63: 11
RICHARDSON, JACK
  Gallows Humor, Sep 62: 38–39 (illus)
  Prodigal, The, Mar 61: 46–47
RICHARDSON, JONATHAN, painting by, Sep 61: 72
RICHARDSON, RALPH, Nov 59: 31, Jan 60: 96, Nov 60: 52, May 61: 57
RICHARDSON, SAMUEL, Clarissa Harlowe, Mar 59: 118, Jan 62: 60–61, 63–64
RICHARDSON, TONY, Mar 61: 103, Jan 63: 26, 27, 32, 86
  Photograph of, Jan 63: 28
RICHELIEU, CARDINAL, Sep 59: 120, 121, Jan 60: 85, Jul 60: 38, 64, Sep 60: 67, Jul 61: 90, May 62: 60, Jul 63: 82, 83
  Portraits of Sep 59: 29, Jul 60: 40
RICHELIEU, DUC DE, Jan 60: 85, 88, Mar 61: 118, 119
  Portrait of, Jan 60: 87
"RICHESSE OBLIGE," editorial by Lucius Beebe reprinted from The Territorial Enterprise, Nov 58: 148
RICHIE, DONALD, "Dostoevsky with a Japanese Camera," article by, Jul 62: 42–47
RICHIER, GERMAINE, Sep 62: 24
RICHMOND, DUKE OF (JAMES STUART), Jul 61: 95
  In painting by Van Dyck, Jul 61: 78
RICHTER, G. M. A., on Ganymedes sculpture, quoted, May 59: 122
RICHTER, HANS, May 63: 43
  Thomas Beecham quoted on, Mar 62: 104
RICKETT, R. J., Nov 62: 66
RICKOVER, HYMAN GEORGE, Jan 60: 10
"RICOTTA, LA," motion picture, Jan 63: 91
RIDING, HORSEBACK. See HORSEMANSHIP
RIDING, LAURA, Jan 62: 53–54
RIEGGER, WALLINGFORD, Jul 59: 20
RIESMAN, DAVID, Nov 58: 12, Nov 59: 23, Sep 62: 16
  Lonely Crowd, The, quoted, Jul 60: 69, 71
  Quoted: on college students of late 1950's, May 63: 87; on efficiency of Americans, May 60: 9; on higher education, Jul 59: 111; on "other-directed" man, Sep 60: 32
RIETI, VITTORIO, Mar 61: 75
"RIGHTS OF MAN, THE," painting by René Magritte, Jan 62: 82; illus, Jan 62: 83
"RIGOLETTO," opera, Anna Moffo in, Jul 61: 97
RIIS, JACOB, Nov 63: 69
RILKE, RAINER MARIA, Jan 63: 78
  On angel of Chartres, quoted, Jul 62: 80
RIMBAUD, ARTHUR, Nov 59: 72
  Quoted, Mar 59: 72; on color of vowels, May 62: 120
"RIME OF THE ANCIENT MARINER, THE," poem by Coleridge, and story of Fletcher Christian, Mar 63: 47–48
RIMSKY-KORSAKOV, NIKOLAI, Nov 62: 44
  Igor Stravinsky quoted on, Sep 58: 82
"RING DES NIBELUNGEN, DER," opera cycle, Nov 58: 27, 133, May 63: 40–45
"RING ROUND THE MOON," play, Nov 58: 62, Nov 60: 52
RIN TIN TIN, Mar 60: 127
RIO DE JANEIRO, BRAZIL

Ministry of Education building, Nov 60: 16, 125
U.S. embassy building, Jun 60: 25
RIPLEY, GEORGE, Mar 63: 77
"RISE AND FALL OF THE THIRD REICH, THE," book by William L. Shirer, reviewed, Nov 60: 119–21
"RISE OF CHRISTIANITY, THE," book by Edward W. Barnes, Sep 63: 8–9
RITCHARD, CYRIL, Nov 58: 120, Jan 59: 139
RITCHIE, JEAN, Sep 62: 66
RITT, MARTIN, Sep 60: 88
RITZ, CÉSAR, May 61: 125
RIVA, EMMANUELLE, May 60: 54
RIVAFLECHA, MARTIN DE, Nov 60: 94
"RIVALRY, THE," play, Jan 63: 88
RIVERA, DIEGO, May 60: 113, Nov 60: 6
"RIVER COVE," painting by Andrew Wyeth, Sep 61: 101; illus, Sep 61: 96
"RIVER JOURNEY AT FIRST SNOWFALL, A," painting by Chao Kan, Jan 61: 25; illus, Jan 61: 23
RIVER OAKS, TEX., May 61: 18
RIVERS, LARRY, Jan 59: 105, Jul 60: 120, Mar 61: 14, Mar 62: 107, May 63: 18
  On government in art, quoted, Sep 61: 17
  Interview with, Sep 59: 94–102
  Paintings by. See ILLUSTRATIONS INDEX
  Photograph of, Sep 59: 94
RIVERS, STEVEN, Sep 59: 95, 102
RIVERSIDE, ILL., Jul 59: 12
RIVIERA
  French, Mar 59: 83
  Italian, Mar 59: 85
RIZZIO, DAVID, Jul 63: 29
"ROAD, THE," print by Tadashige Ono, May 60: 113; illus, May 60: 106
ROADS and HIGHWAYS
  Architectural solutions proposed for traffic problems, Jan 62: 94–95
  Of baroque city, Jul 61: 52
  Disfigurement of, in America, May 61: 4–18
  In earliest cities, Jul 61: 41
  In Los Angeles, Jul 61: 63
  Montauk Highway, May 63: 6–7
  Of U.S. and U.S.S.R. compared, Jul 62: 112, 116–19
"ROADS & INROADS," article by Bernard Rudofsky, Jan 62: 94–95
"ROAD TO ROME, THE," play, Jul 62: 37
"ROAD TO WIGAN PIER, THE," book by George Orwell, Nov 62: 110
"ROADTOWN," Jan 62: 94
"ROAD TO XANADU, THE," book by John Livingston Lowes, cited, May 63: 115, Sep 63: 48
ROBARDS, JASON, JR., Mar 60: 120, 121, Jul 60: 93
ROBBE-GRILLET, ALAIN, Jan 62: 96–97, 99–100, 110, Sep 62: 109
  On nouveau roman, quoted, Jan 62: 96, 101
  Portrait of, Jan 62: 98
ROBBINS, H. C., on Joseph Haydn, quoted, Mar 62: 80
ROBBINS, JEROME, Nov 59: 56, Sep 60: 94, Jul 61: 98, Jan 63: 32
"ROBE, THE," motion picture, Mar 60: 128
ROBERT, RICHARD, Sep 61: 83
ROBERTS, C. H., Nov 62: 86
ROBERTSON, balloonist, Sep 58: 114
ROBERTSON, ARCHIE, "From 'Bully!' to Vigah!'" article by, Nov 63: 68–71
ROBIN, DANY, Jan 63: 38
ROBINSON, C. A., JR., "The Two Worlds of Alexander," article by, Mar 59: 28–59
ROBINSON, CLIFF, memorandum to, from Jonathan Swift, Nov 59: 64–65
ROBINSON, CORINNE ROOSEVELT, May 60: 46
ROBINSON, DWIGHT E., "The Rules of Fashion Cycles," article by, Mar 59: 62–67, 113–17
ROBINSON, EDWARD, Nov 59: 8
ROBINSON, EDWARD ARLINGTON, May 60: 46, Mar 63: 28–29, 33
  Photograph of, Mar 63: 30
ROBINSON, EDWARD G., Sep 60: 54, 56
ROBINSON, FRANCIS, on prima donnas, quoted, Sep 59: 52, 57
ROBINSON, JOHN A. T.
  Honest to God: comment on, by Douglas Auchincloss, Sep 63: 8–9; excerpt from, Sep 63: 4–7, 104–6; reply to, by Archbishop of Canterbury, Sep 63: 107
  Portraits of, Sep 63: 5, 6
ROBINSON, J. T., May 62: 9
ROBINSON, LENNOX, Mar 59: 88
ROBINSON, PERDITA, May 60: 100
"ROBINSON CRUSOE," motion picture, Nov 62: 110
ROBSON, MARK, May 59: 101
"ROCCO AND HIS BROTHERS, BELL' ANTONIO," motion picture, Jan 63: 38
ROCHESTER, N.Y.
  Design by Louis Kahn for First Unitarian Church, Sep 62: 60, 62

1812 Overture of Tchaikovsky hoax, Jan 61: 71
"ROCK, THE," painting by Peter Blume, Jul 61: 71
ROCKEFELLER, DAVID
  Art program of, for Chase Manhattan Bank, Nov 60: 4–11, Mar 61: 121
  Portrait of, Nov 60: 5
ROCKEFELLER, JOHN D., Mar 60: 31, Nov 60: 98, Jul 62: 4
  Interview with, on David Rockefeller's art-buying program, Nov 60: 6–11
  Photograph of, Nov 60: 6
ROCKEFELLER, JOHN D., JR., Jul 62: 5, 6, Nov 62: 3
ROCKEFELLER, JOHN D. III, Nov 58: 118, Jul 62: 4, 6, 7, 8, 10
  Photograph of, Jul 62: 6
ROCKEFELLER, NELSON, Jul 61: 68, Nov 61: 10, Jul 62: 4
ROCKEFELLER, STEVEN, Jul 60: 122
  Photograph of, Jul 60: 6
ROCKEFELLER, WILLIAM, Nov 58: 119
ROCKEFELLER CENTER, in New York City, Sep 60: 39, Nov 60: 6, May 61: 4
ROCKEFELLER FOUNDATION, study of opera in America financed by, Nov 61: 80
ROCKETS, Guggenheim sponsoring of research on, May 59: 8
ROCKINGHAM, MARQUESS OF, Nov 58: 40, 46
ROCKWELL, NORMAN, May 60: 13
  Photograph of, May 60: 12
ROCOCO STYLE
  Vs. 18th-century neoclassicism, Mar 62: 50, 61–63, 68
  Foreshadowed by Van Dyck, Jul 63: 96
RODDY, JOSEPH, "Seven Keyboard Insurgents," article by, Jan 60: 74–81
RODGERS, EILEEN, photograph of, May 61: 51
RODGERS, RICHARD, Sep 58: 59, 60, 61, May 61: 103, 113
  Score of Oklahoma! by, compared with Ballad of Baby Doe, Jan 60: 14
RODIN, (FRANÇOIS) AUGUSTE, Nov 60: 113
  Isamu Noguchi quoted on, Mar 60: 112
RODMAN, SELDEN, Conversations with Artists, quoted, Mar 59: 135
RODNEY, GEORGE BRYDGES, portrait of, Jul 63: 95
RODRIGO, KING OF THE VISIGOTHS, Sep 62: 74
RODZINSKI, ARTHUR, Jul 59: 18
ROEBLING, PAUL, May 63: 108
ROETTIERS, JACQUES, Nov 62: 65
ROGER I, COUNT OF SICILY, Sep 61: 28, 36
ROGER II, KING OF SICILY, Sep 61: 28, 30, 32, 36
ROGER-MARX, CLAUDE, on American abstract expressionism, quoted, Nov 59: 120
ROGER OF HOVEDEN, on tournaments, quoted, Nov 58: 95
ROGERS, ERNESTO, Nov 59: 50, Nov 60: 125
  Building designed by, Nov 60: 15
ROGERS, GINGER, Jan 61: 46, May 63: 111
ROGERS, H. H., May 59: 6–7
ROGERS, JOHN, Mar 60: 125
ROGERS, PAUL, Nov 59: 123
ROGERS, RANDOLPH, sculpture by, Mar 63: 63
ROGERS, SAMUEL, Mar 59: 92
ROGERS, WILL, Sep 58: 58, Nov 61: 103
  Photograph of, Sep 58: 58
"ROGET'S THESAURUS," use of, by Robert Graves, Mar 63: 85, 86
ROGOSIN, LIONEL, Mar 61: 15, 19
  Photograph of, Mar 61: 15
ROHAN, CARDINAL DE, Jan 60: 85
ROHAN, CHEVALIER DE, Mar 61: 117
ROHAN, ULYSSE, May 61: 125
ROISMAN, JOSEPH, photograph of, Nov 62: 44
ROLAND. See "SONG OF ROLAND, THE"
ROLAND, MME, Nov 61: 35
ROLLAND, ROMAIN, Mar 63: 6
ROLLER, ALBERT F., Jan 60: 120
ROLLER, ALFRED, May 63: 43
ROLLO, DUKE OF NORMANDY, Jul 62: 66
ROLT, L. T. C., "The Great Engineer: Isambard Kingdom Brunel," article by, Jan 59: 32–43, 136
ROMAIN, balloonist, Sep 58: 114
ROMAINS, JULES, Men of Good Will, compared to The Marquise Went Out at Five, May 62: 115
ROMAN CATHOLIC CHURCH
  Influence on stagecraft of José Quintero, Mar 60: 119–20
  Ivory, use by, May 60: 121
  Jansenism and Pascal's beliefs, Jan 63: 100, 102, 104
  Mary, Queen of Scots, vs. John Knox, Jul 63: 28–32
  Sovereign Order of Malta, Mar 61: 70
  On space age, quoted, Jan 59: 122–23
  And Thirty Years' War, Nov 62: 32–41
ROMANESQUE ART, André Malraux quoted on, Nov 58: 112
ROMANO, GIULIO
  Painting by, Jan 62: 30–31

Tapestry from cartoons of, Nov 61: 82; illus, Nov 61: 82
ROMANO, UMBERTO, portrait of, with painting by, Jul 61: 24
"ROMANOFF AND JULIET," play, Nov 58: 65, 82, 83, 84, 139, Sep 59: 86, 88
ROMANOV DYNASTY, Sep 59: 62
ROMANSKAYA, MILA, photograph of, Nov 62: 117
"ROMAN SPRING OF MRS. STONE, THE," novel by Tennessee Williams, Mar 59: 119
Motion picture based on, Jan 62: 104
ROMANTICISM
Vs. classicism, May 61: 60
And Joan of Arc, Mar 62: 97
Junk sculpture as expression of, Mar 61: 113
Romantic revolt of 18th and 19th centuries: in literature, May 61: 58–68, 83; in music, May 61: 66, 82–83, 84; in painting, May 61: 66, 72, 74; in politics, May 61: 66, 85
"ROMANTIC REVOLT, THE," article by Harold Nicolson, May 61: 58–88
ROMANUS IV DIOGENES, BYZANTINE EMPEROR, Nov 63: 31
"ROMAUNT OF THE ROSE, THE," quoted, May 59: 41
ROMBERG, BERNHARD, Nov 62: 46
ROMBERG, SIGMUND, Sep 58: 57
ROMBOLA, JOHN
Bullfight drawings, portfolio by, Jul 60: 129–36
"See Manhattan While It Lasts: A Walking Tour," drawings by, with text by Oliver Jensen, May 63: 116–20
ROME, ITALY
Drawings by Domenico Gnoli, Jul 59: 136, 142–44
Foundations of, May 62: 12, 14, 15, 20–21, 23
Gardens of, May 59: 26–27, 28–29, 32
Olympic Games stadiums, Mar 59: 22–23, 122, 123–24
Piazza Navona, Jul 60: 38
In Poussin's time, Mar 61: 79–80
Risorgimento bridge, Mar 59: 20–21
Role in Grand Tour of 18th and 19th centuries, Nov 59: 94–96
Russian émigrés of 19th century in, Sep 60: 131, 134
Saint Peter's. See SAINT PETER, BASILICA OF
Sovereign Order of Malta in, Mar 61: 70
Tasso's oak, Jul 61: 70–75
Vatican and its treasures, Jan 62: 22–49
ROME, ANCIENT
Aphrodisias, Mar 63: 96–101
Arles, colony at, Jul 59: 95–98, 129–30
Art of, André Malraux quoted on, Nov 58: 15
Baths and sanitary facilities, May 60: 39–41
Bullfight origin in, Jul 60: 128
And Byzantine Empire, Nov 63: 4, 6
Cave of Tiberius, May 59: 102–7, 122–24
City-building of, Jul 61: 44–47
City of Rome under Julius Caesar, Mar 59: 26–27
Coin portraits, Sep 63: 33–41
Empire as first period of unity in Europe, Mar 63: 4
Etruscans and, May 60: 60, 73–74
Frescoes of, Sep 63: 12–13
Hadrian's Villa, May 63: 32–39
Ivory, use in, May 60: 120–21
Leo the Great and Attila the Hun, May 63: 76–80
Love in, Nov 58: 108–11
Nature, attitude toward, Mar 60: 13
Occupation of Sicily, Sep 61: 23, 24–25 (map), 26, 30–31
Painting of 1st century A.D., Jul 60: 114–15, 116
Persian conflicts, Jan 63: 50, 52 (chart)
Pompeii and Herculaneum, their burial and discovery, Mar 62: 42–69
Portraiture, Jan 59: 102
Sardis under, Sep 63: 89
As setting for screen epics, May 61: 53–54, 55, 56–57
Slavery in, May 62: 42–49
Theatre of, Jul 59: 45–46
Wheeled vehicles in, Sep 58: 149, 150, 151
Winged victory of, Nov 60: 28, 29–30
"ROME AND A VILLA," book by Eleanor Clark, quoted, May 63: 34
"ROMEO AND JULIET," play by Shakespeare
Ballet based on, Sep 60: 94
Bowdlerized version, Sep 62: 70, 71
"ROME OF ASIA, THE," article by James Morris, May 62: 84–87
ROMNEY, GEORGE, Nov 62: 114, Mar 63: 69
Painting by, Mar 62: 68
RONCHAMP, FRANCE, Shrine of the Virgin at, Sep 59: 9, Mar 61: 39
RONDET, LAURENT ETIENNE, Mar 61: 116
RONSARD, PIERRE DE, Jul 63: 29
"ROOM AT THE TOP," novel by John Braine, motion picture based on, May 62: 116
"ROOMS FOR IMPROVEMENT," article by Nancy Mitford, Nov 61: 32–37
ROOSA, ROBERT V., Sep 61: 13
ROOSEVELT, ALICE, Nov 63: 68

ROOSEVELT, ARCHIE, Nov 63: 70
ROOSEVELT, EDITH CAROW (MRS. THEODORE), Nov 63: 69, 70
ROOSEVELT, ELEANOR, Nov 63: 68
ROOSEVELT, FRANKLIN D., Jul 59: 11, Nov 60: 120, Jul 61: 66, 67, Sep 61: 9, May 62: 8, 9
As Abundance man, Jul 60: 68
Visit of George VI and Queen Elizabeth, Sep 63: 77 (note)
Washington, D.C., memorial, plan for, May 61: 42–43, Sep 61: 13
ROOSEVELT, JAMES, photograph of, Jul 60: 7
ROOSEVELT, QUENTIN, Nov 63: 70
ROOSEVELT, THEODORE, Sep 61: 13
Compared with John F. Kennedy, Nov 63: 68–71
O'Neill, Eugene, quoted on, Mar 60: 35
Photographs of, Nov 63: 68–69, 70, 71
"ROOSEVELT AND HOPKINS," book by Robert Sherwood, May 62: 8, 9
"ROOTS," play, reviewed, Jul 61: 117–18
"ROOTS, THE," motion picture, Nov 62: 110
ROPPEL, EARL (MALCOLM COWLEY and S. FOSTER DAMON), May 60: 48
ROQUE, JACQUELINE, and Picasso, Jan 60: 97–105
ROREM, NED, Jul 59: 21, Mar 61: 75
RORIMER, JAMES J., on Isabella Stewart Gardner, quoted, Jul 59: 28
ROSA DE LIMA, SAINT, Nov 61: 111
"ROSALIND," play, Nov 58: 134–35
ROSANOFF, MRS. MARIE, photograph of, Nov 62: 42
ROSE, FREDERICK, Nov 62: 65, 66
Photograph of, Nov 62: 62
ROSE, GEORGE, May 62: 110–11
ROSE, LEONARD, Jul 62: 30
ROSECRANS, WILLIAM STARKE, Jan 59: 25
"ROSE MARIE," musical, Sep 58: 57
Compared to *Little Mary Sunshine,* Sep 60: 87
ROSEN, JEROME, Jan 59: 21
ROSENBACH, A. S. W., Nov 60: 96–101
Photograph of, Nov 60: 96
ROSENBACH, PHILIP, Nov 60: 97, 100
"ROSENBACH: A BIOGRAPHY," book by Edwin Wolf 2nd and John F. Fleming, article excerpted from, Nov 60: 96–101
ROSENBERG, ALFRED, Nov 61: 74
ROSENBERG, HAROLD, Alfred Kazin quoted on, Jul 62: 103
ROSENBERG, PAUL, on Picasso, quoted, Nov 61: 7
ROSENBERGER, WALTER, on Leonard Bernstein, quoted, Jul 59: 20
"ROSENKAVALIER, DER," opera, Nov 58: 25, 28, May 63: 42
Conducted by Thomas Beecham, Mar 62: 104
Dresden performance of 1920–21, Jan 61: 27
Lehmann-Jeritza feud during performance of, Sep 59: 56
ROSENQUIST, JAMES, Jan 63: 25
Painting by, Jan 63: 23
ROSENTHAL, M. L., *A Primer of Ezra Pound,* Jan 61: 116
ROSENTHAL, MORIZ, Sep 61: 84
ROSENTHAL, TOBY, Jan 59: 7
"ROSMERSHOLM," play, Jan 62: 108
"ROSS," play, May 62: 111–12, Sep 62: 112
ROSS, DAVID, Sep 62: 111 (note), May 63: 10
On Meacham, Anne, quoted, May 61: 99
Presentation of Ibsen plays, Jan 62: 106
ROSS, HAROLD, Jul 62: 37, 38
ROSS, NANCY WILSON, "The Square Roots of Zen," article by, Jul 59: 70–77, 126–27
ROSSELLINI, ROBERTO, May 59: 99, May 60: 51
General Della Rovere, Mar 61: 99–100
Open City, Mar 61: 98, 99, 100
Paisan, Mar 61: 98
ROSSEN, ROBERT, May 61: 55
ROSSETTI, DANTE GABRIEL, May 62: 64
Poem of, and Zen Buddhism, Jul 59: 126–27
ROSSINI, GIOACCHINO ANTONIO, in painting by Joseph Danhauser, May 61: 84–85
ROSTOW, WALT WHITMAN, Sep 61: 13
Stages of Economic Growth, The, quoted, Nov 62: 6
ROTH, LILLIAN, *I'll Cry Tomorrow,* book about, Jul 60: 120
ROTH, SANFORD, Jan 59: 144
ROTHENSTEIN, JOHN, Nov 59: 32
ROTHENSTEIN, WILLIAM, May 61: 38, 40
ROTHKO, MARK, Sep 58: 44, 110, May 59: 11, Nov 59: 41, 120, Jul 60: 16, Jul 62: 13, Jan 63: 16
Painting by, Nov 59: 35
Wyeth, Andrew, quoted on, Sep 61: 101
ROTTERDAM, NETHERLANDS, sculpture by Naum Gabo, Sep 59: 18–19
ROTTERDAM, FORT. See FORT ROTTERDAM
ROUAULT, GEORGES, Sep 58: 110, Sep 62: 24, Nov 62: 48, 57
Works by. See ILLUSTRATIONS INDEX
ROUCHOMOVSKY, ISRAEL, Mar 59: 105
ROUGEMONT, DENIS DE, Mar 63: 9

On Tristan myth, quoted, Jan 62: 58
ROUND TABLE. See ARTHURIAN LEGEND
ROUND TABLE, of Algonquin Hotel, Jul 62: 36–41
ROUSSEAU, HENRI, May 59: 121
Painting by, May 59: 12
ROUSSEAU, JEAN JACQUES, Nov 59: 86, Jan 60: 30, Mar 61: 114, 115, 116, 117, 118, Mar 63: 73, 76
Day, Thomas, as disciple of, May 59: 96, 128
Gospel of nature preached by, Mar 60: 14
Portrait of, May 61: 60
And romantic revolt, May 61: 60, 64, 65, 66, 67, 70
ROUSSEAU, THEODORE, Nov 58: 9
ROUSSEL, KER-XAVIER, Mar 62: 15
ROUTH, MARTIN JOSEPH, Jan 63: 85
"ROUT OF THE CLASSICAL TRADITION, THE," article by Hugh MacLennan, Nov 60: 17–24
ROVINA, ANNA, Jan 61: 33
ROWAYTON, CONN., House of Worship, Nov 62: 70–73
ROWLAND, BENJAMIN, on painters' attitudes toward nature, quoted, Mar 60: 13
ROWLANDSON, THOMAS, May 62: 64
Drawings by, May 62: 61, Nov 62: 22
ROXANE, wife of Alexander the Great, Mar 59: 52–53
ROXBURY, CONN., May 60: 13 (map), 28
ROXELANA, wife of Suleiman the Magnificent, May 59: 135
"ROYAL ACADEMY, THE," article by John Russell, May 62: 56–79
"ROYAL AFFAIR AT VERSAILLES, A," motion picture, Jul 63: 91
ROYAL ALBERT BRIDGE, Jan 59: 39–40
"ROYAL BOX, THE," play, Mar 62: 119
ROYAL FESTIVAL HALL, London, Nov 58: 118
"ROYAL GAME," book by Stefan Zweig, Nov 63: 62
"ROYAL GEORGE," H.M.S., May 60: 128
"ROYAL GOLD OF MARLIK TEPE, THE," illustrated feature, Nov 62: 100–4
ROYAL OPERA HOUSE, London. See COVENT GARDEN
ROYAL POINCIANA HOTEL, Palm Beach, Fla., Jan 61: 104
ROYAL SOCIETY, May 62: 60
And Formosa hoax of George Psalmanazar, Jan 60: 114, 115–16
ROYCE, JOSIAH, Jan 59: 7, 22
ROYE, RENAUD DE, Nov 58: 106
ROYSTON, ROBERT, Jan 59: 8
RUANDA-URUNDI, value of cattle in, Mar 63: 52
RUBENS, PETER PAUL, Sep 58: 24, Sep 59: 120, 121, Jul 60: 50, Sep 60: 111, Mar 61: 79, Mar 62: 63
Charles I of England as patron of, Jul 61: 79, 80, 89, 90–91, 92, 93, 94
And collection of Isabella Stewart Gardner, Jul 59: 29, 30, 38
Paintings by: in British royal collection, Jul 63: 93, 96, 106; reproduced, see ILLUSTRATIONS INDEX
RUBINSTEIN, AKIBA, Jan 62: 120
Photograph of, Jan 62: 114
RUBINSTEIN, ARTUR, Jan 60: 76, 81
RUDAKI, Jan 63: 53
RUDDOCK, JOHN, Jul 62: 111
RUDE, FRANÇOIS, Mar 62: 97
RUDEL, JULIUS, Jan 60: 14
RUDENKO, S. I., Jan 60: 111–12
RÜDLINGER, ARNOLD, Nov 59: 120
RUDOFSKY, BERNARD, "Roads & Inroads," article by, Jan 62: 94–95
RUDOLF II, HOLY ROMAN EMPEROR, Sep 59: 121, Jul 61: 80, Jan 63: 6–7
Portrait of, Sep 59: 28
RUDOLF, MAX, Sep 61: 83
RUDOLPH, PAUL, May 59: 86–87, Jan 60: 21
Building designed by, Mar 62: 33
RUFFO, VENERABLE GENERAL, Knight of Malta, Mar 61: 64
RUGGLES, CARL, Jul 59: 20
RUGS. See CARPETS
RUISDAEL, JACOB VAN, Sep 58: 26
"RULES OF FASHION CYCLES, THE," article by Dwight E. Robinson, Mar 59: 62–67, 113–17
"RULES OF THE GAME, THE," motion picture, Sep 61: 110
RUMAKER, MICHAEL, Sep 58: 40
RUMI. See JALAL-UD-DIN-RUMI
RUPERT, PRINCE, OF ENGLAND, Jul 61: 95
In painting by Van Dyck, Jul 61: 78
RUPF, HERMANN, Nov 61: 9
"R. U. R.," play, Mar 63: 78
RURIK, GRAND PRINCE OF NOVGOROD, Nov 63: 34
RURIK, HOUSE OF, Sep 59: 62
RUSH, BENJAMIN, Jul 63: 25
RUSK, DEAN, Sep 61: 10
Memorandum from Thomas Jefferson to, Jul 61: 30–31
Sketch of, Jul 61: 31
RUSKIN, JOHN, Mar 62: 36

Forged editions of works by, Mar 59: 107
Quoted: on architecture, Mar 59: 113; on buildings of
  Venice, Mar 63: 15, 16; on Homeric landscapes, Mar
  60: 13; on Whistler, May 62: 78
RUSSELL, physician at Brighton, England, c. 1750, Nov
  62: 21
RUSSELL, BERTRAND, Sep 61: 115, Mar 62: 73, Jan
  63: 86, Jul 63: 75, Nov 63: 105
In painting by Feliks Topolski, Nov 60: 131
Quoted: on aggressive instincts, Nov 63: 108; on American
  culture, May 60: 7; on exceptional man, Nov 63: 109;
  on love of excitement, Jul 59: 111; on public credulity,
  Nov 59: 63
RUSSELL, CHARLIE, Sep 60: 51
RUSSELL, DORA, Nov 63: 105
RUSSELL, FRANCIS, articles by
"Archpoet, The," Nov 60: 66–69
"Frost in the Evening," Nov 58: 34–35
"Sheiks and Shebas, Dance No More," Jul 63: 118–19
"Witch of Beacon Hill, The," Jan 59: 108–11
RUSSELL, GEORGE WILLIAM (AE), Mar 59: 88, Nov
  60: 68
RUSSELL, JOHN, contemporary English critic
Articles by: " 'New American Painting' Captures Europe,
  The," Nov 59: 32, 41, 120–21; "Royal Academy, The,"
  May 62: 56–79
On Baron Haussmann, quoted, May 63: 51
RUSSELL, JOHN, English portrait painter, engraving
  from painting by, Sep 63: 48
RUSSELL, JOHN (1ST EARL RUSSELL)
Portrait of, Mar 59: 90
On Smith, Sydney, quoted, Mar 59: 90
RUSSELL, JOHN SCOTT, Jan 59: 136
RUSSELL, LILLIAN, Nov 58: 148
RUSSIA (see also UNION OF SOVIET SOCIALIST RE-
  PUBLICS)
Byzantine legacy, Nov 63: 33, 34
Crown jewels of, May 63: 94, 96; illus, May 63: 102
Effects of Grand Tour on, Nov 59: 94
European attitudes toward, Sep 59: 60, 62
European vs. Asiatic aspects of, Sep 59: 62, 84
Excess in, Sep 60: 129–36
Humboldt, Alexander von, in, Jul 59: 68
As member of Holy Alliance, Mar 63: 5
In Napoleonic Wars: meeting of Alexander I and Napoleon
  at Tilsit, Sep 63: 28–32
Peter the Great, Sep 59: 58–85
Prehistoric wheeled vehicles in, Sep 58: 147
Roosevelt, Theodore, and, Nov 63: 70, 71
World War I aftermath, Jan 59: 115, 121
"RUSSIAN LITERATURE, HISTORY OF," by Prince
  Mirsky, Mar 62: 110
RUSSO, WILLIAM, Jul 59: 21
RUTILIUS NAMATIANUS, CLAUDIUS, on Rome,
  quoted, Jul 61: 45
RYERSON, MARTIN, Sep 60: 102

S

SAADI (MUSLIH-UD-DIN), May 61: 30, Jan 63: 67
SAARINEN, ALINE (MRS. EERO), Jul 60: 78
SAARINEN, EERO, Sep 58: 99, Mar 59: 113, Jul 59: 48,
  Sep 59: 6, 19, Jan 60: 21, 119, 120, Sep 60: 38, May
  62: 16, Jul 62: 8
Interview with, Jul 60: 76–83, 123
Photographs of, Jul 60: 76, Jul 62: 7
Structures designed by. See ILLUSTRATIONS INDEX
Yale University designs, May 59: 84–87
SAARINEN, ELIEL, Jul 60: 77, 78, Jan 63: 12
SABBATAI ZEVI, Mar 60: 125
SABINA, Hadrian's wife, May 63: 34
SABLÉ, MARQUISE DE, Nov 61: 33
SACCO-VANZETTI CASE, Jan 62: 13
SACK, JOHN, photograph of, Mar 63: 27
SACKVILLE-WEST, VICTORIA, Passenger to Teheran,
  quoted, May 59: 41, Mar 61: 28
"SACRED SERVICE," composition by Ernest Bloch, Jul
  59: 21
"SACRE DU PRINTEMPS, LE," composition by Igor
  Stravinsky, Sep 58: 83
SADE, MARQUIS DE, Jan 60: 85, 86, 88, Jan 62: 60, 64
"SAD END OF THE WORD 'FABULOUS,' THE,"
  article by Stephen White, Jan 61: 119
SADLER, A. J., Sep 59: 118, 120
Portrait of, Jul 59: 118
SAFAVID DYNASTY, of Persia, Jan 63: 52 (chart),
  58, 69, 72
SAFED, PALESTINE, Jul 61: 120
SAFIYEH, favorite of Murad III, May 59: 132
SAGAN, FRANÇOISE
Aimez-Vous Brahms? motion picture based on, May 62:
  116
As satirized by "Compass" players, Jan 62: 70
"SAGA OF JENNY," song by Kurt Weill, parody of, Jul

59: 18
SAGAPONACK, N.Y., May 63: 7 (map), 8, 17
SAGE, KAY, painting by, Sep 63: 27
SAGE, LETITIA ANN, Sep 58: 118–19
SAG HARBOR, N.Y., May 63: 7 (map), 9, 24
SAGRES, PORTUGAL, school of Henry the Navigator at,
  Nov 60: 83
SAHARA DESERT, rock paintings of Tassili plateau, May
  59: 70–83, Sep 62: 11, 12, May 63: 43
SAHL, MORT, Jan 61: 123, Jan 62: 66, 68, May 63: 46
On paying cash, quoted, May 62: 119
"SAILOR ON HORSEBACK," television play, Mar 63:
  35
SAINT, EVA MARIE, Mar 63: 35
SAINT-ANGE, MARQUIS DE, Mar 61: 116
ST. ANGELO, FORT. See FORT ST. ANGELO
SAINT AUGUSTINE, FLA., Ponce de Leon Hotel, Jan 61:
  104, 106–7
"SAINT BARTHOLOMEW," painting by Rembrandt,
  Nov 62: 65–66
SAINT CATHERINE'S MOUNT, Mar 60: 89–90, 91
ST. CLAIR, DAVID, Nov 62: 109
ST. DENIS, on Napoleon relic, quoted, Nov 60: 99
SAINT-DENIS, ABBEY OF, Jan 63: 3
SAINT-DENIS, MICHEL, Jan 63: 26
ST. DENIS, RUTH, May 60: 15
SAINTE-BEUVE, CHARLES AUGUSTIN, Nov 58: 89,
  Nov 61: 36
On Mme de Staël and Mme Récamier, quoted, Nov 58: 143,
  144
Portrait of, Nov 58: 89
ST. ELMO, FORT. See FORT ST. ELMO
ST. EMILION, FRANCE, Sep 58: 104–5, 106
SAINT-EXUPÉRY, ANTOINE DE, quoted, Sep 58: 12,
  135, 137
SAINT-GAUDENS, AUGUSTUS, Jul 59: 29
SAINT-GAUDENS, HOMER, May 60: 46
"SAINT GEORGE AND THE DRAGON," painting by
  Raphael, Jul 61: 80, 90, 95, Jul 63: 93, 96; illus, Jul
  61: 87
SAINT GILES FAIR, Oxford, England, Jan 63: 84
"SAINT JEROME," painting by Leonardo da Vinci, Jan
  62: 48
"SAINT JOAN," play by Shaw
Motion picture based on, May 62: 81
Quoted, Mar 62: 89, 93, 94, 96
"ST. JOAN OF THE STOCKYARDS," play, May 62:
  36, 38
"SAINT JOHN," painting by Leonardo da Vinci, Jul 63:
  96
ST. JOHN, KNIGHTS OF. See KNIGHTS OF ST. JOHN
ST. JOHN, OLIVER, Mar 60: 102
ST. JOHN AMBULANCE ASSOCIATION, Mar 61: 70
ST. JOHN'S HOSPITAL, Jerusalem, Mar 61: 48, 51, 52,
  56, 70
"SAINT JOHN THE BAPTIST," painting by Leonardo
  da Vinci, Jul 61: 90, 94, 95
SAINT-LAMBERT, JEAN FRANÇOIS DE, Mar 61:
  117–18
ST. LOUIS, MO., Jefferson National Expansion Memorial,
  Jul 60: 79, 82
SAINT MARK, SQUARE OF, Venice, Jul 61: 3, 56–57
"SAINT MARTIN," painting by Van Dyck, Nov 63: 105
ST. MARY'S COLLEGE OF CALIFORNIA, Jan 59: 19
"SAINT OF BLEECKER STREET, THE," opera, Jan
  60: 15, 122
SAINTPERE, CLAUDE, Sep 58: 63
SAINT PETER, BASILICA OF, Vatican City, Rome, Mar
  59: 124, Jul 60: 50, Jan 62: 22–32, 41–45, 48–49
ST. PETERSBURG, RUSSIA, Sep 59: 79, 81–83
ST.-PIERRE, BERNARDIN DE, Mar 63: 7
SAINT-SIMON, COMTE DE (CLAUDE HENRI DE
  ROUVROY), Mar 62: 35, Mar 63: 7
On Peregrina pearl, quoted, May 63: 95
SAINT-TROPHIME, CATHEDRAL OF, Jul 59: 90, 132
SAITAPHERNES, TIARA OF, Mar 59: 105
SAITO, KIYOSHI, May 60: 113, 114
Print by, May 60: 106
SALACROU, ARMAND, May 61: 91
SALADIN, Mar 61: 56, Jul 62: 56
In painting by Solomon Alexander Hart, Jan 59: 86
Richard I and, Sep 59: 86–91, 130–31
SALAMANCA, DIEGO DE, Sep 58: 114
"SALAMMBÔ," novel by Flaubert, May 61: 53
SALEM, MASS., witch mania in, Nov 59: 63
SALERNO, JOSEPH, Rowayton, Conn., House of Wor-
  ship, designed by, Nov 62: 70–73; illus, Nov 62: 70–71
SALINGER, J. D., Jul 59: 71, Jul 60: 121, Mar 62:
  84, May 62: 100–7, Mar 63: 31, Jul 63: 71, 75
Drawing of, May 62: 100
Kazin, Alfred, quoted on, Jul 62: 102
"Seymour, an Introduction," Mar 61: 42–43, 44, 46
SALINGER, PIERRE, Sep 61: 10
Photographs of, Sep 61: 8
SALISBURY, CONN., May 60: 13 (map), 18

SALK, JONAS, Sep 62: 62
SALK INSTITUTE FOR BIOLOGY, Torrey Pines, Calif.,
  Sep 62: 62
SALLES, GEORGES, on Alexander Calder, quoted, Nov
  62: 16
"SALOME," opera, Nov 58: 120
SALON DES REFUSÉS, May 63: 70
SALONS OF PARIS, Nov 61: 32–37
SALTER, GEORGE, Sep 59: 128
SALTIKOV, COUNTESS, Sep 60: 130
SALT LAKE CITY, UTAH, visit of Richard Francis Bur-
  ton, Jul 63: 114–16, 117
SALTONSTALL, LEVERETT, Jul 62: 34
SALUCES, THOMAS DE, Mar 61: 50
SALVI, NICOLA, May 62: 15
SALZBURG, AUSTRIA
Music festival, Mar 59: 85
Witch burning in, Nov 59: 61
SAMOA, Jan 60: 124, 125
SAMUELY, F. J., Sep 59: 19
"SAMURAI, WITH SWORD, WON'T TRAVEL," article
  by Jean Stafford, May 61: 114–15
SANCHO, KING OF LEÓN, Sep 62: 79
"SANCTUARY," motion picture Sep 60: 88
SAND, GEORGE, Nov 61: 36, Jan 62: 111, May 61: 81,
  Sep 62: 20
Frédéric Chopin by Franz Liszt quoted on, May 63: 109–
  10
In painting by Joseph Danhauser, May 61: 84–85
Portraits of, May 61: 80, 81
"SANDBOX, THE," play, Sep 62: 34–35 (illus), 37, 38–
  39 (illus), 40
SANDBURG, CARL, Jul 63: 69
On present day, quoted, Jul 60: 67
"SAND CASTLE, THE," motion picture, reviewed, Jul
  61: 106–7
SAND CASTLES, Jul 61: 108–9
SANDER, AUGUST, Mar 60: 43
"Timeless Teutons," album of photographs by, Mar 60:
  41–45
SANDERS, CHRISTOPHER, painting by, May 62: 77
SANDERS, GEORGE, Sep 63: 75
SANDERSON, IVAN T., "A Passion for Ivory," article by,
  May 60: 88–95, 120–21
"SAND GARDEN," print by Okiie Hashimoto, May 60:
  113–14; illus, May 60: 110
SAN DIEGO, CALIF., Hotel del Coronado, Jan 61: 104,
  109
SANDO, GYORGY, Jan 62: 14
SANDS, DIANA, May 63: 108
SANDWICH, EARL OF (JOHN MONTAGU), May 60:
  128
SANDYS, LORD, Nov 58: 52
SAN FRANCISCO, CALIF.
Actor's Workshop, Jan 62: 9, 13
Alcoholism in, Nov 63: 106
Architecture, Jan 59: 8–12
Beat Generation of, Sep 58: 38–43
Billboard industry and, May 61: 5
Federal court and office building, Jan 60: 120
Fine arts, Jan 59: 12–15
Flowering of, Jan 59: 4–23
Hilton Hotel, Mar 63: 117
Literature, Jan 59: 16–19
Maiden Lane, Jul 59: 10, 13
Masonic Memorial Temple, Jan 60: 120
Music in, in 1920's and 1930's, Jul 60: 74–75
Performing arts, Jan 59: 20–23
SAN FRANCISCO BALLET, Jan 59: 6
SAN FRANCISCO MUSEUM OF ART, Jan 59: 4–5, 13
SAN FRANCISCO OPERA HOUSE, Jan 59: 6
SAN FRANCISCO STATE COLLEGE, Jan 59: 19, Mar
  60: 71
SAN FRANCISCO SYMPHONY, Jan 59: 6, 21, 22
SANITATION
In ancient Rome, May 60: 39–41, Jul 61: 45
In earliest cities, Jul 61: 41
Turkish hammams, Sep 60: 125–26
In U.S. and U.S.S.R. compared, Jul 62: 116
"SANJURO TSUBAKE," motion picture, Jul 62: 46–47
"SANSHIRO SUGATA," motion picture, Jul 62: 43
SANTA CHIARA, CONVENT OF, Jan 60: 68
SANTA CRUZ, MARQUÉS DE, Jul 63: 50, 53, 57, 58
SANTAYANA, GEORGE, quoted
On Creation and Fall, Mar 62: 9
On critic's values, Jul 62: 103
On Englishmen, Jan 60: 119
SANT' ELIA, ANTONIO, city design by, Mar 62: 39;
  illus, Mar 62: 39
SANTIAGO DE COMPOSTELA, SPAIN, Moslem raid on
  shrine of St. James, Sep 62: 82
SANTIAGO MATAMOROS, Nov 61: 111
SANZI, GIOVANNI, Jan 60: 68
SANZI, RAPHAEL. See RAPHAEL
SAOLOTE, QUEEN OF TONGA, in painting by Feliks

Topolski, Nov 60: 132–33
SAPHADIN, Jan 59: 89, 90, 91, 130, 131
SAPIR, EDWARD, Jul 63: 44
SAPPHO, Sep 63: 85
SARAB. See TEPE SARAB
SARACENS. See MOSLEMS
SARA M. ROBY FOUNDATION, Sep 58: 109–10
SARASWATHI, BALA, Sep 63: 66, 72
  Photograph of, Sep 63: 66
SARATOGA, N.Y., Yaddo colony, Mar 63: 27, 32
SARDIS, ancient city in Asia Minor, Sep 63: 82–89
SARDOU, VICTORIEN, Nov 61: 36
SARGEANT, WINTHROP, articles by
  "I Hear America Singing—Abroad," Nov 61: 76–81
  "New Life in the Old Opera House," Jan 60: 12–17, 122–23
SARGENT, JOHN SINGER, Jan 59: 99, Sep 60: 102, Jul 63: 18
  Gardner, Isabella Stewart, and, Jul 59: 29, 30, 133, 134
  Works by. See ILLUSTRATIONS INDEX
SARGENT, MALCOLM, photograph of, May 62: 59
SARK, ENGLAND, Mar 61: 32–33
SARNOFF RESEARCH CENTER. See DAVID SARNOFF RESEARCH CENTER
SAROYAN, WILLIAM, Jan 59: 6, 7, Sep 59: 124, Sep 63: 79
  Quoted: on ideal repertory, Jan 63: 107; on *Waiting for Godot*, Nov 58: 64
SARRAUTE, NATHALIE, Jan 62: 97–99
  Portrait of, Jan 62: 99
SARTO, ANDREA DEL, Jul 61: 95, Jul 63: 94
SARTRE, JEAN-PAUL, Nov 61: 99, 115, Jan 62: 97, 112
  And Camus, Albert, Nov 59: 69, 72
  Ionesco, Eugène, quoted on, May 61: 93
  Kean, Mar 62: 13, 117, 118, 119
  No Exit (*Huis Clos*), Jul 61: 117, Nov 62: 111, Mar 63: 107
  Quoted: on Calder, Alexander, Nov 62: 12; on novel, Jan 62: 96; on Right Wing plays, Jan 63: 33; on Sarraute, Nathalie, Jan 62: 98
SASAKI, RUTH FULLER, Jul 59: 72, 73, 127
SASANIAN DYNASTY, of Persia, Jan 63: 49–52, 58
SASKATCHEWAN, childhood of Wallace Stegner in, Sep 62: 94–95
SASSOON, SIEGFRIED, Jan 62: 51
SASSUOLO DA PRATO, Jan 60: 61
SATELLITES, COMMUNICATIONS, social consequences of, Jan 62: 16–21
SATIE, ERIK, Igor Stravinsky quoted on, Sep 58: 83
"SATORI," Jul 59: 71, 73, 74, 127
SATTERLEE, NICHOLAS, Jan 60: 21
"SATURDAY NIGHT," musical, Jul 61: 98
"SATURDAY NIGHT AND SUNDAY MORNING," motion picture, Mar 63: 36
"SATURDAY REVIEW," periodical, Mar 59: 112
SAUGUET, HENRI, Mar 61: 72
SAULNIER, RAYMOND J., Jul 60: 67, 68, 71
SAUSALITO, CALIF., Jan 59: 7
SAUSSURE, FERDINAND DE, Jul 63: 44
"SAVAGE EYE, THE," motion picture, Mar 61: 14, 19
"SAVAGE HITS BACK, THE," book by Julius E. Lips, quoted, Sep 60: 11–12
SAVARY, ANNE JEAN MARIE RENÉ, Nov 58: 145
SAVILLE, VICTOR, Nov 61: 115
SAVONAROLA, GIROLAMO, Jan 62: 31
SAVOY, ITALY, and Thirty Years' War, Nov 62: 34, 35, 36, 37
SAVOY, DUKES OF, Sep 61: 38
SAVOY HOTEL, London, May 61: 125–26
SAWYER, RALPH, May 59: 9
SAXONS, in Britain, May 60: 41
SAYERS, DOROTHY, Sep 63: 7
SAYLER, OLIVER M., on cost of repertory, quoted, Jan 63: 108
SAYN-WITTGENSTEIN, CAROLYNE, PRINCESS, May 63: 109–10
SAYRE, NORA, and ROBERT B. SILVERS, "An Interview with Paddy Chayefsky," article by, Sep 60: 49–56
SCALA, ALESSANDRA, Jan 60: 62
SCARCITY ECONOMY, vs. abundance economy, Jul 60: 67
"SCARF, THE," opera, Jan 60: 123
"SCARLET LETTER, THE," novel by Nathaniel Hawthorne, Mar 59: 15
"SCARLET SISTER MARY," novel by Julia Peterkin, Jul 63: 71
SCARRON, PAUL, Jul 63: 83
SCARSDALE, LORD, Nov 58: 47
SCHAEFFER, PIERRE, Jan 59: 54
  Photograph of, Jan 59: 53
SCHALK, FRANZ, Nov 58: 25
SCHANZ, WENZL, Mar 62: 81
SCHAPIRO, MEYER, Sep 59: 97
SCHAWINSKY, XANTI, Nov 61: 73, Nov 59: 48
  Photograph of, Nov 61: 62
"SCHEHEREZADE," ballet, Jan 61: 27

SCHEPER, HINNERK, Nov 61: 73
  Photograph of, Nov 61: 58
SCHERCHEN, HERMANN, Jan 59: 52
SCHEUER, JAMES H., Nov 59: 109
SCHEVILLE, JAMES, Jan 59: 18
SCHICK, CONRAD, Nov 59: 5
SCHILLER, JOHANN CHRISTOPH FRIEDRICH VON, May 61: 84, Mar 62: 97
  Portrait of, May 61: 64
SCHINKEL, KARL FRIEDRICH, Mar 62: 62
SCHIPPER, EMIL, Sep 59: 57
SCHLEICH, HANS, reliquary executed by, May 59: 2, 3
SCHLEIERMACHER, FRIEDRICH E. D., quoted, Sep 63: 5
SCHLEMMER, OSKAR, Nov 61: 61, 62, 68, 71, 73
  Photograph of, Nov 61: 59
  Works by, Nov 61: 63
SCHLESINGER, ARTHUR M., JR., Nov 60: 119, Sep 61: 10
SCHLESINGER, HENRI, painting by, Mar 60: 62
SCHLESINGER, HERBERT, Sep 59: 122
SCHLESINGER, MARION (MRS. ARTHUR M., JR.), Sep 61: 10
SCHLIEMANN, HEINRICH, Jan 61: 77, 78, 91, 94
  Portrait of, Jan 61: 76
SCHMIDT, JOOST, Nov 61: 73
  Photograph of, Nov 61: 58
SCHMIDT, WILLIAM M., on automobile design, quoted, Mar 59: 116
SCHNABEL, ARTUR, Jan 60: 76, 79, 81, Sep 61: 83, 84
  Glenn Gould quoted on, Jan 62: 91, 93
SCHNEIDER, ALAN, Sep 60: 114, Jan 62: 9, 14
  Measure for Measure directed by, Nov 60: 117, 118
SCHNEIDER, ALEXANDER, Sep 61: 87
  Photographs of, Sep 61: 86, Nov 62: 44
  On Stern, Isaac, quoted, Jul 60: 127
SCHNEIDER, MISCHA, photograph of, Nov 62: 44
SCHNEIDER, PIERRE, articles by
  "Miró," Mar 59: 70–81, 126–27
  "Poussin," Mar 61: 76–93
  "Simple Seer, The," Mar 62: 14–27
  "Well-Loved River, The," Jul 62: 52–79
SCHNEIDER-ESLEBEN, PAUL, Mannesmann building, designed by, Nov 60: 124, 125; illus, Nov 60: 12–13
SCHNITGER, ARP, Mar 60: 76, 80
SCHOENBERG, ARNOLD, Jan 59: 21, Sep 61: 83–84, 86, Jan 63: 77
SCHOLANDER, SVEN, May 60: 17
"SCHOLAR ADVENTURERS, THE," book by Richard D. Altick, Mar 59: 107 (note)
"SCHOLARS, THE," poem by William Butler Yeats, quoted, Jan 59: 19
SCHONBERG, HAROLD C.
  "Nice and Abstruse Game, A," article by, Jan 62: 114–20
  On Philharmonic Hall programs, quoted, Jul 62: 8
SCHONGAU, GERMANY, witch mania in, Nov 59: 61
"SCHOOL FOR FATHERS, THE," play, Nov 60: 54
"SCHOOL FOR WIVES, THE," play, Jan 60: 96
SCHOPENHAUER, ARTHUR, May 61: 66
  On arts, quoted, Sep 60: 34
SCHORER, MARK, Jan 59: 19
  On painting by Elmer Bischoff, quoted, Jul 60: 115
SCHOSTAL, JOSEF, Sep 59: 56
SCHOUTEN, WILLEM, Sep 58: 19
"SCHRAUBTHALER," Sep 61: 3; illus, Sep 61: 2
SCHROETER, REBECCA, Mar 62: 82
SCHUBERT, FRANZ, May 61: 66
  Chamber music of, Nov 62: 46, 47; B flat trio, Jan 62: 116
  Portrait of, May 61: 66
SCHUKL CANNERY, Sunnyvale, Calif., Jan 59: 8
SCHULBERG, BUDD, Sep 59: 118
SCHUMAN, WILLIAM, Jul 62: 7, 11
  Portrait of, Jul 62: 9
SCHUMANN, CLARA, on Franz Liszt, quoted, Jan 60: 81
SCHUMANN, ELISABETH, Jan 61: 27
SCHUMANN, ROBERT
  Chamber music of, Nov 62: 46
  Gould, Glenn, quoted on, Jan 62: 92
SCHUMANN-HEINK, ERNESTINE, Sep 59: 53, 54
SCHUPPANZIGH, IGNAZ, Nov 62: 44, 46
SCHUURMAN, ANNA MARIA VAN, Sep 58: 26
  Portrait of, Sep 58: 28
SCHUYLER, JAMES, Sep 61: 119
SCHWARTZ, DELMORE, Sep 61: 117
SCHWARZENBERG, KARL PHILIPP VON, Nov 62: 44
SCHWEITZER, ALBERT, Sep 58: 102, 138–39, Mar 60: 74, 76
"SCHWOURTZ, LE," play, May 61: 95
SCIENCE
  In Age of Leisure, Nov 63: 107, 108–9
  Vs. classical tradition, in education, Nov 60: 18, 21, 23–24
  Ghana claim to origin of chemistry, Jan 63: 117
  Humboldt, Alexander von, as scientist, Jul 59: 56–69, 128

  IQ and, Mar 62: 72–73
  Jargon of, Jul 63: 38
  In Moslem Spain, Sep 62: 89, 92
  As motivation in adventure, Sep 58: 138
  Pascal's contributions, Jan 63: 97, 99–100
  In 17th-century Holland, Sep 58: 23
  Social responsibilities of scientists, Jul 61: 4–9
  Wedgwood, Josiah, and his friends as exponents of, May 59: 88–97, 128–30
SCIENCE FICTION, May 61: 53
  Of Lewis, C. S., May 59: 64–67, 125–27
  Utopia in, Mar 63: 79
"SCIENTIFIC AMERICAN," journal, investigation of "Margery," Jan 59: 108, 109
"SCIENTISTS, THE," novel by Eleazar Lipsky, Sep 60: 118
SCOFIELD, PAUL, May 62: 110, Nov 62: 106
  Photograph of, May 62: 111
SCOT, MICHAEL, Sep 62: 89
SCOT, REGINALD, Nov 59: 60
SCOTLAND
  Mary, Queen of Scots, and John Knox, Jul 63: 28–32
  Witch mania in, Nov 59: 58, 59, 61, 62–63
SCOTT, GEORGE C., Nov 60: 116, Jul 60: 93, May 63: 107
  Portrait of, Jul 60: 92
SCOTT, ROBERT FALCON, Sep 58: 9, 139
  Photograph of, Sep 58: 9
SCOTT, WALTER, Nov 58: 107, Jan 59: 97, Mar 59: 92, May 61: 68, 70
  Quoted: on pictures collected by George IV, Jul 63: 92; on Watt, James, May 59: 92, 94
  Talisman, The, quoted, Jan 59: 86
SCOTT, WINFIELD TOWNLEY, "The Errand from My Heart—," article by, Jul 61: 100–5
SCOTTISH NATIONAL PLAYERS, Tyrone Guthrie with, Nov 63: 35
"SCREWTAPE LETTERS, THE," book by C. S. Lewis, Jan 59: 122, May 59: 66, 67, 125
SCRIABIN, ALEXANDER, Nov 62: 80, May 63: 109
SCRIPTURES, HEBREW, Septuagint manuscript, Nov 62: 78
SCRUGGS, EARL, Sep 62: 66
SCUDÉRY, MAGDELEINE DE, Nov 61: 32–33, Jul 63: 83
  Clélie, Jan 62: 58
  Portrait of, Nov 61: 34
SCULL, MR. and MRS. ROBERT, May 61: 119
SCULPTURE
  Aegina marbles, Sep 59: 30–49
  Of African cultures, Mar 63: 40, 44, 46–53, 56–58
  Of Angkor, Jan 59: 60–81
  Of Aphrodisias, Mar 63: 98–99, 100
  And architecture, Sep 59: 18–19
  Birth of an art form, Jan 59: 144
  Bronze statues found at Piraeus, Mar 60: 6–11
  Calder, Alexander, Nov 62: 10–17
  From Çatal Hüyük, Nov 63: 66–67
  Cave-dwellers of Safadi and Abu Matar, and their ivory figurines, Jan 62: 72–75
  In Cave of Tiberius, May 59: 102–7, 122–24
  Etruscan, May 60: 77; illus, Mar 60: 76, 77, 78–79
  Ford Foundation aid to, Jan 62: 8–9
  Gargoyles from junk, Mar 61: 104–13
  Gislebertus, Master of Autun, Sep 61: 46–57
  Gods in, Nov 58: 4–17, 112–13
  Of Hadrian's Villa, May 63: 35–36, 37
  In ivory, May 60: 89, 94, 120–21
  Marisol's mannequins, Mar 63: 102–4
  From Marlik, Iran, Nov 62: 102–4
  Moore, Henry, Nov 60: 102–15
  Mourners of Dijon, Sep 58: 62–63
  Noguchi, Isamu, Mar 60: 104–12
  Persian, Jan 63: 44, 49
  Portraiture in, Jan 59: 99, 102
  Roman: at Arles, Jul 59: 98, 129; imperial portrait busts, Sep 63: 34–35
  In San Francisco Bay Region, Jan 59: 14
  Shiva Nataraja figures, Sep 63: 68, 72; illus, Sep 63: 64, 65
  Of southern Gaul, Jul 59: 93–95
  Sumerian: new treasures from Nippur, Nov 61: 84–87
  Underwater discoveries, Nov 58: 66–77
  Vatican masterpieces, Jan 62: 45, 48; illus, Jan 62: 22, 36, 46–47, 48
  At World's Columbian Exposition, Sep 60: 127
SCYLLA MYTH, sculptural prototype, May 59: 122, 123–24
SCYTHIANS, Jan 60: 112
"SEABIRD IN THE RAIN," drawing by Morris Graves, Jul 60: 105; illus, Jul 60: 108–9
SEABORG, GLENN T., quoted, May 63: 29
SEABURY, PAUL, on teaching assistants, quoted, Sep 62: 16
SEA COW, as source of mermaid legend, Jan 60: 135
SEAGRAM, SONS OF, buildings, Nov 60: 16, 124, 125

SEAGRAM BUILDING, New York City, Sep 59: 6–7, Sep 60: 39, Nov 60: 16

SEAGRAM DISTILLERS, Sep 58: 110

SEAL, artifact, as evidence of Bronze Age trade, Jul 60: 86–87

SEAL, mammal, as source of mermaid legend, Jan 60: 135

SEAL, ELIZABETH, photograph of, May 61: 50

SEA MONSTERS, Nov 58: 70

"SEA OIL AND SOAPSTONE," illustrated feature, Mar 63: 120

SEARLE, RONALD, May 59: 109, 110
"Paris Preserved," portfolio of drawings by, Mar 62: 120–28

SEARS, PAUL B., on man's responsibility toward nature, quoted, Mar 60: 16

"SEATED WOMAN," painting by Picasso, Nov 61: 12; illus, Nov 61: 9

SEATTLE, WASH.
Billboards in, May 61: 5
Century 21 Exposition, May 62: 16

SEAVER, GEORGE, on Antarctic exploration, quoted, Sep 58: 9

SEBERG, JEAN, May 62: 81
Photograph of, May 62: 80

"SECOND AVENUE WITH T H E," painting by Larry Rivers, Sep 59: 95, 100–1; illus Sep 59: 101

"SECOND CITY, THE." See "FROM THE SECOND CITY"

"SECRETS OF SAN MEN, THE," article by Nigel Cameron with photographs by Brian Brake, Jan 61: 4–13, 124

"SECRETS OF THE HORIZON," painting by René Magritte, Jan 62: 82; illus, Jan 62: 86

SEEGER, PETE, Sep 62: 66

"SEEING SPOTS?" illustrated feature, Sep 61: 66–67

"SEE MANHATTAN WHILE IT LASTS: A WALKING TOUR," text by Oliver Jensen, with drawings by John Rombola, May 63: 117–20

SEGESTA, ITALY, Greek temple at, Sep 61: 24

SEGONZAC, DUNOYER DE, May 62: 78

SEGRAIS, JEAN REGNAULT DE, Nov 61: 34

SEIDL, ANTON, Nov 58: 119–20

SEIFFERT, MARJORIE ALLEN, as "Elijah Hay," May 60: 43, 47

SEINE RIVER, May 61: 4, Jul 62: 52–79

SELDEN, JOHN, Nov 59: 60

SELDES, GILBERT, as critic of mass culture, Jan 60: 6–7, 10

SELEUCUS and SELEUCIDS, Sep 63: 86

"SELF-PORTRAIT," painting by Dürer, Jul 61: 95, Jul 63: 93

"SELF-PORTRAIT," painting by Rubens, Jul 61: 94, Jul 63: 94

SELFRIDGE, GORDON, Nov 60: 13

SELIM I, SULTAN OF TURKEY (SELIM THE GRIM), May 59: 59, Jul 63: 50

SELIM II, SULTAN OF TURKEY (SELIM THE SOT), May 59: 135

SELIM III, SULTAN OF TURKEY, May 59: 62

SELJUK TURKS
Attacks on Byzantine Empire, Nov 63: 28, 31
Invasion of Persia, Jan 63: 52 (chart), 53

SELLERS, PETER, Mar 62: 110, Jan 63: 38

SELZ, PETER, on abstract expressionism, quoted, Sep 60: 122

SEMANTICS, *The Measurement of Meaning*, book by Charles E. Osgood, Mar 60: 122

SEMBRICH, MARCELLA, Sep 59: 54

SENATE OFFICE BUILDING, Washington, D.C., Jan 60: 21

SENECA, LUCIUS ANNAEUS
Memorandum from, to Tennessee Williams, May 59: 54–55
Quoted: on slaves, May 62: 48; on Tuscans, May 60: 61
In Renaissance curriculum, Jan 60: 62

SENNETT, MAX, Jan 62: 109

SENOFSKY, BERYL, Jan 60: 76

"SENSE AND NONSENSE," article by Gilbert Highet, Sep 58: 129–31

SENZAKI, NYOGEN, Jul 59: 72, 126

SERAGLIO OF OTTOMAN SULTANS, May 59: 56–63, 131–35

SERANGELI, GIOACCHINO, painting by, Sep 60: 68

"SERGEANT, THE," novel by Dennis Murphy, Jan 59: 18, Mar 59: 118, 119

SERIAL TECHNIQUE, in music, Sep 60: 32
Total serialism, Jan 63: 77–78

"SERIOUS CALL TO A DEVOUT AND HOLY LIFE," book by William Law, Jan 60: 117

"SERJEANT MUSGRAVE'S DANCE," play, Jul 62: 91, 92–93, 94, Jan 63: 31, 32

SERKIN, PETER, Sep 61: 87

SERKIN, RUDOLF, Jan 60: 76, 79, 81, Sep 61: 82–87
Photographs of, Sep 61: 82, 84, 86, 87

SERT, JOSÉ LUIS, Mar 59: 127
Building designed by, Mar 59: 75

SÉRUSIER, PAUL, Mar 62: 15

"SERVANT OF TWO MASTERS," play, Mar 61: 47

SERVIEN, COMTE DE, Jul 63: 82

SESSHU, Jul 59: 71
Painting by, Jul 59: 70

SESSIONS, ROGER, Jan 59: 21, Jul 59: 20–21
Symphony No. 2, Igor Stravinsky quoted on, Sep 58: 132

"SET THIS HOUSE ON FIRE," novel by William Styron, May 60: 28

SEURAT, GEORGES, painting by, Sep 60: 80

"SEVEN DEADLY SINS, THE," ballet, Nov 59: 56

"SEVEN DEADLY SINS, THE," cycle of plays by Thornton Wilder, Mar 60: 121

"SEVEN GOTHIC TALES," book by Isak Dinesen, Sep 59: 111

"SEVEN KEYBOARD INSURGENTS," article by Joseph Roddy, Jan 60: 74–81

"SEVEN PILLARS OF WISDOM," book by T. E. Lawrence, Jul 62: 109

"SEVEN SAMURAI," motion picture, May 61: 114–15, Jul 62: 46

"SEVENTEEN," magazine, advertising in, Nov 59: 114, 116

SEVERN, JOSEPH, painting by, May 61: 58–59

SEVERUD, FRED, Mar 59: 123

SÉVIGNÉ, MME DE, Nov 61: 33, 34

SEWALL, SAMUEL, Mar 60: 124–25
On Plum Island, Mass., quoted, Mar 60: 15

SEWARD, ANNA
As member of Josiah Wedgwood's group, May 59: 90–96, 128–30
Portrait of, May 59: 90

SEWARD, WILLIAM HENRY, on cupidity of pioneer, quoted, Sep 59: 10

SEYMOUR, THOMAS, Sep 59: 132

"SEYMOUR, AN INTRODUCTION," story by J. D. Salinger, Mar 61: 42–43, 44, 46, May 62: 105–6, 107

SFORZA, BATTISTA, Jan 60: 68
Portrait of, Jan 60: 72

SFORZA, FRANCESCO, Nov 61: 88

SFORZA, LUDOVICO, Jan 60: 66

SHACKLETON, ERNEST, Sep 58: 8, 9–10

"SHADOW OF HEROES," play, Jan 62: 103

"SHADOWS," motion picture, Mar 61: 16, 19

SHAH JAHAN, EMPEROR OF HINDUSTAN, Mar 61: 21, May 62: 15, 84

SHAHN, BEN, Sep 58: 110, 113, Jul 62: 13, 15
"Gallic Laughter of André François, The," article by, May 59: 108–21
Paintings by, Sep 58: 111, Jul 62: 12

"SHAH NAMEH," Persian epic, Jan 63: 51, 62, 67, 72

SHAKESPEARE, WILLIAM
Attitude toward nature, Mar 60: 14
As Baroque poet, Jul 60: 38, 42, 50, 64
Bowdler's *The Family Shakespeare,* Sep 62: 68–71
Chayefsky, Paddy, quoted on, Sep 60: 53, 54
Hamlet, Sep 62: 33, 36, Sep 63: 104; quoted, May 59: 41; Tyrone Guthrie Theatre production, Nov 63: 38–39, 40, 41
Handwriting of, Sep 59: 126
Hemingway, Ernest, quoted on, Jan 59: 132, 133
Henry V, Sep 60: 61
Historical plays, Archibald MacLeish quoted on, Jan 60: 50
Humor in tragedies of, Mar 63: 106–7
On Italic handwriting, quoted, Sep 59: 127
Joan of Arc of, Mar 62: 95
King Lear, Jul 59: 47, May 60: 101
Macbeth, Japanese motion picture based on, Jul 62: 44
Merry Wives of Windsor, The, quoted, Nov 62: 94
Portraits of, Sep 62: 69, 71
Richard III, Jan 61: 29–30
Royal crowns in plays of, May 63: 92
Shakespeareana handled by A. S. W. Rosenbach, Nov 60: 97, 98–99, 100–1
Shylock, riddle of, Jan 60: 89–96
Tempest, The, Isak Dinesen quoted on, Sep 59: 111
Theatre of, Jul 59: 44–45, 46
Twelfth Night, quoted, Mar 62: 13
Use of words in poetry of, Mar 63: 84, 88
Voltaire's opinion of, May 61: 61
"Way the French Need Shakespeare," article by Jean-Louis Barrault, Sep 61: 102–9
Winter's Tale, The, Jan 63: 88

SHAKESPEARE FESTIVAL OF NEW YORK, Nov 60: 116–18, Jan 63: 107, 108

SHAKESPEARE FESTIVAL THEATRES. See AMERICAN SHAKESPEARE FESTIVAL THEATRE; STRATFORD, ONT.; FESTIVAL THEATRE

SHALIMAR, GARDENS OF, Mar 61: 31, 32

SHAN CH'IU KAI, Nov 60: 32

SHANNON, CLAUDE, Jul 59: 107, Mar 60: 48–49

SHAPERO, HAROLD, Mar 63: 29

"SHAPES FROM THE ANCIENT EARTH," statues found at Çatal Hüyük, Turkey, Nov 63: 66–67

SHAPIRO, KARL, Nov 61: 105, Jan 62: 14, Jul 63: 69

SHAPIRO, MEYER, on Jackson Pollock, quoted, Sep 60: 121–22

SHAPLEY, HARLOW, *Of Stars and Men,* quoted, Jan 59: 28, 123

SHAPUR I, KING OF PERSIA, Jan 63: 51, 52

SHAW, DAVE, Sep 60: 51

SHAW, GEORGE BERNARD, Mar 59: 88, Jul 59: 47–48, Nov 60: 128, Jul 61: 116, 118, Mar 62: 73, May 62: 92, Mar 63: 6, Jul 63: 13, 75
Biography by Hesketh Pearson, writing of, Nov 58: 18–21, 134–37
As caricatured and commented upon by Max Beerbohm, May 61: 34, 35, 37, 38, 40
Defense of Ibsen, Jan 62: 106–7, 108
And Don Juan story, Jan 62: 61–62, 62–63
Heartbreak House, Jul 63: 87
Major Barbara, Jan 63: 88
Portrait of, Nov 58: 19
Pygmalion, Sep 58: 144
Quoted: Sep 60: 39; on Americans, May 60: 5–6; on Patti, Adelina, Sep 59: 54; on youth, Mar 63: 32
Saint Joan: motion picture based on, May 62: 81; quoted, Mar 62: 89, 93, 94, 96

SHAW, MRS. GEORGE BERNARD, on Erica Cotterill, quoted, Nov 58: 135–36

SHAW, GLEN BYAM, May 62: 112

SHAW, HOWARD, *The Crime of Giovanni Venturi,* Nov 60: 85

SHAW, IRWIN, *The Gentle People,* Nov 62: 106

SHAW, ROBERT, May 62: 112

SHAWN, TED, May 60: 15
Photograph of, May 60: 14

SHCHUKINE, SERGEI I., Nov 61: 10

SHEAR, THEODORE LESLIE, Sep 63: 86

SHEBA, KINGDOM OF, Nov 59: 118, 119

SHEELER, CHARLES, Jul 63: 18

SHEFFIELD, ENGLAND, May 60: 94

SHEFFIELD, MRS. E. CHAPPELL, on Eugene O'Neill's family, quoted, Mar 60: 31–32

"SHEIKS AND SHEBAS, DANCE NO MORE," article by Francis Russell, Jul 63: 118–19

SHELL BUILDING, London, Nov 60: 124–25

SHELLEY, MARY WOLLSTONECRAFT (MARY GODWIN), Nov 60: 97

SHELLEY, PERCY BYSSHE, Sep 58: 139, May 61: 58–59, 65, Mar 62: 75, 116, Nov 63: 46–47
"Mont Blanc," Mar 60: 14
"Ozymandias of Egypt," quoted, Jul 60: 8
Portraits of, May 61: 58–59, Nov 63: 47
Queen Mab, copy in H. B. Smith's "Sentimental Library," Nov 60: 97
Quoted: on Byron, May 63: 85; on poets, Nov 59: 66; on radiance of eternity, Nov 63: 54

SHELTON, ROBERT, on Joan Baez, quoted, Sep 62: 66

SHEPHERD, DAVID, Jan 62: 66–70
Photograph of, Jan 62: 67

"SHEPHERD'S CHAMELEON, THE," play by Eugène Ionesco, May 61: 95
Excerpt from, May 61: 92, 94, 96

"SHEPHERDS OF ARCADY," painting by Poussin, Mar 61: 89

SHEPLEY, HENRY R., Jan 60: 119, Jul 62: 8

SHEPPARD, EUGENIA, Jul 60: 121–22

SHERATON MOTOR INN, New York City, Mar 63: 117

SHERIDAN, ELIZABETH ANN (MRS. RICHARD BRINSLEY), May 60: 101

SHERIDAN, RICHARD BRINSLEY, Mar 59: 92, 125, Jul 59: 47, May 60: 101

SHERMAN, CONN., May 60: 13 (map), 22, 25

SHERMAN, GEORGE, Jul 60: 71
On David Hurst, quoted, Jan 61: 101

SHERRARD, PHILIP, "Byzantium: The Other Half of the World," article by, Nov 63: 4–34

SHERRINGTON, CHARLES, Sep 63: 101

SHERWOOD, PHILIP BURR, Sep 59: 19

SHERWOOD, ROBERT, Nov 58: 65, Jul 63: 119
Biography by John Mason Brown, excerpts from, May 62: 4–9, Jul 62: 32–41
Caricature of, Jul 62: 32
Portrait of, May 62: 4

SHERWOOD, MILLS AND SMITH, Sep 59: 19

SHEVCHENKO, TARAS, Sep 61: 13

SHIA SECT, in Persia, Jan 63: 59, 69

SHIFRIN, SEYMOUR, Jan 59: 21

SHIKLER, AARON, Jan 59: 99, 105
In group painting, Sep 60: 107
Painting by, Jan 59: 101

SHINAGAWA, TAKUMI, May 60: 114
Print by, May 60: 103

SHINNECOCK INDIANS, May 63: 8

"SHIPBUILDER AND HIS WIFE," painting by Rembrandt, Jul 63: 106; illus, Jul 63: 95

SHIPS and SHIPPING
Brunel, I. K., ships designed by, Jan 59: 40–43, 136
Bullion salvaged, Nov 58: 77

Galleass introduced, July 63: 50, 52, 57, 58
In Golden Age of Dutch Republic, Sep 58: 19–20
Great Western-Sirius race, Jan 59: 40–41
Roman, shown in bas-relief, Nov 58: 76–77
SHIPTON, ERIC, Sep 58: 135, 139
SHIRER, WILLIAM L., *The Rise and Fall of the Third Reich*, reviewed, Nov 60: 119–21
SHIVA, myths of, and dance of India, Sep 63: 64–73
"SHOEMAKER'S HOLIDAY, THE," play, Jul 63: 87
"SHOESHINE," motion picture, May 59: 99, Mar 61: 98, 100
"SHOOT THE PIANO-PLAYER," motion picture, May 63: 111
SHOPPING CENTERS, street furniture of, Nov 59: 107, 108
"SHOPPING WITH KAFKA," article by John Keats, Mar 59: 110–11
"SHOREBIRDS," drawing by Morris Graves, Jul 60: 105; illus, Jul 60: 106–7
SHORTHAND, Ghana claim to invention of, Jan 63: 116, 117
"SHORT HAPPY LIFE, A," play, Jan 62: 103
"SHORT HISTORY OF WHEELED VEHICLES, A," article by E. M. Jope and V. Gordon Childe, Sep 58: 146–51
"SHOW BOAT," musical, Sep 58: 59, Jan 60: 14
SHREVEPORT, LA., theatre of Orlin and Irene Corey, Jan 63: 88
SHREWSBURY, COUNTESS OF. See ELIZABETH, COUNTESS OF SHREWSBURY
SHRINER, HERB, May 63: 46
SHRIVER, R. SARGENT, JR., Sep 61: 10
SHURTLEFF, MICHAEL, *Call Me by My Rightful Name*, Jul 61: 118
SHYLOCK, Jan 60: 89–96
SIBELIUS, JEAN, May 63: 109
SIBYLLA, QUEEN OF JERUSALEM, Jan 59: 88
SICA, VITTORIO DE, Mar 61: 98, 99–100
"How They Live and Die in Naples," text by, with photographs by Herbert List, Sep 63: 49–59
Photographs of, Mar 61: 99, Sep 63: 49
SICANS, Sep 61: 23
SICELS, Sep 61: 22, 23, 24
SICILIAN VESPERS, Sep 61: 32, 34, 37
SICILY
Chronology, Sep 61: 24
History and monuments of, Sep 61: 20–45
Maps, Sep 61: 24–25
People of, Sep 61: 42–43, 44
"SICILY," article by M. I. Finley and D. Mack Smith, Sep 61: 20–45
SICILY, ANCIENT, Sep 61: 22–26
Slavery in, Sep 61: 26, May 62: 46
SICKERT, WALTER RICHARD, May 62: 78
SIDDONS, SARAH, Mar 59: 91
"SIDE-STREET PAINTER, OR SHOPPING WITH SIVARD," paintings by Robert Sivard, Nov 63: 84–91
SIDNEY, PHILIP, Nov 59: 75, Nov 63: 43, 44
"SIEGFRIED," opera, May 63: 45
"SIEGFRIED," play, Nov 60: 54, 55
SIEPI, CESARE, Sep 59: 91
"SIGHT THAT MUSIC MAKES, THE," album by Robert Osborn, May 62: 120–28
SIGISMUND, KING OF POLAND, Sep 59: 60
SIGNAC, PAUL, Jul 62: 69
Painting by, Jul 62: 69
"SIGN OF THE CROSS, THE," motion picture, May 61: 53
"SIGN OF THE FISH, THE," book by Peter Quennell, excerpt from, Jan 60: 108–9
SIGNORELLI, LUCA, painting by, Nov 60: 44
"SILENT LANGUAGE, THE," book by Edward T. Hall, Mar 60: 122–23
Excerpt from, May 59: 136
"SILENT TRAVELLER DRAWS THE WEST, THE," excerpts and paintings from books by Chiang Yee, Nov 59: 129–36
SILK, golden age of, in Persia, Jan 63: 52
SILLS, MR. and MRS. KENNETH CHARLES MORTON, Nov 60: 66, 68
SILLS, PAUL, Jan 62: 66–70, Jul 62: 49
Photograph of, Jan 62: 67
SILOAM, TUNNEL OF, Nov 59: 5–6
SILVER MINES, Guggenheim interests in, May 59: 6–7
SILVERS, PHIL, Sep 58: 58, Mar 60: 126
SILVERS, ROBERT B. (see also SAYRE, NORA, coauthor)
"Alfred Kazin: The Critic as Creator," interview by, Jul 62: 98–103
SILVIUS, AENEAS. See PIUS II, POPE
SIMMONS, J., on David Livingstone, quoted, Sep 58: 136
SIMMONS, JEAN, May 61: 57, Sep 63: 80
SIMON, ABBY, in painting by John Koch, Sep 60: 108
SIMON, ANDRÉ L., on Escoffier, quoted, May 61: 121
SIMON, EDITH, "The Knights of the Maltese Cross," article by, Mar 61: 48–71

SIMON, HERBERT A., Nov 63: 61
SIMON, JOHN, "The Sour Truth About the Sweet Life," article by, Sep 61: 110–12
SIMONETTI, MICHELANGELO, Jan 62: 45
SIMONIDES OF CEOS, Sep 61: 24
"SIMPLE SEER, THE," article by Pierre Schneider, Mar 62: 14–27
"SIMPLICISSIMUS," German satiric romance, Mar 63: 112
SIMPSON, LOUIS, on "Beat" poetry, quoted, Sep 61: 121
SIMPSON, N. F., Sep 62: 34, Jan 63; 26, 29, 32, 33
Photograph of, Jan 63: 31
SINAI. See MOUNT SINAI
SINCLAIR, UPTON, Mar 63: 27, Jul 63: 71, 75
"SINÉ BY THE SEA," drawings by Maurice Siné, May 62: 108–9
SINGER, CHARLES, Sep 58: 146
SINISGALLI, LEONARDO, Nov 59: 48
"SIN OF JESUS, THE," motion picture, Mar 61: 14
SINSHARISHKIN, KING OF ASSYRIA, Sep 59: 103
SIRENS, Jan 60: 134
"SIRIUS," S.S., Jan 59: 40–41
SIROCCO, MOHAMMED, Jul 63: 57–58
SISLEY, ALFRED, Jul 62: 58, 64
Painting by, Jul 62: 58
"SISTER CARRIE," novel by Theodore Dreiser, Jan 62: 63
SISTINE CHAPEL, Jan 62: 31, 41
"SISTINE MADONNA," painting by Raphael, Mar 62: 50
SISYGAMBIS, mother of Darius III, Mar 59: 38, 39, 41
SITWELL, EDITH, Jan 60: 108–9, Mar 61: 22
Photograph of, Jan 60: 108
SITWELL, OSBERT, Jan 60: 108, 109
On Angkor, quoted, Jan 59: 79
Photograph of, Jan 60: 108
SITWELL, SACHEVERELL, Jan 60: 109
Photograph of, Jan 60: 108
SIVARD, ROBERT, "Side-Street Painter, or Shopping with Sivard," paintings by, Nov 63: 84–91
SIXTEEN-STRING JACK, Nov 62: 23
"SIXTH YEAR, THE," television play, Sep 60: 55
SIXTUS IV, POPE, Sep 58: 95, Jan 62: 31
In painting by Melozzo da Forlì, Jan 62: 44
"SIXTY-TWO CURSES OF ESARHADDON, THE," transcribed by Donald J. Wiseman, Sep 59: 103–5
SJÖBERG, ALF, Sep 60: 8
SKAVRONSKY, COUNT, Sep 60: 130
SKELTON, RED, Mar 63: 35
SKIBINE, GEORGE, on George Balanchine, quoted, Jan 61: 44
SKIDMORE, OWINGS & MERRILL, Sep 58: 91, Jan 59: 11, Sep 59: 18, Jan 60: 120, Nov 60: 4, May 62: 16, Jul 62: 8, May 63: 14
Buildings designed by. See ILLUSTRATIONS INDEX
SKINNER, JAMES, May 62: 86
SKIRA, ALBERT, Jan 61: 16
Portfolio from book published by, Jan 62: 32–40
SKOLSKY, SIDNEY, Jul 60: 120
"SKYSCRAPER," motion picture, Mar 61: 16
SKYSCRAPERS, invasion of Europe by, Nov 60: 12–16, 124–25
"SLAUGHTER ON TENTH AVENUE," ballet, Sep 58: 60
SLAVE EMANCIPATION SOCIETY, seal of, May 59: 96
SLAVERY
In ancient Greece and Rome, May 62: 42–49
In ancient Sicily, Sep 61: 26, May 62: 46
In Grand Seraglio of Ottoman Empire, May 59: 58
Humboldt, Alexander von, quoted on, Jul 59: 67–68, 128
In Moslem Spain, Sep 62: 82
In utopias, Mar 63: 75, 76
Wedgwood, Josiah, and his friends and, May 59: 129
SLAVE TRADE, David Livingstone vs., Sep 58: 136
SLEEP, problem of, and communications satellites, Jan 62: 21
"SLEEPING ANTIOPE," painting by Correggio, Jul 61: 94
"SLEEPING CRANE," print by Tadashi Nakayama, May 60: 114; illus, May 60: 112
"SLEEPING PRINCE," play, Jan 61: 30
"SLEEP OF PRISONERS, A," play, Jan 63: 88
SLOANE, SAMUEL, home designed by, Mar 62: 35
SLOCUM, JOSHUA, Sep 58: 8, 139
SLUTER, CLAUS, Sep 58: 62
SMALL, WILLIAM, as member of Josiah Wedgwood's group, May 59: 92, 128, 129
SMETANA, AUGUSTIN, *From My Life*, Nov 62: 45, 47
SMILEY, DR. and MRS. LEONARD, in painting by John Koch, Sep 60: 106
SMITH, ADAM
And Grand Tour, Nov 59: 77, 96
Portrait of, Nov 59: 94
SMITH, ALEXANDER, Sep 63: 47, 48
SMITH, ALISON, Jul 62: 37
SMITH, BESSIE, Jul 61: 116, Jan 63: 75
SMITH, BRADFORD, Jan 59: 122

"A Fabulous Visitor from Formosa," article by, Jan 60: 113–18
SMITH, C. AUBRY, Sep 63: 76, 77, 80
Photographs of, Sep 63: 74, 78
SMITH, CHLOETHIEL, Jan 60: 21
SMITH, DAVID, Sep 58: 110
SMITH, D. MACK. See FINLEY, M. I., co-author
SMITH, ELIZABETH. See SOANE, ELIZABETH SMITH
SMITH, HARRY B., "Sentimental Library" of, Nov 60: 97
SMITH, HASSEL, Jan 59: 13, 14
Paintings by, Jan 59: 4–5, 13
Portrait of, Jan 59: 13
SMITH, HOMER W., on Cartesian mechanism, quoted, Jul 61: 8
SMITH, HUSTON, Jul 59: 71
SMITH, JOSEPH, Jul 63: 105
SMITH, JOSEPH LINDON, Jul 59: 30
SMITH, LEON POLK, Jan 63: 25
SMITH, LOGAN PEARSALL, on pursuit of perfection, quoted, Jan 60: 10
SMITH, MATTHEW, May 62: 60
SMITH, OLIVER, May 62: 113
Sketch by, May 61: 102
SMITH, RED, portrait of, Jan 60: 9
SMITH, RICHARD JOHN, tinsel print picturing, Sep 63: 2, 3
SMITH, SYDNEY, Mar 59: 90–95, 124–25
On American literature, quoted, May 60: 5
Portraits of, Mar 59: 90, 125
SMITH, WILLIAM ANDERSON, on handwriting, quoted, Sep 59: 128
SMITH, WILLIAM JAY, "The Spectral Poets of Pittsburgh," article by, May 60: 42–48
SMITHSON, HARRIET, portraits of, Sep 61: 105
SMOLLETT, TOBIAS, on Englishmen in Europe, quoted, Nov 59: 84
SMYRNA, TURKEY, messianic year of 1666 in, Mar 60: 125
SMYSLOV, VASSILY, Jan 62: 118, 119–20
SNEAD, SAM, Nov 62: 113
SNOW, C. P., Jul 61: 9, Sep 61: 10, Mar 63: 108
Affair, The, Sep 60: 118
On economic development, quoted, May 60: 7, 9
Masters, The, Sep 60: 119
SNOW, ROGER VINTON, Maine song by, quoted, Nov 61: 119
SNOWDON, EARL OF. See ARMSTRONG-JONES, ANTHONY
"SNOW FLURRIES," painting by Andrew Wyeth, Sep 61: 101
SOANE, ELIZABETH SMITH (MRS. JOHN), Nov 63: 74
SOANE, GEORGE, Nov 63: 74, 75, 76
SOANE, JOHN, Nov 63: 72–83
Portrait of, Nov 63: 75
SOANE, JOHN, JR., Nov 63: 74, 75, 76
SOAP, merchandising of, Jan 63: 113
SOBIESKI, JOHN. See JOHN III SOBIESKI
SOBY, JAMES THRALL, on Georges Rouault, quoted, Nov 62: 48
SOCIAL CLASSES. See CLASSES IN AMERICA
"SOCIAL CONSEQUENCES OF THE COMMUNICATIONS SATELLITES, THE," article by Arthur C. Clarke, Jan 62: 16–21
SOCIAL DEMOCRATS, in World War I aftermath, Jan 59: 121
SOCIALISTS, UTOPIAN, Mar 63: 76–77, 79
SOCIAL REALISM, in painting, Sep 58: 109
SOCIAL SCIENCES, jargon of, Jul 63: 38
SOCIAL SERVICE
In Dutch Republic, Sep 58: 21
In Olivetti enterprises, Nov 59: 50–51
"SOCIETY," publicity-seeking in, Jul 60: 121–22
SOCIETY FOR PSYCHICAL RESEARCH, séance by "Margery" for, Jan 59: 110
SOCIETY OF DILETTANTI, Mar 62: 55
SOCIOLOGY
Future American class system, May 59: 20–23
Sociologists at work, Mar 60: 122–23
Status system in America, Nov 59: 20–25, 128
Thought among sociologists, Mar 59: 135
"SOCRATE," composition by Erik Satie, Igor Stravinsky quoted on, Sep 58: 83
SOCRATES, Jan 60: 45
Erasmus quoted on, May 62: 91
Guilt or innocence of, Jul 60: 100–4, 117
In painting by Jacques Louis David, Jul 60: 101
SOEDERLUND, PETER, "Letters from Denmark," drawings by, Jul 63: 120
SOGDIANA, PERSIA, Mar 59: 47, 52
SOISSONS, LOUIS DE, May 62: 59
SOLANGE, MARTHE. See MELIGNY, MARTHE DE
"SOLDIER VIRGIN," book by W. P. Yancy, Mar 62: 98
SOLECKI, RALPH, Sep 62: 5, 8
"SOLER FAMILY LUNCHING ON THE GRASS,"

painting by Picasso, Nov 61: 9–10; illus, Nov 61: 10–11
SOLERI, PAOLO, city design by, Sep 63: 24–25
SOLITUDE
Cult of unthink and, Sep 58: 38, 134
Huxley, Aldous, quoted on, Sep 58: 53
As motivation in adventure, Sep 58: 12
"Privacy Lost," article by William K. Zinsser, Jul 60: 4–7, 120–22
SOLOMON, KING OF ISRAEL
Archaeological discoveries pertaining to, Nov 59: 9–10, 118–19
Song of, quoted, Nov 59: 113
SOLOMON, ABRAHAM, May 62: 73
SOLOMON R. GUGGENHEIM FOUNDATION, May 59: 7, 10–11, 14–15
SOLOMON R. GUGGENHEIM MUSEUM, New York City, May 59: 10–11, 14–15, Sep 60: 96, 128
Saarinen, Eero, quoted on, Jul 60: 82
SOLON, Sep 63: 84
SOMALILAND, Richard Francis Burton in, Jul 63: 112–13
SOMBART, WERNER, Mar 60: 100
"SOME LIKE IT HOT," motion picture, Jan 61: 123
SOMERSET, 1ST DUKE OF (EDWARD SEYMOUR), Sep 59: 130
SOMERSET, 6TH DUKE OF (CHARLES SEYMOUR), Mar 63: 69
"SOMETHING ABOUT A SOLDIER," novel by Mark Harris, Jan 59: 19
SONDHEIM, STEPHEN, Jul 61: 98
Portrait of, Jul 61: 99
"SONG OF ROLAND, THE," Sep 62: 89
"SONG OF SONGS, THE," composition by Lukas Foss, Jan 63: 78
"SONIC CONTOURS," tape recorder composition by Vladimir Ussachevsky, Jan 59: 51, 53
SONNENBERG, BENJAMIN, Jul 60: 121
"SONNETS FROM THE PORTUGUESE," by Elizabeth Barrett Browning, forged private edition of, Mar 59: 107–9
SONTAG, HENRIETTE, Sep 59: 56
SOPHIA, REGENT OF RUSSIA, Sep 59: 66
SOPHIA PALAEOLOGINA, Nov 63: 34
SOPHIE, PRINCESS, OF RUSSIA, Sep 60: 131, 134
SOPHIE, WITTELSBACH PRINCESS, Jan 61: 41–42
SOPHISTS, Jul 60: 104, 117
SOPHOCLES
Oedipus, quoted, Nov 62: 118
In Renaissance curriculum, Jan 60: 62
Survival of works by, Nov 62: 80
SOREL, CLAUDETTE, Jan 62: 14
SOREL, EDWARD, "Men Into Monuments," gallery by, Sep 61: 122–28
———— and PAUL DAVIS, "A Modern Bestiary," portfolio by, Jul 62: 120–28
SORIANO, RAPHAEL, Jan 59: 10
"SORRY STATE OF HISTORY, THE," article by J. H. Plumb, Sep 63: 97–100
Comment on, by Allan Nevins, Sep 63: 101
"SORTILÈGE D'AMOUR," anonymous Flemish painting, Jan 62: 81–82; illus, Jan 62: 80
SOTHEBY & CO., London, Nov 60: 100, Nov 62: 58–67
"SOTHEBY'S" article by William K. Zinsser, Nov 62: 58–67
"SOT-WEED FACTOR, THE," novel by John Barth, Jan 63: 37
SOUFFLOT, JACQUES GERMAIN, Sep 60: 72
"SOUR TRUTH ABOUT THE SWEET LIFE, THE," article by John Simon, Sep 61: 110–12
"SOUS LES TOITS DE PARIS," motion picture, May 63: 111
SOUTH, AMERICAN
Fine arts in, Jan 60: 5–6
Motion picture versions of, May 59: 100
Political parties in, Jul 61: 68
Philadelphians' admiration for, Jul 63: 13
SOUTH AFRICA, UNION OF
Come Back, Africa, motion picture about, Mar 61: 15, 19
N'debele people and their villages, Nov 60: 56–65
SOUTH AMERICA, Alexander von Humboldt in, Jul 59: 62–68, 128
SOUTHAMPTON, N.Y., May 63: 6 (map), 8
SOUTH CAROLINA, UNIVERSITY OF, dormitory buildings, Sep 59: 20
SOUTH DEVON RAILWAY, Jan 59: 39
SOUTHERN, TERRY
Flash and Filigree, Mar 59: 17, 117, 118
Photograph of, Mar 59: 15
SOUTHERN RHODESIA, Zimbabwe, Mar 63: 41 (map), 57 (illus)
SOUTHEY, ROBERT, Mar 62: 97
"SOUTH PACIFIC," musical, Sep 58: 60
"SOUTHPAW, THE," book by Mark Harris, Jan 59: 19
SOUTH SEAS

Dream of, Jan 60: 28–31, 124–27
Gauguin, Paul, in, Jan 60: 32, 124
"SOUTH SEA TALES," book by Jack London, Jan 60: 125
SOUTINE, CHAIM, Sep 58: 110
Larry Rivers quoted on, Sep 59: 98
SOWERS, ROBERT, Sep 59: 19
"SOWING," book by Leonard Woolf, quoted, Jan 61: 113
SOYER, RAPHAEL, Jul 62: 15
In painting by John Koch, Sep 60: 107
SPACE. See OUTER SPACE
"SPACE AND THE SPIRIT OF MAN," article by Arthur C. Clarke, Jan 59: 26–31, 122–23
SPACEMEN, memorandum from Voltaire to, Sep 61: 18–19
"SPACE MERCHANTS, THE," book by Frederik Pohl and C. M. Kornbluth, Mar 63: 79
SPAIN (see also BARCELONA; MADRID)
American abstract expressionism in, Nov 59: 120
And Battle of Lepanto, Jul 63: 50, 52, 53, 57, 58
Bullfighting, Jul 60: 128
Gardens of, May 59: 27, 48–49
Hotels in, Mar 59: 120
Humboldt, Alexander von, political essays of, Jul 59: 67–68
Literary prizes, Jul 63: 73
Memorandum from Don Quixote to Francisco Franco, Jul 59: 24–25
Moslems in, Sep 62: 72–93
Netherlands vs., Sep 58: 18–19, 20
Occupation of Sicily, Sep 61: 22, 24–25 (map), 34, 37, 38
Organ (musical instrument) in, Mar 60: 74
And Thirty Years' War, Nov 62: 33–41
Two Spains of *Don Quixote,* Nov 61: 106–13
Witch mania in, Nov 59: 58, 62
SPALDING, ALBERT, Sep 59: 89
"SPANISH ISLAM," book by Reinhart Dozy, Sep 62: 87
SPANISH LANGUAGE, origin of, Sep 62: 79
SPARHAWK-JONES, ELIZABETH, Mar 63: 29
SPARTA
Alterations at, Mar 59: 133
Peloponnesian War, Jul 60: 102; Thucydides' account of, Jan 60: 41–45
Thirty Tyrants, Jul 60: 102–3
SPARTACISTS, Jan 59: 121
SPARTACUS, Sep 61: 26, Mar 62: 44, May 62: 47
"SPARTACUS," motion picture, May 61: 52, 53, 56–57, Jan 63: 112, Mar 63: 109
SPEAR, RUSKIN, painting by, May 62: 76
"SPECTATOR, THE," periodical, on George Psalmanazar, quoted, Jan 60: 117
"SPECTRAL POETS OF PITTSBURGH, THE," article by William Jay Smith, May 60: 42–48
SPEE, FRIEDRICH VON, Nov 59: 60, 62
SPEECH, FREEDOM OF. See FREEDOM OF SPEECH
SPEKE, JOHN HANNING, Jul 63: 113–14
SPENCE, BASIL, May 62: 61
SPENCER, CHARLES. See MARLBOROUGH, 3D DUKE OF
SPENCER, GEORGE. See MARLBOROUGH, 4TH DUKE OF
SPENCER, HERBERT, on Doge's Palace, Venice, quoted, Mar 63: 15
SPENCER, PLATT ROGERS, Sep 59: 124–25, 128
SPENGLER, OSWALD, Mar 59: 6, 10, 11, Jan 61: 62, 63–64, Sep 63: 99
On Baroque age, quoted, Jul 60: 35
Malraux, André, compared to, Nov 58: 8–9
Portrait of, Mar 59: 11
SPERLONGA, ITALY, Cave of Tiberius, May 59: 102–7, 122–24
SPEYER, LEONORA, Mar 63: 30
SPHINX, André Malraux quoted on, Nov 58: 12–13
SPICER, JACK, "Berkeley in Time of Plague," quoted, Jan 59: 19
SPIEGELTHAL, German consul in Turkey, 1853, Sep 63: 88
SPILLANE, MICKEY, Jan 62: 64
SPINOLA, AMBROGIO DI, Nov 62: 37
SPINOLA, CATTOCCHIA DI MARCO, Sep 58: 92
"SPIRIT OF THE DEAD WATCHES, THE," painting by Paul Gauguin, Jan 60: 32; illus, Jan 60: 36–37
SPIRITUALISM, "Margery," Jan 59: 108–11
SPITTELER, CARL, *Olympian Spring,* Jan 63: 111
SPIVAKOVSKY, TOSSY, Jul 59: 21
"SPLENDOR IN THE GRASS," motion picture, Jan 62: 104, May 62: 82, Jul 62: 49
"SPLENDOR OF PERSIA, THE," book by Robert Payne, quoted, Jan 63: 67
"SPLIT-LEVEL" HOUSE, definition, Mar 59: 114
SPOFFORD, CHARLES M., Jul 62: 5–6, 7
Portrait of, Jul 62: 8
SPOONER, WILLIAM A., quoted, Jan 63: 85
"SPORT OF KNIGHTS, THE," article by Jay Williams,

Nov 58: 92–107
"SPORT OF MY MAD MOTHER, THE," play, Jan 63: 31, 32
SPORTS and GAMES
Archery, Zen style, Jul 59: 75
Bowling, Mar 63: 89–95
Chess. See CHESS
Cricket, Nov 58: 53 (illus), Sep 63: 77, 80
Poker, and American character, Nov 63: 56–62
Polo, in Persia, Jan 63: 51, 58; illus, Jan 63: 63
On television, and development of armchair athletes, Nov 62: 112–13
Tournaments of Middle Ages, Nov 58: 92–107
Yachting, Jul 62: 96–97
Yale University hockey rink, May 59: 84–87
"SPRING," painting by Poussin, Mar 61: 93
SPRINGFIELD "REPUBLICAN," Jul 61: 101
SPRING-RICE, CECIL, on Theodore Roosevelt, quoted, Nov 63: 70
SPRINGS, THE, N.Y., May 63: 7 (map), 9, 13, 22, 26
"SPY'S BEDSIDE BOOK, THE," edited by Graham Greene, May 61: 117
"SQUARE, THE," novel by Marguerite Duras, Jan 62: 101
"SQUARE ROOTS OF ZEN, THE," article by Nancy Wilson Ross, Jul 59: 70–77, 126–27
STAAL DE LAUNAY, BARONNE DE, Jan 60: 87–88
STAATSOPER, East Berlin, Nov 58: 23–24, 133
STAATSOPER, Vienna, Nov 58: 23–25
Jeritza-Lehmann feud, Sep 59: 56–57
"STABAT MATER," composition by Pergolesi, Jul 59: 21
STABILES, of Alexander Calder, Nov 62: 12, 16
STACPOOLE, HENRY DE VERE, Jan 60: 125
STADIATIS, ELIAS, Nov 58: 72
STAËL, AUGUSTE DE, Nov 58: 145, 146
STAËL, GERMAINE DE, May 61: 81, Nov 61: 35
Attitude toward nature, Nov 60: 14
Napoleon, Mme Récamier, and, Nov 58: 86–89, 142–46
Portrait of, Nov 58: 86
Quoted: on Americans, Nov 59: 100; on Marie Antoinette's boudoir, Mar 62: 64; on Russians, Sep 60: 136
Riding, Laura, compared to, Jan 62: 53
STAFFORD, JEAN, May 63: 21
"Isak Dinesen: Master Teller of Tales," article by, Sep 59: 110–12
"Movies," articles by, on current motion pictures: "Hindu Trilogy, The," Jan 61: 115; "Neo-realismo Revisited," Mar 61: 98–100; "Samurai, With Sword, Won't Travel," May 61: 114–15; "Three Orphans and Their Patron Saint," Sep 60: 116–17; "War and Peace in Two Foreign Films," Nov 60: 121–22
Photograph of, May 63: 21
STAHLMAN, SYLVIA, photograph of, Nov 61: 78
STAHR, ELVIS J., Sep 61: 13
STAINED-GLASS REVIVAL, Sep 62: cover, 3, 22–32
STAIRCASE, as architectural feature, Jul 60: 42, 50
STALIN, JOSEPH, Jul 62: 113, Nov 63: 62
Lady Astor-G. B. Shaw visit to, Nov 58: 20
STALLINGS, LAURENCE, Jul 62: 37, 40
STAMBOLISKI, ALEXANDR, Mar 63: 6
STAMFORD, CONN., First Presbyterian Church, Sep 59: 19, Sep 62: 24
STAMOS, THEODOROS, Sep 58: 44, Mar 62: 107
Portrait of, Sep 58: 45
STANDARD, PAUL, Sep 59: 128
STANDARD OIL COMPANY, Mar 60: 31
"STANDING COUPLE," painting by David Park, Jul 60: 115; illus, Jul 60: 17
STANFORD, LELAND, Nov 58: 148
STANFORD UNIVERSITY, Jan 59: 19
STANHOPE, HESTER, Sep 58: 136–37
STANISLAS I, KING OF POLAND, Mar 61: 118
STANISLAVSKY, KONSTANTIN, Jan 61: 32, May 62: 39
And Actors Studio, Nov 62: 106–8
STANISLAVSKY METHOD (see also METHOD ACTING), Sep 58: 42, 44
"STANLEY," television show, Sep 61: 80
STANLEY, HENRY M., on ivory trade, quoted, May 60: 90–91
STANLEY, KIM, Sep 60: 55, 56
STARK, FREYA
On Aphrodisias, quoted, Mar 63: 99
"Timeless Home of the Mother Goddess," article by, Sep 58: 86–87, 140–42
"STARRY NIGHT," painting by Van Gogh, Sep 60: 121
STARS, evolution of, Nov 63: 53
"STARTLED CONFESSOR, THE," painting by Jehan Georges Vibert, Mar 60: 56; illus, Mar 60: 65
"START OF A LONG DAY'S JOURNEY," excerpts from *The Life of Eugene O'Neill,* by Arthur and Barbara Gelb, Mar 60: 25–40
STATE DEPARTMENT, U.S.
Building program of, Jan 60: 19–21, 24–27, 119–20

And Hungarian Crown of Saint Stephen, May 63: 95
Memorandum from Thomas Jefferson to Dean Rusk on buildings of, Jul 61: 30–31
Washington, D.C., building of, Jan 60: 120
"STATELY MANSIONS OF THE IMAGINATION, THE," article by John Maass with portfolio of paintings and designs, Sep 63: 10–27
"STATE OF SIEGE," book by Albert Camus, Nov 59: 70–71
"STATE OF THE UNION," play, Nov 58: 65
STATE SONGS, Nov 61: 118–19
STATIRA, wife of Darius III, Mar 59: 38, 39
"STATUS SEEKERS, THE," book by Vance Packard, Nov 59: 21, 22, 24
STATUS SYSTEM, wreck of, Nov 59: 20–25, 128
STAVORDALE, LORD, Nov 58: 56
STAZEWSKI, HENRYK, May 61: 21–22
Portrait of, May 61: 22
STEEGMULLER, FRANCIS, "Twilight in the Hammam," article by, Sep 60: 125–26
STEEL, ANTHONY, Sep 63: 79
STEELE, WILBUR DANIEL, Jul 61: 13
STEEN, JAN, Sep 58: 28, Sep 60: 34
Painting by, Sep 58: 31
STEFFENS, LINCOLN, Ernest Hemingway quoted on, Jan 59: 133
STEGNER, WALLACE, Jan 59: 19, Jan 62: 14
"Child of the Far Frontier," article excerpted from *Wolf Willow*, book by, Sep 62: 94–95
On college students, quoted, May 63: 87
STEIG, WILLIAM, Nov 61: 57
STEIGER, ROD, Sep 58: 42, Sep 60: 56
STEIN, CLARENCE, Jul 59: 11, 12
STEIN, EDWIN, Nov 62: 98
STEIN, GERTRUDE, Jul 63: 40
Hemingway, Ernest, quoted on, Jan 59: 132
Wyeth, Andrew, quoted on, Sep 61: 100
STEINBECK, JOHN, Jan 59: 7, Jul 63: 69, 75
On literacy and the government, quoted, Sep 61: 5
STEINBERG, LEO, on Jasper Johns, quoted, Jan 63: 25
STEINBERG, SAUL, May 59: 109, Nov 61: 57, May 63: 13
Cartoon detail by, Nov 63: 53
Photograph of, May 63: 13
STEINER, GEORGE, quoted
On American literary criticism, May 62: 106
On Salinger, J. D., May 62: 100
STEINHAUSER, JOHN, Jul 63: 116
STEINITZ, WILLIAM, Jan 62: 116–17, 118, 120
STELLER'S SEA COW, as source of mermaid legend, Jan 60: 135
STENDHAL (MARIE HENRI BEYLE), May 61: 70, Jan 62: 62, Sep 62: 20
Quoted: on politics in art, Sep 61: 107; on Shakespeare, Sep 61: 106
STEPHEN I, KING OF HUNGARY, May 63: 95
STEPHEN, LESLIE, Sep 58: 139
STEPHEN, VIRGINIA. See WOOLF, VIRGINIA
STEPHENS, JAMES, Nov 60: 68
STEPHENSON, GEORGE, Jan 59: 37, 39
STEPHENSON, ROBERT, Jan 59: 37, 38
STERLING, GEORGE, Sep 59: 7, May 60: 46
STERN, BERT, Mar 61: 18
Photograph of, Mar 61: 18
STERN, ISAAC, Jul 60: 73–75, 126–27, Jul 62: 30
Photographs of, Jul 60: 73, 75
STERN, VERA, (MRS. ISAAC), Jul 60: 126
STEVENS, ROGER L., Nov 62: 108
STEVENS, WALLACE, Sep 61: 119
STEVENSON, ADLAI, Jul 60: 120
STEVENSON, ELIZABETH, photograph of, May 59: 17
STEVENSON, ROBERT LOUIS
In South Seas, Jan 60: 30, 124; photograph of, Jan 60: 31
Treasure Island, compared with motion picture based on, May 62: 116
STEWART, ALEXANDER T., Jul 59: 12
STEWART, DAVID, father of Isabella Stewart Gardner, Jul 59: 12, 32
STEWART, DONALD. See PLIMPTON, GEORGE, co-author
STEWART, DONALD OGDEN, Jul 62: 37
STEWART, FRED, Nov 62: 108
STEWART, GEORGE R., Jan 59: 19
"STEWED PRUNES," cabaret show, Jan 62: 66, 70
"STIFF COMPETITION," drawings by Paul Flora, Sep 59: 92–93
STILES, EZRA, May 60: 21
STILL, CLYFFORD, Sep 58: 44, 134, Jan 59: 13, May 59: 11, Nov 59: 120, Jul 60: 16, 115
STILLER, JERRY, Nov 60: 116
"STILL LIFE WITH APPLES," painting by Cézanne, Sep 60: 121
STILLWELL, RICHARD, photograph of, Sep 59: 27
STIMSON, HENRY L., *On Active Service in Peace and War*, Sep 61: 10

STIRLING, JANE, May 63: 110
STOCKBRIDGE, MASS., May 60: 13, 17
STOCKHAUSEN, KARLHEINZ, Jan 59: 51, 54, Jul 59: 21, Sep 60: 31, 122
Composition by, Sep 60: 123
Photograph of, Jan 59: 50
STOCKHOLM, SWEDEN
"Mechanical hotel" in, Mar 63: 117
Mobile by Alexander Calder in National Museum, Nov 62: 16
STODDARD, CHARLES WARREN, Jan 60: 125
STODDARD, GEORGE D., Jul 59: 48
STOFFER, BRYAN SEWALL, Sep 59: 123
STOIC CREED, as formulated by Malebranche, Mar 61: 92
STOKOWSKI, LEOPOLD, Jan 59: 51, 52
STOLOFF, CAROLYN, photograph of, Mar 63: 33
STÖLZL, GUNTA, photograph of, Nov 61: 59
STONE, EDWARD DURRELL, Sep 58: 88–91, Mar 59: 113, Sep 59: 19–20, Jan 60: 20, 119, 120, May 62: 16, Mar 63: 90, 91, May 63: 26
Buildings designed by. See ILLUSTRATIONS INDEX
National Cultural Center design, Sep 61: 14, 17
Photographs of, Sep 58: 89, May 63: 27
Quoted, Sep 60: 35, 39
STONE, FRANK, May 62: 73
STONE, IRVING
Lust for Life, Jan 63: 75
"Perfect Beauty, The," article by, Sep 58: 92–95, 142
STONE, PETER, Mar 62: 117–18, 119
STONE AGE, in Africa, Mar 63: 40, 43–44
STONEHENGE, ENGLAND, Jul 60: 90
"STONES OF VENICE, THE," portfolio of photographs by Alexander Liberman, Mar 63: 16–24
STONOROV, OSCAR, Sep 62: 58
"STORM," novel by George R. Stewart, Jan 59: 19
STOTESBURY, ED, Nov 58: 148
"STOVER AT YALE," novel by Owen Johnson, Sep 60: 119
STRABO, on Sperlonga, Italy, quoted, May 59: 104
STRACHEY, LYTTON, Jan 61: 113
Beerbohm, Max, quoted on, May 61: 40
Portrait of, Jan 60: 106
Proposal of marriage to Virginia Stephen, Jan 60: 107
"STRADA, LA," motion picture, May 59: 99, May 60: 51, Mar 61: 98
STRAFFORD, 1ST EARL OF (THOMAS WENTWORTH), Sep 59: 120, 121
"STRANGE ORDEAL OF THE NORMANDIER, THE," television production, Mar 60: 4–5
"STRANGER, THE," novel by Albert Camus, Nov 59: 70, 71
"STRANGER IN THE ROOM," motion picture, Nov 62: 110, 112
STRASBERG, LEE, Jan 62: 14, 103
And Actors Studio and proposed theatre, Nov 62: 106–8
"STRATEGY IN POKER, BUSINESS, AND WAR," book by John McDonald, Nov 63: 57 (note), 58–59, 61
STRATFORD, CONN., May 60: 13 (map), 28
Shakespeare Festival. See AMERICAN SHAKESPEARE FESTIVAL THEATRE
STRATFORD, ONT., FESTIVAL THEATRE, Jul 59: 44–45, Mar 60: 120, Nov 63: 36, 41
Established by Tyrone Guthrie, Nov 63: 36, 41
Merchant of Venice, The, at, Jan 60: 91
STRATFORD-ON-AVON, ENGLAND, Shakespeare Memorial Theatre, Jul 59: 44
STRAUS, NOEL, in painting by John Koch, Sep 60: 107
STRAUSS, JOHANN, Jul 59: 32, 133
STRAUSS, RICHARD, Nov 58: 25, Jul 59: 22–23, Sep 59: 56, Jan 60: 12, Mar 62: 104
Don Quixote, Jan 25: 125
Gould, Glenn, quoted on, Jan 62: 91
Salome, Nov 58: 120
Stravinsky, Igor, quoted on, Sep 58: 84
STRAVINSKY, IGOR, Jan 59: 21, Jul 59: 21, Nov 61: 70, 71, May 63: 109
Balanchine, George, quoted on, Jan 61: 47
Ballet music by, Nov 59: 54, 56
Conversations with Stravinsky, book by, with Robert Craft, excerpts from, Sep 58: 82–84, 132
On creative process, quoted, Sep 60: 122
Portraits of, Sep 58: 82, Jan 59: 53
Rake's Progress, The, Jan 60: 12
STRAWBERRY HILL, home of Horace Walpole, Mar 62: 62
"STRAY DOG," motion picture, Jul 62: 45
STREAMLINING, as fashion cycle, Mar 59: 115
"STREETCAR NAMED DESIRE, A," play, Sep 58: 38, May 59: 54, 55
STREETCARS, Mar 59: 134–35
"STREET FURNITURE," article by Ada Louise Huxtable, Nov 59: 105–12
"STREET SCENE," opera, Jan 60: 16, 123

STRICK, JOSEPH, Mar 61: 14
STRINDBERG, AUGUST, Jul 61: 116, Nov 63: 109
Influence on Ingmar Bergman, Sep 60: 8
STROEHLING, P. E., Jul 63: 106
STRONG, L. CORRIN, Sep 61: 3
STRUCTURAL LINGUISTICS, Jul 63: 34, 35, 41, 43–48
STRUNK, WILLIAM, JR., *The Elements of Style*, Jul 63: 40
STUART, JAMES, and NICHOLAS REVETT, *Antiquities of Athens*, Mar 62: 55
STUART COMPANY BUILDING, Pasadena, Calif., Sep 58: 88–91
STUBBS, GEORGE, May 59: 92, 129, May 62: 64, Jul 63: 96, 106
Paintings by. See ILLUSTRATIONS INDEX
Self-portrait, May 59: 97
"STUDENT PRINCE, THE," musical, Sep 58: 57
"STUDY OF HISTORY, A," book by Arnold J. Toynbee, Mar 59: 13, Jan 61: 57
STUEMPFIG, WALTER, Jul 62: 15, Jul 63: 18
Painting by, Jul 62: 18, Jul 63: 22
STURGES, JOHN, *The Magnificent Seven*, May 61: 114–15
STYLE. See FASHION
STYRON, WILLIAM, May 60: 28, May 62: 55
Photograph of, May 60: 28
SUARÈS, ANDRÉ, Nov 62: 57
Portrait of, Nov 62: 57
SUBLIME PORTE, May 59: 132
SUBLIMINAL ADVERTISING, Nov 58: 146, 147
"SUBTERRANEANS, THE," novel by Jack Kerouac, Sep 58: 40, 41
SUBURBIA, May 61: 4, 18–19, Jul 61: 62–63
Mass migration to, Jul 59: 6
"SUBVERSE," book by Marya Mannes, May 63: 17
"SUDDEN END OF THE RENAISSANCE, THE," article by H. R. Trevor-Roper, Sep 59: 28–29, 120–21
"SUDDENLY LAST SUMMER," play, May 59: 55, May 61: 99
"SUDDEN SHOWER AT OHASHI," print by Hiroshige, May 60: 103, 104; illus, May 60: 102
SUDERMANN, HERMANN, *The Mad Professor*, Sep 60: 119
SUETONIUS, on Tiberius, quoted, May 59: 103, 107
SUFFOLK, DUKES OF, Nov 58: 51
SUFISM, Jan 63: 58, 59, 67
"SUITE FROM KING LEAR," tape recorder composition by Otto Luening and Vladimir Ussachevsky, Jan 59: 54
SULEIMAN I, SULTAN OF TURKEY (SULEIMAN THE MAGNIFICENT), May 59: 58, 60, 134, 135, Jul 63: 50
Attack by, on Maltese islands, Mar 61: 61, 65
Drawing of, Sep 58: 47
SULLA, LUCIUS CORNELIUS, Sep 58: 140, Mar 60: 6, Mar 63: 99
SULLAVAN, MARGARET, May 63: 110–11
SULLIVAN, ARTHUR. See GILBERT, W. S.
SULLIVAN, DANIEL, Mar 60: 38
SULLIVAN, FRANK, Jul 62: 37
SULLIVAN, JOHN L., Jul 59: 133, Mar 60: 30
SULLIVAN, LOUIS, Sep 59: 6, Jan 60: 23, Sep 60: 99, 101, 102, 127, Mar 62: 36
Quoted: on architecture, Mar 59: 113; on historical eclecticism, Sep 59: 5
Saarinen, Eero, quoted on, Jul 60: 78
SULLIVAN, TIM, Mar 60: 27
SULLY, DUC DE (MAXIMILIEN DE BÉTHUNE), Sep 59: 60, Mar 63: 6–7
SULLY, KATHLEEN, Jan 63: 32
SULLY, THOMAS, Jul 63: 18
"SULTAN," locomotive, Jan 59: 39
SULTANS, of Ottoman Empire, May 59: 62–63, 131–35
SUMER
Bronze Age trade of, Jul 60: 86–87
Cities of, Jul 61: 38–41, 62
Love songs from, Jul 63: 108–9
Nippur, new treasures from, Nov 61: 84–87
Wheeled vehicles in, Sep 58: 146–47
"SUMMER," painting by Rubens, Jul 63: 96
"SUMMER, OR RUTH AND BOAZ," painting by Poussin, Mar 61: 93; illus, Mar 61: 84–85
"SUMMER AND SMOKE," play by Tennessee Williams, Mar 60: 98, 120
Motion picture based on, Jan 63: 112
"SUMMER OF THE SEVENTEENTH DOLL, THE," play, Sep 62: 97
SUMMERS, HOLLIS, Jan 62: 14
"SUMMERTIME," motion picture, Jul 62: 109
"SUMMER TO REMEMBER, A," motion picture, Mar 62: 110, 111–12
SUMMIT HOTEL, New York City, Mar 63: 115
SUMNER, JAMES B., May 59: 9
Photograph of, May 59: 16

SUN, radiations and evolution of, Nov 63: 48–55
"SUN ALSO RISES, THE," novel by Ernest Hemingway, Jan 59: 132, 133, Jan 62: 64, Jul 63: 71
SUNDERLAND LIBRARY, Sep 61: 77
SUNDGAARD, ARNOLD, Jan 60: 122
SUNNYVALE, CALIF., Schuckl cannery building, Jan 59: 8
"SUNRISE AT CAMPOBELLO," play, Nov 58: 65
"SUNSET," song-poem, May 60: 48
SUPERMARKETS, Mar 59: 110–11
"SUPPRESSED DESIRES," play, Jul 61: 13
SUPREME COURT, U.S., on legislating beauty, quoted, May 61: 18
"SURFEIT OF HONEY, A," book by Russell Lynes, quoted, Jul 60: 67
"SURPRISED BY JOY," book by C. S. Lewis, May 59: 66
"SURPRISE IN THE SAHARA," article based on Henri Lhote's *A la découverte des fresques du Tassili*, May 59: 70–83
SURREALISM
Miró, Joan, and, Mar 59: 78, 126
Nude in, Sep 63: 95, 96
SURREY, EARL OF. See HOWARD, HENRY
SURYAVARMAN II, KING OF CAMBODIA, Jan 59: 64
SUSA, IRAN, Jan 63: 44, 59 (map)
"SUSANNAH," opera, Jan 60: 122
SUSSKIND, DAVID, Jan 60: 7, Mar 60: 126, Sep 62: 114, Jan 63: 74
SUSTERMAN (SUTTERMANS), JUSTUS, *A Young Commander*, Jul 59: 30
SUTHERLAND, ELIZABETH, "New York's New Wave of Movie Makers," article by, Mar 61: 12–19
SUTHERLAND, GRAHAM, Jan 59: 103, 105, 107
Paintings by, Jan 59: 103, 107
SUTHERLAND, JOAN, Jul 61: 97
SUTTON, DENYS, on American art, quoted, Nov 59: 32, 41
SUZUKI, DAISETZ TEITARO, Jul 59: 127
Photographs of, Jul 59: 72, 73
On Zen Buddhism, quoted, Sep 60: 122
"SWALLOW," H.M.S., Sep 63: 46
SWAMMERDAM, JAN, Sep 58: 23
SWANBERG, W. A., *Citizen Hearst*, Jul 63: 71
"SWAN LAKE," ballet, Allegra Kent in, Nov 59: 54, 56
SWEDEN
Motion picture version of, May 59: 98
Ocean-going fleets of Bronze Age, Jul 60: 91
Peter the Great and, Sep 59: 79, 80
Rock carvings of, Jul 60: 90
Street lights of Vällingby, Nov 59: 106
And Thirty Years' War, Nov 62: 36, 38
SWEDENBORG, EMANUEL, Sep 58: 116
SWEENEY, JAMES JOHNSON, May 59: 11, Nov 60: 9
On Alexander Calder, quoted, Nov 62: 12, 15
"SWEET BIRD OF YOUTH," play, May 62: 55
"SWEET SMELL OF SUCCESS," motion picture, May 59: 101
SWIFT, DAVID, Sep 60: 116
SWIFT, JONATHAN
On English language, quoted, Jul 63: 34
Hoax by, Jan 61: 71
Memorandum to Cliff Robinson from, Nov 59: 64–65
SWIFT, PAGE, photograph of, Nov 61: 79
SWIMMING POOLS, as status symbols, Nov 59: 25
SWINBURNE, ALGERNON CHARLES, Mar 61: 32, May 63: 85
On Bowdler, Thomas, quoted, Sep 62: 71
Goncourt *Journal* quoted on, Sep 62: 113
Portrait of, May 63: 85
SWITZERLAND
American abstract expressionism in, Nov 59, 120
Witch mania in, Nov 59: 59, 62
"SYLPHIDE, LA," ballet, Sep 60: 94
"SYLPHIDES, LES," ballet, Sep 60: 94
Tyrone Guthrie quoted on, Jan 61: 27
SYLVESTER I, POPE, in painting by Giulio Romano, Jan 62: 30
SYLVESTER II, POPE, May 63: 95
SYMMACHUS, POPE, Jan 62: 27
SYMONDS, JOHN ADDINGTON, on Venice, quoted, Mar 63: 14–15
SYMONS, ARTHUR, on Richard Francis Burton, quoted, Jul 63: 112
"SYMPHONIE FANTASTIQUE," composition by Berlioz, May 61: 82
"SYMPHONIE PASTORALE," motion picture, Mar 61: 98
SYMPHONY ORCHESTRAS
Of American South, Jan 60: 5–6
Boston Pops, Sep 59: 123
Ford Foundation and, Jan 62: 9, 12–13
New York Philharmonic. See NEW YORK PHILHARMONIC

Of Provincetown, Mass., Jul 61: 16
Topeka Civic, Sep 59: 86, 91, 122, 123
"SYMPOSIUM," dialogue by Xenophon, quoted, May 62: 42
SYNAGOGUES. See CHURCHES and SYNAGOGUES
SYNCHROTRON, at Princeton University, Sep 59: 26, 27
SYNGE, JOHN MILLINGTON, Mar 59: 87, 88, Jul 59: 47–48
SYOSSET, N.Y., style show for bowlers, Mar 63: 94
SYRACUSE, city-state, Sep 61: 22, 23, 24, 26, 28
SYRACUSE, CATHEDRAL OF, Nov 60: 29
"SYSTEMATIC THEOLOGY," book by Paul Tillich, quoted, Jan 59: 122
SZELL, GEORGE, Sep 61: 83, Jan 62: 9

T

TACITUS, CORNELIUS, Mar 63: 27, Sep 63: 97
Survival of works by, Nov 62: 87, 89, 94
On Tiberius, quoted, May 59: 107
TADA, NIGERIA, Tsoede bronzes found at, Mar 63: 51
TAFT, ROBERT A., Nov 63: 69
TAGES, Etruscan deity, May 60: 62
TAGGARD, GENEVIEVE, on Emily Dickinson, quoted, Jul 61: 104
TAGGETT, balloonist, Sep 58: 114
TAGLIONI, MARIE, Sep 60: 94
TAGORE, SARMILA, Jan 61: 115
TAGUA, as source of "ivory," May 60: 91
TAHITI, Jan 60: 30–31, 124, 125, 127
Gauguin, Paul, in, Jan 60: 32, 124
Melville, Herman, quoted on, Mar 61: 27
And mutiny on H.M.S. *Bounty*, Sep 63: 43, 45
"TAHITI: ISLE OF DREAMS," book by Robert Keable, Jan 60: 125
TAIFA KINGDOMS, Sep 62: 87–88
TAILLIEZ, PHILLIPPE, Nov 58: 71
TAINE, HIPPOLYTE ADOLPHE, Nov 61: 36
On romanticism, quoted, May 61: 60
"TAKE HER, SHE'S MINE," play, Mar 63: 108
"TAKE 3," New York City cabaret, Jan 62: 66, 70
TAL, MIKHAIL, Jan 62: 118, 120
Photograph of, Jan 62: 117
"TALE FOR A DEAF EAR," opera, Jan 60: 123
"TALE FROM BALI, A," novel by Vicki Baum, Mar 61: 24, 31
"TALE OF GENGI, THE," novel by Lady Murasaki, Mar 61: 9
TALENT, class system based on, May 59: 20–23
"TALES OF HOFFMANN," motion picture, Jan 60: 10
"TALES OF THE SOUTH PACIFIC," book by James Michener, Jan 60: 126
"TALISMAN, THE," novel by Walter Scott, quoted, Jan 59: 86
TALLCHIEF, MARIA, Nov 59: 54, Sep 60: 94, Jan 61: 49 (note)
TALMA, FRANÇOIS JOSEPH, portrait of, Sep 61: 104
TALMA, LOUISE, Mar 63: 31
TAMERLANE, Jan 63: 52, 67, Sep 63: 89, Nov 63: 31
In Persian miniature, Jan 63: 61
"TAMING OF THE SHREW," opera, Jan 60: 122–23
TANCRED, KING OF SICILY, Sep 61: 32
"TANCRED AND ERMINIA," painting by Poussin, Mar 61: 79, 80; illus, Mar 61: 81
TANDY, JESSICA (MRS. HUME CRONYN), Nov 63: 37, 41
TANGANYIKA, Edward Francis Twining as governor of, May 63: 92, 93
TANGANYIKA, LAKE, discovery of, Jul 63: 110, 113
TANGE, KENZO, Mar 60: 111, Sep 61: 58–63
Buildings designed by, Sep 61: 59, 61, 62
Photograph of, Sep 61: 59
TANGIERS, MOROCCO, Mar 61: 22
TANIGUCHI, YOSHIRO, May 61: 42
Monument by, May 61: 48
"TANNHÄUSER," opera, May 63: 69
TANYU. See KANO TANYU
TAPE RECORDER MUSIC, Jan 59: 50–55, 124–27
"TAPESICHORD" MUSIC. See TAPE RECORDER MUSIC
TARIFA, SPAIN, Moslem capture of, Sep 62: 74
TARIK, Moslem general, Sep 62: 74
TARQUINIA, ITALY, necropolis at, May 60: 59–60, 77
TASMAN, ABEL, Sep 58: 15, 19
TASSILI ROCK PAINTINGS, of Sahara, May 59: 70–83, Sep 62: 11, 12, Mar 63: 43
TASSO, TORQUATO
Childhood of, May 60: 33, 34, 36
Portrait of, May 60: 32
Tasso's oak, Jul 61: 70–75
"TASSO'S OAK," painting by Peter Blume, Jul 61: 70–71,

74–75; illus, Jul 61: 72–73
"TASTEMAKERS, THE," book by Russell Lynes, quoted, Mar 59: 113, 114
"TASTE OF HONEY, A," play, May 61: 51
Reviewed, Mar 61: 102, 103
TATE, ALLEN, Jul 61: 75, Sep 61: 117, Jul 63: 72
Quoted: on Adams, Léonie, May 60: 22; on arts and the Kennedy administration, Sep 61: 5
"TATTOOED SAILOR, THE," book by André François, May 59: 112, 118
TAUBER, RICHARD, Jan 61: 27
TAUBMAN, HOWARD, on *Advise and Consent*, quoted, May 62: 117
TAVERNIER, Bastille prisoner, Jan 60: 88
TAVERNIER, JEAN BAPTISTE, Jul 62: 53
TAWDRY, derivation of word, May 60: 128
TAX, INCOME. See INCOME TAX
TAX, POLL, in England, Mar 61: 65
TAXATION, Federal tax laws vs. the individual, Nov 62: 118–19
TAYLOR, British engineer, Jul 62: 66
TAYLOR, A. J. P., memorandum from Adolf Hitler to, Mar 62: 28–29
TAYLOR, BAYARD, Jan 59: 25
TAYLOR, BENJAMIN, Washington, D.C., home of, Sep 61: 14
TAYLOR, DEEMS, Jul 62: 37
TAYLOR, ELIZABETH, May 59: 55, Jan 63: 112
TAYLOR, FRANCIS HENRY, on Walters Art Gallery, quoted, Jul 59: 31
TAYLOR, LAURETTE, Jan 61: 31, May 61: 99
Photograph of, Jan 61: 31
TAYLOR, PETER, Jan 62: 10, 14
TAYLOR, THOMAS, Nov 59: 90
TCHAIKOVSKY, PÊTR ILICH
1812 Overture hoax at Rochester, N.Y., Jan 61: 71
Interpretation of Joan of Arc, Mar 62: 97
Stravinsky, Igor, quoted on, Sep 58: 82
TCHELITCHEW, PAVEL, Jan 61: 46
TEACHERS, IQ of, Mar 62: 74
TEACHING. See EDUCATION
TEAGUE, ROBERT, Nov 62: 68
TEALE, EDWIN WAY, on wilderness, quoted, Mar 60: 16
TEASDALE, SARA, Mar 63: 28
TEBALDI, RENATA, Sep 59: 53, 56
At Metropolitan Opera House, Nov 58: 118, 120
TEBTUNIS PAPYRI, Nov 62: 93
TECHNOLOGY
American, spread and effects of, May 60: 6–9, 122–23
Concrete, use of, Mar 59: 19–21
Ferro-cemento, Mar 59: 21, 122–24
Future of machine civilization, Jan 59: 92–94, 128–29
Princeton, N.J., research projects in, Sep 59: 25–27, 118
Wheeled vehicles, Sep 58: 146–51
TEEN-AGERS, tyranny over motion pictures, radio, and records, Jan 59: 137–39
"TÉLÉMAQUE," French ship, Jul 62: 66
TELEPHONE
Communications satellites and, Jan 62: 18–19, 21
"Don't Call Me; I Won't Call You Either," Jan 63: 118–19
Unlisted, in New York City, Jul 60: 5
TELEVISION (see also CRITIC'S VIEW: CHANNELS; CRITIC'S VIEW: TELEVISION)
Bernstein, Leonard, Jul 59: 18
Burnett, Carol, Sep 61: 80
Chayefsky, Paddy, interview with, Sep 60: 49–56
Children's attitude toward, Mar 62: 40, 41
Cigar commercials, Sep 60: 120
Communications satellites and, Jan 62: 16–21
Creative vs. borrowed forms in, Mar 60: 4–5, 126–28
Effects of Togetherness cult, Nov 58: 146, 147
Federal Trade Commission complaints against commercials, Nov 60: 123
Garry Moore Show, Sep 61: 80
Invasion of privacy by, Jul 60: 5–6, 120, 121
Man's need of novelty and, Jul 59: 108–9, 111
Mass media and imaginary audience, Mar 60: 46–51
"Mr. Eliot Revisits the Waste Land," poem by W. H. Armstrong, Jan 63: 92–93
Nonconformist taste in, Mar 59: 112
Radio vs., Nov 61: 102–3
Talent shown in commercials, Mar 61: 101
Teen-agers and, Jan 59: 139
Ustinov, Peter, Nov 58: 82–84
"Word from Our Sponsors, A," miniature satirical revue, Jul 61: 77
"TELEVISION CULTURE IN ROUND NUMBERS," article by Stephen White, Jul 62: 94–95
TELFORD, THOMAS, Jan 59: 36–37
TELL AGRAB, wheeled vehicles from, Sep 58: 147, 148
TELL EL-AMARNA, Nov 58: 13
TELL EL-KHALIFA, JORDAN, identification with Ezion-geber, Nov 59: 10
TELL EL-QUEDAH, PALESTINE, archaeological site,

Nov 59: 10, 118

TEMKO, ALLAN, articles by
"Arles," Jul 59: 90–98, 129–32
"Dawn of the 'High Modern,' The," Sep 59: 4–21
"Flowering of San Francisco, The," Jan 59: 4–23
"Lifting the Federal Façade," Jan 60: 18–27, 119–21
"Louvre, The," Sep 60: 57–69, 72, 81
Saarinen, Eero, interview, Jul 60: 76–83, 123
"World's Most Daring Builder, The," Mar 59: 18–25, 121–24

TEMPELS, PLACIDE, on Bantu animism, quoted, Mar 63: 106

"TEMPEST, THE," play by Shakespeare, Jul 60: 38
Isak Dinesen quoted on, Sep 59: 111

TEMPLARS. See KNIGHTS OF THE TEMPLE

TEMPLE, 1ST EARL (RICHARD TEMPLE GRENVILLE), May 59: 47

TEMPLE, WILLIAM, on Dutch, quoted, Sep 58: 26

TEMPLETON, JOHN, Sep 59: 55

"TEMPS MODERNES, LES," journal, Nov 59: 69, 72

"TEMPTATION OF ST. ANTHONY, THE," painting by Jacques Callot, Nov 60: 31; illus, Nov 60: 44–45

"TENANT FARMER," painting by Andrew Wyeth, Sep 61: 88, 99; illus, Sep 61: 90–91

"TEN AUTHORS IN PURSUIT OF ONE SUBJECT," article by Malcolm Cowley, Mar 59: 14–17, 117–19

"TENDER IS THE NIGHT," novel by F. Scott Fitzgerald, Jul 62: 100

"TENDERLOIN," musical, May 61: 51

TENERIFE, CANARY ISLANDS, exploration by Alexander von Humboldt, Jul 59: 60, 62

TENIERS, DAVID, Jul 63: 96, 106

"TEN INDIANS," story by Ernest Hemingway, Jan 59: 133

TENLEY, THEODORE, Nov 58: 83

TEN LOST TRIBES OF ISRAEL, theories concerning, Mar 60: 102–3, 124–25

TENN, WILLIAM, "Null P," Mar 63: 79

TENNESSEE VALLEY AUTHORITY, Jan 60: 120

TENNIEL, JOHN, drawing of Jabberwock, Sep 58: 130

TENNYSON, ALFRED, Nov 63: 44–46
On mermaids, quoted, Jan 60: 130
Portrait of, Nov 63: 46

"TEN PAINS OF DEATH, THE," book by Gavin Maxwell, quoted, Sep 61: 43

"TENSEGRITY MAST," work by Buckminster Fuller, Mar 60: 108

"TENTH MAN, THE," play, Sep 60: 49, 53–55, 56

"TEN THOUSAND THINGS, THE," book by Maria Dermoût, Mar 61: 22

TEPE SARAB, IRAN, archaeological site, Sep 62: 4, 7 (map)

TER-ARUTUNIAN, ROUBEN, Sep 62: 110

TER BORCH, GERARD, Sep 58: 26, Jul 63: 106
Painting by, Jul 63: 95

TERENCE
In Renaissance curriculum, Jan 60: 62
Survival of works by, Nov 62: 76, 80

TERESA, SAINT, Nov 61: 109, 111

"TERRITORIAL ENTERPRISE, THE," editorial by Lucius Beebe reprinted from, Nov 58: 148

TERRY, ELLEN, Jul 59: 28

TERRY, WALTER, "Denmark's Royal Ballet," article by, Sep 60: 90–95

TERTULLIAN, quoted
On Hadrian, May 63: 33
On Septuagint manuscript, Nov 62: 78

TESIO, FAUSTO, Nov 62: 45

TEXAS
Source of souvenir cattle horns sold in, Mar 63: 52
Suburbia in, May 61: 18, 19

TEXTILE RESEARCH INSTITUTE, Princeton, N.J., Sep 59: 27

THACKERAY, WILLIAM MAKEPEACE, Nov 61: 35
Vanity Fair, Jan 62: 62, 64

THAIS, Mar 59: 47

THALAMAS, PAUL, May 61: 126

THALBERG, SIGISMOND, Jan 60: 81

THALER, MICHAEL, "A History of Art," drawings by, Jan 61: 120–21

THAMES RIVER, England, tunnel under, from Rotherhithe to Wapping, Jan 59: 34–35

THAMES RIVER, at New London, Conn., Mar 60: 26

"THAT HIDEOUS STRENGTH," novel by C. S. Lewis, May 59: 64, 125–26

THEATRE (see also "ON STAGE")
Absurd. See THEATRE OF THE ABSURD
After-dark satire, Jan 62: 66–71
Alienation theory, Mar 61: 44, 46
Ancient sites used for performances, Jul 62: 27–31
Anouilh, Jean, and his plays, Nov 60: 50–55, 126–27
At Bauhaus, Nov 61: 62, 68, 71
Brecht, Bertolt, May 61: 34–41
Camelot, May 61: 102–13

Chance as principle of creation in, Sep 60: 124, Mar 61: 45–46
Chayefsky, Paddy, Sep 60: 49–56
Circle in the Square, New York City, Mar 60: 94–99, 119–21
Corey, Orlin and Irene, and their theatre, Jan 63: 88–91
Crawling Arnold, play by Jules Feiffer, Nov 61: 49–56
"Crazy Gang," English vaudeville comics, Jan 61: 122–23
Current, articles by Robert Hatch on: "Actors Studio Goes Legit, The," Nov 62: 106–8; "Arise, Ye Playgoers of the World," Jul 61: 116–18; "Case for Repertory, The," Jan 63: 106–9; "Coming Talent Casts Its Shadow Before, A," Jul 62: 91–94; "Disturbing? Jean Genet Is Downright Terrifying," Nov 61: 98–102; "Human Beings and Substitutes," Mar 61: 102–3; "Hunt for Heroes, The," May 62: 110–12; "Laugh Now, Pay Later," Mar 63: 106–9; "Laughter at Your Own Risk," Sep 60: 112–16; "Melodrama on Broadway: Our Secret Lives Are Showing," May 63: 106–8; "On Being Upstaged by Scenery," Sep 62: 110–12; "Persistence of Ibsenism, The," Jan 62: 106–8; "Roaring Presence of Brendan Behan, The," Jan 61: 113–14; "This Blessed Plot, This Shakespeare in the Park," Nov 60: 116–18; "Where There Is Total Involvement," Mar 62: 106–9
Dyskolos, The, of Menander, Jul 59: 78–79; translation by Gilbert Highet, Jul 59: 80–88
English Stage Company and revolt against West End, Jan 63: 26–33
Ford Foundation aid to, Jan 62: 9–10, 13
Form and anti-form in, Mar 61: 42–47
Gang-and-girl show, Sep 58: 58, 59
Greatness in, Jan 63: 26–33
Guthrie, Tyrone, and Minneapolis theatre, Nov 63: 35–41
Hollywood influence on, Mar 60: 128
Humor on Broadway, Jan 61: 123
Of India: Kathakali, Nov 63: 66–68, 72
Ionesco, Eugène, May 61: 89–97
Japanese, Jul 59: 126
Kean, Edmund, and plays based on his life, Mar 62: 12–13, 114–19
MacLeish, Archibald, on being a poet in the theatre, interview, Jan 60: 48–56
Memorandum from Lucius Annaeus Seneca to Tennessee Williams, May 59: 54–55
Monk, Julius, and miniature late-evening satirical revue, Jul 61: 76–77
Mostel, Zero, May 62: 50–53
Musical comedy, Sep 58: 56–61, 143–44
"Nothing" plays, Nov 58: 62–65
Off-Broadway theatres, Jul 59: 41–42, Mar 60: 98–99, 119, Sep 62: 111
O'Neill, Eugene, New London, Conn., youth of, Mar 60: 25–40
In Provincetown, Mass., Jul 61: 13, 16
Pulitzer Prizes in drama, Jul 63: 71
Roman theatre at Arles, Jul 59: 129
In San Francisco Bay Region, Jan 59: 22
Scott, George C., Jul 60: 92–93
Shortage of theatres, Sep 58: 143
Shylock, riddle of, Jan 60: 89–96
Strumpets on Broadway, May 61: 50–51
Survival of Greek and Roman plays, Nov 62: 76, 80, 83, 88–89
Theatre and stage forms, Jul 59: 41–48
In Topeka, Kans., Sep 59: 86, 88, 122–23
Topical show, Sep 58: 58–59
Tyranny of teens in, Jan 59: 138
Tyrone Guthrie Theatre, Minneapolis, Nov 63: 35–41
Unthink cult in, Sep 58: 38, 42–43
Ustinov, Peter, Nov 58: 82–85, 137–39
Vaudeville, Jul 59: 112–20
Welles, Orson, career of, Jul 63: 86–87
"Why the French Need Shakespeare," article by Jean-Louis Barrault, Sep 61: 102–9

"THEATRE ARTS MONTHLY," on repertory, quoted, Jan 63: 107, 108

"THEATRE BREAKS OUT OF BELASCO'S BOX, THE," article by Walter Kerr, Jul 59: 41–48

THEATRE DE LYS, New York City, Mar 60: 98

"THEATRE OF CHANCE, THE," Sep 60: 124, Mar 61: 45–46

"THEATRE OF FORM AND ANTI-FORM, THE," article by Walter Kerr, Mar 61: 42–47

THEATRE OF THE ABSURD, Sep 62: 33–41, 111
Melodrama and, May 63: 106, 107

THÉAULON, Mar 62: 118

"THEIR NAMES ARE WRIT IN WEBSTER," article by Gilbert Highet, May 60: 126–28

THEOCRITUS, in Renaissance curriculum, Jan 60: 62

THEODORA, BYZANTINE EMPRESS, Sep 60: 126, Nov 63: 10, 11, 12
Portrait of, Nov 63: 18–19

THEODOSIUS, monk, on Syracuse cathedral, quoted, Sep 61: 22

THEODOSIUS I, ROMAN EMPEROR, May 63: 78

THEODOSIUS II, BYZANTINE EMPEROR, May 63: 78, Nov 63: 11

THEODOSIUS III, BYZANTINE EMPEROR, Nov 63: 26

"THEORY OF THE COIFFURED LASSES, A," drawings by Marcello Mariotti, Mar 63: 118–19

"THERE SHALL BE NO NIGHT," play, May 62: 6, 8

THERON, TYRANT OF ACRAGAS, Sep 61: 23

"THESE THOUSAND HILLS," motion picture, Sep 60: 88

THESSALONICA, KINGDOM OF, Nov 63: 31

"THETIS," ship, bullion salvaged from, Nov 58: 77

"THEY ALL ADD UP TO ZERO," article by Thomas Meehan, May 62: 50–53

"THEY KEPT THE OLD FLAG FLYING," article by Geoffrey Bocca, Sep 63: 74–81

THIANGES, MARQUISE DE, Nov 61: 34

THIBLE, MME., Sep 58: 118

THICKNESSE, PHILIP, Nov 59: 90

THIEBAUD, WAYNE, Jan 63: 25

"THIEF'S JOURNAL, A," book by Jean Genet, Nov 61: 98, 99

THIEL, RUDOLF, And There Was Light, quoted, Jul 62: 86

THIERRY, AMÉDÉE, Mar 63: 7

THINKOMETER, Nov 58: 32, 33, 147

"THIN MAN, THE," motion picture, Mar 60: 127

"THIRD MAN, THE," novel by Graham Greene, May 61: 117
Motion picture based on, Nov 59: 31, 126, Mar 61: 98, Jul 63: 91

THIRTY TYRANTS, Jul 60: 102–3

THIRTY YEARS' WAR, Nov 62: 32–41
Millenarism and philo-Semitism during, Mar 60: 101–2

"THIS IS YOUR LIFE," television program, Jul 60: 6

"THIS MUSIC CREPT BY ME UPON THE WATERS," radio play, Jan 60: 54

THOMAS, DYLAN, Sep 61: 119
Sketch of, Sep 58: 84
Stravinsky, Igor, quoted on, Sep 58: 84

THOMAS, HENRI, Jul 63: 74

THOMAS, ROBERT, photograph of, Nov 61: 79

THOMPSON, FRANCIS, Mar 61: 12, 19
Photograph of, Mar 61: 12

THOMPSON, MARCIA, Jan 62: 12

THOMPSON, RANDALL, Jul 59: 20

THOMSON, VIRGIL, Jul 59: 72
Mother of Us All, The, Jul 59: 20
On Stern, Isaac, quoted, Jul 60: 126

THOREAU, HENRY DAVID, Mar 60: 13, 15, May 63: 115, Sep 63: 100
Quoted: on being awake, Mar 62: 75; on man's flying, May 61: 16; on man's view of past and present, Jul 60: 32; on Walden Pond, Sep 58: 51

THORNDIKE, SYBIL, Jan 61: 30

THORWALDSEN, BERTEL, Sep 59: 49

"THOSE STRANGE AMERICANS ACROSS THE HUDSON," article excerpted from The Waist-High Culture, book by Thomas Griffith, Jul 59: 121–25

"THOUSAND CLOWNS, A," play, Mar 63: 108

"THREE FRIENDS AND HUNDRED BIRDS," painting by Pien Wen-chin, Jan 61: 25; illus, Jan 61: 24

"THREE MEN ON A HORSE," play, Mar 63: 106

"THREE MUSICIANS," painting by Picasso, Nov 61: 10, 12; illus, Nov 61: 13

"THREE ORPHANS AND THEIR PATRON SAINT," article by Jean Stafford, Sep 60: 116–17

"THREEPENNY OPERA," musical, Nov 58: 62, Jan 60: 123, May 62: 35

"THREE SISTERS, THE," play, Tyrone Guthrie Theatre production, Nov 63: 38, 39–40, 41

"THRONE OF BLOOD," motion picture, Jul 62: 44

"THROUGH THE AGES IN THE BEST BEDS," illustrated feature, May 60: 129–36

"THROUGH THE GLASS BRIGHTLY," article by Wolf Von Eckardt, Sep 62: 22–32

"THROUGH THE LOOKING GLASS," book by Lewis Carroll, quoted, Jul 63: 34

THUCYDIDES, Sep 63: 97, 101
Quoted: on corruption of language by war, Jul 63: 37; on military divers, Nov 58: 71
Survival of works by, Nov 62: 78

"THUCYDIDES' WAR," article by M. I. Finley, Jan 60: 41–45

THURBER, JAMES, May 60: 21, May 63: 46
Hemingway, Ernest, quoted on, Jan 59: 133
On oral culture, quoted, Jul 63: 35
Photograph of, May 60: 21

THURSTONE, L. L., Mar 62: 71

THYNNE, THOMAS, house of, Nov 58: 38–39

TIAMAT, Mesopotamian deity, Jul 61: 37

TIARA OF SAITAPHERNES, Mar 59: 105

TIBBETT, LAWRENCE, Sep 59: 55

TIBERIUS, ROMAN EMPEROR, Sep 63: 3
  Cave of, May 59: 102–7, 122–24
  Coin portraits of, Sep 63: 36, 38
  Coins from reign of, Sep 63: 38–39
TIBERIUS CLAUDIUS NERO, Jul 59: 95
TIBET, traditional Paradise of, Nov 60: 31
TIDSWELL, CHARLOTTE, Mar 62: 13, 114, 115
TIEPOLO, GIOVANNI BATTISTA, works by, Jan 61: 2,
  3, Mar 61: 66–67
TIERNEY, GENE, May 62: 118
TIETJENS, EUNICE, on *Spectra*, quoted, May 60: 43
TIGER, mechanical man-eating, of Sultan of Mysore, Sep
  60: 13; illus, Sep 60: 20–21
"TIGER, THE," play, May 63: 10
"TIGER BAY," motion picture, Sep 60: 116
"TIGER, TIGER, BURNING BRIGHT," play, May 63:
  107–8
"TIGHT LITTLE ISLAND," motion picture, May 59: 99
TILLICH, PAUL, Sep 63: 8, 9, 105, 106
  MacLeish, Archibald, quoted on, Jan 60: 56
  Photograph of, Sep 63: 8
  Systematic Theology, quoted, Jan 59: 122
TILSIT (SOVETSK), U.S.S.R., meeting of Napoleon and
  Alexander I at, Sep 63: 28–32
TIME
  Communications satellites and, Jan 62: 21
  Tyranny of, Jul 62: 80–88
"TIME," magazine
  And American poetry, Sep 61: 117, 119
  "Cover" stories of, Jul 60: 120
  On Japanese use of tranquilizers, quoted, Mar 61: 6
"TIME CYCLE," musical creation by Lukas Foss, Jan 63:
  78
"TIMELESS HOME OF THE MOTHER GODDESS,"
  article by Freya Stark, Sep 58: 86–87, 140–42
"TIMELESS TEUTONS," album of photographs by
  August Sander, Mar 60: 41–45
TIME-LIFE BUILDING, London, Eero Saarinen quoted
  on, Jul 60: 79
"TIME MACHINE, THE," book by H. G. Wells, Jul 62:
  85, Mar 63: 78–79
"TIME OF MAN, THE," article by Loren Eiseley, Mar 62:
  4–11
TIME PARADOX, Jul 62: 87
"TIME REMEMBERED," play, Nov 60: 51, 52, 54, 127
"TIMES, THE," of London, quoted on Edmund Kean, Mar
  62: 116
TIME TRAVEL, Jul 62: 84–86, 88
TIMEWELL, R. S., Nov 62: 65, 66
TIMOTHEUS, Greek poet, Nov 62: 93
TIMOTHEUS, AULUS KAPREILIUS, May 62: 42–43,
  46, 47–48
TIMURID DYNASTY, of Persia, Jan 63: 52 (chart), 57,
  58, 67, 68–69
"TIN DRUM, THE," novel by Günter Grass, Jul 63: 73
  Reviewed, Mar 63: 111–13
TINSEL PRINTS, Sep 63: 3
TINTORETTO, Jul 61: 90, 94
  Lady in Black, Jul 59: 30
TIPU SAHIB, SULTAN OF MYSORE, mechanical man-
  eating tiger of, Sep 60: 13; illus, Sep 60: 20–21
TIRES, medieval, Sep 58: 151
TIRO, Cicero's slave and secretary, Jan 63: 116, 117
TIROL, and Thirty Years' War, Nov 62: 34, 36, 37
TIRSO DE MOLINA, *The Trickster of Seville and the Guest
  of Stone,* Jan 62: 58–59
TISCHENDORF, KONSTANTIN VON, Nov 62: 94
  Portrait of, Nov 62: 82
TISHMAN BUILDING, New York City, motion picture
  about, Mar 61: 16–17
TISSIER, JEAN BAPTISTE ANGE, painting by, Sep 60:
  68
TISSOT, JAMES, painting by, May 62: 74–75
"TITANIC," White Star liner, May 59: 7
"TITANS, THE," composition by William Russo, Jul 59:
  21
TITIAN, Jan 59: 103, Jul 59: 29, Sep 60: 34, 62, Nov 61:
  7, 12
  Charles I as collector of paintings by, Jul 61: 89, 90, 94,
  95, Jul 63: 93–94, 96
  Influence on Poussin, Mar 61: 80, 91, 92
  Judgment of Cercyon, forgery of, Mar 59: 105
  Paintings by. See ILLUSTRATIONS INDEX
TIVOLI, ITALY
  Hadrian's Villa, May 63: 32–39
  Villa d'Este, May 63: 35; water gardens of, May 59: 29,
  May 62: 12, 13–14, 18–19, 22–23
"TO BE A POLITICIAN," book by Stimson Bullitt, ex-
  cerpt from, May 59: 20–23
TOBEY, MARK, Sep 58: 113, Jan 59: 13, Jul 59: 76, Jul
  60: 114, Sep 60: 122
  Painting by, Jul 59: 76
"TOBY TYLER," motion picture, reviewed, Sep 60: 117
TOCH, ERNST, Mar 63: 30

TOCQUEVILLE, ALEXIS DE, May 60: 6
  Democracy in America, quoted, Nov 62: 112
"TODAY IS FRIDAY," story by Ernest Hemingway, Jan
  59: 133
"TODAY'S TEMPLE OF TALENT," article by Stephen
  White, Mar 61: 101
TODD, MABEL LOOMIS, Jul 61: 104
TODD SCHOOL, Jul 63: 86
TOGETHERNESS
  Chayefsky, Paddy, quoted on, Sep 60: 55
  Revolt against, Nov 58: 30–33, 146–47
  In tourism, Mar 59: 83
TOGLIATTI, PALMIRO, Sep 61: 37
TOKYO, JAPAN
  Highway-building-carpark unit, Jan 62: 94, 95
  Hiroshige's prints of, May 60: 104
  Imperial Hotel, Sep 59: 8
TOLEDAN TABLES, Sep 62: 80, 92
"TO LIVE," motion picture, Jul 62: 45–46
TOLKIEN, J. R. R., May 59: 66
TOLSTOY, LEO, Mar 62: 110, 111
  Anna Karenina, Jan 62: 62
  As caricatured by Max Beerbohm, May 61: 38
  Gorky, Maxim, quoted on, May 62: 51
  War and Peace, Jan 62: 62; Andrew Wyeth quoted on, Sep
  61: 100
  What Is Art? quoted, Nov 60: 56
TOMB CHAMBERS
  Of Bronze Age (passage graves), Jul 60: 87, 89
  Of Marlik Tepe, Iran, Nov 62: 102
TOMB PAINTINGS
  Egyptian, to illustrate Bible passages, illus, Nov 59: cover,
  3, 14–19
  Etruscan, May 60: 59–60, 77–78; illus, May 60: 62, 63,
  65–72
"—TO ME, IT SOUNDS LIKE NEWSPEAK," comment
  by William Harlan Hale, Mar 61: 97
"TOMORROW IS ALREADY HERE," book by Robert
  Jungk, quoted, May 60: 8
TONE, FRANCHOT, Jul 59: 42
TONE-ROW, in music. See TWELVE-TONE ROW
TOOHEY, JOHN PETER, Jul 62: 37
"TOO MUCH, TOO SOON," book about Diana Barry-
  more, Jul 60: 120
TOOTHPASTE, advertising of, Nov 60: 123
"TOPAZ," American sealing ship, Sep 63: 47
TOPEKA, KANS., cultural development of, Sep 59: 86–91,
  122–23
TOPEKA CIVIC SYMPHONY ORCHESTRA, Sep 59:
  86, 91, 122, 123
TOPKAPI MUSEUM, Istanbul, May 59: 56, 131
TOPOLSKI, FELIKS, Nov 60: 128
  Murals by, Nov 60: 129–36
"TOPOLSKI'S CORONATION," article by Timothy
  Green, Nov 60: 128–36
"TOPPER," television show, Jul 61: 98
TORAH CEREMONY, Nov 62: 76
"TORCH OF LIFE, THE," book by René Dubos, excerpt
  from, Nov 62: 5–9
TORELLI, GIACOMO, Jul 63: 82
TORN, RIP, Nov 62: 108, May 63: 107
TORRE VELASCA, Milan, Nov 60: 125; illus, Nov 60: 15
TORRICELLI, EVANGELISTA, experiment of, Jan 63:
  99–100
TORRIO, JOHNNY, Sep 61: 44
TORROJA, EDUARDO, Sep 59: 19, Mar 59: 123
TORTONA, ITALY, parabolic warehouses in, Mar 59: 122
"TOSCA," opera, Mar 61: 72
  Welitsch-Tibbett performance of, Sep 59: 55
TOSCANINI, ARTURO, Nov 58: 24, 120, Jul 59: 18,
  Sep 59: 52, 55, Sep 61: 84, 85
  Thomas Beecham and, Mar 62: 104, 105
TOSHIHITO, PRINCE, Sep 61: 65
TOTA, QUEEN OF NAVARRE, Sep 62: 79
"TOTAL REVOLUTION IN THE NOVEL," article by
  Richard Gilman, Jan 62: 96–101
TOTAL SERIALISM, in music. See under SERIAL
  TECHNIQUE
TOTO, Mar 61: 100
TOUCHAGUES, French painter, Mar 62: 99
"TOUCH OF EVIL," motion picture, Jul 63: 90
"TOUCH OF THE POET, A," play, New London, Conn.,
  background of, Mar 60: 31
TOULOUSE-LAUTREC, HENRI DE, May 60: 104, Sep
  60: 34, Mar 62: 15, 16, 25
TOUREL, JENNIE, Sep 58: 134
TOURETTE, LE COUVENT SAINTE-MARIE DE LA,
  Mar 61: 34–41
TOURISM
  Englishmen in Europe, Tobias Smollett quoted on, Nov 59:
  84
  Established in Paris, May 63: 70–71
  Of Europeans, Mar 63: 8
  Grand Tour of 18th and 19th centuries, Nov 59: 73–104,

  Mar 62: 55, 56
  In Japan, Mar 61: 7
  Visit U.S.A. program, Sep 62: 116–19
  Vulgarization of cities by, Sep 58: 54
  What not to see in Europe, Mar 59: 82–85, 120
TOURNACHON, G. F. See NADAR
TOURNAMENTS, of Middle Ages, Nov 58: 92–107
TOURS, FRANCE, Battle of Poitiers, Sep 62: 74–75
"TO WAKEN AN OLD LADY," poem by William Carlos
  Williams, quoted, Sep 61: 120
"TOWARD NEW TOWNS FOR AMERICA," book by
  Clarence Stein, Jul 59: 12
TOWER OF BABEL, Jan 62: 94
TOWNLEY, CHARLES, Nov 59: 102
TOWNSEND, JAMES, Jul 62: 40
TOYNBEE, ARNOLD J., Mar 59: 6, 10, 13, May 60: 5,
  Nov 60: 99, Sep 61: 10, Sep 63: 99
  On Angkor, quoted, Jan 59: 61
  "Historian's Struggle with Religion, The," article excerpted
  from *Reconsiderations,* book by, Jan 61: 57–65
  Malraux, André, compared to, Nov 58: 8–9
  Portrait of, Mar 59: 13
"TOYS ON A FIELD OF BLUE," motion picture, Nov
  62: 98
"TRACK OF THE CAT, THE," novel by Walter Van Til-
  burg Clark, Jan 59: 19
TRADE. See COMMERCE; FOREIGN TRADE
TRADESCANT, JOHN, Nov 63: 73
"TRAFALGAR," painting by Turner, Jul 63: 106
TRAFFIC
  In ancient Rome, Jul 61: 45
  In baroque city, Jul 61: 52
  In Italy, Nov 61: 125–27
  In Los Angeles, Jul 61: 63
  Memorandum from Julius Caesar to Robert Moses, Mar 59:
  26–27; comment on, May 63: 105
  Regulations in U.S.S.R., Jul 62: 116–17
"TRAGEDY OF GOOD INTENTIONS, THE," play,
  Nov 58: 137
TRAGER, GEORGE L., Mar 60: 123
  On phoneme and morpheme, quoted, Jul 63: 45
TRAHERNE, THOMAS, on gardening, quoted, May 59:
  25
"TRAIL OF THE SPLENDID GYPSY, THE," article
  by Stanley Kauffmann, Mar 62: 12–13, 114–19
TRAJAN, ROMAN EMPEROR, May 63: 34
  Coinage during reign of, Sep 63: 38, 39; illus, Sep 63: 36
TRAJAN LETTERS, Sep 59: 125, 126
TRANQUILIZERS, Japanese use of, Mar 61: 6
"TRANSATLANTIC REVIEW," periodical, Jan 59: 132
  Article by William Burroughs in, quoted, Jul 63: 39–40
TRANSPORTATION
  "Law of diminishing transportation," Sep 58: 152
  Wheeled vehicles, Sep 58: 146–51
TRANSVAAL, UNION OF SOUTH AFRICA, N'debele vil-
  lages of, Nov 60: 56–65
TRANS-WORLD AIRLINES, terminal at New York Inter-
  national Airport, Sep 59: 19, Jul 60: 82
TRASK, WILLARD R., articles translated by
  "Abu Simbel: The Seal on the Gate of Egypt," Jul 60: 10–
  15, 124–25
  "In Search of the Etruscans," May 60: 56–79
  "Surprise in the Sahara," May 59: 70–83
"TRAUERFLORA," book of drawings by Paul Flora, Sep
  59: 92
TRAVEL (see also TOURISM)
  Advertising of, Nov 59: 115
  Burton, Richard Francis, Jul 63: 110–17
  Communications satellites and, Jan 62: 18
  Humboldt, Alexander von, as traveler, Jul 59: 62–68
  Influence of Grand Tour of 18th century on, Nov 59: 94
  Non-hotels, Mar 63: 115–17
  Peter the Great in Europe, Sep 59: 66–74
  Pilgrimage of Friar Felix Fabri to Mount Sinai, Mar 60:
  81–93
  Qualifications for, Edward Gibbon quoted on, Nov 59: 84
  Search for hammams, during Mediterranean cruise, Sep 60:
  125–26
  Search for paradise, Mar 61: 20–33
  Silent Traveller draws the West, Nov 59: 129–36
  U.S. and U.S.S.R. compared, Jul 62: 112–19
**"TRAVELING AMONG STREAMS AND MOUN-
  TAINS,"** painting by Fan K'uan, Jan 61: 16; illus, Jan
  61: 19
"TRAVIATA, LA," opera
  Moffo, Anna, in, Jul 61: 97
  Patti performance of, in Boston, Sep 59: 54
TREACHER, ARTHUR, Sep 58: 76
"TREASURE ISLAND," novel by Stevenson, and motion
  picture based on, compared, May 62: 116
"TREASURE OF THE SIERRA MADRE, THE," mo-
  tion picture, Jul 63: 90
TREATY OF NYSTADT, Sep 59: 80
TREATY OF WESTPHALIA, Sep 59: 60

TREDREE, H. L., *The Strange Ordeal of the Normandier,* on television, Mar 60: 4–5

"TREE OF COOLE, THE," article by Robert Emmett Ginna, Mar 59: 86–89

TREITSCHKE, HEINRICH VON, Mar 59: 6

"TRELAWNY OF THE 'WELLS,' " play, quoted, Mar 62: 117

TRENCH, HERBERT, May 61: 37

TRENTON, N.J., Jewish Community Center bathhouse, Sep 62: 59; illus, Sep 62: 60

"TRÈS RICHES HEURES." See BOOK OF HOURS

TRESSART, JOHN, on Joan of Arc, quoted, Mar 62: 94

TREVELYAN, GEORGE MACAULAY, on cricket, quoted, Nov 58: 53

TREVOR-ROPER, H. R., articles by
 "Case of Coexistence, A: Christendom and the Turks," reprinted from *Men and Events,* book by, Sep 58: 46–47
 "Europe's Brief Flood Tide of Philo-Semitism," Mar 60: 100–3, 124–25
 "Great Confrontations III: Mary, Queen of Scots, and John Knox," Jul 63: 28–32
 " 'Last Universal Man, The,' " Jul 59: 56–69, 128
 "Persecution of Witches, The," Nov 59: 57–63
 "Sudden End of the Renaissance, The," Sep 59: 28–29, 120–21
 "Two Spains of Don Quixote, The," Nov 61: 106–13
 "Why Do Great Wars Begin?" Nov 62: 32–41

"TRIAL, THE," novel by Kafka, motion picture based on, Jul 63: 85, 89, 90, 91

"TRICKSTER OF SEVILLE AND THE GUEST OF STONE," play, Jan 62: 58–59

TRIER, GERMANY, Jul 59: 130
 Witch mania in, Nov 59: 60, 61

TRIGETIUS, prefect of Italy, 452, May 63: 79

TRILLING, LIONEL, Alfred Kazin quoted on, Jul 62: 103

"TRIMALCHIO'S DINNER," satire by Petronius, Nov 62: 86, May 63: 81

TRINITY ALTARPIECE, painting by Hugo van der Goes, Jul 63: 94; illus, Jul 63: 95

TRINQUETAILLE, FRANCE, Jul 59: 97

"TRIO," stories by Somerset Maugham, motion picture based on, May 62: 116

TRIPOLI, during Crusades, Jan 59: 87

"TRIP TO THE MOON, A," motion picture, Nov 62: 97

TRISTAN MYTH, Denis de Rougemont quoted on, Jan 62: 58

TRISTAN UND ISOLDE," opera, Mar 62: 104, May 63: 41, 42, 45
 Liebestod from, Sep 60: 121

TRISTRAM and ISOUD, versions of James Knowles and Thomas Malory, May 60: 117–18

TRITONS, Jan 60: 134

"TRIUMPH OF CAESAR," painting by Mantegna, Jul 61: 90, 94, Jul 63: 94; illus, Jul 63: 95

"TRIUMPH OF ST. JOAN, THE," opera, Jan 60: 123

"TROJAN HORSE, THE," radio play, Jan 60: 54

"TROJAN HORSELESS CARRIAGE, THE," article by Oliver Jensen, Jan 60: 118–19

TROJAN WAR, Jul 60: 85, 113
 Historical light on, Jan 61: 73–99

TROLLEY CARS. See STREETCARS

TROLLOPE, ANTHONY, Jul 63: 13
 In painting by W. P. Frith, May 62: 62

TROLLOPE, FRANCES, on Italian streets, quoted, Nov 61: 120

TROMP, MARTIN, Sep 58: 15, 20

"TROPIC OF CANCER," book by Henry Miller, Nov 61: 104–5, May 62: 55

"TROPIC OF CAPRICORN," book by Henry Miller, Nov 61: 104, 105, May 62: 55

"TROPISMES," novel by Nathalie Sarraute, Jan 62: 97

TROPPAU, PROTOCOL OF, Mar 63: 5

TROTSKY, LEON, Jan 59: 115

TROTTA, GERI, "On Stage: Edward Albee," article by, Sep 61: 78–79

"TROVATORE, IL," opera, Mar 62: 119

"TROVE OF PAZYRYK, THE," illustrated feature, Jan 60: 110–12

TROY, HUGH, hoaxes by, Jan 61: 68, 72

TROY, WILLIAM, May 60: 22

TRUAX, HAWLEY, Jul 62: 37

"TRUE GLORY, THE," motion picture, Sep 60: 50

TRUFFAUT, FRANÇOIS, May 60: 51–52, 53, Mar 61: 19, Jan 62: 109
 Portrait of, May 60: 54

TRUMAN, HARRY S., Jul 61: 66, Mar 63: 7, Nov 63: 58
 In 1948 election, predictions concerning, Mar 60: 49

TRUMBO, DALTON, May 62: 117

TRURO, MASS., Jul 61: 12, 13

"TRY 'MASSACHUSETTS' ON YOUR PIANO," article by Gilbert Highet, Nov 61: 118–19

TS'AO CHIH-PAI, painting by, Mar 60: 12

TSOEDE FIGURES, Mar 63: 46, 51

TS'UI PO, Jan 61: 16, 25

Painting by, Jan 61: 17

TUAREGS, Sep 62: 88

TUBUAI ISLAND, Sep 63: 45

TUCCI, NICCOLO, "Domenico Gnoli's World of Fantasy," article by, Jul 59: 135–36

TUILERIES, Sep 60: 65–66, 69, 72, 81

TUKEY, JOHN W., Nov 63: 61

TULIPS, May 59: 41, 60

TULLY, GORDON, photograph of, Jan 63: 11

TULLY, RICHARD WALTON, Jan 60: 125

"TUNES OF GLORY," motion picture, Nov 61: 115

TUNNELS
 Box Hill, near Bath, England, Jan 59: 38
 Thames River, Rotherhithe to Wapping, Jan 59: 34–35

TURGENEV, IVAN, Sep 59: 79

TURIN, ITALY
 Exhibition halls, Mar 59: 22, 24, 121–22
 Street furniture, Nov 59: 107
 Tourney staged in, Nov 58: 107

"TURKENSPIEL," play, Sep 58: 46

TURKEY
 Aphrodisias and its ruins, Mar 63: 96–101
 Archaeological sites at Beldibi, Hacilar, and Çatal Hüyük, Sep 62: 7 (map), 8; sculptures found at Çatal Hüyük, Nov 63: 66–67; wall paintings at Çatal Hüyük, Sep 62: 10–13
 Ephesus, Sep 58: 85–87, 140–42
 Iron smelting developed in, Jul 60: 113
 Prehistoric wheeled vehicles in, Sep 58: 147
 Sardis, Sep 63: 82–89

TURKISH BATHS, of Near East, Sep 60: 125–26

TURKISH EMPIRE. See OTTOMAN EMPIRE

TURKS. See OTTOMAN TURKS; SELJUK TURKS

TURNER, J. M. W., May 60: 104, May 62: 59, 64, 73, Jul 63: 92, 106
 Egremont as patron of, Mar 63: 62–71
 Portrait of, Mar 63: 65
 Works by. See ILLUSTRATIONS INDEX

TURNER, PETE, N'debele life, photographs by, Nov 60: 57–64

TURNER, P. W., *Cry Dawn in Dark Babylon,* Jan 63: 88

TURNEY, MATT, Nov 62: 68, 98
 Portrait of, Nov 62: 69

"TURN OF THE SCREW, THE," story by Henry James, television version, Mar 60: 127, Mar 63: 35

TUSCANY (see also ETRUSCANS)
 Etruscan heritage in language, May 60: 64
 Lawrence, D. H., in, May 60: 59

TUTUOLA, AMOS, *The Palm-Wine Drinkard,* Nov 62: 109

TUTWILER, JULIA S., Alabama song, quoted, Nov 61: 119

TWAIN, MARK, Jan 59: 7, 25, May 60: 134, Jul 63: 114
 Captain Stormfield's Visit to Heaven, May 59: 126
 Hemingway, Ernest, quoted on, Jan 59: 132, 133
 Huckleberry Finn: characterization of "Jim," Jan 60: 96; compared to *The Catcher in the Rye,* May 62: 101, 102, 103; quoted, Sep 59: 27
 Joan of Arc, Mar 62: 98
 In Paris, May 63: 70, 72
 Quoted, Nov 60: 21; on Basilica in Venice, Mar 63: 15; on river boats, Mar 63: 94
 In South Seas, Jan 60: 124–25

"TWELFTH NIGHT," play by Shakespeare
 Opera based on, May 62: 82
 Quoted, Mar 62: 13

TWELVE-TONE ROW, in music, Jan 63: 77–78, 79, 80

TWENTIES. See NINETEEN-TWENTIES

"TWENTY-FIVE CENTURIES OF PERSIA," article by Terence O'Donnell, Jan 63: 40–72

"TWILIGHT IN THE HAMMAM," article by Francis Steegmuller, Sep 60: 125–26

TWINING, EDWARD FRANCIS
 And his book, *A History of the Crown Jewels of Europe,* May 63: 92–96
 Photograph of, May 63: 93

TWINING, HELEN MARY (LADY TWINING), May 63: 93, 96

TWITCHELL, KARL S., Nov 59: 119

"TWO CHEERS FOR MEDIOCRITY," article by Stephen White, Sep 62: 114–15

"TWO FIGURES WITH VERMILION LIGHT," painting by Elmer Bischoff, Jul 60: 115; illus, Jul 60: 23

"TWO GENTLEMEN OF VERONA," play by Shakespeare, Nov 60: 118

"TWO HANIWA," print by Kiyoshi Saito, May 60: 113, 114; illus, May 60: 106

TWORKOV, JACK, Jul 61: 23, Jan 63: 16
 Portrait of, with paintings by, Jul 61: 22

"TWO SPAINS OF DON QUIXOTE, THE," article by H. R. Trevor-Roper, Nov 61: 106–13

"TWO WORLDS OF ALEXANDER, THE," article by C. A. Robinson, Jr., Mar 59: 28–59

TYLER, WILLIAM D., on advertising as reflection of

American society, quoted, Nov 62: 114

TYNAN, KENNETH, Jan 63: 86
 Quoted: on *Death of Bessie Smith, The,* Jul 61: 116; on English Stage Company productions, Jan 63: 29

"TYPEE," story by Herman Melville, Jan 60: 124
 Quoted, Mar 61: 27

TYPE STYLES
 Bauhaus influence on, Nov 61: 69
 Futura, Sep 59: 128
 Origins in handwriting, Sep 59: 125–26

TYPEWRITERS, Adriano Olivetti, manufacturer of, Nov 59: 45–51, 127

"TYPISTS, THE," play, May 63: 10

"TYRANNY OF THE TEENS, THE," article by William K. Zinsser, Jan 59: 137–39

TYRE
 Destruction by Alexander the Great, Mar 59: 40, 42
 In Third Crusade, Jan 59: 88

TYRO. See TIRO

TYROL. See TIROL

"TYRONE GUTHRIE: THE ARTIST AS MAN OF THE THEATRE," article by Robert Hatch, Nov 63: 35–41

TYRRHENIANS. See ETRUSCANS

TYRRHENUS, PRINCE OF LYDIA, May 60: 61

U

"UBU ROI," play, May 61: 89

UDALL, STEWART, Sep 61: 5, 10, 13, 17
 Photograph of, Sep 61: 8

UFFIZI GALLERY, Florence, Jul 59: 28

UGANDA, Edward Francis Twining in, May 63: 93

"UGLY AMERICA, THE," article by Peter Blake, May 61: 4–19

"UGLY AMERICAN, THE," novel by Eugene Burdick, Jan 59: 19

UHDE, WILHELM, Nov 61: 9

ULBRICHT, WALTER, May 62: 41

ULLMAN, JAMES RAMSEY, "The Dream of the South Seas," article by, Jan 60: 28–31, 124–27

ULTRAVIOLET RAYS, Nov 63: 51–52

ULUCH ALI, DEY OF ALGIERS, Jul 63: 53, 57, 58

"ULYSSES," motion picture, May 61: 57

"ULYSSES," novel by James Joyce, Jan 61: 116, Jan 62: 64
 Hemingway, Ernest, quoted on, Jan 59: 132
 Jung, Carl G., quoted on, Nov 61: 105
 Marquise Went Out at Five compared to, May 62: 115
 Quoted, Sep 58: 131

"ULYSSES IN NIGHTTOWN," play, May 62: 51

UMANO. See MEALE, GAETANO

UMAYYAD CALIPHATE OF DAMASCUS, Sep 62: 75

"UMBERTO D.," motion picture, Mar 61: 98, 100

"UNCOMMON THOUGHTS IN A COMMON PLACE," article by Gilbert Highet, Sep 61: 114–15

"UNDER THE SYCAMORE TREE," play, Jan 61: 101

"UNEXPECTED ANSWER, THE," painting by René Margritte, Jan 62: 82; illus, Jan 62: 86

UNGERER, TOMI, Jan 61: 128
 Photographs of, Jan 61: 129, 130, 132–33
 Works by, Jan 61: 128–36

UNILATERAL DEDENSIFICATION, FALLACY OF, Jul 59: 5–6, 10, 11

UNION OF SOVIET SOCIALIST REPUBLICS
 Changes in style of, Nov 62: 116–17
 Chess and Cold War strategy, Nov 63: 61–62
 Education in: reading ability in schools of U.S. and U.S.S.R. compared, Jul 63: 42–43
 Painting in, Sep 60: 37
 Pazyryk burial finds discoveries, Jan 60: 110–12
 Teaching of humanities in, Nov 60: 23
 "Uncultured," meaning in, Jan 60: 6
 And United States, compared, Jul 62: 112–19

UNITED AIRLINES HANGAR, San Francisco, Jan 59: 11

UNITÉ D'HABITATION (also called RADIANT CITY), in Marseilles, Nov 60: 125, Mar 61: 36

UNITED NATIONS, Mar 63: 6
 Buildings of, in New York City, Jan 60: 27, Sep 60: 39, Mar 61: 36

UNITED NATIONS EDUCATIONAL, SCIENTIFIC, AND CULTURAL ORGANIZATION (UNESCO)
 Paris headquarters of, Mar 59: 122–23, Sep 59: 18; gardens at, Mar 60: 110–11; monument by Alexander Calder, Nov 62: 16
 Project to save ancient temples threatened by Aswan Dam, Jul 60: 10

UNITED STATES. See AMERICAN CIVILIZATION

UNITED STATES AIR FORCE ACADEMY, buildings of, Jan 60: 120

UNITED STATES MILITARY ACADEMY, buildings of, Jan 60: 120

UNITED STATES STEEL CORPORATION, May 63: 113

UNITED STATES TRAVEL SERVICE, Sep 62: 116

UNIVERSITIES. See COLLEGES and UNIVERSITIES

"UNNAMABLE, THE," novel by Samuel Beckett, Sep 60: 113

UNTERMEYER, LOUIS, May 60: 28
Photograph of, May 60: 28

UNTHINK, CULT OF, Sep 58: 38–45, 134–35

UPDIKE, JOHN, Mar 62: 84, Jul 63: 70
Photograph of, Mar 62: 85
On Salinger, J. D., quoted, May 62: 103, 104, 106

UPJOHN COMPANY, administration center in Kalamazoo, Mich., May 62: 16

"UPPER DEPTHS, THE," play, May 63: 14

"UPSTAIRS AT THE DOWNSTAIRS," New York City cabaret, Jan 62: 66, 68, 71

UR, Mesopotamian city, Jul 61: 41, 62
Evidence of Bronze Age trade found at, Jul 60: 86–87

URARTU, conflict with Assyria, Nov 62: 102

URBAN II, POPE, Jan 59: 87

URBAN VIII, POPE, Nov 60: 31, Jul 61: 89, Jan 62: 43, 45, Nov 62: 34, Nov 63: 63
Portraits of, Jul 60: 39, Nov 63: 63

URBAN, JOSEPH, Nov 58: 118

URBAN RENEWAL
In New York City, May 63: 52, 105
In Paris under Napoleon III, May 63: 50–75, 105
In Philadelphia, Sep 62: 62, Jul 63: 9, 26–27
Saarinen, Eero, quoted on, Jul 60: 82, 123

URBINO, ITALY, Renaissance court at, Jan 60: 66, 68

URBINO, DUKES OF. See MONTEFELTRO

UREY, HAROLD, Jul 62: 84

URSINS, JEAN JOUVENEL DES, on reign of Charles VII of France, quoted, Mar 62: 91–92

URUK. See ERECH

USAGE, of language, defined, Jul 63: 35

"USES OF ADVERSITY, THE," article by Stephen White, Sep 60: 120

USSACHEVSKY, VLADIMIR, Jan 59: 51, 54, Sep 60: 32
Photograph of, Jan 59: 52

USSHER, ARLAND, on William Butler Yeats, quoted, Nov 60: 66

USSHER, JAMES, Jan 59: 122

USTINOV, IONA (KLOP) VON, Nov 58: 84–85

USTINOV, NADIA BENOIS, Nov 58: 84–85

USTINOV, PETER, Nov 58: 82–85, 137–39, May 61: 53, Jul 61: 112, Sep 63: 75, 80
Photographs of, Nov 58: 83–85
Romanoff and Juliet, Nov 58: 65, Sep 59: 86, 88

USTINOV, SUZANNE CLOUTIER, Nov 58: 138–39

UTHER PENDRAGON, versions of James Knowles and Thomas Malory, May 60: 115–16

"UTOPIA," book by Thomas More, Mar 63: 74–75

"UTOPIAN ESSAYS AND PRACTICAL PROPOSALS," book by Paul Goodman, Mar 63: 79

UTOPIAN SOCIALISTS. See SOCIALISTS, UTOPIAN

UTOPIAS
And anti-utopias, Mar 63: 72–79
Buildings originating in movements toward, Mar 62: 35
As created by scientists, Jul 61: 6–7, 9

UTRECHT, UNIVERSITY OF, Sep 58: 23

UTRILLO, MAURICE, Mar 59: 105

UTSON, JÖRN, building designed by, Sep 59: 15

UZZIAH, KING OF JUDAH, Nov 59: 118

V

VAA, DYRE, fountain designed by, May 62: 29

VADIM, ANNETTE, May 60: 53 (note)

VADIM, ROGER, May 60: 49, 53 (note), Sep 61: 110, May 62: 55

"VAGABOND KING, THE," musical, Sep 58: 57

"VAILIMA," home of Robert Louis Stevenson, Jan 60: 124

VAKHTANGOV, EUGENE, Jan 61: 32–33

VALENTIJN, FRANÇOIS, and mermaid legend, Jan 60: 130–31

VALENTIN, MONELLE, Nov 60: 54

VALENTINIAN III, ROMAN EMPEROR, May 63: 79

VALÈRE, SIMONE, May 61: 93

VALERIAN, ROMAN EMPEROR, Jan 63: 50, 52 (chart)
Capture of, shown in rock carving, Jan 63: 51

VALERIUS MAXIMUS, on Volsinii, quoted, May 60: 74

VALÉRY, PAUL, Nov 59: 67, 72, Sep 61: 103, 104, May 62: 113
On the sea, quoted, Nov 62: 12

VALK, FREDERICK, Jan 60: 91
Portrait of, Jan 60: 93

VALLA, LORENZO, May 62: 90

VALLETTA, MALTA, Nov 61: 61, 65

VALLEY OF THE FALLEN, THE, May 61: 42; illus. May 61: 47

VALTELLINE, and Thirty Years' War, Nov 62: 34–35, 37, 41

VAN ALLEN, JAMES A., photograph of, May 59: 16

VANBRUGH, JOHN, Nov 58: 60
And building of Blenheim Palace, Sep 61: 70, 73–76
Portraits of, Nov 58: 60, Sep 61: 72

VAN BUREN, ABIGAIL, memorandum to, from Eleanor of Aquitaine, May 60: 30–31

VANCE, NINA, Jan 62: 13, 14

VANDALS, Sep 61: 24, 26, May 63: 78, 80

VAN DEN HAAG, ERNEST, Jan 60: 7

VANDERBEEK, STAN, Nov 62: 97

VANDERBILT, AMY, on endorsements, quoted, Jul 60: 122

VANDERBILT, CONSUELO (DUCHESS OF MARLBOROUGH), Sep 61: 77
Photograph of, Sep 61: 77

VANDERBILT, CORNELIUS, Jan 61: 104

VANDERBILT, WILLIAM H., Nov 58: 118–19

VANDERBILT FAMILY, Nov 58: 148

VAN DER POST, LAURENS, The Dark Eye in Africa, quoted, Mar 63: 106

VAN DE VELDE, HENRI, Nov 61: 63, 64

VAN DOREN, CARL, May 60: 21, Jul 62: 99

VAN DOREN, DOROTHY, May 60: 21

VAN DOREN, IRITA, May 60: 21

VAN DOREN, MARK, May 60: 21, Jul 63: 70
On Byron's Don Juan, quoted, Jan 62: 61
Photograph of, May 60: 21

VAN DYCK, ANTHONY, Jul 61: 90, 91, 92, 95, Nov 62: 61, 66, Mar 63: 69
Paintings by: in British royal collection, Jul 63: 92, 93, 96, 105, 106; in Gardner Museum, Jul 59: 29, 30, 38; reproduced, see ILLUSTRATIONS INDEX
Portrait of Charles I sold, Sep 61: 77

VAN DYKE, DICK, Sep 62: 115

VAN ENS, Dutch engineer, Jul 59: 132

"VANESSA," opera, Nov 58: 120, Jan 60: 15, 17, 122, 123

VAN EYCK. See EYCK

"VAN GOGH," motion picture, May 60: 54

VAN GOGH, VINCENT, Sep 58: 110, Jan 59: 103, Nov 59: 121, Sep 60: 34, 102, 121, Nov 62: 64, Jan 63: 75
At Arles, Jul 59: 132
Influence on Joan Miró, Mar 59: 74
Japanese influence, May 60: 103, 104, 113, 114
Paintings by. See ILLUSTRATIONS INDEX

"VANISHING BOFFOLA, THE," article by William K. Zinsser, Jan 61: 122–23

"VANITY FAIR," magazine, career of Robert Sherwood on, Jul 62: 33–36

"VANITY FAIR," novel by Thackeray, Jan 62: 62, 64

VANLOO, JEAN BAPTISTE, Jul 63: 96

VanORDEN, BIANCA
Photograph of, Mar 59: 15
Water Music, Mar 59: 117, 118, 119

VANSITTART, ROBERT GILBERT, Sep 58: 129–30

VANVITELLI, LUIGI and CARLO, May 62: 15

VARÈSE, EDGARD, Jan 59: 53
Arcana, Jul 59: 20
Ionisation, Igor Stravinsky quoted on, Sep 58: 132
Photograph of, Jan 59: 52

VARIN, QUANTIN, Mar 61: 79

VARTHEMA, LODOVICO DI, Sep 58: 8

VASARI, GIORGIO, quoted
On Innocent VIII and Mantegna, Jan 62: 31
On Michelangelo, Jan 62: 41
On Vespucci, Simonetta, Sep 58: 94, 95

VASSE, W. W. See EDWARDS, J. H., co-author

VATEL, 17th-century chef, May 61: 77, Jul 63: 77, 81, 82

"VATICAN, THE," article by Alfred Werner with portfolio from Skira book, Jan 62: 22–49

VAUBAN, MARQUIS DE (SÉBASTIEN LE PRESTRE), Jul 61: 53

VAUDEVILLE, Jul 59: 112–20
English team, "The Crazy Gang," Jan 61: 122–23

VAUGHAN, DOROTHY, Europe and the Turk, quoted, Sep 58: 47

VAUGHAN, STUART, Nov 60: 118

VAUVENARGUES, CHATEAU DE, Jan 60: 98, 104

VAUX, CALVERT, Jul 59: 12

VAUX-LE-VICOMTE, castle of Nicolas Fouquet, May 62: 14, Jul 63: 76–83

VEBLEN, THORSTEN, Nov 59: 128

VECCHIO, PALMA, Sep 59: 31

VEENI, A. KRISHNA, photographs of, Sep 63: 70, 71

VEGA, LOPE DE, Jul 60: 42, 50

VEGETARIANISM, G. B. Shaw quoted on, Nov 58: 135

VELÁZQUEZ, DIEGO RODRÍGUEZ DE SILVA Y, Sep 58: 19, Jan 59: 103, May 59: 121, Jul 59: 29, 31, Jul 60: 38, 50, Jul 63: 93
Paintings by. See ILLUSTRATIONS INDEX

VELDES, WILLEM VAN DE, SR. and JR., Jul 63: 96, 106

VENCE, FRANCE, chapel designed by Matisse, Mar 61: 39

VENEZUELA
Caràcas shopping center, Jan 62: 94
Humboldt, Alexander von, in, Jul 59: 62

VENGEROVA, ISABELLE, Jan 60: 76, 81

VENICE, ITALY, Mar 63: 14–25
Boat traffic in, Nov 61: 125
Domestic architecture of, Nov 58: 41
In Grand Tour of 18th and 19th centuries, Nov 59: 87
Hoax by Horace de Vere Cole in, Jan 61: 72
As model city, Jul 61: 3, 56–57
As port for pilgrims to Holy Land, Mar 60: 82–84, 91
Square of St. Mark's, Napoleon quoted on, Jul 59: 15
Squares and quays of, Nov 61: 122
Suburbs of, Jul 61: 62
And Thirty Years' War, Nov 62: 35–36, 37, 39, 40
Tourism and, Sep 58: 54, Mar 59: 83, 120

VENICE, REPUBLIC OF, and Battle of Lepanto, Jul 63: 50, 52, 53, 57–58

VENIERO, SEBASTIAN, Jul 63: 50, 57

VENNE, ADRIAEN VAN DER, Sep 58: 26
Painting by, Nov 62: 32

VENTRIS, MICHAEL, Jan 61: 81, Nov 62: 90
Portrait of, Jan 61: 76

VENTURI, LIONELLO, Jul 59: 31, Jan 60: 68
On Georges Rouault, quoted, Nov 62: 57

VENUS, goddess, in art, André Malraux quoted on, Nov 58: 114

VENUS, planet, Jan 59: 29

VENUS OF ARLES, sculpture, Jul 59: 129

"VENUS OF PARDO," painting by Titian, Jul 61: 89, 94, Jul 63: 94

VERDI, GIUSEPPE, Jan 60: 123, Mar 62: 97, 119
Balanchine, George, quoted on, Jan 61: 47, 56
String quartet of, Nov 62: 46, 47

VERDON, GWEN, May 63: 13
Photographs of, Sep 58: 60, May 63: 12

VERGA, GIOVANNI, Sep 61: 44

VERGERIUS, Jan 60: 61, 62, 64

VERGIL, Nov 63: 43
In Renaissance curriculum, Jan 60: 62
Survival of Aeneid, Nov 62: 76, 80

VERHAEREN, EMILE, Mar 63: 6

VERLAINE, PAUL, on water, quoted, Jul 62: 60

VERMEER, JAN, Sep 58: 34, Jul 59: 29, Sep 60: 34, Jul 63: 105
Forgeries by Hans van Meegeren, Mar 59: 109
Malraux, André, quoted on, Nov 58: 116, 117
Paintings by. See ILLUSTRATIONS INDEX

VERNE, JULES, The Begum's Fortune, Mar 63: 77–78

VERONA, ITALY, Mar 59: 85

VERONESE, PAOLO, Jul 61: 95, Jan 62: 26

VERSAILLES, PALACE OF, Sep 60: 67, 69, 72, Jul 63: 77, 82, 83
Gardens of, May 59: 29, 32, May 62: 12, 14

VERUS, LUCIUS AURELIUS, ROMAN EMPEROR, Sep 63: 89

VESALIUS, ANDREAS, drawing by, Nov 62: 4

VESPASIAN, ROMAN EMPEROR
Coinage during reign of, Sep 63: 33–34, 38, 39
Coin portraits of, Sep 63: 34, 35

VESPASIANO DA BISTICCI, Sep 59: 126

VESPUCCI, AMERIGO, Nov 60: 97–98
Surviving letter by, Nov 60: 97–98

VESPUCCI, GIORGIO ANTONIO, Nov 60: 97–98

VESPUCCI, MARCO, Sep 58: 92

VESPUCCI, SIMONETTA, Sep 58: 92–95, 142
Portrait of, Sep 58: 92

VESTIER, ANTOINE, painting by, Jan 60: 82

VESTRIS, AUGUSTE, Sep 60: 94

VESUVIUS, MOUNT, earthquake and eruptions from, Mar 62: 45, 49, 50

VETTII, HOUSE OF THE, at Pompeii, Mar 62: 45

VEUILLOT, LOUIS FRANÇOIS, May 63: 72

VIAN, BORIS, May 61: 95

VIBERT, JEHAN GEORGES, Mar 60: 56
Painting by, Mar 60: 65

VICENTINO, LUDOVICO DEGLI ARRIGHI, Sep 59: 127

"VICIOUS CIRCLE, THE," book by Margaret Case Harriman, quoted, Jul 62: 37

VICTORIA, QUEEN OF ENGLAND, Nov 60: 13, May 63: 101, Nov 63: 59
As collector of paintings, Jul 63: 107
Desk presented to President Hayes by, Sep 61: 13
In Paris, May 63: 70–71
Parodies by Max Beerbohm, May 61: 38, 40
Portraits of, Jul 63: 94, 95

VICTORIA, LAKE, discovery of, Jul 63: 113–14

VICTORIA DE NEMOURS, portrait of, Jul 63: 95

VICTORIA MARY LOUISA, DUCHESS OF KENT, Jul 63: 107

VICTORIAN AGE
Composite paintings of eminent men and women made in 1857, Jan 59: 140–43

Handwriting during, Sep 59: 128

"VICTORS, THE," motion picture, May 63: 10

VICTORY, WINGED, Nov 60: 28, 29–30

"VICTORY AT SEA: 1571: LEPANTO," article adapted from *Great Sea Battles*, book by Oliver Warner, Jul 63: 49–61

VIDAL, GORE, May 61: 56

VIEIRA, ANTONIO, Mar 60: 102–3, 124, 125

VIEL-CASTEL, HORACE DE, May 63: 70

VIENNA, AUSTRIA
"Circa 1400" exhibition, Mar 63: 8
Heuriger, Mar 59: 84
Musical life of 1920's, Sep 61: 84
Staatsoper, Nov 58: 23–25; Jeritza-Lehmann feud, Sep 59: 56–57
Turkish attacks on, Jul 63: 50, 52, 60
World War I aftermath, Jan 59: 117, 121

VIERECK, PETER, Mar 63: 30

"VIEWS OF THE BIBLICAL WORLD," illus from, Nov 59: 11–19

VIGÉE-LEBRUN, MARIE ANNE ÉLISABETH, Nov 58: 88

VIGNALI, ABBÉ, Nov 60: 99

VIGNOLA, GIACOMO DA, church designed by (with Giacomo della Porta), Jul 60: 52

VIGO, JEAN, May 60: 51, Jan 62: 110

VILAR, JEAN, Sep 61: 102
Photograph of, Sep 61: 109

VILLA ALDOBRANDINI, cascades at, May 62: 12, 13

VILLA D'ESTE, Tivoli, Italy, May 63: 35
Water gardens of, May 59: 29, May 62: 12, 13–14, 18–19, 22–23

"VILLAGE VOICE, THE," newspaper, Jules Feiffer's works for, Nov 61: 48

VILLARD, HENRY, Jan 59: 25

VILLARET, FULK DE, Mar 61: 62

VILLEGAS, JOSÉ, painting by, Mar 60: 59

VILLIERS, JEAN DE, Mar 61: 60

VILLON, FRANÇOIS, Nov 61: 88
On Joan of Arc, quoted, Mar 62: 95

VINCENTINO, *Battle of Lepanto*, Mar 63: 14

VINCI, LEONARDO, Jul 60: 62

VINCI, LEONARDO DA, Sep 58: 116, Jan 59: 103, Sep 60: 34, 61, Jan 62: 94, Mar 62: 72, May 63: 91, Jul 63: 96
Last Supper, Sep 60: 121
Paintings by, illus, Sep 60: 70, 71
On painting vs. sculpture, quoted, Nov 60: 103
Saint Jerome, Jan 62: 48
Saint John the Baptist, Jul 61: 90, 94, 95
Sketches by, Henry Moore quoted on, Nov 60: 113
Virgin and Saint Anne, May 62: 78

VIOLLET-LE-DUC, EUGÈNE EMMANUEL, May 61: 113, Sep 61: 57, May 63: 71

VIOT, JACQUES, Mar 59: 70

VIRGIL. See VERGIL

"VIRGIN AND CHILD WITH SAINT JOHN," relief by Michelangelo, May 62: 78

"VIRGIN AND SAINT ANNE," cartoon by Leonardo da Vinci, May 62: 78

"VIRIDIANA," motion picture, Nov 62: 110, 111–12

VISCONTI, FILIPPO MARIA, Jan 60: 66

VISCONTI, LODOVICO, Sep 60: 81

VISCONTI, LOUIS, May 63: 68

VISIGOTHS
In Roman Empire, May 63: 78
Votive crowns of, May 63: 104

"VISIT, THE," play, Nov 58: 63, 65

"VISIT U.S.A." PROGRAM, Sep 62: 116–19

VISSCHER, ANNA and MARIA, Sep 58: 26

VITELLIUS, AULUS, ROMAN EMPEROR, Sep 63: 38

"VITELLONI," motion picture, May 59: 99, Mar 61: 98

VITRUVIUS POLLIO, MARCUS, on architecture, quoted, Jul 60: 82

VITTORINO DA FELTRE
Portrait medal of, Jan 60: 59
School at Mantua, Jan 60: 59–68

VIVIAN BEAUMONT THEATER, Jan 63: 106, 109

VLADIMIR I, OF RUSSIA (SAINT VLADIMIR), May 63: 102, Nov 63: 34

VLADIMIR II, of RUSSIA (VLADIMIR MONOMAKH), May 63: 102

VLAMINCK, MAURICE DE, Jul 62: 65

"VOGUE," magazine, Mar 60: 50

"VOICES OF SILENCE, THE," book by André Malraux, quoted, Nov 58: 6, 8, 116

VOIGT, WILHELM, impersonation of army captain by, Jan 61: 68–71, 72

VOITURE, VINCENT, Nov 61: 32

VOLCANOES, studies of Alexander von Humboldt, Jul 59: 62–67

VOLKOV, ALEXANDER, Mar 62: 119

VOLKOVA, VERA, Sep 60: 94

VOLKSWAGEN, advertising of, Jan 62: 113

VOLLARD, AMBROISE, Nov 62: 48, 57

VOLNEY, C. F., Jan 63: 116, 117

"VOLPONE," play, Nov 63: 41

VOLSINII, ITALY, May 60: 74
Valerius Maximus quoted on, May 60: 74

VOLTAIRE, Nov 59: 67, 68, Sep 60: 72, May 61: 58, 61, 64, May 63: 54
And age of reason, Mar 61: 114–19
Attitude toward Joan of Arc, Mar 62: 95, 96
In Bastille, Jan 60: 85, 88
Childhood of, May 60: 33, 34, 35
Criticism of Shakespeare, Sep 61: 102, 104
At Ferney, France, Nov 59: 80
Memorandum to the Spacemen from, Sep 61: 18–19
In painting by Huber, Mar 61: 119
Portraits of, May 60: 32, Mar 61: 114
Quoted: on Blenheim Palace, Sep 61: 69; on history, Mar 62: 90; on Sicily, Sep 61: 22–23, 24, 26

VOLTERRA, DANIELE DA, Jan 62: 41

VONDEL, JOOST VAN DEN, Sep 58: 15, 24, 26

VON ECKARDT, WOLF, articles by
"All But Lost Art of Handwriting, The," Sep 59: 124–28
"Bauhaus, The," Nov 61: 58–75
"Man Who 'Destroyed' Paris, The," May 63: 50–75; comment on, May 63: 105
"Through the Glass Brightly," Sep 62: 22–32

VON NEUMANN, JOHN. See MORGENSTERN, OSKAR, co-author

VORSE, MARY HEATON, Jul 61: 13

VOSSIUS, GERARD, Sep 58: 26

VOUET, SIMON, Jul 61: 90

"VOYEUR, THE," novel by Alain Robbe-Grillet, Jan 62: 96, 99–100

VOYNICH, WILFRID M., Jan 63: 5, 7

VOYNICH, MRS. WILFRID M., Jan 63: 5

VUILLARD, EDOUARD, Mar 62: 15, 16

"VULGARIANS, THE," book by Robert Osborn, Sep 60: 43

W

WADSWORTH, CHARLES, Jul 61: 100, 102, 104–5
Portrait of, Jul 61: 102

WAGENFELD, WILHELM, lamp designed by, Nov 61: 71

WAGER, MICHAEL, Nov 62: 108

WAGNER, COSIMA (see also BÜLOW, COSIMA VON), May 63: 41

WAGNER, RICHARD, May 61: 66, 83, 84, Nov 61: 4, Mar 63: 25, 109
Beecham, Thomas, quoted on, Mar 62: 103
Liebestod, Sep 60: 121
Ludwig II of Bavaria as patron of, Jan 61: 39–42, 125–26
Operas of: at Bayreuth, Nov 58: 27; at Paris, Nov 58: 133; staging of, May 63: 40–45
In Paris, May 63: 69, 70

WAGNER, ROBERT, Mar 63: 36

WAGNER, SIEGFRIED, May 63: 45

WAGNER, WIELAND, Nov 58: 27, May 63: 40, 42, 44–45
Photograph of, May 63: 44

WAGNER, WOLFGANG, Nov 58: 27, May 63: 44–45

WAIN, JOHN, Jan 63: 86

"WAIST-HIGH CULTURE, THE," book by Thomas Griffith, essay from, Jul 59: 121–25

"WAITING AT THE CHURCH," song, Mar 60: 28

"WAITING FOR GODOT," play, Nov 58: 62, 63–64, Jan 59: 22, Sep 60, 114
Quoted, Sep 62: 35–36

WAKE ISLAND, Jan 60: 127

WALDEN POND, in 1957, Sep 58: 51

WALDMÜLLER, FERDINAND, painting by, Mar 60: 64

WALDSTEIN, FERDINAND VON, COUNT, Mar 62: 81

WALKER, FRANCIS, Jul 59: 133

WALKER, RALPH T., Jan 60: 27, 119

"WALKER IN THE CITY, A," book by Alfred Kazin, Jul 62: 98, 103

"WALKÜRE, DIE," opera, May 63: 41–42, 43, 45
Jeritza-Lehmann feud during performance of, Sep 59: 56–57

WALL, BERRY, Nov 58: 148

WALLACE, ALFRED RUSSEL, Mar 62: 9

WALLACE, DAVID, Jul 62: 37

WALLACE, EDGAR, Nov 59: 126

WALLACE, LEW, *Ben Hur*, Mar 63: 110

WALLACE, MIKE, Jan 60: 7, Mar 60: 126, Jul 60: 6

WALLACH, ELI, Sep 60: 56, Jan 62: 14, Nov 62: 107, May 63: 10
In *Magnificent Seven, The*, May 61: 114
Photograph of, May 63: 11

WALLENSTEIN, ALBRECHT VON, Sep 59: 121, Mar 60: 101, Nov 62: 38
Portrait of, Sep 59: 29

WALLENSTEIN, ALFRED, Jan 59: 52, Jan 62: 9

WALLER, EDMUND, on English language, quoted, Jul 63: 34

"WALL STREET JOURNAL," on boom in bowling, quoted, Mar 63: 95

WALN, NORA, *The House of Exile*, Nov 63: 107

WALPOLE, HORACE, May 60: 38, Nov 61: 35, Mar 62: 56, 62
Quoted, Mar 61: 116; on ballooning, Sep 58: 117–18, 119; on Blenheim Palace, Sep 61: 69; on Fox, Charles James, May 60: 98, 99, 100; on gambling, May 60: 98; on George III, Jul 63: 105; on Kent, William, Nov 58: 60; on landscape gardening, May 59: 47

WALPOLE, HUGH, Jan 63: 75

WALPOLE, ROBERT, Nov 58: 42, Nov 59: 75, 86, 94, 96
Home of, Nov 58: 46, 52, 53, 56
Portrait of, Nov 58: 43

WALRUS, as source of ivory, May 60: 91, 92, 94

WALSH, CHAD, May 59: 67

WALTER, BRUNO
Beecham, Thomas, quoted on, Mar 62: 104
Brenner, Engelbert, quoted on, Jul 59: 17

WALTER, THOMAS U., Jan 60: 22

WALTERS, HENRY, Jul 59: 31

WALTERS ART GALLERY, Baltimore, Jul 59: 31

WALTHER, PAUL, Mar 60: 85

WALTON, IZAAK
Epitaph to second wife, facsimile, Sep 59: 133
Portrait of, Sep 59: 133

WALTON, WILLIAM, Jan 60: 12, Sep 61: 5, 10, 14
Paintings by, Sep 61: 7
Photographs of, Sep 61: 6, 7

"WALTZ OF THE TOREADORS, THE," play, Nov 58: 62, Nov 60: 51, 52, 126, Mar 61: 46

"WAR AND PEACE," novel by Tolstoy, Jan 62: 62
Andrew Wyeth quoted on, Sep 61: 100

"WAR AND PEACE IN TWO FOREIGN FILMS," article by Jean Stafford, Nov 60: 121–22

WARBURG, ABY, quoted, Sep 62: 114

WARBURG, FELIX, Nov 58: 118

WARBURTON, WILLIAM, Mar 61: 116

WARD, BARBARA, May 60: 5

WARD, JAMES, painting by, May 62: 76

WARD, ROBERT, Jan 60: 123, Jan 62: 10

WARDLE, IRVING, "Revolt Against the West End," article by, Jan 63: 26–33

WARE, GREAT BED OF, May 60: 129; illus, May 60: 131

WARFARE
Adventure in, Sep 58: 137
Causes of great wars, Nov 62: 32–41
Balloons used in, Sep 58: 120
Beginnings of organized medical services, Mar 61: 70
Chariotry in, Sep 58: 147–49
Divers in, Nov 58: 70–71
Elephants used in, May 63: 3
Jousts in, Nov 58: 106
Man's weapons instinct, Nov 61: 38–41
Military machine of Alexander the Great, Mar 59: 33–37
Origin of, Jul 61: 39
Slavery and, in ancient world, May 62: 44–46
Women warriors of Sahara rock paintings, May 59: 83

WARFIELD, SANDRA, photographs of, Nov 61: 79, 81

WARFIELD, WILLIAM, Mar 61: 72, Jan 62: 14

WARHOL, ANDY, Jan 63: 25

WARING, FRED, Sep 61: 9

"WAR IS NO DAMN GOOD!" book by Robert Osborn, Sep 60: 43

"WAR LOVER, THE," motion picture, Mar 63: 36

WARNECKE, JOHN CARL, Jan 60: 120
Buildings designed by, Jan 60: 21, 23

WARNER, H. B., Sep 63: 77

WARNER, OLIVER, "Victory at Sea: 1571: Lepanto," article adapted from *Great Sea Battles*, book by, Jul 63: 49–61

WARNER, W. LLOYD, studies on American classes by, Nov 59: 22–23, 24

"WAR OF THE WORLDS, THE," novel by H. G. Wells, broadcast by Orson Welles, Jul 63: 87–88

WARREN, MICH., General Motors Technical Center, Jul 60: 82

WARREN, LILLIAN (DUCHESS OF MARLBOROUGH), Sep 61: 77

WARREN, ROBERT PENN, Jul 63: 72
Photograph of, May 59: 16

WARREN, SAMUEL D., debate on right to privacy, Jul 60: 122

WARREN, WILLIAM C., on reading and writing abilities of college graduates, quoted, Jul 63: 41

WARRINER, FREDERIC, Nov 60: 118

WARS OF RELIGION. See RELIGIOUS WARS

WASHBURN MUNICIPAL UNIVERSITY OF TOPEKA, Sep 59: 123

WASHINGTON, billboards in Seattle environs, May 61: 5

WASHINGTON, D.C.
  Arena Stage, Jan 62: 9, 13, May 62: 35
  Dulles International Airport, Jul 60: 77, 123
  Federal architecture, Jan 60: 21–24, 120
  Hotel advertising, Mar 63: 116
  Lafayette Square, preservation as proposed by Kennedy administration, Sep 61: 14
  Monuments and memorials in, May 61: 42, Sep 61: 13; Eero Saarinen quoted on, Jul 60: 79, 82
  National Cultural Center project, Sep 61: 14–15
  White House. See WHITE HOUSE, THE
  World's Fair, proposed plan, Sep 60: 80–87
WASHINGTON, BOOKER T., Nov 63: 70
WASHINGTON, GEORGE, Sep 58: 119, Jul 63: 14
"WASHINGTON CROSSING THE DELAWARE," painting by Larry Rivers, Sep 59: 98; illus, Sep 59: 96
WASHINGTON MONUMENT, Washington, D.C., Jan 60: 21–22
  Saarinen, Eero, quoted on, Jul 60: 79
"WASPS," play by Aristophanes, Jul 60: 102
WASSERSTEIN, JULIUS, Jan 59: 14
"WAS SOCRATES GUILTY AS CHARGED?" article by M. I. Finley, Jul 60: 100–4, 117
"WASTE LAND, THE," poem by T. S. Eliot, Jul 63: 39
  Influence in Japan, Mar 61: 11
  Marquise Went Out at Five compared to, May 62: 115
  "Mr. Eliot Revisits the Waste Land," poem by W. H. Armstrong, Jan 63: 92–93
  Quoted, Sep 61: 117
WATERFORD, 3D MARQUESS OF (HENRY DE LA POER), Nov 58: 107
"WATER LILIES," painting by Monet, Sep 58: 84
WATER MILL, N.Y., May 63: 6 (map), 8, 14, 18
"WATER MUSIC," novel by Bianca VanOrden, Mar 59: 117, 118, 119
"WATER MUSIC," tape recorder compostion by John Cage, Jan 59: 125
WATERS, EDWARD N., Frédéric Chopin by Franz Liszt, translated by, May 63: 109–10
"WATERS OF BABYLON, THE," play, Jan 63: 32
"WATER: THE WINE OF ARCHITECTURE," article by Ada Louise Huxtable, May 62: 10–33
WATKINS, FRANKLIN C., Jan 59: 96, Jul 63: 18
  Paintings by, Jan 59: 100, Jul 63: 23
WATKINS, GINO, Sep 58: 10
WATKINS, JOHN, Jul 63: 105
WATSON, H. D., Latin version of "The Hunting of the Snark," quoted, Jul 61: 114
WATSON, THOMAS J., JR., Jul 63: 70 (note)
WATT, JAMES
  As member of Josiah Wedgwood's group, May 59: 88–96, 128–30
  Portrait of, May 59: 91
WATTEAU, JEAN ANTOINE, Nov 61: 4, 6, Mar 62: 63
  Painting by, Nov 59: 102
WATTS, ALAN, Jul 60: 114
  On Zen Buddhism, quoted, Jul 59: 74, Sep 60: 32, 122
WATUTSI TRIBE, of Africa, value of cattle among, Mar 63: 52
WAUGH, EVELYN, Jul 63: 13, 73
"WAY AHEAD, THE," motion picture, Nov 58: 137
WAYNE STATE UNIVERSITY, McGregor Center, May 62: 16
"WAY OF THE WORLD, THE," play, Sep 62: 111
WEAKLAND, REMBERT, Nov 60: 94
WEAPONS
  Greek fire, Nov 63: 24, 26
  Guns of white man as pictured by native artists, Sep 60: 13–14
WEAPONS INSTINCT OF MAN, Nov 61: 38–41
WEAVER, JOHN V. A., Jul 62: 37
WEAVER, ROBERT C., on urban renewal program, quoted, Sep 61: 17
WEAVER, WARREN, definition of information, quoted, Jul 57: 107
WEBER, BEN, Jan 62: 9
WEBER, KARL, Mar 62: 61
WEBERN, ANTON VON, Nov 59: 56, May 62: 82
  Igor Stravinsky quoted on, Sep 58: 84
WEBSTER, MARGARET, Nov 58: 120
WEBSTER, NOAH, on a standard in speaking, quoted, Jul 63: 35
"WEBSTER'S THIRD NEW INTERNATIONAL DICTIONARY," Jul 63: 34, 35, 40–41, 43, 45
WECHSBERG, JOSEPH, articles by
  "Behind the Golden Curtain," Nov 58: 23–27, 133
  "Haydn: A Presence More Vivid than Ever," Mar 62: 76–83
  "Hot-Tempered High C, The," Sep 59: 50–57
  "Music of Friends, The," Nov 62: 42–47
  "New Look in Valhalla, The," May 63: 40–45
  "What Not to See in Europe," Mar 59: 82–85, 120
"WEDDING DANCE," painting by Bruegel, Sep 60: 121

"WEDDINGS AND BABIES," motion picture, Mar 61: 19, Sep 62: 108, 109–10
WEDGWOOD, C. V., articles by
  "Golden Age of the Dutch Republic, The," Sep 58: 14–35
  "Great Confrontations II: Leo the Great and Attila the Hun," May 63: 76–80
  "Prince of Patrons, The," Jul 61: 78–95
WEDGWOOD, EMMA, May 59: 130
WEDGWOOD, JOSIAH, Nov 59: 96
  And classical revival, Mar 62: 61, 67
  And his friends, May 59: 88–97, 128–30
  And Portland vase, Nov 63: 64
  Portrait medallion of, May 59: 89, Nov 63: 63
WEDGWOOD, SUSANNAH, May 59: 130
WEESE, HARRY, Jan 60: 21, 119
WEIDNER, EDWARD E., The World Role of Universities, quoted, Sep 62: 15
WEIGEL, HELENE, May 62: 39
  Photograph of, May 62: 36
WEILL, KURT, Nov 58: 62, Nov 59: 56, Jan 60: 123, May 62: 39
  Portrait of, Jan 60: 14
  Saga of Jenny, parody of, Jul 59: 18
WEIMAR, GERMANY
  Bauhaus in, Nov 61: 60–72
  Goethe's period, Jul 59: 59
WEINGARTNER, FELIX VON, Thomas Beecham quoted on, Mar 62: 104
WEINSTEIN, ARNOLD, The Red Eye of Love, Sep 62: 41
WELDON, JOAN, photograph of, Mar 62: 12
WELFARE, SOCIAL. See SOCIAL SERVICE
WELITSCH, LJUBA, Sep 59: 55
WELLES, ORSON, May 60: 51, Jul 61: 97, Jul 63: 84–91
  Photographs of, Jul 63: 84–91
WELLES, RICHARD H., Jul 63: 76
"WELL-LOVED RIVER, THE," article by Pierre Schneider, with photographs by Henri Cartier-Bresson, Jul 62: 52–79
WELLS, H. G., May 61: 104, Mar 63: 6, Sep 63: 98
  Grisly Folk, The, Jul 62: 84
  On Lady Astor-Stalin visit, quoted, Nov 58: 20
  Time Machine, The, Jul 62: 85
  Utopias of, Mar 63: 78–79, Nov 63: 106
  War of the Worlds, The, broadcast by Orson Welles, Jul 63: 87–88
WELLS, MICHAEL, Nov 61: 115
WELWYN, ENGLAND, Sep 59: 11, 12
"WENDINGEN," Dutch magazine, Nov 60: 16
WENIG, R., painting by, Jan 61: 36–37
WENTWORTH WOODHOUSE, Nov 58: 40, 51
"WE'RE NO ANGELS," motion picture, Nov 58: 138
WERFEL, ALMA MAHLER, Nov 61: 61
WERFEL, FRANZ, on St. Peter's, Rome, quoted, Jan 62: 48
"WERKBUND," Nov 61: 62
WERNER, ALFRED, articles by
  "Most Mysterious Manuscript, The," Jan 63: 4–9
  "Vatican, The," Jan 62: 22–32, 41–49
WERTENBAKER, LAEL TUCKER, Death of a Man, Jul 60: 120, Jan 62: 111–12
WERTENBAKER, THOMAS JEFFERSON, Sep 59: 118
WERVE, CLAUS DE, Sep 58: 62
WESKER, ARNOLD, Jan 63: 26, 32, 33
  Portrait of, Jan 63: 31
  Roots, reviewed, Jul 61: 117–18
WESLEY, JOHN, Mar 51: 116
  On witchcraft, quoted, Nov 59: 61
WESSELMANN, TOM, painting by, Sep 63: 92
WEST, AUBREY, Sep 59: 128
WEST, BENJAMIN, May 62: 62–63, Jul 63: 18, 105
  Painting by, Jul 63: 95
WEST, JAMES M., Nov 58: 148
WEST, JESSAMYN, Jan 59: 18
WEST, NATHANAEL, Jan 62: 64
WEST, REBECCA, quoted, Nov 58: 6
WEST, RICHARD, letter from Horace Walpole to, quoted, Mar 62: 56
WEST CORK, IRELAND, Jul 60: 105
WEST CORNWALL, CONN., May 60: 21
WESTERNERS, American, Jul 59: 121–23
"WESTERN INTELLECTUAL TRADITION, THE," book by J. Bronowski and Bruce Mazlish, excerpt from, May 62: 89–95
"WESTERN SYMPHONY," ballet, Nov 59: 56
WESTHAMPTON, N.Y., May 63: 6, 7, 8
WESTHAMPTON BEACH, N.Y., May 63: 6 (map), 8, 18
WEST INDIES
  Dutch in, in 17th century, Sep 58: 20
  And Thirty Years' War, Nov 62: 41
WESTON, MARYBETH, "On Stage: David Hurst," article by, Jan 61: 100–1
WEST POINT. See UNITED STATES MILITARY ACADEMY

WESTPORT, CONN., May 63: 91
"WEST SIDE STORY," musical, Sep 58: 144, Jan 59: 138, Jul 61: 98, Jan 63: 32
WEST VIRGINIA, state hymn, quoted, Nov 61: 119
WEYHE, E., Mar 61: 123
WHALE, as source of ivory, May 60: 91, 92
WHARTON, EDITH, Jul 59: 32, May 60: 13, Jan 62: 64
  The House of Mirth, Mar 59: 15
WHATELEY, RICHARD, Jan 63: 85
"WHATEVER BECAME OF MONEY?" article by Stephen White, May 62: 118–19
"WHATEVER BECAME OF PERSONAL ETHICS?" article by Louis Kronenberger, Mar 63: 60–61
"WHAT GOOD IS TELEVISION," article by Walter Kerr, Mar 60: 4–5, 126–28
"WHAT NEXT IN ART?" article by Irwin Glusker, Jan 63: 16–25
"WHAT NOT TO SEE IN EUROPE," article by Joseph Wechsberg, Mar 59: 82–85, 120
"WHAT PRICE GLORY?" play, Jul 62: 40
"WHAT WILL THE ROBIN DO THEN, POOR THING?" article by Walter Kerr, Mar 62: 40–41
WHEAT, prehistoric, at Jarmo, Iraq, Sep 62: 5 (illus), 8
WHEELED VEHICLES, Sep 58: 146–51
  In ancient Rome, and ban of Julius Caesar on, Mar 59: 26–27, Jul 61: 45
  Role in development of city, Jul 61: 52
WHEELER, BERT, Jul 59: 114
  Photograph of, Jul 59: 116
WHEELER, CHARLES, May 62: 59
  Photograph of, May 62: 58
WHEELER, MRS. GEORGE 2ND, photograph of, Sep 61: 12
WHELAN, DENNIS, "Mr. Wright Makes Himself Clear," a recollection by, Sep 60: 128
"WHEN FORGERY BECOMES A FINE ART," article by Gilbert Highet, Mar 59: 105–9
"WHEN FOUND, MAKE A VERSE OF," book by Helen Bevington, Sep 61: 115
"WHEN GOVERNMENT WENT ALL OUT FOR THE ARTS," article by William Harlan Hale, Nov 62: 18–19
"WHEN ISLAM RULED IBERIA," article by Gerald Brenan, Sep 62: 72–93
"WHEN MAN FIRST LEFT THE EARTH," article by Peter Lyon, Sep 58: 114–28
"WHEN WE DEAD AWAKEN," play, Jan 62: 106
"WHERE KURSK AND KANSAS MEET," article by Mervyn Jones, Jul 62: 112–19
"WHERE NOTHING SUCCEEDS LIKE EXCESS," article by Lesley Blanch, Sep 60: 129–36
"WHERE TALENT IS TRIED AND TESTED," article by Charles L. Mee, Jr., Nov 62: 96–99
"WHERE THE DANCE ENACTS DAILY LIFE," photographs from Les Hommes de la Danse, book by Michel Huet, Jul 59: 49–55
"WHERE THERE IS TOTAL INVOLVEMENT," article by Robert Hatch, Mar 62: 106–9
"WHERE THE ROMANS ENJOYED 'OMNIA COMMODA,'" article by Lawrence Wright, May 60: 39–41
"WHERE WILL THE BOOKS GO?" article by John Rader Platt, Sep 62: 42–47
  Comment on, Nov 62: 105
WHICHER, GEORGE F., Jul 61: 100
"WHIMS OF CUPID AND THE BALLET MASTER, THE," ballet, Sep 60: 94
WHIRLING WILSONS, vaudeville act, Jul 59: 115
WHISTLER, JAMES A. McNEILL, Jul 59: 30, May 60: 104, Sep 60: 102
  Painting by, Sep 60: 70
  Quoted: on art, Jan 60: 5; on painting, May 63: 90; on taste in art, Jan 63: 73
  And Royal Academy, May 62: 78
WHISTLER, REX, painting by, Nov 62: 23
WHITE, BYRON R., Sep 61: 13
WHITE, E. B., quoted
  On advertising jargon, Jul 63: 36
  On writing, Jul 63: 40
WHITE, HARVEY E., photograph of, May 59: 16
WHITE, PAUL DUDLEY, Jul 60: 120
WHITE, STEPHEN, articles by
  "Abolish the Armchair Athlete," Nov 62: 112–13
  "Creative Man at Work, The," Mar 62: 112–13
  "Culture in the Wee Hours," Sep 61: 113–14
  "Glass That Wasn't There, The," Nov 60: 123
  "Hershey Bar, The: Is Advertising Really Necessary?" May 63: 112–13
  "Moment of Truth, The," Jul 60: 128
  "No Deposit, No Return," May 61: 118
  "O for the Days of Amos 'n' Andy," Nov 61: 102–3
  "Sad End of the Word 'Fabulous,' The," Jan 61: 119
  "Suds in Your Eye," Jan 63: 113–14
  "Television Culture in Round Numbers," Jul 62: 94–95

"Today's Temple of Talent," Mar 61: 101
"21-inch Smokescreen, The," Mar 63: 113–14
"Two Cheers for Mediocrity," Sep 62: 114–15
"Uses of Adversity, The," Sep 60: 120
"Whatever Became of Money?" May 62: 118–19
"Who Put the Alphabet into the Soup?" Jan 62: 112–13
"Would You Want Your Sister to Marry Rosser Reeves?" Jul 61: 118–19
WHITE, T. H., Mar 61: 32
  Once and Future King, The, May 61: 103–4
WHITE, THEODORE H., "The Making of a Master," article by, Jul 60: 73–75, 126–27
WHITE, WILLIAM A., Nov 60: 98–99
WHITE, WILLIAM ALLEN, May 62: 6
WHITEBAIT, WILLIAM, Mar 62: 119
"WHITE COLLAR," book by C. Wright Mills, Nov 59: 23, 25
"WHITE GODDESS, THE," book by Robert Graves, Jan 62: 54
WHITEHALL CONFERENCE OF 1655, Mar 60: 125
WHITEHEAD, ALFRED NORTH, Nov 58: 31, Nov 59: 21
  On Byzantine culture, quoted, Nov 63: 6
WHITEHEAD, ROBERT, Jul 62: 7, Jan 63: 106, 109
"WHITE HORSE, THE," painting by Paul Gauguin, Jan 60: 32; illus, Jan 60: 38
WHITE HOUSE, THE, changes made by Mrs. John F. Kennedy, Sep 61: 13–14
WHITE MAN, as portrayed by artists of colored races in early contacts, Sep 60: 10–29
WHITEMUD RIVER, childhood of Wallace Stegner on, Sep 62: 94–95
"WHITE PAPER," television program, Sep 61: 113
"WHITE SHADOWS IN THE SOUTH SEAS," book by Frederick O'Brien, Jan 60: 125
WHITESIDE, WALKER, Mar 62: 119
"WHITE SISTER, THE," play, Mar 60: 32
WHITMAN, ROBERT, *Ball,* Nov 62: 114
WHITMAN, WALT, May 61: 66, Jul 61: 103
  Kazin, Alfred, quoted on, Jul 62: 99, 101
  Portrait of, Mar 61: 125
  Quoted: on monuments, May 61: 42; on New York City, Jul 59: 5; on poets, Mar 60: 49; on self-contradiction, Jan 59: 25
"WHITMAN PORTRAIT, A," woodcut book by Antonio Frasconi, Mar 61: 123; illus from, Mar 61: 125
WHITNEY, HARRY PAYNE, Mar 60: 33
WHITNEY, JOHN HAY, memorandum to, from Horace Greeley, Jan 59: 24–25
WHITNEY MUSEUM OF AMERICAN ART, Sep 58: 110
WHITTEMORE, THOMAS, Jul 59: 30
WHITTY, MAY, Sep 63: 77 (note)
"WHO IS BEHIND THE ASSAULT ON ENGLISH?" article by Lincoln Barnett, Jul 63: 33–48
"WHO PUT THE ALPHABET INTO THE SOUP?" article by Stephen White, Jan 62: 112–13
"WHO'S AFRAID OF VIRGINIA WOOLF?" play, Sep 61: 79, Mar 63: 107–8, Sep 63: 98–99
"WHO'S UNDERDEVELOPED?" article by Oliver Jensen, Jan 63: 116–17
"WHY DO GREAT WARS BEGIN?" article by H. R. Trevor-Roper, Nov 62: 32–41
"WHY ENGLAND SLEPT," book by John F. Kennedy, Sep 61: 5
"WHY I MAKE MOVIES," article by Ingmar Bergman, Sep 60: 4–9
"WHY MEN SEEK ADVENTURE," article by Wilfrid Noyce, Sep 58: 6–13, 135–39
WHYTE, WILLIAM H., JR., Nov 58: 147, Jul 59: 7, Nov 59: 23
  Organization Man, The, Jul 60: 68, 69
  On the young, quoted, May 63: 87
"WHY THE FRENCH NEED SHAKESPEARE," article by Jean-Louis Barrault, Sep 61: 102–9
WICHITA, KANS., American art in, Sep 58: 113
WICKWIRE, NANCY, Jan 62: 14
WIDDEMER, MARGARET, Mar 63: 30
WIDENER, FIFI, Jul 63: 22
WIDENER, JOSEPH E., Jul 63: 22
  Photograph of, Jul 63: 22
  Portrait by Augustus John, Jan 59: 105
WIDENER, PETER and JOSEPH, Nov 60: 98
WIDENER, PETER A. B., Jul 59: 29, Jul 63: 9
"WIDOW OF WASDALE HEAD, THE," play, Nov 58: 134–35
WIEDLINGER, PAUL, Mar 59: 123
WIELAND, CHRISTOPH MARTIN
  Childhood of, May 60: 34, 36, 38
  Portrait of, May 60: 32
WIENER, NORBERT, May 59: 9, Jul 59: 107, Mar 60: 48–49
  On IQ in industry, quoted, Nov 63: 104
  Photograph of, May 59: 16

WIERTZ, ANTOINE, Jan 62: 80–81
  Painting by, Jan 62: 78
WIG, in Baroque age, Jul 60: 38
WIGGLESWORTH, MICHAEL, on wilderness, quoted, Mar 60: 14–15
WIGHAM, H. J., Mar 60: 33
WIGHTWICK, GEORGE, Nov 63: 75–76
WIJDEVELD, THEO VAN DE, Nov 60: 16
WILBUR, RICHARD, Sep 61: 117, 118, 121, Jan 62: 10, Jul 63: 72
  "Parable," quoted, Sep 61: 118
WILDE, OSCAR, Jan 59: 133, Jul 59: 47–48, Jan 60: 109, Nov 60: 68, Jul 63: 118
  Beerbohm, Max, and, May 61: 34, 38, 39
  Kennedy, Mrs. John F., quoted on, Sep 61: 9
  In painting by W. P. Frith, May 62: 63
  Quoted: on cynics, Jul 61: 9; on intelligibility, Jul 63: 37; on marriages, Sep 62: 113; on Niagara Falls, May 60: 5
WILDENSTEIN, GEORGES, Sep 61: 14
WILDER, ALEC, Jul 61: 107
WILDER, BILLY, Jan 61: 123
WILDER, THORNTON, Jan 59: 84, Mar 61: 44, Mar 63: 28, 31, Jul 63: 73, 86
  And Circle in the Square, Mar 60: 98, 121
  Our Town, May 59: 101
  Photograph of, Mar 63: 30
  Quoted: on American theatrical directors, Jan 63: 107; on crisis and creativity, Sep 61: 5; on Dickens, Charles, Jan 61: 31–32
WILDERNESS
  Congressional bill to preserve, Mar 60: 16
  Man's need of, Sep 58: 51–52, Mar 60: 16
  Man's way with, Mar 60: 12–16
  Photographs by Ansel Adams, Mar 60: 16–24
"WILD ONE, THE," motion picture, Sep 58: 42
"WILD RIVER," motion picture, Sep 60: 88
"WILD SWANS AT COOLE, THE," poems by William Butler Yeats, Mar 59: 87
WILKIE, DAVID, Jul 63: 106
WILKINSON, C. S., *The Wake of the Bounty,* Sep 63: 47
WILLIAM V, DUKE OF BAVARIA, reliquary commissioned by, May 59: 2, 3
WILLIAM I, EMPEROR OF GERMANY, Sep 62: 21
WILLIAM II, EMPEROR OF GERMANY, Jan 61: 71, May 61: 120, Nov 61: 6, Mar 62: 29, May 63: 96
WILLIAM III, KING OF ENGLAND, Sep 58: 34, Jul 63: 96
  In painting by Daniel Maclise, Sep 59: 73
  Peter the Great and, Sep 59: 66, 74
WILLIAM IV, KING OF ENGLAND, Jul 63: 106–7
WILLIAM I, PRINCE OF ORANGE-NASSAU (WILLIAM THE SILENT), Sep 58: 19, 21, 23
WILLIAM II, PRINCE OF ORANGE-NASSAU, Sep 58: 34
WILLIAM III, PRINCE OF ORANGE-NASSAU, Sep 58: 34
WILLIAM OF TYRE, illus based on chronicles of, Jan 59: 88–89, 91
WILLIAMS, CHARLES, May 59: 66
WILLIAMS, HARRISON, Sep 61: 17
WILLIAMS, JAY, "The Sport of Knights," article by, Nov 58: 92–107
WILLIAMS, JOHN, Sep 63: 48
WILLIAMS, TENNESSEE, Nov 58: 65, May 59: 100, Jul 59: 48, Nov 60: 51, Jul 61: 116, Nov 62: 108
  Chayefsky, Paddy, quoted on, Sep 60: 56
  Glass Menagerie, The, Jan 61: 31, May 61: 99
  Kazin, Alfred, quoted on, Jul 62: 101
  Memorandum to: from Freud, May 62: 54–55; from Seneca, May 59: 54–55
  Milk Train Doesn't Stop Here Anymore, The, May 63: 108
  Night of the Iguana, The, Sep 62: 111–12
  Period of Adjustment, reviewed, Mar 61: 102–3
  Roman Spring of Mrs. Stone, The, Mar 59: 119, Jan 62: 104
  Streetcar Named Desire, A, Sep 58: 38
  Suddenly Last Summer, May 61: 99
  Summer and Smoke, Mar 60: 98, 120; motion picture based on, Jan 63: 112
WILLIAMS, VAUGHAN, Thomas Beecham quoted on, Mar 62: 103
WILLIAMS, WILLIAM CARLOS, Sep 61: 117, 120, 121
  Drawing of, May 60: 47
  Homage to, by Paul Engle, Mar 59: 60–61
  Many Loves, Mar 62: 106, 107
  Photograph of, May 60: 47
  And Spectric poets, May 60: 44, 47
  "To Waken an Old Lady," quoted, Sep 61: 120
  Travesty on, by Edward Adler, Jul 62: 65
WILLIAM THE MARSHAL, Nov 58: 106
WILLOW GROVE, PA., bowling in, Mar 63: 90–92, 93, 94
WILLOW RUN, MICH., Sep 62: 58
"WILL WE LOSE GOD IN OUTER SPACE?" article in *Christian Herald* by C. S. Lewis, May 59: 126

"WILSON," motion picture, Mar 61: 98
WILSON, ALEXANDER, Mar 60: 15
WILSON, ANGUS, Jan 63: 27
WILSON, CARROLL, May 59: 8
WILSON, CHARLES, Sep 61: 10
WILSON, EDMUND
  Kazin, Alfred, quoted on, Jul 62: 99, 103
  Photograph of, May 59: 17
WILSON, EDWARD, Sep 58: 8, 9, 12, 138, 139
WILSON, JACK, Jul 59: 118
WILSON, JANE, May 63: 14, 18
  Photograph of, May 63: 19
WILSON, PETER, Nov 62: 63–64, 66
WILSON, RICHARD, May 62: 60
WILSON, SOL, Jul 61: 23
  Portrait of, with painting by, Jul 61: 23
WILSON, WOODROW, Jan 59: 121
  At Princeton University, Sep 59: 24, 25, 118
  And Roosevelt, Theodore, Nov 63: 71
WILTON DIPTYCH, Jul 63: 96
WINCHELL, WALTER, Jul 60: 6
  On Hollywood Englishmen, quoted, Sep 63: 79
WINCKELMANN, JOHANN JOACHIM, Mar 62: 50, 55, 56, 61, 63
  Portrait of, Mar 62: 62
WINDGASSEN, WOLFGANG, May 63: 42
"WINDOW IN THRUMS, A," book by J. M. Barrie, quoted, Mar 63: 26–27
WINDSOR CASTLE, Nov 62: 23, 29, 30
WINE, Sep 58: 104–7, 145
WINGATE, JOHN, Jul 60: 122
WINGED BULL, as motif in ancient cultures of Near East, Nov 62: 102–4, Jan 63: 3
WINGED VICTORY, Nov 60: 28, 29–30
"WINNIE ILLE PU," translation by Alexander Lenard, reviewed, Jul 61: 112–15
WINOGRON, BLANCHE, Nov 60: 91
WINSTON, BOB, Jan 59: 14
  Silver jewelry by, Jan 59: 5
WINSTON, HARRY, Nov 58: 120
WINSTON, RICHARD and CLARA, translation of *Memories, Dreams, Reflections,* reviewed, Jan 63: 109–11
"WINTER," painting by Rubens, Jul 63: 96
WINTERHALTER, F. X., Jul 63: 107
  Painting by, Jul 63: 95
WINTERICH, JOHN T., Jul 62: 37
WINTERS, YVOR, Jan 59: 16, Sep 61: 117
"WINTERSET," play, Mar 60: 127
"WINTER'S TALE, THE," play by Shakespeare, Jan 63: 88
WINTHROP, JOHN (1588–1649), Mar 60: 102
WINWAR, FRANCES, in painting by John Koch, Sep 60: 107
WIRKKALA, TAPIO and RUT BRYK, Jul 63: 63–66
  Objects designed by, Jul 63: 62, 64–65, 66, 67
  Photographs of, Jul 63: 62–63, 64
WISCONSIN, UNIVERSITY OF, Spectric poetry at, May 60: 47
WISCONSIN DANCE GROUP, Nov 62: 68
"WISDOM OF THE HEART," book by Henry Miller, quoted, Jul 60: 72
WISE, HENRY, Sep 61: 73–74, 76, 77
WISE, THOMAS J., Mar 59: 108–9
  Portrait of, Mar 59: 108
WISEMAN, DONALD J., "The Sixty-Two Curses of Esarhaddon," transcribed by, Sep 59: 103–5
WISTER, OWEN, on Philadelphians, quoted, Jul 63: 12
WITCHES, PERSECUTION OF, Nov 59: 57–63
"WITCH OF BEACON HILL, THE," article by Francis Russell, Jan 59: 108–11
WITHERING, WILLIAM
  As member of Josiah Wedgwood's group, May 59: 90, 92, 130
  Portrait of, May 59: 90
"WITHIN A BUDDING GROVE," novel by Marcel Proust, Jul 63: 75
WITT, HAROLD, Jan 59: 18
WITT-DIAMANT, RUTH, Jan 59: 18, 19
WOBURN ABBEY, Nov 58: 46, 50, Jan 59: 59
WODEHOUSE, P. G., "My World and What Happened to It," article by, Jan 59: 56–59, 127
WOJCIECHOWSKI, ALEKSANDER, May 61: 22
WOLF, BEN, portrait of, with painting by, Jul 61: 25
WOLF, MRS. C. A., Sep 59: 88
WOLF, EDWIN 2ND, and JOHN F. FLEMING, *Rosenbach: A Biography,* article excerpted from, Nov 60: 96–101
WOLFE, BERTRAM D., photograph of, May 59: 17
WOLFE, THOMAS, May 59: 5, Nov 61: 105, Jul 63: 71, 75
  Photograph of, May 59: 16
WOLFF, KURT, Jan 63: 109
WÖLFFLIN, HEINRICH, Jul 60: 38
WOLFSON, VICTOR, *American Gothic,* Mar 60: 98, 120

"WOLF WILLOW," book by Wallace Stegner, excerpt from, Sep 62: 94–95
WOLKONSKY, ZENEÏDE, Sep 60: 134
WOLKONSKY FAMILY, Sep 60: 131
WOLSEY, THOMAS, CARDINAL, Mar 63: 85
Letter from Henry VIII to, Sep 59: 130
"WOMAN IN WHITE," painting by Picasso, Nov 61: 12; illus, Nov 61: 9
WOMEN
"Come, Girls, Art Can Be Fun!" excerpt from *A Modern Demonology,* by Frank Getlein, Sep 61: 64–65
Mental differences between men and women, Mar 62: 71–72
Position of: in Dutch Republic, Sep 58: 26; in Elam, Nov 62: 104; among Etruscans, May 60: 57, 62; in Marlik, Nov 62: 104; in neolithic cultures, Jul 61: 37
Warriors of Sahara rock paintings, May 59: 83
"WOMEN OF TRACHIS," play, Sep 60: 124
WOMEN'S CONGRESS ON HOUSING, Nov 58: 147
"WONDROUS SURVIVAL OF RECORDS, THE," article by Gilbert Highet, Nov 62: 74–95
Comment on, Nov 62: 105
WOOD, GRANT, Nov 59: 121, Jul 60: 114
WOOD, JOHN THE ELDER, Jul 61: 54
WOOD, JOHN THE YOUNGER, Jul 61: 54
WOOD, J. T., Sep 58: 140
WOOD, NATALIE, Jan 59: 139
Photograph of, Jul 63: 88
WOOD, PEGGY, Jul 62: 37, 38
WOODHAM-SMITH, MRS. CECIL, Sep 63: 98
The Reason Why, book by, May 60: 128
WOODSTOCK MANOR, near Oxford, England, Sep 61: 71, 73, 74–76
WOODWARD, JOANNE, Nov 62: 107
WOODWORTH, ROBERT A., on Eugene O'Neill, quoted, Mar 60: 34
WOOLF, LEONARD, Jan 60: 107
Sowing, quoted, Jan 61: 113
WOOLF, VIRGINIA, Jan 61: 68
Portrait of, Jan 60: 107
Strachey's proposal of marriage to, Jan 60: 107
WOOLLCOTT, ALEXANDER, Jul 62: 37, 38–39, 40, Jul 63: 86
Caricature of, Jul 62: 32
WOOLLEY, LEONARD, Nov 62: 90
On Mesopotamian cities, quoted, Jul 61: 41, 62
WOOLWICH, ENGLAND, Peter the Great in, Sep 59: 74
WOOLWICH, BISHOP OF. See ROBINSON, JOHN A. T.
WOOTTON, JOHN, Jul 63: 96
"WORD FROM OUR SPONSORS, A," miniature satirical revue, Jul 61: 77
WORDSWORTH, WILLIAM, Nov 59: 90, Mar 60: 14, May 61: 65–66, 68, Sep 63: 47–48, 101
Portrait of, May 61: 65
On youth, quoted, May 62: 103
WORLD AGRICULTURAL FAIR, New Delhi, India, American exhibit, Jan 60: 121
"WORLD CRISIS, THE," book by Winston S. Churchill, quoted, Jan 59: 121
"WORLD OF APU, THE," motion picture, Nov 62: 109
Reviewed, Jan 61: 115
"WORLD OF PAUL SLICKEY, THE," musical, Jan 63: 31
"WORLD OF WALTER PAEPCKE, THE," article by Marquis W. Childs, Sep 58: 96–103, 133–34
WORLD'S COLUMBIAN EXPOSITION (CHICAGO WORLD'S FAIR OF 1893), Jan 60: 22–23, May 60: 80–81, 87
Painting and sculpture at, Sep 60: 102, 127
WORLD'S FAIRS (see also by name), May 60: 80
Plan of Victor Gruen for 1964 fair, May 60: 80–87
"WORLD'S MOST DARING BUILDER, THE," article by Allan Temko, Mar 59: 18–25, 121–24
"WORLDS OF ROBERT SHERWOOD, THE," excerpt from biography by John Mason Brown, May 62: 4–9
WORLD WAR I
Aftermath in Europe, political posters, Jan 59: 112–21
Causes of, Nov 62: 41
Effects: on ideal of European unity, Mar 63: 6; on philosophy, Mar 63: 9
Joan of Arc as symbol during, Mar 62: 98
Roosevelt, Theodore, and, Nov 63: 71
WORLD WAR II
Address by Robert Sherwood at Milton Academy, June 14, 1940, May 62: 6–7
Causes of, Nov 62: 33, 41
D-day deception, Jan 61: 71–72
Effects: on ideal of European unity, Mar 63: 6; on philosophy, Mar 63: 9; in South Seas, Jan 60: 126–27
And Joan of Arc cult, Mar 62: 98, 99
Origins of, memorandum from Adolf Hitler to A. J. P. Taylor, Mar 62: 28–29
Poker-playing in, Nov 63: 60
Teaching of foreign tongues during, Jul 63: 46–47

WORLOCK, FREDERIC, Jan 63: 106
WORSLEY, T. C., quoted
On Guthrie, Tyrone, Nov 63: 38
On Ustinov, Peter, Nov 58: 138
"WOULD YOU WANT YOUR SISTER TO MARRY ROSSER REEVES?" article by Stephen White, Jul 61: 118–19
WOUWERMAN (or WOUVERMANS), PHILIPS, Sep 58, 26, Jul 63: 106
"WOZZECK," opera, Nov 58: 26, Jan 60: 12–13
Beecham, Thomas, quoted on, Mar 62: 103
Stravinsky, Igor, quoted on, Sep 58: 132
"WOZZECK," play by Georg Büchner, Jan 60: 12–13
"WRECK OF THE STATUS SYSTEM, THE," article by Eric Larrabee, Nov 59: 20–25, 128
WREN, CHRISTOPHER, Nov 58: 41, Sep 60: 69, Sep 61: 73, May 62: 60
WRENN, JOHN HENRY, Mar 59: 107
WRIGHT, FRANK LLOYD, Jan 59: 8, May 59: 11, 87, Sep 59: 6, 7–8, 19, Jan 60: 23, 119, Jul 60: 5, 77, Mar 61: 36, May 61: 42, Jul 61: 64, Nov 61: 45, 70, Jan 62: 94, Mar 62: 32, 33, 39, Sep 62: 62, Mar 63: 91
Buildings designed by. See ILLUSTRATIONS INDEX
Design for Ellis Island, Sep 63: 24–25
On New York City, quoted, Jul 59: 5, 10–11
Portrait of, Sep 60: 96
Saarinen, Eero, quoted on, Jul 60: 82
War on fine arts by, Sep 60: 96–103, 127–28
WRIGHT, HENRY, Jul 59: 11
WRIGHT, JAMES, Sep 61: 121
WRIGHT, JOSEPH, May 59: 94
Painting by, May 59: 92–93
WRIGHT, LAWRENCE, *Clean and Decent,* excerpt from, May 60: 39–41
WRIGHT, LOUIS B., photograph of, May 59: 17
WRIGHT, ROBERT, Mar 62: 119
WRIGHT, THOMAS, on Richard Francis Burton, quoted, Jul 63: 115
"WRITERS AT WORK," book of interviews, Jan 59: 82
WRITING (see also HANDWRITING)
Changes in script, and survival of ancient books, Nov 62: 83, 86
Mycenaean script (Linear B), Jan 61: 77, 81, 98
WURSTER, WILLIAM W., Jan 59: 8, 22, Jan 63: 13
WÜRZBURG, GERMANY, Bishop's Palace, Jul 60: 50
WURZBURG, FRANCIS L., Jul 62: 35
"WUTHERING HEIGHTS," novel by Emily Brontë, opera based on, Jan 60: 122
WYATT, JAMES, Nov 61: 44, Mar 62: 36
Building designed by, Mar 62: 36
WYCHERLEY, WILLIAM, *The Country Wife,* Jan 63: 29
WYCK, JAN, Jul 63: 96
WYETH, ANDREW, Sep 58: 109, 110, 113, Jan 59: 105, Jul 62: 15, Jul 63: 88
Interview with, Sep 61: 88, 97–101
Photographs of, Sep 58: 113, Sep 61: 98
Works by. See ILLUSTRATIONS INDEX
WYETH, N. C., Sep 58: 110, 113, Sep 61: 88, 99–100
WYLIE, ELEANOR, Mar 63: 28, 32
WYLIE, I. A. R., Sep 59: 118
WYLIE, PHILIP, Jan 62: 64
Generation of Vipers, quoted, Mar 59: 134
WYNDHAM, EARLS OF. See EGREMONT
WYNDHAM, "MRS.," Mar 63: 67, 69
WYNN, ED, Sep 58: 58, 60, Sep 61: 80
WYOMING, state song, quoted, Nov 61: 119

X

XANTHOS, Sep 63: 85–86
XENOPHANES, quoted, Sep 63: 85
XENOPHON
Apology, Jul 60: 102, 103, 104
On poverty, quoted, May 62: 42
In Renaissance curriculum, Jan 60: 62
XERXES I, KING OF PERSIA, May 59: 31, May 62: 49, Jan 63: 72
Gate at Persepolis, Nov 62: 104; illus, Jan 63: 48
Herodotus quoted on, Sep 63: 85
"Pomegranate Brigade" of, Nov 62: 104
In stone relief at Persepolis, Jan 63: 44
X RAYS, Nov 63: 52–53

Y

YACHTING, "Amateurs All," by Oliver Jensen, Jul 62: 96–97
YADDO, colony at Saratoga, N.Y., Mar 63: 27, 32
YADIN, YIGAEL, Nov 59: 10, 118
Photograph of, Nov 59: 9

YALE UNIVERSITY
Architectural revolution at, May 59: 84–87
Art Gallery and Design Center, Sep 62: 57, 58–59; illus, Sep 62: 59, 61
Colleges designed by Eero Saarinen, Jul 60: 78, 123; sculptures by Constantino Nivola for, May 63: 26
Hockey rink designed by Eero Saarinen, May 59: 84–86; player quoted on, Jul 60: 82
Kahn, Louis, at, Sep 62: 58–59
Study on "brainstorming," Nov 58: 33
Teaching situation at, Sep 62: 17
YAMAGUCHI, GEN, May 60: 113, 114
Print by, May 60: 108
YAMASAKI, MINORU, Mar 59: 123, Jan 60: 21, 120, 121, May 62: 16
Buildings designed by. See ILLUSTRATIONS INDEX
YANCY, W. P., *Soldier Virgin,* Mar 62: 98
YANGSHAO CULTURE, of China, Jan 61: 11
"YANKEE CITY," series of books by W. Lloyd Warner, Nov 59: 22–23, 24
"YANKEES IN PARADISE," book by Bradford Smith, Jan 59: 122
YATER, GEORGE, portrait of, with painting by, Jul 61: 24
YAYOI, Japanese culture, Sep 61: 60, 63
YEATS, JACK BUTLER, Mar 59: 88
YEATS, WILLIAM BUTLER, Mar 59: 87–88, Nov 60: 66–69, Sep 61: 117, 119, Jan 63: 110, Nov 63: 44
As caricatured by Max Beerbohm, May 61: 38
Frost, Robert, compared to, Nov 58: 34
MacLeish, Archibald, quoted on, Jan 60: 53
Portraits of, Nov 60: 67, 69
Quoted: on Byzantium, Nov 63: 33; on public art, Jan 60: 120; on writing, Jul 63: 40
"Scholars, The," quoted, Jan 59: 19
Thomas, Dylan, quoted on, Sep 58: 84
YEFREMOV, I., Nov 63: 106
YELLOW RIVER, CHINA, San Men Dam and archaeological rescue project, Jan 61: 4–13, 124
YELLOWSTONE NATIONAL PARK, Mar 60: 16
"YES—AND AFTER," play, Jan 63: 32
"YESTERDAY," book by Maria Dermoût, Mar 61: 22
"YOJIMBO," motion picture, Jul 62: 46
YOLANDE (YELANDE), EMPRESS OF CONSTANTINOPLE, Nov 63: 31
YORK, DUKE OF (FREDERICK), Nov 62: 23
YORK, SUSANNAH, Nov 61: 115
Photograph of, Nov 61: 114
YORUBA CIVILIZATION, of Africa, and its ancestors, Mar 63: 41 (map), 44, 46–58
YOSEMITE VALLEY, Mar 60: 16
YOSHIDA, HODAKA, May 60: 113, 114
Prints by, May 60: 109, 111
"YOU ARE THERE," television show, Mar 63: 35
"YOU CAN'T TAKE IT WITH YOU," play, Jan 62: 110, Mar 63: 106
YOUNG, BRIGHAM, interviewed by Richard Francis Burton, Jul 63: 114, 116
YOUNG, CHIC, Jul 60: 5
YOUNG, EDGAR B., Jul 62: 7–8, 9
YOUNG, EDWARD, Sep 63: 48
YOUNG, G. M., on art in England, quoted, May 62: 73
YOUNG, LESTER, Sep 59: 96, Jan 63: 75
YOUNG, PHILIP, Jan 59: 84–85
YOUNG, ROLAND, Sep 63: 77 (note)
YOUNG, STARK, on drama, quoted, May 63: 106, 107
YOUNG, WILLIAM H., Jul 61: 14
"YOUNG AND THE DAMNED, THE," motion picture, Nov 62: 110
"YOUNG IDEA, THE," book edited by Lloyd Morris, May 60: 44, 47
"YOUNG LADY OF FASHION," painting, Jul 59: 31
"YOUNG ONE, THE," motion picture, Nov 62: 110
"YOUNG SAVAGES, THE," motion picture, May 62: 82, Mar 63: 35
YOUNGSTEIN, MAX E., Nov 62: 108
"YOUNG STRANGER," motion picture, Mar 63: 35
YOURCENAR, MARGUERITE, *Hadrian's Memoirs,* quoted, May 63: 35
"YOUR FRIENDLY FIDVCIARY," article by Oliver Jensen, Mar 61: 120–21
YÜ, EMPEROR OF CHINA, Jan 61: 5
Temple of, Jan 61: 11, 124
YUSUF IBN-TASHFIN, Sep 62: 88
YVON, ADOLPHE, painting by, May 63: 50

Z

ZAANDAM, NETHERLANDS, Peter the Great in, Sep 59: 74
ZAGROS MOUNTAINS
Archaeological sites in foothills of, Sep 62: 4–9
Urartu-Assyria contest for control of passes, Nov 62: 102

ZAMBOANGA, PHILIPPINE ISLANDS, Mar 61: 23
ZAMPA, LUIGI, Mar 61: 98
ZAND DYNASTY, of Persia, Jan 63: 52 (chart), 72
ZANTE, GREECE, Aegina Marbles at, Sep 59: 32, 49
ZANZIBAR, Mar 61: 33
ZARKALI, AL-. See ARZACHEL
ZARNECKI, GEORGE, and DENIS GRIVOT, *Gislebertus: Sculpteur d'Autun*, Sep 61: 48
ZASLAVSKY, DORA. See KOCH, DORA ZASLAVSKY
ZATURENSKA, MARYA, Mar 63: 30
"ZAZIE DANS LE MÉTRO," book by Raymond Queneau, May 61: 90
ZECKENDORF, WILLIAM, Jul 59: 10
Caricature of, Jul 62: 126; letter to editor about, Jan 63: 115
Structures built by, Jan 63: 115
ZEHRFUSS, BERNARD, Mar 59: 122–23
ZEISLER, PETER, Nov 63: 36
ZELTER, CARL FRIEDRICH, Nov 60: 90
ZEN BUDDHISM, Jul 59: 70–77, 126–27, Sep 60: 32, 122
Besoyan, Rick, quoted on, Sep 60: 87
Bodhidharma and Japanese folk tales about, Sep 62: 2
Gardens of, May 59: 50
Zen telegrams of Paul Reps, Jan 60: 46–47
"ZEN IN ENGLISH LITERATURE," book by R. H. Blyth, quoted, Jul 59: 126–27
ZENO, Mar 59: 54
ZENON, FLAVIUS, Mar 63: 98
"ZEN TELEGRAMS," drawings by Paul Reps, Jan 60: 46–47
ZERBE, KARL, Jan 62: 8
"ZERO FOR CONDUCT," motion picture, May 60: 51, Jan 62: 110

ZERVOS, CHRISTIAN, Nov 61: 6
ZETTERLING, MAI, May 61: 99
ZEUS, bronze found off Artemisium, Nov 58: 76; illus, Nov 58: 75
ZEUS AMMON, ORACLE OF, visit of Alexander the Great to, Mar 59: 40, 43
ZEUS-GANYMEDES MYTH, in sculpture, May 59: 122, 123, 124
ZEVI, SABBATAI. See SABBATAI ZEVI
ZIEGFELD, FLORENZ, Sep 58: 58
ZILBOORG, GREGORY, Sep 58: 60
ZIMBABWE, SOUTHERN RHODESIA, archaeological site, Mar 63: 41 (map), 57 (illus), 58
"ZINJANTHROPUS," Mar 62: 10
ZINSSER, WILLIAM K., articles by
   "Camelot," May 61: 102–13
   "Encode Me, My Sweet Encodable You," Sep 62: 120
   "Far Out on Long Island," May 63: 4–27
   "Is It True What the Movies Say About . . . ," May 59: 98–101
   "Little Flight Music, A," Mar 62: 100–1
   "On Stage: Stephen Sondheim," Jul 61: 98–99
   "Privacy Lost," Jul 60: 4–7, 120–22
   "Sotheby's," Nov 62: 58–67
   "Tyranny of the Teens, The," Jan 59: 137–39
   "Vanishing Boffola, The," Jan 61: 122–23
ZIRYAB, Sep 62: 77
ZIYARID KINGS, of Persia, Jan 63: 60
ZOFFANY, JOHN, Jul 63: 105
   Paintings by. See ILLUSTRATIONS INDEX

"ZOHAR," Mar 60: 102, 103, 125
ZOLA, ÉMILE, Nov 59: 68, May 63: 70
ZONING, May 61: 18, Jul 62: 115
"ZOO STORY, THE," play, Jul 61: 117, Sep 61: 79, Sep 62: 34
ZORILLA Y MORAL, JOSÉ, *Don Juan Tenorio*, Jan 62: 60
ZORINA, VERA, Nov 59: 54, Jan 61: 49 (note)
ZORN, ANDERS, Jul 59: 40, 134, Sep 63: 96
   Painting by, Jul 59: 27
ZOROASTER and ZOROASTRIANISM, Jan 61: 62–63, Jan 63: 43–44, 58, 59
ZOSER, KING OF EGYPT, André Malraux quoted on statue of, Nov 58: 13, 116
ZOUSMER, JESSE, Jul 60: 6
ZUCKER, PAUL, on style, quoted, Sep 59: 125
ZUKERTORT, JOHANNES, Jan 62: 116–17, 120
ZUKOR, ADOLPH, Mar 60: 38
"ZULEIKA DOBSON," novel by Max Beerbohm, Sep 60: 119, May 61: 38
"ZULU," train, Jan 59: 39
ZÚÑIGA, BALTASAR DE, Nov 62: 38, 41
ZURARA, Portuguese chronicler, quoted on explorations sponsored by Henry the Navigator, Nov 60: 76, 83
ZURBARÁN, FRANCISCO DE, Jul 59: 29
   Painting by, Jul 60: 46
ZURICH, SWITZERLAND, American singers at Stadttheater, Nov 61: 80
ZWEIG, STEFAN, May 62: 39
   Royal Game, Nov 63: 62
ZYWNY, ADALBERT, May 63: 110

INDEX OF ILLUSTRATIONS

A LISTING OF ALL ILLUSTRATIONS BY SUBJECT, ARTIST, AND TITLE

A

ABBAS I, SHAH OF PERSIA (ABBAS THE GREAT), painting of, Jan 63: 69

"ABDUCTION OF REBECCA, THE," painting by Delacroix, May 61: cover, 3

ABRAHAM AND LOT, painting by Shalom Moskovitz, Jul 61: 124–25

"ABSINTHE," painting by Degas, Sep 60: 78

ABU SIMBEL, EGYPT, temples of Ramses II at, Jul 60: 10–11, 15

ACAPULCO, MEXICO, Las Brisas, Jan 61: 104

ACHELOUS, river-god, in Etruscan pendant, May 60: cover, 3

ACHILLES, Greek picturizations of, Jan 61: 80, Jan 62: 47

"ACROBATS, THE," woodcut by Antonio Frasconi, Mar 61: 124–25

ACROPOLIS, Athens, Jul 61: 42–43

"ACROPOLIS MAIDEN," painting by Harry Engel, Jul 61: 25

ACTON, LORD. See DALBERG-ACTON, JOHN EMERICH EDWARD

ADAM, ROBERT
Mantelpiece at Syon House, Mar 62: 67
Portraits of, Nov 58: 60, Mar 62: 62
Rooms designed by, Nov 58: 50, 54, 61

ADAM AND EVE, painting by Shalom Moskovitz, Jul 61: 123

ADAMS, ANSEL, photographs of wilderness by, Mar 60: 17–24

ADAMS, JOHN QUINCY (1767–1848), portrait of, May 60: 32

ADAMS, LÉONIE, photograph of, May 60: 23

ADDAMS, CHARLES, photograph of, May 63: 18

ADDISON, JOSEPH, portrait of, Nov 63: 45

ADELARD OF BATH, page from Euclid's *Elements* translated by, Sep 62: 81

ADEMUWAGUN ADESIDA II, DEJI OF AKURE, portrait of, Mar 63: 59

ADLER, EDWARD, photograph of, Sep 62: 64

ADLER, MORTIMER J., photographs of, Sep 58: 98, 99

"ADORATION OF THE MAGI," illumination by Girolamo of Cremona, Nov 58: 2, 3

"ADORATION OF THE MAGI," painting by Ghirlandaio, detail from, Nov 60: 26–27

"ADORATION OF THE MAGI, THE," illumination by Jean Fouquet, Nov 61: 89

ADVERTISING
Art of André François, May 59: 116–17
Preparation of TV commercial, Jan 60: 10

AEGINA MARBLES, Sep 59: cover, 3, 30, 31, 33–48

AFRICA (see also NORTH AFRICA; SOUTH AFRICA, UNION OF)
Ancient cities of, Mar 63: 43, 57
Cattle of, ancient and modern, Mar 63: 52
Dance of, Jul 59: 49–55
Gold ornaments from, Mar 63: 56
Maps: historical, Mar 63: 41; northwest coast, 1468, Nov 60: 79; southwest coast, 1555, Nov 60: 82
Sculpture of, Mar 63: 38–39, 46–52, 58
Tribal chieftain, Ademuwagun Adesida II, Deji of Akure, Mar 63: 59
White man in, early portrayals, Sep 60: 22–23

"AFRICAN IMAGE," painting by Umberto Romano, Jul 61: 24

AGAMEMNON, MASK OF, Jan 61: 90

"AGON," ballet, scene from, Jan 61: 50–51

AGOSTINO DI DUCCIO, *Virgin,* Sep 60: 70

AGRIPPINA THE ELDER, coin portrait of, Sep 63: cover, 3

AGRIPPINA THE YOUNGER, Nero calling on, drawing by Philippe Julian, Mar 63: 80

AHERNE, BRIAN, in *My Fair Lady,* Sep 58: 59

"AH WILDERNESS!" play, scene from, Mar 60: 35

AIR FORCE ACADEMY. See UNITED STATES AIR FORCE ACADEMY

AJAX, in Athenian vase painting, Jan 62: 47

AKHNATON, colossus, Nov 58: 4

AKIHITO, with bride, photograph, May 60: 7

AL-, in Arabian names. See second element of name

"ALALAHA," painting by Tadeusz Kantor, May 61: 20

ALAMEDA, CALIF., Coast Guard swimming pool, Jan 60: 24

ALASKA, Mount McKinley, Mar 60: 22–23

ALBEE, EDWARD, photograph of, Sep 61: 78

ALBERS, ANNI, wall hanging designed by, Nov 61: 70

ALBERS, JOSEF
Armchair designed by, Nov 61: 71
City, Nov 61: 64
Homage to the Square: Obvious, Nov 61: 75
In Late Day (Homage to the Square), Nov 60: 10
Photographs of, Nov 61: 58, 75

"ALBERT'S SON," painting by Andrew Wyeth, Sep 61: cover, 3

ALBRIGHT, IVAN LE LORRAINE, portrait of Mrs. Leigh Block by, Jan 59: 102

ALCESTIS MYTH, sarcophagus sculpture, Jan 62: 46–47

ALDREDGE, TOM, at "The Premise," Jan 62: 69

ALEXANDER I, CZAR OF RUSSIA, received by Napoleon, painting by Adolphe Roehn, Sep 63: 28–29

ALEXANDER VI, POPE, portrait of, from *The Resurrection* by Pinturicchio, Jan 62: 32, 38

"ALEXANDER'S ENTRY INTO BABYLON," painting by Charles Lebrun, Mar 59: 50–51

"ALEXANDER'S VICTORY AT ARBELA," painting by Albrecht Altdorfer, Mar 59: 48–49

ALEXANDER THE GREAT
At Battle of Issus, sarcophagus sculpture, Jan 63: 50
Coin portrait of, Nov 63: 63
Descent into sea, painting, Nov 58: 68–69
And Diogenes, painting from 15th-century French manuscript, Mar 63: 10–11
Head of, sculpture, Mar 59: 28
Scenes from life of, Mar 59: 31–55, 59

ALFONSO X, KING OF CASTILE AND LEÓN, illus from works by, Sep 62: 83–86

ALGONQUIN ROUND TABLE, caricatures, Jul 62: 32, 41

ALHAMBRA, THE
Court of the Lions, May 62: 26
Towers of, Sep 62: 93

"ALHAMBRA INTERIOR," painting by José Villegas, Mar 60: 59

"ALIEN CHILD," painting by Carroll Cloar, Nov 58: 79

ALI PASHA, Turkish commander at Battle of Lepanto, pictured in Nuremberg broadside, Jul 63: 57

ALK, HOWARD, in *From the Second City,* Jan 62: 67

ALLAN, DAVID, painting by, of Lord Cathcart's family, Nov 58: 53

ALLEGORY, painting by Lorenzo Costa, Jan 60: 67

"ALLEGORY: H.R.H. THE PRINCE REGENT AWAKENING THE SPIRIT OF BRIGHTON," painting by Rex Whistler, Nov 62: 23

"ALLEGORY OF THE PEACE OF MUENSTER," painting by Adriaen van Nieulandt, Sep 58: 35

ALLEN, GEORGE V., with USIA publications, painting by Robert Sivard, Nov 63: 91

ALLEN, STEPHEN, portrait of, Jan 59: 9

ALLEN, WOODY, photograph of, May 63: 47

"ALL'S WELL THAT ENDS WELL," play by Shakespeare, scene from, Nov 63: 38

ALMA-TADEMA, LAWRENCE, *A Reading from Homer,* painting by, Mar 60: 64

"ALONE IN THE STUDIO," painting by Henri Schlesinger, Mar 60: 62

ALPHABET, decorated letters by Peter Soederlund, Jul 63: 120

ALTDORFER, ALBRECHT
Alexander's Victory at Arbela, Mar 59: 48–49
Forest Landscape with St. George, detail from, Mar 60: 12
Susannah and the Elders of Babylon, Sep 63: 15

"AMBASSADOR OF AUTUMN, THE," painting by Paul Klee, Nov 61: 65

AMERICAN AIRLINES, terminal at New York International Airport, Sep 59: 10–11

AMERICAN PRESIDENT LINES TOWER, San Francisco, model of, Jan 59: 9

"AM I NOT A MAN AND BROTHER," Wedgwood medallion, May 59: 96

AMMAN, JOST, woodcut by, Sep 58: 151

"AMORINI," paintings from Pompeii, Nov 60: 36–37

AMRAM, DAVID, photograph of, May 62: 83

AMSTERDAM, NETHERLANDS
Flower Market, painting by Gerrit Berckheyde, Jul 61: 58
Maps, Jul 61: 58–59
Peter the Great and Dutch vessels at, Sep 59: 70–71

ANDERSON, LENNART, *Large Reclining Nude,* Sep 63: 94

ANDERSON, T. J., photograph of, Mar 63: 29

"AND GOD CREATED WOMAN," motion picture, Brigitte Bardot in, May 60: 49

ANDOVER, MASS., Laaff house, Nov 61: 74

ANDREWS, JULIE, in *My Fair Lady,* Sep 58: 59

ANDREWS, MR. and MRS. ROBERT, portrait of, by Gainsborough, May 62: 66–67

ANGELICO, FRA (GIOVANNI DA FIESOLE)
Annunciation, detail from, Nov 60: 35
St. Lawrence Distributing Alms, Jan 62: 32, 40

ANGELS AND THEIR ANTECEDENTS, Nov 60: cover, 3, 26–27, 29, 33–49

"ANGELS IN THE MOON," stonecut by Natsivaar, Mar 63: 120

ANGKOR, CAMBODIA
  Aerial view of Angkor Vat, Jan 59: 64
  Image on wall at, Jan 59: 60
  Portfolio of photographs by Ernst Haas, Jan 59: 65–80

ANKARA, TURKEY, record of Augustus inscribed on temple wall, Nov 62: 79

ANNE, QUEEN OF ENGLAND, in allegorical painting by Godfrey Kneller, Sep 61: 72

ANNE OF AUSTRIA, in group portrait, engraving by Matthew Merian, Sep 60: 66

ANNIGONI, PIETRO, portraits by
  Queen Elizabeth II, Jul 63: 93
  Venerosi-Pesciolini, Countess Paola, Jan 59: 104

ANNIUS VERUS. See VERUS, ANNIUS

"ANNUNCIATION," painting by Carlo Crivelli, Sep 63: 14

"ANNUNCIATION," painting by Fra Angelico, detail from, Nov 60: 35

"ANNUNCIATION, THE," illumination by Jean Fouquet, Nov 61: 91

ANOUILH, JEAN
  Photograph of, Nov 60: 50
  Scenes from plays by, Nov 60: 50, 52, 53, 55, Mar 61: 42

ANSHEN, ROBERT, portrait of, Jan 59: 9

ANSHEN & ALLEN, pavilion at Dinosaur National Monument, designed by, Jan 60: 25

"ANTIGONE," play by Anouilh, scene from, Nov 60: 53

ANTINOË, EGYPT, Coptic intarsia found at, May 62: 2, 3

ANTINOÜS, sculptured head of, May 63: 34

"ANTINOUS WITH HIS JOCKEY AND TRAINER," painting by George Stubbs, detail from, May 62: cover, 3

ANTLERED MONARCH, of Persia, Jan 63: 57

APHRODISIAS, ruins of, Mar 63: 96–101

APHRODITE, torso from Aphrodisias, Mar 63: 98

"APOCALYPSE OF ST. SEVER," 11th-century French manuscript, illus from, Nov 60: 95

APOLLO, bronze statues
  Archaic-classic, found at Piraeus, Mar 60: 8–9
  In Temple of Apollo, at Pompeii, Mar 62: 51

APOLLO BELVEDERE, Roman copy in Vatican, Jan 62: 47; head of, Mar 59: 56

APOLLO FROM PAROS, sculpture, Sep 60: 71

APOLLONIA, SAINT, martyrdom of, illumination by Jean Fouquet, Nov 61: 94

APOLLONIUS, Belvedere Torso, Jan 62: 32, 36

APOXYOMENOS, sculpture by Lysippus, Nov 58: 7

APPIAN WAY, tombs along, Nov 58: 111

APSARAS, Japanese sculpture, wood, Nov 60: 38

APULEIUS, LUCIUS, The Golden Ass
  Page from, Nov 62: 89
  Works inspired by, Nov 62: 91

ARABIA, city of Medina, Jul 63: 113

ARBELA
  Battle of, painting by Albrecht Altdorfer, Mar 59: 48–49
  Plains of, photograph, Mar 59: 47

ARCADIA, fresco at Herculaneum, Mar 62: 66

ARCHAEOLOGICAL SITES IN NEAR EAST, map, Sep 62: 7

"ARCHDUKE CHARLES OF AUSTRIA," painting by Thomas Lawrence, Jul 63: 95

ARCHER, WILLIAM, in Ibsen caricature by Max Beerbohm, Jan 62: 107

ARCHIMEDES, relief portrait of, Sep 61: 26

"ARCHITECT'S DREAM, THE," painting by Thomas Cole, Jul 61: 32

ARCH OF TITUS, painting by Frederick Church, Jervis McEntee, and G. P. A. Healy, Nov 59: 101

ARCIMBOLDO, GIUSEPPE, Trojan horse, painting by, Nov 60: 2, 3

ARDEN, JOHN, photograph of, Jan 63: 30

ARGYLL, 11TH DUKE OF (IAN DOUGLAS CAMPBELL), and his home (Inveraray Castle), photograph, Nov 61: 26

ARIAS, ANTONIO, double portrait, of Charles V and Philip II, by, Nov 61: 108

ARISTOTLE
  And Alexander, medieval painting, Mar 59: 32
  Portion of Constitution of Athens by, on papyrus, Nov 62: 80

ARIZONA
  Home of Barry M. Goldwater near Phoenix, Sep 63: 103
  Taliesin West, home of Frank Lloyd Wright, Sep 59: 8–9

ARLES, FRANCE
  Paintings by Van Gogh, Jul 59: 92, 93, 99–105
  Photographs of people and scenes, Jul 59: 92–96
  Seal of, 13th century, Jul 59: 90
  In 17th century, painting, Jul 59: 91

ARLISS, FLORENCE, in House of Rothschild, Sep 63: 78

ARLISS, GEORGE

In House of Rothschild, Sep 63: 78
  As Shylock, Jan 60: 93

ARMSTRONG, LOUIS, in Jazz on a Summer's Day, Mar 61: 19

ARONSON, DAVID, Conjuror I, Jul 62: 25

"ARRANGEMENT IN GRAY AND BLACK," painting by Whistler, detail from, Sep 60: 70

ARSINOË, QUEEN OF EGYPT, sculpture, Jan 62: 47

ARTEMIS, bronze statue found at Piraeus, Mar 60: 7

ARTEMIS OF EPHESUS, sculpture, Sep 58: 85

"ARTIST IN HIS STUDIO, THE," painting by Vermeer, Sep 58: 29

"ARTIST'S FAMILY, THE," painting by Henry Lamb, May 62: 77

ARUNDELL, ISABEL. See BURTON, MRS. RICHARD FRANCIS

ARZACHEL (AL-ZARKALI), Toledan Tables of, Sep 62: 80

"ASCENT," painting, Adolph Gottlieb at work on, Mar 59: 135

ASHANTI MASK, of gold, Mar 63: 56

ASHBRIDGE, BRYAN, at Baalbek Festival, Jul 62: 31

ASHURBANIPAL, KING OF ASSYRIA, bed of, May 60: 130

ASHURNASIRPAL, KING OF ASSYRIA, amber statuette of, Jul 61: 38

ASIA MINOR, archaeological sites, map, Sep 63: 85

ASPEN, COLO., Sep 58: 98–103
  Marble garden, Nov 61: 74

ASSYRIAN SCULPTURE
  Guardian spirit, Nov 60: 33
  King Ashurnasirpal, Jul 61: 38
  Man's head, Sep 60: 71

ASTARTE, Phoenician goddess, gold relief, Jul 61: 41

ASTROLABE, Arabian, Sep 62: 81

ATHENA, bronze sculpture found at Piraeus, Mar 60: 11

ATHENIAN VOTING DISKS, Jul 60: 103

ATHENS, GREECE
  Acropolis, Jul 61: 42–43
  American Embassy, Nov 61: 72
  New York Philharmonic in Roman theatre, Jul 62: 30

ATHLETE, bronze sculpture from Herculaneum, Mar 62: 45

"AT HOME THROUGH THE AGES," drawings by Philippe Julian, Mar 63: 80–83

ATTILA, KING OF THE HUNS, encounter with Leo I, painting by Raphael, May 63: 76–77

"AU BORD DE L'EAU," painting by Cézanne, Sep 61: 15

AUBUSSON, PIERRE D', painting of, Mar 61: 49

AUDEN, W. H., photograph of, Nov 60: 90

AUDLEY END, Nov 58: 41

AUGUSTINE, SAINT, in 15th-century French miniature, Nov 62: 81

AUGUSTUS, ROMAN EMPEROR
  Bust of, Sep 60: 70
  Coin portraits of, Sep 63: 36, 39
  5th-century statue at Vatican, Jan 62: 46
  Inscription of, on temple wall at Ankara, Nov 62: 79

AUGUSTUS WILLIAM, PRINCE OF PRUSSIA, and Mme Récamier, portrait, Nov 58: 89

AUSTRIA
  Eisenstadt, rooms associated with Joseph Haydn, Mar 62: 76, 78–79
  Forchtenstein residence of Esterházys, Mar 62: 80
  University of Vienna, Mar 62: 83

AUTOMOBILES
  Cabriolet designed by Walter Gropius, Nov 61: 71
  Junk yards, May 61: 14–15, Nov 62: 114

"AUTUMN IN FRANCE," poster by André François, May 59: 113

AVERROËS, Latin-manuscript portrait of, Sep 62: 79

AVERY, MILTON
  Dunes and Sea, Jul 61: 28
  Interlude, Jul 62: 20
  Portrait of, Jul 61: 28

"AVVENTURA, L','" motion picture, scenes from, Sep 61: 111

AZECHI, UMETARO, Stand on the Snow Gorge, print by, May 60: 107

AZTEC SUN CALENDAR, Nov 63: 52

B

BAALBEK FESTIVAL, ballet at, Jul 62: 31

BABEL, TOWER OF. See TOWER OF BABEL

BABIN, VICTOR, photograph of, Sep 58: 98

BABYLON
  Appearance today, Mar 59: 50–51

Hanging gardens of, Renaissance conception, May 59: 28

BABYLONIAN ART, Nov 59: 11, 13, Jan 60: 130

BACCHANTE, Campanian fresco, Mar 62: 68

BACH, JOHANN SEBASTIAN, ms. page of B minor prelude, Jul 60: 62

BACON, FRANCIS, portrait of, Nov 60: 19

BAEZ, JOAN, photograph of, Sep 62: 67

BAHRAM V, KING OF PERSIA, hunting deer, Persian miniature, Jan 63: 65

"BALADINS, LES," painting by Picasso, Nov 61: 5

BALANCHINE, GEORGE
  Backstage with Mrs. John F. Kennedy and ballet, photograph, Sep 61: 16
  Portrait of, Jan 61: 44–45

"BALCONY, THE," play, Arnette Jens in, May 61: 50

BALI, landscapes, Sep 58: 48–49, Mar 61: 29

BALINESE CONCEPT OF ECLIPSE, Jan 59: 29

BALINESE DANCING GIRL, Mar 61: cover, 3

"BALL," "happening" by Robert Whitman, Nov 62: 114

"BALLAD OF A SOLDIER," motion picture, scene from, Mar 62: 111

"BALLAD OF BABY DOE," opera, set for, Jan 60: 16

BALLET. See DANCE

"BALL ON SHIPBOARD," painting by James Tissot, May 62: 74–75

BALLOONS, Sep 58: cover, 5, 114–28

BANGKOK, THAILAND, U.S. embassy design, Jan 60: 21

BARBER, SAMUEL, portrait of, Jan 60: 14

BARBERINI CASKET, May 60: 75

BARBERINI IVORY, Nov 63: 14; detail from, Sep 60: 71

BARBERINI VASE. See PORTLAND VASE

BARCELONA, SPAIN
  Apartment house designed by Antonio Gaudí, Mar 59: 79
  Casa Batlló, Mar 62: 38
  Church of Sagrada Familia, Sep 59: 7
  German Pavilion, Sep 59: 12
  Parapet seats, Nov 59: 109

BARDOT, BRIGITTE, in And God Created Woman, May 60: 49

BARNES, ALBERT C., photograph of, Jul 63: 22

BARRAULT, JEAN-LOUIS
  In Julius Caesar, Sep 61: 108
  Portrait of, Sep 61: 102–3

BARRYMORE, JOHN, in Romeo and Juliet, Sep 63: 78

BARTH, JOHN, photograph of, Jan 63: 36

BARTÓK, BÉLA, drawing by Robert Osborn, May 62: 127

BASTILLE, drawing by Pierre François Palloy, Jan 60: 84

BATE, STANLEY, with painting Resting Warrior, May 60: 15

BATH, ENGLAND
  Promenade at, print, Jul 61: 54
  Royal Crescent, Jul 61: 54–55

"BATHERS, THE," painting by Fragonard, Sep 60: 75

BATHS OF CARACALLA, May 60: 39, 40

"BATTLE OF BOUVINES," painting by Georges Mathieu, Sep 60: 30

BAUHAUS, THE
  Buildings of, at Weimar and Dessau, Nov 61: 58
  Curriculum, Nov 61: 61
  Designs created at, Nov 61: 61
  Domestic arts at, Nov 61: 71
  Graphic arts at, Nov 61: 68–69
  Masters of, c. 1925, Nov 61: 58–59
  Theatre at, Nov 61: 62–63
  Workshop at Dessau, Nov 61: 60

BAULÉ ORNAMENTS, of gold, Mar 63: 56

BAVARIA, GERMANY
  Castles of Ludwig II, Jan 61: 34–35, 38–43, May 62: 24
  Memorials of victory at Lepanto: monstrance at Ingolstadt, Jul 63: 58, 59; pulpit at Irsee, Jul 63: 60

BAWDEN, EDWARD, The De Lank Quarry, No. 1, May 62: 77

BAXLEY, BARBARA, in Period of Adjustment, Mar 61: 103

BAYER, HERBERT
  Buildings at Aspen, Colo., designed by, Sep 58: 101, 102, 103
  Invitation to Bauhaus party by, Nov 61: 69
  Marble garden designed by, Nov 61: 74
  Photographs of, Nov 61: 59, 74
  Type style designed by, Nov 61: 69

BAYEUX TAPESTRY, sketch from, Jan 59: 122

BAYON, TEMPLE OF, photographs by Ernst Haas, Jan 59: 70–75

BAZAINE, JEAN, windows of church of Sacré Coeur, Audincourt, France, designed by, Sep 62: 25

BEACH COSTUMES, drawings by Maurice Siné, May 62: 108–9

"BEAST X," sculpture by Lynn Chadwick, Mar 61: 106

BEATNIK, WITH PAD, May 60: 136

BEATON, CECIL
  Photograph of the Sitwells by, Jan 60: 108
  Set for Vanessa, designed by, Jan 60: 17

BEATTY, WARREN, photograph of, Jan 62: 105

BEAUTY SALON, mechanized, Nov 62: 115
BEAUVAIS, FRANCE, New York Pro Musica at, Nov 60: 93
"BECKET," play, scenes from, Nov 60: 50, 55
BECKFORD, WILLIAM
  Fonthill Abbey, designed for, Mar 62: 36
  At home in Fonthill Abbey, drawing by Philippe Julian, Mar 63: 81
BEDS THROUGH THE AGES, May 60: 129–36
BEECHAM, THOMAS, photograph of, Mar 62: 102
BEERBOHM, MAX
  Ibsen Receiving Mr. William Archer in Audience, Jan 62: 107
  "Improvements" made in books owned by, May 61: 34–39
  Self-caricature, May 61: 33
BEER CAN SCULPTURE, May 61: 119
BEERSHEBA FIGURINES, Jan 62: 73–75
BEETHOVEN, LUDWIG VAN
  Drawing by Robert Osborn, May 62: 126–27
  Letter from Count Waldstein to, Mar 62: 81
  Ninth symphony, opening bars, ms., May 61: 84
  Spell of, painting by Joseph Danhauser, May 61: 84–85
"BEGUM'S FORTUNE, THE," book by Jules Verne, illus for, Mar 63: 76
BEHAN, BRENDAN, scene from *The Quare Fellow,* play by, Mar 60: 98
BELCLAIR BROTHERS, vaudeville act, Jul 59: 117
BELGIOIOSO, L. B., E. PERESSUTTI, and ERNESTO ROGERS, memorial to World War II dead, May 61: 48
BELLA, STEFANO DELLA, equestrian ballet, drawing by, Nov 59: 2, 3
BELL IDOL, Greek, Sep 60: 70
BELLINI, GENTILE
  Mohammed II, portrait by, May 59: 61
  Turkish Artist, A, Jul 59: 40
BELLOC, H., *The Cruise of the "Nona,"* "improved" by Max Beerbohm, May 61: 39
BELMONDO, JEAN-PAUL, photograph of, Nov 61: 117
BELOV, GRIGORI, in *Life in Bloom,* Mar 62: 111
BELVEDERE TORSO, sculpture by Apollonius, Jan 62: 32, 36
BENÉT, STEPHEN VINCENT, photograph of, May 59: 16
BENGAL COLONIST, painting by Dip Chand, Sep 60: 18
BENINCASA, GRAZIOSO, map by, Nov 60: 79
BENIN SCULPTURE, Mar 63: 48, 49, 50, 58
BENTHAM, JEREMY, portrait of, May 60: 32
BENTLEY, THOMAS, portrait medallion of, May 59: 90
BERCKHEYDE, GERRIT, *The Flower Market at Amsterdam,* Jul 61: 58
BERENSON, BERNARD, photographs of, Jul 59: 28, 29
BERKELEY, CALIF., Christian Science Church, Jan 59: 10
BERLIN, GERMANY
  Airlift Memorial, May 61: 45
  Kaiser Wilhelm Memorial Church, May 61: 45
BERLIOZ, HECTOR
  Contemporary caricature of, May 61: 82
  Portrait by Courbet, May 61: 82
BERNARD OF CLAIRVAUX, SAINT, in illumination by Jean Fouquet, Nov 61: 95
BERNHARDT, SARAH
  As Hamlet, Sep 61: 107
  In her studio, May 60: 135
  As Lady Macbeth, Sep 61: 106–7
  Portrait of, Jan 61: 28
BERNINI, GIOVANNI LORENZO, works by
  Colonnades, piazza of St. Peter's, Rome, Jul 60: 52
  Fountain at Blenheim Palace, Sep 61: 71
  Fountain of the Four Rivers, Rome, May 62: 20
  Mourning Angel, Jul 60: 36
  Piazza Navona, Rome, Jul 60: 51
BERNSTEIN, LEONARD
  Photographs of, Jul 59: 16, 20–21, Jan 60: 9
  Sketch of, by Al Hirschfeld, Jul 59: 19
BERRUGUETE, PEDRO, painting of Federigo da Montefeltro, Duke of Urbino, attributed to, Jan 60: 63
BERTELLI, FERRANDO, Battle of Lepanto, engraving by, Jul 63: 54–55
BERTOIA, HARRY, screen designed by, Sep 59: 13
BESOYAN, RICK, photograph of, Sep 60: 86
BIBLE
  Early manuscripts, Nov 62: 74, 82
  13th-century Old Testament, Jan 62: 45
"BICYCLE THIEF, THE," motion picture, scene from, May 59: 99, Mar 61: 100
BIDDLE, NICHOLAS, JR., photograph of, Jul 63: 16
BIDDLE FAMILY, of Philadelphia, in 1931, Jul 63: 16–17
BIEDERMEIER STYLE, drawing by Philippe Julian, Mar 63: 82
BIENEFELD, HEINZ, stained-glass wall designed by, at Church of St. Mary the Queen, Cologne, Germany, Sep 62: 30–31
BIGGS, E. POWER, photographs of, Mar 60: 78

BIG SUR, CALIF., photograph, Jan 59: 16–17
BINGHAM, ANNE WILLING (MRS. WILLIAM), portrait by Gilbert Stuart, Jul 63: 9
"BIRD," sculpture by Elisabeth Frink, Mar 61: 111
"BIRDIE IN THE GARDEN," painting by Larry Rivers, Sep 59: 97
"BIRDS FROM MY HOMELAND," woodcut book by Antonio Frasconi, illus from, Mar 61: 126–27
"BIRD SINGING IN THE MOONLIGHT," painting by Morris Graves, Jul 59: 77
"BIRTH OF VENUS," painting by Botticelli, detail from, Sep 58: 94, Sep 63: 90
BISCHOFF, ELMER
  Cityscape with Orange Light, Nov 60: 11
  Drawing of, by David Park, Jul 60: 115
  Girl Wading, Jul 60: 24
  Landscape with Bare Tree, Jul 60: 22
  Portrait of Richard Diebenkorn by, Jul 60: 115
  Two Figures with Vermilion Light, Jul 60: 23
BITTER, KARL, *Glorification of War,* Sep 60: 103
"BLACKCOCK," painting by Edwin Landseer, Mar 60: 68
"BLACK LINES, NO. 189," painting by Kandinsky, May 59: 14
BLACKMUR, R. P., photograph of, Sep 59: 24
"BLACK ON OCHRE," painting by Morris Davidson, Jul 61: 24
"BLACK ORPHEUS," motion picture, scene from, May 60: 53
"BLACKS, THE," play, scenes from, Nov 61: 100, 101
BLAKE, PETER, photograph of, May 63: 16–17
BLAKE, WILLIAM
  God the Creator, Sep 63: 4
  Inferno, May 61: 72
BLANKENBURG, HEINZ, photograph of, Nov 61: 78
BLENHEIM PALACE, Sep 61: 69, 70, 71
  House party, 1896, Sep 61: 77
  Plan of, c. 1710, Sep 61: 74
BLIGH, WILLIAM
  Motion picture portrayals of, Sep 63: 42
  Mutiny against, engravings, Sep 63: 44, 45
  Portrait of, from painting by John Russell, Sep 63: 48
BLOCK, MRS. LEIGH
  Photograph of, Jan 59: 102
  Portrait by Ivan Le Lorraine Albright, Jan 59: 102
"BLOOD MOON," opera, rehearsals of, Jan 62: 5, 10
"BLUE AND BLACK," painting by Sam Francis, Nov 59: 33
"BLUE DENIM," play, scene from, Nov 58: 65
"BLUE DIAMOND," painting by George Ortman, Jan 63: 24
"BLUE GIRL," painting by Cornelisz Verspronck, Sep 58: 30
"BLUE TONGUED FISH," stabile by Alexander Calder, Nov 62: 13
"BLUE VASE, THE," painting by Cézanne, Sep 60: 70
BLUME, PETER
  Eternal City, The, Mar 59: 11
  Photographs of, May 59: 16, May 60: 25, Jul 61: 74
  Tasso's Oak, Jul 61: 72–73; sketches for, Jul 61: 70–71
BLUMENFELD, ERWIN, photograph of Eugene O'Neill by, Mar 60: 39
BOABDIL EL CHICO, likenesses of, Sep 62: 92
BOAR, Near Eastern statuette, Sep 62: 8
BOAR HUNT, wall painting from Tiryns, Greece, Jan 61: 82–83
BOCCACCIO, GIOVANNI, portrait of, by Andrea del Castagno, Nov 62: 87
BOCCIONI, UMBERTO, *Unique Forms of Continuity in Space,* Nov 62: 4
BÖCKLIN, ARNOLD, *Sport of the Waves,* Jan 60: 132
BODHIDHARMA
  Ivory sculpture, Sep 62: 2, 3
  Portrait of, by Sesshu, Jul 59: 70
BOETHIUS, *De Arithmetica, De Musica,* illus from, Jan 59: 2, 3
BOHROD, AARON, *Cyrano,* Jul 62: 18
BOLEYN, THOMAS, brass-plate effigy of, Sep 60: 2, 3
BOLÍVAR, SIMÓN, portrait of, Jul 59: 62
BOLOGNA, ITALY, tobacco factory, Mar 59: 23
BOLSHEVISM, posters on, after World War I, Jan 59: 114–17
"BOLTON LANDING," painting by Willem de Kooning, Sep 58: 108
BONAPARTE, MATHILDE, PRINCESSE, salon of, Nov 61: 37
BONAPARTE, NAPOLEON. See NAPOLEON I
BONNARD, PIERRE
  Dining Room on the Garden, Mar 62: 18–19
  Home of, Mar 62: 26, 27
  In Front of the Window, Mar 62: 17
  Luncheon, Mar 62: 22
  Madame Natanson and Marthe Bonnard, Mar 62: 18
  Nude in Front of a Mirror, Mar 62: 23
  Nude in the Bathtub, Mar 62: 20–21

Portraits of, Mar 62: 14, 27
  Walk by the Sea, Mar 62: 24
BONPLAND, AIMÉ, portrait of, Jul 59: 62
BOOK COVER, jeweled, from Venice, Mar 63: cover, 3
BOOK OF HOURS
  Of Berry, Duc de, miniature from, showing Louvre, Sep 60: 63
  Of Chevalier, Etienne, illuminations by Jean Fouquet from, Nov 61: 89–96
"BOOK OF JOB, THE," play, cast of, Jan 63: 89, 90
"BOOK OF MANY SUNS, A," woodcut book by Antonio Frasconi, illus from, Mar 61: 128
"BOOK OF THE DEAD, THE," papyrus scroll, Nov 62: 83
BOOKS
  Largest and smallest in Vatican Library, Jan 62: 45
  Mass and class appeal in, Jan 60: 9
  Paperbacks, Jan 60: 4
"BOON," painting by Jack Tworkov, Jul 61: 22
BORKIN, HAROLD J. See WEHRER, JOSEPH J., associate
BORY, JEAN-MARC, in *The Lovers,* May 60: 51
BOSCH, HIERONYMUS
  Garden of Earthly Delights, The, Mar 63: 72
  Temptation of St. Anthony, detail from, Jan 62: 78
BOSTON, MASS.
  City Hall designs, Jan 63: 10–15
  Jamaica Pond, Nov 59: 136
  Louisburg Square, Nov 59: 130
  Park Street Church, Nov 59: 129
  Street lamp, Nov 59: 106
BOTKIN, HENRY
  Portrait of, Jul 61: 25
  Transition No. 2, Jul 61: 25
BOTT, FRANCIS, window for chapel of Château de Reux, Normandy, designed by, Sep 62: 29
BOTTICELLI, SANDRO
  Birth of Venus, detail from, Sep 58: 94, Sep 63: 90
  Exodus in *Scenes from the Life of Moses,* detail from, Jan 62: 32, 39
  Primavera, La, Sep 58: 95
  Tragedy of Lucretia, Jul 59: 36–37
BOTVINNIK, MIKHAIL, photograph of, Jan 62: 117
BOUCHER, FRANÇOIS
  Medallions from designs by, Nov 58: 61
  Miss O'Murphy, Sep 63: 92
BOUGUEREAU, ADOLPHE WILLIAM, *Les Oréades,* Mar 60: 61
BOULEZ, PIERRE, photograph of, Jan 59: 53
BOULLÉE, ETIENNE, design for Isaac Newton cenotaph, Mar 62: 35
BOULTON, MATTHEW, portrait of, May 59: 91
BOVARY. See MADAME BOVARY
BOWLES, SAMUEL, portrait of, Jul 61: 105
BOX TUNNEL, near Chippenham, England, Jan 59: 38–39
BOYARS, print, Sep 59: 64
BRADBURY, RAY, *Fahrenheit 451,* illus for, Mar 63: 79
BRAKE, BRIAN, photographs by
  Of China, Sep 62: 48–56; at San Men Dam, Jan 61: 4–10, 12–13
  Dance of India, Sep 63: 64–67, 69–71, 73
BRANCUSI, CONSTANTIN
  Maiastra, May 59: 19
  Sorceress, May 59: 14
BRANDO, MARLON
  In *Mutiny on the Bounty,* Sep 63: 42
  Photograph of, Sep 58: 38
BRANDT, M., teapot designed by, Nov 61: 71
BRASSEUR, PIERRE, as Edmund Kean, Mar 62: 118
BRASS-PLATE EFFIGY, of Thomas Boleyn, Sep 60: 2, 3
BRATBY, JOHN, *Gloria and Sunflowers,* May 62: 76
BRAUN, KARL, as Wotan, May 63: 40
BRAZIL
  Brasilia cathedral, model for, Sep 59: 15
  Church of St. Francis at Pampulha, Sep 59: 9
BREAKERS, THE, Palm Beach, Fla., Jan 61: 108–9
"BREAKWATER AT HONFLEUR, THE," painting by Monet, Jul 62: 78–79
BRECHT, BERTOLT
  Portrait of, used in *Brecht on Brecht,* May 62: 34
  Scenes from plays by, Mar 61: 47, May 62: 36, 37, 38, 39, 41
BREEN, ADAM VAN, ice skating at The Hague, painting by, Sep 58: 16–17
BRENNEISEN, M., polar landscape, photograph by, Sep 58: 68–69
BRETTON WOODS, N.H., Mount Washington Hotel, Jan 61: 108–9
BREUER, HANS, as Mime, May 63: 43
BREUER, MARCEL
  Laaff house, designed by, Nov 61: 74
  Photographs of, Nov 61: 59, 74
BRICE, FANNIE, as Baby Snooks, Sep 58: 58
BRICK MAKING, in Egyptian tomb painting, Nov 59: 16–

17

"BRIDGE, THE," painting by Winston S. Churchill, May 62: 76

"BRIDGE AT MAINCY," painting by Cézanne, Jul 62: 57

"BRIDGE AT MANTES, THE," painting by Corot, Jul 62: 72–73

BRIDGES
Clifton Bridge, over Avon River, England, Jan 59: 36–37
Concord Bridge, Nov 59: 131
Covered, at West Cornwall, Conn., May 60: 10
In Hiroshima Peace Park, Mar 60: 111
Khaju, at Isfahan, Iran, May 61: 24–29, 31
At Maincy, France, Jul 62: 57
At Rapallo, Italy, Jul 60: 97
Of Seine River, Jul 62: 61–66, 69, 72–75
Soane, John, design by, Nov 63: 76

BRIDOU, LUCIENNE, in *The Heyer Things of Life*, Jan 62: 71

BRIGHTON, ENGLAND
Hippodrome Theatre, Jul 59: 119
Photographs by Bruce Davidson, Nov 61: 22, 23
Royal Pavilion, Mar 62: 35, Nov 62: 31; aquatints by John Nash, Nov 62: 20–21, 25–28

BRILL, REGINALD, *Dustmen*, May 62: 77

BRINCKERHOFF, BURT, in *Blue Denim*, Nov 58: 65

BROADUS, JOHN, in *Reynard the Fox*, Jan 63: 91

BROCA, PHILIPPE DE, photograph of, Jan 62: 109

BROCKBANK, American view of British, cartoon by, Jan 59: 57

BRODERSON, ROBERT, *Memory of Childhood*, Jul 62: 22

BROOK, ALEXANDER
Malagueña, Jul 62: 17
Photograph of, May 63: 24–25
Portrait by, of Danny Fillin, Jan 59: 101

BROOK, CLIVE, photographs of, Sep 63: 76

BROOK, MRS. CLIVE, photograph of, Sep 63: 76

BROOKS, VAN WYCK, photograph of, May 60: 26

BROWN, LANCELOT ("CAPABILITY"), portrait of, May 59: 46

BROWNE, BYRON
Night Sail, Jul 61: 24
Portrait of, Jul 61: 24

BROWNING, COLLEEN, *Comtesse Lucine and Sabine Savelli*, Jul 62: 24

BROWNING, JOHN, portrait of, Jan 60: 79

BROWNING, ROBERT, portrait of, May 63: 82

"BROWNISH," painting by Kandinsky, Jan 59: 12

BRUCE, NIGEL, in *Sherlock Holmes*, Sep 63: 79

BRUEGEL, PIETER THE ELDER
Caravel from *Landscape with the Fall of Icarus*, Sep 58: 2
Dulle Griet (*Mad Maggie*), Jan 59: 45–49
Tower of Babel, Sep 63: 10–11

BRUGES, JEAN DE, illus from *Le Livre des Tournois*, Nov 58: cover, 3

BRUHN, ERIK, photograph of, Sep 60: 95

BRUNEL, ISAMBARD KINGDOM
Engineering achievements of: Box Tunnel, Jan 59: 38–39; Clifton Bridge, Jan 59: 36–37; *Great Eastern*, S.S., Jan 59: 42–43; *Great Western*, S.S., Jan 59: 40–41; Thames Tunnel, Jan 59: 34, 35
Portrait of, Jan 59: 32

BRUSSELS, BELGIUM
Manneken-Pis, May 62: 23
U.S. pavilion at 1958 Exposition, Sep 58: 91

BUCKINGHAM PALACE, Jul 63: 106

BUDAPEST QUARTET, Nov 62: 44

BUDDHA, sculpture of, Mar 59: 57

"BUDDHA HEAD," print by Un'ichi Hiratsuka, May 60: 113

BUDDHIST MONKS, in meeting at Sian, China, Sep 62: 55

BUDDHIST PRIEST, at Angkor, photograph by Ernst Haas, Jan 59: 77

BUDDHIST SUN MEDALLION, Nov 63: 51

BULL (see also WINGED BULL)
Cave painting at Lascaux, Sep 62: 12

BULLFIGHTING, drawings by John Rombola, Jul 60: 129–36

BULTMANN, RUDOLPH, photograph of, Sep 63: 8

BUNNAGE, AVIS, in *The Hostage*, May 61: 50–51

BUNSHAFT, GORDON, photograph of, May 63: 14

BURGESS HILL SCHOOL, Sep 62: 105–7

BURGHERS, painting by Rembrandt, Sep 58: 27

BURGKMAIR, HANS, woodcut by, showing Paul Hofhaimer playing organ, Mar 60: 75

BURGOS, SPAIN, statue of El Cid, Sep 62: 88

"BURIAL OF ATALA, THE," painting by Girodet, May 61: 67

BURLIN, PAUL, photograph of, Mar 63: 32

BURLINGTON HOUSE, London, May 62: 57

BURNE-JONES, EDWARD, *The Golden Stairs*, Mar 60: 56

BURNETT, CAROL, photograph of, Sep 61: 80

BURRI, ALBERTO, and new art form, photographs, Jan 59: 144

BURTON, DECIMUS, Palm Stove at Kew Gardens, designed by, Mar 62: 36

BURTON, RICHARD FRANCIS
Portraits of, Jul 63: 111, 114, 115, 117
Received by African king, print, Jul 63: 112

BURTON, MRS. RICHARD FRANCIS (ISABEL ARUNDELL), portraits of, Jul 63: 114, 115

BUSA, PETER
Oil Anchors, Jul 61: 25
Portrait of, Jul 61: 25

BUSCH, ADOLF, photograph of, Sep 61: 84

BUSCH, HERMANN, photograph of, Sep 61: 84

BUTLER, FANNY KEMBLE, portrait of, Mar 59: 90

BUTOR, MICHEL, portrait of, Jan 62: 100

BYNNER, WITTER, drawing of, May 60: 46

BYRON, GEORGE GORDON, BARON, portraits of, Mar 59: 90, May 61: 60

BYZANTINE ART and ARCHITECTURE
Hagia Sophia, Nov 63: 20, 21, 32
Icon, with Saint Michael, Nov 60: 43
Illus from manuscripts, Nov 63: 7, 22, 24
Ivory plaque (Barberini), Nov 63: 14; detail from, Sep 60: 71
Kariye Çami, Nov 63: 28
Mosaics. See under MOSAICS
Reliquary cross, Nov 63: 15
Sculpture: bronze horses from Hippodrome, Nov 63: 12; relief showing Theodosius and family, Nov 63: 13

BYZANTINE EMPIRE, map, Nov 63: 8–9

"BYZANTINE EMPRESS," painting by Larry Rivers, Sep 59: 97

C

CABOT, CEIL, in *Dressed to the Nines*, Jul 61: 76

CAESAREA FESTIVAL, Jul 62: 30

"CAFÉ TERRACE AT NIGHT," painting by Van Gogh, Jul 59: 102

CAGE, JOHN, photograph of, Jan 59: 55

CAIN, INTERROGATION OF, sculpture by Gislebertus, Sep 61: 49

CALDER, ALEXANDER
Blue Tongued Fish, Nov 62: 13
Ceiling of Aula Magna, Caracas, Jul 59: 23
Eleven Red, Nov 62: 12
Photograph of, Nov 62: 11; in courtyard of home, Nov 62: 14; in studio, Nov 62: 17
White Flower, Red Flower, Nov 62: 13
Works by, miscellaneous, Nov 62: 10, 14, 17

CALDWELL, BARRY, in *The Sand Castle*, Jul 61: 106–9

CALIFORNIA (see also SAN FRANCISCO)
Alameda, Coast Guard swimming pool, Jan 60: 24
Big Sur, Jan 59: 16–17
Death Valley sand dunes, Mar 60: 24
Hotel del Coronado, near San Diego, Jan 61: 109
Los Angeles, Tamarind Workshop, Jan 62: 4
Stanford University Medical Center, May 62: 15

CALIGULA'S BARGES, Nov 58: 72–73

CALLAS, MARIA MENEGHINI, portrait of, Sep 59: 50

CALLOT, JACQUES, prints by
Miseries of War, The and *The Miseries and Glories of War*, details from, Nov 62: 34–41
Pantalone, Jan 60: 95
Play-ballet, Jan 60: 95
Temptation of St. Anthony, The, Nov 60: 44–45

"CALVARY," painting by Andrea Mantegna, Sep 60: 70

"CAMEL BUGGY," painting by Sidney Nolan, Sep 62: 98

"CAMELOT," musical
Costume designs by Tony Duquette, May 61: 105–13
Sketch for, by Oliver Smith, May 61: 102

CAMPANIAN ANTIQUITIES (see also HERCULANEUM; POMPEII)
Bacchante, fresco, Mar 62: 68
Melpomene, sculpture, Mar 62: 67
Thalia, sculpture, Mar 62: 67
Villa Boscoreale mural, Sep 63: 13

CAMPIDOGLIO, PIAZZA DEL, in Rome, painting by Pannini, Nov 59: 91

CAMUS, ALBERT, drawing of, Nov 59: 70

CAMUS, MARCEL, photograph of, May 60: 53

CANALETTO, ANTONIO
Piazzetta, The, Venice, Jul 63: 104
Roman Forum, detail from painting by, Nov 59: 74
Square of St. Mark's, The, Jul 59: 14–15

CANARY ISLANDS, map by Alexander von Humboldt, Jul 59: 60–61

"CAN-CAN," ballet, scene from, Sep 58: 60

CANDELA, FÉLIX, buildings designed by
Church of the Miraculous Virgin, Mexico City, Sep 59: 16
Xochimilco restaurant, Mar 59: 25

CANDELL, VICTOR
Midnight Growth, Jul 61: 21
Portrait of, Jul 61: 21

"CANDIDE," musical, scene from, Nov 63: 39

CANTERBURY, ARCHBISHOP OF. See RAMSEY, MICHAEL

CANTERBURY PILGRIMS, Jul 61: 49

CAPA, ROBERT, GI's at Palermo, photograph by, May 60: 4

CAPRI, ITALY, scenes, Mar 61: 24, 25

"CAPRICCIO," painting by William Marlow, Sep 63: 19

"CAPTAIN AND CREW," painting by Karl Knaths, Jul 61: 19

CARACALLA, ROMAN EMPEROR
Baths of, May 60: 39, 40
Coin portrait of, Sep 63: 37

CARACAS, VENEZUELA
Aula Magna, Jul 59: 23
Shopping center, Jan 62: 95

CARAVAGGIO, MICHELANGELO DA, *The Conversion of St. Paul*, Jul 60: 46

CARAVAQUE, LOUIS, portrait of Peter the Great by, Sep 59: 58

CARAVELS
From *Landscape with the Fall of Icarus*, painting by Pieter Bruegel the Elder, Sep 58: 2
From "Miller Atlas" of 1519, Nov 60: 75

"CARBURETOR," painting by Walter Murch, Nov 60: 9

CARCASSONNE, FRANCE, Jul 61: 50–51

"CARCERI D'INVENZIONE," engraving by Piranesi, Sep 63: 22–23

CARDINALE, CLAUDIA, photograph of, Jan 63: 39

CARDWELL, SYLVIA, in *Reynard the Fox*, Jan 63: 91

CARLYLE, THOMAS, portrait of, Mar 59: 90

CARNÉ, MARCEL, photograph of, May 60: 55

CARPACCIO, VITTORE, episode from "Legend of Saint Ursula," painting by, Sep 63: 18–19

CARPETS, PERSIAN, May 59: 44, Jan 63: 70–71
From tomb at Pazyryk, Jan 60: 110–11

CARRACCI, ANTONIO MARZIALE, *Deluge*, Nov 61: 83

CARRÈRE, JOHN MERVEN, Ponce de Leon Hotel, designed by (with Thomas Hastings), Jan 61: 106–7

CARROLL, DIAHANN, photograph of, Nov 60: 87

CARTHAGINIAN FUNERAL MONUMENTS, Sep 61: 28, 29

CASALS, PABLO, photograph of, Sep 61: 86

CASINO PIO, Vatican City, Jan 62: 49

CASSAVETES, JOHN, photograph of, Mar 61: 16

CASSON, LIONEL, photograph of, May 59: 17

CASTAGNO, ANDREA DEL, portrait of Boccaccio by, Nov 62: 87

CASTIGLIONE, BALDASSARE, portrait of, by Raphael, Jan 60: 65, Nov 61: 83

CASTIGLIONE, COUNTESS, portraits of, May 63: 64, 65

"CASTLE IN THE DOWNSE," Sandown, Kent, May 60: 2, 3

"CASTLE OF THE PYRENEES," painting by René Magritte, Jan 62: 76

CASTROL HOUSE, London, Nov 60: 14

ÇATAL HÜYÜK, TURKEY
Sculptures, Nov 63: 66–67
Wall paintings, Sep 62: 10, 12, 13

CATHCART FAMILY, painting by David Allan, Nov 58: 53

CATHER, WILLA, photograph of, Mar 63: 30

CATHERINE II, EMPRESS OF RUSSIA (CATHERINE THE GREAT), greeting peasants, Sep 60: 135

CATTLE, African, ancient and modern, Mar 63: 52

"CAVALRY CHARGE," painting by Géricault, Sep 60: 70

CAVERNS, at Lascaux, France, Jul 61: 34–35

CAVE VILLAGE, in China, Jan 61: 6–7

CAYAMBE VOLCANO, Jul 59: 63

CEDAR, Oriental region, illus from *Secrets de l'Histoire Naturelle*, Jan 62: 2, 3

CENSER, BAROQUE, Jul 60: 42

"CENTIPEDE," sculpture by Isamu Noguchi, Mar 60: 107

CENTURY 21 EXPOSITION, pavilion designed by Minoru Yamasaki, Mar 62: 32

CERAMICS
By Miró, Joan, Mar 59: 71
By Prieto, Antonio, Jan 59: 5
By Wirkkala, Rut Bryk, Jul 63: 66, 67

CERVANTES SAAVEDRA, MIGUEL DE (see also DON QUIXOTE)
At Battle of Lepanto, Nov 61: 108–9
Portrait of, attributed to Juan de Jauregui, Nov 61: 107

CÉSAR (CÉSAR BALDACCINI)
Galactic Insect, Mar 61: 106–7
Winged Figure, Mar 61: 110–11

CEYLON DANCERS, Sep 59: 106–9

CÉZANNE, PAUL
Au bord de l'eau, Sep 61: 15
Blue Vase, The, Sep 60: 70
Bridge at Maincy, Jul 62: 57
Impersonation by Zero Mostel, May 62: 53

CHABROL, CLAUDE, photograph of, May 60: 52
CHADWICK, LYNN, *Beast X,* Mar 61: 106
CHAGALL, MARC
Impersonation by Zero Mostel, May 62: 53
Windows of synagogue of Hadassah-Hebrew University Medical Center, Jerusalem, designed by, Sep 62: cover, 3, 26–27
"CHAIRING THE MEMBER," engraving by Hogarth, Nov 63: 81
"CHALK CLIFFS AT RÜGEN," painting by Caspar David Friedrich, May 61: 73
CHAMBERLAIN, JOHN, *Wildroot,* Mar 61: 112
CHAMBLESS, EDGAR, architectural design by, Jan 62: 95
CHAMPAIGNE, PHILIPPE DE, painting of Cardinal Richelieu by, Jul 60: 40
CHAND, DIP, painting of Bengal colonist by, Sep 60: 18
CHANDELIER DESIGN, by Dürer, Jan 60: 132
CHAO KAN, *A River Journey at First Snowfall,* Jan 61: 23
CHAO YEN, *Eight Riders in Spring,* Jan 61: cover, 3
CHAPLIN, CHARLES SPENCER
In *One A.M.,* May 60: 136
In *Shoulder Arms,* Jan 60: 8
CHARDIN, TEILHARD DE, photograph of, Sep 63: 8
"CHARGE OF THE LIGHT BRIGADE, THE," motion picture, scene from, Sep 63: 81
CHARIOTS
Chinese, Jan 61: 8
Mycenaean, Jan 61: 81
Prehistoric, Sep 58: 148–49
Roman, Jul 61: 44
CHARLEMAGNE
Entering Arles, miniature, Jul 59: 132
Portrait of, Sep 59: 129
CHARLEMONT, EDUARD, *Moorish Chief,* painting by, Mar 60: 69
CHARLES V, HOLY ROMAN EMPEROR, portraits of
By Arias, Antonio, Nov 61: 108
By Titian, Jul 61: 83
CHARLES I, KING OF ENGLAND
Banqueting House, built by, Jul 61: 90–91, 95
Execution of, Jul 61: 95
Portraits of, Sep 59: 28, 133, Jul 63: 94; by Van Dyck, equestrian, on which Cromwell's head was substituted, Jul 61: 93, *Roi à la chasse,* Jul 61: 78
CHARLES VII, KING OF FRANCE, in illumination from *The Vigils of Charles VII,* Mar 62: 94
CHARLES X, KING OF FRANCE, presenting awards, painting by François Joseph Heim, Mar 60: 54–55
CHARLESTON, S.C., cypress and azalea garden, May 59: 53
CHARLOTTE SOPHIA, QUEEN OF ENGLAND, with children, portrait by Zoffany, Jul 63: 95
CHARMATZ, WILLIAM, drawings by, on "Visit U.S.A." program, Sep 62: 116–19
CHARTRES CATHEDRAL, angel bearing sundial, Jul 62: 80
CHASE MANHATTAN BANK BUILDING, New York City, Nov 60: 4
CHATEAUBRIAND, FRANÇOIS RENÉ DE, portraits of, Nov 58: 89, May 61: 67
CHATHAM, EARL OF. See PITT, WILLIAM THE ELDER
CHATTERTON, THOMAS, portrait of, May 60: 32
CHAUNCEY, HENRY, photograph of, Sep 59: 27
CHAYEFSKY, PADDY, drawing of, Sep 60: 52–53
"CHEATS, THE," motion picture, scene from, May 60: 55
CHEN CHI, *Metropolitan Opera House,* Nov 58: 22–23
CHEN JUNG, dragons in scroll painted by, Nov 60: 29
CHERUBIM, from altarpiece at Champagny, Savoy, Nov 60: 36–37
CHESS
Chess pieces, portfolio photographed by Lee Boltin, Jan 62: 121–28
Great players, Jan 62: 114–15, 117, 118
Illus from *Book of Chess,* by Alfonso X of Castile and León, Sep 62: 83
CHEVALIER, ETIENNE, illuminations from Book of Hours of, Nov 61: 89–96
CHEVREUL, MARIE-EUGÈNE, and Nadar, in picture interview, Mar 59: 68–69
CHEW, SAMUEL, photograph of, Jul 63: 14
CHIANCIANO, ITALY, health resort, Mar 59: 22–23
CHIANG YEE
Sketch of, Nov 59: 129
Water colors and drawings of Boston, New York, Oxford, Edinburgh, and Paris by, Nov 59: 129–36
CHICAGO, ILL.
Inland Steel building lobby ornament, Sep 59: 12
Midway Gardens, caryatid and mural for, Sep 60: 103
Olivetti store, Nov 59: 46
Robie house, Sep 60: 100–1
State Street lighting, Nov 59: 106–7
Tribune Tower, Jan 63: 12
World's Fair of 1893. See WORLD'S COLUMBIAN EXPOSITION

"CHICKEN WIRE," drawing by Andrew Wyeth, Sep 61: 101
CHIGI, PRICE LUDOVICO, portrait of, Mar 61: 69
"CHILDE HAROLD'S PILGRIMAGE," painting by Turner, May 61: 62–63
"CHILD GOD," print by Hodaka Yoshida, May 60: 111
"CHILDREN OF DARKNESS," play, rehearsal of, Mar 60: 97–98
CHIMBORAZO VOLCANO, Jul 59: 64–65
CHINA
Early portrayals of white man in, Sep 60: 28
Photographs by Brian Brake, Sep 62: 48–56; at San Men Dam, Jan 61: 4–10, 12–13
CHINESE ART
Dragons from scroll by Chen Jung, Nov 60: 29
Flying Taoist saint, Ming drawing, Nov 60: 46
God of Wealth in His Civil Aspect, The, porcelain, Nov 62: 2, 3
Imperial treasures, paintings, Jan 61: cover, 3, 14, 17–24
Man and nature, painting by Ts'ao Chih-Pai, Mar 60: 12
Spring Festival on the River, from scroll, Jul 61: 65
"CHIPS WITH EVERYTHING," play, scene from, Jan 63: 26–27
CHISWICK HOUSE, Nov 58: 58–59
"CHOLMONDELEY FAMILY," painting by William Hogarth, Nov 58: 42
CHOPIN, FRÉDÉRIC FRANÇOIS, portrait by Delacroix, May 61: 81
CHRIST AND APOSTLES, on 10th-century Venetian book cover, Mar 63: cover, 3
"CHRIST DERIDED," painting by William Congdon, Jul 62: 25
CHRISTIAN, LINDA, portrait of, Jul 60: 7
CHRISTMAS, menu of Café Voisin, 1870, May 61: 127
"CHRIST OF LAVAUDIEU," wood sculpture, French, Sep 60: 70
"CHRISTUS," painting by Rouault, Nov 62: 49
CHRISTUS, PETRUS, *Portrait of a Young Girl,* Jan 59: cover, 3
CHURCH, FREDERICK, Arch of Titus, painting by (with Jervis McEntee and G. P. A. Healy), Nov 59: 101
CHURCHES and SYNAGOGUES
In Austria: Karlskirche, Vienna, Jul 60: 63
In Brazil: Brasilia cathedral, model, Sep 59: 15; St. Francis, Pampulha, Sep 59: 9
In California: Christian Science, at Berkeley, Jan 59: 10
In Connecticut: First Presbyterian, Stamford, Sep 59: 20, 21; House of Worship, Rowayton, Nov 62: 70–71
In France: Abbey of Royaumont, Beauvais, Nov 60: 93; Chartres Cathedral, angel with sundial, Jul 62: 80; Notre Dame, Paris, May 63: 53; Sainte-Chapelle, Paris, Nov 59: 82–83; St. Lazare Cathedral, Autun, Sep 61: 48, sculptures at, Sep 61: 46–47, 49–56; Saint-Trophime Cathedral, Jul 59: 92, 95; at Sézanne, May 62: 17; Shrine of the Virgin, Ronchamp, Sep 59: 4–5
In Germany: Kaiser Wilhelm Memorial Church, Berlin, May 61: 45; pulpit of church at Irsee, Jul 63: 60
In Italy: Gesù, Rome, Jul 60: 52; Sant' Agnese, Rome, Jul 60: 51; Sant' Eufemia, Spoleto, Nov 60: 92; San Giovanni degli Eremiti, Palermo, Sep 61: 32; Sant' Ignazio, Rome, ceiling fresco of, Jul 60: 48–49; Santa Maria della Salute, Venice, Mar 63: 24; St. Mark's, Venice, Mar 63: 17, 18, Nov 63: 12; St. Peter's, Rome, see SAINT PETER, BASILICA OF; San Vitale, Ravenna, mosaics in, Nov 63: cover, 3, 16–19; Syracuse cathedral, Sicily, Sep 61: 27
In Mexico: Church of the Miraculous Virgin, Mexico City, Sep 59: 16
In Michigan: Methodist, at Warren, Nov 62: 72
Of Mount Sinai, Mar 60: 91, 92–93
Pugin, Augustus Welby, designs by, Mar 62: 37
In Russia: Holy Trinity, outside Moscow, Sep 59: 65; Saint Basil's Cathedral, Moscow, Sep 60: 133
Soane, John, designs by, Nov 63: 78–79
In Spain: Córdoba cathedral, Sep 62: 73; El Tránsito, Toledo, Sep 62: 90; in Seville, Giralda tower bell and Patio of the Oranges, Sep 62: 91; Sagrada Familia, Barcelona, Sep 59: 7; Santiago de Compostela, Jul 60: 54
Stained-glass windows in: Château de Reux chapel, Normandy, Sep 62: 29; Christ Church, Bochum, Germany, Sep 62: 28; Dominican chapel, Le Havre, France, Sep 62: 32; Hadassah-Hebrew University Medical Center synagogue, Jerusalem, Sep 62: cover, 3, 26–27; Hem, France, chapel, Sep 62: 28; Sacré Coeur, Audincourt, France, Sep 62: 25; St. Mary the Queen, Cologne, Germany, Sep 62: 30–31; St. Rémy, Baccarat, France, Sep 62: 22
In Turkey: Church of the Chora, Istanbul, Nov 63: 28, mosaics in, Nov 63: 29, 30; Hagia Sophia, Istanbul, Nov 63: 20, 21, 32, mosaics in, Nov 63: 5, 23; at Sardis, Sep 63: 87
In Washington: Episcopal, at Burien, Nov 62: 72
In Wisconsin: Greek Orthodox, at Wauwatosa, Nov 62: 72
CHURCHILL, RANDOLPH, photograph of, Jul 60: 6

CHURCHILL, WINSTON S.
Bridge, The, painting by, May 62: 76
Portraits of: at age 15, Nov 60: 25; by Karsh, Yousuf, Jan 59: 103; by Sutherland, Graham, Jan 59: 103
"CHURCH OF THE MINORITIES, II," painting by Lyonel Feininger, Nov 61: 66
CIBORIUM, from Limoges, Sep 60: 71
CID, EL, statue of, at Burgos, Spain, Sep 62: 88
"CIRCUS, THE," mechanized play, scene from, Nov 61: 63
"CITÉ INDUSTRIELLE," design by Tony Garnier, Mar 62: 38
"CITTÀ NUOVA," design by Antonio Sant' Elia, Mar 62: 39
"CITY," sandblasted glass by Josef Albers, Nov 61: 64
"CITY LIFE," painting by Grace Hartigan, Nov 59: 40
"CITYSCAPE WITH ORANGE LIGHT," painting by Elmer Bischoff, Nov 60: 11
CLARK, BOBBY, photograph of, Sep 58: 58
CLARKE, SHIRLEY, photograph of, Mar 61: 16–17
CLAUDIUS I, ROMAN EMPEROR, coin portraits of, Sep 63: 33, 36
CLEMENTINUM LIBRARY, Prague, Czechoslovakia, Jul 60: 34
CLERICI, FABRIZIO
Minotaur Accusing His Mother, Sep 63: 26
Venice Without Water, Sep 63: 18
CLEVELAND, OHIO, Longwood Village "exedra," Nov 59: 109
CLIBURN, VAN, portrait of, Jan 60: 81
"CLIFTON BRIDGE," painting by I. K. Brunel, Jan 59: 36–37
CLIO, with Liberty and Father Time paying their respects, lithograph, Sep 63: 97
CLOAR, CARROLL
Alien Child, Nov 58: 79
Garden of Love, Nov 58: 80–81
Gibson Bayou Anthology, Nov 58: 78
My Father Was Big as a Tree, Nov 58: 79
Self Encounter, Nov 58: 79
CLOSTERMAN, JOHN, portrait of Duke of Marlborough by, Sep 61: 68
CLOUET, JEAN, portrait of Francis I by, Sep 60: 70
COCKER, E., calligraphic sun by, Nov 63: 53
"COCKTAIL PARTY," painting by John Koch, Sep 60: 106–7
CODEX AZCATITLAN, illus from, Sep 60: 25
CODEX PEREZ, page from, Nov 62: 92
CODEX SINAITICUS, page from, Nov 62: 82
CODEX VATICANUS LATINUS 3738, illus from, Sep 60: 24
"COFFEE," painting by Richard Diebenkorn, Jul 60: 19
COGHLAN, CHARLES F., as Edmund Kean, Mar 62: 119
COHAN, GEORGE M., in *Ah Wilderness!* Mar 60: 35
COINS
Byzantine, Sep 63: 82
Cretan, Jul 60: 87
Of Roman Empire, Sep 63: 33–41
COLE, THOMAS
Architect's Dream, The, Jul 61: 32
Consummation of Empire, The, Sep 63: 20–21
COLERIDGE, SAMUEL TAYLOR, portraits of, May 60: 32, May 61: 61
COLI, FRANÇOIS, Escoffier creation for, May 61: 127
COLLAGE, by Conrad Marca-Relli, Nov 60: 8
COLMAN, RONALD, photographs of, Sep 63: 76, 78
COLOGNE, GERMANY, radio station at, Jan 59: 52–53
COLOMBIA, air volcanoes at Turbaco, Jul 59: 66
COLORADO (see also DENVER)
Aspen, Nov 58: 98–103; marble garden at, Nov 61: 74
U.S. Air Force Academy at Colorado Springs, May 62: 10–11
COLUMBO, IGNAZIO, human pyramid, engraving by, Jul 63: 2, 3
COLUMBUS MEMORIAL LIGHTHOUSE, in Dominican Republic, May 61: 47
"COME BACK, AFRICA," motion picture, scene from, Mar 61: 15
COMET, sketch from Bayeux Tapestry, Jan 59: 122
"COMIC HISTORY OF ROME, THE," illus from, by John Leech, May 61: 52, 54, 55, 56, 57
COMMODUS, LUCIUS AELIUS AURELIUS, coin portrait of, Sep 63: 39
COMPTON, ARTHUR H., photograph of, May 59: 16
"COMTESSE LUCINE AND SABINE SAVELLI," painting by Colleen Browning, Jul 62: 24
CONCORD BRIDGE, painting by Chiang Yee, Nov 59: 131
CONCORDIA SENIOR COLLEGE CHAPEL, Jul 60: 80
CONGDON, WILLIAM, *Christ Derided,* Jul 62: 25
"CONJUROR I," painting by David Aronson, Jul 62: 25
CONNECTICUT (see also HOUSATONIC RIVER)
Hartford, Mutual Insurance Company building, Sep 59: 14

New Canaan home of Philip Johnson, Nov 58: 33
New London views, Mar 60: 29, 32, 33
"CONNECTION, THE," play, scene from, Mar 61: 43
CONNELL, GORDON, in *Dressed to the Nines*, Jul 61: 76
CONSTABLE, JOHN
  Cornfield, The, May 61: 69
  Leaping Horse, The, May 62: 70–71
CONSTANTINE I, ROMAN EMPEROR (CONSTANTINE THE GREAT)
  Coin portraits of, Sep 63: 40, 41
  Constantine's Donation, painting by Giulio Romano, Jan 62: 30–31
  Mosaic portrait in Hagia Sophia, Nov 63: 5
  Roman statue, broken, Mar 59: 4–5
  Vision seen by, and defeat of Maxentius, from 9th-century manuscript, Nov 63: 7
CONSTANTINOPLE (see also ISTANBUL)
  Attack by Ottoman Turks, 15th-century French miniature, Nov 63: 32
  Taken by Crusaders, painting by Delacroix, Nov 63: 26–27
CONSTANTIUS I, ROMAN EMPEROR, medallion portrait of, Sep 63: 37
"CONSTRUCTION A II," painting by Moholy-Nagy, Nov 61: 64
"CONSUMMATION OF EMPIRE, THE," painting by Thomas Cole, Sep 63: 20–21
CONTAINERS, mass and class appeal in, Jan 60: 9
"CONTESA DEI NUMI, LA," opera, scene from, Jul 60: 62–63
"CONTES BARBARES," painting by Gauguin, Jan 60: 33
CONTI, PRINCE DE, salon of, Nov 61: 33
"CONTINUOUS ON RED," painting by Alexander Liberman, Sep 61: 66–67
"CONVERSION OF ST. PAUL, THE," painting by Michelangelo da Caravaggio, Jul 60: 46
COOK, JEAN, photograph of, Nov 61: 79
COOPER, PETER, *Philadelphia in 1720's*, painting by, Jul 63: 6–7
COPÀN, HONDURAS, Mayan stele, Jul 62: 87
COPENHAGEN, DENMARK
  Louisiana Museum pool, May 62: 30
  Tivoli Gardens shop signs, Nov 59: 111
COPLAND, AARON
  Drawing by Robert Osborn, May 62: 124
  Photographs of, May 59: 16, Mar 63: 30
COPTIC GLASS INTARSIA, fragment, May 62: 2, 3
CÓRDOBA, SPAIN
  Great Mosque, Sep 62: 73
  Madinat al-Zahra remains, Sep 62: 77
  Plaza de las Flores, May 59: 48
COREY, IRENE
  Costumes and masks designed by, Jan 63: 89–91
  Photograph of, Jan 63: 88
COREY, ORLIN, photographs of, Jan 63: 88, 90
CORNEILLE, PIERRE, portrait of, Jul 60: 39
CORNELL, KATHARINE, in *Antigone*, Nov 60: 53
"CORNFIELD, THE," painting by Constable, May 61: 69
CORONADO, HOTEL DEL, near San Diego, Calif., Jan 61: 109
CORONATION, murals by Feliks Topolski, Nov 60: 129–36
COROT, CAMILLE, *The Bridge at Nantes*, Jul 62: 72–73
CORREGGIO, *The Mystic Marriage of Saint Catherine*, Nov 61: 82
CORSO, GREGORY, in *Pull My Daisy*, Mar 61: 14–15
CORTES, HERNANDO, encounter with Montezuma
  Paintings by Miguel Gonzales, Nov 63: 92
  Sketch by Aztec artist, Nov 63: 94
COSIMO, PIERO DI, portrait of Simonetta Vespucci by, Sep 58: 93
"COSMOS," painting by Ben Shahn, Sep 58: 111
COSSACKS COMPOSING LETTER, painting by Repin, Sep 60: 136
COSTA, LORENZO, allegorical painting by, Jan 60: 67
COSTA, MARY, in rehearsal of *Blood Moon*, May 62: 10
COT, PIERRE AUGUSTE, *The Storm*, Mar 60: cover, 3, 60
COURBET, GUSTAVE, portrait of Hector Berlioz by, May 61: 82
"COURTHOUSE STEPS," painting by William Walton, Sep 61: 7
"COUSINS, THE," motion picture, scene from, May 60: 52
COUSTEAU, JACQUES-YVES, photograph of, Sep 58: 11
COUTURIER, M.-A., window of Dominican chapel, Le Havre, France, designed by, Sep 62: 32
COVENT GARDEN, London, Nov 58: 27
COW, HUMPED, sculpture from Marlik, Iran, Nov 62: 102
COWARD, NOËL, *Look After Lulu*, scene from, Jan 63: 33
COWLES, RUSSELL, photograph of, May 60: 24
COWLEY, MALCOLM, photograph of, May 60: 22
COZINE, RUTHANNE, in *Reynard the Fox*, Jan 63: 91
CRANACH, LUCAS THE ELDER, *Venus with Cupid as*

a Honey Thief, detail from, Sep 63: 92
CRANBROOK ACADEMY OF ART, Orpheus fountain, May 62: 28–29
"CREATION OF ADAM, THE," painting by Michelangelo, detail from, Sep 58: 80
CREATOR MEASURING THE WORLD, from 13th-century illuminated French manuscript, Jan 59: 26
"CRESCENT WRENCH," painting by Jim Dine, Jan 63: 22
CRESQUES, ABRAHAM, map from Catalan atlas of, Mar 63: 45
CRETAN COIN, Jul 60: 87
"CRINOLINE, JOYS AND WOES OF," German print, Mar 59: 2, 3
CRIVELLI, CARLO
  Annunciation, Sep 63: 14
  Saint George and the Dragon, Jul 59: 32, 33
CROESUS, KING OF LYDIA, pictured on Greek vase, Sep 63: 84
CROMWELL, OLIVER
  Faked portrait of, by Pierre Lombart, Jul 61: 93
  Portraits of, Sep 59: 29, Mar 60: 103
CROSS
  Byzantine, of silver gilt, Nov 63: 15
  Gold and enamel, 6th to 9th centuries, Jan 62: 32, 33
CROWNS OF EUROPE, May 63: 94, 97–104
"CRUCIFIXION," painting by Duccio di Buoninsegna, Jul 63: 97
"CRUCIFIXION," painting by Raphael, Jul 60: 44
"CRUCIFIXION," painting by Rouault, Nov 62: 55
"CRUCIFIXION" ALTAR, painting by Rubens, Jul 60: 45
CRUIKSHANK, GEORGE
  Cartoon of Charles James Fox by, May 60: 101
  Satire on balloon craze, Sep 58: 126–27
  Sketches of Edmund Kean by, Mar 62: 114, 115
CRUSADE, THIRD, illus from French manuscript, Jan 59: 88–89, 91
CRUSADER CHIEFTAINS, Mar 61: 50
CRYSTAL PALACE, London, 1851, May 60: 87, Mar 62: 37
CUERNAVACA, MEXICO, park benches, Nov 59: 108
CUEVAS, GEORGE DE, photograph of, Jul 60: 7
CUPID and PSYCHE, works inspired by romance of, Nov 62: 91
  Painting by Van Dyck, Jul 63: 95
CUPS
  Of Khosrau I, Jan 63: 56
  Mycenaean, Jan 61: 87–89
  Nautilus shell, Baroque period, May 61: 2
CURTIN, PHYLLIS, photograph of, Nov 61: 79
CYCLADIC IDOL, Sep 60: 71
CYLINDER SEAL, Near Eastern, Sep 62: 9
"CYRANO," painting by Aaron Bohrod, Jul 62: 18
"CYRANO DE BERGERAC," play, scene from Nov 63: 37
CYRUS THE GREAT, tomb of, Jan 63: 42

D

DAGGER, MYCENAEAN, Jan 61: 73–75
DALBERG-ACTON, JOHN EMERICH EDWARD (LORD ACTON), photograph of, Mar 59: 7
DALE, CHESTER, portrait of, by Salvador Dali, Jan 59: 98
DALI, SALVADOR
  Don Quixote, Nov 61: 113
  Portrait of Chester Dale by, Jan 59: 98
  Set for *Don Juan Tenorio*, Jan 62: 64
DALLAS, TEX., Bruno Graf home, Sep 58: 91, May 62: 31
DALY, JAMES, in *Period of Adjustment*, Mar 61: 103
DANCE
  Of Africa, Jul 59: 49–55
  Baalbek Festival: Beryl Gray and Bryan Ashbridge, Jul 62: 31
  Balinese dancing girl, Mar 61: cover, 3
  Bruhn, Erik, Sep 60: 95
  Ceylon National Dancers, Sep 59: 106–9
  Danish Ballet in *The Whims of Cupid*, Sep 60: 92–93
  Equestrian ballet, Nov 59: 2, 3
  Etruscan, for the dead, May 60: 70
  Halprin, Ann, Jan 59: 22
  Of India, Sep 63: 64–67, 69–71, 73
  Indian girls forming palanquin, Jan 60: 2, 3
  Jacob's Pillow, with Ted Shawn, May 60: 14–15
  Kennedy, Mrs. John F., and New York City Ballet, Sep 61: 16
  Kent, Allegra, Nov 59: 52–53, 55
  Louis XIV costumed for, Jul 60: 60
  Marines jitterbugging in New Britain, May 60: 9
  Mass and class appeal in, Jan 60: 8
  Minuet, diagrams, Nov 59: 98–99
  Modern, model of theatre for, Jan 62: 6

Musical Clown, by Oskar Schlemmer, rehearsal, Nov 61: 63
  New York City Ballet: in *Agon*, Jan 61: 50–51; backstage, Sep 61: 16; in *Figure in the Carpet*, Jan 61: 52–55
  Of Nikolais, Alwin, Nov 58: 90–91
  Play-ballet of 1616, Jul 60: 60
  Verdon, Gwen, in *Can-Can*, Sep 58: 60
  Zorina, Vera, in *Slaughter on Tenth Avenue*, Sep 58: 61
"DANCING HOURS, THE," jasper plaque by John Flaxman, May 59: 88, 130
DANHAUSER, JOSEPH, *The Spell of the Master*, May 61: 84–85
"DANIEL, PLAY OF." See "PLAY OF DANIEL, THE"
DANIEL, SONG OF, from *Apocalypse of St. Sever*, Nov 60: 95
D'ANNUNZIO, GABRIELE, sketch of, Sep 58: 83
DANRY, JEAN (HENRI MASERS DE LATUDE), portrait of, by Antoine Vestier, Jan 60: 82
DANTE ALIGHIERI, portrait of, Nov 60: 18
DARDEN, SEVERN, in *From the Second City*, Jan 62: 67
DARIUS I, KING OF PERSIA, inscription of, Nov 62: 79
DARLING, JOAN, at "The Premise," Jan 62: 69
DARUMA. See BODHIDHARMA
DARWIN, CHARLES, portrait of, Jul 59: 62
DARWIN, ERASMUS, portrait medallion of, May 59: 91
"DASH, HECTOR, NERO, AND LOREY," painting by Landseer, Jul 63: 95
DAUMIER, HONORÉ
  Don Quixote, Nov 61: 111
  Drawing by, at Louvre, Sep 60: 71
  International Exposition of 1855, cartoon, May 63: 57
  Pygmalion and Galatea, Mar 60: 53
  Rebuilding of Paris, cartoons, May 63: 57
DAVENPORT, MARY, photograph of, Nov 61: 79
DAVID, KING OF ISRAEL, playing organ, illus from Rutland Psalter, Mar 62: 75
DAVID, JACQUES LOUIS
  Portraits by: Napoleon I, Nov 58: 88, Sep 60: cover, 3; Récamier, Mme, Nov 58: 87
  Socrates reaching for hemlock, painting by, Jul 60: 100–1
DAVIDSON, MORRIS
  Black on Ochre, Jul 61: 24
  Portrait of, Jul 61: 24
DA VINCI. See VINCI
DAVIS, DONALD, in *Krapp's Last Tape*, Sep 60: 112
DAVIS, MILES, portrait of, May 61: 101
DAVIS, PAUL, and EDWARD SOREL, "A Modern Bestiary," portfolio by, Jul 62: 120–28
DAVISON, MRS. HENRY P., family of, painting by Simon Elwes, Jan 59: 104–5
DAVY, GLORIA, in *Midsummer Night's Dream*, Nov 61: 81
DAWN, MARPESSA, in *Black Orpheus*, May 60: 53
DAY, THOMAS, portrait of, May 59: 90
"DAY OF THE GOD, THE," painting by Gauguin, Jan 60: 38–39
DEAN, JAMES, in *Rebel Without a Cause*, Sep 58: 42
"DEATH OF SARDANAPALUS, THE," painting by Delacroix, May 61: 76–77
"DEATH OF SENECA, THE," drawing by Tiepolo, Jan 61: 2
"DEATH OF SIMON MAGUS, THE," painting by Benozzo Gozzoli, Jul 63: 95
DEATH VALLEY, sand dunes in, Mar 60: 24
DEBUCOURT, PHILIBERT LOUIS, Palais-Royal gardens, painting by, Nov 59: 80–81
DECIUS, ROMAN EMPEROR, coin portrait of, Sep 63: 36
"DEEP ATTACHMENT," print by Gen Yamaguchi, May 60: 108
DEGAS, EDGAR, *Absinthe*, Sep 60: 78
DE KOONING, WILLEM
  Bolton Landing, Sep 58: 108
  Photograph of, Sep 58: 108
  Portrait of Marilyn Monroe by, Jul 62: 14
DELACROIX, EUGÈNE
  Abduction of Rebecca, The, May 61: cover, 3
  Chopin, Frédéric François, portrait by, May 61: 81
  Death of Sardanapalus, The, May 61: 76–77
  Don Juan, Jan 62: 61
  Hamlet, Sep 61: 106
  Liberty Leading the People, Mar 59: 7
  Lion Hunt, The, May 61: 78–79
  Massacre at Scio, The, May 61: 74–75
  Portrait of, May 61: 74
  Sand, George, portrait, May 61: 80
  Taking of Constantinople by the Crusaders, The, Nov 63: 26–27
DELANEY, SHELAGH, *A Taste of Honey*, scene from, Mar 61: 103, May 61: 51
"DE LANK QUARRY, NO. 1," painting by Edward Bawden, May 62: 77
DE LA TOUR, GEORGES, *St. Joseph the Carpenter*, detail from, Sep 60: 70
DE LA TOUR, QUENTIN, *Madame Pompadour*, Sep 60: 74

DELAUNAY, R., *Sun and Moon*, Nov 63: 54
DE LAVALLADE, CARMEN, photograph of, May 63: 48
DELHI, INDIA
American Embassy Chancellery, Sep 58: 91, Jan 60: 20
American exhibit at World Agricultural Fair, Jan 60: 26–27
Red Fort, Mar 61: 20
DE LIAGRE, ALFRED, JR., photograph of, May 63: 4–5
"DELIGHTS OF COUNTRY LIFE," screen, Nov 58: 48–49
DELLO JOIO, NORMAN, photographs of, Jan 62: 5, Mar 63: 30
DELPHI, GREECE, Mar 59: 33
Slave, sculpture of Siphnian Treasury, May 62: 43
DELPHIC SIBYL, painting by Michelangelo, Jan 62: cover, 3
"DELUGE," painting by Carracci, Nov 61: 83
DELVAUX, PAUL
Penelope, Sep 63: 94–95
Prisonnière, La, Jan 62: 81
DEMETER, bronze statue, Nov 58: 67
"DEMOISELLES D'AVIGNON, LES," painting by Picasso, Nov 61: 8
DENNY, REGINALD, photographs of, Sep 63: 77, 78
DENVER, COLO.
Denver Hilton, Jan 63: 115
Mile High Center, Jan 63: 115
Zeckendorf Plaza, Nov 59: 107
"DEPARTURE OF REGULUS, THE," painting by Benjamin West, Jul 63: 95
"DEPARTURE OF THE BUCENTAUR," painting by Francesco Guardi, Nov 59: 88–89
DEPTFORD, ENGLAND, Peter the Great at, painting by Daniel Maclise, Sep 59: 72–73
"DERBY DAY," painting by William Powell Frith, Mar 60: 66–67
DESCARTES, RENÉ, portrait of, Jul 60: 39
"DE SPIRITU SANCTO," book by Didymus Alexandrinus, portrait of Saint Jerome from, Nov 62: cover, 3
DESSAU, GERMANY, Bauhaus, Nov 61: 58
DETROIT, MICH.
McGregor Center at Wayne State University, May 62: 33
Reynolds Metals Company sales office, May 62: 32
DEVATA, carvings at Angkor, Jan 59: 76, 78
DEVERIA, ACHILLE, portrait of Victor Hugo by, May 61: 83
DEVINE, GEORGE, photograph of, Jan 63: 28
DEWHURST, COLLEEN
In *Children of Darkness*, Mar 60: 96–97
Portrait of, Jul 60: 95
DIAGHILEV, SERGEI, sketch of, Sep 58: 132
DIANA OF EPHESUS, statues of, Sep 58: 85, Nov 63: 80
DICKENS, CHARLES, portrait of, Mar 59: 90
DICKINSON, EDWIN, portrait of, Jul 61: 29
DICKINSON, EMILY, portrait of, Jan 61: 100
DICKSEE, FRANK, *Startled*, May 62: 74
DIDYMUS ALEXANDRINUS, portrait of Saint Jerome from *De Spiritu Sancto* by, Nov 62: cover, 3
DIEBENKORN, RICHARD
Coffee, Jul 60: 19
Drawing of, by Elmer Bischoff, Jul 60: 115
July, Jul 60: cover, 3
Ocean View from Window, Jul 60: 18
Park, David, portrait by, Jul 60: 115
Portrait of, with painting by, Jan 59: 15
DIGGES, DUDLEY, in *Raffles*, Sep 63: 79
DIJON, MOURNERS OF, sculpture, Sep 58: 62–63
DILLMAN, BRADFORD, in *Long Day's Journey into Night*, Mar 60: 38
DILLON, DOUGLAS, at Chateau Haut-Brion vineyard, photograph, Sep 61: 12
DINE, JIM, *Crescent Wrench*, Jan 63: 22
DINESEN, ISAK, portrait of, Sep 59: 110
"DINING ROOM ON THE GARDEN," painting by Pierre Bonnard, Mar 62: 18–19
DINOSAUR NATIONAL MONUMENT, pavilion at, Jan 60: 25
DIOCLETIAN, ROMAN EMPEROR, coin portrait of, Sep 63: 37
DIOGENES, and Alexander the Great, painting from 15th-century French manuscript, Mar 63: 10–11
DIONYSIAC MYSTERY CULT, Pompeian frescoes, Mar 62: cover, 3, 57–60
DISCOBOLUS, sculpture by Myron, Roman copy, Jan 62: 47
DISNEYLAND, Jan 60: 8
DISRAELI, BENJAMIN, portrait of, Mar 59: 90
DOBSON, THOMAS, Newcastle train shed, designed by, Mar 62: 36–37
"DOCUMENTARY, NO. 1," painting by James Fitton, May 62: 76
"DOG AND COCK, THE," painting by Picasso, Nov 61: 9
"DOG BARKING AT THE MOON," painting by Joan Miró, Mar 59: 76

DOGE'S PALACE, Venice, Mar 63: 19–21
"DOLCE VITA, LA," motion picture, scenes from, Sep 61: 111
DOLPHIN, from Roman mosaic at Sardis, Sep 63: 82
DOMINICAN REPUBLIC, Columbus Memorial Lighthouse, May 61: 47
DOMITIAN, ROMAN EMPEROR, coin portrait of, Sep 63: 37
"DOM JUAN," play by Molière, title page of first edition, Jan 62: 58
DONAT, ROBERT, in *Goodbye, Mr. Chips*, Sep 63: 79
"DON GIOVANNI," opera
Illus from 1801 edition, Jan 62: 59
19th-century costume design for, Jan 62: 56
DON JOHN OF AUSTRIA. See JOHN OF AUSTRIA
"DON JUAN," painting by Delacroix, Jan 62: 61
"DON JUAN," poem by Byron, illus for, Jan 62: 60
"DON JUAN," print by Goya, Jan 62: 62
"DON JUAN TENORIO," play
Illus from 1844 version, Jan 62: 63
Set for 1959 production, designed by Dali, Jan 62: 64
DONKEY CARTS, of Sicily, and their decorations, Sep 61: 34–37
DONLEAVY, J. P., photograph of, Mar 59: 15
DONNE, JOHN, portrait of, Jul 60: 58
"DON QUIXOTE DE LA MANCHA," novel by Cervantes
Illus for: Czech, Nov 61: 112; by Dali, Salvador, Nov 61: 113; by Daumier, Nov 61: 111; by Doré, Gustave, Nov 61: 110; earliest, Nov 61: 109; by Frasconi, Antonio, Nov 61: 113; by Goya, Nov 61: 110; Japanese, Nov 61: 112
Title page of first edition, Nov 61: 109
DORÉ, GUSTAVE
Don Quixote, Nov 61: 110
London slum, Jul 61: 61
"DORMITION OF THE VIRGIN, THE," painting by Mantegna, Jul 61: 81
"DOUBLE PORTRAIT," painting by Marcia Marcus, Jan 63: 18
DOUGLAS, PAUL H., photograph of, May 59: 17
DOW, ALDEN, home of, May 62: 30–31
DRAGONS, in scroll painted by Chen Jung, Nov 60: 29
DRAKE, ALFRED, as Edmund Kean, Mar 62: 12
DRAKE, JOHN, photographs of fire escapes by, Nov 63: 110–12
DRAPER, WILLIAM F., portrait of C. W. Mayo by, Jan 59: 104
DRESDEN, GERMANY, Zwinger Palace, Mar 59: 62
"DRESSED TO THE NINES," revue, Jul 61: 76, Jan 62: 71
DRESSELHUYS, LORRAINE MANVILLE, photograph of, Jul 60: 7
DUBUFFET, JEAN, *Knight of Darkness*, Mar 61: 110
DUCCIO DI BUONINSEGNA
Crucifixion, Jul 63: 97
Temptation of Christ, Nov 60: 44
DUCHAMP, MARCEL, *Nude Descending a Staircase*, Mar 60: 56, Sep 63: 90
DUCIS, JEAN FRANÇOIS, portrait of, Sep 61: 104
"DUEL AFTER THE MASQUERADE," painting by Jean Léon Gérôme, Mar 60: 68
"DULLE GRIET," painting by Pieter Bruegel the Elder, Jan 59: 48–49; details from, Jan 59: 45–47
DULLES INTERNATIONAL AIRPORT, in Washington, D.C., Jul 60: 83
DUNCAN, ANDREW, in *From the Second City*, Jan 62: 67
DUNCAN, DAVID DOUGLAS, photographs by, of Picasso and his works and of Jacqueline Roque, Jan 60: 97, 99–105, Nov 61: 13
"DUNE," painting by Joe Kaplan, Jul 61: 25
"DUNES AND SEA," painting by Milton Avery, Jul 61: 28
DUNSTON, BERNARD, *The Zip-Fastener*, May 62: 77
DUQUETTE, TONY, costume designs for *Camelot*, May 61: 105–13
DURAS, MARGUERITE, portrait of, Jan 62: 101
DÜRER, ALBRECHT
Chandelier designed by, Jan 60: 132
Portrait of, Sep 59: 131
Woodcut of sun by, Nov 63: 52
DURHAM, ANDERSON & FREED, church at Burien, Wash., designed by, Nov 62: 72
DÜSSELDORF, GERMANY
Mannesmann building, Nov 60: 12–13
Phoenix-Rheinrohr building, Nov 60: 14
"DUSTMEN," painting by Reginald Brill, May 62: 77
"DYBBUK, THE," play, scene from, Jan 61: 33
DYER-BENNET, RICHARD, photograph of, May 60: 16

E

EAKINS, THOMAS
Fairman Rogers Four-in-Hand, The, Jul 63: 21
Gross Clinic, The, Jul 63: 20

Schmitt, Max, rowing on Schuylkill, Jul 63: 21
"EARTH AND GREEN," painting by Mark Rothko, Nov 59: 35
EAST, JAMES, photograph of, Sep 62: 107
EASTBOURNE TERRACE, in London, Nov 60: 14
EASTLAKE, CHARLES LOCK, *Hagar and Ishmael*, May 62: 74
"ECCE DOLOR," painting by Rouault, Nov 62: 53
"ECHECS AMOUREUX, LES," illus from, Nov 58: 14, 15
ECKERMANN, JOHANN PETER, at Weimar, drawing by Philippe Julian, Mar 63: 82
ECLIPSE OF MOON, Balinese concept, Jan 59: 29
ECLIPSE OF SUN, photograph, Sep 58: 65
ECUADOR, volcanoes of, in paintings from sketches by Alexander von Humboldt, Jul 59: 63–65
EDGEWORTH, RICHARD LOVELL, portrait of, May 59: 91
EDINBURGH, SCOTLAND, Lady Stair's house, Nov 59: 134
"EDUCATION OF MARIE DE MÉDICI, THE," painting by Rubens, Jul 60: 37
EDWARD IV, KING OF ENGLAND, portrait of, Jul 63: 95
EDWARD VI, KING OF ENGLAND, portrait of, Sep 59: 130
EDWARDS, RALPH, photograph of, Jan 60: 9
EGREMONT, 3D EARL OF, portrait of, Mar 63: 65
"EIGHT RIDERS IN SPRING," painting by Chao Yen, Jan 61: cover, 3
EISENSTADT, AUSTRIA
Concert hall at Esterházy palace, Mar 62: 78–79
Rooms in Haydn's home, Mar 62: 76
EKBERG, ANITA, in *La Dolce Vita*, Sep 61: 111
ELDRIDGE, FLORENCE, in *Long Day's Journey into Night*, Mar 60: 38
ELEPHANT OF PARIS, Mar 59: 136
ELEPHANTS, Sep 58: 78–79, May 60: 88
Armor for, May 63: 2, 3
Hunting of, early prints, May 60: 90, 91
"ELEVEN RED," mobile by Alexander Calder, Nov 62: 12
"ELF," bronze by William Goscombe John, May 62: 74
EGYPT, ANCIENT
Book of the Dead, papyrus scroll, Nov 62: 83
Monuments in Nubia, Jul 60: 9–11, 14, 15
Mortuary chapel decoration, May 62: 2, 3
Roman mosaic floor from, Nov 63: 49
Sculpture: army officer, Nov 59: 16; "Hathor" cow in bas-relief, Mar 63: 52; in Louvre, Sep 60: 71; Queen Arsinoë, Jan 62: 47; torso of girl, Mar 61: 2
Ship of 18th Dynasty, Jul 60: 84
Sun, concept of, Jan 59: 29, Nov 63: 49
Tomb of Seti I, Nov 63: 80
Tomb paintings, Nov 58: 9, May 59: 25, Nov 59: cover, 3, 14–19, Jul 60: 15, 91, Mar 63: 42
Zodiac, Jul 62: 84–85
ELFRETH'S ALLEY, Philadelphia, Jul 63: 10–11
ELIZABETH I, QUEEN OF ENGLAND
Cradle of, May 60: 134
Portraits of, Sep 59: 132, Jul 63: 95
ELIZABETH II, QUEEN OF ENGLAND
Coronation of, murals by Feliks Topolski, Nov 60: 129–36
Portrait of, by Pietro Annigoni, Jul 63: 93
ELIZABETH PETROVNA, EMPRESS OF RUSSIA, painting of, Sep 60: 134
ELLIOTT, GEORGE P., photograph of, Mar 59: 16
ELLIS ISLAND, design by Frank Lloyd Wright for, Sep 63: 24–25
ELSOM, CECIL, Eastbourne Terrace, designed by, Nov 60: 14
ELTENBERG RELIQUARY, May 60: 95
ELWES, SIMON, *Sunday Lunch at Peacock Point*, Jan 59: 104–5
"EMBARCATION OF THE QUEEN OF SHEBA," painting by Claude Lorrain, Jul 60: 47
EMERSON, RALPH WALDO, portrait of, May 61: 66
EMINENT MEN, composite painting by W. Warman, Jan 59: 142–43
EMINENT WOMEN, composite painting by W. Warman, Jan 59: 140–41
"EMPEROR MING-HUANG'S JOURNEY TO SHU," Chinese painting, Jan 61: 18
"ENCLOSURE," collage by Lily Harmon, Jul 61: 25
"ENDGAME," play, scene from, Nov 58: 63
ENGEL, HARRY
Acropolis Maiden, Jul 61: 25
Portrait of, Jul 61: 25
ENGLAND (see also GREAT BRITAIN; LONDON)
Bath, Jul 61: 54–55
Blenheim Palace, Sep 61: 69, 70, 71
Brighton. SEE BRIGHTON
Burgess Hill School, Sep 62: 105–7
Church designs of Augustus Welby Pugin, Mar 62: 37
Comic history of, colored etchings by John Leech, Mar 60: 129–36
Fonthill Abbey, Mar 62: 36

Gardens of, May 59: 46–47
Newcastle train shed, Mar 62: 36–37
Noble houses of 18th century, Nov 58: 38–54, 58–59, 61
Oxford University, views, Nov 59: 133, Jan 63: 83, 85, 86, 87
Petworth House, Mar 63: 62–64; in water colors by Turner, Mar 63: 66, 68, 70, 71
Stonehenge, Jul 60: 86, Jul 62: 82–83
ENGLE, PAUL, photograph of, Mar 59: 61
ENSOR, JAMES, *Skeletons Arguing Over a Corpse*, Jan 62: 79
"ENTOMBMENT, THE," painting by Poussin, Mar 61: 88
EPHESUS
Diana of, statues, Sep 58: 85, Nov 63: 80
Sacred Way, Sep 58: 86
"EPIC OF MAN, THE," drawings by Fernando Krahn, Sep 63: 108–12
EPPING, FRANC, with sculpture *The Musician*, May 60: 15
ERASMUS, DESIDERIUS, portrait by Hans Holbein the Younger, May 62: 88
ERIDU, Mesopotamian city, cemetery at, Jul 61: 34
ERLACH, FISCHER VON, Karlskirche, in Vienna, designed by, Jul 60: 53
ERNST, MAX, painting by, May 59: 18
ESARHADDON'S TREATY, cuneiform tablet, Sep 59: 105
ESCHER, MAURITS, *Relativity*, Sep 63: 22
ESCOBAR, MARISOL
Mannequins by, Mar 63: 102–4
Photograph of, Mar 63: 103
Self-portrait, Mar 63: 103
ESCOFFIER, GEORGES AUGUSTE
Creations by, May 61: 127
Menus by, May 61: 123, 128
Portrait of, May 61: 120
ESTERHÁZY PALACE, concert hall, Mar 62: 78–79
"ETERNAL CITY, THE," painting by Peter Blume, Mar 59: 11
ETRUSCAN ART, May 60: cover, 3, 56–57, 62, 63, 65–72, 75–79
Horse's head, sculpture, Jan 62: 46
Tragliatella vase, Jul 60: 87
Votive statue of child, Jan 62: 46
ETTING, EMLEN, portrait of Mrs. Etting by, Jul 63: 9
EUCLID'S "ELEMENTS," page from translation by Adelard of Bath, Sep 62: 81
EUGÉNIE, EMPRESS OF FRANCE, with Napoleon III, painting by Tissier, Sep 60: 68
"EULA II," painting by Larry Rivers, Sep 59: 99
"EVANGELISTS STONING THE POPE, THE," painting attributed to Girolamo da Treviso, Jul 63: 95
EVANS, EDITH, as Rosalind, Jan 61: 31
EVANS, MAURICE, in *Man and Superman*, Jan 62: 65
EVE, sculpture by Gislebertus, Sep 61: 54–55
"EVENING IMAGES," painting by Kyle Morris, Nov 60: 7
EVERGOOD, PHILIP, *Threshold to Success*, Sep 58: 111
"EXODUS," detail of, from *Scenes from the Life of Moses*, by Botticelli, Jan 62: 32, 39
EYCK, HUBERT VAN, Heaven and Hell, painting by, Sep 63: 7
EYCK, JAN VAN
Saint Barbara, Jul 61: 48
Virgin and Chancellor Rolin, The, Nov 58: 17

F

"FAHRENHEIT 451," book by Ray Bradbury, illus for, Mar 63: 79
FAIRBANKS, DOUGLAS, JR., in *Gunga Din*, Sep 63: 80
"FAIRMAN ROGERS FOUR-IN-HAND, THE," painting by Thomas Eakins, Jul 63: 21
FALKENSTEIN, CLAIRE, portrait of, with construction by, Jan 59: 14
"FAMILY," mannequins by Marisol Escobar, Mar 63: 103
"FAMILY GROUP," sculpture by Henry Moore, Nov 60: 111
"FAMILY GROUP," sculpture by Isamu Noguchi, Mar 60: 110
"FAMILY OF DARIUS BEFORE ALEXANDER, THE," painting by Veronese, Mar 59: 38–39
"FAMILY OF SALTIMBANQUES," painting by Picasso, Nov 61: 8
FAN K'UAN, *Traveling Among Streams and Mountains*, Jan 61: 19
"FARM, THE," painting by Joan Miró, Mar 59: 73
"FARM AT LAEKEN, THE," painting by Rubens, Jul 63: 98–99
FASHION CYCLES, Mar 59: 62, 64–65, 67, 114, 115
"FATATA TE MITI," painting by Gauguin, detail from, Jan 60: cover, 3
FAUQUEZ, ARTHUR, cast of *Reynard the Fox*, play by,

Jan 63: 90–91
FAUSTINA THE ELDER, coin portrait of, Sep 63: 38
FAUSTINA THE YOUNGER, coin portrait of, Sep 63: 38
FEDER, MRS. HENRY, portrait by Larry Rivers, Jan 59: 101
"FEEDING THE BIRDS," painting by Sidney Nolan, Sep 62: 99
FEIFFER, JULES, drawings by, Nov 61: 49, 51, 52, 54
FEININGER, LYONEL, *Church of the Minorities, II*, Nov 61: 66
FELTRE, VITTORINO DA. See VITTORINO DA FELTRE
"FEMME ASSISE AU CAPUCHON," painting by Picasso, Nov 61: 6
"FEMME AU MIROIR," lithograph by Joan Miró, Mar 59: 80–81
FENCING, in gentlemen's curriculum, Nov 59: 98
FENWAY COURT, Boston, Jul 59: 26
FERDINAND V, KING OF CASTILE, at surrender of Granada, bronze relief, Sep 62: 92
FERGUSSON, FRANCIS, cast of *The King and the Duke*, musical by, Mar 60: 98
FERRIS, JAMES, photograph of, Jan 59: 8
FERRIS WHEEL, Indian forerunner of, Jul 61: 2, 3
FERTILITY GODDESS
From Çatal Hüyük, Turkey, Nov 63: 66
Near Eastern statuette, Sep 62: 8
FERTILITY SYMBOL, neolithic, Jul 61: 37
FERZETTI, GABRIELE, in *L'Avventura*, Sep 61: 111
"FÊTE AT RAMBOUILLET," painting by Fragonard, Nov 59: 85
"FÊTE CHAMPÊTRE," painting attributed to Giorgione, Jul 61: 84–85
FEYDEAU, GEORGES, *Look After Lulu*, scene from, Jan 63: 33
FICKE, ARTHUR DAVISON
Drawing of, May 60: 46
Sketches by, May 60: 42
FIELD, SHIRLEY ANNE, photograph of, Mar 63: 36
"FIELD OF THE CLOTH OF GOLD, THE," painting, Jul 63: 95
FIELDS, W. C., photograph of, Sep 58: 58
"FIGHTING COCK, THE," play, scene from, Nov 60: 53
"FIGURE IN THE CARPET, THE," ballet, scenes from, Jan 61: 52–55
"FIGURES IN A STREET," painting by L. S. Lowry, May 62: 76
"FIGURE WITH FLOWERS," painting by David Park, Jan 59: 5
FILLIN, DANNY, portrait of, by Alexander Brook, Jan 59: 101
"FIRE AND APPARITIONS," painting by José Guerrero, Nov 60: 5
FIRE ESCAPES, photographs by John Drake, Nov 63: 110–12
FIRSTBORN OF EGYPT, SMITING OF, painting by Shalom Moskovitz, Jul 61: 121
"FIRST SINNERS," painting by Rouault, Nov 62: 50
FISCHER, BOBBY, photograph of, Jan 62: 118
"FISHING FOR SOULS," painting by Adraen van de Venne, Nov 62: 32
FITTON, JAMES, *Documentary No. 1*, May 62: 76
FITZHERBERT, MARIA ANNE (MRS. FITZHERBERT)
In caricature by Thomas Rowlandson, Nov 62: 22
In print, *The Wedding Night*, Nov 62: 22
FIZDALE, ROBERT, portrait of, Mar 61: 74
FLAXMAN, JOHN, *The Dancing Hours*, plaque by, May 59: 88, 130
FLEISHER, LEON, portrait of, Jan 60: 76
FLOATING DEITY, from Japanese scroll, Nov 60: 47
FLORA, PAUL, drawings by
Latin-American revolution, May 60: 120–23
Trauerflora, Sep 59: 92–93
FLORENCE, ITALY
Baptistry, detail from Ghiberti's doors, Nov 60: 47–48
Foundling Hospital, detail from Ghirlandaio's *Adoration of the Magi* in, Nov 60: 26–27
Laurentian Library, Nov 62: 88
Tribuna of Uffizi Gallery, painting by John Zoffany, Nov 59: 92–93
FLORIDA
Home designed by Bruce Goff, Nov 61: 45
Resort hotels, Jan 61: 102–3, 106–7, 108–9
Sarasota high school, Mar 62: 33
"FLOWER MARKET AT AMSTERDAM, THE," painting by Gerrit Berckheyde, Jul 61: 58
"FLOWING ARCH," painting by Carl Morris, Jan 62: 15
FLOYD, CARLISLE, portrait of, Jan 60: 15
FLYING TAOIST SAINT, Chinese drawing, Nov 60: 46
FLYNN, ERROL, in *The Charge of the Light Brigade*, Sep 63: 81
FONTAINE. See LA FONTAINE
FONTAINEBLEAU CHÂTEAU, boudoir of Marie Antoinette, Mar 62: 65
FONTAINEBLEAU HOTEL, Miami Beach, Fla., Jan 61:

102–3
FONTANA, DOMENICO, portrait of, May 59: 32
FONTHILL ABBEY, Mar 62: 36
Drawing by Philippe Julian, Mar 63: 81
"FOOL'S HOUSE," painting by Jasper Johns, Jan 63: 19
FOPPA, VINCENZO, young scholar reading, fresco by, Jan 60: 57
FORCHTENSTEIN, AUSTRIA, Esterházy residence, Mar 62: 80
"FOREST LANDSCAPE WITH ST. GEORGE," painting by Albrecht Altdorfer, detail from, Mar 60: 12
FORLÌ, MELOZZO DA, Sixtus IV receiving a new librarian, fresco by, Jan 62: 44
"FORMOSA, DESCRIPTION OF," book by George Psalmanazar, illus from, Jan 60: 113–18
FORRESTER, MAUREEN, photograph of, Mar 62: 86
FORT WAYNE, IND., Concordia Senior College chapel, Jul 60: 80
FORT WORTH, TEX., development plan, Jul 59: 8–9
FOSS, LUKAS, photographs of, Jan 63: 76, 81
FOUCHÉ, JOSEPH, portrait of, Nov 58: 88
FOUNTAINS, May 62: 10–15, 17–29, 33
Of Apollo, Versailles, Nov 59: 38–39
Baroque, design for, May 59: 40
At Blenheim Palace, Sep 61: 71
Of Peterhof Palace, Sep 59: 85
Of Philip V at La Granja, Spain, Jul 60: 56
Of Piazza Navona, Rome, Jul 60: 51
FOUQUET, JEAN
Illuminations from Book of Hours, Nov 61: 89–96
Portrait of, Nov 61: 88
FOUQUET, NICOLAS
Castle of, Jul 63: 76–77, 78–79, 83
Portrait of, Jul 63: 76
"400 BLOWS, THE," motion picture, scene from, May 60: 54
"FOUR LANE ROAD," painting by Edward Hopper, Sep 58: 113
"FOUR MEN," painting by David Park, Jul 60: 20–21
FOURTH OF JULY, Escoffier creation for, May 61: 127
FOX, CHARLES JAMES
Cartoons on, May 60: 100, 101
Portrait of, by Karl Anton Hickel, May 60: 97
FRA ANGELICO. See ANGELICO, FRA
FRAGONARD, JEAN HONORÉ
Bathers, The, Sep 60: 75
Fête at Rambouillet, Nov 59: 85
FRANCE (see also PARIS)
Carcassonne, Jul 61: 50–51
Carpentras, detail from 1st-century arch, May 62: 44
Caverns at Lascaux, Jul 61: 34–35, Sep 62: 12
Champagny, detail from baroque altarpiece, Nov 60: 36–37
Chaux, design for, *c.* 1775, Mar 62: 34
Clermont-Ferrand, slopes of Puy de Dôme, Jan 63: 96
Crown of Louis XV, May 63: 103
Fontainebleau, Marie Antoinette's boudoir, Mar 62: 65
Louvre. See LOUVRE, THE
St. Lazare Cathedral, Autun, Sep 61: 48; sculptures of, Sep 61: 49–56
Seine River. See SEINE RIVER
Sézanne, church and fountain, May 62: 17
Suburban home near Paris, 1772, May 62: 76
Vaux-le-Vicomte, Jul 63: 76–77, 78–79, 83
Versailles. See VERSAILLES, PALACE OF
FRANCESCA, PIERO DELLA, Urbino diptych, paintings by, Jan 60: 69–72
FRANCESCATTI, ZINO, photograph of, May 60: 17
FRANCIS I, KING OF FRANCE, portrait by Jean Clouet, Sep 60: 70
FRANCIS, SAM
Blue and Black, painting by, Nov 59: 33
At work, silhouette of, Nov 59: 32
FRANCO, FRANCISCO, monument of, near Madrid, May 61: 47
FRANÇOIS, ANDRÉ
Advertising art by, May 59: 116–17
Drawings by, May 59: 108; from *Adventures du Bon Roy Luys XI, Les*, May 59: 114–15; from *Half-Naked Knight, The*, May 59: 118, 119; from *Tattooed Sailor, The*, May 59: 118
Paintings by, May 59: 109–11; *Autumn in France*, May 59: 113; *Men Just Don't Understand*, May 59: 120
Photograph of, May 59: 112
FRANK, ROBERT, photograph of, Mar 61: 15
FRANKENHEIMER, JOHN, photograph of, Mar 63: 34
FRANKLIN, BENJAMIN, portraits of, May 59: 91, Sep 59: 135
FRASCONI, ANTONIO
Acrobats, Mar 61: 124–25
Bestiary, Mar 61: 122–23
Birds from My Homeland, illus from, Mar 61: 126–27
Book of Many Suns, illus from, Mar 61: 129
Don Quixote, Nov 61: 113
Frasconi, Pablo, portrait, Mar 61: 122
Photograph of, May 59: 16

Printing with Dough, Mar 61: 124
Self-portrait, Mar 61: 122
Sun design, Nov 63: 54
Whitman Portrait, A, illus from, Mar 61: 125
FRAWLEY, JIM, at "The Premise," Jan 62: 69
FREDE, RICHARD, photograph of, Mar 59: 15
FREDERICK HENRY, PRINCE OF ORANGE-NASSAU, painting by Paulus van Hillegaert, Sep 58: 14
FREDERICK WILLIAM IV, KING OF PRUSSIA, portrait of, Jul 59: 59
FREEMAN, DOUGLAS SOUTHALL, photograph of, May 59: 17
FRIEDRICH, CASPAR DAVID, *Chalk Cliffs at Rügen,* May 61: 73
FRINK, ELISABETH, *Bird,* Mar 61: 111
FRITH, WILLIAM POWELL
Derby Day, Mar 60: 66–67
Mary, Queen of Scots, John Knox and John Erskine, painting by, Jul 63: 28–29
Private View of the Royal Academy, May 62: 62–63
Ramsgate Sands, detail from, Jul 63: 95
"FROG EATING A LIZARD," sculpture by Eduardo Paolozzi, Mar 61: 105
FROG HIEROGLYPH, Nov 59: 17
"FROM THE SECOND CITY," revue, scenes from, Jan 62: 67
FROST, ROBERT, photographs of, Nov 58: 34–35, Sep 61: 8
FULLER, BUCKMINSTER, chromium head of, by Isamu Noguchi, Mar 60: 111
FULLER, EDMUND, photograph of, May 60: 22
"FUNERAL OF ETIENNE CHEVALIER, THE," illumination by Jean Fouquet, Nov 61: 92
FURNITURE
Bauhaus designs, Nov 61: 71
Mass and class appeal in chairs, Jan 60: 8
FUSELI, HENRY, *Midsummer Night's Dream,* May 61: 72
FUTURAMA CITY, of New York World's Fair, Jul 59: 6

G

GABLE, CLARK, in *Mutiny on the Bounty,* Sep 63: 42
GABO, NAUM, steel construction by, Sep 59: 17
GAGARIN, YURI, photograph of, Nov 62: 116
GAINSBOROUGH, THOMAS
Honorable Mrs. Graham, The, Nov 58: 55
Mr. and Mrs. Robert Andrews, May 62: 66–67
Portraits of British royal family, Jul 63: 95
"GALACTIC INSECT," sculpture by César, Mar 61: 106–7
GALBA, SERVIUS SULPICIUS, ROMAN EMPEROR, coin portrait of, Sep 63: 37
GALBRAITH, JOHN KENNETH, photograph of, May 59: 17
"GALILEO," play, scene from, May 62: 41
GALLIENUS, PUBLIUS, ROMAN EMPEROR, coin portrait of, Sep 63: 36
GALLUP, GEORGE, photograph of, Sep 59: 25
GANDHARA SCULPTURE, Mar 59: 57
GANDY, J. M.
Church designs of John Soane, drawing by, Nov 63: 78–79
John Soane Museum, water color by, Nov 63: 72
GANNETT, LEWIS, color photograph of, May 60: 20
GANYMEDES SEIZED BY EAGLE, sculpture, May 59: 103, 105
"GARDEN OF EARTHLY DELIGHTS, THE," painting by Hieronymus Bosch, Mar 63: 72
"GARDEN OF FIDELITY," of Babur, May 59: 45
"GARDEN OF LOVE, THE," painting by Carroll Cloar, Nov 58: 80–81
GARDENS, May 59: cover, 3, 25–28, 33–40, 42–53
Marble garden at Aspen, Colo., Nov 61: 74
Of prefectural hall, Kagawa, Japan, Sep 61: 62
At UNESCO headquarters, Paris, Mar 60: 109
GARDNER, ISABELLA STEWART
Paintings in collection of, Jul 59: cover, 3, 32–40
Photograph of, Jul 59: 31
Portraits of: by Sargent, Jul 59: 30; by Zorn, Jul 59: 27
GARGOYLES, Mar 61: 104, 113
GARIBALDI, GIUSEPPE, portraits of, Sep 61: 38, 39
GARNERAY, JEAN FRANÇOIS, climax of "July Days," painting by, May 61: 86–87
GARNIER, TONY, *Cité Industrielle,* Mar 62: 38
"GATE OF HELL," motion picture, scene from, May 59: 99
GAUDÍ, ANTONIO, architectural works of, in Barcelona
Apartment house, Mar 59: 79
Casa Batlló, Mar 62: 38
Church of Sagrada Familia, Sep 59: 7
Parapet seats, Park Güell, Nov 59: 109
GAUGAMELA, BATTLE OF. See ARBELA, Battle of
GAUGUIN, PAUL
Contes Barbares, Jan 60: 33
Day of the God, The, Jan 60: 38–39

Fatata te Miti, detail from, Jan 60: cover, 3
Ia Orana Maria, Jan 60: 40
Landscape with Peacocks, Jan 60: 35
Maruru, Jan 60: 126
Noa Noa, Jan 60: 127
Spirit of the Dead Watches, The, Jan 60: 36–37
Tahitian Carrying Bananas, Jan 60: 125
Te Arii Vahine, Jan 60: 127
White Horse, The, Jan 60: 38
Woman with Fruit, Jan 60: 34
GELB, JAN
Portrait of, Jul 61: 26
Sunset Chord, Jul 61: 26
GELBER, JACK, *The Connection,* scene from, Mar 61: 43
GELLER, ABRAHAM, AND ASSOCIATES, design for memorial to F. D. Roosevelt, May 61: 43
"GENERAL DELLA ROVERE," motion picture, scene from, Mar 61: 99
GENERAL MOTORS TECHNICAL CENTER, in Warren, Mich., Jul 60: 80–81
"GENERALS, THE," mannequins by Marisol Escobar, Mar 63: 102
"GENESIS," mural by Rico Lebrun, Jul 62: 15
"GENESIS," nature photographs, Sep 58: 64–81
GENET, JEAN
Balcony, The, Arnette Jens in, May 61: 50
Blacks, The, scenes from, Nov 61: 100, 101
GENEVA, SWITZERLAND, League of Nations Palace, Jan 63: 12
GENTILESCHI, ORAZIO, *Holy Family,* Nov 61: 83
"GEOFFREY SHARP," painting by Ruskin Spear, detail from, May 62: 76
GEOFFRIN, MME, SALON OF, painting by Lemonnier, Nov 59: 81
GEORGE III, KING OF ENGLAND
Equestrian statue by Turnerelli, Nov 63: 80
Portraits of, Mar 59: 90, Jul 63: 94
GEORGE IV, KING OF ENGLAND
In *Allegory,* by Rex Whistler, Nov 62: 23
Bed of, May 60: 133
In caricature by Thomas Rowlandson, Nov 62: 22
Portraits of, Mar 59: 90, Jul 63: 94
In print, *The Wedding Night,* Nov 62: 22
GEORGE V, KING OF ENGLAND, coronation menu, May 61: 123
GEORGETOWN UNIVERSITY, graduation ritual, May 63: 86–87
GERARD, FRANÇOIS, portrait of Mme de Staël by, Nov 58: 86
GÉRICAULT, THÉODORE, *Cavalry Charge,* Sep 60: 70
GERMANY (see also BAVARIA; BERLIN; DÜSSELDORF)
Bauhaus. See BAUHAUS, THE
Crowns of, May 63: 97, 98, 99
Einstein Tower, Potsdam, Mar 62: 39
GÉRÔME, JEAN LÉON
Duel after the Masquerade, Mar 60: 68
Pygmalion and Galatea, Mar 60: 52
GEYRE, TURKEY, Mar 63: 100
GHANA, postcard reproductions of *Ancient African History,* murals at Accra, Jan 63: 116–17
GHIBERTI, LORENZO, detail from doors of San Giovanni baptistry, Florence, Nov 60: 48–49
GHIRLANDAIO, DOMENICO, *Adoration of the Magi,* detail from, Nov 60: 26–27
GIANNINI, VITTORIO, portrait of, Jan 60: 15
GIBBONS, GRINLING
Doorways by, Sep 61: 71
Petworth House carvings, Mar 63: 64
GIBEON, POOL OF, Nov 59: 8
"GIBSON BAYOU ANTHOLOGY," painting by Carroll Cloar, Nov 58: 78
GIELGUD, JOHN, as Hamlet, Jan 61: 30
GIEROWSKI, STEFAN, abstract painting by, May 61: 23
GILBERT, W. S., and ARTHUR SULLIVAN
Drawing by Robert Osborn, May 62: 121
H.M.S. Pinafore, scene from, Nov 63: 39
GILL, BOB, "Jazz!" drawing by, Jan 63: 120
GINSBERG, ALLEN
Photograph of, Sep 58: 41
In *Pull My Daisy,* Mar 61: 14–15
GIORDANI, JOHN N., photograph of, May 60: 9
GIORGIONE, IL, *Fête Champêtre,* Jul 61: 84–85
GIOTTO, impersonation by Zero Mostel, May 62: 52
GIOVANNI and NICCOLÒ, *The Last Judgment,* Jan 62: 32, 35
GIRARD, ALEXANDER, sun design by, Nov 63: 53
"GIRL BEFORE A MIRROR," painting by Picasso, May 59: 12
"GIRL IN A FUR WRAP," painting by Titian, Jul 61: 82
"GIRL ON THE VIA FLAMINIA, THE," play, scene from, Mar 60: 98
"GIRL WADING," painting by Elmer Bischoff, Jul 60: 24
"GIRL WITH GREEN EYES," painting by Matisse, Jan 59: 12
GIRODET-TRIOSON (ANNE LOUIS GIRODET DE

ROUCY)
Burial of Atala, The, May 61: 67
Chateaubriand, François-René de, portrait, May 61: 67
GIROLAMO OF CREMONA, *Adoration of the Magi,* Nov 58: 2, 3
GIROLAMO OF TREVISO, *The Evangelists Stoning the Pope,* attributed to, Jul 63: 95
GISLEBERTUS, sculptures of St. Lazare Cathedral at Autun, France, Sep 61: 46–47, 49–56
GLACIER NATIONAL PARK HOTEL, Jan 61: 112
GLADIATORS, May 62: 46, 47
GLARNER, FRITZ, non-objective tondo by, Nov 60: 4
GLASS
Designs of Tapio Wirkkala, Jul 63: 62, 64, 65
Portland vase, Nov 63: 65
"GLORIA AND SUNFLOWERS," painting by John Bratby, May 62: 76
"GLORIFICATION OF WAR," sculpture by Karl Bitter, Sep 60: 103
"GLORIOUS GLUTTON," Russian cartoon, Sep 60: 129
GNOLI, DOMENICO, drawings by
Cities of Italy, Jul 59: 137–44
Lucien's cage, Jul 60: 2, 3
"GODDESS MUSIC AND HER DISCIPLES, THE," Italian miniature painting, Jan 59: 2, 3
"GOD OF WEALTH IN HIS CIVIL ASPECT, THE," Chinese porcelain, Nov 62: 2, 3
GODOWSKY, LEOPOLD, and string quartet, Nov 62: 42
GOD THE CREATOR, painting by William Blake, Sep 63: 4
GODWIN, FRANCIS, *The Man in the Moone,* illus for, Mar 63: 75
GOES, HUGO VAN DER, detail from Trinity Altarpiece, painting by, Jul 63: 95
GOETHE, JOHANN WOLFGANG VON
Portraits of, May 60: 32, May 61: 61
At Weimar: drawing by Philippe Julian, Mar 63: 82; lithograph, Jul 59: 58
GOFF, BRUCE, homes designed by, Nov 61: 42–47
GOHEEN, ROBERT F., photograph of, Sep 59: 24
GOLD, ARTHUR, portrait of, Mar 61: 74
GOLDBERG, MRS. ARTHUR
Heine's Moses, Sep 61: 11
Photograph of, with paintings by, Sep 61: 11
"GOLDEN ASS, THE." See APULEIUS, LUCIUS
"GOLDEN BOY," play, scene from, Jan 61: 32
"GOLDEN STAIRS, THE," painting by Burne-Jones, Mar 60: 56
GOLDSMITH, MYRON, portrait of, Jan 59: 8
GOLDWATER, BARRY M.
Arizona home of, Sep 63: 103
Monument to, design by Edward Sorel, Sep 61: 128
GOLLINS, MELVIN AND WARD, Castrol House, designed by, Nov 60: 14
GOLUB, LEON, head, painting by, Nov 60: 4
GONZAGA, ELISABETTA, portrait probably by Mantegna, Jan 60: 65
GONZAGA, LUDOVICO, MARQUIS OF MANTUA, and his family, fresco by Mantegna, Jan 60: 58–59
GONZALES, MIGUEL, Cortes riding into Mexico City, paintings by, Nov 63: 92
GOODALL, EDWARD, Thames Tunnel, painting by, Jan 59: 35
"GOODBYE, MR. CHIPS," motion picture, scene from, Feb 63: 79
GOODNOUGH, ROBERT, *The Survivors,* Nov 60: 4
"GOOD WOMAN OF SETZUAN, THE," play, scene from, Mar 61: 47
GORDONI, VIRGINIA, photographs of, Nov 61: 79, 81
GORSLINE, DOUGLAS, characters in "absurd" plays, drawings by, Sep 62: 34–35, 38–39
GOTTLIEB, ADOLPH
Side Pull, Nov 59: 39
At work on *Ascent,* Mar 59: 135
GOULD, GLENN, photographs of, Jan 60: 75, Jan 62: 88, 92, 93
GOYA, FRANCISCO JOSÉ DE
Don Juan, Jan 62: 62
Don Quixote, Nov 61: 110
Massacre of May 3, May 61: 70
Sleep of Reason, Jul 61: 4
GOZZOLI, BENOZZO
Angels, painting by, Nov 60: cover, 3
Death of Simon Magus, The, Jul 63: 95
GRACES. See THREE GRACES
GRADUATION RITUAL, at Georgetown University, May 63: 86–87
GRAESNER, GEORG WILHELM, *The Victory at Lepanto,* Jul 63: 51
GRAF, BRUNO, home of, designed by Edward D. Stone, Sep 58: 91, May 62: 31
GRAF, HERBERT, photograph of, Nov 61: 79
GRAFFMAN, GARY, portrait of, Jan 60: 76
GRAHAM, MARY, portrait of, by Gainsborough, Nov 58: 55

GRAHAM, RONNY, photograph of, Nov 60: 84
GRANADA, SPAIN
    Alhambra towers, Sep 62: 93
    Surrender by Moslems to Ferdinand and Isabella, bronze relief, Sep 62: 92
GRAND HOTEL, on Mackinac Island, Mich., Jan 61: 108
GRAND OPERA
    American, designs for, Jan 60: 16–17
    Opera houses, Nov 58: 22–29
GRAND TETON RANGE, Mar 60: 18–19
GRAND TOUR
    Curriculum during, Nov 59: 98–99
    Father greeting son after, Nov 59: 104
    Paintings illustrating, Nov 59: 74, 78–83, 85, 88, 91–93, 97, 100–3
    Travel incidents during, Nov 59: 76–77, 86–87
GRAND UNION HOTEL, Saratoga Springs, N.Y., Jan 61: 105
GRANT, CARY, in Gunga Din, Sep 63: 80
GRANVILLE, J. J., cartoon on Hernani by, May 61: 83
GRAU, SHIRLEY ANN, photograph of, Mar 59: 16
GRAVES, MORRIS
    Bird Singing in the Moonlight, Jul 59: 77
    Hedgerow Animal, Jul 60: 105
    Hibernation, 1954, Jul 60: 110–11
    Night Hedgerow Animal, Jul 60: 112
    Seabird in the Rain, Jul 60: 108–9
    Shorebirds, Jul 60: 106–7
GRAVES, ROBERT, portraits of, Jan 62: 52, 53
GRAY, BERYL, at Baalbek Festival, Jul 62: 31
"GREAT AMERICAN NUDE NO. 39," painting by Tom Wesselmann, Sep 63: 92
GREAT BRITAIN (see also ENGLAND)
    Coronation of Elizabeth II, murals by Feliks Topolski, Nov 60: 129–36
    Crown jewels of, May 63: 100–1
    Hanley before World War II, Jul 61: 60
    New face of Britain, photographs by Bruce Davidson, Nov 61: 15, 18–31
"GREAT BRITAIN," S.S., Jan 59: 42–43
"GREAT EASTERN," S.S., Jan 59: 42–43
"GREAT WESTERN," S.S., Jan 59: 40–41
GREAT WESTERN RAILWAY, England, Jan 59: 38–39
GREECE (see also ATHENS)
    Mount Olympus, Jan 61: 99
    Sparta, ideals old and new, Mar 59: 133
GREECE, ANCIENT
    Hand-to-hand combat, shown on Greek plate, Jan 63: 50
    Mycenaean civilization as shown by ruins and artifacts, Jan 61: 73–75, 77–85, 87–90, 92–95
    Philosophers of, on Roman sarcophagus, Jul 61: 43
    Remains at Sardis, Sep 63: 88
    Sculpture: Apollo from Paros, Sep 60: 70; bell idol, Sep 60: 70; Belvedere Apollo, Roman copy in Vatican, Mar 59: 56, Jan 62: 47; bronze statues recovered from Aegean, Nov 58: 74, 75; from Cave of Tiberius, May 59: 102, 103, 106; Cnidian Venus of Praxiteles, Roman copy, Jan 62: 46; Discobolus of Myron, Roman copy, Jan 62: 47; Laocoön, May 59: 105, 106, Jan 62: 47; Nile, The, Roman copy, Jan 62: 46; from Piraeus, Mar 60: 7–11; slave, sculpture at Delphi, May 62: 43; stele of slave trader, May 62: 42; sun-god from Italy, Nov 63: 52; Venus de Milo, Sep 60: 70; Victory of Samothrace, Sep 60: 71
    Vases, Jan 61: 80, 81, 94, 96, 98, Jan 62: 47, Sep 63: 84; Portland vase, Nov 63: 65
GREEK FIRE, Nov 63: 24
GREENBELT, MD., Jul 61: 62
GREENBERG, NOAH, photographs of, Nov 60: 89, 90
GREENBIE, BARRIE, theatre design by, with Elizabeth Harris and Seth Hiller, Jan 62: 6
GREENE, MILTON H., "A Flourish of Strumpets," photographs by, May 61: 50–51
GREENHAM, PETER, portrait of Brian Horrocks by, May 62: 77
GREENLAND FJORD, photograph by Werner Lüthy, Sep 58: 70
"GREEN ON BLUE," painting by Ellsworth Kelly, Jan 63: 20
GREGORY OF NAZIANZUS, miniature from manuscript of homilies by, Nov 63: 7
GREY, CHARLES, portrait of, Mar 59: 90
GRILLER QUARTET, Jan 59: 20
GRIST, RERI, photographs of, Nov 61: 79, 81
GRIZZARD, GEORGE, in Hamlet, Nov 63: 41
GROPIUS, WALTER
    Adler cabriolet designed by, Nov 61: 71
    American Embassy, Athens, designed by, Nov 61: 72
    Chicago Tribune Tower design, Jan 63: 12
    Photographs of, Nov 61: 59, 73
GROS, ANTOINE-JEAN, Napoleon at Battle of Arcola, painting by, May 61: 71
GROSS, CHAIM
    Portrait of, Jul 61: 26
    Young Acrobats, Jul 61: 26

"GROSS CLINIC, THE," painting by Thomas Eakins, Jul 63: 20
GROTIUS, HUGO, portraits of, Sep 58: 33, May 60: 32
"GROUND HOG DAY," painting by Andrew Wyeth, Sep 61: 92
GRUEN, VICTOR
    Photograph of, May 60: 84
    Plans for 1964 World's Fair, May 60: 80–85
GUADALQUIVER RIVER, SPAIN, ruins of mill built by Moslems on, Sep 62: 76
GUARDI, FRANCESCO
    Departure of the Bucentaur, Nov 59: 88–89
    Piazza San Marco, detail from painting by, Jul 61: cover, 3
GUERNSEY, LORD, photograph of, Mar 60: 78
GUERRERO, JOSÉ, Fire and Apparitions, Nov 60: 5
GUEST, MRS. WINSTON, photograph of, Jul 60: 7
GUGGENHEIM, MEYER, and his sons, photograph of, May 59: 6–7
GUGGENHEIM, OLGA HIRSCH (MRS. SIMON), photograph of, May 59: 13
GUGGENHEIM, PEGGY
    Museum of, May 59: 4, 18, 19
    Photograph of, May 59: 18
GUGGENHEIM, SOLOMON R.
    Museum of, May 59: 14–15
    Photographs of, May 59: 7, 15
GUGGENHEIM FELLOWS
    Cartoons on, May 59: 8, 9
    Photographs of, May 59: 16–17
GUGGENHEIM MUSEUM. See SOLOMON R. GUGGENHEIM MUSEUM
GUILDFORD, HENRY, portrait by Holbein, Jul 63: cover, 3
GUINNESS, ALEC
    In Hamlet, Nov 63: 41
    At rehearsals of Our Man in Havana, Nov 59: 28, 29, 30
GUISE, DUC DE, in pageant of 1662, Jul 60: 61
GULFPORT, MISS., home designed by Bruce Goff, Nov 61: 45
GULLIKSEN, HAROLD, photograph of, Sep 59: 25
GUNEYA, NITTAWALA MULYAKDESSALAGE, photograph of, Sep 59: 107
"GUNGA DIN," motion picture, scene from, Sep 63: 80
GUNN, HOMER, with sculpture Wind, May 60: 15
GUNS, of white man, pictured by native artists, Sep 60: 10, 22, 26
GUSTAVUS II, KING OF SWEDEN (GUSTAVUS ADOLPHUS), portraits of, Jul 60: 39, Sep 61: 2, 3
GUSTON, PHILIP, The Return, Nov 59: 34
GUTHRIE, TYRONE
    Photographs of, Jan 61: 26, Nov 63: 35
    Top of the Ladder, play by, scene from, Nov 63: 37

H

HACKWOOD, WILLIAM, Wedgwood medallions designed by, May 59: 89, 96
HADRIAN, ROMAN EMPEROR
    Coin portrait of, Sep 63: 36
    Sculptured head of, May 63: 35
    Villa of, May 63: 32, 36, 37, 38–39; contents of, in painting by John Zoffany, Nov 59: 103
"HAGAR AND ISHMAEL," painting by Charles Lock Eastlake, May 62: 74
HAGIA SOPHIA, Istanbul, Nov 63: 20, 21, 32
    Mosaics in, Nov 63: 5, 23
HAGUE, THE, NETHERLANDS, ice skating at, in painting by Adam van Breen, Sep 58: 16–17
HAIGH, KENNETH, in Look Back in Anger, Jan 63: 33
"HALF-NAKED KNIGHT, THE," book by André François, drawings from, May 59: 118–19
HALPRIN, ANN, photograph of, Jan 59: 23
HALS, FRANS, The Women Guardians of the Haarlem Alsmhouse, Sep 58: 31
HALSMAN, PHILIPPE, photographs by
    Albee, Edward, Sep 61: 78
    Nixon, Richard M., Jul 60: 4
    York, Susannah, Nov 61: 114
"HAMBLETONIAN; RUBBING DOWN," painting by George Stubbs, May 62: 68–69
HAMBURG MUNICIPAL CODE OF 1497, miniature from, Sep 59: 61
HAMILTON, EMMA (LADY HAMILTON), portraits of
    In "Grecian attitude," by Romney, Mar 62: 69
    As Muse of Comedy, Nov 59: 95
HAMILTON, WILLIAM, portraits of, Nov 59: 94, Mar 62: 62, Nov 63: 63
"HAMLET," lithograph by Delacroix, Sep 61: 106
"HAMLET," play by Shakespeare, scenes from, Nov 63: 40, 41
HAMMACK, WARREN, in The Book of Job, Jan 63: 89
HAMMURABI'S CODE, on diorite stele, Nov 62: 79

HAMPTON COURT, Jul 63: 107
HANDWRITING, portfolio of historic manuscripts, Sep 59: 129–36
HANDY, W. C., drawing by Robert Osborn, May 62: 123
HANISCH, ARTHUR, portrait of, Sep 58: 88
"HANIWA" HOUSE, Sep 61: 61
HANKIN, LARRY, in The Heyer Things of Life, Jan 62: 71
HANLEY, ENGLAND, Jul 61: 60
"HAN PALACE, THE," Chinese painting of 12th century, Jan 61: 20
HAN PALACE WITH ARTIST PAINTING, Chinese painting, Jan 61: 14
HANSEATIC MERCHANTS, miniature, Sep 59: 61
"HAPPY HAVEN, THE," play, scene from, Jul 62: 93
HARDWICK HALL, Nov 58: 40–41
"HARE AND JAYS," painting by Ts'ui Po, Jan 61: 17
HAREM OF GRAND SERAGLIO, May 59: 58–59, 62–63
HARMON, BOB, in Reynard the Fox, Jan 63: 91
HARMON, LILY
    Enclosure, Jul 61: 25
    Portrait of, Jul 61: 25
HARRIMAN, W. AVERELL, photograph of, Sep 61: 15
HARRIS, BARBARA, in From the Second City, Jan 62: 67
HARRIS, ELIZABETH, theatre design by, with Barrie Greenbie and Seth Hiller, Jan 62: 6
HARRIS, JULIE, in The Lark, Nov 60: 52
HARRIS, MARK, photograph of, Mar 63: 29
HARRISON, REX
    In Fighting Cock, The, Nov 60: 53
    In My Fair Lady, Sep 58: 59
HARRISON, WALLACE K., First Presbyterian Church, Stamford, Conn., designed by, Sep 59: 20, 21
HARRISON & ABRAMOVITZ, assembly hall designed by, Mar 59: 25
HART, SOLOMON ALEXANDER, Saladin at bedside of Richard, painting by, Jan 59: 86
HARTFORD, CONN., Mutual Insurance Company building, Sep 59: 14
HARTIGAN, GRACE, City Life, painting by, Nov 59: 40
HASHIMOTO, OKIIE, Sand Garden, print by, May 60: 110
HASTINGS, THOMAS, Ponce de Leon Hotel, designed by (with John Merven Carrère), Jan 61: 106–7
HAUSSMANN, GEORGES EUGÈNE, BARON, with Napoleon III, painting by Adolphe Yvon, May 63: 50
HAVANA, CUBA
    Police and police station, Nov 59: 30
    Side street, painting by Robert Sivard, Nov 63: 88
HAVOC, JUNE, photographs of, Jul 59: 112, 113, 119
HAWTHORNE, CHARLES W., with art class, Jul 61: 12
HAYDN, JOSEPH, rooms at Eisenstadt, Austria, associated with, Mar 62: 76, 78–79
HAYES, ALFRED, scene from The Girl on the Via Flaminia, play by, Mar 60: 98
HAYWORTH, RITA, in The Lady from Shanghai, Jul 63: 89
HEADDRESSES, drawings by Marcello Mariotti, Mar 63: 118–19
"HEADS, FIGURES AND IDEAS," sketchbook by Henry Moore, drawings from, Nov 60: 102, 106–7
HEALY, G. P. A., Arch of Titus, painting by (with Frederick Church and Jervis McEntee), Nov 59: 101
HEAVEN AND HELL, painting by Hubert Van Eyck, Sep 63: 7
"HEDGEROW ANIMAL," drawing by Morris Graves, Jul 60: 105
HEIM, FRANÇOIS JOSEPH, Charles X presenting awards, painting by, Mar 60: 54–55
"HEINE'S MOSES," painting by Mrs. Arthur Goldberg, Sep 61: 11
HELD, JOHN, JR., sheiks and shebas, cartoons by, Jul 63: 118, 119
HELENA, SAINT, in miniature from 9th-century manuscript, Nov 63: 7
HELLMUTH, OBATA & KASSABAUM, design by, for Washington, D.C., office block "Number 9," Jan 60: 22–23
HELMET, of boar's teeth, Mycenaean, Jan 61: 82
HEMINGWAY, ERNEST, portraits of, Jan 59: 82, 85
HENRY IV, HOLY ROMAN EMPEROR, portrait of, Sep 59: 129
HENRY VIII, KING OF ENGLAND, portraits of, Sep 59: 130, Jul 63: 94
HENRY THE NAVIGATOR, portrait of, Nov 60: 72
HENSCHE, HENRY
    Portrait of, Jul 61: 24
    Sunlight, Jul 61: 24
HENTRICH AND PETSCHNIGG, Phoenix-Rheinrohr building, designed by, Nov 60: 14
HERCULANEUM, ITALY, antiquities
    Arcadia, fresco in Basilica, Mar 62: 66
    Athlete, bronze sculpture, Mar 62: 45
    Christian altar, Jul 61: 45

Room in House of the Bronze Hercules, Mar 62: 52
Room in Suburban Thermae, Mar 62: 53
HERRENCHIEMSEE, castle in Bavaria, Jan 61: 38–39
HEVENINGHAM HALL, orangery of, Nov 58: 47
HEYER, BILL, in *The Heyer Things of Life*, Jan 62: 71
"HEYER THINGS OF LIFE, THE," revue, scenes from, Jan 62: 71
HEYN, PIET, bust of, Sep 58: 20
"HIBERNATION, 1954," drawing by Morris Graves, Jul 60: 110–11
HICKEL, KARL ANTON, portrait of Charles James Fox by, May 60: 97
HIGHET, GILBERT, photograph of, May 63: 23
HILL, JEROME, photograph of, Jul 61: 107
HILLEGAERT, PAULUS VAN, Frederick Henry of Orange-Nassau, painting by, Sep 58: 14
HILLER, SETH, theatre design by, with Barrie Greenbie and Elizabeth Harris, Jan 62: 6
HILLMER, JACK, house designed by, Jan 59: 11
HIMALAYAN LANDSCAPE, photograph, Sep 58: 6
HINDU VIEW OF UNIVERSE, Jan 59: 29
HINGLE, PAT, in *J.B.*, Jan 60: 54
HINNANT, BILL, in *Dressed to the Nines*, Jul 61: 76
HIRATSUKA, UN' ICHI, *Buddha Head*, print by, May 60: 113
HIROHITO, EMPEROR OF JAPAN, with Gen. Douglas MacArthur, photograph, May 60: 7
HIROSHIGE, ICHIRYUSAI, *Sudden Shower at Ohashi*, May 60: 102
HIROSHIMA, JAPAN
Bridge in Peace Park, Mar 60: 111
Peace Center, Sep 61: 61
"HIROSHIMA MON AMOUR," motion picture, scene from, May 60: 50
HIRSCHFELD, AL, sketch of Leonard Bernstein by, Jul 59: 19
HISTORY, Liberty and Father Time paying their respects to Clio, lithograph, Sep 63: 97
"HISTORY OF ART, A," drawings by Michael Thaler, Jan 61: 120–21
"H.M.S. PINAFORE," comic opera, scene from, Nov 63: 39
HOBBES, THOMAS, portrait of, Jul 60: 39
HOFFNUNG, GERARD, cartoons by, Jul 62: 104–7
HOFHAIMER, PAUL, in woodcut by Hans Burgkmair, Mar 60: 75
HOFMANN, HANS
Portrait of, Jul 61: 17
String Quartet, Jul 61: 17
HOGARTH, WILLIAM
Chairing the Member, Nov 63: 81
Cholmondeley Family, Nov 58: 42
Lord Hervey and His Friends, Nov 58: 40
HOLBEIN, HANS THE YOUNGER
Erasmus, portrait by, May 62: 88
Guildford, Henry, portrait of, Jul 63: cover, 3
Illus for *The Praise of Folly*, May 62: 91, 93, 95
HOLKHAM HALL, Nov 58: 44–45
HOLLYWOOD STONE, Jul 60: 87
"HOLY FAMILY," drawing by Poussin, Mar 61: 91
"HOLY FAMILY," painting by Gentileschi, Nov 61: 83
HOLY FAMILY'S ESCAPE INTO EGYPT, sculpture by Gislebertus, Sep 61: 54–55
"HOMAGE TO THE SQUARE: OBVIOUS," painting by Josef Albers, Nov 61: 75
HOMEM, DIOGO, Prester John pictured by, Nov 60: 76
HOMEM, LOPO, illus from "Miller Atlas" by, Nov 60: 75
HOMER
Bust of, Jan 61: 76
Iliad, illus from early manuscript, Nov 62: 84–85
HOMER, WINSLOW, *On the Beach*, detail from, May 63: cover, 3
HONDIUS, GERRIT
Portrait of, Jul 61: 25
Still Life with Flowers, Jul 61: 25
HONDURAS, Mayan stele at Copán, Jul 62: 87
HOOD, RAYMOND, Chicago *Tribune* Tower, designed by, Jan 63: 12
HOOVER, HERBERT, as scarcity man, cartoon, Jul 60: 68
HOPI INDIAN SUN-GOD, Nov 63: 50
HOPKINSON, EDWARD, JR., photograph of, Jul 63: 4
HOPPER, EDWARD
Four Lane Road, Sep 58: 113
Portrait of, Jul 61: 10
Rooms by the Sea, Jul 61: 11
"HORLOGÈRE, L'," trades engraving, Nov 61: 2, 3
HORROCKS, BRIAN, portrait of, by Peter Greenham, May 62: 77
HORSE
Etruscan sculpture, Jan 62: 46
Lydian terra-cotta relief, Sep 63: 82
HORSEMANSHIP, lessons in, Nov 59: 98–99
HORSEMEN OF NIGERIA, Mar 63: 53–55
HORSES, WINGED, Etruscan terra cotta, May 60: 78–79
HORTA, VICTOR, Van Eetvelde salon, designed by, Mar 62: 38

"HOSTAGE, THE," play, Avis Bunnage in, May 61: 50–51
HOUDINI, HARRY, photograph of, Jul 59: 116
HOUET, Louis XVI returning to Paris, painting by, Sep 60: 66–67
HOUGHTON, ARTHUR A., JR., portrait of, Jul 62: 8
HOUGHTON HALL, Nov 58: 42, 51
HOUSATONIC RIVER
Celebrities and scenes near by, May 60: 12, 14–29
Covered bridge at West Cornwall, Conn., May 60: 10
Map, May 60: 13
HOUSE, ERIC, in *H.M.S. Pinafore*, Nov 63: 39
"HOUSE OF ROTHSCHILD," motion picture, scene from, Sep 63: 78
HOUSING DEVELOPMENTS, cartoon from *Punch*, Sep 58: 53
HOUSTON, TEX., Alley Theatre play, Jan 62: 5
HOWARD, LESLIE, photographs of, Sep 63: 77, 78
HOWARD, TREVOR, in *Mutiny on the Bounty*, Sep 63: 42
HOWES, SALLY ANN, in *My Fair Lady*, Sep 58: 59
HUBER, JOHANN, painting of Voltaire by, Mar 61: 119
HUGO, VICTOR
Cartoon by Granville on *Hernani*, May 61: 83
Funeral cortege of, Nov 59: 66–67
Portrait of, by Achille Deveria, May 61: 83
HULA-HOOP, May 60: 6
"HUMAN CONDITION II, THE," painting by René Magritte, Jan 62: 87
HUMAN PYRAMID, Venice, 1806, Jul 63: 2, 3
HUMBOLDT, ALEXANDER VON
Aquarelle of, Jul 59: 69
Paintings from sketches by, Jul 59: 60–61, 63–66
Portrait by Rembrandt Peale, Jul 59: 56
HUMPHREY, WILLIAM, photograph of, Mar 59: 15
HUNGARY, crown of Saint Stephen, May 63: 95
HUNT, in Persian miniature, Jan 63: 65
HUNTING PACK OF PETER BECKFORD, painting, Nov 58: 52
HUNTING SCENE, 19th century, Nov 60: 4
HURST, DAVID, portrait of, Jan 61: 100
HUTCHINS, ROBERT M., photograph of, Sep 58: 99
HUYGENS, CONSTANTIJN, portrait of, Sep 58: 33
HYPERIDES, portion of speech by, on papyrus, Nov 62: 80

I

"IA ORANA MARIA," painting by Gauguin, Jan 60: 40
IBEX, silver, from Persia, Jan 63: 55
IBSEN, HENRIK
Caricatures of, Jan 62: 107
Inscription by, to Max Beerbohm (by Max Beerbohm), May 61: 37
"ICEMAN COMETH, THE," play, scene from, Mar 60: 99
ICE SKATING AT THE HAGUE, painting by Adam van Breen, Sep 58: 16–17
ICON, Sep 59: 64–65
ICON CONTROVERSY, illuminations from 11th-century Greek psalter, Nov 63: 22
IDRI-MI, KING OF ALALAKH, statue of, with autobiography, Nov 62: 79
IDRISI, AL-, map of world by, Sep 62: 80–81
IFE SCULPTURE, Mar 63: 47, 51
"ILIAD," illus from early manuscript, Nov 62: 84–85
ILLINOIS (see also CHICAGO)
Home designed by Bruce Goff, Nov 61: 44
ILLINOIS, UNIVERSITY OF, assembly hall, Mar 59: 25
ILLUMINATED MANUSCRIPTS, pages from, Nov 62: 74, 95
IMMACULATE HEART TRIO, Nov 62: 47
IMPROVISATION CHAMBER ENSEMBLE, Jan 63: 81
Diagrams used by, Jan 63: 76, 79, 80, 81
"INAUGURATION," painting by Jack Levine, Sep 58: 111
INDIA (see also DELHI)
Buddhist sun medallion, Nov 63: 51
Dance of, Sep 63: 64–67, 69–71, 73
Early portrayals of white man in, Sep 60: 10, 18–21
Jhelum River, in Kashmir: mirror lake of, Mar 61: 30; tourist boats on, Mar 61: 31
Jodhpur palace fountain, May 62: 27
Sun wheel from, Nov 63: 50
Temple tanks at Jambukeshwar, May 62: 27
INDIANA
Fort Wayne, Concordia chapel, Jul 60: 80
Memorial to utopian communities of, May 61: 49
INDIANS, AMERICAN
Aztec sun calendar, Nov 63: 52
Early portrayals of white man by, Sep 60: 26–27
Hopi sun-god, Nov 63: 50
Mochican kingfisher from Peru, Mar 62: 2, 3

Montezuma's encounter with Cortes, Nov 63: 92, 94
"INFERNO," painting by William Blake, May 61: 72
"IN FRONT OF THE WINDOW," painting by Pierre Bonnard, Mar 62: 17
INGERSOLL, R. STURGIS, portrait of, by Franklin C. Watkins, Jul 63: 23
INGHIRAMI, TOMMASO, portrait of, by Raphael, Jul 59: 35
INGOLSTADT, GERMANY, monstrance commemorating victory at Lepanto, Jul 63: 58, 59
INGRES, JEAN AUGUSTE DOMINIQUE
Portraits by: Mme Moitessier, Mar 62: 66; *Mademoiselle Rivière*, Sep 60: 73; *Monsieur Bertin*, Jan 59: 95; self-portrait, Sep 60: 70
Turkish bath, painting by, May 59: 62–63
INLAND STEEL BUILDING, Chicago, lobby of, Sep 59: 12
"IN LATE DAY (HOMAGE TO THE SQUARE)," painting by Josef Albers, Nov 60: 10
"IN MEMORIAM II," painting by Theodoros Stamos, Sep 58: 45
INSCRIPTIONS, FAKE, by Max Beerbohm, May 61: 36, 37
"INSPIRATION OF THE POET," painting by Poussin, Mar 61: 76–77
INSURANCE PLAQUES, of Philadelphia's Hand-in-Hand, Jul 63: 24
"INTERIOR," painting by Turner, Mar 63: 63
"INTERIOR IN VENICE, AN," painting by John Singer Sargent, May 62: 74
"INTERLUDE," painting by Milton Avery, Jul 62: 20
INTERNATIONAL LABOR SYNDICATE POSTER, Jan 59: 120
"IN THE JUNGLE OF CITIES," play, scene from, May 62: 39
IONESCO, EUGENE, portrait of, May 61: 94
IRAN (see also ISFAHAN; PERSIAN ART and ARCHITECTURE)
Persepolis, Mar 59: 52–53, Jan 63: 45–48
Tepe Sarab, archaeological site, Sep 62: 4
IRAQ
Cemetery at Eridu, Jul 61: 34
Marsh dwellers at Kirsuwa, Jul 61: 36
Tablet found at Kish, Nov 62: 75
Wheat, prehistoric and modern, from Jarmo, Sep 62: 5
"IRMA LA DOUCE," musical, Elizabeth Seal in, May 61: 50
"IRON PICTURE, THE," painting by Al Leslie, Jan 63: 21
IRSEE, GERMANY, pulpit commemorating victory at Lepanto, Jul 63: 60
IRVING, WASHINGTON, portrait of, Nov 59: 100
ISABELLA I, QUEEN OF CASTILE, at surrender of Granada, bronze relief, Sep 62: 92
ISFAHAN, IRAN
Khaju bridge, May 61: 24–29, 31
Madreseh, Jan 63: 41; court of, Mar 61: 28
Masjid-i-Shah, Jan 63: 68–69
ISRAEL
Archaeological sites in, Nov 59: 4–5, 7, 9
Beersheba figurines, Jan 62: 73–75
Caesarea festival, Jul 62: 30
Underground chambers at Safadi, Jan 62: 72
ISSUS, BATTLE OF, Roman mosaic, Mar 59: 34
ISTANBUL, TURKEY
Hagia Sophia, Nov 63: 20, 21, 32; mosaics in, Nov 63: 5, 23
Hippodrome site, with obelisks, Nov 63: 13
Kariye Çami, Nov 63: 28; mosaics in, Nov 63: 29, 30
Pavement from Great Palace, details, Nov 63: 11
ISTOMIN, EUGENE, portrait of, Jan 60: 77
ITALIAN SCULPTURE, bust of woman, Sep 60: 71
ITALY (see also cities of, by name; HERCULANEUM; POMPEII; SICILY)
Capri scenes, Mar 61: 24, 25
Caserta fountain, May 62: 21
Hadrian's Villa, May 63: 32, 36, 37, 38–39
Neolithic village in Foggia Plain, Jul 61: 36
Rapallo, reflections at, Jul 60: 96–99
Street scenes, drawings by Nicholas Solovioff, Nov 61: 120–28
Tuscan scene, May 60: 58
Villa Aldobrandini cascade, May 62: 13
Villa d'Este fountains, May 62: 18–19, 22–23
"ITALY, CITIES OF," drawings by Domenico Gnoli, Jul 59: 137–44
ITTEN, JOHANNES, photograph of, Nov 61: 62
IVAN IV, CZAR OF RUSSIA (IVAN THE TERRIBLE), with son's body, painting by Repin, Sep 60: 131
IVASHOV, VLADIMIR, in *Ballad of a Soldier*, Mar 62: 111
IVES, BURL, photographs of, Nov 59: 28, 29
IVORY ART OBJECTS, May 60: 92–93, 95
Barberini plaque, Nov 63: 14; detail from, Sep 60: 71
Box carved by Khalaf, Sep 62: 74
IVREA, ITALY, Olivetti plant at, Nov 59: 46–47

J

JACKSON, ANNE, photograph of, May 63: 11
JACKSON, C. D., portrait of, Jul 62: 8
JACKSON, JOE, photograph of, Jul 59: 117
JACOBS, JANE, photograph of, Jul 62: 51
JACOB'S MEETING WITH THE ANGEL, 13th-century Sicilian mosaic, Nov 60: 42
JACOB'S PILLOW, May 60: 14–15
JACQUES, MAURICE, wall designs by, Nov 58: 61
JACQUES DE VERONA, sketch of Mount Sinai's shrines by, Mar 60: 91
JAMES, HENRY, "portrait" of, by Max Beerbohm, May 61: 36
JANE, LADY DALKEITH, portrait of, by John R. Merton, Jan 59: 96–97
JAPAN
    Apsaras, wood sculpture, Nov 60: 38
    Early portrayals of white man in, Sep 60: 15–17, 29
    Floating deity, from scroll, Nov 60: 47
    Hiroshima. See HIROSHIMA
    Kagawa prefectural hall, Sep 61: 59, 62
    Katsura villa, Sep 61: 61
    Kobe, U.S. Consulate, Jan 60: 18
    Kurashiki city hall, Sep 61: 62
    Kyoto scene, Mar 61: 27
    Railroad of 1870's, Mar 61: 4–5
    Street scenes, Mar 61: 4, 6, 9, 10
    Temple gardens, May 59: 50, 51
    Tokyo's highway-parking-building unit, Jan 62: 95
JARMO, IRAQ, wheat, prehistoric and modern, from, Sep 62: 5
JAUREGUI, JUAN DE, portrait of Cervantes attributed to, Nov 61: 107
JAY, JOHN, portrait of, Nov 60: 22
"JAZZ!" design by Bob Gill, Jan 63: 120
"JAZZ ON A SUMMER'S DAY," motion picture, scenes from, Mar 61: 18–19
"JEDERMANN," play, scene from, Jan 61: 32
JEFFERS, ROBINSON, portrait of, Jan 59: 19
JEFFERSON, THOMAS
    Letter to Alexander von Humboldt, facsimile, Jul 59: 69
    Portraits of, Nov 60: 23, Jul 61: 30
JEFFERSON ARCH, St. Louis, Mo,, Jul 60: 79
JEFFERSON MEMORIAL, Washington, D.C., Jul 60: 78
JELLICOE, ANN, photograph of, Jan 63: 31
JENS, ARNETTE, in The Balcony, May 61: 50
JENS, SALOME, photograph of, Jan 62: 102
JEROME, SAINT, portrait from De Spiritu Sancto, book by Didymus Alexandrinus, Nov 62: cover, 3
JERUSALEM
    Capture of, 1099, Mar 61: 53
    In 15th century, woodcuts by Erhard Reuwich, Mar 60: 84–85, 88
    St. John's Hospital, Mar 61: 69
"JESTER, THE," painting by Gerald Kelly, Jan 59: 106
JESUS CHRIST, in Romanesque and Gothic sculpture, Nov 58: 12–13
JHAM, MINARET OF, Nov 59: 42–43
JINNAH, MOHAMMED ALI, designs for memorial to, May 61: 46
JOAN OF ARC
    Contemporary portrait sketch, Mar 62: 97
    In illuminations from The Vigils of Charles VII, Mar 62: 90, 91, 94, 95, 96, 99
    Portrait of, from manuscript of poems by Charles d'Orléans, Mar 62: 88
"JOB, BOOK OF." See "BOOK OF JOB, THE"
"JOB AND HIS COMFORTERS," illumination by Jean Fouquet, Nov 61: 93
"JOB NO. 2," painting by Abraham Rattner, Jul 62: 19
"JOHN," mannequin by Marisol Escobar, Mar 63: 104
JOHN VII, POPE, portrait of, in mosaic, Jan 62: 32, 34
JOHN, AUGUSTUS, self-portrait, May 62: 79
JOHN OF AUSTRIA
    In engraving by Bertelli, Jul 63: 54
    Portrait on medal, Jul 63: 52
    Sword of, Jul 63: 49
JOHNS, JASPER
    Fool's House, Jan 63: 19
    Two Beer Cans, May 61: 119
JOHNSON, BEN, Red Hat, Sep 63: 93
JOHNSON, PHILIP
    Home of, Nov 58: 33
    Memorial to utopian communities of Indiana, designed by, May 61: 49
    —— and LUDWIG MIES VAN DER ROHE, Seagram building, designed by, Sep 59: 6, Nov 61: 73
JOHN THE BAPTIST, in Retable du Parlement, painting by Flemish master, Sep 60: 58
"JOKER, THE," motion picture, scenes from, Jan 62: 110
JOLLAIN, NICOLAS RENÉ, illus for Les Amours de

Psyché et de Cupidon, Nov 62: 91
JONES, INIGO, Banqueting House of Whitehall Palace, designed by, Jul 61: 90–91, 95
JORDAN, Pool of Gibeon, Nov 59: 8
JOSEPH RELATES HIS DREAMS, painting by Shalom Moskovitz, Jul 61: 126
"JOSIAH WEDGWOOD AND HIS FAMILY," painting by George Stubbs, May 59: 95
JUDAS ISCARIOT, sculpture by Gislebertus, Sep 61: 52–53
"JUDGMENT OF SOLOMON," painting by Poussin, Mar 61: 92–93
JUILLIARD QUARTET, Sep 58: 99
JULIA DOMNA, coin portrait of, Sep 63: 38
JULIA MAESA, coin portrait of, Sep 63: 39
JULIAN, PHILIPPE, "At Home Through the Ages," drawings by, Mar 63: 80–83
JULIUS II, POPE, with his uncle, Sixtus IV, in fresco by Melozzo da Forlì, Jan 62: 45
"JULIUS CAESAR," play by Shakespeare, scene from Barrault production, Sep 61: 108
"JULY," painting by Richard Diebenkorn, Jul 60: cover, 3
"JULY DAYS" CLIMAX, engraving by Garneray, May 61: 86–87
JURY TRIAL DISKS, ATHENIAN, Jul 60: 103
JUSTINIAN, BYZANTINE EMPEROR, mosaic portraits of, in Church of San Vitale, Ravenna, Nov 63: cover, 3, 16–17

K

KAHN, LOUIS
    Buildings designed by: Jewish Community Center bathhouse, Trenton, N.J., Sep 62: 60; Richards Medical Research Building, Philadelphia, Mar 62: 31, Sep 62: 58, 62, 63; University of Pennsylvania laboratory, Mar 62: 31; Yale Art Gallery and Design Center, Sep 62: 59, 61
    Photograph of, Sep 62: 59
KAHN & JACOBS, American Airlines terminal designed by, Sep 59: 10–11
KAHNWEILER, DANIEL-HENRY, portrait by Picasso, Nov 61: 9
KAI KHOSRAU, KING OF PERSIA, preparations for coronation of, Persian miniature, Jan 63: 64
KALLMAN, GERHARD M.
    Boston City Hall design by (with Noel Michael McKinnell and Edward F. Knowles), Jan 63: 10, 12–15
    Photograph of, Jan 63: 11
KAMIHIRA, BEN, Miyo, Jul 62: 23
KANDINSKY, VASILY
    Black Lines, No. 189, May 59: 14
    Brownish, Jan 59: 12
    Two Sides Red, No. 437, Nov 61: 67
KANDLER, JOHANN JOACHIM, centerpiece designed by, Jul 59: 2, 3
KANE, ART, "Rapallo's Reflections," photographs by, Jul 60: 96–99
KANO TANYU, painting by, Jul 59: 74–75
KANSAS, musical life of Topeka, Sep 59: 86–89
KANTOR, TADEUSZ
    Alalaha, May 61: 20
    Portrait of, May 61: 22
KAPLAN, JOE
    Dune, Jul 61: 25
    Portrait of, Jul 61: 25
"KARL," painting by Andrew Wyeth, Sep 61: 89
KARLOFF, BORIS, photograph of, Sep 63: 77
KARSH, YOUSUF, photograph of Winston Churchill by, Jan 59: 103
KASHMIR, INDIA, Jhelum River scenes, Mar 61: 30, 31
KATAVOLOS, WILLIAM, city design by, Sep 63: 25
KATSELAS, TASSO, design for memorial to F. D. Roosevelt, May 61: 43
KATSURA VILLA, near Kyoto, Japan, Sep 61: 61
KAZAN, ELIA, monument to, design by Edward Sorel, Sep 61: 122–23
KAZIN, ALFRED, photograph of, May 59: 17
KAZIS, NICOLAS, wall of church of St. Rémy, Baccarat, France, designed by, Sep 62: 22
"KEAN," musical, scene from, Mar 62: 12
KEAN, EDMUND
    Actors in role of, Mar 62: 12, 118
    Playbill for Othello, Mar 62: 115
    Portrait of, Mar 62: 13
    Sketches of, by G. R. Cruikshank, Mar 62: 114, 115
KEATS, JOHN, portrait of, May 61: 64
KEERE, PIETER VAN DEN, map by, Sep 58: 22–23
"KELLY," painting by Sidney Nolan, Sep 62: 100
KELLY, ELLSWORTH, Green on Blue, Jan 63: 20
KELLY, GERALD, portraits of Somerset Maugham by, Jan 59: 106

"KELLY AT GLENROWAN," painting by Sidney Nolan, Sep 62: 101
KENNEDY, JOHN FITZGERALD
    Composite photographs with Theodore Roosevelt, Nov 63: 68–69, 70, 71
    Photographs of, Sep 61: 6
    Virginia house of, Sep 63: 102
KENNEDY, MRS. JOHN FITZGERALD, with New York City Ballet, photograph, Sep 61: 16
KENT, ADALINE, Presence, sculpture by, Jan 59: 12
KENT, ALLEGRA, photographs of, Nov 59: 52–53, 55
KENT, DUKE OF, photograph of, Jan 59: 59
KENT, WILLIAM
    Houses designed by, Nov 58: 42, 44–45, 51, 58–59
    Portraits of, Nov 58: 60, May 59: 46
KENYA, archaeological discoveries in Olduvai Gorge, Mar 62: 9, 10
KEPLER, JOHANNES, portrait of, Jul 60: 39
KERNS, ROBERT, photograph of, Nov 61: 79
KEROUAC, JACK, photograph of, Sep 58: 40
KEW, ENGLAND, Royal Botanical Gardens, May 59: 46, 47
    Palm Stove, Mar 62: 36
KEY, BAROQUE, Jul 60: 50
"KEY PROJECT," design by Frank Lloyd Wright, Sep 63: 24–25
KHAJU BRIDGE, in Isfahan, Iran, May 61: 24–29, 31
KHALAF, ivory box carved by, Sep 62: 74
KHOSRAU I, KING OF PERSIA, cup of, Jan 63: 56
KHOSRAU II, KING OF PERSIA, visiting Armenian princess, Persian miniature, Jan 63: 66
KIERZKOWSKI, BRONISLAW, abstract painting by, May 61: 23
KILGALLEN, DOROTHY, portrait of, Jan 60: 9
"KING AND QUEEN," sculpture by Henry Moore, Nov 60: 112; detail from, Nov 60: 110
"KING AND THE DUKE, THE," musical, scene from, Mar 60: 98
KINGFISHER, Mochican, of cast copper, Mar 62: 2, 3
KINOSHITA, MOKUTARO, memorial to, by Yoshiro Taniguchi, May 61: 48
KIPLING, RUDYARD
    Caricature of, by Max Beerbohm, May 61: 37
    Portrait of, May 63: 83
KIP'S BAY PLAZA, New York City, Jan 63: 115
KIRCHNER, LEON, photograph of, Jan 59: 21
KIRSTEIN, LINCOLN, portrait of, Jul 62: 9
KLEE, PAUL
    Ambassador of Autumn, The, Nov 61: 65
    Senecio, Nov 61: cover, 3
KLINE, FRANZ, photograph of, Jul 61: 18
KNATHS, KARL
    Captain and Crew, Jul 61: 19
    Portrait of, Jul 61: 19
KNELLER, GODFREY
    Anne, Queen of England, allegorical painting by, Sep 61: 72
    Sarah, Duchess of Marlborough, portrait by, Sep 61: 72
"KNICK-KNACK PEDDLER, THE," painting by Li Sung, Jan 61: 21
"KNIGHT OF DARKNESS," sculpture by Jean Dubuffet, Mar 61: 110
KNIGHTS OF ST. JOHN, Mar 61: 49, 50, 58, 59, 63, 66–67, 68–69, 71
KNISH, ANNE, "portrait" of, by Arthur Davison Ficke, May 60: 42
KNOWLES, EDWARD F., Boston City Hall design by (with Gerhard M. Kallmann and Noel Michael McKinnel), Jan 63: 10, 12–15
KOBE, JAPAN, U.S. Consulate, Jan 60: 18
KOCH, JOHN
    Cocktail Party, Sep 60: 106–7
    Movers, The, Sep 60: 109
    Music, Sep 60: 108
    Self-portrait, with Mrs. Koch, Sep 60: 110
    Still Life with Angels, Sep 60: 104
    Studio End of Day, The, Sep 63: 94
    Studio Interior, Sep 60: 108
    Three Musicians, Sep 60: 109
KOENIG, OTTO, photograph by, Sep 58: 77
KOFI KAKARI, ASHANTI KING, gold mask of, Mar 63: 56
KOLB, MINA, in From the Second City, Jan 62: 67
KOLBE, GEORGE, statue by, in German Pavilion, Barcelona, Sep 59: 12
KORAN, page from 14th-century copy made in Granada, Sep 62: 78
KORE OF EUTHYDIKOS, sculpture, Nov 58: 6
"KOUROS," sculpture by Isamu Noguchi, Mar 60: 107
KOUROS OF MILO, sculpture, Nov 58: 7
KOZOL, JONATHAN, photograph of, Mar 59: 15
KRACHMALNICK, SAMUEL, photographs of, Nov 61: 79, 81
KRAHN, FERNANDO, "The Epic of Man," drawings by, Sep 63: 108–12

KRAK OF THE KNIGHTS, Mar 61: 54–55
KRASNER, LEE, photograph of, May 63: 22
KRESGE AUDITORIUM, at Massachusetts Institute of Technology, Jul 60: 80–81
KUMP, ERNEST J., U.S. Coast Guard swimming pool shelter, designed by, Jan 60: 24
KUROSAWA, AKIRA, photograph of, Jul 62: 42
KYOTO, JAPAN, scene, Mar 61: 27

L

LAAFF HOUSE, Andover, Mass., Nov 61: 74
LABYRINTH MOTIF, Jul 60: 87
"LADY IN PINK, THE," painting by Turner, Mar 63: 67
"LADY WITH A FAN, THE," painting by Rembrandt, Jul 63: 101
LA FONTAINE, JEAN DE, Les Amours de Psyché et de Cupidon, illus for, Nov 62: 91
LA GRANJA, SPAIN, fountains of Philip V, Jul 60: 56
LAHR, BERT
    Photograph of, Sep 58: 58
    In Waiting for Godot, Nov 58: 64
LALLI, interpreting song to Shiva in mudras, Sep 63: 70–71
LAMARTINE, ALPHONSE MARIE LOUIS DE, portrait of, May 61: 65
LAMB, HENRY
    Artist's Family, The, May 62: 77
    Portrait of Lytton Strachey by, Jan 60: 106
LAMB, WILLIAM. See MELBOURNE, 2D VISCOUNT
LAMI, LOUIS EUGÈNE, ball at Hôtel de Ville, Paris, painting by, May 63: 69
LA MONTAINE, JOHN, photograph of, Mar 63: 30
LAMP DESIGNS
    By Noguchi, Isamu, Mar 60: 106, 111
    By Wagenfeld, Wilhelm, Nov 61: 71
    By Wirkkala, Tapio, Jul 63: 66
LAMPEDUSA, GIULIO DI, portrait of, Sep 61: 40
LAMPERT, ZOHRA, photograph of, Jul 62: 48
LANCOME, FRED, with sculpture Hindu Rhythm, May 60: 15
"LANDING OF MARIE DE MÉDICIS AT MARSEILLES, THE," painting by Rubens, mermaid detail from, Jan 60: 132–33
LANDIR, HELMUT, windows of Christ Church, Bochum, Germany, designed by, Sep 62: 28
LANDON, MR. and MRS. ALFRED M., photograph of, Sep 59: 90–91
"LANDSCAPE," painting by Sidney Nolan, Sep 62: 102
"LANDSCAPE WITH BARE TREE," painting by Elmer Bischoff, Jul 60: 22
"LANDSCAPE WITH PEACOCKS," painting by Gauguin, Jan 60: 35
"LANDSCAPE WITH POLYPHEMUS," painting by Poussin, Mar 61: 86–87
"LANDSCAPE WITH THE FALL OF ICARUS," painting by Pieter Bruegel the Elder, detail from, Sep 58: 2
LANDSEER, EDWIN
    Blackcock, Mar 60: 68
    Old Shepherd's Chief Mourner, The, Mar 60: 63
    Dash, Hector, Nero, and Lorey, Jul 63: 95
LANDUYT, OCTAVE, Petrifaction, Jan 62: 79
LANE, HARRY, with painting Façade, May 60: 15
LANGNER, LAWRENCE, photograph of, May 60: 29
LANSBURY, ANGELA, in A Taste of Honey, May 61: 51
LANSDOWNE, MARQUESS OF, portrait of, Mar 59: 90
LAOCOÖN GROUP, sculpture, May 59: 105, 106, Jan 62: 47
LAPIDUS, MORRIS, Fontainebleau Hotel, designed by, Jan 61: 102–3
"LARGE RECLINING NUDE," painting by Lennart Anderson, Sep 63: 94
"LARK, THE," play, scene from, Nov 60: 52
LA SCALA, Milan, Nov 58: 24
LASCAUX, FRANCE, caverns at, Jul 61: 34–35
    Painting of bull in, Sep 62: 12
"LAST JUDGMENT," painting by Signorelli, detail from, Nov 60: 44
"LAST JUDGMENT, THE," altarpiece by Giovanni and Niccolò, Jan 62: 32, 35
"LAST JUDGMENT, THE," sculpture by Gislebertus, Sep 61: 46–47
"LA STRADA," motion picture, scene from, Mar 61: 100
LATUDE. See MASERS DE LATUDE, HENRI
LAUGHTON, CHARLES
    In Advise and Consent, May 62: 117
    In Mutiny on the Bounty, Sep 63: 42
LAURENCIN, MARIE, portrait of Somerset Maugham by, Jan 59: 106
LAURENTIAN LIBRARY, Florence, Italy, Nov 62: 88
"LAVENDER HILL MOB, THE," scene from, May 59: 98

LAWRENCE, THOMAS
    Archduke Charles of Austria, Jul 63: 95
    Soane, John, portrait, Nov 63: 75
    Princess Lieven, May 62: 65
"LAWRENCE OF ARABIA," motion picture, scene from, Jul 62: 108
LEACOCK, RICHARD, photograph of, Mar 61: 17
LEAGUE OF NATIONS PALACE, Jan 63: 12
    Design for, by Le Corbusier, Jan 63: 12
LEAN, DAVID, photograph of, Jul 62: 110
"LEAPING HORSE, THE," painting by Constable, May 62: 70–71
LÉAUD, PIERRE, in The 400 Blows, May 60: 54
LEBANON, Baalbek Festival ballet, Jul 62: 31
LEBENSTEIN, JAN, Personnage, May 61: 23
LeBLOND, JEAN-BAPTISTE, plan for St. Petersburg by, Sep 59: 81
LEBRUN, CHARLES
    Alexander's Entry Into Babylon, Mar 59: 50–51
    Ceiling painting The Triumph of Truth, Jul 63: 81
    Portrait of, Jul 63: 81
    Rooms decorated by: at Vaux-le-Vicomte, Jul 63: 79; at Versailles, Jul 63: 81
LEBRUN, RICO, Genesis, Jul 62: 15
LE CORBUSIER
    Couvent Sainte-Marie de la Tourette, designed by, Mar 61: 34–39, 41
    Design for League of Nations Palace, Jan 63: 12
    Design for rebuilding Paris, Mar 62: 38–39
    Shrine of the Virgin, Ronchamp, France, designed by, Sep 59: 4–5
LEDOUX, CLAUDE-NICOLAS, forge design for Chaux, France, Mar 62: 34
LEECH, JOHN, etchings by
    From Comic History of England, Mar 60: 129–36
    From Comic History of Rome, May 61: 52, 54, 55, 56, 57
LEEUWENHOEK, ANTON VAN, portrait of, Sep 58: 33
LÉGER, FERNAND, window of church of Sacré Coeur, Audincourt, France, designed by, Sep 62: 25
LEIBNIZ, GOTTFRIED WILHELM VON, portrait of, May 60: 32
LEIGH, VIVIAN, in Look After Lulu, Jan 63: 33
LEMONNIER, ANICET-CHARLES-GABRIEL, salon of Mme Geoffrin, painting by, Nov 59: 81
LENIN, NIKOLAI, design for memorial to, May 61: 46
LENINGRAD, U.S.S.R., Peterhof, Sep 59: 84, 85
LE NÔTRE, ANDRÉ
    Gardens and landscaping designed by: at Vaux-le-Vicomte, Jul 63: 76–77, 78–79; at Versailles, May 59: 38–39
    Portrait of, May 59: 32
LENYA, LOTTE, in Brecht on Brecht, May 62: 34
LEO I, POPE (LEO THE GREAT), encounter with Attila, painting by Raphael, May 63: 76–77
LEOCHARES, copy of head of Alexander by (?), Mar 59: 28
LEONIDAS, statue of, Mar 59: 133
LEOPARD, Benin bronze, Mar 63: 48
LEOPARDI, GIACOMO, portrait of, May 60: 32
LEPANTO, BATTLE OF
    Engravings, Nov 61: 108–9, Jul 63: 53, 54–55
    Map, Jul 63: 52
    Memorials of: broadside showing Ali Pasha, Jul 63: 57; medal with portrait of Don John of Austria, Jul 63: 52; monstrance (Bavarian), Jul 63: 58, 59; pulpit at Irsee, Germany, Jul 63: 60; stained-glass window at Wettingen, Switzerland, Jul 63: 61
    Paintings, Jul 63: 51, 56
LERICI, CARLO M., using Nistri periscope, May 60: 61
LES ALICAMPS CEMETERY, Arles, France, Jul 59: 94
LESLIE, AL, The Iron Picture, Jan 63: 21
LESPINASSE, MLLE DE, portrait of, Nov 61: 35
LE TESTU, GUILLAUME, map by, Nov 60: 82
"LETTER, THE," painting by Ter Borch, Jul 63: 95
"LETTERS FROM DENMARK," drawn by Peter Soederlund, Jul 63: 120
LE VAU, LOUIS, buildings designed by
    At Louvre, Sep 60: 64–65
    Vaux-le-Vicomte, Jul 63: 76–77, 78–79, 83
LEVER HOUSE, New York City, Jan 60: 9
LEVINE, JACK
    Inauguration, Sep 58: 111
    Photographs of, Sep 58: 111, May 59: 16
    Spanish Prison, The, Jul 62: 16
LEVITTOWN, N.Y., Jul 61: 63
LEVY, HENRY, photographs by, Sep 63: 70–71
LEWIS, C. S.
    Illus from books of, May 59: 66–69, 126
    Portrait of, May 59: 65
LHOTE, HENRI, photograph of, May 59: 81
LIBBY, WILLARD FRANK, photograph of, May 59: 16
LIBERMAN, ALEXANDER
    Continuous on Red, Sep 61: 66–67
    "Stones of Venice, The," portfolio of photographs by, Mar 63: 16–24

"LIBERTY LEADING THE PEOPLE," painting by Delacroix, Mar 59: 7
LIBYAN SIBYL, painting by Michelangelo, Jan 62: 32, 37
LIEBLING, A. J., photograph of, May 63: 21
"LIFE IN BLOOM," motion picture, scene from, Mar 62: 111
LILLIE, BEATRICE, photograph of, Sep 58: 58
LINCOLN, ABRAHAM, portrait of, Nov 58: 32
LINCOLN CENTER FOR THE PERFORMING ARTS, in New York City
    Architects of, group photograph, Jul 62: 7
    Opera house, Nov 58: 28–29
    Plan for, Nov 58: 119
    Projected buildings, Jul 62: 10–11
LINDBERGH, CHARLES A., photograph of, Sep 58: 10
LINDERHOF, castle in Bavaria, Jan 61: 40–41, 43
LINDISFARNE GOSPELS, page from, Nov 62: 74
LINDSAY, CATHERINE, photograph of, Mar 63: 26
LINDSTROM, ROY, with painting Roadside Barn, May 60: 15
LINEAR B SCRIPT, Jan 61: 77
"LINES WERE DEEPLY ETCHED ON THE MAP OF HER FACE, THE," painting by James Rosenquist, Jan 63: 23
LING, Chinese archaeologist, portrait of, Jan 61: 4
LION, WINGED, on Persian drinking vessel of gold, Jan 63: 54
LION HUNT, on Mycenaean dagger, Jan 61: 74–75
"LION HUNT, THE," painting by Delacroix, May 61: 78–79
LIONNI, LEO, "exedra" in Cleveland designed by, Nov 59: 109
LIPCHITZ, JACQUES
    Man with a Guitar, Sep 60: 103
    Sculpture in memorial to utopian communities of Indiana, May 61: 49
LIPKIN, SEYMOUR, portrait of, Jan 60: 78
LIPPI, ANNIBALE, garden designed by, May 59: 36–37
LIPPMANN, WALTER, portrait of, Jan 60: 9
LIPPOLD, RICHARD
    Rod-and-wire construction by, Sep 59: 12
    Sun, The, Nov 63: 55
LISBON, PORTUGAL
    Disaster of 1755, German print, Mar 61: 117
    Garden of Palace of Fronteira, May 59: 48–49
LI SHAO CH' UAN, in Journey to the West, Sep 62: 54
LIST, HERBERT, photographs of Naples by, Sep 63: 49–59
"LISTENING TO THE WIND IN THE PINES," painting by Ma Lin, Jan 61: 22
LI SUNG, The Knick-knack Peddler, Jan 61: 21
"LITTLE-LITTLE," painting by Christopher Sanders, May 62: 77
"LITTLE STREET, THE," painting by Vermeer, Sep 58: 32
"LIVE LIKE PIGS," play, scene from, Jul 62: 93
LIVIA, EMPRESS OF ROME
    Garden room of, May 59: 26–27
    Mosaic pavement from villa of, Jul 59: 26
LIVING THEATRE, THE
    Lobby of, Mar 62: 108
    Scene from In the Jungle of Cities, May 62: 39
"LOHENGRIN," opera, scene from, May 63: 41
LOKESVARA, sculpture, Jan 59: 65
LOMBART, PIERRE, engravings of Van Dyck portrait of Charles I by, Jul 61: 93
LONDON, ENGLAND
    Bank of England, Nov 63: 82
    Banqueting House of Whitehall Palace, Jul 61: 90–91, 95
    Castrol House, Nov 60: 14
    Court of Chancery designed by John Soane, Nov 63: 82–83
    Covent Garden, Nov 58: 27
    Crystal Palace, May 60: 87, Mar 62: 37
    Eastbourne Terrace, Nov 60: 14
    Hyde Park Corner, Jul 61: 53
    John Soane Museum, Nov 63: 72, 73, 74, 75, 77, 80–81
    Kew Gardens. See KEW, ENGLAND
    Photographs by Bruce Davidson, Nov 61: 15, 20, 21, 22, 29, 31
    Piccadilly Circus, building proposed for, Nov 60: 16
    Planting boxes, Nov 59: 111
    Slum area, 1870's, Jul 61: 61
    U.S. Embassy, model, Jan 60: 20, Jul 60: 81
LONDON, GEORGE, as Flying Dutchman, May 63: 44
"LONG DAY'S JOURNEY INTO NIGHT," play, scene from, Mar 60: 38
LONGFELLOW, HENRY WADSWORTH, with daughter Edith in painting of Arch of Titus, Nov 59: 101
LONG ISLAND, N.Y.
    Map, May 63: 6–7
    Personalities living on eastern end, and their homes, May 63: 4–5, 11–27
"LONGLEAT," painting by Jan Siberechts, Nov 58: 38–39
"LOOK AFTER LULU," play, scene from, Jan 63: 33

"LOOK BACK IN ANGER," play, scene from, Jan 63: 33
LORD, OTIS P., portrait of, Jul 61: 103
"LORD HERVEY AND HIS FRIENDS," painting by William Hogarth, Nov 58: 40
LORRAIN, CLAUDE, *Embarcation of the Queen of Sheba*, painting by, Jul 60: 47
LOS ANGELES, CALIF., Tamarind Workshop, Jan 62: 4
LOUIS IX, KING OF FRANCE, in *Retable du Parlement*, painting by Flemish master, Sep 60: 58
LOUIS XIII, KING OF FRANCE, in group portrait, engraving by Matthew Merian, Sep 60: 66
LOUIS XIV, KING OF FRANCE, portrait of, Jul 63: 77
LOUIS XV, KING OF FRANCE, bed of, May 60: 132
LOUIS XVI, KING OF FRANCE, returning to Paris, painting by Houet, Sep 60: 66–67
LOUISIANA MUSEUM, near Copenhagen, pool, May 62: 30
LOUVRE, THE, views of, Sep 60: 57, 58, 63, 64–65, 66–67, 82–85
    Ladies of, paintings, Sep 60: 73–80
    Treasures of, Sep 60: 70–71
"LOUVRE SEEN FROM THE PONT-NEUF, WINTER," painting by Pissarro, Jul 62: 68–69
"LOVERS, THE," motion picture, scene from, May 60: 51
"LOWER DEPTHS, THE," motion picture, scene from, Jul 62: 46
LOWRY, L. S., *Figures in a Street*, May 62: 76
LOWRY, W. McNEIL, photograph of, Jan 62: 4
"LOW TIDE," painting by Sol Wilson, Jul 61: 23
LUDEKENS, FRED, house of, designed by Jack Hillmer, Jan 59: 11
LUDWIG II, KING OF BAVARIA
    Castles of, Jan 61: 34–35, 38–43, May 62: 24
    In painting by R. Wenig, Jan 61: 36–37
LUENING, OTTO, photograph of, Jan 59: 52
"LUNCHEON," painting by Pierre Bonnard, Mar 62: 22
"LUNCHEON OF THE BOATING PARTY," painting by Renoir, Jul 62: cover, 8
LUTHER, MARTIN, in *Schraubthaler* miniatures, Sep 61: 2, 3
LÜTHY, WERNER, photograph by, Sep 58: 70
LYDIA, remains at Sardis, Sep 63: 82–83, 87, 88
LYNES, RUSSELL, color photograph of, May 60: 19
LYNLEY, CAROL, in *Blue Denim*, Nov 58: 65
LYSIPPUS, Apoxyomenos, sculpture by, Nov 58: 7

M

MacARTHUR, DOUGLAS, with Hirohito, photograph, May 60: 7
MACAULAY, THOMAS BABINGTON, portraits of, Mar 59: 90, May 60: 32
MacAVOY, EDOUARD, portrait of Somerset Maugham by, Jan 59: 106
"MACBETH," play by Shakespeare, scene from Vilar production, Sep 61: 109
McCRACKEN, JAMES
    As Otello, Nov 61: 77, 79
    At rehearsal, Nov 61: 81
McCUTCHEON, BILL, in *Dressed to the Nines*, Jan 62: 71
MacDOWELL, EDWARD
    Bust of, Mar 63: 31
    Drawing by Robert Osborn, May 62: 125
MacDOWELL, MARIAN NEVINS (MRS. EDWARD), photograph of, Mar 63: 31
MacDOWELL COLONY, photographs taken at, Mar 63: 26–29, 31–33
McENTEE, JERVIS, Arch of Titus, painting by (with Frederick Church and G. P. A. Healy), Nov 59: 101
MacINNES, HELEN, photograph of, May 63: 23
MacIVER, LOREN, *Manhattan*, Jul 62: 21
McKAIN, BRUCE
    Portrait of, Jul 61: 25
    Shore Line, Jul 61: 25
MACKINAC ISLAND, MICH., Grand Hotel, Jan 61: 108
McKINLEY, MOUNT, Mar 60: 22–23
McKINNELL, NOEL MICHAEL
    Boston City Hall design by (with Gerhard M. Kallman and Edward F. Knowles), Jan 63: 10, 12–15
    Photograph of, Jan 63: 11
MACKLIN, CHARLES, as Shylock, Jan 60: 90
McLAGLEN, VICTOR, in *Gunga Din*, Sep 63: 80
MacLEISH, ARCHIBALD, drawing of, Jan 60: 48
MACLISE, DANIEL
    Peter the Great at Deptford, England, painting by, Sep 59: 72–73
    Sketch of Sydney Smith by, Mar 59: 125
MacLOW, JACKSON, *The Marrying Maiden*, scene from, Mar 61: 45
MACREADY, W. C., as Shylock, Jan 60: 90
MADAME BOVARY, at home, drawing by Philippe Julian, Mar 63: 82

"MADAME NATANSON AND MARTHE BONNARD," painting by Pierre Bonnard, Mar 62: 18
"MAD MAGGIE." See "DULLE GRIET"
"MADONNA," in glass, by Tapio Wirkkala, Jul 63: 64
"MADONNA WITH THE RABBIT," painting by Titian, detail from, Jul 61: 86
MAGI, SLEEP OF, sculpture by Gislebertus, Sep 61: 50–51
"MAGICIAN, THE," motion picture, scene from, Sep 60: 7
"MAGNIFICENT SEVEN, THE," motion picture, scene from, Jul 62: 44
MAGRITTE, RENÉ
    Castle of the Pyrenees, Jan 62: 76
    Human Condition II, The, Jan 62: 87
    Mental Calculus, Sep 63: 26
    Night at Pisa, Jan 62: 86
    Personal Values, The, Jan 62: 84
    Plagiarism, The, Jan 62: 85
    Rights of Man, The, Jan 62: 83
    Secrets of the Horizon, The, Jan 62: 86
    Unexpected Answer, The, Jan 62: 86
MAHARAJ, BRIJMOHAN, photograph of, Sep 63: 66
"MAIASTRA," sculpture by Brancusi, May 59: 19
MAILLOL, ARISTIDE, *The River*, May 59: 13
"MALAGUEÑA," painting by Alexander Brook, Jul 62: 17
MA LIN, *Listening to the Wind in the Pines*, Jan 61: 22
MALLE, LOUIS, photograph of, May 60: 51
MALTA
    Grand Council of Knights of Malta, Mar 61: 66–67
    Siege of, 1565, Mar 61: 63–64
    Valletta, harbor area, Mar 61: 69
MALTA, SOVEREIGN ORDER OF
    Grand Council at Malta, 1740, Mar 61: 66–67
    Grand Council at Rome, c. 1951, Mar 61: 69
    Priory in Rome, Mar 61: 68–69
MAN, EPIC OF, drawings by Fernando Krahn, Sep 63: 108–12
"MAN AND SUPERMAN," play, scene from, Jan 62: 65
MANESSIER, ALFRED, stained-glass wall of chapel at Hem, France, designed by, Sep 62: 28
MANET, ÉDOUARD
    Musique aux Tuileries, La, May 63: 74–75
    Olympia, Sep 60: 76–77
"MANHATTAN," painting by Loren MacIver, Jul 62: 21
MAN IN THE IRON MASK, Jan 60: 86
"MAN IN THE MOONE, THE," romance by Francis Godwin, illus for, Mar 63: 75
MANN, THEODORE, photograph of, Mar 60: 94
MANNES, MARYA, photograph of, May 63: 16
MANNESMANN BUILDING, in Düsseldorf, Nov 60: 12–13
MAN'S FAMILY TREE, Mar 62: 7
MAN SINGH, MAHARAJAH OF MARWAR, in *zula*, Jul 61: 2, 3
MANSO, LEO
    Portrait of, Jul 61: 20
    Soldia, Jul 61: 20
MANSOURI, LOFTI, photograph of, Nov 61: 79
MANTEGNA, ANDREA
    Calvary, Sep 60: 70
    Dormition of the Virgin, The, Jul 61: 81
    Gonzaga, Elisabetta, portrait, Jan 60: 65
    Marquis of Mantua and his family, portrait, Jan 60: 58–59
    Triumph of Caesar, Jul 63: 95
MANTUA, ITALY, Jan 60: 60–61
MANUFACTURERS TRUST COMPANY BUILDING, New York City, Sep 59: 13
MANUSCRIPTS, ILLUMINATED. See ILLUMINATED MANUSCRIPTS
"MAN WITH A GUITAR," sculpture by Lipchitz, Sep 60: 103
"MAN WITH GLOVE," painting by Titian, Sep 60: 71
MAPS
    Africa: from Catalan atlas of Abraham Cresques, Mar 63: 45; historical, showing early cultures, Mar 63: 41; North Africa, showing Tassili-N-Ajjer plateau, May 59: 83; northwest coast, 1468, by Grazioso Benincasa, Nov 60: 79; southwest coast, 1555, by Guillaume le Testu, Nov 60: 82
    Alexander the Great, route of, Mar 59: 36–37
    Amsterdam, Jul 61: 58–59
    Aphrodisias, related to ancient Rome, Mar 63: 98
    Arles, France, and vicinity, Jul 59: 131
    Asia Minor, archaeological sites, Sep 63: 85
    Bible lands, archaeological discoveries in, Nov 59: 119
    Byzantine Empire, Nov 63: 8–9
    Canary Islands, by Alexander von Humboldt, Jul 59: 60–61
    Cantino Planisphere of 1502, Nov 60: 78, 80–81
    European travels of Peter the Great, Sep 59: 68–69
    Fossil man's origins, Mar 62: 11
    Holy Land, route of Richard I, Jan 59: 131
    Housatonic River valley, May 60: 13

Lepanto, Battle of, Jul 63: 52
Long Island, N.Y., May 63: 6–7
Marlik, Iran, and neighboring cultures, Nov 62: 104
Mycenaean world, c. 1400 B.C., Jan 61: 93
Near East archaeological sites, Sep 62: 7
Netherlands, by Pieter van den Keere, Sep 58: 22–23
Nile River valley monuments threatened by Aswan Dam, Jul 60: 125
Paris, 1847, May 63: 54–55
Persian Empire, Jan 63: 58–59
Roman Empires, Eastern and Western, 4th century, Nov 63: 8
Seine River, Jul 62: 74
Sicily, with chronology, Sep 61: 24–25
South Sea Islands, Jan 60: 124
Trade routes, prehistoric, Jul 60: 88–89
Venice in 1500, Jul 61: 56–57
Of world (1154), by al-Idrisi, Sep 62: 80–81
MARANTZ, IRVING
    Portrait of, Jul 61: 25
    Yellow Cloud Over Race Point, Jul 61: 25
"MARATHON BOY," sculpture, Nov 58: 74
MARCA-RELLI, CONRAD, collage by, Nov 60: 8
MARCH, FREDRIC, in *Long Day's Journey into Night*, Mar 60: 38
MARCUS, MARCIA, *Double Portrait*, Jan 63: 18
MARCUS AURELIUS, ROMAN EMPEROR
    Coin portrait of, Sep 63: 36
    Detail from column of, May 62: 45
    Leading a triumph, sculpture, Jul 61: 44
MARGO, BORIS
    Portrait of, Jul 61: 27
    Pulsation of Oneness, Jul 61: 27
"MARGUERITE OF PROVENCE," sculpture, Sep 60: 70
MARI, Mesopotamian city, Jul 61: 39
MARIA AMALIA, QUEEN OF NAPLES, portrait of, Mar 62: 62
"MARIA GOLOVIN," opera, set for, Jan 60: 17
MARIE ANTOINETTE, QUEEN OF FRANCE
    Bed of, May 60: 132
    Boudoir of, at Fontainebleau, Mar 62: 65
    Sèvres portrait bust of, Mar 62: 65
MARINI, MARINO, sculpture by, May 59: 4
MARIOTTI, MARCELLO, "A Theory of the Coiffured Lasses," drawings by, Mar 63: 118–19
MARISOL'S MANNEQUINS, Mar 63: 102–4
MARITAIN, JACQUES, photograph of, Sep 59: 26
MARKS, HENRY STACY, *Science Is Measurement*, May 62: 74
MARLBOROUGH, 1ST DUKE OF, portrait of, by John Closterman, Sep 61: 68
MARLBOROUGH, SARAH, DUCHESS OF, portrait of, by Godfrey Kneller, Sep 61: 72
MARLBOROUGH COAT OF ARMS, Sep 61: 71
MARLIK, IRAN, ancient objects found at
    Figurines, Nov 62: 102
    Of gold: pomegranate necklace, Nov 62: 101; torso, Nov 62: 100; vase, Nov 62: 103
MARLOW, WILLIAM, *Capriccio*, Sep 63: 19
"MARRIAGE OF ROXANE AND ALEXANDER," painting by Il Sodoma, Mar 59: 54–55
"MARRIAGE OF THE VIRGIN, THE," illumination by Jean Fouquet, Nov 61: 90
"MARRYING MAIDEN, THE," play, scene from, Mar 61: 45
MARSHALL, HERBERT, photograph of, Sep 63: 76
MARSH DWELLERS, at Kirsuwa, Iraq, Jul 61: 36
MARSICANO, NICHOLAS, *Seated Figure in Green*, Sep 63: 92
MARTEL, CHARLES, in miniature from 15th-century Flemish manuscript, Sep 62: 75
MARTIN, JEROME, *Mitosis*, Nov 62: 120
MARTIN, JUDY, in *The Heyer Things of Life*, Jan 62: 71
MARTIN, NAN, as Sarah in *J.B.*, Jan 60: 55
"MARTY," motion picture, scene from, Jan 60: 8
"MARTYRDOM OF SAINT APOLLONIA, THE," illumination by Jean Fouquet, Nov 61: 94
"MARURU," woodcut by Gauguin, Jan 60: 126
MARX, KARL, portrait of, Mar 59: 9
MARY, VIRGIN. See ST. MARY; VIRGIN
MASERS DE LATUDE, HENRI, portrait of, by Antoine Vestier, Jan 60: 82
MASKS
    African, Mar 63: 49, 56
    Of Agamemnon, Jan 61: 90
    Created by Irene Corey, Jan 63: 90–91
    Roman water spout, Nov 63: 81
    Studies by Oskar Schlemmer, Nov 61: 63
    Used in *The Happy Haven*, Jul 62: 93
MASSACHUSETTS (see also BOSTON; HOUSATONIC RIVER)
    Concord Bridge, Nov 59: 131
    Home of John Greenleaf Whittier, Nov 58: 33

Laaff house at Andover, Nov 61: 74
MASSACHUSETTS INSTITUTE OF TECHNOLOGY, Kresge Auditorium, Jul 60: 80–81
"MASSACRE AT SCIO, THE," painting by Delacroix, May 61: 74–75
"MASSACRE OF MAY 3," painting by Goya, May 61: 70
MASSEY, RAYMOND, as Mr. Zuss in J.B., Jan 60: 52
MASTROIANNI, MARCELLO, in La Dolce Vita, Sep 61: 111
MATERNA, AMALIE, as Brünnhilde, May 63: 42
MATHIEU, GEORGES, painting Battle of Bouvines, Sep 60: 30
MATHIEU, WILLIAM, Jan 62: 67
MATISSE, HENRI
    Girl with Green Eyes, Jan 59: 12
    Glimpse of Notre-Dame in the Late Afternoon, Jul 62: 67
    Photograph of, May 60: 134
    Sarah Stein, Jan 59: 12
MATT, LEONARD VON, photographs of Aegina Marbles by, Sep 59: cover, 3, 33–48
MATTHEWS, GERRY, in Dressed to the Nines, Jul 61: 76
MATZENAUER, MARGARETE, as Brünnhilde, May 63: 40
MAUGHAM, SOMERSET, portraits of, by various artists, Jan 59: 106, 107
MAXIMINUS I, ROMAN EMPEROR, coin portrait of, Sep 63: 37
MAXIMINUS II, ROMAN EMPEROR, coin portrait of, Sep 63: 37
MAXWELL, ELSA, photograph of, Jul 60: 7
MAYAN CULTURE
    Page from Codex Perez, Nov 62: 92
    Stele at Copán, Jul 62: 87
MAYBECK, BERNARD
    Church at Berkeley, Calif., designed by, Jan 59: 10
    Ponce de Leon Hotel, designed by (with John Merven Carrère and Thomas Hastings), Jan 61: 106–7
MAYER, EDWIN JUSTUS, rehearsal of Children of Darkness, play by, Mar 60: 96–97
MAYER, RALPH, and BENA FRANK, photograph of, Mar 63: 28
MAYO, C. W., portrait of, by William F. Draper, Jan 59: 104
MAZARIN, JULES, CARDINAL
    Portrait of, Nov 61: 83
    Works from collection of, Nov 61: 82–83
MAZET, JEAN CLAUDE, design for an industrial city, Jul 61: 64
MAZZONI, SEBASTIANO, The Temple of Janus, painting by, Jul 60: 43
"ME," painting by Larry Rivers, Sep 59: 94
MEACHAM, ANNE, portrait of, May 61: 98
MÉDICIS, MARIE DE
    Education of, painting by Rubens, Jul 60: 37
    In group portrait, engraving by Matthew Merian, Sep 60: 66
    Landing at Marseilles, painting by Rubens, mermaid detail from, Jan 60: 132–33
    Portrait of, Sep 59: 28
MEDINA, ARABIA, Jul 63: 113
MEISSEN WARE, "Temple of Love," Jul 59: 2, 3
MELANCHTHON, PHILIPP, portrait of, May 60: 32
MELBA, NELLIE, portraits of, Jan 61: 28, May 61: 124
MELBOURNE, 2D VISCOUNT (WILLIAM LAMB), riding with Queen Victoria, painting, Mar 59: 95
MELK, AUSTRIA, Benedictine monastery, Jul 60: 55
MELPOMENE, Campanian sculpture, Mar 62: 67
MEMLING, HANS, The Passion of Christ, Sep 63: 16–17
"MEMORY OF CHILDHOOD," painting by Robert Broderson, Jul 62: 22
MENANDER, sculpture of, Jul 59: 78, 89
MENASSEH BEN ISRAEL, portrait by Rembrandt, Mar 60: 102
MENCKEN, H. L., portrait of, Nov 60: 70
MENDELSOHN, ERIC, Einstein Tower, designed by, Mar 62: 39
MENDELSSOHN, FELIX, drawing by Robert Osborn, May 62: 124–25
"MEN JUST DON'T UNDERSTAND," painting by André François, May 59: 120
MENLO PARK, CALIF., Parke-Davis building, Mar 59: 25
MENORAH, found at Sardis, Sep 63: 87
MENOTTI, GIAN-CARLO, photographs of, May 59: 16, Jan 60: 15
"MENTAL CALCULUS," painting by René Magritte, Sep 63: 26
MENUS
    For Duke of Newcastle's dinner, 1761, Nov 58: 57
    By Escoffier, May 61: 123, 128
MEREDITH, BURGESS, in Plaster Bambino, Jan 62: 12
MERIAN, MATTHEW, Louis XIII and his family, engraving by, Sep 60: 66
MERMAIDS IN ART, Jan 60: 129–36
MEROË, ancient Nubian city, Mar 63: 43

MERRILL, ELMER D., photograph of, May 59: 16
"MERRY COMPANY," painting by Jan Steen, Sep 58: 31
MERTON, JOHN R., portrait of Jane, Lady Dalkeith, by, Jan 59: 96–97
"MESA CITY," design by Paolo Soleri, Sep 63: 24–25
METOCHITES, THEODORE, mosaic portrait of, in Kariye Çami, Nov 63: 29
METROPOLITAN OPERA HOUSE, New York City
    Old and new, Nov 58: 28–29, 119
    Painting by Chen Chi, Nov 58: 22–23
MEXICO
    Acapulco, Las Brisas Hotel, Jan 61: 104
    Aztec sun calendar, Nov 63: 52
    Codex Perez from Yucatan, page from, Nov 62: 92
    Conquest of, illus from Codices, Sep 60: 24–25
    Cortes and Montezuma, Nov 63: 92, 94
    Cuernavaca, park benches, Nov 59: 108
MEXICO, UNIVERSITY OF, library building, Sep 59: 8
MEXICO CITY, MEXICO, Church of the Miraculous Virgin, Sep 59: 16
MEYERS, SIDNEY, photograph of, Mar 61: 14
MICHAELS, SIDNEY, Plaster Bambino, scene from, Jan 62: 12
MICHELANGELO
    Creation of Adam, detail from, Sep 58: 80
    Delphic Sibyl, Jan 62: cover, 3
    Libyan Sibyl, Jan 62: 32, 37
    Piazza del Campidoglio, designed by, Nov 59: 91
    With Pope Paul IV and model of St. Peter's dome, painting, Jan 62: 24
    Slave, Sep 60: 70
MICHIGAN (see also DETROIT)
    Mackinac Island, Grand Hotel, Jan 61: 108
    Midland, home of Alden Dow, May 62: 30–31
    Orpheus fountain at Cranbrook Academy of Art, May 62: 28–29
    Warren, General Motors Technical Center, Jul 60: 80–81
MIDDLETON, JOHN IZARD, View from the Summit of Monte Cavo, painting by, Nov 59: 100
"MIDNIGHT GROWTH," painting by Victor Candell, Jul 61: 21
"MIDSUMMER NIGHT'S DREAM," opera, scene from, Nov 61: 81
"MIDSUMMER NIGHT'S DREAM," painting by Henry Fuseli, May 61: 72
MIDWAY GARDENS, in Chicago, caryatid and mural for, Sep 60: 103
MIELZINER, JO, set for Street Scene, designed by, Jan 60: 16–17
MIES VAN DER ROHE, LUDWIG
    Buildings designed by: German Pavilion, Barcelona, Sep 59: 12; Seagram building, New York City (with Philip Johnson), Sep 59: 6, Nov 61: 73
    Photograph of, Nov 61: 73
MIFUNE, TOSHIRO, in Throne of Blood, Jul 62: 45
MILAN, ITALY
    La Scala, Nov 58: 24
    Memorial to World War II dead, May 61: 48
    Pirelli building, Nov 60: 15
    Torre Velasca, Nov 60: 15
MILHAUD, DARIUS, photograph of, Sep 58: 98
MILI, GJON, photographs of Circle in the Square by, Mar 60: 94–95, 96–97, 98, 99
MILL, Moslem, on Guadalquivir River, Spain, Sep 62: 76
MILL, JOHN STUART, portrait of, May 60: 32
MILLER, HENRY, photograph of, Jan 59: 17
MILLER, LEA, textile by, Jan 59: 4
"MILLER ATLAS," by Lopo Homem, illus from, Nov 60: 75
MILLES, CARL, Orpheus fountain at Cranbrook Academy of Art, May 62: 28–29
MILLS, JOHN
    In Ross, May 62: 111
    In Top of the Ladder, Nov 63: 37
MILTON, JOHN, portraits of, Sep 59: 134, Jul 60: 39
MINARET OF JHAM, Nov 59: 42–43
MINERVA, Roman mosaic, Jan 62: 46
MINNEAPOLIS, MINN., Southdale shopping center, Jul 59: 12, 13
"MINOTAUR ACCUSING HIS MOTHER," painting by Fabrizio Clerici, Sep 63: 26
MINOW, NEWTON
    In Modern Bestiary, Jul 62: 127
    Photograph of, Sep 61: 12
MIRABEAU, COMTE DE (HONORÉ RIQUETI), portrait of, May 60: 32
MIRÓ, JOAN
    Ceramics by, Mar 59: 71
    Dog Barking at the Moon, Mar 59: 76
    Farm, The, Mar 59: 73
    Femme au Miroir, Mar 59: 80–81
    Mural at UNESCO headquarters, Paris, Sep 59: 16
    Personnages devant le Soleil, Mar 59: cover, 3
    Photographs of, Mar 59: 71, 73, 75

Poetess, The, Mar 59: 76–77
Studio of, designed by José Luis Sert, Mar 59: 75
"MISERIES OF WAR" and "MISERIES AND MISFORTUNES OF WAR," etchings by Jacques Callot, details from, Nov 62: 34–41
MISSAL, smallest book in Vatican Library, Jan 62: 45
"MISSES DE SCHAUENSEE AND MUFFIN," painting by Franklin C. Watkins, Jan 59: 100
MISSISSIPPI
    Gulfport home designed by Bruce Goff, Nov 61: 45
    Moorish home at Natchez, Mar 62: 35
"MISS O'MURPHY," painting by François Boucher, Sep 63: 92
"MISTAKEN VIEW OF THE BRITISH," cartoon by Brockbank, Jan 59: 57
MITCHELL, ROCCO, photograph of, May 60: 9
"MITOSIS BY MARTIN," cartoons by Jerome Martin, Nov 62: 120
"MIYO," painting by Ben Kamihira, Jul 62: 23
MOCHICAN ART, cast copper kingfisher, Mar 62: 2, 3
"MODEL IN PROFILE," painting by Seurat, Sep 60: 80
"MODERN BESTIARY, A," portfolio by Edward Sorel and Paul Davis, Jul 62: 120–28
MODIGLIANI, AMADEO, Nude of 1917, May 59: 14
MOE, HENRY ALLEN, photograph of, May 59: 17
MOFFETT, ROSS
    Portrait of, Jul 61: 24
    Provincetown Historical Museum, Jul 61: 24
MOFFO, ANNA, portrait of, Jul 61: 96
MOHAMMED II, portrait by Gentile Bellini, May 59: 61
MOHAMMED REZA PAHLAVI, SHAH OF IRAN, photograph of, Jan 63: 43
MOHAMMED'S ASCENT, 17th-century miniature, Nov 60: 40–41
MOHOLY-NAGY, LÁSZLÓ
    Construction A II, Nov 61: 64
    Photogram, Nov 61: 68
MOHONK, LAKE, N.Y., Mountain House, Jan 61: 110–11
MOITESSIER, MME, portrait by Ingres, Mar 62: 66
MOLIÈRE, Psyché, scene from, Nov 62: 91
"MONA LISA," painting by Da Vinci, detail, Sep 60: 70
MONASTERY OF LA TOURETTE, Mar 61: 34–39, 41
MONET, CLAUDE
    Breakwater at Honfleur, The, Jul 62: 78–79
    Manet's boat, Jul 62: 72
    Sketch of, Sep 58: 132
MONK, JULIUS, photograph of, Jul 61: 76
MONROE, MARILYN, portrait by Willem de Kooning, Jul 62: 14
"MONSIEUR BERTIN," portrait by Ingres, Jan 59: 95
MONSTRANCE, commemorating Battle of Lepanto, Jul 63: 58, 59
MONTAGU, ASHLEY, portrait of, Jan 60: 9
MONTANA, Glacier National Park Hotel, Jan 61: 112
MONTEFELTRO, FEDERIGO DA, DUKE OF URBINO, portraits of
    By Francesca, Piero della, Jan 60: 69
    By Berruguete, Pedro, (?), Jan 60: 63
MONTEFELTRO, GUIDOBALDO DA, DUKE OF URBINO
    As child, in painting attributed to Pedro Berruguete, Jan 60: 63
    Portrait of, Jan 60: 65
MONTEVERDI, CLAUDIO, portrait of, Jul 60: 39
MONTEZUMA II, AZTEC EMPEROR, encounter with Cortes. See CORTES, HERNANDO
MONTOYA, CARLOS, photograph of, May 63: 20
MONTSERRAT MOUNTAIN, SPAIN, Mar 59: 79
MONUMENTS, designs by Edward Sorel, Sep 61: 122–28
MONVILLE, MAZIÈRE DE, suburban house design, Mar 62: 30, 31
MOON
    Eclipse of, Balinese concept, Jan 59: 29
    Rise of, Greek concept, Jan 59: 123
"MOON FOR THE MISBEGOTTEN, A," play, scene from, Mar 60: 36
MOORE, DOUGLAS, portrait of, Jan 60: 14
MOORE, HENRY
    Brick wall in Rotterdam, sculptured by, Sep 59: 14
    Family Group, Nov 60: 111
    King and Queen, Nov 60: 112: detail from, Nov 60: 110
    Photograph of, Nov 60: 105
    Reclining figures, Nov 60: 107, 108–9, 110; sketches for, Nov 60: 106–7
    Seated Figure (sketch), Nov 60: 102
    UNESCO headquarters sculpture, Reclining Figure, Nov 60: 106–7
    Upright Exterior and Interior Form, Nov 60: 105
    Warrior with Shield, Nov 60: 110
MOORE, THOMAS, portrait of, Mar 59: 90
"MOORISH CHIEF," painting by Eduard Charlemont, Mar 60: 69
MORE, THOMAS, Utopia, frontispiece for 1518 edition, Mar 63: 74

MOREAU, JEANNE, in *The Lovers*, May 60: 51
MORGAN, EMANUEL, sketch of, by Arthur Davison Ficke, May 60: 42
MORGAN, GLADYS, poster, Jul 59: 114
MORGAN, J. PIERPONT, photograph of, Jul 60: 4
MORGAN, MAC, photograph of, May 60: 17
MORGENSTERN, OSKAR, photograph of, Sep 59: 25
MORLEY, GRACE McCANN, portrait of, Jan 59: 12
MORNY, DUC DE, portraits of, May 63: 64, 71
MORRIS, CARL
   Flowing Arch, Jan 62: 15
   Portrait of, Jan 62: 15
MORRIS, C. C., photograph of, Jul 63: 15
MORRIS, HILDA
   Portrait of, Jan 62: 15
   Vaulted Echo, Jan 62: 15
   Wind Tides, Jan 62: 15
MORRIS, KYLE, *Evening Images*, Nov 60: 7
MORRIS, WILLIAM, *News from Nowhere*, frontispiece for, Mar 63: 77
MORROW, JO, photographs of, Nov 59: 28, 29
MORROW, MRS. MUNI, portrait by Aaron Shikler, Jan 59: 101
MOSAICS
   Byzantine, at Istanbul: Constantine the Great, in Hagia Sophia, Nov 63: 5; Enos, Abel and Adam, in Kariye Çami, Nov 63: 30; Leo VI, in Hagia Sophia, Nov 63: 23; Metochites, in Kariye Çami, Nov 63: 29; pavement details, from Grand Palace, Nov 63: 11
   Byzantine, of Ravenna: Justinian and Theodora, Nov 63: cover, 3, 16–19; mermaid, Jan 60: 129; zealot, Nov 58: 5
   Byzantine icon, Saint Michael the Archangel, Nov 60: 43
   By Piza, A. L. Toledo, Nov 63: 54
   Roman: Battle of Issus, Mar 59: 34–35; dolphin, from Sardis, Sep 63: 82; floor, sun motif, Nov 63: 51; gladiators, May 62: 46; John VII, Pope, Jan 62: 32, 34; Minerva, head, Jan 62: 46; pavement from Empress Livia's villa, Jul 59: 26
   Sicilian, Jacob's meeting with angel, Nov 60: 42
"MOSAIC #34," by A. L. Toledo Piza, Nov 63: 54
MOSCOW, U.S.S.R.
   Domes of Saint Basil's Cathedral, Sep 60: 133
   Side streets, paintings by Robert Sivard, Nov 63: 88, 90
MOSES, ROBERT
   In *Modern Bestiary*, Jul 62: 126
   Monument to, designed by Edward Sorel, Sep 61: 124
"MOSES, SCENES FROM THE LIFE OF," painting by Botticelli, detail from, Jan 62: 32, 38
MOSES DESCENDS FROM MOUNT SINAI, painting by Shalom Moskovitz, Jul 61: 122
MOSKOVITZ, SHALOM
   Old Testament paintings by: Abraham and Lot set out from Haran, Jul 61: 124–25; Adam and Eve, Jul 61: 123; Joseph relates his dreams, Jul 61: 126; Moses descends from Mount Sinai, Jul 61: 122; Noah and the ark, Jul 61: 128; slaughter of the firstborn, Jul 61: 121; Tower of Babel, Jul 61: 127
   Photograph of, Jul 61: 120
MOSLEY, OSWALD, one-man demonstration for, in Trafalgar Square, Nov 61: 21
MOSTEL, ZERO
   Impersonations of artists by, May 62: 52–53
   Photograph of, May 62: 50
   In *Rhinoceros*, Sep 62: 35
"MOTHER, THE," play, scene from, May 62: 37
"MOTHER COURAGE," play, scene from, May 62: 36
MOTHERWELL, ROBERT, *The Voyage*, painting by, Nov 59: 38
MOTION PICTURES, mass and class appeal in, Jan 60: 8
MOULINS, MASTER OF, *St. Madeleine and Donor*, detail from, Sep 60: 72
MOUNTAIN GOAT, bronze, from Marlik, Iran, Nov 62: 102
MOUNTAIN HOUSE, Lake Mohonk, N.Y., Jan 61: 110–11
MOUNT RAINIER NATIONAL PARK, undergrowth in, Mar 60: 17
MOUNT WASHINGTON HOTEL, Bretton Woods, N.H., Jan 61: 108–9
"MOURNERS OF DIJON," sculpture, Sep 58: 62, 63
MOURNING ANGEL, sculpture by Bernini, Jul 60: 36
MOUSSORGSKY, MODEST, sketch of, Sep 58: 83
"MOVERS, THE," painting by John Koch, Sep 60: 109
MOY, SEONG
   Portrait of, Jul 61: 24
   Stolen Kiss, The, Jul 61: 24
MOZART, WOLFGANG AMADEUS, at salon of Prince de Conti, Nov 61: 33
MUCZYNSKI, ROBERT, rehearsing high school trio, Jan 62: 8
MULHARE, EDWARD, in *My Fair Lady*, Sep 58: 59
MULLER, HERMANN J., photograph of, May 59: 16
MÜLLER, ROBERT
   Roasting Spit, The, Mar 61: 108–9
   Stele for a Termite, Mar 61: 107
MULLIGAN, GERRY, in *Jazz on a Summer's Day*, Mar 61: 18

MURCH, WALTER, *Carburetor*, Nov 60: 9
MURPHY, DENNIS, photographs of, Jan 59: 17, Mar 59: 16
MUSES, Thalia and Melpomene, Campanian sculptures, Mar 62: 67
"MUSIC," painting by John Koch, Sep 60: 108
"MUSICAL CLOWN," ballet, rehearsal, Nov 61: 63
MUSICAL INSTRUMENTS, medieval, Jan 59: 2, 3
MUSIC DIAGRAMS
   For tape recorder music, Jan 59: 50–51, 55, 125
   For Improvisation Chamber Ensemble, Jan 63: 76, 79, 80, 81
"MUSIC LESSON, THE," painting by Vermeer, Jul 63: 100
"MUSIQUE AUX TUILERIES, LA," painting by Manet, May 63: 74–75
MUSSET, ALFRED DE
   Portrait of, May 60: 32
   Self-portrait, with George Sand, May 61: 81
MUTINEERS, 1790 engraving, Sep 63: 43
MUTINY ON H.M.S. "BOUNTY"
   In contemporary engravings, Sep 63: 44, 45
   In motion pictures, Sep 63: 42
MUTUAL INSURANCE COMPANY, Hartford, Conn., Sep 59: 14
MYCENAE, GREECE
   Artifacts showing civilization of, Jul 60: 86, Jan 61: 73–75, 80–85, 87–90, 92, 94
   Lion Gate, Jan 61: 78
   Map of Mycenaean world, *c.* 1400 B.C., Jan 61: 93
   Ruins at, Jan 61: 78–79
MYERS, LOU, "Philosophical Primer," drawings by, Jul 61: 110–11
"MY FATHER WAS BIG AS A TREE," painting by Carroll Cloar, Nov 58: 79
MYLLER, ROLF, design for memorial to F. D. Roosevelt, May 61: 43
MYRON, Discobolus, Roman copy, Jan 62: 47
"MYSTIC MARRIAGE OF SAINT CATHERINE, THE," painting by Correggio, Nov 61: 82
"MYTH RIDER, THE," painting by Sidney Nolan, Sep 62: 103

N

NAARDEN, NETHERLANDS, Jul 61: 52
NABOKOV, VLADIMIR, photograph of, May 59: 16
NADAR, in picture interview with Marie-Eugène Chevreul, Mar 59: 68–69
NAGA, ancient Nubian city, Mar 63: 43
NAKAYAMA, TADASHI, *Sleeping Crane*, print by, May 60: 112
NAMUTH, HANS, photographs of Alexander Calder and his creations by, Nov 62: 10–11, 14, 17
NAPLES, ITALY
   Drawings by Domenico Gnoli, May 59: 137–41
   Photographs by Herbert List, Sep 63: 49–59
   Street scene, Nov 59: 51
NAPOLEON I
   At Battle of Arcola, painting by Antoine-Jean Gros, May 61: 71
   Camp bed of, May 60: 134
   Coronation ceremonies, painting by Serangeli, Sep 60: 68
   Portrait and handwriting of, Sep 59: 136
   Portraits of, by David, Nov 58: 88, Sep 60: cover, 3
   Receiving Alexander I, painting by Adolphe Roehn, Sep 63: 28–29
NAPOLEON III
   With Eugénie, painting by Tissier, Sep 60: 68
   With Haussmann, painting by Adolphe Yvon, May 63: 50
NASH, JOHN, Brighton Pavilion, designed by, Mar 62: 35, Nov 62: 20–21, 25–28, 31
NATCHEZ, MISS., Moorish residence designed by Samuel Sloane, Mar 62: 35
NATIONAL CULTURAL CENTER, design by Edward D. Stone, Sep 61: 16
NATSIVAAR, *Angels in the Moon*, Mar 63: 120
NATWICK, MILDRED, in *The Waltz of the Toreadors*, Nov 60: 53
NAUTILUS SHELL CUP, May 61: 2
NAVONA, PIAZZA, in Rome, Jul 60: 51
NAZIS, poster opposing, Jan 59: 119
N'DEBELE VILLAGE, photographs by Pete Turner, Nov 60: 57–64
NECKER, JACQUES, portrait of, Nov 58: 88
"NEIGHBORLY ENCOUNTER," sculpture by Uli Nimptsch, May 62: 77
NEILSON, JACQUES, tapestries by, Nov 58: 61
NEOLITHIC FERTILITY SYMBOL, Jul 61: 37
NEOLITHIC VILLAGE, in Foggia Plain, Italy, Jul 61: 36
NERO, ROMAN EMPEROR
   Calling on Agrippina, drawing by Philippe Julian, Mar 63: 80

Coin portrait of, Sep 63: 37
NERVI, PIER LUIGI
   Photograph of, Mar 59: 20
   Structures designed by, Mar 59: 20–23, 122, 123; Pirelli building, Milan (in collaboration), Nov 60: 15; Rome Sports Palace, Mar 62: 32
NESTOR, KING OF PYLOS, palace and bathtub of, Jan 61: 84–85
NESTOR'S CUP, Jan 61: 87
NETHERLANDS (see also AMSTERDAM; ROTTERDAM)
   Arnhem memorial to British and Canadian paratroops, May 61: 44
   Naarden, Jul 61: 52
   Sun's setting, photograph by Emil Schulthess, Sep 58: 71
NEUMANN, BALTHASAR, stairwell at Wurzach Palace, designed by, Jul 60: 56–57
NEUSCHWANSTEIN, castle of, in Bavaria, Jan 61: 34–35, 42
NEW CANAAN, CONN., home of Philip Johnson, Nov 58: 33
NEWCASTLE, ENGLAND, train shed, Mar 62: 36–37
NEWCASTLE, DUKE OF, cartoon, Nov 58: 57
NEW DELHI, INDIA. See DELHI
NEW GUINEA SCENE, Jan 60: 29
NEW HAMPSHIRE
   Bretton Woods, Mount Washington Hotel, Jan 61: 108–9
   MacDowell Colony. See MacDOWELL COLONY
NEW JERSEY
   Ocean Grove, Spray View House, Jan 61: 112
   Radburn, aerial view, Jul 59: 7
   Trenton, Jewish Community Center Bathhouse, Sep 62: 60
NEW LONDON, CONN.
   Harbor, in Eugene O'Neill's day, Mar 60: 29
   Home of Gordon Nonie, Mar 60: 33
   Home of O'Neill family, Mar 60: 32
"NEWS FROM NOWHERE," romance by William Morris, frontispiece for, Mar 63: 77
NEWTON, ISAAC
   Cenotaph design for, by Etienne Boullée, Mar 62: 35
   Portrait of, Nov 60: 20
NEW YORK
   Lake Mohonk, Mountain House, Jan 61: 110–11
   Saratoga Springs, Grand Union Hotel, Jan 61: 105
NEW YORK, N.Y.
   Chase Manhattan Bank building, Nov 60: 4
   Fort Tryon Park, Nov 59: 132
   Impressions by John Rombola, May 63: 116–20
   Kip's Bay Plaza, Jan 63: 115
   Lever House, Jan 60: 9
   Manufacturers Trust Company building, Sep 59: 13
   112 West 34th Street, Jan 63: 115
   139 East 33rd Street, Jan 63: 115
   Park West Village, Jan 63: 115
   Pepe's Live Poultry Market, painting by Robert Sivard, Nov 63: 89
   Photographs by Ruth Orkin, Mar 59: 96–104
   Seagram building, Sep 59: 6, Nov 61: 73
   Skyscrapers, Jul 59: 4
   Solomon R. Guggenheim Museum, Sep 60: 97
   Street furniture, Nov 59: 105–12
   U.S. Mission to United Nations, design for, Jan 60: 23
"N.Y., N.Y.," motion picture, scenes from, Mar 61: 12–13
NEW YORK CITY BALLET, Jan 61: 50–55, Sep 61: 16
NEW YORK INTERNATIONAL AIRPORT
   American Airlines terminal, Sep 59: 10–11
   Street lighting, Nov 59: 107
   TWA terminal, Jul 60: 80, Mar 62: 33
NEW YORK PHILHARMONIC
   At Athens festival, Jul 62: 30
   At Caracas, Jul 59: 23
NEW YORK PRO MUSICA, Nov 60: 88–89, 92–93, 95
NICCOLÒ and GIOVANNI, *The Last Judgment*, Jan 62: 32, 35
NICHOLSON, VIRGINIA, photograph of, Jul 63: 86
"NICKY," painting by Andrew Wyeth, Sep 61: 93
NICOLLE, V. J., view of Seine from Louvre, painting by, Sep 60: 57
NIEBUHR, BARTHOLD GEORG, portrait of, May 60: 32
NIEMEYER, OSCAR
   Cathedral at Brasilia, Brazil, model designed by, Sep 59: 15
   Church of St. Francis, Pampulha, Brazil, designed by, Sep 59: 9
NIEULANDT, ADRIAEN VAN, *Allegory of the Peace of Münster*, Sep 58: 35
NIGERIA
   Art objects from medieval kingdoms, Mar 63: 46–51, 58
   Cavalry of, Mar 63: 53–55
"NIGHT AT PISA," painting by René Margritte, Jan 62: 86
"NIGHT FISHING AT ANTIBES," painting by Picasso, May 59: 12
"NIGHT HEDGEROW ANIMAL," drawing by Morris Graves, Jul 60: 112

"NIGHT LAND," sculpture by Isamu Noguchi, Mar 60: 110

"NIGHT SAIL," painting by Byron Browne, Jul 61: 24

NIKOLAIS, ALWIN, dances of, Nov 58: 90–91

NILE, THE, Roman copy of Hellenistic sculpture, Jan 62: 46

NIMPTSCH, ULI, *Neighborly Encounter*, May 62: 77

NIPPUR, Mesopotamian city, Jul 61: 40–41
Clay tablet from, Jul 63: 109

NIVEN, DAVID, photographs of, Sep 63: 76, 78, 79

NIVOLA, CONSTANTINO
Photograph of, May 63: 26
Sculptured wall designed by, Sep 59: 14

NIXON, RICHARD M., photograph of, Jul 60: 4

NOAH AND ARK, painting by Shalom Moskovitz, Jul 61: 128

"NOA NOA," woodcut by Gauguin, Jan 60: 127

NOGUCHI, ISAMU
Bridge at Hiroshima designed by, Mar 60: 111
Garden at UNESCO headquarters, Paris, designed by, Mar 60: 109
Lamps designed by, Mar 60: 106, 111
Photographs of, May 59: 16, Mar 60: 105, 106
Sculpture by: *Centipede*, Mar 60: 107; *Family Group*, Mar 60: 110; Fuller, Buckminster, chromium head, Mar 60: 111; *Kouros*, Mar 60: 107; *Night Land*, Mar 60: 110
Studio-home of, Mar 60: 104

NOH SINGER, painting by Mark Tobey, Jul 59: 76

NOK SCULPTURE, head, Mar 63: 46

NOLAN, SIDNEY
Camel Buggy, Sep 62: 98
Feeding the Birds, Sep 62: 99
Kelly, Sep 62: 100
Kelly at Glenrowan, Sep 62: 101
Landscape, Sep 62: 102
Myth Rider, The, Sep 62: 103
Photograph of, Sep 62: 97
Ram Caught in Flood, Sep 62: 96

NOLAND, KENNETH, *Noon Afloat*, Jan 63: 17

NONIE, GORDON, New London, Conn., home of, Mar 60: 33

"NOON AFLOAT," painting by Kenneth Noland, Jan 63: 17

"NO PASSING," painting by Kay Sage, Sep 63: 27

NORMAN, OKLA., home designed by Bruce Goff, Nov 61: 46–47

NORTH AFRICA, Tassili rock paintings, May 59: 73–80, Sep 62: 12

NORTHWEST ORIENT AIRLINES, advertisement of, Mar 59: 133

NORWAY
Swan fountain at Oslo, May 62: 29
U.S. embassy building, detail, Jul 60: 81

NOTRE DAME CATHEDRAL, Paris, May 63: 53
Coronation of, Nov 58: 16

"NOTRE-DAME IN THE LATE AFTERNOON," painting by Matisse, Jul 62: 67

NOVAK, STEFAN, sculpture by, Jan 59: 4

NOVARINA, MAURICE, church of Sacré Coeur at Audincourt, France, designed by, Sep 62: 25

NOYCE, WILFRID, photograph of, Sep 58: 8

"NUDE," painting by David Park, Sep 63: 91

"NUDE DESCENDING A STAIRCASE," painting by Marcel Duchamp, Mar 60: 56, Sep 63: 90

"NUDE IN FRONT OF A MIRROR," painting by Pierre Bonnard, Mar 62: 23

"NUDE IN THE BATHTUB," painting by Pierre Bonnard, Mar 62: 20–21

"NUDE OF 1917," painting by Modigliani, May 59: 14

"NUMBER 12," painting by Jackson Pollock, Sep 63: 92

NUNGESSER, CHARLES, Escoffier creation for, May 61: 127

"NUT TREES AT THOMERY," painting by Sisley, Jul 62: 58

"NYDIA, THE BLIND GIRL OF POMPEII," sculpture by Randolph Rogers, Mar 60: 63

O

"OARSMEN AT CHATOU," painting by Renoir, Jul 62: 70–71

OATES, WHITNEY J., photograph of, Sep 59: 26

OBATA, GYO, design by, for Washington, D.C., office block "Number 9," Jan 60: 22–23

OBERON, MERLE, photograph of, Sep 63: 76

"OBJET NO 2," print by Koshiro Onchi, May 60: 105

OCEAN GROVE, N.J., Spray View House, Jan 61: 112

"OCEAN VIEW FROM WINDOW," painting by Richard Diebenkorn, Jul 60: 18

ODYSSEUS
Homeland of, Jan 61: 97

Sculpture, May 59: 102
Ship of, Jan 61: 96

"OEDIPUS REX," play by Sophocles, scene from, Nov 63: 36

OENSLAGER, DONALD, set for *Ballad of Baby Doe*, designed by, Jan 60: 16

OESTERLEN, DIETER, Christ Church, Bochum, Germany, designed by, Sep 62: 28

O'GORMAN, JUAN, University of Mexico library, designed by, Sep 59: 8

O'HARA, MAUREEN, photographs of, Nov 59: 30, Jul 60: 6

OHIO, Longwood Village "exedra," at Cleveland, Nov 59: 109

"OIL ANCHORS," painting by Peter Busa, Jul 61: 25

OKADA, EJIE, in *Hiroshima Mon Amour*, May 60: 50

OKLAHOMA, homes designed by Bruce Goff, Nov 61: 42–43, 46–47

"OLD GUITARIST, THE," painting by Picasso, Nov 61: 8

"OLD SHEPHERD'S CHIEF MOURNER, THE," painting by Edwin Landseer, Mar 60: 63

OLD TESTAMENT EVENTS, paintings by Shalom Moskovitz, Jul 61: 121–28

OLIVARES, COUNT-DUKE OF
Painting by Velázquez, Jul 60: 41
Portrait of, Sep 59: 29

OLIVETTI, ADRIANO, portrait of, Nov 59: 44

OLIVETTI COMPANY, buildings, machines, and advertising designs of, Nov 59: 46–47, 48–49, 51, 127

OLIVIER, LAURENCE
In *Hamlet*, Nov 63: 40
As Richard III, Jan 61: 30

OLLIVIER, MARIE, in *Kean*, Mar 62: 118

"OLYMPIA," painting by Édouard Manet, Sep 60: 76–77

OLYMPUS, MOUNT, Jan 61: 99

ONCHI, KOSHIRO, *Objet No 2*, print by, May 60: 105

"ONE," painting by Jackson Pollock, Nov 59: 36–37

"ONE A.M.," motion picture, scene from, May 60: 136

O'NEILL, ELLA QUINLAN (MRS. JAMES), portrait of, Mar 60: 30

O'NEILL, EUGENE
New London, Conn., home of, Mar 60: 32
Photographs of, Mar 60: 26, 28, 34, 39
Scenes from plays by, Mar 60: 35, 36, 38, 99

O'NEILL, JAMES, photographs of, Mar 60: 31, 34

O'NEILL, JAMIE, photographs of, Mar 60: 34, 36

"ONE SUMMER OF HAPPINESS," motion picture, scene from, May 59: 98

ONO, TADASHIGE, *The Road*, May 60: 106

"ON THE BEACH," painting by Winslow Homer, detail from, May 63: cover, 3

OPERA. See GRAND OPERA

OPPENHEIM, DAVID, photograph of, May 63: 15

"ORÉADES, LES," painting by Adolphe William Bouguereau, Mar 60: 61

OREGON, coast south from Cape Sebastian, Mar 60: 20–21

ORGAN, musical instrument, Mar 60: 72, 74, 75, 77–78

ORINOCO RIVER, painting, Jul 59: 63

ORKIN, RUTH
Photograph of, Mar 59: 96
Photographs of New York City by, Mar 59: 96–104

"ORPHEUS AND EURYDICE," painting by Poussin, Mar 61: 82–83

ORPHEUS FOUNTAIN, by Carl Milles, May 62: 28–29

ORRERY, LECTURE ON, painting by Joseph Wright, May 59: 92–93

ORTMAN, GEORGE, *Blue Diamond*, Jan 63: 24

OSBORN, ROBERT
Drawings by, Sep 60: 41–48
Photograph of, May 60: 18
"Sight That Music Makes, The," album of composers by, May 62: 121–28

OSBORNE, JOHN
Look Back in Anger, scene from, Jan 63: 33
Photograph of, Jan 63: 30

OSLO, NORWAY
Swan fountain by Dyre Vaa, May 62: 29
U.S. embassy building, detail, Jul 60: 81

OSTERLEY PARK PINK ROOM, Nov 58: 61

O'TOOLE, PETER, in *Lawrence of Arabia*, Jul 62: 108

"OUR MAN IN HAVANA," motion picture, scenes during making of, Nov 59: 26–30

OVID, portrait of, Nov 63: 44

OXFORD UNIVERSITY, ENGLAND
Radcliffe Square, painting by Chiang Yee, Nov 59: 133
Views drawn by John Glashan, Jan 63: 83, 85, 86, 87

P

PACIFIST POSTER, British, Jan 59: 119

PAEPCKE, WALTER, portrait of, Sep 58: 96–97

PAGE, GERALDINE, in *Summer and Smoke*, Mar 60: 98

PAHLAVI SYMBOL, Jan 63: 40

"PAINTER ON THE ROAD TO TARASCON, THE," self-portrait by Van Gogh, Jul 59: 99

"PAINTER WITH CAT AND MODEL," painting by James Ward, May 62: 76

"PAISAN," motion picture, scene from, Mar 61: 100

PAKISTAN, designs for memorials to Mohammed Ali Jinnah, May 61: 46

PALAIS-ROYAL GARDENS, Paris, painting by Philibert Louis Debucourt, Nov 59: 80–81

PALAZZO VENIER DEI LEONI, May 59: 4, 18, 19

PALERMO, ITALY
Church of San Giovanni degli Eremiti, Sep 61: 32
Palazzo Gangi ballroom, Sep 61: 40–41
Pictured in donkey-cart panels, Sep 61: 36, 37

PALESTINE (see also JERUSALEM)
Holy Land views, 15th-century woodcuts by Erhard Reuwich, Mar 60: 2, 81, 84–89

PALIMPSEST, Nov 62: 77

PALLAS ATHENE, cast, Nov 63: 80

PALLOY, PIERRE FRANÇOIS, drawing of Bastille by, Jan 60: 84

PALM BEACH, FLA., The Breakers, Jan 61: 108–9

PALMYRAN RELIEF, Nov 59: 14

PANNINI, GIOVANNI PAOLO, paintings by
Campidoglio, Rome, Nov 59: 91
Concert at French embassy, Rome, Jul 60: 62–63
St. Peter's, Rome, Nov 59: 97

PANOFSKY, ERWIN, photograph of, Sep 59: 26

PANTALONE, Jan 60: 89, 95

PAOLOZZI, EDUARDO, *Frog Eating a Lizard*, Mar 61: 105

PAPERBACK BOOKS, Jan 60: 4

PAPYRUS SCROLLS, Nov 62: 80, 83

"PARADISE LOST," by John Milton, facsimile page from first edition, Sep 58: 81

PARIS, FRANCE
Attack by Joan of Arc on, Mar 62: 95
Drawings by Ronald Searle, Mar 62: 121–28
Étoile radiating from Arc de Triomphe, Jul 61: 53
Hôtel de Sully, painted ceiling of, Nov 62: 91
Le Corbusier design for rebuilding, Mar 62: 38–39
Louvre, views of, Sep 60: 57, 58, 63, 64–65, 66–67, 82–85
Map, 1847, May 63: 54–55
Palais des Expositions Mar 59: 25
Palais-Royal gardens, Nov 59: 80–81
Place de Furstemberg, Nov 59: 135
Place des Vosges, Jul 61: 55
Port-Royal convent, Jan 63: 100
Sainte-Chapelle, Nov 59: 82–83
Second Empire scenes, May 63: 50, 52–53, 56, 59–62, 66–75
Seine River views, Jul 62: 62–69
Side-street paintings by Robert Sivard, Nov 63: 84, 86–87, 90
Street furniture, Nov 59: 110
Théâtre National de l'Opéra, Nov 58: 25
UNESCO headquarters. See under UNITED NATIONS

"PARISIENNE, LA," motion picture, scene from, May 59: 98

"PARIS PRESERVED," drawings by Ronald Searle, Mar 62: 121–28

PARK, DAVID
Drawing of, by Richard Diebenkorn, Jul 60: 115
Figure with Flowers, Jan 59: 5
Four Men, Jul 60: 20–21
Nude, Sep 63: 91
Portrait of Elmer Bischoff by, Jul 60: 115
Standing Couple, Jul 60: 17

"PARK SCENE WITH FIGURES," painting by Turner, Mar 63: 66

PARR, JACK, monument to, design by Edward Sorel, Sep 61: 125

PARTRIDGE, BERNARD, *Mr. Punch's Pocket Ibsen*, Jan 62: 107

PASADENA, CALIF., Stuart Company building, Sep 58: 88–90

PASCAL, BLAISE
Photographs by Erich Lessing commemorating, Jan 63: 95–101, 103
Portraits of, May 60: 32, Jul 60: 39, Jan 63: 94

"PASSAGE OF THE ST. GOTHARD, FROM THE CENTER OF DEVIL'S BRIDGE, THE," painting by Turner, May 62: 72

"PASSION OF CHRIST, THE," painting by Hans Memling, Sep 63: 16–17

PATAY, BATTLE OF, Mar 62: 93

PATEL, PIERRE, painting of Versailles by, Nov 59: 78–79

PATEN, from Abbey of Saint-Denis, Jan 63: 2, 3

"PATHER PANCHALI," motion picture, scene from, May 59: 99

PAUL IV, POPE, with Michelangelo, painting, Jan 62: 24

PAULING, LINUS, photograph of, May 59: 16

PAXTON, JOSEPH, Crystal Palace, designed by, May 60: 87, Mar 62: 37

PAZYRYK, U.S.S.R., rug and art objects found at, Jan 60: 110–11, 112

PEACOCK THRONE, at Linderhof, Jan 61: 43

PEALE, CHARLES WILLSON, and his museum, self-portrait, Jul 63: 19

PEALE, REMBRANDT, portrait of Alexander von Humboldt by, Jul 59: 56

PEARY, ROBERT, portrait of, Sep 58: 13

PEASE, JAMES, in *Midsummer Night's Dream,* Nov 61: 81

PEDERSEN, WILLIAM F., BRADFORD S. TILNEY AND ASSOCIATES, design by, for memorial to F. D. Roosevelt, May 61: 41, 43

PEI, I. M., buildings designed by
  Kip's Bay Plaza, New York City, Jan 63: 115
  Zeckendorf Plaza, Denver, Nov 59: 107

PEKING, CHINA, National Museum, Sep 62: 56

"PENELOPE," painting by Paul Delvaux, Sep 63: 94–95

PENNSYLVANIA, UNIVERSITY OF
  Laboratory designed by Louis Kahn, Mar 62: 31
  Richards Medical Research Building, Mar 62: 31, Sep 62: 58, 62, 63

PERESSUTTI, E. See BELGIOIOSO, L. B., associate

"PERFECT WAGNERIAN, THE," drawing by Robert Osborn, May 62: 122–23

PERI, Persian 16th-century miniature, Nov 60: 41

"PERIOD OF ADJUSTMENT," play, scene from, Mar 61: 103

PERSEPOLIS, IRAN, ruins at, Mar 59: 52–53, Jan 63: 45–48

PERSIAN ART and ARCHITECTURE
  Carpets, May 59: 44, Jan 60: 110–11, Jan 63: 70–71
  Cup of Khosrau I, Jan 63: 56
  Gold and silver objects, Jan 63: cover, 3, 54, 55
  Miniatures, Nov 60: 40–41, Jan 63: 61–66
  Mosques at Isfahan, Mar 61: 28, Jan 63: 41, 68–69
  Persepolis, Jan 63: 45–48
  Sculpture, Jan 63: 45, 48, 50, 51, 57, 70–71
  Tombs: of Cyrus the Great, Jan 63: 42; of Qabus, Jan 63: 60

PERSIAN EMPIRE, map, Jan 63: 58–59

"PERSONAL VALUES, THE," painting by René Magritte, Jan 62: 84

"PERSONNAGE," painting by Jan Lebenstein, May 61: 23

"PERSONNAGES DEVANT LE SOLEIL," painting by Joan Miró, Mar 59: cover, 3

PERU
  Cord bridge, Jul 59: 66
  Mochican cast copper kingfisher from, Mar 62: 2, 3

PETER I, CZAR OF RUSSIA (PETER THE GREAT)
  Cartoons on, Sep 59: 75–78
  Portraits of, Sep 59: 58, 63, 67
  Scenes from life of, Sep 59: 63, 65, 67, 70–74, 81–85

PETERHOF, villa of Peter the Great, Sep 59: 82, 84, 85, May 62: 24–25

PETERS, ROBERTA, photographs of, Sep 59: 89, 90–91

PETERSON, GLADE, photographs of, Nov 61: 79, 81

PETRA, TRANSJORDAN, Jul 62: 26–29

"PETRIFACTION," painting by Octave Landuyt, Jan 62: 79

PETRONIUS, facsimile of error in translation of work by, Nov 62: 86

PETWORTH HOUSE
  Grinling Gibbons room, Mar 63: 64
  Paintings by Turner, Mar 63: 63, 66–71
  Photograph of, Mar 63: 62–63

"PETWORTH HOUSE FROM THE LAKE, DEWY MORNING," painting by Turner, Mar 63: 70

"PEYTON PLACE," motion picture, scene from, May 59: 101

PHELPS, ROBERT, photograph of, Mar 59: 16

PHILADELPHIA, PA.
  Citizens of, past and present, photographs and paintings, Jul 63: 4, 9, 14–17, 19–24
  Cliveden, Jul 63: 14
  Elfreth's Alley, Jul 63: 10–11
  Lynnewood Hall foyer, Jul 63: 8
  Pennsylvania Academy of Fine Arts, Jul 63: 18
  Photographic views, Jul 63: 6–7, 12–13, 27
  Richards Medical Research Building, Mar 62: 31, Sep 62: 58, 62, 63
  In 1720's, Jul 63: 6–7

PHILAE, EGYPT, inundation of temple of Isis, Jul 60: 14–15

PHILIP II, KING OF MACEDON, coin portrait of, Mar 59: 31

PHILIP II, KING OF SPAIN, portrait by Antonio Arias, Nov 61: 108

PHILIP III, KING OF SPAIN, portrait of, Sep 59: 28

PHILIP V, KING OF SPAIN, fountains of, Jul 60: 56

PHILIP THE ARAB, ROMAN EMPEROR, coin portrait of, Sep 63: 37

PHILLIPS, KYLE, photograph of, Sep 59: 27

"PHILOSOPHER GIVING THAT LECTURE ON THE ORRERY IN WHICH A LAMP IS PUT IN THE PLACE OF THE SUN," painting by Joseph Wright, May 59: 92–93

"PHILOSOPHICAL PRIMER," drawings by Lou Myers, Jul 61: 110–11

PHOENIX-RHEINROHR BUILDING, Düsseldorf, Nov 60: 14

"PHOTOGRAM," by Moholy-Nagy, Nov 61: 68

PIAZZA ARMERINA, ITALY, Roman villa near, Sep 61: 30, 31

PIAZZA SAN MARCO, Venice, Jul 59: 14–15, Jul 61: cover, 3

"PIAZZETTA, VENICE, THE," painting by Canaletto, Jul 63: 104

PICASSO, PABLO
  Baladins, Les, Nov 61: 5
  Demoiselles d'Avignon, Les, Nov 61: 8
  Dog and Cock, The, Nov 61: 9
  Family of Saltimbanques, Nov 61: 8
  Femme Assise au Capuchon, Nov 61: 6
  Girl Before a Mirror, May 59: 12
  Impersonation by Zero Mostel, May 62: 53
  Kahnweiler, Daniel-Henry, portrait by, Nov 61: 9
  Mural by, Jan 60: 104
  Night Fishing at Antibes, May 59: 12
  Old Guitarist, The, Nov 61: 8
  Photographs of, Jan 60: 97, 101, 105, Nov 61: 13
  Roque, Jacqueline, paintings of, Jan 60: 99–103
  Seated Woman, Nov 61: 9
  Soler Family Lunching on the Grass, The, Nov 61: 10–11
  Studio at Cannes, Jan 60: 101
  Three Musicians, Nov 61: 13
  Woman in White, Nov 61: 9
  Woman with Loaves, Nov 61: 8

"PICNIC," motion picture, scene from, May 59: 100

"PICTURE BOX MAN, THE," painting by Ferdinand Waldmüller, Mar 60: 64

PICTURE INTERVIEW, origin of, Mar 59: 68–69

PICTURE WRITING, oldest example, Nov 62: 75

PIEN WEN-CHIN, *The Three Friends and Hundred Birds,* detail from, Jan 61: 24

"PIETÀ," illumination by Jean Fouquet, Nov 61: 96

"PIETA," painting by Rouault, Nov 62: 56

PIG, Near Eastern statuette, Sep 62: 8

PIKE, JAMES A., photograph of, Sep 63: 8

PILÂTRE DE ROZIER, FRANÇOIS, portrait of, Sep 58: 125

PINDAR, sculpture of, Nov 63: 43

PINTER, HAROLD, photograph of, Jan 63: 30

PINTORI, GIOVANNI, designs by
  Billboard, Nov 59: 47
  Booklet cover, Nov 59: 48–49
  Frieze, Nov 59: 44

PINTURICCHIO (BERNARDINO BETTI, or DI BETTO), paintings by
  Alexander VI, detail from *The Resurrection,* Jan 62: 32, 38
  Ideal Knight of St. John, Mar 61: 71

PIRANESI, FRANCESCO, tourists at Pompeii, etching by, Mar 62: 63

PIRANESI, GIAMBATTISTA, engravings by
  Carceri d'Invenzione, Sep 63: 22–23
  Eruption of Mount Vesuvius, Mar 62: 46–47
  St. Peter's, Rome, Jul 60: 52

PIRELLI BUILDING, Milan, Nov 60: 15

PISANELLO, IL, portrait medal of Vittorino da Feltre by, Jan 60: 59

PISCES, sculpture by Gislebertus, Sep 61: 53

PISSARRO, CAMILLE, *Louvre Seen from the Pont-Neuf, Winter,* Jul 62: 68–69

PITCAIRN ISLAND, Sep 63: 46–47

PITOËFF, GEORGES and LUDMILLA, as Romeo and Juliet, Sep 61: 109

PITT, WILLIAM THE ELDER (EARL OF CHATHAM), portrait of, Nov 60: 21

PITT, WILLIAM THE YOUNGER, portrait of, May 60: 32

PIUS V, POPE, portrait of, on Bavarian monstrance, Jul 63: 59

PIZA, A. L. TOLEDO, *Mosaic #34,* Nov 63: 54

"PLAGIARISM, THE," painting by René Magritte, Jan 62: 85

"PLASTER BAMBINO," play, scene from, Jan 62: 12

PLATES
  Greek, Jan 63: 50
  Hispano-Moresque, Sep 60: 70

"PLAY OF DANIEL, THE," 12th-century musical play
  Manuscript of, Nov 60: 91
  Scenes from, Nov 60: 92–93, 95

PLEASENCE, DONALD, in *The Caretaker,* May 62: 111

PLOWRIGHT, JOAN, in *A Taste of Honey,* Mar 61: 103

PLUMMER, CHRISTOPHER
  In *J.B.,* Jan 60: 51

In *Lark, The,* Nov 60: 52

PLUTO'S REALM, from *Les Echecs Amoureux,* Nov 58: 15

"POETESS, THE," painting by Joan Miró, Mar 59: 77

POITIERS, BATTLE OF, miniature from 15th-century Flemish manuscript, Sep 62: 75

POLAR LANDSCAPE, photograph by M. Brenneisen, Sep 58: 68–69

POLLOCK, JACKSON
  Number 12, Sep 63: 92
  One, Nov 59: 36–37
  Shadowed, Sep 58: 109

POLO, in Persian miniature, Jan 63: 63

POMEGRANATE NECKLACE, from Marlik, Iran, Nov 62: 101

POMPADOUR, MARQUISE DE, portrait of, by Quentin de La Tour, Sep 60: 74

POMPEII, ITALY, antiquities
  Apollo, bronze sculpture, Mar 62: 51
  Casts of the dead, Mar 62: 48, 49
  Dancing figures, in Villa of Cicero, Mar 62: 64
  Frescoes: Dionysiac mystery cult, Mar 62: cover, 3, 57–60; from House of Lucretius Fronto, Mar 62: 44; from House of the Vettii, Nov 60: 36–37, Mar 62: 64; Three Graces, Mar 62: 67; Vesuvius, Mar 62: 42
  Tourists at, etching by Francesco Piranesi, Mar 62: 63
  Tripod, bronze, Mar 62: 66
  Vico Storto, Mar 62: 54

PONCE DE LEON HOTEL, St. Augustine, Fla., Jan 61: 106–7

"POND IN A GARDEN, A," Egyptian tomb painting, May 59: 25

"PONGO THE MONSTER," painting by André François, May 59: 117

"PONT DE L'ANGLOIS," painting by Van Gogh, Jul 59: 103

PONTI, GIO, Pirelli building, Milan, designed by (in collaboration), Nov 60: 15

"PONT LOUIS-PHILIPPE," painting by Paul Signac, Jul 62: 69

POPE, ALEXANDER, portrait of, May 60: 32

PORPHYRY, Latin-manuscript portrait of, Sep 62: 79

PORTA, GIACOMO DELLA, Gesù, church designed by (with Giacomo da Vignola), Jul 60: 52

PORTER, ENDYMION, with Van Dyck, in portrait by Van Dyck, Jul 61: 88

PORTINARI, CANDIDO, tile mural designed by, Sep 59: 9

PORTLAND, DUCHESS OF, portrait of, Nov 63: 63

PORTLAND VASE, Nov 63: 65

"PORTRAIT OF A YOUNG GIRL," painting by Petrus Christus, Jan 59: cover, 3

PORT-ROYAL CONVENT
  De Paris, Jan 63: 100
  Des Champs: farm building and windlass, Jan 63: 98–99; Pascal's room, Jan 63: 97

PORTUGAL, Sagres, Nov 60: 75

PORTUGUESE TRADERS IN JAPAN, screen detail, Sep 60: 15

POSTERS
  For Bauhaus exhibition, Nov 61: 68
  Political, from aftermath of World War I, Jan 59: 112–20
  Of "Visit U.S.A." program, Sep 62: 116–19
  For Werkbund exhibition, Nov 61: 70

POTSDAM, GERMANY, Einstein Tower, Mar 62: 39

POUSSIN, NICOLAS
  Entombment, The, Mar 61: 88
  Holy Family, Mar 61: 91
  Inspiration of the Poet, Mar 61: 76–77
  Judgment of Solomon, Mar 61: 92–93
  Landscape with Polyphemus, Mar 61: 86–87
  Orpheus and Eurydice, Mar 61: 82–83
  Self-portrait, Mar 61: 78
  Summer, or Ruth and Boaz, Mar 61: 84–85
  Tancred and Erminia, Mar 61: 81
  Triumph of Galatea, Mar 61: 90

POWELL, LOVELADY, in *Dressed to the Nines,* Jul 61: 76, Jan 62: 71

POZZO, ANDREA, ceiling fresco by, Jul 60: 48–49

POZZUOLI, ITALY, Olivetti factory entrance, Nov 59: 46

PRAGUE, CZECHOSLOVAKIA, Clementinum Library, Jul 60: 34

"PRAISE OF FOLLY, THE," book by Erasmus
  Illus for, by Hans Holbein the Younger, May 62: 91, 93, 95
  Title page, May 62: 91

PRANDTAUER, JAKOB, Benedictine monastery of Melk, designed by, Jul 60: 55

PRAXITELES, head of Cnidian Venus by, Jan 62: 46

"PRAYER, THE," painting by Rouault, Nov 62: 51

"PRECIPITATE BURIAL," painting by Antoine Wiertz, Jan 62: 78

PREMINGER, OTTO
  Directing *Advise and Consent,* photograph, May 62: 117
  Sketch by Louis Lomonaco, May 62: 116

"PRESENCE," sculpture by Adaline Kent, Jan 59: 12

PRESLEY, ELVIS, photograph of, Sep 58: 43
PRESTER JOHN, picture by Diogo Homem, Nov 60: 76
PRESTOPINO, GREGORIO and ELIZABETH, photograph of, Mar 63: 28
PRICE, LEONTYNE, portrait of, Mar 61: 73
PRIESTLEY, JOSEPH, portrait medallion of, May 59: 90
PRIETO, ANTONIO, ceramics by, Jan 59: 5
"PRIMAVERA, LA," painting by Botticelli, Sep 58: 95
"PRINCE OF WALES' PHAETON," painting by George Stubbs, Jul 63: 102–3
"PRINCESS LIEVEN," painting by Thomas Lawrence, May 62: 65
PRINCETON UNIVERSITY, buildings and projects at, Sep 59: 22
"PRINTING WITH DOUGH," woodcut by Antonio Frasconi, Mar 61: 124
"PRISONER OF ZENDA, THE," motion picture, scene from, Sep 63: 78
"PRISONNIÈRE, LA," painting by Paul Delvaux, Jan 62: 81
"PRIVATE TRADER," painting by Robert Sivard, Nov 63: 88
"PRIVATE VIEW OF THE ROYAL ACADEMY," painting by W. P. Frith, May 62: 62–63
PROKHORENKO, SHANNA, in Ballad of a Soldier, Mar 62: 111
PROSKE, HAL, in Reynard the Fox, Jan 63: 91
PROUST, MARCEL, sketch of, Sep 58: 84
PROVINCETOWN, MASS., harbor view, Jul 61: 14–15
"PROVINCETOWN HISTORICAL MUSEUM," painting by Ross Moffett, Jul 61: 24
PSYCHE. See CUPID and PSYCHE
PTOLEMY'S "GEOGRAPHY," title page, Nov 62: 95
PUGIN, AUGUSTUS WELBY, churches designed by, Mar 62: 37
"PULL MY DAISY," motion picture, scene from, Mar 61: 14–15
"PULSATION OF ONENESS," painting by Boris Margo, Jul 61: 27
"PUNCH," magazine, cartoons from
    American view of the British, Jan 59: 57
    Housing developments, Sep 58: 53
PUNT, MEN OF, Egyptian tomb painting, Jul 60: 91
"PYGMALION AND GALATEA," cartoon by Daumier, Mar 60: 53
"PYGMALION AND GALATEA," painting by Jean Léon Gérôme, Mar 60: 52

Q

QABUS, KING OF PERSIA, tomb of, Jan 63: 60
"QUARE FELLOW, THE," play, scene from, Mar 60: 98
"QUEEN," magazine, illus from, Nov 62: 115
"QUEEN FOR A DAY," television program, Jul 60: 7
QUENNELL, PETER, portrait of, Jan 60: 109
QUILT, EARLY AMERICAN, sunflower pattern, Nov 63: 51
QUINTERO, JOSÉ, photographs of, Mar 60: 95, 96–97

R

RA, EGYPTIAN SUN-GOD, Nov 63: 49
RADBURN, N.J., aerial view, Jul 59: 7
"RAFFLES," motion picture, scene from, Sep 63: 79
RAILROAD, JAPANESE, Jul 61: 4–5
"RAIN, STEAM AND SPEED," painting by Turner, May 61: 88
"RALLY," painting by William Walton, Sep 61: 7
"RAM CAUGHT IN FLOOD," painting by Sidney Nolan, Sep 62: 96
RAMSES II, KING OF EGYPT, temples at Abu Simbel built by, Jul 60: 10–11, 15
RAMSEY, MICHAEL, ARCHBISHOP OF CANTERBURY, photograph of, Sep 63: 107
"RAMSGATE SANDS," painting by W. P. Frith, detail from, Jul 63: 95
RAND, AYN, in A Modern Bestiary, Jul 62: 121
"RAPALLO'S REFLECTIONS," photographs by Art Kane, Jul 60: 96–99
"RAPE OF EUROPA, THE," painting by Titian, Jul 59: cover, 3, 38–39
    Copies by Rubens and Van Dyck, Jul 59: 38
RAPHAEL
    Attila turned back by Leo I, painting, May 63: 76–77
    Castiglione, Baldassare, portrait, Jan 60: 65, Nov 61: 83
    Crucifixion, Jul 60: 44
    Inghirami, Tommaso, portrait, Jul 59: 35
    Saint George and the Dragon, Jul 61: 87
    Tapestry cartoon, detail from, Jul 63: 95

"RASHOMON," motion picture, scene from, Jul 62: 43
RASPONI, LANFRANCO, photograph of, Jul 60: 7
RASPUTIN, GRIGORI, portrait of, Sep 60: 130
RATHBONE, BASIL, photographs of, Sep 63: 78, 79
RATTNER, ABRAHAM, Job No. 2, Jul 62: 19
RAUBITSCHEK, ANTONY E., photograph of, Sep 59: 25
RAVENNA, ITALY, Church of San Vitale mosaics, Nov 63: cover, 3, 16–19
RAY, ANDREW, in A Taste of Honey, Mar 61: 103
RAY, MAN, photograph of Picasso by, Nov 61: 13
"READING FROM HOMER, A," painting by Lawrence Alma-Tadema, Mar 60: 64
"REBEL WITHOUT A CAUSE," motion picture, scene from, Sep 58: 42
RÉCAMIER, JEANNE FRANÇOISE JULIE ADÉLAÏDE (JULIETTE)
    Pictured in portrait of Augustus William of Prussia, Nov 58: 89
    Portrait of, by David, Nov 58: 87
RECLINING FIGURES, sculptures by Henry Moore, Nov 60: 107, 108–9, 110
    Sketches for, Nov 60: 106–7
"RED HAT," painting by Ben Johnson, Sep 63: 93
REED, CAROL, photographs of, Nov 59: 26–30
REIMER, GEORG, as Edmund Kean, Mar 62: 118
"RELATIVITY," lithograph by Maurits Escher, Sep 63: 22
REMBRANDT VAN RIJN
    Burghers, Sep 58: 27
    Lady with a Fan, The, Jul 63: 101
    Menasseh ben Israel, portrait, Mar 60: 102
    Self-portrait, Sep 60: 70
    Shipbuilder and His Wife, Jul 63: 95
    Storm on the Sea of Galilee, Jul 59: 34
    Supper at Emmaus, Jul 60: 47
REMICK, LEE, photograph of, Sep 60: 89
RENÉ, DUKE OF ANJOU, illus from Tournament book of, Nov 58: cover, 3, 92–104
RENOIR, PIERRE AUGUSTE
    Luncheon of the Boating Party, Jul 62: cover, 3
    Oarsmen at Chatou, Jul 62: 70–71
    Swing, The, Sep 60: 79
REPIN, ILYA EFIMOVICH, paintings by
    Ivan the Terrible with son's body, Sep 60: 131
    Zaporog Cossacks, Sep 60: 136
REPS, PAUL, "Zen Telegrams," drawings by, Jan 60: 46–47
RESHEVSKY, SAMUEL, photograph of, Jan 62: 118
RESNAIS, ALAIN, photograph of, May 60: 50
RESNIK, REGINA, photograph of, Nov 61: 79
RESORTS
    Luxury hotels, Jan 61: 102–12
    Mass and class appeal in, Jan 60: 8
"RETABLE DU PARLEMENT," painting by Flemish master, Sep 60: 58
"RETURN, THE," painting by Philip Guston, Nov 59: 34
"RETURN OF THE FLY, THE," motion picture, scene from, Jan 60: 8
REUTHER, WALTER P., photograph of, Sep 58: 99
REUWICH, ERHARD, woodcuts by
    Holy Land, Mar 60: 2, 81, 84–89
    Venice, Mar 60: 82–83
"REYNARD THE FOX," play, cast of, Jan 63: 90–91
REYNOLDS, JOSHUA
    Portrait of Admiral Rodney by, Jul 63: 95
    Self-portraits, Nov 59: 95, May 62: 56
REYNOLDS METALS COMPANY, sales office at Detroit, May 62: 32
"RHEINGOLD, DAS," opera, scene from, May 63: 42–43
RHODES, GREECE, Mar 61: 68–69
    Great Hall at, Mar 61: 49
    Siege of, Mar 61: 57–59
RHODESIA. See SOUTHERN RHODESIA
RIBICOFF, ABRAHAM, photograph of, Sep 61: 8
RICE PADDY, near Chengtu, China, Sep 62: 52–53
RICHARD AND SALADIN, painting by Solomon Alexander Hart, Jan 59: 86
RICHARDS MEDICAL RESEARCH BUILDING, Philadelphia, Mar 62: 31, Sep 62: 58, 62, 63
RICHARDSON, JONATHAN, portrait of John Vanbrugh by, Sep 61: 72
RICHARDSON, RALPH
    In Cyrano de Bergerac, Nov 63: 37
    In Waltz of the Toreadors, The, Nov 60: 53
RICHARDSON, TONY, photograph of, Jan 63: 28
RICHELIEU, CARDINAL, portrait of, Sep 59: 29; by Philippe de Champaigne, Jul 60: 40
RICHELIEU, DUC DE, in Bastille, with his mistresses, Jan 60: 87
RIGAUD, J. F., The Three Favorite Aerial Travellers, painting by, Sep 58: cover, 5
"RIGHTS OF MAN, THE," painting by René Magritte, Jan 62: 83
"RING ROUND THE MOON," play, scene from, Nov 60: 52

RIVA, EMMANUELLE, in Hiroshima Mon Amour, May 60: 50
"RIVER, THE," sculpture by Aristide Maillol, May 59: 13
RIVERA, DIEGO, mural by, Mar 59: 9
"RIVER COVE," painting by Andrew Wyeth, Sep 61: 96
"RIVER JOURNEY AT FIRST SNOWFALL, A," painting attributed to Chao Kan, Jan 61: 23
RIVERS, LARRY
    Birdie in the Garden, Sep 59: 97
    Byzantine Empress, Sep 59: 97
    Eula II, Sep 59: 99
    Feder, Mrs. Henry, portrait, Jan 59: 101
    ME (with artist), Sep 59: 94
    Saxophonist Jay Cameron, The, Sep 59: 99
    Second Avenue with T H E, Sep 59: 101
    Washington Crossing the Delaware, Sep 59: 96
RIVIÈRE, MADEMOISELLE, painting by Ingres, Sep 60: 73
"ROAD, THE," print by Tadashige Ono, May 60: 106
ROADSIDE SCENES, U.S.A., May 61: 6–17
"ROASTED CHESTNUTS," painting by Andrew Wyeth, Sep 58: 112
"ROASTING SPIT, THE," sculpture by Robert Müller, Mar 61: 108–9
ROBARDS, JASON, JR.
    In Iceman Cometh, The, Mar 60: 99
    In Long Day's Journey into Night, Mar 60: 38
ROBBE-GRILLET, ALAIN, portrait of, Jan 62: 98
ROBIE HOUSE, in Chicago, Sep 60: 100–1
ROBINSON, BILL, photograph of, Jul 59: 116
ROBINSON, EDWARD ARLINGTON, photograph of, Mar 63: 30
ROBINSON, JOHN A. T.
    Cartoons on, Sep 63: 9
    Portraits of, Sep 63: 5, 6
ROCKEFELLER, DAVID, portrait of, Nov 60: 5
ROCKEFELLER, JOHN D., photograph of, Nov 60: 6
ROCKEFELLER, JOHN D. III, photograph of, Jul 62: 6
ROCKEFELLER, STEVEN, photograph of, Jul 60: 6
ROCKEFELLER CENTER, New York City, Jul 59: 11
ROCK PAINTINGS OF SAHARA, May 59: 73–80, Sep 62: 12
ROCKWELL, NORMAN, photograph of, May 60: 12
RODGERS, EILEEN, in Tenderloin, May 61: 51
RODNEY, GEORGE BRYDGES, portrait of, by Reynolds, Jul 63: 95
ROEHN, ADOLPHE, Napoleon receiving Alexander I, painting by, Sep 63: 28–29
ROGERS, ANN, in My Fair Lady, Sep 58: 59
ROGERS, ERNESTO (see also BELGIOIOSO, L. B., associate)
    Torre Velasca, Milan, designed by, Nov 60: 15
ROGERS, RANDOLPH, Nydia, the Blind Girl of Pompeii, sculpture by, Mar 60: 63
ROGERS, WILL, photograph of, Sep 58: 58
ROGOSIN, LIONEL, photograph of, Mar 61: 15
"ROI À LA CHASSE," portrait of Charles I of England by Van Dyck, Jul 61: 78
ROLAND. See "SONG OF ROLAND, THE"
ROMAN EMPIRES, EASTERN AND WESTERN, in 4th century, map, Nov 63: 8
ROMANO, GIULIO
    Constantine's Donation, Jan 62: 30–31
    Tapestry representing Scipio, from cartoons by, Nov 61: 82
ROMANO, UMBERTO
    African Image, Jul 61: 24
    Portrait of, Jul 61: 24
ROMBOLA, JOHN
    Bullfight drawings by, Jul 60: 129–36
    Impressions of New York, May 63: 117–20
ROME, ITALY
    Arch of Titus, Nov 59: 101
    Campidoglio, Nov 59: 91
    Forum, detail, Nov 59: 74
    Fountains of, May 62: 20, 21, 23
    Palazzetto dello Sport, Mar 59: 22–23, Mar 62: 32
    Piazza Navona, Nov 60: 51
    Priory of Knights of Malta, Mar 61: 68–69
    St. Peter's church. See SAINT PETER, BASILICA OF
    Side street, painting by Robert Sivard, Nov 63: 88
    Stadio Flaminio, Mar 59: 23
    Street scenes, drawings by Domenico Gnoli, May 59: 142–44
    Tasso's oak, Jul 61: 75; as painted by Peter Blume, Jul 61: 72–73
ROME, ANCIENT
    Arena at Arles, Jul 59: 96, 97
    City of Rome in time of Constantine, scale model, Jul 61: 46–47
    Coin portraits of, Sep 63: 33–41
    Comic History of Rome, The, illus from, by John Leech, May 61: 52, 54, 55, 56, 57
    Garden, fresco, May 59: 26–27
    Memorial inscription, Nov 58: 109

Mosaic floor, sun motif, Nov 63: 51
Mosaic pavement from Villa Livia, Jul 59: 26
Mural from Campanian villa Boscoreale, Sep 63: 13
Relics in John Soane Museum, Nov 63: 80–81
Remains at Sardis, Sep 63: 82–83, 88
Sculpture: Alcestis myth, on sarcophagus, Jan 62: 46–47; Antinoüs, head, May 63: 34; from Aphrodisias, Mar 63: 97–101; Augustus, bust, Sep 60: 70, statue, Jan 62: 46; Greek philosophers, on sarcophagus, Jul 61: 43; Hadrian, head, May 63: 35; at Hadrian's Villa, May 63: 36, 38–39; Marcus Aurelius leading a triumph, Jul 61: 44; married couple, Jan 62: 47; sea trade, bas-relief, Nov 58: 76–77; slaves depicted in, May 62: 44, 45, 47, 48, 49; winged victory from Leptis Magna, Nov 60: 34
"ROMEO AND JULIET," motion picture, scene from, Sep 63: 78
ROMNEY, GEORGE, portrait by, of Lady Hamilton in Grecian attitude, Mar 62: 69
RONCHAMP, FRANCE, shrine of the Virgin, Sep 59: 4–5
"ROOMS BY THE SEA," painting by Edward Hopper, Jul 61: 11
ROOSEVELT, FRANKLIN D.
As abundance man, cartoon, Jul 60: 68
Designs for memorial to, May 61: 41, 43
ROOSEVELT, JAMES, photograph of, Jul 60: 7
ROOSEVELT, THEODORE, composite photographs with John F. Kennedy, Nov 63: 68–69, 70, 71
ROQUE, JACQUELINE
Paintings of, by Picasso, Jan 60: 99–103
Photographs of, Jan 60: 97, 100, 105
ROSE, FRED, photograph of, Nov 62: 62
ROSENBACH, A. S. W., photograph of, Nov 60: 96
ROSENQUIST, JAMES, The Lines Were Deeply Etched on the Map of Her Face, Jan 63: 23
ROSTAND, EDMOND, Cyrano de Bergerac, scene from, Nov 63: 37
ROTHKO, MARK, Earth and Green, Nov 59: 35
ROTHSCHILD FAMILY, at home, drawing by Philippe Julian, Mar 63: 83
ROTTERDAM, NETHERLANDS
Department store ornamentation, Sep 59: 17
Memorial to heroism during 1940 bombardment, May 61: 45
Sculptured wall, Sep 59: 14
ROUAULT, GEORGES
Christus, Nov 62: 49
Crucifixion, Nov 62: 55
Ecce Dolor, Nov 62: 53
First Sinners, Nov 62: 50
Pieta, Nov 62: 56
Prayer, The, Nov 62: 51
Self-portrait, Nov 62: 48
Suarès, André, portrait, Nov 62: 57
To Golgotha, Nov 62: 52
Veronica's Veil, Nov 62: 54
ROUND TABLE, of Algonquin Hotel, caricatures, Jul 62: 32, 41
ROUSSEAU, HENRI
Impersonation by Zero Mostel, May 62: 53
Sleeping Gypsy, The, May 59: 12
ROUSSEAU, JEAN JACQUES, portrait of, May 61: 60
ROWLANDSON, THOMAS
George IV and Mrs. Fitzherbert, caricature by, Nov 62: 22
Staircase at Royal Academy exhibition, drawing by, May 62: 61
ROYAL ACADEMY OF ARTS, London, May 62: 57
Annual Dinner, 1961, May 62: 58–59
Exhibition of 1787, engraving, May 62: 61
Staircase during exhibition, drawing by Thomas Rowlandson, May 62: 61
Students of the schools, May 62: 58
"ROYAL ROSE, THE," engraving by P. W. Tomkins, Sep 59: 2, 3
RUBENS, PETER PAUL
Copy by, of The Rape of Europa, Jul 59: 38
Crucifixion altar, Jul 60: 45
Education of Marie de Médici, The, Jul 60: 37
Farm at Laeken, The, Jul 63: 98–99
Landing of Marie de Médicis at Marseilles, mermaid detail from, Jan 60: 132–33
RUDOLF II, HOLY ROMAN EMPEROR, portrait of, Sep 59: 28
RUDOLPH, PAUL, Sarasota, Fla., high school, designed by, Mar 62: 33
RUGS. See CARPETS, PERSIAN
RUSK, DEAN, sketch of, Jul 61: 31
RUSSELL, JOHN, portrait of William Bligh from painting by, Sep 63: 48
RUSSELL, JOHN (1ST EARL RUSSELL), portrait of, Mar 59: 90
RUSSIA (see also UNION OF SOVIET SOCIALIST REPUBLICS)
Crown, Monomakh's Cap, May 63: 102
St. Petersburg in time of Peter the Great, Sep 59: 81–83

S

SAARINEN, EERO
Photograph of, Jul 60: 76
Structures designed by, Jul 60: 76, 79, 80–81, 83; TWA terminal, New York International Airport, Mar 62: 33; U.S. embassy building, London, Jan 60: 20; Yale hockey rink, May 59: 84–85
SACK, JOHN, photograph of, Mar 63: 27
SADLER, A. J., portrait of, Jul 59: 118
SAGE, KAY, No Passing, Sep 63: 27
SAGRES, PORTUGAL, Nov 60: 75
SAHARA DESERT
Artificial oasis in, Sep 58: 54–55
Rock paintings of Tassili plateau, May 59: 73–80, Sep 62: 12
SAINT AUGUSTINE, FLA., Ponce de Leon Hotel, Jan 61: 106–7
"SAINT BARBARA," painting by Jan Van Eyck, Jul 61: 48
SAINT BASIL'S CATHEDRAL, Moscow, domes of, Sep 60: 133
SAINT CATHERINE'S MONASTERY, on Mount Sinai, Mar 60: 89, 91, 92–93
SAINTE-BEUVE, CHARLES AUGUSTIN, portrait of, Nov 58: 89
"ST. FRANCIS KNEELING," painting by Francisco Zurbarán, Jul 60: 46
"SAINT GEORGE AND THE DRAGON," painting by Crivelli, Jul 59: 32, 33
"SAINT GEORGE AND THE DRAGON," painting by Raphael, Jul 61: 87
ST. GOTTHARD PASS, SWITZERLAND, Nov 59: 86, May 62: 72
ST. JAMES PALACE, Jul 63: 107
ST. JOHN, VIRGIN ISLANDS, Caneel Bay Plantation, Jan 61: 103
ST. JOHN AMBULANCE BRIGADE, Mar 61: 68
ST. JOHN'S HOSPITAL, Jerusalem, Mar 61: 69
"ST. JOSEPH THE CARPENTER," painting by Georges de La Tour, detail from, Sep 60: 70
ST. JULIET, Catalan painting, Mar 59: 79
"ST. LAWRENCE DISTRIBUTING ALMS," painting by Fra Angelico, Jan 62: 32, 40
ST. LOUIS, MO.
Air terminal, Mar 59: 25
Jefferson Arch, Jul 60: 79
SAINT LUKE, paintings from Gospel manuscripts, Nov 58: 10, 11
"ST. MADELEINE AND DONOR," painting by Master of Moulins, detail from, Sep 60: 71
ST. MARK'S SQUARE, Venice. See PIAZZA SAN MARCO
SAINT MARY, in sculpture, Sep 58: 87, Nov 58: 8, 16
SAINT MICHAEL, on Byzantine icon, Nov 60: 43
SAINT PAUL, sculpture, Nov 58: 8
SAINT PETER, BASILICA OF, Vatican City, Rome, Jul 60: 52, Jan 62: 25, 49
Floor plans, Jan 62: 26, 27, 43
Interior, Nov 59: 97, Jan 62: 42
Views of Old St. Peter's, Jan 62: 22, 26–27, 30–31
ST. PETERSBURG, RUSSIA, in time of Peter the Great, Sep 59: 81–83
SAITO, KIYOSHI, Two Haniwa, print by, May 60: 106
SALADIN AT BEDSIDE OF RICHARD, painting by Solomon Alexander Hart, Jan 59: 86
SALERNO, JOSEPH
House of Worship at Rowayton, Conn., designed by, Nov 62: 70–71
Photograph of, Nov 62: 71
SALINGER, J. D., drawing of, by R. M. Ziering, May 62: 100
SALINGER, PIERRE, photographs of, Sep 61: 8
SALINGER, STEPHEN, photograph of, Sep 61: 8
SAND, GEORGE, portraits of
By Delacroix, May 61: 80
By Musset, Alfred de, May 61: 81
SAND, PAUL, in From the Second City, Jan 62: 67
"SAND CASTLE, THE," motion picture, scenes from, Jul 61: 106–9
SANDER, AUGUST, "Timeless Teutons," album of photographs by, Mar 60: 41–45
SANDERS, CHRISTOPHER, Little-Little, May 62: 77
"SAND GARDEN," print by Okiie Hashimoto, May 60: 110
SAN FRANCISCO, CALIF., Jan 59: 4–5
Art festival, Jan 59: 7
Federal building, design for, Jan 60: 23
Maiden Lane, Jul 59: 10
Nob Hill, Jan 59: 6
North Beach bar, Sep 58: 38
SAN MEN DAM, China, scenes at, Jan 61: 4–10, 12–13
SANT' ELIA, ANTONIO, Città Nuova, Mar 62: 39

"SARAH STEIN," painting by Matisse, Jan 59: 12
SARASOTA, FLA., high school, Mar 62: 33
SARASWATHI, BALA, photograph of, Sep 63: 66
SARATOGA SPRINGS, N.Y., Grand Union Hotel, Jan 61: 105
SARDIS, remains at, Sep 63: 82–83, 87, 88
SARGENT, JOHN SINGER
Interior in Venice, An, May 62: 74
Portraits by: of Gardner, Isabella Stewart, Jul 59: 30; of Yeats, William Butler, Nov 60: 69
SARRAUTE, NATHALIE, portrait of, Jan 62: 99
SASAKI-WALKER-LUDERS ASSOCIATES, design by, for memorial to F. D. Roosevelt, May 61: 43
"SAVAGE EYE, THE," motion picture, scene from, Mar 61: 14
"SAXOPHONIST JAY CAMERON, THE," painting by Larry Rivers, Sep 59: 99
SAYER, JAMES, cartoon of Charles James Fox by, May 60: 100
SCHAEFFER, PIERRE, photograph of, Jan 59: 53
SCHAWINSKY, XANTI, photograph of, Nov 61: 62
"SCHEHEREZADE," ballet, scene from, Jan 61: 29
SCHILLER, JOHANN CHRISTOPH FRIEDRICH VON, portrait of, May 61: 64
SCHLEMMER, OSKAR
Mask studies by, Nov 61: 63
Musical Clown, ballet by, rehearsal, Nov 61: 63
SCHLESINGER, ARTHUR M., JR., in A Modern Bestiary, Jul 62: 128
SCHLESINGER, HENRI, Alone in the Studio, painting by, Mar 60: 62
SCHLIEMANN, HEINRICH, portrait of, Jan 61: 76
SCHMITT, cartoonist, Jubilee Banquet to Dr. Ibsen, Jan 62: 107
SCHMITT, MAX, rowing on Schuylkill River, painting by Thomas Eakins, Jul 63: 21
SCHNEIDER, ALEXANDER, photograph of, Sep 61: 86
SCHNEIDER-ESLEBEN, PAUL, Mannesmann building, Düsseldorf, designed by, Nov 60: 12–13
SCHOOLBOY READING, fresco by Vincenzo Foppa, Jan 60: 57
"SCHRAUBTHALER," Sep 61: 2, 3
SCHUBERT, FRANZ, portrait of, May 61: 66
SCHULTHESS, EMIL, photographs by, Sep 58: 66–67, 71, 74–75, 76, 78–79
SCHUMAN, WILLIAM, portrait of, Jul 62: 9
SCHUURMAN, ANNA MARIA VAN, portrait of, Sep 58: 28
SCHUYLKILL RIVER, painting by Thomas Eakins, Jul 63: 21
SCHWANENBURG, HANS VON, reliquary designed by, May 59: 2, 3
"SCIENCE IS MEASUREMENT," painting by Henry Stacy Marks, May 62: 74
"SCIPIO," tapestry from cartoons by Giulio Romano, Nov 61: 82
SCOFIELD, PAUL, in A Man for All Seasons, May 62: 111
"SCORE OF WHITE PIGEONS, A," painting by Ben Shahn, Jul 62: 12
SCORPIO, sculpture by Gislebertus, Sep 61: 53
SCOTLAND, photographs by Bruce Davidson, Nov 61: 18–19, 23, 26
SCOTT, GEORGE C., portrait of, Jul 60: 92
SCOTT, ROBERT FALCON, and Antarctic party of 1912, photograph of, Sep 58: 9
SCRIBE, Egyptian sculpture, Sep 60: 71
SCUDÉRY, MAGDELEINE DE, portrait of, Nov 61: 34
"SEABIRD IN THE RAIN," drawing by Morris Graves, Jul 60: 108–9
SEA COW, STELLER'S, Jan 60: 135
SEAGRAM BUILDING, New York City, Sep 59: 6, Nov 61: 73
SEAL, ELIZABETH, in Irma la Douce, May 61: 50
SEALS
Babylonian, showing fish deities, Jan 60: 130
Cylindrical, Near Eastern, Sep 62: 9
SEARLE, RONALD, "Paris Preserved," drawings by, Mar 62: 121–28
"SEATED FIGURE," sketch by Henry Moore, Nov 60: 102
"SEATED FIGURE IN GREEN," painting by Nicholas Marsicano, Sep 63: 92
"SEATED WOMAN," painting by Picasso, Nov 61: 9
SEATTLE, WASH., WORLD'S FAIR. See CENTURY 21 EXPOSITION
SEBERG, JEAN, photograph of, May 62: 81
"SECOND AVENUE WITH T H E," painting by Larry Rivers, Sep 59: 101
"SECRETS DE L'HISTOIRE NATURELLE," illus from, Jan 62: 2, 3
"SECRETS OF THE HORIZON, THE," painting by René Magritte, Jan 62: 86
SEGESTA, ITALY, landscape with Greek temple, Sep 61: 20–21
SÉGUIER, PIERRE, funeral of, Jul 60: 59
SEINE RIVER

Map, Jul 62: 74

Paintings, Sep 60: 57, Jul 62: 57, 58, 67, 68–73, 78–79

Photographs, Jul 62: 52, 53–54, 60–66, 74–77

"SELF ENCOUNTER," painting by Carroll Cloar, Nov 58: 79

SENECA, DEATH OF, drawing by Tiepolo, Jan 61: 2

"SENECIO," painting by Paul Klee, Nov 61: cover, 3

SERAGLIO OF OTTOMAN SULTANS, May 59: 56–59, 62–63, 132–33

SERANGELI, GIOACCHINO, coronation ceremonies of Napoleon I, painting by, Sep 60: 68

SERKIN, RUDOLF, photographs of, Sep 61: 82, 84, 86, 87

"SERMON OF SAINT BERNARD OF CLAIRVAUX, THE," illumination by Jean Fouquet, Nov 61: 95

SERT, JOSÉ LUIS, studio designed by, Mar 59: 75

"SERVIO TULLIO," opera, scene from, Jul 60: 61

SESSHU, painting of Bodhidharma by, Jul 59: 70

SEURAT, GEORGES, Model in Profile, painting by, Sep 60: 80

"SEVENTH SEAL, THE," motion picture, scene from, Sep 60: 4–5

SEVERN, JOSEPH, Shelley Composing "Prometheus Unbound" in the Baths of Caracalla, May 61: 58–59

SEVERUS, SEPTIMIUS, ROMAN EMPEROR, detail from Arch of, May 62: 45

SEVILLE, SPAIN

Council of war at Alcázar, 12th century, Sep 62: 84

Giralda tower bell and Patio of the Oranges, Sep 62: 91

SEWARD, ANNA, portrait of, May 59: 90

SFORZA, BATTISTA, paintings of, by Piero della Francesca, Jan 60: 71, 72

"SHADOWED," painting by Jackson Pollock, Sep 58: 109

"SHADOWS," motion picture, scene from, Mar 61: 16

SHAHN, BEN

Cosmos, Sep 58: 111

Score of White Pigeons, A, Jul 62: 12

SHAKESPEARE, WILLIAM

All's Well That Ends Well, scene from, Nov 63: 38

Hamlet, scenes from, Nov 63: 40, 41

Julius Caesar, scene from Barrault production, Sep 61: 108

Macbeth: scene from Japanese motion picture based on, Jul 62: 45; scene from Vilar production, Sep 61: 109

Portraits of, Sep 62: 69, 71

Taming of the Shrew, The, scene from, Nov 63: 38

Title page of first complete translation into French, Sep 61: 103

Twelfth Night, scene from, Nov 63: 37

SHALOM OF SAFED. See MOSKOVITZ, SHALOM

SHAPUR I, KING OF PERSIA, capture of Valerian, rock carving, Jan 63: 61

SHARAKU, TŌSHŪSAI, impersonation by Zero Mostel, May 62: 52

SHAW, GEORGE BERNARD

Caricatures of, by Max Beerbohm, May 61: 34, 35

Corrections on manuscript, facsimile, Nov 58: 21

Man and Superman, scene from, Jan 62: 65

Portrait of, Nov 58: 19

SHAWN, TED, at Jacob's Pillow, photograph, May 60: 14–15

SHEIKS and SHEBAS, cartoons by John Held, Jr., Jul 63: 118, 119

SHELLEY, PERCY BYSSHE, portrait of, Nov 63: 47

"SHELLEY COMPOSING 'PROMETHEUS UNBOUND' IN THE BATHS OF CARACALLA," painting by Joseph Severn, May 61: 58–59

SHERIDAN, JIM, in Dressed to the Nines, Jan 62: 71

"SHERLOCK HOLMES," series of motion pictures, scene from, Sep 63: 79

SHERMAN, GARRY, in From the Second City, Jan 62: 67

SHERWOOD, ROBERT, portrait of, May 62: 4

SHIKLER, AARON, portrait of Mrs. Muni Morrow by, Jan 59: 101

SHINAGAWA, TAKUMI, Yellow and Purple, print by, May 60: 103

"SHIPBUILDER AND HIS WIFE," painting by Rembrandt, Jul 63: 95

SHIPS and BOATS

America's Cup races, Mar 61: 18–19

Balsa raft on Orinoco River, Jul 59: 63

Barca, Nov 60: 75

At Battle of Lepanto, Nov 61: 108–9, Jul 63: 51, 54–56, 61

Bounty mutiny, Sep 63: 44, 45

Caligula's barges, Nov 58: 72–73

Caravels: from "Miller Atlas" of 1519, Nov 60: 75; from painting by Bruegel, Sep 58: 2

Carrack, Portuguese, Sep 60: 16–17

Chinese junks, Sep 62: 50

Coca-cola barge, Venice, Sep 58: 50

Of conquistadores, Sep 60: 25

Doge's craft, Bucentaur, Venice, Nov 59: 88–89

Dutch: at Amsterdam, as seen by Peter the Great, Sep 59: 70–71; East Indiamen, Sep 58: 24–25

Egyptian, of 18th Dynasty, Jul 60: 84

Galleys on the Neva, 1753, Sep 59: 82–83

Great Britain, Jan 59: 42–43

Great Eastern, Jan 59: 42–43

Great Western, Jan 59: 40–41

Of Hanseatic merchants (Hansekoggen), 1497, Sep 59: 61

Maltese galleys, Mar 61: 61, 64

Odysseus' ship, Jan 61: 96

At Philadelphia, c. 1723, Jul 63: 6–7

At Pitcairn Island, 1856, Sep 63: 46–47

Roman, in bas-relief, Nov 58: 76–77

On Seine River, Jul 62: 70–71, 72

Spanish Moslem warships, Sep 62: 86

Spanish Silver Fleet, Sep 58: 21

Storm on the Sea of Galilee, painting by Rembrandt, Jul 59: 34

Tourist boats on Jhelum River, Mar 61: 31

Turkish galleys, Mar 61: 59, 64

Turkish warships, 1565, Mar 61: 64

SHIVA SCULPTURES, Sep 63: 64, 65

SHOLES, STEVE, photograph of, Sep 58: 43

"SHOREBIRDS," drawing by Morris Graves, Jul 60: 106–7

"SHORE LINE," painting by Bruce McKain, Jul 61: 25

"SHOULDER ARMS," motion picture, scene from, Jan 60: 8

SIBELIUS, JEAN, drawing by Robert Osborn, May 62: 128

SIBERECHTS, JAN, Longleat, Nov 58: 38–39

SIBYLS, of Michelangelo, Jan 62: cover, 3, 32, 37

SICA, VITTORIO DE

In General Della Rovere, Mar 61: 99

Photograph of, Sep 63: 49

SICILY

Ballroom of Palazzo Gangi, Palermo, Sep 61: 40–41

Carthaginian funeral monuments, Sep 61: 28, 29

Church of San Giovanni degli Eremiti, Palermo, Sep 61: 32

Donkey carts and their decorations, Sep 61: 34–37

Maps, with chronology, Sep 61: 24–25

Roman villa near Piazza Armerina, Sep 61: 30, 31

Scenes, Sep 61: 42–43, 44, 45

Segesta, landscape with Greek temple, Sep 61: 20–21

Trinacria, Sep 61: 22, 45

"SIDE PULL," painting by Adolph Gottlieb, Nov 59: 39

SIGNAC, PAUL, Pont Louis-Philippe, Jul 62: 69

"SIGN OF GERSAINT," painting by Watteau, Nov 59: 102

SIGNORELLI, LUCA, Last Judgment, detail from, Nov 60: 44

SILENT TRAVELLER. See CHIANG YEE

SILVER FLEET, of Spain, Sep 58: 21

SIMPSON, N. F., portrait of, Jan 63: 31

SIMS, ZOOT, mannequin portrait by Marisol Escobar, Mar 63: 104

SINAI, MOUNT, Mar 60: 89, 91, 92–93

SINATRA, FRANK, and pack, in A Modern Bestiary, Jul 62: 124–25

SINÉ, MAURICE, beach costumes, drawings by, May 62: 108–9

SISLEY, ALFRED, Nut Trees at Thomery, Jul 62: 58

SISTINE CHAPEL, frescoes, Jan 62: cover, 3, 32, 37, 39

SITWELL, OSBERT, SACHEVERELL and EDITH, photograph by Cecil Beaton, Jan 60: 108

SIVARD, ROBERT, side-street paintings by, Nov 63: 84, 86–91

SIXTUS IV, POPE, receiving a new librarian, fresco by Melozzo da Forlì, Jan 62: 44

SIYAWUSH, KING OF PERSIA, playing polo, Persian miniature, Jan 63: 63

SKATING AT THE HAGUE, painting by Adam van Breen, Sep 58: 16–17

"SKELETONS ARGUING OVER A CORPSE," painting by James Ensor, Jan 62: 79

SKIDMORE, OWINGS & MERRILL, buildings designed by

Deering Milliken plant, Spartanburg, S.C., May 62: 33

Lever House, New York City, Jan 60: 9

Manufacturers Trust Company building, New York City, Sep 59: 13

U.S. Air Force Academy, Jan 60: 22–23

SKULLS, primate, Mar 62: 8

SKYLITZES, JOHN, illus from 14th-century manuscript of chronicles, Nov 63: 24

"SKYSCRAPER," motion picture, scene from, Mar 61: 16–17

"SLAUGHTER ON TENTH AVENUE," ballet, scene from, Sep 58: 61

"SLAVE," sculpture by Michelangelo, Sep 60: 70

SLAVES, depicted in ancient Greek and Roman art, May 62: 42–49

SLAVE TRADER'S STELE, May 62: 42

"SLEEPING CRANE," print by Tadashi Nakayama, May 60: 112

"SLEEPING GYPSY, THE," painting by Henri Rousseau, May 59: 12

"SLEEP OF REASON," etching by Goya, Jul 61: 4

SLOANE, SAMUEL, Moorish home designed by, Mar 62: 35

"SMILES OF A SUMMER NIGHT," motion picture, scene from, Sep 60: 6

SMITH, ADAM, portrait of, Nov 59: 94

SMITH, C. AUBREY, photographs of, Sep 63: 74, 78

SMITH, HASSEL

Paintings by, Jan 59: 4–5, 13

Portrait of, Jan 59: 13

SMITH, OLIVER, sketch for Camelot, May 61: 102

SMITH, RED, photograph of, Jan 60: 9

SMITH, RICHARD JOHN, as buccaneer, tinsel print, Sep 63: 2, 3

SMITH, SYDNEY

Portrait of, Mar 59: 90

Sketch of, by Daniel Maclise, Mar 59: 125

SMITHSON, HARRIET

As Desdemona, Sep 61: 105

As Ophelia, Sep 61: 105

SNAKE RIVER, in Wyoming, color photograph, Mar 60: 18–19

SOANE, JOHN

Bank of England, reconstructed by, Nov 63: 82

Bridge design by, Nov 63: 76

Church designs by, Nov 63: 78–79

Court of Chancery designed by, Nov 63: 82–83

Museum and home of, Nov 63: 72, 73, 74, 75, 77, 80–81

Portrait by Thomas Lawrence, Nov 63: 75

SOCRATES, sculpture of, Mar 59: 57

SOCRATES REACHING FOR HEMLOCK, painting by Jacques Louis David, Jul 60: 100–1

SODOMA, IL, The Marriage of Roxane and Alexander, Mar 59: 54–55

SOEDERLUND, PETER, decorated alphabet letters by, Jul 63: 120

SOLAR SYSTEM, 18th-century chart after Copernicus, Jan 59: 30–31

"SOLDIA," painting by Leo Manso, Jul 61: 20

"SOLER FAMILY LUNCHING ON THE GRASS, THE," painting by Picasso, Nov 61: 10–11

SOLERI, PAOLO, Mesa City, Sep 63: 24–25

SOLOMON, IZLER, photograph of, Sep 58: 99

SOLOMON R. GUGGENHEIM MUSEUM, New York City, May 59: 15, Sep 60: 97

SOLOVIOFF, NICHOLAS, Italian street scenes, drawings by, Nov 61: 120–28

SONDHEIM, STEPHEN, portrait of, Jul 61: 99

"SONG OF ROLAND, THE," illus from 14th-century version, Sep 62: 88

SOPHOCLES, Oedipus Rex, scene from, Nov 63: 36

"SORCERESS," sculpture by Brancusi, May 59: 14

SOREL, EDWARD, monument designs by, Sep 61: 122–28

—— and PAUL DAVIS, "A Modern Bestiary," portfolio by, Jul 62: 120–28

"SORTILÈGE D'AMOUR," anonymous Flemish painting, Jan 62: 80

SOTHEBY'S, London, scenes at, Nov 62: 58, 60–62, 64, 65, 67

SOTHERN, E. H., as Shylock, Jan 60: 93

SOUTH AFRICA, UNION OF, N'debele village life, photographs by Pete Turner, Nov 60: 57–64

SOUTH CAROLINA

Charleston, cypress and azalea garden, May 59: 53

Spartanburg, Deering Milliken plant, May 62: 33

SOUTHERN, TERRY, photograph of, Mar 59: 15

SOUTHERN RHODESIA, Zimbabwe, Mar 63: 57

SOWERS, ROBERT, airlines terminal window designed by, Sep 59: 10–11

SPAIN (see also BARCELONA)

Alhambra, May 62: 26, Sep 62: 93

Moslem rule, relics and reminders of, Sep 62: 73–81, 83–86, 88–93

Valley of the Fallen, May 61: 47

Votive crown of Recevinthus, May 63: 104

"SPANISH PRISON, THE," painting by Jack Levine, Jul 62: 16

SPARTA, GREECE, ideals old and new, Mar 59: 133

SPARTANBURG, S.C., Deering Milliken textile plant, May 62: 33

SPEAR, RUSKIN, Geoffrey Sharp, detail from, May 62: 76

SPECTACULARS, of Baroque age, Jul 60: 60–65

"SPECTRA," book of poems by Emanuel Morgan and Anne Knish, cover of, May 60: 44

"SPELL OF THE MASTER, THE," painting by Joseph Danhauser, May 61: 84–85

SPENGLER, OSWALD, portrait of, Mar 59: 11

SPHINX, at Wadi es-Sebua, Jul 60: 9

"SPIRIT OF THE DEAD WATCHES, THE," painting by Gauguin, Jan 60: 36–37

SPOFFORD, CHARLES M., portrait of, Jul 62: 8

SPOLETO, ITALY, New York Pro Musica at, Nov 60: 88–89, 92

"SPORT OF THE WAVES," painting by Arnold Böcklin,

Jan 60: 132

SPRAY VIEW HOUSE, in Ocean Grove, N.J., Jan 61: 112

"SPRING FESTIVAL ON THE RIVER," Chinese scroll, Jul 61: 65

"SQUARE OF ST. MARK'S, THE," painting by Canaletto, Jul 59: 14–15

SQUIRE, RAGLAN, & PARTNERS, design by, for memorial to Mohammed Ali Jinnah, May 61: 46

STAËL, GERMAINE DE
Château at Coppet, Nov 58: 144
Portrait of, by François Gérard, Nov 58: 86

STAFFORD, JEAN, photograph of, May 63: 21

STAG, red pottery, from Marlik, Iran, Nov 62: 102

STAGE DESIGN, development of, Jul 59: 42–47

STAHLMAN, SYLVIA, photograph of, Nov 61: 78

STAINED-GLASS WINDOWS. See under CHURCHES and SYNAGOGUES

STAMFORD, CONN., First Presbyterian Church, Sep 59: 20, 21

STAMOS, THEODOROS, portrait of, Sep 58: 45

"STANDING COUPLE," painting by David Park, Jul 60: 17

"STAND ON THE SNOW GORGE," print by Umetaro Azechi, May 60: 107

STANFORD UNIVERSITY MEDICAL CENTER, May 62: 15

"STARTLED," painting by Frank Dicksee, May 62: 74

"STARTLED CONFESSOR, THE," painting by Jehan Georges Vibert, Mar 60: 65

STATE DEPARTMENT, U.S., buildings of, Jul 61: 30–31

STAZEWSKI, HENRYK, portrait of, May 61: 22

STEEN, JAN, *Merry Company,* Sep 59: 31

STEFFANI, AGOSTINO, scene from *Servio Tullio,* opera by, Jul 60: 61

STEICHEN, EDWARD, photograph of William Butler Yeats by, Nov 60: 67

STEINBERG, SAUL
Photograph of, May 63: 13
Sun, cartoon detail by, Nov 63: 53

STEINLEN, THÉOPHILE ALEXANDRE, posters by, Jan 59: 113, 120

"STELE FOR A TERMITE," sculpture by Robert Müller, Mar 61: 107

"STELE OF THE VULTURES," Sumerian sculpture, Jul 61: 39

STERN, BERT, photograph of, Mar 61: 18

STERN, ISAAC, photographs of, Jul 60: 73, 75

STEVENSON, ELIZABETH, photograph of, May 59: 17

STEVENSON, ROBERT LOUIS, and household, in Samoa, Jan 60: 31

STILL LIFE, of 1910, painting, Nov 60: 4

"STILL LIFE WITH ANGELS," painting by John Koch, Sep 60: 104

"STILL LIFE WITH FLOWERS," painting by Gerrit Hondius, Jul 61: 25

STILLWELL, RICHARD, photograph of, Sep 59: 27

STOCKHAUSEN, KARLHEINZ
Compositions by, Jan 59: 50–51, Sep 60: 123
Photograph of, Jan 59: 50

"STOLEN KISS, THE," painting by Seong Moy, Jul 61: 24

STOLOFF, CAROLYN, photograph of, Mar 63: 33

STONE, EDWARD D.
Buildings designed by: Sep 58: 88–90, 91; Graf home, dining room, May 62: 31; Stanford University Medical Center, May 62: 15; U.S. embassy building, New Delhi, Jan 60: 20
Design by, for a national cultural center, Sep 61: 16
Photographs of, Sep 58: 89, May 63: 27

STONE AGE LIFE, 15th-century miniature, Jan 62: 2, 3

STONEHENGE, ENGLAND, Jul 60: 86, Jul 62: 82–83

"STORM, THE," painting by Pierre Auguste Cot, Mar 60: cover, 3, 60

"STORM ON THE SEA OF GALILEE," painting by Rembrandt, Jul 59: 34

STRACHEY, LYTTON, portrait of, by Henry Lamb, Jan 60: 106

"STRADA, LA," motion picture, scene from, Mar 61: 100

STRASBERG, SUSAN, in *Time Remembered,* Nov 60: 53

STRATFORD, CONN., American Shakespeare Festival Theatre, May 60: 29

STRATFORD, ONT., Festival Theatre, Jul 59: 42–43

STRAVINSKY, IGOR
Photograph of, Jan 59: 53
Sketch of, Sep 58: 82

"STREET SCENE," opera, set for, Jan 60: 16–17

STREET FURNITURE, Nov 59: 105–12

"STRELTSY," print, Sep 59: 65

"STRING QUARTET," painting by Hans Hofmann, Jul 61: 17

STUART, GILBERT, portrait of Anne Willing Bingham by, Jul 63: 9

STUART COMPANY BUILDING, Pasadena, Calif., Sep 58: 88–90

STUBBS, GEORGE
Antinous with His Jockey and Trainer, detail from, May 62: cover, 3
Hambletonian; Rubbing Down, May 62: 68–69
Prince of Wales' Phaeton, Jul 63: 102–3
Self-portrait, May 59: 97
Wedgwood, Josiah, and his family, May 59: 95

"STUDIO END OF DAY, THE," painting by John Koch, Sep 63: 94

"STUDIO INTERIOR," painting by John Koch, Sep 60: 108

STUEMPFIG, WALTER
Industrial scene, Jul 63: 22
Waterworks, The, Jul 62: 18

STYRON, WILLIAM, photograph of, May 60: 28

SUARÈS, ANDRÉ, portrait of, by Rouault, Nov 62: 57

"SUDDEN SHOWER AT OHASHI," print by Hiroshige, May 60: 102

SULEIMAN THE MAGNIFICENT, Sep 58: 47

SULLIVAN, ARTHUR. See GILBERT, W. S.

SULLY, HÔTEL DE, Paris, painted ceiling in, Nov 62: 91

SUMER
Cemetery at Eridu, Jul 61: 34
King list, Nov 59: 12
Sculpture, Nov 61: 84–87; *Stele of the Vultures,* Jul 61: 39
Sun design, Nov 63: 50
Tablet with love song, Jul 63: 109

"SUMMER, OR RUTH AND BOAZ," painting by Poussin, Mar 61: 84–85

"SUMMER AND SMOKE," play, scene from, Mar 60: 98

SUMNER, JAMES B., photograph of, May 59: 16

SUN
Eclipse of, Sep 58: 65
Egyptian concept, Jan 59: 29
As motif in art, Nov 63: 49–55
Photograph of, Nov 63: 48
Sunset, Holland, Sep 58: 71

"SUN, THE," painting by Richard Lippold, Nov 63: 55

"SUN AND MOON," painting by R. Delaunay, Nov 63: 54

"SUNDAY LUNCH AT PEACOCK POINT," painting by Simon Elwes, Jan 59: 104–5

SUNFLOWER QUILT PATTERN, Nov 63: 51

SUN-GODS, Nov 63: 49, 50, 52

"SUNLIGHT," painting by Henry Hensche, Jul 61: 24

"SUN, NO. 14," construction by Claire Falkenstein, Jan 59: 14

"SUNSET CHORD," painting by Jan Gelb, Jul 61: 26

"SUPPER AT EMMAUS, THE," painting by Rembrandt, Jul 60: 47

SURGICAL INSTRUMENTS, illus from treatise by Abulcasis, Sep 62: 81

"SURRENDER OF BREDA, THE," painting by Velázquez, Sep 58: 18

"SURVIVORS, THE," painting by Robert Goodnough, Nov 60: 4

SUSANNAH AND THE ELDERS OF BABYLON, painting by Albrecht Altdorfer, Sep 63: 15

SUSSKIND, DAVID, in *A Modern Bestiary,* Jul 62: 123

SUTHERLAND, GRAHAM, portraits by
Churchill, Winston S., Jan 59: 103
Maugham, Somerset, Jan 59: 107

SUZUKI, DAISETZ, photographs of, Jul 59: 72, 73

SWAN FOUNTAIN, by Dyre Vaa, May 62: 29

SWEDEN, Vällingby street lighting, Nov 59: 107

SWIFT, JONATHAN, drawing of, Nov 59: 64

SWIFT, PAGE, photograph of, Nov 61: 79

SWINBURNE, CHARLES ALGERNON, portrait of, May 63: 85

"SWING, THE," painting by Renoir, Sep 60: 79

SWITZERLAND
Geneva, League of Nations Palace, Jan 63: 12
St. Gotthard Pass, Nov 59: 86, May 62: 72
Wettingen, window commemorating Lepanto, Jul 63: 61

SYDNEY, AUSTRALIA, opera house design, Sep 59: 15

SYON HOUSE, Nov 58: 50, 54, May 59: 46
Mantelpiece by Robert Adam, Mar 62: 67

SYRACUSE, ITALY, cathedral, Sep 61: 27

T

TAHITI
Girls of, Mar 61: 26
Paintings and woodcuts by Paul Gauguin, Jan 60: 34–38, 40, 125–27
Punaauia scene, Jan 60: 28

"TAHITIAN CARRYING BANANAS," woodcut by Gauguin, Jan 60: 125

"TAKING OF CONSTANTINOPLE BY THE CRUSADERS, THE," painting by Delacroix, Nov 63: 26–27

TAL, MIKHAIL, photograph of, Jan 62: 117

"TALE OF TWO BROTHERS, THE," portion of, on papyrus, Nov 62: 80

TALIESIN EAST, Wisconsin home of Frank Lloyd Wright, living room of, Sep 60: 98

TALIESIN WEST, Arizona home of Frank Lloyd Wright, Sep 59: 8–9

TALLMAN, RANDOLPH, in *Reynard the Fox,* Jan 63: 90

TALMA, FRANÇOIS JOSEPH, as Hamlet, Sep 61: 104

TAMERLANE, in Persian miniature, Jan 63: 61

"TAMING OF THE SHREW, THE," play by Shakespeare, scene from, Nov 63: 38

"TANCRED AND ERMINIA," painting by Poussin, Mar 61: 81

TANGE, KENZO
Buildings designed by, Sep 61: 59, 61, 62
Photograph of, Sep 61: 59

TANGUAY, EVA, photograph of, Jul 59: 116

TANIGUCHI, YOSHIRO, memorial to Mokutaro Kinoshita, designed by, May 61: 48

TANYU. See KANO TANYU

TAOIST SAINT, FLYING, Chinese drawing, Nov 60: 46

TAPE RECORDER MUSIC DIAGRAMS, Jan 59: 50–51, 55, 125

TAPESTRIES
French, Sep 60: 70; detail showing woman at organ, Mar 60: 72
Scipio, from cartoons by Giulio Romano, Nov 61: 82

TARQUINIA, ITALY, aerial photograph of necropolis, May 60: 60

TASSILI ROCK PAINTINGS, May 59: 73–80, Sep 62: 12

TASSO, TORQUATO, portrait of, May 60: 32

TASSO'S OAK, Rome
Painting of, by Peter Blume, Jul 61: 72–73: sketches for, Jul 61: 70–71
Photograph of, Jul 61: 75

"TASTE OF HONEY, A," play, scene from, Mar 61: 103, May 61: 51

"TATTOOED SAILOR, THE," book by André François, drawing from, May 59: 118

TAYLOR, ELIZABETH, in *A Modern Bestiary,* Jul 62: 122

TAYLOR, LAURETTE, in *The Glass Menagerie,* Jan 61: 31

TEAPOT, designed by M. Brandt, Nov 61: 71

"TE ARII VAHINE," woodcut by Gauguin, Jan 60: 127

TELEVISION
Mass and class appeal of personalities in, Jan 60: 9
Preparation of commercial, Jan 60: 10

"TEMPLE OF JANUS, THE," painting by Sebastiano Mazzoni, Jul 60: 43

"TEMPLE OF LOVE," Meissen ware centerpiece, Jul 59: 2, 3

"TEMPTATION OF CHRIST," painting by Duccio di Buoninsegna, Nov 60: 44

"TEMPTATION OF ST. ANTHONY," painting by Hieronymus Bosch, detail from, Jan 62: 78

"TEMPTATION OF ST. ANTHONY, THE," painting by Jacques Callot, Nov 60: 44–45

"TENANT FARMER," painting by Andrew Wyeth, Sep 61: 90–91

"TENDERLOIN," musical, Eileen Rodgers in, May 61: 51

TENERIFE, map by Alexander von Humboldt, Jul 59: 60–61

TENNYSON, ALFRED, portrait of, Nov 63: 46

TEPE SARAB, IRAN, archaeological site, Sep 62: 4

TER-ARUTUNIAN, ROUBEN, set for *Maria Golovin,* designed by, Jan 60: 17

TER BORCH, GERARD, *The Letter,* Jul 63: 95

TETON RANGE, photograph, Mar 60: 18–19

TEUTONS. See "TIMELESS TEUTONS"

TEXAS
Dallas, Bruno Graf home, Sep 58: 91, May 62: 31
Fort Worth development plan, Jul 59: 8–9
Houston, Alley Theatre play, Jan 62: 5

THALER, MICHAEL, *A History of Art,* Jan 61: 120–21

THALIA, Campanian sculpture, Mar 62: 67

THAMES TUNNEL, paintings of, Jan 59: 34, 35

THEATRE, model designed by Barrie Greenbie, Elizabeth Harris and Seth Hiller, Mar 62: 6

THEATRE OF THE ABSURD, characters in, drawings by Douglas Gorsline, Sep 62: 34–35, 38–39

THEODORA, BYZANTINE EMPRESS, mosaic portrait of, in Church of San Vitale, Ravenna, Nov 63: 18–19

THEODOSIUS II, BYZANTINE EMPEROR, coin portrait of, Sep 63: 82

THIRTY YEARS' WAR, etchings by Jacques Callot on horrors of, Nov 62: 34–41

THOMAS, DYLAN, sketch of, Sep 58: 84

THOMAS, ROBERT, photograph of, Nov 61: 79

THOMPSON, FRANCIS, photograph of, Mar 61: 12

"THREE FAVORITE AERIAL TRAVELLERS, THE," painting by J. F. Rigaud, Sep 58: cover, 5

"THREE FRIENDS AND HUNDRED BIRDS, THE," painting by Pien Wen-chin, detail from, Jan 61: 24

THREE GRACES, Pompeian fresco, with Adam adaptation, Mar 62: 67

"THREE MUSICIANS," painting by John Koch, Sep 60: 109

"THREE MUSICIANS," painting by Picasso, Nov 61: 13

"THREEPENNY OPERA," musical, scene from, May 62: 38

"THRESHOLD TO SUCCESS," painting by Philip Evergood, Sep 58: 111

"THRONE OF BLOOD," motion picture, scene from, Jul 62: 45

THURBER, JAMES, photograph of, May 60: 21

TIARA OF SAITAPHERNES, Mar 59: 106

TIBERIUS, ROMAN EMPEROR
Cave of, May 59: 105; sculpture from, May 59: 102–3, 106
Coin portraits of, Sep 63: 36, 38
Portrait sculpture of, May 59: 123

TIBETAN PARADISE, 18th-century banner, Nov 60: 39

TIEPOLO, GIOVANNI BATTISTA
Death of Seneca, The, Jan 61: 2
Grand Council at Malta, Mar 61: 66–67

TIGER, mechanical man-eating, Sep 60: 20–21

TIGER HUNT, painting by Indian artist of bazaar school, Sep 60: 10

TILLICH, PAUL, photograph of, Sep 63: 8

TILNEY, BRADFORD S. See PEDERSEN, WILLIAM F., associate

"TIMELESS TEUTONS," album of photographs by August Sander, Mar 60: 41–45

"TIME REMEMBERED," play, scene from, Nov 60: 53

TINSEL PRINT, showing Richard John Smith as buccaneer, Sep 63: 2, 3

TIRYNS, GREECE, artifacts found at, Jan 61: 82–83, 92

TISCHENDORF, KONSTANTIN VON, portrait of, Nov 62: 82

TISSIER, JEAN BAPTISTE ANGE, Napoleon III and Eugènie, painting by, Sep 60: 68

TISSOT, JAMES, Ball on Shipboard, May 62: 74–75

TITIAN
Emperor Charles V with dog, portrait by, Jul 61: 83
Girl in a Fur Wrap, Jul 61: 82
Madonna with the Rabbit, detail from, Jul 61: 86
Man with Glove, Sep 60: 71
Rape of Europa, The, Jul 59: cover, 3, 38–39
Venus, Nov 61: 82

TOBEY, MARK, Noh singer, painting by, Jul 59: 76

"TO GOLGOTHA," painting by Rouault, Nov 62: 52

TOKYO, JAPAN, highway-carpark-building combination, Jan 62: 95

TOLEDO, SPAIN, El Tránsito, Sep 62: 90

TOMKINS, P. W., The Royal Rose, engraving by, Sep 59: 2, 3

TONE, FRANCHOT, in A Moon for the Misbegotten, Mar 60: 36

TOPEKA, KANS., musical life of, Sep 59: 86–89

"TOP OF THE LADDER," play, scene from, Nov 63: 37

TOPOLSKI, FELIKS, coronation of Elizabeth II of England, murals by, Nov 60: 129–36

TORRE VELASCA, Milan, Nov 60: 15

TOTEM POLE, of Haida Chief Skowl, Sep 60: 27

TOULOUSE-LAUTREC, HENRI DE, impersonation by Zero Mostel, May 62: 52

TOURNAMENT, from King René's Le Livre des Tournois, Nov 58: cover, 3, 92–104

TOWER OF BABEL
Painting by Pieter Bruegel the Elder, Sep 63: 10–11
Painting by Shalom Moskovitz, Jul 61: 127
17th-century engraving, Jan 62: 94

TOYNBEE, ARNOLD, portrait of, Mar 59: 13

TRADES ENGRAVINGS, 18th-century
Horlogère, Nov 61: 2, 3
Jardinier, May 59: 33

"TRAGEDY OF LUCRETIA, THE," painting by Botticelli, Jul 59: 36–37

TRAJAN, ROMAN EMPEROR
Coin portrait of, Sep 63: 36
Temple built by, in Nubia, Jul 60: 12–13

"TRANSITION NO. 2," painting by Henry Botkin, Jul 61: 25

TRANSJORDAN, scenes at Petra, Jul 62: 26–29

TRANS-WORLD AIRLINES (TWA), terminal at New York International Airport, Jul 60: 80, Mar 62: 33

"TRAP BOAT AT DAWN," painting by George Yater, Jul 61: 24

TRAVEL
Episodes of Grand Tour, Nov 59: 76–77, 86–87
"Visit U.S.A." program, posters and drawings, Sep 62: 116–19

"TRAVELING AMONG STREAMS AND MOUNTAINS," painting by Fan K'uan, Jan 61: 19

"TRAVIATA," opera, scene from, Nov 61: 81

TREE OF COOLE, Mar 59: 86, 89

TRENTON, N.J., Jewish Community Center bathhouse, Sep 62: 60

TREZZINI, DOMENICO, Summer Palace of Peter the Great, designed by, Sep 59: 82

TRIAL IN CALCUTTA, bazaar-school painting, Sep 60: 19

"TRICHEURS, LES," motion picture, scene from, May 60: 55

"TRIMALCHIO'S DINNER," satire by Petronius, facsimile of error in translation of, Nov 62: 86

TRINITY ALTARPIECE, painting by Hugo van der Goes, detail from, Jul 63: 95

TRIPOD, BRONZE, Pompeian, with Russian adaptation, Mar 62: 66

"TRISTAN UND ISOLDE," opera, 1962 décor, May 63: 45

TRISTRAM and ISOUD, May 60: 116, 117, 118

"TRIUMPH OF CAESAR," painting by Mantegna, Jul 63: 95

"TRIUMPH OF GALATEA," sketch by Poussin, Mar 61: 90

"TRIUMPH OF TRUTH, THE," ceiling painting by Charles Le Brun, Jul 63: 81

TROJAN HORSE, painting by Giuseppe Arcimboldo, Nov 60: 2, 3

TROJAN WAR, site of, Jan 61: 95

TROOBNICK, EUGENE, in From the Second City, Jan 62: 67

TRUFFAUT, FRANÇOIS, photograph of, May 60: 54

TS'AO CHIH-PAI, landscape by, Mar 60: 12

TSOEDE BRONZES, Mar 63: 51

TS'UI PO, Hare and Jays, Jan 61: 17

TULLY, GORDON, photograph of, Jan 63: 11

TURBACO, COLOMBIA, air volcanoes, Jul 59: 66

TURIN, ITALY, Exhibition Hall, Mar 59: 22

TURKEY (see also ISTANBUL)
Ankara, record of Augustus inscribed on temple wall, Nov 62: 79
Aphrodisias, Mar 63: 96–101
Çatal Hüyük: sculptures, Nov 63: 66–67; wall paintings, Sep 62: 10, 12, 13
Ephesus: Sacred Way, Sep 58: 86; statues found at, Sep 58: 85, 87
Sardis, Sep 63: 82–83, 85 (map), 87, 88

"TURKISH ARTIST, A," color drawing by Gentile Bellini, Jul 59: 40

TURKISH BATH, painting by Ingres, May 59: 62–63

TURNER, J. M. W.
Childe Harold's Pilgrimage, May 61: 62–63
Passage of the St. Gothard, from the Center of Devil's Bridge, The, May 62: 72
Petworth water colors, Mar 63: 63, 66–71
Portrait of, Mar 63: 65
Rain, Steam and Speed, May 61: 88

TURNER, PETE, N'debele village of Transvaal, photographs by, Nov 60: 57–64

TURNERELLI, statue of George III by, Nov 63: 80

TURNEY, MATT, photograph of, Nov 62: 69

TUTANKHAMEN, KING OF EGYPT, tomb painting from reign of, Mar 63: 43

TUSCANY, ITALY, scene, photograph, May 60: 58

TWA. See TRANS-WORLD AIRLINES

"TWELFTH NIGHT," play by Shakespeare, scene from, Nov 63: 37

TWINING, EDWARD FRANCIS, photograph of, May 63: 93

"TWO BEER CANS," sculpture by Jasper Johns, May 61: 119

"TWO FIGURES WITH VERMILION LIGHT," painting by Elmer Bischoff, Jul 60: 23

"TWO HANIWA," print by Kiyoshi Saito, May 60: 106

TWORKOV, JACK
Boon, Jul 61: 22
Portrait of, Jul 61: 22

"TWO SIDES RED, NO. 437," painting by Kandinsky, Nov 61: 67

TYPE STYLES, showing Bauhaus influence, Nov 61: 69

U

UDALL, STEWART, photograph of, Sep 61: 8

UFFIZI GALLERY, Tribuna of, painting by John Zoffany, Nov 59: 92–93

"UMBERTO D.," motion picture, scene from, Mar 61: 100

UNDERWATER GLOVE AND FLIPPERS, drawing by Leonardo da Vinci, Nov 58: 70

UNDERWATER WARRIOR, from Vegetius' De Re Militari, Nov 58: 71

"UNEXPECTED ANSWER, THE," painting by René Magritte, Jan 62: 86

UNGERER, TOMI
Photographs of, Jan 61: 129, 130, 132–33
Works by, Jan 61: 128–36

UNION OF SOVIET SOCIALIST REPUBLICS
Ancient treasures found at Pazyryk, Jan 60: 110–11, 112
Changes in style of, photographs, Nov 62: 116–17
Gymnasts at Sports Day demonstration, Sep 60: 132
Peterhof, Sep 59: 82, 84, 85, Nov 62: 24–25

"UNIQUE FORMS OF CONTINUITY IN SPACE," sculpture by Umberto Boccioni, Nov 62: 4

UNITED NATIONS
UNESCO headquarters, in Paris: ceramic mural by Joan Miró, Sep 59: 16; garden designed by Isamu Noguchi, Mar 60: 109; sculpture by Henry Moore, Nov 60: 106–7
U.S. Mission headquarters, New York City, design for, Jan 60: 23

UNITED STATES AIR FORCE ACADEMY, Jan 60: 22–23, May 62: 10–11

UNITED STATES TRAVEL SERVICE PROGRAM, posters and drawings, Sep 62: 116–19

UNIVERSE, Hindu view, Jan 59: 29

UNTERMEYER, LOUIS, photograph of, May 60: 28

UPDIKE, JOHN, photograph of, Mar 62: 85

"UPRIGHT EXTERIOR AND INTERIOR FORM," sculpture by Henry Moore, Nov 60: 105

URBAN VIII, Pope, portraits of, Jul 60: 39, Nov 63: 63

"URBINO DIPTYCH, THE," paintings by Piero della Francesca, Jan 60: 69–72

URE, MARY, in Look Back in Anger, Jan 63: 33

URSULA, SAINT, episode from legend of, painting by Vittore Carpaccio, Sep 63: 18–19

USSACHEVSKY, VLADIMIR, photograph of, Jan 59: 52

USTINOV, PETER, photographs of, Nov 58: 83–85

UTAH, Dinosaur National Monument pavilion, Jan 60: 25

"UTOPIA," book by Thomas More, frontispiece for 1518 edition, Mar 63: 74

UTSON, JÖRN, opera house designed by, Sep 59: 15

V

VAA, DYRE, swan fountain at Oslo, designed by, May 62: 29

VALDARES SISTERS, photograph of, Jul 59: 117

VALERIAN, ROMAN EMPEROR, surrender to Shapur I, rock carving, Jan 63: 51

VALK, FREDERICK, as Shylock, Jan 60: 93

VALLEY OF THE FALLEN, monument near Madrid, May 61: 47

VAN ALLEN, JAMES A., photograph of, May 59: 16

VANBRUGH, JOHN, portrait of, Nov 58: 60; by Jonathan Richardson, Sep 61: 72

VAN DOREN, MARK, photographs of, Sep 58: 98, May 60: 21

VAN DYCK, ANTHONY
Copy by, of The Rape of Europa, Jul 59: 38
Cupid and Psyche, Jul 63: 95
Equestrian portrait of Charles I of England, Jul 61: 93; with head of Cromwell substituted, Jul 61: 93
Roi à la chasse, Jul 61: 78
Self-portrait, with Endymion Porter, Jul 61: 88

"VANESSA," opera, set for, Jan 60: 17

VAN EYCK. See EYCK

VAN GOGH, VINCENT
Impersonation of, by Zero Mostel, May 62: 52
Paintings by: Arles, springtime view, Jul 59: 100–1; Arlesian, Jul 59: 92; Café Terrace at Night, Jul 59: 102; garden of hospital at Arles, Jul 59: 104–5; home in Arles, Jul 59: 103; Painter on the Road to Tarascon, The, self-portrait, Jul 59: 99; Pont de l'Anglois, Jul 59: 103; White Roses, Sep 61: 15; Zouave, Jul 59: 93

VanORDEN, BIANCA, photograph of, Mar 59: 15

VAPHIO CUPS, Jan 61: 88–89

VARÈSE, EDGARD, photograph of, Jan 59: 52

VATICAN CITY
Bronze pine cone, Jan 62: 48
Casino Pio, Jan 62: 49
Fresco by Raphael of encounter between Leo I and Attila, May 63: 76–77
St. Peter's. See SAINT PETER, BASILICA OF
Treasures of, Jan 62: 32–40, 45, 48

VAUDEVILLIANS
Cemetery plot for, Jul 59: 112
Photographs of, Jul 59: 113–18

"VAULTED ECHO," sculpture by Hilda Morris, Jan 62: 15

VAUX-LE-VICOMTE, Jul 63: 76–77, 78–79, 83

VEENI, A. KRISHNA, photographs of, Sep 63: 70, 71

VEGETIUS, De Re Militari, illus from, Nov 58: 71

VELÁZQUEZ, DIEGO RODRÍGUEZ DE SILVA Y
Olivares, Count-Duke of, portrait by, Jul 60: 41
Surrender of Breda, The, Sep 58: 18

VENEROSI-PESCIOLINI, COUNTESS PAOLA, portrait of, by Pietro Annigoni, Jan 59: 104

VENEZUELA, Caracas shopping center, Jan 62: 95

VENICE, ITALY
Book cover, 10th-century, from, Mar 63: cover, 3

Buildings and monuments, photographs by Alexander Liberman, Mar 63: 16–24
Coca-Cola barge, photograph, Sep 58: 50
Departure of the Bucentaur, painting by Francesco Guardi, Nov 59: 88–89
In 1500, map, Jul 61: 56–57
In 15th century, Mar 60: 82–83
Gondoliers, as seen on Grand Tour, Nov 59: 87
Human pyramid, 1806, Jul 63: 2, 3
Imaginary views of, Sep 63: 18–19
Piazza San Marco: horses above doorway of church, Nov 63: 12; paintings of, Jul 59: 14–15, Jul 61: cover, 3
Piazzetta, The, Jul 63: 104
"VENICE WITHOUT WATER," painting by Fabrizio Clerici, Sep 63: 18
VENNE, ADRIAEN VAN DE, *Fishing for Souls*, Nov 62: 32
VENTRIS, MICHAEL, portrait of, Jan 61: 76
VENUS
Cnidian, of Praxiteles, head, Jan 62: 46
De Milo, Sep 60: 70
From *Echecs Amoureux, Les*, Nov 58: 14
From painting by Botticelli, Sep 58: 94
Painting by Titian, Nov 61: 82
"VENUS WITH CUPID AS A HONEY THIEF," painting by Lucas Cranach the Elder, detail from, Sep 63: 92
VERDON, GWEN, photographs of, Sep 58: 60, May 63: 12
VERMEER, JAN
Artist in His Studio, The, Sep 58: 29
Little Street, The, Sep 58: 32
Music Lesson, The, Jul 63: 100
VERMONT, Federal-style post office and courthouse, Jan 60: 22
VERNE, JULES, *The Begum's Fortune*, illus for, Mar 63: 76
VERONESE, PAOLO, *The Family of Darius Before Alexander*, Mar 59: 38–39
"VERONICA'S VEIL," painting by Rouault, Nov 62: 54
VERSAILLES, PALACE OF
Festival of Louis XIV, Jul 60: 60–61
Fountains, May 62: 14
Galerie des Glaces, Jul 63: 81
Gardens, May 59: 38–39
Hameau, Mar 62: 34
Open-air ballroom, May 62: 12
Painting of, by Pierre Patel, Nov 59: 78–79
VERSPRONCK, CORNELISZ, *Blue Girl*, Sep 58: 30
VERUS, ANNIUS, coin portrait of, Sep 63: 39
VESALIUS, ANDREAS, *De Humani Corporis Fabrica*, detail from, Nov 62: 4
VESPASIAN, ROMAN EMPEROR, coin portraits of, Sep 63: 34, 35
VESPUCCI, SIMONETTA, portrait of, by Piero di Cosimo, Sep 58: 92
VESTIER, ANTOINE, portrait of Henri Masers de Latude by, Jan 60: 82
VESUVIUS, MOUNT
Eruption of 79 A. D., engraving by Giambattista Piranesi, Mar 62: 46–47
Pompeian fresco, Mar 62: 42
As seen on Grand Tour, Nov 59: 87
VIBERT, JEHAN GEORGES, *The Startled Confessor*, painting by, Mar 60: 65
VICTORIA, QUEEN OF ENGLAND
Inscription by, to Max Beerbohm (by Max Beerbohm), May 61: 36
With Lord Melbourne, painting, Mar 59: 95
In Paris, May 63: 70–71
Portrait of, Jul 63: 94; by F. X. Winterhalter, Jul 63: 95
VICTORIA DE NEMOURS, with Queen Victoria, portrait by F. X. Winterhalter, Jul 63: 95
VICTORY, WINGED
From Leptis Magna, Libya, relief, Nov 60: 34
From Samothrace, Greece, sculpture, Sep 60: 71
VIENNA, AUSTRIA
Karlskirche, Jul 60: 53
Staatsoper, Nov 58: 26
VIENNA, UNIVERSITY OF, Mar 62: 83
"VIEW FROM THE SUMMIT OF MONTE CAVO," painting by John Izard Middleton, Nov 59: 100
"VIGILS OF CHARLES VII, THE," illus from, Mar 62: 90–91, 93–96, 99
VIGNOLA, GIACOMO DA, Gesù, church designed by (with Giacomo della Porta), Jul 60: 52
VILAR, JEAN, as Macbeth, Sep 61: 109
VILLA ALDOBRANDINI, cascade, May 62: 13
VILLA D'ESTE, fountains, May 62: 18–19, 22–23
VILLA-LOBOS, HEITOR, drawing by Robert Osborn, May 62: 126
VILLEGAS, JOSÉ, *Alhambra Interior*, painting by, Mar 60: 59
VINCI, LEONARDO, scene from *La Contesa dei Numi*, opera by, Jul 60: 62–63

VINCI, LEONARDO DA
Mona Lisa, detail from, Sep 60: 70
Virgin of the Rocks, The, detail from, Sep 60: 71
Webbed glove and flippers, drawing by, Nov 58: 70
"VIRGIN," sculpture by Agostino di Duccio, Sep 60: 70
"VIRGIN AND CHANCELLOR ROLIN, THE," painting by Jan Van Eyck, Nov 58: 17
VIRGINIA, Atoka home of John F. Kennedy, Sep 63: 102
"VIRGIN OF THE ROCKS, THE," painting by Da Vinci, detail from, Sep 60: 71
"VIRGIN SPRING, THE," motion picture, scene from, Sep 60: 8
VISHNU, on palanquin of dancing girls, Jan 60: 2, 3
VITTI, MONICA, in *L'Avventura*, Sep 61: 111
VITTORINO DA FELTRE, portrait medal of, by Il Pisanello, Jan 60: 59
VOLCANOES
Air, in Turbaco, Colombia, Jul 59: 66
Cayambe, Ecuador, Jul 59: 63
Chimborazo, Ecuador, Jul 59: 64–65
Crater, photograph by Emil Schulthess, Sep 58: 66–67
Vesuvius. See VESUVIUS, MOUNT
VOLTAIRE
Bust of, crowned at Théâtre, Français, Nov 59: 69
Candide, musical version, scene from, Nov 63: 39
At Ferney, print, Nov 59: 80
In painting by Johann Huber, Mar 61: 119
Portraits of, May 60: 32, Mar 61: 114
VOLVELLE, of 16th century, Mar 63: 2, 3
"VOYAGE, THE," painting by Robert Motherwell, Nov 59: 38
VROOM, H. C., return of Cornelis de Houtman's ship, painting by, Sep 58: 24–25
"VULGARIANS, THE," book by Robert Osborn, drawings from, Sep 60: 41, 44, 45

W

WADSWORTH, CHARLES, portrait of, Jul 61: 102
WAGENFELD, WILHELM, lamp designed by, Nov 61: 71
WAGNER, RICHARD, drawing by Robert Osborn, May 62: 122–23
WAGNER, WIELAND, photograph of, May 63: 44
"WAITING FOR GODOT," play, scene from, Nov 58: 64
WALDEN POND, in 1957, Sep 58: 51
WALDMÜLLER, FERDINAND, *The Picture Box Man*, painting by, Mar 60: 64
WALDSTEIN, FERDINAND VON, COUNT, letter to Beethoven from, Mar 62: 81
"WALK BY THE SEA," painting by Pierre Bonnard, Mar 62: 24
WALLACH, ELI, photograph of, May 63: 11
WALLENSTEIN, ALBRECHT EUSEBIUS WENZEL VON (DUKE OF FRIEDLAND), portrait of, Sep 59: 29
WALLER, FATS, drawing by Robert Osborn, May 62: 123
WALL HANGING, designed by Anni Albers, Nov 61: 70
WALPOLE, ROBERT, portrait by John Wootton, Nov 58: 43
WALTON, IZAAK, portrait of, Sep 59: 133
WALTON, WILLIAM
Courthouse Steps, Sep 61: 7
Photographs of, Sep 61: 6, 7
Rally, Sep 61: 7
"WALTZ OF THE TOREADORS, THE," play, scenes from, Nov 60: 53, Mar 61: 42
"WAR AND PEACE," motion picture, scene from, Jan 60: 8
WARD, JAMES, *Painter with Cat and Model*, May 62: 76
WARE, BED OF, May 60: 131
WARFIELD, SANDRA, photographs of, Nov 61: 79, 81
"WAR IS NO DAMN GOOD!" book by Robert Osborn, drawings from, Sep 60: 46–47
WARMAN, W., composite paintings by, Jan 59: 140–43
WARNECKE, JOHN CARL, building designs by
Federal building, San Francisco, Jan 60: 23
U.S. Embassy, Bangkok, Jan 60: 21
WARREN, MICH., General Motors Technical Center, Jul 60: 80–81
WARREN, ROBERT PENN, photograph of, May 59: 16
"WARRIOR WITH SHIELD," sculpture by Henry Moore, Nov 60: 110
WARSAW ART STUDENTS, May 61: 21
WASHINGTON
Mount Rainier National Park, virgin undergrowth in, Mar 60: 17
Seattle Fair. See CENTURY 21 EXPOSITION
WASHINGTON, D.C.
Dulles International Airport, Jul 60: 83
Jefferson Memorial, Jul 60: 78
National Cultural Center, design for, Sep 61: 16
"Number 9" office block, Jan 60: 22–23

Senate Office Building, Jan 60: 19
State Department buildings, Jul 61: 30–31
State, War and Navy Building, Jan 60: 121
"WASHINGTON CROSSING THE DELAWARE," painting by Larry Rivers, Sep 59: 96
"WATCHDOGS OF THE WEST," cartoon by Peter Ustinov, Nov 58: 138
"WATCHMAKER'S WIFE, THE," trades engraving, Nov 61: 2, 3
WATER ORGAN, at Villa d'Este, May 62: 19
"WATERWORKS, THE," painting by Walter Stuempfig, Jul 62: 18
WATKINS, FRANKLIN C.
Ingersoll, R. Sturgis, portrait by, Jul 63: 23
Misses De Schauensee and Muffin, The, Jan 59: 100
WATSON, LUCILE, in *Ring Round the Moon*, Nov 60: 52
WATT, JAMES, portrait of, May 59: 91
WATTEAU, JEAN ANTOINE, *Sign of Gersaint*, Nov 59: 102
"WAVERLEY," novel by Scott, illus from, May 61: 68
WAYNE STATE UNIVERSITY, McGregor Center, May 62: 33
WEBBER, ROBERT, in *Period of Adjustment*, Mar 61: 103
WEBSTER, JOHN, *The White Devil*, scene from, Nov 63: 36
"WEDDING NIGHT, THE," or "THE FASHIONABLE FROLIC," print, Nov 62: 22
WEDGWOOD, JOSIAH
And his family, painting by George Stubbs, May 59: 95
Articles produced by, May 59: 88–91, 96, 130, Mar 62: 67
Portrait medallion of, by William Hackwood, May 59: 89, Nov 63: 63
Pottery works of, May 59: 95
WEHRER, JOSEPH J., and HAROLD J. BORKIN, design by, for memorial to F. D. Roosevelt, May 61: 43
WEIGEL, HELENE, in *Mother Courage*, May 62: 36
WEILL, KURT, portrait of, Jan 60: 14
WEIMAR, GERMANY
Bauhaus, Nov 61: 58
Goethe and Eckermann at home in, drawing by Philippe Julian, Mar 63: 82
WELDON, JOAN, in *Kean*, Mar 62: 12
WELLES, ORSON, photographs of, Jul 63: 84–91
WELLS, H. G., *When the Sleeper Wakes*, illus for, Mar 63: 78
WENIG, R., painting of Ludwig II by, Jan 61: 36–37
WENTWORTH WOODHOUSE, Nov 58: 40
WESKER, ARNOLD
Chips with Everything, scene from, Jan 63: 26–27
Photograph of, Jan 63: 31
WESSELMAN, TOM, *Great American Nude No. 39*, Sep 63: 92
WEST, BENJAMIN, *The Departure of Regulus*, Jul 63: 95
WEST CORNWALL, CONN., covered bridge at, May 60: 10
WETTINGEN, SWITZERLAND, window commemorating victory at Lepanto, Jul 63: 61
WHEAT, prehistoric and modern, from Jarmo, Iraq, Sep 62: 5
WHEELED VEHICLES
Development of, Sep 58: 146–51
Sun wheel from India, Nov 63: 50
WHEELER, BERT, photograph of, Jul 59: 116
WHEELER, MRS. GEORGE 2ND, photograph of, Sep 61: 12
"WHEN THE SLEEPER WAKES," fantasy by H. G. Wells, illus for, Mar 63: 78
"WHIMS OF CUPID, THE," ballet, scene from, Sep 60: 92–93
WHISTLER, JAMES ABBOTT McNEILL, *Arrangement in Gray and Black*, painting by, detail from, Sep 60: 70
WHISTLER, REX, *Allegory: H.R.H. The Prince Regent Awakening the Spirit of Brighton*, Nov 62: 23
WHITBY, ENGLAND, photographs by Bruce Davidson, Nov 61: 24–25, 30
WHITE, HARVEY E., photograph of, May 59: 16
"WHITE DEVIL, THE," play, scene from, Nov 63: 36
"WHITE FLOWER, RED FLOWER," mobile by Alexander Calder, Nov 62: 13
"WHITE HORSE, THE," painting by Gauguin, Jan 60: 38
WHITE MAN, as portrayed by artists of colored races in early contacts, Sep 60: 10, 15–29
"WHITE ROSES," painting by Van Gogh, Sep 61: 15
WHITMAN, ROBERT, *Ball*, Nov 62: 114
"WHITMAN PORTRAIT, A," woodcut by Antonio Frasconi, illus from, Mar 61: 125
WHITTIER, JOHN GREENLEAF, home of, Nov 58: 33
WIDENER, JOSEPH E., photograph of, Jul 63: 22
WIELAND, CHRISTOPHER MARTIN, portrait of, May 60: 32
WIENER, NORBERT, photograph of, May 59: 16
WIERTZ, ANTOINE, *Precipitate Burial*, Jan 62: 78

WILDE, OSCAR, caricatures of, by Max Beerbohm, May 61: 38–39
WILDER, THORNTON, photograph of, Mar 63: 30
WILDERNESS, photographs by Ansel Adams, Mar 60: 16–24
"WILDROOT," construction by John Chamberlain, Mar 61: 112
"WILD STRAWBERRIES," motion picture, scene from, Sep 60: 9
WILLIAM III, KING OF ENGLAND, in painting by Daniel Maclise, Sep 59: 73
WILLIAMS, TENNESSEE
Monument to, design by Edward Sorel, Sep 61: 126–27
Period of Adjustment, scene from, Mar 61: 103
Summer and Smoke, scene from, Mar 60: 98
WILLIAMS, WILLIAM CARLOS
Drawing of, May 60: 47
Photograph of, Mar 59: 60
WILSON, EDMUND, photograph of, May 59: 17
WILSON, JANE, photograph of, May 63: 19
WILSON, MARY LOUISE, in *Dressed to the Nines*, Jul 61: 77
WILSON, SOL
Low Tide, Jul 61: 23
Portrait of, Jul 61: 23
WILSON BROTHERS, vaudevillians, photograph of, Jul 59: 115
WINCKELMANN, JOHANN JOACHIM, portrait of, Mar 62: 62
WINDSOR CASTLE, Jul 63: 106–7
"WIND TIDES," sculpture by Hilda Morris, Jan 62: 15
WINGED BULL, as motif in art objects of ancient Near East, Nov 62: 103, Jan 63: cover, 3
"WINGED FIGURE," sculpture by César, Mar 61: 110–11
WINGED VICTORY. See VICTORY, WINGED
WINSTON, BOB, silver jewelry designed by, Jan 59: 5
WINTERHALTER, F. X., portrait of Queen Victoria and Victoria de Nemours by, Jul 63: 95
WIRKKALA, TAPIO and RUT BRYK
Objects designed by, Jul 63: 62, 64–65, 66, 67
Photographs of, Jul 63: 62–63, 64
WISCONSIN, buildings designed by Frank Lloyd Wright, Sep 60: 98, Nov 62: 72
WISE, THOMAS J., portrait of, Mar 59: 108
WITCHES and WITCHCRAFT, prints, Nov 59: 57–63
WITHERING, WILLIAM, portrait of, May 59: 90
WOBURN ABBEY, Chinese dairy of, Nov 58: 46
WOLF, BEN
Aunt Mary's Pond, Wellfleet, Jul 61: 25
Portrait of, Jul 61: 25
WOLFE, BERTRAM D., photograph of, May 59: 17
WOLFE, THOMAS, photograph of, May 59: 16
"WOMAN IN WHITE," painting by Picasso, Nov 61: 9
"WOMAN WITH FRUIT," painting by Gauguin, Jan 60: 34
"WOMAN WITH LOAVES," painting by Picasso, Nov 61: 8
"WOMEN GUARDIANS OF THE HAARLEM ALMS-HOUSE, THE," painting by Frans Hals, Sep 58: 31
WOOD, NATALIE, in *Tomorrow Is Forever*, Jul 63: 88
"WOODS," print by Hodaka Yoshida, May 60: 109
WOOLF, VIRGINIA
Common Reader, The, "improved" by Max Beerbohm, May 61: 39
Portrait of, Jan 60: 107
WOOTTON, JOHN, portrait of Robert Walpole by, Nov 58: 43
WORDSWORTH, WILLIAM, portrait of, May 61: 65
WORLD'S COLUMBIAN EXPOSITION, May 60: 86
WORLD'S FAIR OF 1964, plans of Victor Gruen for, May 60: 80–85
WORLD WAR II
GI's at Palermo, photograph by Robert Capa, May 60: 4
GI's dancing, New Britain, May 60: 9
WRIGHT, FRANK LLOYD
Key Project, Sep 63: 24–25
Portrait of, Sep 60: 96
Works by, Sep 60: 97, 98, 100–1, 103; Solomon R. Guggenheim Museum, May 59: 15; Taliesin West, Sep 59: 8–9; Wauwatosa, Wis., church, Nov 62: 72
WRIGHT, JOSEPH, *A Philosopher giving that Lecture on the Orrery*, May 59: 92–93
WRIGHT, LOUIS B., photograph of, May 59: 17
WRITING
Handwriting, examples, Sep 59: 125–36
Linear B script, Jan 61: 77
Picture writing, oldest example, Nov 62: 75
Sumerian, Jul 63: 108, 109
WURZACH PALACE, stairwell of, Jul 60: 56–57
WYATT, JAMES, Fonthill Abbey, designed by, Mar 62: 36
WYETH, ANDREW
Albert's Son, Sep 61: cover, 3
Chicken Wire, Sep 61: 101
Ground Hog Day, Sep 61: 92
Karl, Sep 61: 89
Nicky, Sep 61: 93
Photographs of, Sep 58: 113, Sep 61: 98
River Cove, Sep 61: 96
Roasted Chestnuts, Sep 58: 112
Tenant Farmer, Sep 61: 90–91
Young America, Sep 61: 94–95
WYOMING, Snake River and Grand Teton Range, Mar 60: 18–19

X

XERXES I, KING OF PERSIA
Gate of, at Persepolis, Jan 63: 48
Portrait sculpture of, in stone relief, Jan 63: 45
XOCHIMILCO, MEXICO, restaurant designed by Félix Candela, Mar 59: 25

Y

YADIN, YIGAEL, photographs of, Nov 59: 9
YALE UNIVERSITY
Architecture of, May 59: 86–87
Art Gallery and Design Center, Sep 62: 59, 61
Hockey rink, May 59: 84–85
YAMAGUCHI, GEN, *Deep Attachment*, May 60: 108
YAMASAKI, MINORU, buildings designed by
McGregor Center, Wayne State University, May 62: 33
Parke-Davis building, Menlo Park, Calif., Mar 59: 25
Reynolds Metals Company sales office, May 62: 32
St. Louis air terminal, Mar 59: 25
Seattle Fair pavilion, Mar 59: 25
U.S. consulate, Kobe, Jan 60: 18
U.S. exhibit, World Agricultural Fair, New Delhi, Jan 60: 26–27
Warren, Mich., church, Nov 62: 72
YATER, GEORGE
Portrait of, Jul 61: 24
Trap Boat at Dawn, Jul 61: 24
YEATS, WILLIAM BUTLER, portraits of
By Sargent, John Singer, Nov 60: 69
By Steichen, Edward, Nov 60: 67
"YELLOW AND PURPLE," print by Takumi Shinagawa, May 60: 103
"YELLOW CLOUD OVER RACE POINT," painting by Irving Marantz, Jul 61: 24
"YOJIMBO," motion picture, scene from, Jul 62: 47
YORK, SUSANNAH, photograph of, Nov 61: 114
YOSHIDA, HODAKA
Child God, May 60: 111
Woods, May 60: 109
"YOUNG ACROBATS," sculpture by Chaim Gross, Jul 61: 26
"YOUNG AMERICA," painting by Andrew Wyeth, Sep 61: 94–95
YVON, ADOLPHE, painting of Napoleon III and Baron Haussmann by, May 63: 50

Z

ZAANDAM, NETHERLANDS, cottage of Peter the Great, Sep 59: 67
ZADKINE, OSSIP, World War II memorial at Rotterdam, designed by, May 61: 45
ZAHL, PAUL A., photograph by, Sep 58: 72
ZARKALI, AL-. See ARZACHEL
ZECKENDORF, WILLIAM
Caricature of, Jul 62: 126
Structure built by, Jan 63: 115
ZEN IDEAL, painting by Kano Tanyu, Jul 59: 74–75
"ZEN TELEGRAMS," drawings by Paul Reps, Jan 60: 46–47
ZEUS, bronze statue, Nov 58: 75
ZIMBABWE, SOUTHERN RHODESIA, Mar 63: 57
"ZIP-FASTENER, THE," painting by Bernard Dunston, May 62: 77
ZODIAC, from Dendera, Egypt, Jul 62: 84–85
ZOFFANY, JOHN, paintings by
Art objects from Hadrian's Villa, Nov 59: 103
Queen Charlotte Sophia and children, Jul 63: 95
Tribuna of Uffizi Gallery, Nov 59: 92–93
"ZOOT," mannequin by Marisol Escobar, Mar 63: 104
ZORINA, VERA, in *Slaughter on Tenth Avenue*, Sep 58: 61
ZORN, ANDERS, portrait of Isabella Gardner by, Jul 59: 27
ZURBARÁN, FRANCISCO, *St. Francis Kneeling*, painting by, Jul 60: 46

Index prepared by Isabel Garvey